James Fuller

About the Author

CARL SFERRAZZA ANTHONY, the author of nine books, is considered the nation's expert on the subject of presidential wives and families. He has written extensively for publications, including the *New York Times*, *Los Angeles Times*, *Washington Post*, *Vanity Fair*, *American Heritage*, *Smithsonian*, and *Town & Country*, and also writes screenplays. He lives in Los Angeles.

ALSO BY CARL SFERRAZZA ANTHONY

First Ladies: The Saga of the Presidents' Wives and Their Power, 1789–1990
(2 volumes)

*Florence Harding: The First Lady, the Jazz Age, and the Death
of America's Most Scandalous President*

*America's First Families: An Inside View of 200 Years
of Private Life in the White House*

The Kennedy White House: Family Life and Pictures, 1961–1963

America's Most Influential First Ladies

*As We Remember Her: Jacqueline Kennedy Onassis
in the Words of Her Family and Friends*

*"This Elevated Position . . .": A Catalogue and Guide to the National
First Ladies Library and the Importance of First Lady History*
(editor and contributor)

*Heads of State: The Presidents as Everyday, Useful Household Items in
Pewter, Plastic, Porcelain, Copper, Cork, Chalk, China, Wax, Walnut & More*

NELLIE TAFT

THE UNCONVENTIONAL FIRST LADY OF THE RAGTIME ERA

Carl Sferrazza Anthony

HARPER PERENNIAL

NEW YORK ● LONDON ● TORONTO ● SYDNEY ● NEW DELHI ● AUCKLAND

Security Public Library
715 Aspen Drive
Colorado Springs, CO 80911

For Olivia Sferrazza, Kendall Sullivan,
Grace Campbell-McGuire, and Eva Cullen,
those little girls who can now all grow up
to be President on their own

HARPER ● PERENNIAL

A hardcover edition of this book was published in 2005 by William Morrow, an imprint of HarperCollins Publishers.

NELLIE TAFT. Copyright © 2005 by Carl Sferrazza Anthony. All rights reserved. Printed in the United States of America. No part of this book may be used or reproduced in any manner whatsoever without written permission except in the case of brief quotations embodied in critical articles and reviews. For information address HarperCollins Publishers, 10 East 53rd Street, New York, NY 10022.

HarperCollins books may be purchased for educational, business, or sales promotional use. For information please write: Special Markets Department, HarperCollins Publishers, 10 East 53rd Street, New York, NY 10022.

First Harper Perennial edition published 2006.

Designed by Mary Speaker

The Library of Congress has catalogued the hardcover edition as follows:

Anthony, Carl Sferrazza.
   Nellie Taft : the unconventional first lady of the ragtime era / Carl Sferrazza
   Anthony.—1st ed.
      p.   cm.
   Includes bibliographical references.
   ISBN 0-06-051382-9 (acid-free paper)
   1. Taft, Helen Herron, 1861–1943. 2. Presidents' spouses—United States—
   Biography. 3. Taft, William H. (William Howard), 1857–1930. I. Title.

E762.1.T12.A57 2005
973.91'2'092—dc22
[B]   2004052553

ISBN-10: 0-06-051383-7 (pbk.)

ISBN-13: 978-0-06-051383-2 (pbk.)

06 07 08 09 10 ❖/RRD 10 9 8 7 6 5 4 3 2 1

Yo no naka wa
Mikka minu ma ni
Sakura kana

Life is short, like the three-day
Glory of the cherry blossom

—JAPANESE PROVERB,
ATTRIBUTED TO MASSO YOSHIKAWA, 1926

CONTENTS

ACKNOWLEDGMENTS

There are several individuals I would especially like to acknowledge who helped me to see this book to completion. First and foremost is Michael Bromley, a historian of American transportation, generally, and the Tafts, specifically. Michael most generously shared everything he had already researched, which was extensive. This extraordinary act of generosity included not only Taft papers but various other publications.

Nan Card of the Rutherford Hayes Presidential Center provided the full breadth of that institution's archives regarding Nellie Taft's parents and siblings, the Herrons, and their relationship with President Hayes and his family, and Gil Gonzales of that institution expedited the photographs of their collection.

Lori McConnell, cultural resource specialist of the National Park Service, National Capital Parks, Central Division, made an extensive survey of that institution's archives regarding Nellie Taft, the development of West Potomac Park, and the Japanese cherry blossom trees. Ms. McConnell went above and beyond the call of duty in this regard, providing me with a full and definitive mini-archive.

Master Gunnery Sergeant D. Michael Ressler, chief librarian of the U.S. Marine Band, also went above and beyond with his great assistance in tracking down the details of Mrs. Taft's band concerts at West Potomac Park.

As usual, my good friend, the gentle and beautiful Mary

Wolfskill of the Manuscript Division at the Library of Congress, was of great help.

Francesca Di Meglio of the *Ladies' Home Journal* took her own time to research and copy articles for me from that publication related to or written by the Tafts.

I cannot begin to express how much I appreciated the help and enthusiasm at the Pilgrim Monument and Provincetown Museum, of Jeffory Morris, curator of collections, and Chuck Turley, executive director. Special thanks to artist John Dowd who permitted me to use his private Provincetown history collection on the Taft visit.

Among the Taft family I would first like to thank the current first lady of Ohio and the great-granddaughter-in-law of Will and Nellie, Hope Taft. Mrs. Taft led me to the engaging Seth Taft who seems to embody much of the character of his late father, Charlie Taft, with whom, incidentally, I had some brief conversations and correspondence in the late 1970s when I was beginning to take a professional interest in the political aspects of presidential marriages and families.

Ray Henderson of the William Howard Taft National Historic Site provided many photographs I had never seen before, and I appreciate his help.

I also thank Supreme Court Justice Sandra Day O'Connor and Linda H. Neary, administrative assistant, for providing the Justice's speech on Mrs. Taft.

I would also like to thank my agent, Lisa Bankoff of ICM, and her aides-de-camp, Patrick Price and Tina Dubois. At William Morrow, Claire Wachtel recognized the value of telling the Taft story through Nellie's perspective, and whenever I phoned, her assistant, Jennifer Pooley, was always cheerful and helpful. Ditto to Kevin Callahan, who saw the project to its end. Finally, the often unthanked production and management team handled the multiple drafts and rewrites with utter professionalism: Kim Lewis, executive managing editor; Andrea Molitor, production editor; Aryana Hendrawan, production manager; and—with nerves of steel—copy editor Rose Ann Ferrick.

Prologue: Being First

Nobody who didn't know Cincinnati life could describe it. It was a town with a great sense of its own importance. Not a common, vulgar, Midwestern town at all. . . . They were all terribly nice and civilized. They traveled to Europe and promenaded along with the Anglais and they got presented at court and bought inferior pictures. They were very much that way. They considered Boston and Philadelphia to be all right, but New York was just a place one sailed to Europe from.

—ALICE ROOSEVELT LONGWORTH

In the black of the night on November 3, 1908, its columns, portico, and wings made ghostly by the dancing shadows of the torchlight parade, the Taft mansion resembled the most famous building in America. It had what Mrs. William Howard Taft called "the same classic lines" as the White House and was even said to be designed by the same architect, James Hoban. But the Taft mansion—as imposing as the Newport "cottages" and Palm Beach palaces where wealthy Easterners summered and wintered—was not quite grand enough to be confused with the White House. "Not quite grand enough" sometimes seemed to be the rally cry which drove the ambitions of Nellie Taft.

She was neither the prettiest nor the eldest of the eight children in the Herron family. Her father had not been quite rich enough to provide her with the complete education she wanted. She began to follow the path she had determined to in her teens—that of the independent single woman who supported herself with a profession. Her confidence, however—undermined by her mother's warning that she not become an impoverished old maid—often abandoned her. But she did not give up on herself entirely, for she harbored an even more impossible teenage fantasy of her future life. To achieve this she would ostensibly follow a traditional path and marry—but only a man who accepted her as an intellectual equal and career partner. Her sisters and many of her friends married into families of great industrial wealth, while Nellie wed Will Taft from a clan renowned for its altruistic public service. Before she had even begun to date him, Nellie had determined that she would marry a man who would someday be elected President of the United States.

What Nellie thought and felt, however, might change several times in the course of a day. She often wanted many things that were impossible to have at the same time: privacy and recognition, beautiful possessions without the obligation of any permanent home, derivative power yet the right to veto her husband's decisions. She loved to smash precedent, but she also highly valued tradition. She thrived on her independence, yet took refuge in her family. Intellectually progressive in her notion of civil racial equality, she could out-snob the worst of snobs. She was known for both her ability to laugh at danger and for her utterly humorless attitude. She was adventurous and curious while also cautious and conservative, lavish yet frugal; she was fully certain of her own capabilities but often overwhelmed by insecurity and frequently found herself seeing the value of both sides of an argument. She was, thus, often inwardly conflicted about the "right" thing to do.

Despite the fact that she often thought what was fashionable was ridiculous, she also wanted her social peers to know that she could conform. While never relying on her zodiac guide as seriously as they did, for example, the self-conscious Nellie knew just what it meant to be a Gemini.

■

Even on this night when she finally achieved the great goal of her life, it would be hard for Nellie Taft to entirely submerge her sense of being "not quite good enough." It seemed drawn out by a certain type of person—a Roosevelt.

Tonight the most famous house in Cincinnati was animated with sound and light and that smug sense of finally being first. Men in bowlers and their wives in cartwheel hats hoisted the fringed "Taft" banners and held high their torchlights. They chanted "Taft! Taft! Taft!" while the otherwise droning songs of the Citizen's Taft Club were peppered with a dash of ragtime, that jumpy new sound created by the African American denizens of Storyville in New Orleans. Boisterously clustered around the portico, they were anticipating the great man himself, now the President-elect. They had already affectionately dubbed him "Big Bill," referring to his fat and jolly image. Friends and family loved him as "Will."

The mansion on Pike Street had been owned by a string of Cincinnati's leading families. It was built in 1820 in the Federal style for one Martin Baum, but *not* by the White House architect James Hoban. Baum had been one of many entrepreneurial Germans to find success in the grimy city by the Ohio River that was initially dominated by Revolutionary War officers. Baum sold the mansion to the city's "first millionaire," Nicholas Longworth, in 1829. Longworth was the eccentric patriarch of an educated and refined clan that became the city's leading art patrons. In 1871 the Longworths sold the mansion to David Sinton, an Irish immigrant who made millions in iron and real estate. Sinton left the house to his only child, Annie, who married Will Taft's half-brother Charles in 1873. With the Sinton money, Charles—always known as Charley—and Annie quite outshone the Longworths, filling the mansion with Chinese porcelains, European and American portrait and landscape paintings, French Renaissance enamels, and Italian decorative arts.

At this moment, with national reporters watching every move from the house, the Tafts were not only Cincinnati's but also the nation's leading family. Not even the oldest residents of Cincinnati would call it the

Longworth or Sinton house any longer. It was now the "Taft mansion." Inside, the portrait of the late American ambassador to Austria Alphonso Taft gazed benignly on the room buzzing with his sons, Charley and William, and their family and friends.

It seemed like the latest move in a chess game among this circle of Cincinnati high society. The Longworths may not have had priceless artwork like the Tafts did, but their most recent acquisition was the world's greatest treasure at the time. Two years earlier, Nick Longworth, grandson of the original owner of the Taft mansion, had married the famous "Princess Alice," not only a President's daughter but a Roosevelt. But the Tafts called the checkmate now, seizing the White House itself from the Roosevelts. At least the Roosevelts thought so.

This night was a triumphant one for Cincinnati, too, at least in the mind of Nellie Taft. With its location right on the Ohio River, between New Orleans and Pittsburgh, it had rapidly developed in the decades following the American Revolution; but even in its pioneer beginnings, it had a sense of its own importance, being named after the Society of the Cincinnati, the elite organization of male descendants of officers who had served with George Washington. First settled in 1788, it was later dubbed Porkopolis, with its status as the world's leading packing center for pork.

If the soot from the numerous manufacturing plants—glass, furniture, wood pulp, cotton, and lead, among many other products—fell on the shoulders of every class of citizens, the benefit generated from the factories did likewise. Civic duty ran high in Cincinnati: Its hospitals, parks, welfare institutions, and schools were founded and augmented by altruistic captains of local industry. Early social leaders immediately sought to establish the city as a refined one with cultural tastes and opportunities as fine as those back East, and they created literary societies, art exhibitions, and music salons. Nellie Taft would be among them.

The focus on the arts in a city that was considered the Far West to eastern colonists was prompted by Cincinnati's early and large German immigrant population. Throughout the nineteenth century, succeeding generations of Germans helped make Cincinnati a city that appreciated fine music—as much as it did its beer gardens and halls. Beer, first brewed there in 1821, was even consumed by proper young music student Nellie Herron, a lifelong connoisseur of the drink. Even with respect to its breweries, the city compared itself favorably to the East. In *Cincinnati,* published in 1826 by locals B. Drake and E. D. Mansfield, it was pointed out that Cincinnati's beer, porter, and ale were "of a quality at least equal to that of the Atlantic states."

The truth was, no matter how sophisticated its museums or fine its parks, Cincinnati would always be viewed as a backwater by the social elite of New York and Boston. That tended to make the Cincinnatians strive all the more to prove their sophistication. The Storers, the Findlays, the Tafts, the Sintons, the Longworths, and the Andersons made their tours of Europe, held debutante balls for their daughters, and kept summer homes in New England. Still, while many leading families helped establish the quality of higher education at regional institutions such as Miami University with generous donations, they sent their own sons to Harvard and Yale, proving themselves as worthy as their Yankee counterparts. In their efforts to prove themselves equal to eastern snobs, however, dullness seemed to mark the leading Cincinnatians. With stiff and pretentious manners, many leaders—most notably the Anglophilic Bellamy Storers— merely reinforced their conventionality and inward sense of inferiority compared to the Astors and Rockefellers. Even with wealth often greater than many New York social families, the Cincinnatians could not buy effervescence. Still, no one seemed to resent the assumption that those cities were better than her own than Nellie Taft.

It wasn't that Nellie had any sentiment about Cincinnati. When she moved on physically in her life, she also moved on emotionally. As a young woman she wanted out of the grimy city and made her escapes early and often—to the nation's capital, to a palace in the jungles of Asia, and every summer to a cottage in Canada. Still, she was extremely sensitive to the remarks of Alice Roosevelt Longworth, who derided the denizens of

"Cin-cin-nasty" for their obvious efforts. Despite being Alice's senior by twenty years, Nellie had always been uncomfortable around her. Alice brought out Nellie's deepest insecurities. And whenever Alice went into one of her tirades against Cincinnati, Nellie took it personally, as if she herself was being belittled. No matter how eagerly Nellie gallivanted to New York, she was defensive when her city was demeaned.

Nellie admitted that Cincinnati was "noisy," had "unlovely" buildings and "badly paved and as badly kept" streets, all of it "under a pall of soft coal smoke which left its sooty mark upon everything—inhabitants included." Yet, she boasted, Chicago—at least when she was growing up in Cincinnati—was not as prosperous, and Cleveland "was not even spoken of as a rival." Most important was that it "boasted an unusual society . . . young men of good stock . . . families of wealth and culture . . . educated . . . public-spirited. . . ." Without specifying how, she simply declared Cincinnati "in advance of any other city . . . in culture and refinement."

When it came to comparing it to New York, she parsed her words a bit more carefully. Cincinnati, Nellie believed, was the most "important center west of New York," with "musical advantages . . . better than any city . . . with the exception of New York or Boston." It was perhaps not insignificant that New York and Boston were socially ruled, respectively, by Alice's paternal and maternal families, the Roosevelts and the Lees (and through them the Lodges and the Cabots). If the Roosevelts had seemed to conquer Cincinnati as well with the marriage of Alice to the Longworths, it was a temporary victory. As of this night, Cincinnati would hereafter be known as the city not of Longworths but of Tafts.

The root of Nellie Taft's insecurity, as well as the force driving her ambition to reach the pinnacle of political power and social prestige, was not spurred, however, by a resentment of Roosevelts or New York. Going back to her childhood, her sense of being somehow secondary seemed to emanate from the very house she now stood in. Annie and Charles Taft were wealthy beyond the imagination of most Americans, let alone the Cincinnati elite. Even the Larz Andersons, who lived next door in the redbrick mansion that Nellie said "had an air of great dignity," weren't as rich. Across the street in a cramped three-story gray brick row house, lawyer John Williamson Herron, his wife, Harriet, and their six daughters and two sons could never hope to be in the same league.

The morning after the 1908 election, Americans reading about the "Taft mansion" election party and the presence there of Mrs. William Howard Taft would assume it referred to her house. Nellie Taft was painfully conscious of the fraudulence of such a supposition. The former Nellie Herron would later confess that the "striking and imposing" mansion "across the street from us . . . lent distinction to the neighborhood. Our house was none too large for the family. . . . We had our share of the happy-go-lucky and somewhat crowded existence of a large family on a moderate income." Nellie had spent her girlhood fixated on the status afforded to the names Anderson, Sinton, Longworth, and Taft. At least the Herrons lived on the "fashionable end" of Pike Street.

Her father had been friend to two Presidents and was a highly respected member of Cincinnati legal, literary, and artistic circles. Her mother, the granddaughter and daughter of congressmen, possessed an intelligence rare among women. These bragging points, contrasting with the realities of her status, fueled her idealized notion of what she should be, what she must have. Ever after, forty-seven-year-old Nellie was rarely satisfied with what she had achieved. So, as her lifelong dream was being realized on this night, Nellie Taft admitted she was "nervous." Any reasonable person would have declared her the winner of the greatest prize of all, but she still felt uneasy and worried that somehow it would be taken away from her.

Rationally, there was nothing to fear. Everything had gone as she had planned five months earlier on Notification Day, when candidates were officially notified that their party had chosen them as standard-bearers. That June day Will Taft had stood under a tented platform set up at the "Taft mansion," making his acceptance speech. For months before the nomination, Nellie had stage-managed Will—judging his speeches, making light of his misgivings, cultivating potentially helpful political connections and contributors, and promoting his candidacy so he emerged as the best choice.

Nellie was always in the process of winning something—a political dispute with Will; a point of principle with her children, Robert, Helen, and Charles (always known as Charlie, with an "ie," to distinguish him from his uncle); a bill of goods with a merchant; a bridge game with political wives; and now a presidential election. Perhaps her nervousness came from a fear that she had won too much and that she, not Will, would suffer for it. She had spent much of her life striving to be first, and now that had been achieved. There seemed to be no place else to go.

As if it were vulgar to acknowledge her efforts, Nellie behaved as if Will's victory was simply the natural progression of her grand scheme. "The Republican confidence grew stronger and stronger, so when we were assembled finally under the hospitable roof of Mr. and Mrs. Charley Taft, with a company of friends to receive the dispatches on election night," she recalled, "the news of the great success that came did not surprise us."

Nellie Taft had even managed to win over a man as famous around the world for his unrelenting righteousness as for his love of winning, Theodore Roosevelt. Within the last five years Nellie had twice managed to coax sensitive Will out of fulfilling his own ambition to sit on the Supreme Court and instead following her plan. His love for her and his respect for her astuteness often resulted in his acquiescence to her views. Part of Nellie's success had come in refusing to be intimidated by the gnashing teeth of the bully President Roosevelt. Confronted with his polite suggestion that someone other than Will might get his support, she had manipulated Teddy around to fully anoint Will as his successor. Brilliant, disciplined, pushy, generous, intense, honest, and, above all, adventurous—that was Nellie Taft at her best.

Nellie had reason to be nervous. Although Teddy was back home in the White House, after weeks of promoting Taft as his heir and then voting for him in New York, his daughter, Alice, had her eye on Nellie. She had been invited to the Taft mansion on election night as the wife of

Congressman Longworth, but this fooled no one. She was there as her father's great defender, his spy, his unofficial ambassador, and loyal enforcer. She resented anyone who might replace him, anointed or not, and it showed. She might surrender the White House to the Tafts on March 4, 1909, but she would not leave Washington.

An international celebrity, Alice would continue to draw attention to herself just when Nellie was seeking the recognition she had so longed for. They detested each other. Nellie would be First Lady for four years, but Alice would always be Princess. Alice later abstractly termed the "unmistakable attitude on the part of members of his [Taft's] family" as prompting an enduring element of her persona: "I rather think that then and there I began to indulge in a proclivity toward malice that occasionally comes over me." On election night she strangely remarked to Nellie: "I'm quite good at casting spells. Don't get on my wrong side."

As early returns forecasted a Taft victory and champagne corks popped—Nellie always drank champagne—Alice overheard remarks made by Mrs. Taft that seemed to belittle her father: "We don't owe so very much to Roosevelt anyway; he could have got along quite as well without him." Nick's sisters, Nan Wallingford and Clara de Chambrun, were equally smug. Alice recalled, "They had known him all their lives and were close and affectionate friends. But to me there was something not quite pleasing in the idea of 'my dear Mr. Taft' as a great man, and, still less pleasing, as a great President, rubbed in by my in-laws too!"

Several hours before the Longworths and other guests arrived, Will Taft had roused his lumbering frame from the exquisite bedroom suite he and Nellie occupied, two rooms down to the right of the entrance foyer. He had reached Cincinnati at eight that morning, returning from an exhausting western tour. Will hated everything about campaigning, most particularly having to extol his qualifications. Beneath a happy armor of avoirdupois he carried in his most sensitive heart a realization that he was not meant to be President—not that he couldn't get elected, but that it was not right for him. A subtle depression settled over him. When he went into dark moods, Will often turned to his three brothers, Charley, Horace, and Henry (sometimes called Harry), the latter two sharing the same mother as Will.

With his snowy beard and thin build, half-brother Charley looked like a cross between Santa Claus and John D. Rockefeller. He was all that and more, helping to fund the campaign with his and Annie's millions and serving as a spur and sounding board. Nellie appreciated his generosity, but they were only really close when sketching out plans for Will. Harry, a wealthy lawyer, always had the business world view, and while his wife, Julia, could be a bit too hysterical for Nellie at times, she enjoyed partying with them at their luxurious New York brownstone. Horace, founder of the Connecticut boarding school for boys Taft School, was less of a yes-man and the most liberal of the four brothers. Although Horace's wife, Winnie, was not close to any of the Tafts, Nellie and Horace loved teasing each other and remained friends throughout their lives.

Nellie and Annie seemed to get on all right, but entirely different desires drove them. Annie loved entertaining and showing off her fabulous treasures. Nellie always had some challenging goal to accomplish. On this night the exuberant Annie hosted her guests with the lighthearted nature that a privileged childhood had afforded. Nellie may not have had an affluent upbringing like her sister-in-law, but she did enjoy more influence over Will than anyone else within or without the Taft family.

With them in the mansion this election night were Will and Nellie's two sons, Bob and Charlie. Polar opposites, Bob was shy, which made him remote, cautious, and conventional, focused on proving himself worthy of his adored father's expectations. Charlie, the youngest, was blessed with a Twain-like wit. He explored, questioned, and offered his unsolicited sense of merry ridiculousness. Unlike Bob, who kept his distance from Nellie, Charlie and his mother were tightly bound to each other. Balancing the boys was middle child Helen, a freshman at Bryn Mawr, where she was this night. Studious yet soulful, she had the same determination to achieve something beyond marriage and motherhood as Nellie had at her age, yet she had more confidence to strike out on an independent path. Exceedingly thoughtful and gentle, Helen stood in stark contrast to her predecessor, Alice. She was blissfully uninterested in fame.

Two of Nellie's five sisters were also at the mansion: the unmarried Maria Herron, who lived with their aged father, and Jennie Anderson, who had married into the wealthy Anderson family. With their two other sisters in Pittsburgh, Eleanor More and Lucy Laughlin, they formed a loyal protective club of their own, supporting one another through thick and thin. The only sister Nellie did not like was Emily, apparently for no reason other than that she had been born first—and was perceived by the President-elect's wife to have been blessed with beauty and showered with flattery. When Nellie's family finally recognized her intelligence, it made this fourth of six daughters stand out as such an unusual individual that she could no longer be ignored. Lovely Emily couldn't have been more different.

To keep his guests updated of the latest election returns, Charley had seen to it that extra telegraph wires and telephones were installed in the house. The Citizen's Taft Club blared "Beautiful Ohio" into the clear night outside as campaign manager Gus Karger ran between the "Gray Room" and the "Music Room" where the guests awaited the returns. New York, Roosevelt's state, went for Taft. Massachusetts went for Taft. New Jersey, Connecticut, Michigan, Tennessee, and Wisconsin all went Taft. Will himself read aloud the good news from Maryland.

"The returns came in without a setback anywhere steadily, piling up his enormous majority," Alice Longworth recalled. And then her sisters-in-law began to fawn. Alice added that "there was much comparing them with the returns of 1904. Whenever Taft ran ahead of Father's figures, they fairly gloated, so as far as I was concerned, the stage was set for the first steps that led to the 'breaking up of a beautiful friendship'" between Teddy and Will.

Had the Longworth sisters scrutinized the numbers more carefully, their giddiness might have stopped short. Yes, technically Taft got some fifty thousand more votes than Roosevelt had—out of nearly 15 million votes—but it was a foolish number to hang popularity on. Despite having the enthusiastic support of a beloved President and the party machinery, Taft won with only 51.6 percent of the vote (Roosevelt had gotten 56.4 percent four years earlier). The states where he failed to get the majority had all voted for Roosevelt in 1904. They were all "progressive" Republican states: Colorado, Nebraska, Nevada, and Oklahoma. Did that wing of the party believe Taft would be less progressive than Roosevelt would have been had the incumbent President run for a third term? There were no exit polls to suggest the reason specifically, but those four progressive states did go for William Jennings Bryan, the radical Democratic candidate.

Bryan was branded a socialist for suggesting that the railroads be publicly owned, thus driving big business resolutely behind Taft. Bryan clarified that he meant this only in theory but added that he was actually more of the genuine heir to Roosevelt's progressivism than Taft because Teddy had commandeered and adapted the Bryan ideas on reform. Most dismissed Bryan's allegations as those of a desperate politician seeking to ride the coattails of a populist President. The western "progressive" states, however, did not; they went Democratic.

The entire premise of Will's candidacy was based on his promise to continue Roosevelt's reform policies. Roosevelt presumably trusted that Taft knew what kind of reforms he was expected to continue, and Taft apparently saw value in the reforms. When Taft self-deprecatingly told voters that they'd be disappointed because he wouldn't be as dynamic a President as Teddy, the worst it suggested was that Taft would focus on bolstering and entrenching the existing Roosevelt reforms rather than initiating a new flurry of them.

If some other Republican candidate promised to vigorously initiate progressive reforms even more closely to Roosevelt's vision, would Taft have still been nominated? Wouldn't Roosevelt have preferred just such a candidate? Indeed, Nellie had insisted, Roosevelt was secretly undermining Taft before the convention by trying to spur a draft movement for this candidate who could not seek the nomination openly. Reminded at the time that this prospective candidate would surely honor a promise he made not to run, she wasn't convinced. She knew that promises could be broken.

And that Roosevelt was just the man to do it.

Will teased Nellie that she was too mistrustful of Roosevelt; he professed "love" for his friend Teddy. Even after Taft won the election, however, Nellie would not relent. She concluded that Will's temperament simply disabled his ability to recognize that, beyond policy and politics, ego drove Roosevelt's need to always be noticed and always be first. If Will believed that Nellie was so finely attuned and even obsessed about such traits in Roosevelt because she herself possessed them in such abundance, he never let on. Will hated hurting or disappointing those whose approval he sought.

■

Except for the two nonconsecutive Grover Cleveland terms, the Republican Party had controlled the American Presidency since its first successful election, that of "Father Abraham," the legendary Lincoln, in 1860. It had survived the financial scandals of Grant, the disputed election of Hayes, the assassination of Garfield, the shocking move against patronage by Arthur, the inertia of Harrison, and the assassination of McKinley. In his eight years in the White House, Spanish-American War hero, author, outdoorsman, and living caricature Theodore Roosevelt not only thrust the United States onto the world stage as an imperial power and strained the constitutional limitations of the presidency, but he redefined Republicanism.

In the post–Civil War era, industry boomed. Railroads, coal, mining, oil, lumber, metals, and all their ancillary enterprises drove America into the new century as the world's wealthiest nation, affording more opportunity than any other. By the 1890s, cities were swelling with those who came to work the factories: the rural poor in the South, Asians out West, and millions of southern and eastern Europeans in the Northeast. Improving the deplorable living and working conditions of this new and vast working class became part of the larger crusade in the new century to improve the quality of civil life. Questions regarding big business's responsibility toward labor were no longer ignored. Workers unionized and reformers organized to create protective labor legislation—and industry was threatened.

No President wanted to alienate or weaken industry; the economy was fueled by it. Theodore Roosevelt, however, did want big business to start behaving responsibly, and he would initiate government regulations if that's what it took. Teddy became the first President to preach passionately against the sins of monopolies and trusts driven by greed and wider profit margins. Roosevelt initiated protective legislation for workers in unsafe factories and removed western lands from the grasp of unsavory developers. To great national publicity he had enraged capitalist J. P. Morgan by busting up his Northern Securities railroad holding company in 1902. Five years later, however, Roosevelt placated Morgan by permitting U.S. Steel to absorb the Tennessee Coal and Iron Company with no antitrust law repercussions. Roosevelt cracked big business, but he didn't break it. His image as a trustbuster rested as much on his bravado as his deeds.

There was another piece to the puzzle outside the U.S. borders but sitting on its coasts. Robber barons had found a seat at the President's table since Grant's day, but with McKinley as host, imported treats made their appearance. By the end of the Spanish-American War, the United States had acquired Samoa, Guam, the Hawaiian Islands, and the Philippine Islands in the Pacific; had made Cuba its protectorate; and intervened in the Dominican Republic off its southeastern coast in the Caribbean. With the U.S. government protecting their interests, American industry expanded into and rapidly developed these regions. The Republic of Hawaii, for example, was annexed by McKinley because American business smelled the sweet potential of its sugar crop. After spurring a war with Colombia to free its colony of Panama and then helping to establish it as a republic, Roosevelt bought a ten-mile-wide strip of land there to build a canal that would make the American shipping trade more efficient and profitable. Teddy declared it could be done, and the world believed him.

There had never been a President like Roosevelt. The youngest man to assume the position, he was also the first to be physically active and he regularly preached to his fellow Americans on the virtues of exercise. Other Presidents fished or rode horses; Teddy rowed, boxed, climbed, played tennis, and swam. His ascendance converged with a new industry that would shape the new century and alter civilization's own perception of itself: the "moving picture show." During the eight Roosevelt years, the technology became accessible to even the poorest of immigrants in America. In ornate wood and metal boxes in city streets and arcades, the "nickelodeon" was a wonder to all. For five cents a series of "moving pictures" could be glimpsed through a glass viewer as the patron turned a knob. It became a brilliant vehicle for dramatizing the "Teddy" persona and further building his celebrity cult. Other Presidents had been seen in still images, but Roosevelt's picture literally moved.

William Howard Taft had first come into the public consciousness when he was laying the cornerstone of a civil society in the Philippines. As Roosevelt's War Secretary, he was then sent to quell native troubles in Panama and Cuba for American interests and oversaw the building of the Panama Canal. Despite a misperception that he was unfriendly to organized labor, Taft had a genuinely progressive spirit with a conservative sensibility. He felt that it was duty to fight the "cruel injustice" and "race feeling" committed against African Americans; he believed that "intelligent" women shouldn't be denied the right to vote; he sympathized with the fears and working conditions of the immigrant poor; but he always exercised caution against doing too much too quickly.

At heart Will was judicious. Above all else he honored the laws of the land. To his thinking, slow and careful effort must be made to consider all aspects of an issue before changing laws. He would indeed "bust" the trusts as Roosevelt did. In fact, in his one term Taft would bring ninety suits against trusts. In his two terms, Roosevelt brought only forty-four. It was just that Taft didn't make a lot of noise about doing it.

Roosevelt knew that a good story or picture could often move emotions and perceptions more quickly than the dullness of reality. He pushed the Meat Inspection Act and the Pure Food and Drug Act through Congress, for example, just after Upton Sinclair's *The Jungle,* a popular novel set in the filthy Chicago slaughterhouses, became a national bestseller. Roosevelt posed for publicly released photographs wearing informal, rugged sportswear—a first for Presidents. It was no secret that Roosevelt was a member of the elite ruling class of the old eastern Establishment and even the most exclusive club at the most exclusive of American institutions, Harvard University. That reality was transcended when a picture of him driving a horse over a fence or a story about him boxing in the White House was printed. Taft coming after Roosevelt was like short, bald John Adams coming after monumental, bewigged George Washington. If Teddy was a lean boy wonder, Will was a marzipan sugarplum.

The visual image of Taft simply overpowered rational facts. No matter how many inches of ink were devoted to the eight years and thousands of miles he had spent journeying the globe for his nation, it was the inert caricature of 350-pound "Big Bill" that earned him public recognition. Fat people, it was assumed, were kind. Guided by judicial responsibility, Taft was assiduous in ensuring basic liberties as he structured a colonial government in the Philippines. It was far easier, however, to grasp it as a tropical adventure of Christian benevolence toward exotic "little brown brothers." On the campaign trail the fat man's frequent smile and laugh translated as confidence and happiness. No reporters wondered if this man who widely acknowledged that his driving ambition was to be chief justice was now worried or depressed about having been pressed into the presidency.

Taft had no fire in his belly for the job and no special vision of where to lead his country. Acutely aware that he would never fit into Teddy's David-fighting-Goliath costume, he didn't even try. Will hadn't actively pursued the presidency, and he wasn't going to act as if he had. Indeed, analysts might conclude that a docile Will had displayed passive-aggressive behavior toward Teddy in the last weeks before the election by ignoring Roosevelt's unsolicited advice to stop playing golf because the common man viewed it as a rich man's game. Taft promised to continue the Roosevelt program—but he would not give up golfing.

If the press and public braced for four years of less colorful copy, Taft's inertia was not unappealing to big business and its Republican proponents. Teddy's eventual intent to enact a "square deal for every working man and every working woman" would threaten the wealthy who most benefited from the status quo. While he found support for his rhetoric among newer "insurgent" Republicans from western and farm states, the old guard that still ruled Congress feared that the cowboy routine had been increasingly uncontrollable. Too many reforms and changes to the laws could stir up the small but strong socialist sentiments out there. After eight years of Roosevelt forcing the government to actively regulate business and, in the process, pushing presidential powers just beyond their constitutional limits, the vision of a sugarplum President was welcome.

Roosevelt seemed not to take this personally. He may have privately regretted his impulsive promise on election night 1904 not to run for a third term, but he knew he would irrevocably damage his status if he broke that promise; the risk of being called a liar—and perhaps even losing the election as a result—was not worth it. While cultivating an air of effortless spontaneity, Roosevelt was a genius at cloaking his methodical intention. He had been able to enact much of the reform legislation with his blustery bullying, waving his proverbial warrior's "big stick" as if leading a new American revolution! In fact, by using the government to force at least some industry concessions to labor, he had all along sought to avert socialism.

Once Taft was inaugurated, Teddy would go to Africa and hunt big game for a year. As his admirers bemoaned the sunset of his brilliant presidency, Roosevelt apostles humbly pointed out that this only underscored what a man of honor he was. Even if it meant making the supreme sacrifice of retiring, Roosevelt would be true to his word. Some of the faithful—most notably William Howard Taft himself—felt that Roosevelt was denying his countrymen the blessing of his leadership. The next best scenario was to run a candidate who received Roosevelt's blessing on the promise of maintaining the Roosevelt agenda. Well, concluded the outgoing President's family, friends, and colleagues, it might not be ideal, but Taft would have to suffice. There was never any question in their minds that the only reason Taft became President was that Roosevelt said he could. And Roosevelt expressed faith that Taft would do as he promised. He never knew Taft to be ungrateful—even when he was given gifts he hadn't asked for. If it was clear to those gathered in the Taft mansion that Will and Teddy were different personalities, their bond nevertheless suggested their accord on just what the promise to "continue reforms" meant.

It must have been equally obvious to the Longworths, Herrons, and Tafts that the incoming First Lady was as tactical in her competitiveness and self-conscious of her status as the outgoing President. Jealous of each other's influence over Will, their mutual antipathy would only intensify, and pride would prevent either from seeking a peace. Hammering out a compromise between conservatives and progressives on reform policy for the sake of Republican unity would be more easily obtained than taming the antagonism between Will's wife and best friend. When the Taft White House shunted Roosevelt's people, Teddy attributed this trampling of his kingmaker prerogatives to a wife meddling in her husband's work; Nellie was not his idea of the proper American woman. He would turn vengeful. Nellie saw Teddy's sense of entitlement as arrogant interference with her husband's duty. Her resentment of both his support and his criticism of the Taft White House ballooned into total aversion of all things Roosevelt. To her, Teddy was the antithesis of a real friend.

Without a mediator to force a truce, the mysterious alchemy of emotional animosities can destroy the strongest of political parties, ruin the most innocent of players and their best-laid plans, and redirect the course of history. And Will Taft was a judge, not a broker. Other presidential elections turned on issues like the economy, war, and scandal; the next one would be won and lost on ego as much as reform. Nellie Taft frequently anticipated the future with an imagination that tended to race toward the worst-case scenario. But even she could not imagine the disaster to come four years from this very night.

■

After Roosevelt's telegram of congratulations was received by Taft, the new President-elect wired back a message that said it all: "It is your administration that the victory approves."

If, once it was clear that Taft had won, Alice Roosevelt Longworth felt she was in enemy territory, Nellie was equally uneasy. She hadn't approved Will's telegram to Teddy before it was sent. She usually reviewed all of his important communications. With Alice right there, however, the notion of Nellie rewriting the telegram to somehow reflect her opinion that Will won the election in spite of Roosevelt would have been a call to arms. Nellie knew that Alice would report every innuendo and fact of this night to Teddy the next morning. And Alice knew that Nellie knew. Once again, Nellie was anxious instead of joyous.

The cheers and the band music outside beckoned the victor. His voice was hoarse from endless days on the whistle-stop campaign. He went outside from the foyer to the top step to thank the crowd. Nellie watched from the open door as Will delivered a brief speech that concluded with his pledge to be "a worthy successor of Theodore Roosevelt."

The remark surely sent her blood pressure up. Throughout the campaign she had routinely excised Will's speeches of reverential references to Teddy. It was all the worse coming in Taft's first moment of glory. Even sensitive Will should have felt secure enough that he wouldn't be accused of ingratitude if he failed to mention that cursed name—Roosevelt. The remarks were certain to be quoted directly in the papers. Remembering the crowd of reporters there, however, she instinctively assumed an adoring smile for Will. She had learned her lesson five months earlier on these same steps, on Notification Day.

That day she offered her opinion without a trace of rehearsal; she confessed her support for the suffragette's desire to vote, but opposition to permitting women to run for public office! This from a woman who had openly declared her determination to wed a man whom she could help make President and who would have to accept her as an equal partner in his career's decisions. Politics had taught Nellie irony. Just how "worthy" would Will think the American people considered Roosevelt had they read that private letter he wrote suggesting that if drafted he would break his promise not to seek a third term? That he was, essentially, a liar about his ambitions.

Since her Gilded Age youth, Nellie had been quietly observing not only Presidents but their wives as well. The women appeared as substantial as sweet custard. In the national curio cabinet Edith Roosevelt was maternal goddess, Ida McKinley sentimental invalid, Frances Cleveland bride doll, Carrie Harrison grandma horticulturist, Crete Garfield noble widow, Lucy Hayes Methodist saint, and Julia Grant beribboned fussbudget. Not since the Civil War when "meddling" Mary Lincoln intruded the political club had editors rebuked and socialites snubbed a lady of the White House. After Mrs. Lincoln's overt political machinations, the ladies of the White House could not be lured from the Blue Room. Each one since Lucy Hayes in 1877, for example, avoided the slightest suggestion of endorsing the Women's Christian Temperance Union. Instead, when Lucy Hayes refused to serve alcohol or Frances Cleveland filled her glass with Apollonaris, a presidential secretary would lecture troublemaking lady reporters to respect a woman's right to run her own house—only incidentally the White House—and the wise wives of America quietly winked back. These wives abhorred that appellation created by the newspapers—"First Lady of the Land": it suggested a woman who had a responsibility to set an example for her country and be involved in public life. Dolley Madison had stood as the emulated legend for exactly one full century of successors, and all the candy boxes, powder compacts, and ice cream containers that carried her image never used that vulgar title.

What if there was a First Lady involved in social welfare projects and patronage, one who edited speeches and insisted on inspecting public institutions with the President instead of being sent off to a ladies' tea, or who had her own plan to develop a public land space, or even publicly prompted federal policy?

Nellie, however, had also taken tea behind closed doors. She knew that Lucy Hayes actually held rabidly anti-immigrant views, that Ida McKinley's belief in missionary work factored into the President's decision to retain the Philippines, and that Edith Roosevelt could render powerless a public official who failed to pass her moral superiority standards.

Imagine how the public would react to a First Lady who drank beer, smoked cigarettes, and played poker?

Coming out onto the front landing with Will to wave at the crowd of syncophants, loyal supporters, admirers, and curious observers, Nellie would have had her first steady gaze at them, with a view illuminated by torchlights. This moment was the realization of a dream borne and nurtured long before she had met a Roosevelt or married a Taft. From her current perspective on the top step of the Taft mansion, Nellie could see that cramped three-story gray brick row house across the street. There is no record of her thoughts as she stood there looking into the night, but she had envisioned this very sight some three decades before, in that very house where she had grown up. Back then, Nellie Herron had been stuck in the middle.

As they turned to reenter the house, Will paused, his saucy blue eyes twinkling as he beamed a loving smile at his Nellie. He insisted that she enter before him. She did. Finally, she was first.

34366000010810

One

First Lady of the Land (1861–1878)

Nothing in my life reaches the climax of human bliss I felt
when, as a girl of sixteen, I was entertained at the White House.
—HELEN "NELLIE" HERRON TAFT

To write about one's childhood," Nellie Taft cautiously stated in her memoirs, "is not easy." First she explained she didn't have any memories that were "sufficiently 'early' to have any special value." Then, when she admitted to having a "score" of childhood stories, she decided that they were "hardly worth relating." In what she attempted to pass off as self-deprecation, her reason for keeping her childhood to herself was that it was "quite commonplace."

A superficial glance at her early years would suggest privilege and comfort. It was deceiving. In fact, it was so "not easy" for her to turn back that she kept her childhood to herself. It was in those early years that all the conflicting emotions, ambitions, insecurities, and self-definitions that characterized her as a public figure were set. As always, it began with her parents.

Her father was a brilliant lawyer who could probably have been elected President had his wife "allowed" him to pursue a path to that office as his best friend and a college friend both successfully did. After John had completed the folly of one term as a state senator, Harriet Herron would not relent in her opposition to his taking any further public service posts until five of their six daughters were married off. John's later stint as a U.S.

district attorney lasted only four years. Otherwise, his life was spent working to support the vision she had for herself and her daughters as being part of the Cincinnati upper class. Nothing was more important to John Herron than keeping Harriet Herron happy, and nothing was more important to her than keeping up appearances—despite the anxiety it created over their financial stability. Yet even when she was living the life she thought was best, Harriet would complain. The day after Christmas one year, she wrote that "John is spending it at his office where most of his holidays are spent, engaged in the usual problem of making ends meet at the close of the year."[1]

John was born on May 10, 1827, in Shippensburg, Pennsylvania. His great-grandfather, Francis Herron, had emigrated from County Wexford, Ireland, ninety-seven years earlier, settling in the Pequa Valley, so any trace of a brogue had long faded from the family. John's father, Francis, died when he was fourteen, but the son dutifully made frequent visits from Ohio to his mother, the former Jane Wills, in Lancaster, Pennsylvania, until her death in 1877.[2]

Attending Miami University in Oxford, Ohio, where he became president of the Theta Pi fraternity, John befriended Benjamin Harrison (as President of the United States, it was Harrison who would name Herron to the only appointed public office he held, that of district attorney). A loyal alumnus, he would serve as chairman of the university's board of trustees for fifty years, cultivate potential faculty to build its prestige, and preside over its founding-day celebration. That a woman's gymnasium was later named for him was ironic in light of his belief that "women should never sweat; they might perspire a little bit, become a trifle moist, but never sweat." Of all his daughters it would be Nellie who consistently defied such old-fashioned notions and eventually did so in such dramatic fashion as to seem to be proving a point to him about women's capabilities.[3]

After reading for the law, Herron leased office space in Cincinnati and opened a sole practice. Unable to afford the rent alone, on January 8, 1850, he took in another young attorney with whom he began a lifelong bond. It was a friendship that would prove decisive in shaping the direction of Nellie's ambitions. Herron was a man "of good habits, education, and mind—a good fellow, by accounts and by appearance," according to the diary of his new friend, Rutherford B. Hayes. The duo helped found Cincinnati's Literary Society, and when "Ruddy" was dating Lucy Webb, he even had her stand a "cross-examination" by Herron, who had guessed correctly that they were engaged. "I am inclined to think he is in the same interesting predicament," Hayes surmised, regarding John's lady friend Harriet Collins.[4]

John and Harriet married on March 7, 1854, in the Cleveland home of her brother, William Collins. Lawyer, banker, and later director of the Lake Shore Railroad and East Cleveland Railroad, Willie had come to Ohio to pursue business opportunities a year before with Harriet, their brother Isaac, and widowed mother Maria Clinton. They had migrated from the family seat of Lowville in western New York where, as descendants of the town's founders, they had been the recognized social leaders. Harriet had been born there on September 15, 1833, when her father, Elijah, was forty-seven years old.

The great-great-grandson of a Bramford, England, immigrant, Elijah Collins had been a Democratic congressman from New York's twentieth district, a seat his son Willie later held, both serving one term each (1823–25 and 1847–49, respectively), long enough to earn the title of "honorable." While Willie would become a Republican when that party ran its first presidential candidate (1856), Isaac remained a Democrat, even serving as a delegate to the convention that nominated Samuel Tilden, who ran against Hayes. A Yale graduate, he later became a judge.

Elijah's death had left the family in genteel poverty. In an era when a girl's status was defined by her father's prestige, it was especially hard for fifteen-year-old Harriet. She soon found refuge in heraldry. Her maternal grandfather, Isaac Clinton, was a Revolutionary War hero and minister. Through her grandmother Charity Welles, however, Harriet boasted an astonishing ancestry of Saxon, Celtic, Nordic, Gallic, Roman, and even biblical kings, saints, and nobility, documented in medieval church records and ancient castle guides. Cincinnati elite might whisper about how Harriet strained to keep up, but she always had her blueblood. Nellie found her mother's ancestor worship ridiculous. Only late in life could she be coaxed into joining a heraldic group by a cousin who was lonely for company.[5]

The newlywed Herrons first lived on Longworth Street in the city, but by the time Nellie was a year old, they were boarding in the East Walnut Hill house run by the Walt Whitmore family—"a beautiful place," John thought. The Civil War was raging, and the city came under martial law when the Confederate Army approached southern Ohio after taking nearby Lexington and Frankfort, Kentucky. Nellie remembered none of the war. Shortly after another move to Fourth and Broadway, the Herrons settled permanently on Pike Street. Her earliest memory was of sitting on the steps there, watching Union soldiers marching home from the war in a parade celebrating the peace when she was four years old.[6]

Harriet would give birth to eleven children. Helen Louise was the third of the eight children who survived. Born two months after the firing on Fort Sumter, on June 2, 1861, she was always called "Nellie." Eldest child, Emily, born in 1856, was showered with attention by her parents, and Nellie, seeming to resent this, remained distant from her. It was Jane—"Jennie"—born in 1858, whom Nellie turned to as an older sister and confidante. Two more girls, one born before and the other after Nellie, died in infancy. What effect this had on her can only be surmised, but the death of these two sisters left an age difference of three years between Nellie and the next oldest and next youngest, further reinforcing her easily ignored standing of—as she called it—"number three" and feeling alone in a family large even by Victorian standards. Eventually it seemed to forge a tighter bond between her and the next child, Maria, born in 1864.

Weeks after Maria's birth, Harriet was again pregnant and later that year bore William, the first of two sons. The second, John "Jack," came in 1870 after the death of yet another baby daughter. Finally, there was the patient Eleanor, Nellie's junior by thirteen years, and the beloved "littlest sister,"

Lucy (named after Hayes's wife), an astounding eighteen years younger. It was from Jennie, Maria, and Eleanor that Nellie found her greatest support. Despite the children's age span of twenty-three years, there were always at least six other siblings in the house throughout Nellie's years at home.[7]

Nellie would affectionately recall Harriet's "exceedingly keen wit and a mind alert to the humor in every situation" in the household, and especially recalled how she "made her family circle a very amusing and interesting one in which to grow up." That Harriet maintained her "stimulating personality" in light of her enormous responsibilities of motherhood was all the more remarkable to her daughter. Without nursemaids or nannies, Harriet raised her brood. "So many children to nurse," Nellie recalled, "to scold, to sew for and, sometimes, to cook for—in a word, to bring up on a small income."

If Harriet embraced the traditional role of motherhood, however, she held John responsible for not just the family's well-being but the lifestyle that she expected for them. Remarkably, within two short years John Herron had gone from sleeping on a hard mattress in a corner of the small offices he had shared with Hayes to being named junior partner at King & Anderson. Eventually, he would be lead attorney at Herron, Gatch & Herron, in practice with his son Will. Regardless of how prestigious his standing in the legal community, though, John never made enough money to keep Harriet happy.

Whether it was to avoid her querulous demands or the fact that he was genuinely trying to drum up more business, John always seemed to be at the office—weekends, evenings, and holidays. There was no evidence of marital discord, and the long range of their parenthood certainly attested to a physical intimacy between them. Lonely for his company, Harriet was frequently depressed while her determination to keep up appearances on an uncertain income left her anxious. Silently observing her mother through large brown eyes, Nellie would never voice her disapproval of the role of a woman as exemplified by Harriet, but at some early point in her life she determined to diverge from it.

John Herron remarked that he spent money on his family in the winter and went into debt by the summer. He rented a fashionable cottage on the eastern seaboard or rooms in the cool mountain resorts for his wife and children, although he usually stayed in the city to work. He would hire servants when Harriet wanted to entertain. His sons would receive Yale and Harvard educations, and his daughters were presented to Cincinnati society as debutantes in expensive and beautiful gowns. Still, he was willing to go into debt to keep his family circulating among and behaving like the elite set. The power of perception overtook reality for Harriet. Her sensitivity to suggestions that meeting their financial obligations was anything but effortless was evident even with the family. A wealthy aunt offered to pay half of Lucy's expenses if she accompanied her to Paris, Eleanor reported to Nellie, "although she knew how proud Mama is." Regardless of the relief it would have provided the Herrons, while giving their daughter a social season in the City of Lights, Eleanor continued, "Of course, Mama wouldn't let her do that, but Papa seems willing."

Nellie fully absorbed the contradictory messages about money, status, and appearance that her parents unwittingly instilled throughout her early life. Outside the Herron home Nellie was supposed to enjoy all the comforts and privileges of the wealthy class as a natural part of her entitlement. Inside the house, however, the monetary and emotional sacrifices were obvious: the ever-absent father trying to keep a step ahead of the debt, the toll on her mother's otherwise lighthearted nature, the stress on the young daughters to keep abreast of the latest whim of the fashionables. Nellie was expected to behave coolly, even grandly, in the arena of great wealth, yet she carried within her heart a sense of guilt about driving her father further into debt and having to work that much harder. The overall effect of this was to breed a repressed nervousness in Nellie's very core. For many a decade it would seem that she rarely experienced genuine relaxation.

Being an anxious debutante in summer silks offered greater hope for a different life than did the dull reality of middle-class tedium in the winter. Arctic blasts of wind coming off the nearby river left snowdrifts banked against the three-story Herron house. The structure was utterly indistinguishable from the rows of houses that flanked it, its somber interiors augured by the exterior's grim gray brick and the sad little yard before it, surrounded by black iron fencing and gate. Even when Nellie was inside the house visualizing she was elsewhere, she couldn't escape the intrusion of reality. Her life in the gray house, she later recalled, was "marred by an impression of the clatter and clang" of harnessed workhorses pulling heavy wagons from the river landing up the steep, cobblestone hill, at the bottom of which sat the Herron home. It is no surprise then that her "pleasantest associations" of Cincinnati were in the "striking and imposing" Anderson and Sinton mansions across Pike Street at the top of the hill.

Despite the presence of his ten sons, Larz Anderson's redbrick house always seemed to have "an air of great dignity," but to Nellie the Sinton mansion was the greater of the two. The white colonial mansion had columns, a manicured greensward, and clipped topiary, and she considered it "one of the most beautiful residences" in the United States. In 1873, when she was twelve, Nellie took an interest in the details of Annie Sinton's wedding to Charley Taft, making him an instant millionaire by inheritance. As an adolescent she would be among the many girls invited to come for an informal luncheon several hours before one of Annie Taft's famous evening parties. Becoming familiar with the layout of the mansion, as some of the older girls carried their gowns upstairs to dress, she must also have drawn comparisons with her own home. Nellie never plainly or confidentially stated what she really thought of Annie, but a certain degree of envy would be easily understood.

If Harriet's efforts to integrate her daughters among the young misses and maidens of Cincinnati's upper class was the motivation for enrolling Nellie and her sisters at the most fashionable girl's school in town, she was also providing them with an extraordinarily in-depth education. In a large, old Victorian house on Seventh Street, Edith Nourse of Maine set out to "develop high qualities of character" in her female students. Called "the nursery," the Miss Nourse School for Girls counted the city's daughters of privilege in its roster. Nellie may have been "number three" at home, but when she entered the Nourse school at five years old, she was but one of one hundred. And anonymity at school proved a godsend for the introverted Nellie.

Losing herself in reading and writing, learning numbers and arithmetic, she became an excellent and enthusiastic student, while her skills at drawing left much to be desired. Enrolled in the "primary department" until she was ten years old, Nellie also had weekly lessons in history, mythology, and (to provide "powers of observation and stimulating their curiosity") elemental science. It was when the map was pulled down for geography lessons that her first interest in exploring life beyond Cincinnati was stirred, but a more definitive desire was inspired in her by teacher George Schneider, who came to instruct Nourse students from the Cincinnati Music School. As Nellie proudly recalled many years later, "Music was the absorbing interest of my life in those days, the inspiration of all my dreams and ambitions."

Nellie may have relished the solitude of the city's Mercantile Library, where she studied, or doing calisthenics in the school's "perfectly private playground," but once John Herron bought a piano and hired an instructor to give her vocal and instrumental lessons, his daughter spent all her free time at home banging out her scales so loudly that the entire neighborhood could hear her. Such indulgence—the sort of obvious symbol of wealth that Harriet tended to pursue—spoke not only of her father's respect for Nellie but the level of her passion for music.

While she studied music, however, Nellie continued on an academic course. In the "high department" for girls older than eleven, she took English literature, two branches of natural sciences, and—after excelling in French—German, Latin, and Greek. All of it was intended to make "fit" the graduating young lady of eighteen "for the Harvard Examinations, the Cincinnati University or any college open to women."[8]

There were few outlets available to an upper-middle-class American girl of the late 1870s that would permit her to stand above and beyond her peers. For a young woman with Nellie's interests those possibilities included further education, advancing her study of music into a profession, publishing poetry or novels, leadership in social reform, or earning a salary as a teacher, perhaps a nurse. Convention had it, however, that she find comfort and security as a wife. That there was no example, no compromise, no tradition of perhaps achieving recognition while also being a wife would be the conflict that sent her into emotional turmoil over the next few years.

In looking at her parents' marriage, Nellie had clear evidence that a wife could negatively influence the direction of her husband's career. When Ruddy Hayes had been governor, he had offered Herron a superior court judgeship to fill a vacancy left by Alphonso Taft. John responded that he had to "go for money and leave glory to others." The only glory he took was directorship of Longview Hospital, a state mental institution.

Knowing how much John longed to serve on the bench, Hayes offered him another judgeship before he left his governorship. To this John Herron responded poignantly: "I wish I could accept it. I may never have such another chance. . . . should like the labor. . . . It would benefit me. Like other things when I want them, I can't get them—and when I can get them, I can't take them. At present I don't have one dollar coming in from a single investment that I have made and so I must look to my profession to support my family. And I don't feel that it would be safe to borrow to meet current expenses."[9]

The disappointment her father felt at passing up the judgeships left a lingering impression with Nellie. It also convinced her that the bench could never be anyplace for a husband whose wife had ambitions of her own for him and their family.

John was a delegate to the 1876 Cincinnati convention that nominated Ruddy for the presidency, but Lucy Hayes seemed to garner as much national attention. "How does Lucy like the present publicity given to her face and life?" John quipped in one letter to Ruddy. Once Hayes was President, John would successfully recommend the "honest and . . . deserving" M. A. Jacobi, editor of a Cincinnati German newspaper, artist E. F. Andrews, and his own son-in-law Charles Anderson for federal jobs. For himself, however, John Herron asked only for an invitation to sleep at the White House. His wish would be granted, and—along with Harriet and other family members—Nellie would come along.

The connection between John, Harriet, Ruddy, and Lucy was intense and caring: Lucy cared for John's elderly mother, Harriet was midwife to Lucy in childbirth, Ruddy lent John money, John made a loan to Lucy, Harriet put Ruddy up when he was in town, and Lucy calmed Harriet after a family death. "I have had no other friend with whom there has been such freedom of intimacy," Harriet said of Lucy, telling her that all the Herron children had "genuine love" for her and the President. Nellie called the First Lady "Aunt Lucy" and signed herself as "ever your affectionate niece."[10]

No matter how the sixteen-year-old Nellie might feel connected to Mrs. Hayes, it was the First Lady's namesake, the "littlest sister," however, whose "bewitching" ways captured the fancy of the President. To honor little Lucy, he asked the Herrons to bring the seven-week-old infant to the White House with them when they joined the celebration of the Hayes's silver wedding anniversary. His "little angel," Hayes suggested, could then be baptized in the White House. To add insult to injury for Nellie, her sister Jennie, recently married to Charles Anderson, one of the ten sons of the millionaire clan across Pike Street, was also to be an honored White House guest.

That Nellie was tagging along seemed an afterthought. Still, she felt "intense excitement." In her acceptance letter to Aunt Lucy, Nellie revealed her insecurity about emerging into a world as grand as the White House and her sense of neglect as a middle child in a large family:

"I feel very much complimented that you should have remembered me in the preparations for the holiday festivities. I have been in some doubts as to whether it would do for me to emerge from the chrysalis of school girl existence even for a short time into the butterfly life of young ladyhood, but the temptation has proved too strong for me, and it will give me great pleasure to accept your invitation. Never having known any position but that of number three, I am prepared to enjoy any superior advantages exceedingly."[11]

Before arriving in Washington on December 27, 1877, Nellie filled herself with the negative disappointment she already seemed to have experienced all too frequently. Not yet socially "out" as a debutante, she knew she wouldn't be able to attend the "brilliant parties" in Washington. If her brief sojourn there meant a social life limited to Sunday hymn-singing and the family suppers that followed formal holiday receptions, it was "fortunately, for my peace of mind, [that] the Hayes lived very quietly, so it was not so trying to have to devote myself to the sights of the Capital like any other tourist." She was permitted downstairs to glimpse the New Year's Day Reception, at which the President and First Lady greeted thousands of citizens. In his December 28 diary entry, President Hayes recorded that Nellie Herron helped make "the house alive with laughter, fun, and music."

The Herron family's week at the White House was soon over, but it would make a more indelible mark on history than just a christening for a baby or an honor for a bride. In fact, it would set Nellie Herron on her course with destiny. Though she was barely old enough to recall the ludicrous presidential candidacy of Victoria Woodhull in 1872, Nellie had nevertheless been deeply inculcated with the usefulness of social conformity; she would not have believed it was possible, let alone wise, for a woman to be elected President.

As would prove true with most of the decisions in her life, however, Nellie's thinking was never entirely conventional. It was during her stay at the White House that she realized that there might be a *third* way to fuse her ambition for recognition while achieving the societal expectations of marriage. It would be thirty years before she publicly admitted to it in an interview with journalist George Griswold Hill. After "so enjoyable" a time at the White House, he revealed in a national magazine, Nellie Herron returned to Cincinnati in the new year of 1878 and "confided to some of her girl friends that it was her purpose to marry only 'a man destined to be President of the United States.' "[12]

And if her friends knew anything about Nellie Herron, they knew that she took extremely seriously everything she thought and said about herself.

Two

Beer, Cigarettes, and Gambling (1878–1884)

There is no doubt about it, I am very exacting and at the same time unwilling to make the least advance. . . . I must have something to take me out of my own thoughts—something active to do. . . . I have thought that a woman should be independent and not regard matrimony as the only thing to be desired in life.

—NELLIE HERRON

It was, she said, "the blues" which "calls forth my writings." In a small diary that she kept between 1879 and 1884, from the age of eighteen to twenty-five, Nellie Herron revealed herself more unguardedly than anywhere else. It was more than the usual sort of Victorian teenage diary of social notices, romantic updates, and gossip. In her diary she revealed frightening and hopeful projections, myriad insecurities, ideals of marital partnership, personal aspirations, and spiraling tendencies to depression and anxiety. In finding a place to distance herself somewhat from her darkest thoughts, where she could then try to analyze herself more objectively and thus return to a rational sensibility, Nellie also revealed an unrelenting perfectionism and harsh self-criticism. She wrote of her diary, "If anyone should see this, what an idiot I would seem." In an age that predated Freudian psychology, the diary became the lone solace in the world for the emotions of a teenager blossoming into an adult. Although written when she was young, the lengthy document is a blueprint of a lifetime of habits, characteristics, and thinking patterns—these both helpful and hurtful.

Graduation from Miss Nourse's school had come in June 1879. "To one who feels as I do that I will probably never marry," Nellie wrote forlornly, "the leaving of school seems like settling down in life." There were limited options for a girl like Nellie Herron if she hoped to follow the social expectations of an upper-middle-class white family in the latter nineteenth century. The first inevitability was to "come out" in society as a debutante, signaling the period in which she would now actively be considered in the marriage market, making her accessible to potential suitors at social functions. "It is odd to think that I am really 'coming out,' about to arrive at that state of young ladyhood which I have always dreaded," she wrote in her first entry, on September 5. "I am actually prepared to receive attentions and offers and to wait around calmly to see if my future life will adjust itself."

Nellie knew exactly the sort of man she wanted to marry, and he would have to run through some rigorous testing by her before she would even entertain accepting an offer of marriage if it came. The impossible odds against having all this line up, her diary shows, depressed Nellie. Once she managed to earn some self-esteem by her own efforts of intellect, however, enough confidence filled her that the seemingly impossible task ahead inspired her to meet the challenge she set for herself.

Society women were not supposed to work, pursue a career, or earn even nominal salaries of their own, before or after marriage. That would be an embarrassment to either her parents or her husband, a suggestion that they needed the money. There was no thought of what the woman with aspirations was to do. In 1880 America, most women and men did not have high school educations. The number of women who had college educations was even smaller, and those with any sort of graduate degree in a profession were infinitesimal.

These realities were the core of Nellie Herron's mental turmoil and painful stress, the heart of the constant conflicts within her. "I am very anxious to be busy and accomplish something," she wrote just over two months after graduation, "for it seems as if the serious business of life were beginning." By ultimately following her own ideas on what was right for her, the tough character that later marked Nellie in public life began to emerge from the privileged, intelligent, but insecure girl she was as a teenager.

Seeing the situation both optimistically and pragmatically, she realized that her greatest love and greatest training was in music. If she could somehow find a job using her love of music, it would make her "so happy," abate her depressive tendencies, and distract her self-doubts. It would help in "earning a living should I ever be obliged to make a career of it." She was willing to "make almost any sacrifice to continue with it." Earning a living as a musician would be ideal, but she was not yet expert enough to do this. She knew she needed more training, and she also knew the state of her father's finances. "The prospect of not being able to take lessons makes me almost miserable. Yet I feel as if the sum of money were too great to be spent for a pastime, for such Papa cannot but regard it. . . . I have a good method, touch and some taste. My technical knowledge is small and with the college there is an opening here." In the meanwhile, she continued practicing intensely on her own.

Just before her debutante party in December 1879, Nellie broached the subject with her mother, suggesting that instead of spending money on the expensive gowns expected of her as a young socialite, her parents could let her intensify her musical education. Predictably, Harriet said music lessons were a "useless expense," that Nellie "must have" her new dresses.

Nellie promised to "brace up and try to have a good time." She admitted that "coming out has been my great big bear ever since I have been old enough to think of it," but once she had made her debut, Nellie realized she was capable of enjoying herself at some social events. She credited her bevy of girlfriends with helping to boost her confidence. Miss Herron was now moving in a moneyed crowd of fellow debs. Alice "Allie" Keys seems to have been a frequent companion who, gleaning from Nellie's diary, was properly modest and avidly pursuing a potential husband. Allie carried on a "desperate flirtation" with one John D., but Nellie decided he was "no more to be depended on than most fellows. Almost all are so insincere."

Nellie did not find any of the rich society boys in her circle attractive. She did not care if they excelled at football or the waltz, or whether they were headed off to Harvard or Yale in the autumn. "I hate boys and college youths and society young men," she wrote in one of the many dim assessments she made of them. "A man is not endurable until he is twenty-eight or thirty and not always then." There were "plenty of men" but "so few pleasant ones in Cincinnati."

Her attitude was, of course, caught up with her own sense of esteem. She had liked one boy, for example, who was "quite struck" with her, but "Nina Pugh has cut me out in the sweet youth's affections!" When some suitors called formally on her one night, she felt her "nervousness was truly ridiculous. . . . Imagine sitting up trembling so that I could hardly speak, as stupid as a hitching post, just because I had to converse for half an hour with three old fellows. . . . I would enjoy society if I could only get over my nervousness for after all I was not stupider than most of the girls and why should I not be able to talk as much. I reason and wonder and think the next time I will be composed and the next time am so miserably ill at ease that it is all I can do to appear embarrassed, to say nothing of attempting to appear at my best. I am going to try and overcome it by going [out] as much as possible and reading very little."

Indeed, Nellie pushed herself into constant activity as a way of warding off "the blues." She was a fair swimmer and excellent bowler. She took in baseball games. She played duets and quartets with friends, often to raise money for various charities. She cherished attending concerts of all kinds. Most men, she concluded, "do not like music and I can not be comfortable or feel in the mood at all if the person I am with is not enjoying himself." Nellie also began a lifelong passion for gambling at cards, improving her whist game by constant practice. Within two years Nellie would gleefully be reporting how she and friends "amused ourselves by playing poker for money for the rest of the evening"—fairly outrageous as a pastime for a Victorian debutante. She took in theater and opera, followed by supper club meals. Amateur theatrics became a favorite distraction, Nellie writing original pieces like "Woodcock's Lillie Game" and acting and staging the pieces for such causes as the local widow's home. By June when the show was over, however, she noted that there was "a considerable gap when it was all over and a lamentable dearth of subjects to think of this spring."

"I have not on the whole been very cheerful," she soon admitted again, "my natural disposition is not buoyant." The issue that plagued her the previous autumn returned. "I am beginning to want some steady occupation. I hate being such a good for nothing. . . . I should have some occupation that would require active work moving around and I don't know where to find it." Nellie hoped "to be of use to other people." She had no role in the home: "mama . . . unwilling to trust anything out of her house." Surveying her community, she felt she had "no way to do other good outside of home. . . . I have never taken any interest in church affairs from my feeling a lack of interest in the services of the Presbyterian Church." She had little sense of spirituality within herself. "I shall turn over a new leaf in that respect," she promised herself, "and hope that the chance will be given me to become of actual use in the world." She never did become active in church work.

Nellie came back to the fact that money was freedom and struck on a new idea to make cash. "I believe my greatest desire now is to write a book," she scribbled. "Write it I must confess for money—not that I think that I could ever write anything good, but because I do so want to be independent." She initially decided to pen a novel but couldn't settle on a setting. "America is humdrum as far as I am concerned. I lose all natural interest in a novel as soon as I find that the scene is laid in America." Ever since she had seen the global map at Miss Nourse's school, Nellie had been curious about the wider world. While her new ambition to travel to distant lands might have been born out of a desire to escape her miserable life, it was added to her list of things to accomplish.

That July, Nellie didn't make it out of America, but she did get out of Cincinnati. She joined friends at Yellow Springs, Ohio, including Annie Sinton Taft, the heiress who lived across the street. "[W]e are all rusticating up here doing absolutely nothing," she scribbled, "and I am reduced to a queer state of mind. I am blue as indigo." Swinging in a hammock when she was struck again with depression, Nellie couldn't fathom her emotions. When she decided it was her natural state of being, her mood worsened. "Is it any wonder I have the blues?" she wrote. "Anything but one's own nature can be remedied, but from oneself there is no escape. I am sick and tired of myself. I would rather be anyone else even some one who has not some advantages I have and I am only nineteen. I feel often as if I were fifty."

What triggered her further spiral came after her father made her join him at Narragansett, Rhode Island. On August 14, 1880, she recorded that throughout the summer she had "cried myself to sleep half the time." Nellie brightened considerably, however, after joining a group of rich Cincinnati acquaintances in a beach house, including Sallie Woolly, Bessie Jewett, and John Holmes. She played the piano for sing-alongs, beat most of them at cards, and developed an intense crush on Holmes. She felt he liked Sallie, however, and slinked away, spending long hours sleeping. Another boy asked her to play cards because Bessie had backed out of the game, but when Bessie changed her mind, Nellie cloistered herself with a book. When Holmes teased her "about being always asleep" and often shutting her eyes, she was deeply hurt. It "effectively shut me up," provoking further teasing as to "why I did not talk." She turned her anger into jealousy over "natural born flirt" Bessie. With three women in the house and one man, it was likely that Bessie felt the same way about Nellie at some point during the weekend.

Although Nellie, Sallie, and Bessie all made it to church services, their focus was clearly on having fun: eating clams, having their photographs taken, playing tennis and croquet, and sailing. The girls could write home about such harmless amusements without alarming their proper parents. Out of the clutches of Harriet for the first time in her life, however, Nellie seized on her freedom. She began smoking, and drinking, and stepped up her gambling.

The girl that Harriet Herron would undoubtedly have considered the "bad influence" was Sallie Woolley. Sallie was seasoned in concealing her talent for rolling smelly weed into papers and lighting and smoking it, mixing just enough whiskey into milk to give it "punch" but not so much that its odor could be detected, and winning cash in poker.

Nellie's experimentation with drinking alcohol, smoking cigarettes, and gambling at cards emerges in her diary records of her Newport vacation. Waiting in line for Sunday brunch at Billington's was especially gruesome, because this bad girls' club of three was all hung over from drinking on Saturday night. It was after their meal that Nellie and Sallie broke a rigid taboo enforced not by law but social ostracism. They hid themselves in "a little oasis framed by the rocks," and Nellie took her first puffs of the sinfully addictive tobacco that not even Bessie had the guts to try. Cigarette smoking by women in 1880, wrote historian Paula S. Fass, was limited to "prostitutes and women in liberated bohemian and intellectual sets."

"Sallie and I smoked a cigarette," Nellie confessed to her diary, "but all failed to change me from the stupid state I have been in." If cigarettes failed to lift Nellie's mood, as many said it would, she would keep trying. In fact, she became a lifelong cigarette smoker. While her skill at card games was not yet refined, she would persist in gambling and go on to win higher stakes.

The presence of men—a reminder of the expectations for marriage—seemed to curtail her fun. Three days after Holmes hurt her feelings, Nellie was wounded again. When a couple, Dudley and Eliza, joined the friends, the former cracked to the group, "Oh, you have no idea how entertaining Miss Eliza is in the moonlight. She never said a word all the way home." Holmes chimed in, "She talked about as much as Miss Herron does in daylight!" Humiliated, Nellie went to bed in a silent rage.

The mood changed, however, once Holmes departed the beach house. Again, Nellie, Sallie, and Bessie felt free to behave and speak freely. Harriet would have been horrified at the sight of Nellie in her wool bathing suit doing anything braver than dipping her toes, but with Sallie and Bessie she ran free in the ocean, gleefully knocked over by the heavy surf and having a "spirited discussion as to whether a girl is not acting under a mistaken sense of duty who makes a repugnant marriage to save her family from ruin." After another pitcher of "milk punch," she headed home.

Newport was at least a change of scenery for Nellie, but she was also beginning to get a taste of small adventure. Changing trains to head west, she recorded, "I got my first glimpse of New York City. We got out at Central Depot and took the elevated railway to Jersey City ferry. It was very much as I had expected and I did wish, as we flew along, that I could explore some of the wonders."

Nellie returned to Cincinnati with confidence. Even the train invigorated her faith in humanity again, for she was surprised at how nicely people treated her when she became sick along the way. After her summer experiences, she reaffirmed an important decision: She would devote herself to music and then, the following year, find employment. She would practice piano six hours a day, and it would "make me happier." The plan was "more firmly settled in my mind than any of the other plans I have framed and [it has] come from the persistent attacks of the blues which I have had this summer." Another shift had taken place. After beating two "foolish" men at poker, Nellie concluded that "money" was not as important as "brains."

That autumn of 1880, Nellie was made head of the household—marketing, cooking, washing, and cleaning—when her parents joined the Hayeses on a historic seventy-two-day trip, the first time a President went to the West Coast. The Herrons were gone through November. Feeling "lonely to be left without a man in the house" but "about to start a game of poker" with her inculcated younger siblings Jack and Maria, Nellie was surprised when a male friend, Fenton Lawson, dropped by. With her newfound confidence, she thought she would give flirtation a try, and she happily "seemed to rather succeed."

Over the next few months her confidence in dealing with men grew. There was a Dr. Branning, "an unmitigated ass that . . . matches my sense of the ludicrous." She felt "perfectly at home" with one Tom Mack, "which I never do with the men I admire most." She and Howard Hollister got into "an exceedingly sentimental conversation" about "dying for someone you loved." Within a moment, Nellie said, she was "all afire . . . as I am exceedingly romantic myself but [his remark] came across as an insult after and I accused him of it, that he was only trying to draw me out and making fun of me. 'Make fun of you,' he exclaimed. 'Why Miss Herron there is no one whose good opinion I value as much as yours.'" She would have liked to believe it, but she sensed male condescension. "I have yet to find the man I could fancy," she confessed, "perhaps because he has not fancied me." She found that she had a tendency to see too many "dislikes" in men and that these feelings would "seize" her uncontrollably.

If Nellie's refusal to compromise her ambition to find that "man who would be president" left her without a prospect, it also drove her back to self-criticism. She thought "my own diffident cold manner does not draw forth any warmth" in men. "What a shame that I have not learned to 'lead men on.'" She envied those who did. "Impulsiveness, if graceful, has the strangest attraction for me."

Still, Nellie preferred serious conversations with a "club" of friends including Sallie Woolley, Howard Hollister, and Tom Mack, with the latter two seeming to push the boundary of friendship toward dating. Also with them was the heiress Annie Taft. How it was that Nellie so closely befriended Annie is curious, especially since the latter and her husband, Charley Taft, were a dozen years older. It may have had something to do with Charley's younger brother, a Yale graduate recently returned to Cincinnati and working as a court reporter. His name was Will.

Like the Herrons, the Tafts looked out for one another. Charley and Annie recognized something in Nellie that might appeal to Will. A week before they hosted a dance in their mansion, Nellie was "surprised immensely" to receive an invitation from none other than Will Taft.

"Why he asked me I have wondered ever since," she wrote in her diary, "for it was his one invitation of the winter as he has not been anywhere and I know him very slightly though I like him very much." Whether or not the fellow was the potential husband to fulfill her dream of getting to the White House, Nellie did not have time to discover. At the dance Will was "attentive" to her but "not in the least devoted" and actually "very distant." She appreciated the bouquet he sent her all the more because he was "not accustomed to sending them."

Will had asked Nellie to the dance, it seems, as a favor to Charley or Annie. That no future dates were set seemed not to bother her, yet Nellie was notably irked when she learned that Will Taft found the pretty but empty-headed Sally Smith attractive. "I can not understand it," she admitted.

Still, early summer 1881 found Nellie bolder at flirting, unconcerned about what others thought, for example, of her sitting on her front steps with a man late at night. She liked a Mr. Sanders, "a tawny Adonis," who gave her a "thrilling excitement," about which she scribbled in the diary: "I will not amplify the details." At a July 4 party she happily found herself the only woman present and "had a good deal of fun." At another gathering Nellie was attracted to a "pleasant chatty" man who promised to "taste my Roman Punch which I said was an accomplishment of mine." While "comfortably established in the hammock" with a beau, she was "properly refrained."

Despite the flirting, however, Nellie still failed to find the sort of man she could marry. "I am very exacting," she penned, "so what wonder that I am not always satisfied." As summer went on, she again slipped into depression. "How useless most of my life is," she concluded. "I am so tired of it all." Depression, she decided, was "a nemesis which pursue [sic] some people relentlessly." When she comforted a friend who also suffered from depression, she noted it was "so sad that my eyes fill with tears when she talks of it." Not quite twenty years old, Nellie concluded that it was simply a "fatality" that one was born with. "Oh that I could keep always fresh the feelings that I have when she talks to me and I could never be so impatient and unsympathetic as I often am," she wrote.

She found no solace in organized religion. Although her family attended the Second Presbyterian Church, Nellie often felt that "the sermon did not do much good." Church attendance, she wrote, was an "obligation in the higher sense of the word!" She realized that she "certainly must be in a bad way" for not being "very believing" of what was said from the pulpit or of its provoking "any feeling of sympathy" for the tenets of her religion. Still, she had faith in something larger without believing in "orthodox" stories: "I seem to want to believe and think that I do without having any real belief." When, one night, musing about astrological constellations and "how little we could realize the immensity of it all," a friend asked, "You are not religious, are you?" Nellie responded carefully but simply, "I am not religious." After enduring yet another interminable Sunday church service, Nellie once again found "recreation in the shape of freezing punch."

Nellie's increasingly frequent references to alcoholic punch might suggest that drinking numbed her depression and calmed her anxiety. Throughout the decades of her life, however, there was never even a slightly veiled reference in her writings or those of others that she became intoxicated frequently or in any other way drank to excess. She did have a high tolerance for alcohol. Both of her parents had a taste for fine French champagne, aged Scottish whiskeys, fruity Italian red wines, and summer German whites. Harriet once wrote Hayes: "Speaking of 'good spirits,' I hope you have bottled up an extra supply for my use—I need, and am ready to make friends with them." On a later trip to New York, Nellie noticed that her father had "first taken drink" before meeting her for lunch, with "the effect merely of putting him in a good humor."[1]

That the proper Harriet Herron would serve and drink alcohol might seem incongruous by later preconceptions of the Victorian upper class. As cookbooks, etiquette guides, and newspaper advertisements prove, however, the moderate serving and drinking of cocktails encouraged in the

properly hospitable upper-class Victorian homes was a crucial step in helping to legitimize alcohol consumption for women. As was also made clear
in *Mrs. Beeton's Book of Household Management*, women were considered
somehow genetically impaired at mixing the perfect cocktail of sweet fla-
vors and bright colors. The lady who could "mix" a Brain Duster or Yankee Invigorator was indeed an equal of man. That Nellie Herron was
taking personal pride in her ability to make a superior punch spoke less of
an interest in becoming intoxicated than it did in making a statement of
her modern sense of feminine equality to men and her capability to run an
upper-class home.

Nellie Herron's drinking, however, extended beyond any amount
consumed by her mother to prove herself sophisticated. If her comfort
with the cocktail marked Nellie as a woman who believed herself as capable as a man, her love of beer indicated something far broader. Slipping out
to the boisterous public saloons and bars for steins of lager was neither
fashionable nor acceptable behavior for a teenage girl of Nellie's class. It
would have horrified her parents as well as any potential husbands of the
upper class. Yet it was here that Miss Herron made her stand. It was an unmistakable sign that she would defy authority and convention when and
how she wished—if only behind her parents' back.

Beer had already helped to define the unique character of Cincinnati.
The city's tens of thousands of immigrant, first- and second-generation
Germans grew up with beer as the beverage of choice in their homes, but
much of the city's working- and lower-middle-class men were gathering at
local beer halls, pubs, and saloons after a long day of physical labor.

By the time Nellie Herron was born, Vine Street in Over-the-Rhine,
the German downtown neighborhood of Cincinnati, offered more than
one hundred different beer halls, saloons, and gardens, its fresh beer sup-
plied by the thirty-six nearby breweries, carried in wood barrels through
the cobblestone streets. For every resident some forty gallons of beer were
being consumed annually. In 1879, two years before Nellie entered her first
beer hall, Cincinnati's Morlein brewery ranked eighth in the nation in beer

production, turning out nearly 940,000 barrels. This was remarkable in a nation of 2,520 breweries and a beer production of 10 million barrels. When Carrie Nation came to Cincinnati ready to smash liquor bottles and beer barrels with her famous hatchet, she was so overwhelmed by the number of places that served beer that she didn't even try to swing it. "I would have dropped dead from exhaustion," she confessed.

The saloon was the primary place where beer was dispensed, either being consumed there or taken home in the small tin "growler" pails. Even after beer was pasteurized and bottled, it was purchased from the saloon. For the German Cincinnatian, saloons offered nickel lunches that included foods of the old country such as herring, sardines, wienerwurst, and pumpernickel. Whether it was Wielert's, Tivoli's, Flam's, Shickling's, Schuman's, or Glossner's, saloon clientele was largely devoid of women. The only sort that would have frequented a downtown saloon was the "fast" woman, those engaged in such occupations as dancing for a dime and prostitution who had no reputation to lose. Sallie Woolley apparently introduced Nellie to the crowded, smoky saloons, but these were not their most frequent watering holes.

Newer "resorts" were built on the seven hills of Cincinnati, including Lookout House, Highland House, Bellevue House, and Price Hill House, and thousands of summertime visitors made their way up to these pleasure palaces even if just for the view of the city while enjoying a frosty five cent schooner of a familiar brew. It was not just the *lager* (which were not the brown ales favored by the British Americans) at these resorts that provided the German Americans with *gemütlichkeit*, a sense of familial comfort and community. There was a full range of activities provided for the entire family on Sundays, the one day of the week that the city's industrial workers were all free. From morning on, there was bowling, dancing, concert performances, and running through the fun houses. One resort even had a woman acrobat who set herself on fire and jumped into the river, forty feet below. Cincinnati had its German schools, newspapers, street signs, and even an urban architecture style called Sauerbraten

Gothic, but it was under the shade trees and the tents of the "beer resorts" that its working-class community regularly massed together. It also made the events a natural draw for politicians to stump for votes from the men in the families.

For a young woman trained to associate only with the elite class, foraying into the German American drinking establishments exposed Nellie Herron to a level of society about which she had been entirely ignorant. And she loved every minute of it. "[A] beer saloon," she wrote in her July 2, 1881, diary entry, was her "favorite place of entertainment." She frequently arranged to meet friends at the resorts and seemed to greatly enjoy the lively oompah German brass bands at Highland House and dancing at the bimonthly German polkas at Clifton Hall. While she could blend in more easily at the family-oriented resorts, Nellie drew attention to herself at the saloons, but she was disappointed when one saloon proprietor, "who knew us well," sought to shield her and Sallie from the men at the bar. "Though that was really no drawback in as much as there were always men, still we accepted the offer and went upstairs onto the porch, which overlooks the park. There we sat and drank our beer and ate our cheese sandwiches, its invariable accompaniment, with our feet on the railing in front. It was quite Bohemian and consequently delightful."

If slipping out for a beer with the immigrant working class began to establish within society girl Nellie an egalitarian sensibility that would serve her well, it also bolstered a confidence in her pursuit of an unconventional life. Indeed, she liked being different. Invited to yet another saloon, Nellie wrote, "I agreed [to go], there being something Bohemian about it, which delighted me. . . . We drank beer and ate wienerwurst which would have greatly horrified probably some of my friends." For the rest of her life Nellie would be a connoisseur of beer, a mug of it never far away.

While beer and cigarettes might relax and distract her for a few hours in the summer evenings of 1881, they couldn't mask her frustration with herself. Without any progress nearly a year had passed since she had returned from Newport filled with the confidence that came from her declaration that she would pursue a musical career. It was not entirely her fault. She had spent two months running the Herron household. Then the holiday season had descended upon her, and she had slipped easily into the social life she had promised herself she would eschew. She hadn't entirely abandoned her promise to herself, having continued to practice her piano, but the goals she had laid out for herself were a bit overwhelming. Continuing to search for her ideal husband by socializing was far more in keeping with parental expectations than announcing to Harriet and John that she was going to get a job. In the summer of 1881, however, she knew the roots of her dark moods. "It was simply that I was not busy. . . . Now when my time is not fully occupied I fall back into the same state." She thrived when intellectually stimulated. This time she firmly decided to find a job.

Nellie's brother Will was leaving for Yale, and Mrs. Herron needed to notify his French teacher, Madame Fredin, that he would be stopping his lessons. Nellie volunteered to speak with Fredin, confessing to her diary, "I have taken quite a step. . . . I went to tell her in order to see if I could not interest her in giving me a place in her school some time. It was a very vague idea, but I told her I was very anxious to teach, and she laughed and said she would remember me."

On September 12, after attending a week of concerts, Nellie Herron again resolved to throw herself back into music. Some months later when she saw singer Adeline Patti perform, Nellie "never imagined anything so perfectly beautiful in my life as her voice. I could almost have gushed, unlike me." She returned to intense practicing at her piano. She also determined to take music lessons again, and felt she would work harder with a male teacher. Lessons with any teacher, however, met with resistance from her parents. After the bills came in for his and Harriet's trip to the West Coast with President Hayes, John Herron was again worried about money: "He seems to think that we will have to economize to make up for the California trip, but I hope it may be less expensive than he expects."

The greater problem proved to be her mother. While Nellie ultimately lost her case and gave up her vision of an expensive course of piano study, she still insisted on continuing her education. She enrolled in less costly individual classes in German and chemistry at the University of Cincinnati, Harriet complaining that it was still a waste of time and money. Despite the guilt she knew she would feel, Nellie defied her mother. She simply had to take action for her own sanity: "I have not felt much interest in anything. . . . I have been a good for nothing and useless. . . . I am thoroughly disgusted with myself. I am not in the least what I want to be. . . . I am not satisfied spending the whole day at home in quiet pursuits. I must have something to take me out of my own thoughts—something active. . . . I think it very much better to go to the university than to simply waste my time but I can not persuade Mamma to look upon it in that light . . . [al]though I intend to do it anyway. Still, her opposition makes one uncomfortable. . . . I am so sick of making resolutions to be different [since] they [resolutions] all seem to amount to so little and I am less what I want [to be as a person]."

Change came suddenly. That winter Madame Fredin called at Pike Street when one of her male teachers became ill and asked Nellie to start work immediately as a substitute teacher. Nellie accepted and taught for two weeks. Fredin asked her to continue on with several lessons and then changed her mind, saying she wouldn't be hiring another teacher until the autumn of 1882. "I was provoked," Nellie recorded with obvious anger, "for I thought she had simply put me off and that that was an end of the matter."

On April 1, however, Fredin returned to Pike Street with an offer of teaching French four hours each week for the next two months. Nellie would get the handsome salary of $50. Before she began, though, a teacher in the primary school became ill, and Nellie assumed her position for the rest of the term. The opportunity filled Nellie with a sorely needed sense of confidence and hope in her future: "So here I am probably better as a teacher for life. I have begun now to look forward to having a school of my own as the great ambition of my life. And I can see that already other things are beginning to give place to it in my mind. . . . I think that it [her having taken a teaching job] passes for a whim with the few who know about it at all. It seems strange for anyone who has been as gay. Such a regular society girl as I have been to settle down in this way but I always was queer and I believe that after a while I shall be better satisfied."

Finally, after her first month of working as a teacher, Nellie felt "happy and contented." She had achieved the first great goal of her life— to become a working woman earning her own salary and not relying on her father for cab fare, trinkets, concert tickets—and beer and cigarettes.

It was only a matter of weeks, however, before a letter from a Mr. White arrived at Pike Street for Nellie. It was another employment offer, a permanent position in a new boys school he was opening with a Mr. Sykes. The position was as an assistant teacher of the youngest boys. It was for five days a week, five hours a day, at a salary of $700 for the year. "[T]hough I realized that it was more than ever settling down to drudgery," Nellie recorded, "I accepted of course. The moment I read it, I felt I should."[2]

A need for approval or guilt drove Nellie to immediately write her mother, then in Columbus. Anticipating Harriet's reaction, Nellie wrote that she had already decided to take the job. Mrs. Herron had become especially attached to Nellie as a young woman for her intellectually provocative conversations and witty company, but she still had considerable manipulative powers over her daughter. With rigid standards on how Nellie should make herself appealing to as successful a suitor as possible, and fearing what Cincinnati society would think of the Herrons' financial status if their daughter accepted permanent full-time work at a salary, she responded with little concern for Nellie's own needs:

> I received your business communication yesterday and in the intervening hours since, have given it my serious and thoughtful consideration. Since you seem determined to avail yourself of the privilege of your coming of age and please yourself in any event, I suppose all that remains for me to do is to suggest some things you might not have thought of, or if you have thought of them may not have sufficiently weighed them.
>
> Are you quite sure then—that at the age of not quite twenty-one it is wise for you to decide to devote yourself to school teaching as a

*profession—there being no positive necessity in the case? Do you
realize that you will have to give up society, as you now enjoy it,
and possibly, to a considerable extent, some of your intimate friends
as well—certainly late hours and dancing parties do not promote
the patience and physical endurance required by a teacher. And then
is it quite the thing for a young girl in your position to teach in a
boys school—and where there are no other ladies? I have not much
information about the school, but I admit the offer is
complimentary and the compensation offered seems large. I do not
wish you to be influenced by either of these considerations however
but to think seriously where and how it will all end!*

*You are such a tender, sensitive, darling child—now don't laugh
at this as sentimental—that I own. I shrink from thinking of you as
making your own way in the world in any inconsequential manner.
And school teaching is such a monotonous drudgery, and does not, I
think, beyond a certain point, tend to enlarge one's education or
views. . . . I would far rather have you at home—all to myself. . . .
Why must you be in such haste.*

Nellie did not back down but instead invited Joseph White to come
to the Herron home, unchaperoned, to confer on "matters of business."[3]

Like most young women of her era and class, Nellie had been trained
to strictly obey parental dictation. She was clearly not doing so by accepting
the boys school teaching post. In reaction, she began to second-guess herself.
On May 3 she was unable to sleep, recording a jumbling stream-of-conscious
flow of ideas, emotions, fears, and dreams, often in conflict with one another.

*I feel sort of blue and miserable, more so than I have done since
February when I cried myself to sleep more often than I should like
to say. . . . I have been on the whole happier since I have been
teaching but I can not help it if doubts occasionally come up as to
whether I am doing wisely.*

If I could only feel that I was doing something noble, something that would be of some assistance to some one, if I were, for instance, teaching for nothing . . . [no salary] I would have some consolation but what motive actuates me after all except a desire for an independence of which after all there is no need, and a horror of the thought of waiting around for it certainly does resemble that to be married.

If I were only compelled to teach for my living how I shall thank heaven—but to feel that perhaps I am wasting my best years in a routine which can not benefit me much during which I might be acquiring something of which would enlarge my mind: the idea is dreadful.

And yet there is another side a little more cheerful. I like teaching when I feel well. I really enjoy it. It is certainly a good discipline in patience—and more improving in a certain way than society alone is, but I am not sure that that satisfaction will support me forever and I have no other.

Mamma . . . does not understand my motives in doing it and neither does anybody else, and I think it is that lack which has [undermined] my own belief. If I had been asked before I ever had an opportunity whether I would take it if offered I should have said yes without hesitation and would have argued then that it was right—but now that I have done it, I seem myself to look at myself with pitying wonder and say, "Poor girl, why could you not get along as other girls do?" Some few people admire it because . . . it shows spirit and my wish is not to show spirit. I never had any. The by far greater numbers [of people] look at me indifferently and wonder at my queer task. I am not strong minded in the least except in theory—it takes a little gulp to swallow the idea of always teaching, even if I am successful or should sometime be the head of a school and yet perhaps I am not right in thinking that way. . . .

I do think that she [a woman] is much happier single, and doing some congenial work. I certainly will be much happier than if I lived at home always and did nothing regularly. . . . I was pretty wretched before I [started teaching]. Papa told me I had better not.

I had two dreadful letters from Mamma. Even Maria told me that
she entirely agreed with Mamma. So that I felt as if I were deciding
my whole life without any help. I had not even any one to consult
with who looked upon it the way I did. Since I began to teach
N.H.D. [a suitor] has not been here except in the most formal way
on Tuesday evenings. . . . I cannot help connecting the
circumstances.

Nellie took a summer vacation with other women friends at Yellow Springs, where she felt she could "throw off entirely all the little troubles which make one so ashamed of themselves." She had been "disgusted with myself," she wrote on July 8, for being "selfish and insincere and jealous and wasted my thoughts in making myself uncomfortable—all this when I had time to think and worry—when school was out." Now she was "much better."

Nellie felt none of the competitiveness she did when male friends were along. It made her think about becoming a nun: "I can understand anyone's going into a convent here. And really I am coming to the conclusion that instead of being wrong it is much the best thing for most women to do. . . . [Allie] thoroughly approved of Protestant sisterhoods. It has always been a great idea to belong to one, so we have determined to use all our influence some day to starting one. . . ." Nellie even had her first acquaintance with a woman of a "Boston marriage," a euphemism of the era for lesbianism. On July 11 she and Allie Keyes went to dinner at neighbors, the Bells, where they met "Miss Gilmore who is a lovely girl, poor thing, and a friend Miss Gray—a real Boston girl of the mannish order."

Becoming a nun or entering a Boston marriage, had she been so inclined, were not among the options for Miss Herron, however, especially if she still hoped to fulfill the most impossible of her ambitions: marrying exactly the right man who could theoretically be elected President. She clearly enjoyed her working in a profession where her natural skills were put to use, but if she could share her life with a man willing to share his work with her, that could perhaps be even more fulfilling.

"Of course a woman is happier who marries," she concluded in her diary, "if she marries exactly right, but how many do?"

▪

For more than a year Nellie Herron had been seeking to define her growing friendship with young lawyer Howard Hollister, although they rarely "do smoothly together." His dependency worried her. "He needs too much encouragement," she wrote, "and I can not give encouragement as other girls do even if I want to which I am not sure I do." Her notation of several weeks earlier might have been related to her disenchantment. She and a friend had "walked to the elevator and on the way we met Will Taft whom I had not seen before this summer and started to talk to him for a while." The brief encounter was enough to register "excitement," and consequently "I stayed awake half the night."

Nellie managed to keep Howard as a sort of half-friend, half-beau. By the summer of 1881 when he began showing interest in her friend Agnes, Nellie went out with an old friend, Albert Chatfield. She discovered that she had "outgrown" Howard. "I am losing interest in everybody," she realized. "Instead of growing more charitable . . . I appear to like them less because everything in them is not what I imagined. I have one ideal [beau] left, which I hope will remain. Anyone would think [so,] I believe, from looking at the account of last summer." She was referring to the fellow she had run in to on her way to the elevator.

Becoming closer to her "ideal" became all the more complicated, however, when Howard, in confessing to Nellie that he had called on Agnes, revealed that his friend Will Taft "thought he was doing just right" by not seeing Agnes again. Taft may have unintentionally prolonged what Nellie believed was the inevitable dissolution of Howard's romancing of her, but it also illustrated Taft's values and how much she shared them. Her break with Howard came naturally enough when he came back a second time to tell her that Agnes truly wanted to date him. Nellie was disgusted. Any respect she had for Howard vanished when she realized his lack of resolve. "I think men are perfect fools," she wrote, "and he in par-

ticular is the most thoroughly inconsequent weak person I ever knew. . . .
He must have companionship. . . . It is enough to make one entirely cynical—
to think that anyone could be so wanting in consistency." As a sign of her
growing confidence in herself as a single woman, she wrote in her diary: "I
don't care what he does" and bluntly told him they could remain friends but
she had no interest in dating him. "I do not blame you," he responded, "no
better woman lives." While she helped Allie plan her wedding, Nellie forti-
fied her determination not to settle for milquetoasts like Howard.

Just as Miss Herron was making active strides in creating her own
unique life, she was suddenly brought down by none other than Harriet.
An urgent letter from her father abruptly ended Nellie's vacation and told
her to rush home—her mother had blood poisoning. It was not a serious
health threat, but Harriet made the most of it. As John Herron wrote to
Hayes, she wanted "someone to sit with and talk to her and Nellie was always favorite company."[4] Nellie found her mother to be "helpless and miserable," but she did as she was told. In the process she retreated into
emotional uncertainty as she prepared for her first full year of teaching. It
clearly seemed to be a passive ruse on the part of Harriet to control Nellie,
and it provoked the young woman into renewed fears about remaining unmarried. On September 29, Nellie tied money, work, love, and family guilt
together in a jumble:

> I feel discouraged tonight in that state of mind which always
> attacks me if I think. I began school over a week ago, and settled
> down for the winter to hard work. . . . Mamma is displeased [about
> the return to work] and [the fact] that I am in a chronic state of
> being tired out. I do not get sick, but I have just strength enough for
> it and no more. . . . Sometimes I feel . . . I am never to marry. I
> should be a miserable, apathetic woman without an interest in life
> unless I betroth myself now while I am young and courageous and
> engaged in some real work. The usual puttering which an
> unmarried woman calls work would never satisfy me.
>
> I do not pretend to myself that teaching a primary department

of boys is congenial work. I only say it is the only thing which so far I have found to do—by which I could be in any way independent is [why] I do it. But when I look ahead I am miserable. It seems to me as if I could not teach those dreadful boys another year and yet if I give it up and have no other offer, I give up a principle that I have tried to follow out. I have thought that a woman should be independent and not regard matrimony as the only thing to be desired in life and yet by action I [will] have declared that she is only to work when that work is altogether pleasant.

I do not dislike teaching when the boys behave themselves. I even feel that I rather like it, and if I only felt that I could someday make more money I would have courage to keep on. I am afraid it was a mistake ever leaving Madame [Fredin]. I would perhaps have had a better chance there. If I have another offer I shall certainly leave Mr. White's but if I have none? I don't believe that since I began teaching I have ever had the least sympathy or understanding of my routine—Mamma thinks I am wrong . . . [but] that does not seem to me to be the reason for giving up my opinions. . . .

Why should I take life so hard? Other people seem to get through all right without inconvenient ideas.

That last entry is a pretty low one and represents my state of mind. . . . When I am overworked and tired it occurs to me pretty frequently. I should not be so tired if when I came home from school I could only collapse and rest, but instead I have to pretend to be cheerful and lively or Mamma begins fussing about my being tired to death, of killing myself and really, if I think of it, I have not much to be lively about. So all week I have been in that state when my eyes filled with tears at the least provocation, and I take refuge in silence because I have nothing to say that any one could want to hear.

On at least one front, Nellie had resolution. She was able to go out and drink beer at Highland House with Howard Hollister "quite like a comrade and man." She believed that "a very ordinary love affair may perhaps have become what I have always longed for, a warm friendship between two quite congenial people . . . so much more to be desired than the other." She then mused at length about friendship, love, the companionate marriage, and male passions:

> *Why is it that it is so very rare for a man and woman to be simple intimate friends—that a friendship is infinitely higher than what is usually called love, for in it there is a realization of each others' defects, and a proper appreciation of their good points without that fatal idealization which is so blind and to me so contemptible. A man imagines himself in love with a girl simply because he thinks he has some reason to admire her, and can not understand any other sort of feeling for her. From my point of view a love which is worthy of the name should always have a beginning in the other, and should this friendship rise to something higher, it is a blessed happiness and in it there is no possibility of disappointment or self deception. When a man thinks he loves her [in that] way, [it] is so complicated. He loves a creature of his own imagination who may have no resemblance to you—and he shows besides in so loving, a want of the highest feeling which is a great defect. This moral realization has at least relieved my feelings on a subject I have always felt a good deal upon.*

Nellie Herron had learned to face her "realization" without illusion and hold fast to her principled standards. She would not invest any effort or emotion in a relationship with any man who viewed her simply as an object of romantic love but indicated no real interest in her as a person. When she was around men who did not engage a woman in a meaningful conversation of significant subjects, Nellie admitted, "I am a bump on a log. This not being pleasant, I don't especially enjoy myself, and have a strange feeling all the time of being an onlooker and not a participant."

If she had not yet made her match with a man who would be President, Nellie was equally disappointed in not fulfilling another youthful ambition: A musical career seemed to be an increasingly remote possibility. She had taken her courses in chemistry and German at the university just as she had planned, but her father still refused to pay for more music lessons, and she didn't have enough of her own to cover the cost. "How I wish I could play just a little better than I do," she wrote in the summer of 1883. "I get a good deal, a great deal even, of pleasure from it as it is, but I often bungle it and satisfy myself so little that I don't care much to hear myself play."

If the sound of her own music left her frustrated, Nellie was able to lose herself in pleasure by taking in the performances of others. She seemed especially elated when she could share the experience with a good friend. Nellie was thus delighted when, in February 1883, she went to the first night of the Cincinnati Opera Festival with Will Taft. As absorbed in his work as a new attorney as she was with hers as a teacher, they hadn't seen each other in ten months, ever since he had convinced her to attend a dance with him after he learned that "fancy dress"—to which she had objected—had been dropped as a requirement.

Initially, Nellie Herron may have been smitten with Will Taft, perhaps even had a crush on him, but the more enduring reality was that they were becoming that rare woman and man who could be bona fide "simple friends" without any hint of romance. Nellie was not in love with Will, nor did she deceive herself with that objectifying idealization that she knew was fatal to a friendship. In the four days that followed their night at the opera, for example, Will took four different women to the succeeding performances, and Nellie was not in the least jealous or perturbed. She simply enjoyed his intelligent company and genuinely appreciated his respect for her views in their conversations. It would be another three months before Will and Nellie saw each other again, when he escorted her to a mutual friend's house, but their place in each other's lives already seemed secure. He did not try to play her emotions as Howard Hollister had or treat her with condescension as John Holmes had. Whether she smoked or drank beer didn't seem to matter to him; he was showing increased interest in her ideas. For a "bohemian" like Nellie, Will was the ideal male friend.[5]

When she began her second autumn of teaching, Miss Herron seemed at peace with her unspoken decision to postpone her active pursuit of a musical career. Besides, her mind was fully occupied because she was reading political, economic, historical, and literary works, as well as newspapers that she studied for local, national, and international news. It was all preparation for an intense weekly meeting of heated debate and discussion. Earlier in the year Nellie had organized her more serious friends into a "salon" in the gray Herron house on Pike Street.

The furnishings of the Herron sitting room were of little importance to the young people who gathered there, including Will's brother Horace Taft and Nellie's younger sister Maria—who were openly sweet on each other. This circle, rather than Nellie's old crowd of socialites and pleasure seekers, was where she felt natural; she could speak her mind and be herself. The group took their membership seriously, rarely missing one of the meetings, which were sometimes held at other homes. On November 3, for example, the salon was held at her friend Allie's house, and Nellie indulged Will Taft by making "the sacrifice" to walk with him rather than take a streetcar. By spring 1884 the group had formed a close core of comradery, and they were socializing outside of the meeting.[6]

That season Nellie recorded: "We went on the long deferred salon picnic and had a very good time," taking buggies to a farmhouse, walking to a hilltop, sitting on a fence and singing, and then lunching. "The men then proceeded to make the punch to which we all did full justice." It was at one such picnic that twenty-five-year-old Nellie made an offhanded remark, which someone remembered. When Horace Taft got home that night, he told Will, "I just heard Nellie say that you didn't sing so badly. She must be in love with you."[7]

Three

The Will of Love (1884–1890)

*We boys are all trying to push along toward success if for no
other reason than to convince Father in his ebbing days that he
has not spent a life in vain.*

—CHARLEY TAFT

In light of her later-known teenage intention of someday becoming a
First Lady married to a President who accepted her as an intellectual
equal, it is intriguing to realize she had the forethought even then, as
a young woman writing her diary, that she would read it as an old lady and
clearly see herself as a "foolish goose." Considering how conscious she was
of the intensely private self-analysis she wrote in her diary, it suggests that
it was important enough to always preserve it. Indeed, she kept it with all
her papers. Long before she knew she would be a public figure, Nellie
Taft's ambition was so strong that she, at the least, *sensed* it.

If few First Ladies in history left as emotionally honest, painful, and
private a record of their lives as Nellie Herron Taft did, there is also
evidence that some things were burned instead of left to posterity. While
Nellie didn't mind leaving to history a melodramatic pageant of upper-
class Victorian youth in her diary, her more mature and deeply felt emotions as she grew close to Will Taft were too intense to donate as part of
her papers in the Library of Congress.

Here she was, an upper-middle-class debutante who frequented beer saloons with working-class men. Here she was: a feminist, "bohemian," employed teacher who both feared and relished the idea of living as a single person for the rest of her life. And, always, she harbored a desire for fame, for standing out and being noticed. It was easy to see why Nellie Herron was always filled with the need for that rush she called "exciting" in one situation and "anxious" in another. At no point in her life until the actual moment of truth was Nellie Herron more simultaneously excited and anxious than when she realized that in Will Taft she had finally found exactly what she had always described as her "ideal": a traditional marriage to an untraditional husband.

Nellie Herron must have been stunned when she realized that marrying Will Taft would not mean she had to cease and desist a passionate pursuit of her own ambitions. Whether it was Nellie working on her own again (while also managing a family) or working on his career, Will would never tell Nellie what to do with her life. Nor is there any record of expectations or role-playing that he wished her to conform to. Nellie did not have to choose between husband and career; she could have both. She had achieved perhaps one of the most difficult and specifically defined goals of her young life, and it must have terrified her.

William Howard Taft was what might be characterized as a "conservative feminist" President—that is, one who genuinely believed that women were intellectually equal to men if given full access to education and should be equally salaried and employed, but that most women would probably end up pursuing a traditional role as wife and mother. His views would open further over a lifetime, influenced by especially intelligent women who shared his life: his mother, his wife, and his daughter.

The formidable and blunt Bostonian Louise Torrey Taft must have intimidated the social climbing Harriet Herron, but it is known that they exchanged formal calls in each other's parlors during the social season. What they thought of each other was either never recorded or destroyed. Considering how different their values were, it is probably a case of the latter. More alike were their husbands, both intelligently sensitive and capable. Not only were John Herron and Alphonso Taft both attorneys, but they had worked together to create the local Literary Society. Their daughters, Maria Herron and Fanny Taft, were classmates at Miss Nourse's, and best friends. It was odd, then, that Nellie Herron hadn't met Will Taft until 1879 at a bobsledding party one winter night.

The large, muscular Will had recently enrolled in his first year at Cincinnati Law School after graduating from Yale University the previous June. Warm, sensitive, and gentle, he nevertheless confessed to having no memory of his first meeting with Nellie. She never held it against him. Everyone knew that Will was absolutely obsessed with the great ambition of his life: to become chief justice of the U.S. Supreme Court.

Although she only mentioned him in passing in her diary, and only once with any great interest, Nellie's immediate attraction was the burly, blond Will's looks, but during their first lengthy encounter, a simple act of kindness drew her to his character. At a picnic the day after July 4, 1880, Will kindly offered to cut up meat on her little sister Eleanor's plate. Nellie found this "enchanting as ever." She wrote to Allie Keys of how shy she became when she found herself in his presence—and how he seemed to ignore her: "Who do you think arrived and stayed until Tuesday but that adorable Will Taft—imagine, just think of it. Unfortunately, I did not recover from my surprise and delight soon enough to make that impression which I would have wished. . . . Oh, it was such a splendid opportunity to make an impression . . . but alas! He strikes me with awe, and I could not make any more out of it." That night Nellie once again cried herself to sleep.

Will Taft was "old stock," English American with some gilded genealogy. His great-great-great-great-grandfather, carpenter Robert Taft, had immigrated to Braintree, Massachusetts, in 1678, nearly sixty years after the landing of the *Mayflower*, the ship the Tafts long boasted had brought their ancestors to America. While never known to express even a faintly snobbish remark about their lineage, family tradition and honor were foremost to them. Like Nellie, Will had an aggressive mother who was highly ambitious for her child and a wise, patient, and providing father whose advice was cherished.

Alphonso Taft's grandfather was a Bunker Hill minuteman. His grandfather was a county court judge in Townsend, Vermont, the town where he was born in 1810. The first Taft at Yale, Alphonso graduated in 1833 and then studied law there. He came to Cincinnati in 1839 and went on to serve illustriously as judge of the superior court there from 1865 to 1871. That, however, would be the limit of his judicial career. A Cabinet and ambassadorial career provided a far grander lifestyle for Louise Taft, who relished the social status and privileges that came as the wife of the American minister in the fairy-castle land of Austria, the post held by Alphonso at the time Will and Nellie began courting. Two years later he would occupy the same official position in the equally romantic but more darkly complex czarist Russia.

There is no record of what public office Louise Taft would have ideally wanted for her husband and herself, but she had become a close friend of First Lady Julia Grant when Alphonso was serving as Grant's War Secretary and Attorney-General. Harriet Herron may have been a confidante back home in Ohio for Lucy Hayes, but Louise Taft had intimate familiarity with the White House, where she was often at the family dinner table as a personal guest. Perhaps Louise Taft thought herself better than the bumbling Missouri army wife in the White House, who saw little value in educating women; it is only speculation, but it would be quite in character. It is known, however, that Alphonso aspired to become chief justice. Will long recalled his father's remark that the chief justiceship was "greater than the presidency," which fired his own ambition for the position. The great dream of Alphonso would become the engine that drove Will's supreme yearnings. If Nellie was partially driven in her ambition to achieve and somehow obtain what her father *might* have, so, too, was Will driven by his father's unrequited designs.

Alphonso's first marriage to fellow Vermonter Fanny Phelps ended with her death from tuberculosis at age twenty-nine and left a tragic legacy. Of their six children, only Charley and Peter lived to adulthood, and the latter died at age forty-four. Fourteen years Will's senior, Charley was a father figure to his younger half-brothers, Will, Henry, and Horace, and half-sister Fanny. With the security of Annie Sinton's fortune, Charley was part owner of the *Cincinnati Times-Star*, for which he served as editor and publisher, a powerful political berth.

While the senior Tafts were overseas, Annie Taft assumed a maternal role for Will and Horace. (Henry and his wife, Julia, were living in New York, where he practiced law.) With their parents' house being leased, Will and Horace shared rented rooms on Broadway but spent most of their time and took their meals regularly in Charles and Annie's home.

Despite their widening differences on politics, Will and Horace were particularly close. Horace, though still a Republican, would come to support Grover Cleveland when the former President ran again for the presidency in 1892. He enjoyed good-naturedly needling Will on his staunch Republicanism.

Horace was the first of the Taft boys to fall in love with a Herron girl. In his case it was his sister Fanny's best friend, Maria Herron. Despite her sharp tongue, the tiny, beautiful, and bright Maria with the black braided hair and blue eyes was never to marry. She left no written or spoken reason for remaining single, but in light of her responsibilities as caretaker for her mother and then her father, a sense of obligation to her parents emerges as the most likely reason. Something sad and strange seemed to have happened between Horace and Maria; Horace held out for a long time, long past the marriage of all his siblings, waiting for Maria. She never said yes. Still, the fact is that a powerful force had drawn another female Herron and male Taft together and certainly encouraged the relationship of Will and Nellie, especially since the four of them were all in the "salon" together.

In her weekly salon Nellie finally created the balance she had sought, a way to socialize with her set while also stimulating her intellect. It kept her connected to a larger world of global subjects while maintaining a comfort level with progressive friends. Oftentimes Nellie Herron would read a book to the nine regular members and deliver a lecture to the group, then throw open the subject to discussion. She tended to control things. The salon's intention, Nellie made clear, was "cultivation," not "recreation."[1]

The group generally met on Saturday nights, the members having read "assignments." Then they argued about the works of Voltaire and Rousseau, read aloud the plays of Shakespeare and Marlowe, dissected economic theories, debated the role of national government, or historically assessed the Founding Fathers. They staged plays and played charades. After each weekly session ended, Nellie laid out a feast of oysters and strawberries. Conversations inevitably drifted into gossip and flirtations. Will was teasingly sarcastic on that point. "Tell Maria that I am drinking deep from the fountain of knowledge which her sister has set up in the Salon," Will wrote to his mother in Europe, where Maria was visiting with Fanny. "The lamps and gas are only lit for the sake of conventionality. The phosphorus that scintillates from the brain of each member is quite sufficient to illuminate two or three rooms as large as Mrs. Herron's parlor."

Will Taft unhesitatingly confided in his parents. In an age when emotional distance between parents and sons was the norm, the Tafts were unusual. Alphonso openly expressed his love of and pride in his sons, balanced with his exacting expectations for their success. On the one hand, when Will reluctantly began his law practice, Alphonso wrote Charley, "That is his destiny and he should be in it." On the other hand, after Peter had committed the socially taboo act of divorce, his father wrote him: "You may rely upon one thing, and that is that my heart is always with you."

Alphonso consciously created a strongly knit sensibility in his family, pulling the brothers together as a sort of team and laying the foundation for a dynasty that would rule and improve their city, state, and nation in generations to come. His full partner in this inculcation was his second wife, Louise Torrey Taft, whom he married in 1853. Neither parent was absolute in assuming traditional gender patterns. If Alphonso was as nurturing and comforting as Louise, she was as firm, dictatorial, and commanding as he could be. It was an untraditional marriage for the times, with husband and wife as intellectual equals. Besides dining with the Grants, the Tafts had also met Lincoln, played cards with Garfield, and been entertained by Buchanan. Both mused about one of their sons someday being President.

Of the five children Louise Torrey bore Alphonso, four lived to maturity. Will, the eldest, was born on September 15, 1857, and then Henry, Horace, and Fanny. When Will was a toddler, his father described him as one "to make the best of the ills of this life." With light blue eyes and a soft voice, Will was also thick and sturdy. By the time he met Nellie he was over six feet and more than two hundred pounds.[2] Perhaps the greatest gift he inherited from his father was a willingness to expand his intellect. Alphonso was not a wealthy man able to pursue wild passions, but he quenched his thirst for knowledge by intense research, whether the subject was Cicero, ancient Egypt, Darwinism, astronomy, Halley's comet, or Pittman shorthand. If Nellie had developed a respect for those who were culturally different from her in the German saloons, Will's belief in the equality of civil rights for all races stemmed from his father's vigilant abolitionism. During the Civil War, Alphonso stood up to many of the southern sympathizers in Cincinnati, which was just across the border from Kentucky, parts of which were held by the Confederacy.

The egalitarianism of the Taft family was also rooted in their New England faith of Unitarianism, a basic tenet of which respects the equality of humans. Louise Torrey, born in Boston in 1827, was the bulwark of that belief in her family. Louise read not only the Bible to Will as a child but the classics as well. Her husband actually complained when she neglected intellectual pursuits to perform housekeeping. Intelligence, wit, and a willingness to take control were traits the Taft men respected in women. One of four girls in the Torrey family, Louise was closest to the one who never married, Delia. Delia, in turn, became a second mother to Will. An outspoken suffragette, she was partial to champagne and California. She never married because she made it clear that she cherished her own "strong mind."

The Tafts believed that children should be lavished with love. The results were apparent early. "[H]e means to be a scholar, and studies well," wrote Alphonso of seven-year-old Will. "I have never had any little boy show a better spirit in that respect. . . . He has a kind of zeal that is his own." Will was a happy and active boy. He played baseball, bowled, danced, wrestled, boxed, lifted weights, did calisthenics, sledded, and skated. In summers he climbed arbors and trees to harvest grapes and apples.

Will was an excellent student, graduating second in both his class at the public Woodward High School and at Yale (where he won a prize for his essay "Availability as a Ruling Consideration in the Choice of Presidential Candidates"). At times Will expressed resentment toward his father's high standards. "You expect great things of me," he wrote his father while at Yale, "but you mustn't be disappointed if I don't come up to your expectations."

All the Tafts were exacting. Even Peter once wrote Will, "Never be content until you have done the very best you could have done, for if you always do that you will never be unhappy . . . and do your part in building up the reputation of the family." This took its toll. Henry flourished, and Charley's money-by-marriage fueled his pursuits. However, Peter was left depressed and guilty that he couldn't live up to expectations and was later confined to a sanitarium following a breakdown. When Horace followed his passion for education and gave up law to found the Taft School, Alphonso panicked, as if a great crime had been committed. Although all the boys earned their law degrees and practiced law immediately upon graduation as expected, Will was drawn toward politics like his father. Recognizing Will's potential, Alphonso, who had been defeated in his run for the Republican nomination for governor, did all he could to focus Will on high achievement. "Willie is foremost," he wrote, "and I am inclined to think he will always be so." Even Louise secretly preferred him. "Mediocrity," she said, "will not do for William."

With his dependency on their love, Will greatly needed to please his parents. It was only passively that any subtle resistance to their pressures emerged. When Will slipped out of his law firm (where he worked after stints as a court reporter, assistant prosecutor of Hamilton County, and internal revenue collector for Ohio's First District) to catch a boating race, for example, Alphonso was livid. "You must not feel that you have time enough to while away," he chastised Will. "Our anxiety for your success is very great and I know there is but one way to attain it, & that is by self-denial and enthusiastic hard work in the profession. . . . You will have to be on the alert for business, and for influence among men, if you would hope to accomplish success." When Garfield ran for President, Alphonso even coaxed Will onto the campaign speaking stump. Will had grown accustomed to unconditional love, support, advice, and even guidance. By the end of 1883 he saw such qualities in Nellie Herron.[3]

Nellie hosted a New Year's Eve party for the salon. It kicked off a season of heavy romance. On Valentine's Day, Nellie wrote a poem teasing Will about his work obsession:

> *Leave your dull cases,*
> *Let them grow dusty.*
> *Turn to the graces! Till laughter effaces, their pages musty!*

Hardly romantic, it was enough of an open door for Will to gently prompt his family members to push Nellie a bit further. Nellie received an anonymous valentine, most certainly from Horace, that she saved for years, the first and last stanzas running:

> *St. Valentine the good!*
> *Now cheer and cheer him still!*
> *For giving Will to Nellie,*
> *And giving Nellie to Will. . . .*

> *And over this glass let's pray,*
> *While grinding out love's mill,*
> *He'll give each boy a Nellie.*
> *And give each girl a Will.*

The day after Valentine's, Annie Taft sent "Helen Herron, Spinster" a party invitation: "Should she wish to find her true and only Valentine." Four days later Will followed up, asking Nellie to please attend so they could dance together. Two days later he again wrote her, ostensibly to retrieve his library book, *Culture and Anarchy* by Matthew Arnold, but he confessed to feeling "an aching void" and if the messenger didn't find her home, "I'll call for the book just after supper."[4]

Privately, Will feared that he had neither the salary nor the prestige to be a serious contender for Nellie. Among his circle of fellow lawyers and friends were Howard Hollister and John Holmes, Nellie's two most recent suitors. "[M]uch as I admire her," he wrote his mother of Nellie, he didn't have "the least reason to think that she would be pleased to have me join the number who are struggling for her hand." By March 12, Will drummed up the courage to address her as "Nellie" in his first, careful letter of affection to her, along with flowers. Ostensibly, he apologized for the fact that he had to see his aunt and would miss the next salon: "The excuse for the roses is the note and the excuse for the note is the roses. . . . Aunt Delia can not realize the sacrifice we make to see her. Still less can she appreciate my individual sacrifice."[5]

The budding relationship was almost nipped over a salon disagreement on slavery. When Nellie expressed her staunch abolitionism and Will shot her argument down in a constitutional context, he learned that she was one woman who took her educated and principled opinions seriously. He groveled for forgiveness: "I deeply regret that my manner was such as to leave the impression on your mind that I held your suggestions or arguments lightly or regarded them with contempt. . . . In the discussion I forgot myself and that was inexcusable. . . . So far from holding your opinions lightly, I know no one who attaches more weight to them or who more admires your powers of reasoning than the now humbled subscriber."[6]

Four months later, in his first letter addressed to "My dear Nellie," Will recalled his ride east with her to New York, from where she changed trains to head north to the Adirondacks for a summer sojourn with her family. In his discussion about reading Anthony Trollope's *A Small House at Allington*, he subtly made a point to counteract her perfectionist tendencies:

> *I advise you to read it again. Trollope is a great favorite of mine because of the realistic everyday tone which one finds in every line he writes. He describes real people. His heroes have the failings human character is heir to, and we like them none-the-less on that account. Even your ideal of constancy in friendship Phineas Phim was not without his little foibles, which made no one like him less. . . . You speak of the trouble you gave me . . . I stayed over for the pleasure of coming on with you. . . . The only drawback was that you left so soon. . . . Let me hear from you, how you get on in your mountain retreat. It will relieve the strain on your mind after your study of Darwin, Lyell, Tyndal and your -ologies.*[7]

Will also began to pose to her larger ethical and philosophical questions. When he voted for Howard Hollister's father, John, in his run for a judgeship—an election he lost—it presented a moral dilemma he mused over with Nellie. He admitted that he had voted for the senior Hollister only because of his friendship with Howard. "This is treason but I dare say it to you, knowing as I do your reputation as a Tomb. This suggests a subject for discussion. How far ought a friend to go in carrying out his friend's wishes when those wishes in his opinion are not in accord with the best interests of the community and the party? Ought he to be candid and tell his friend the cold truth and risk his friend's friendship . . . ? Or ought he to bury out of sight his unbiased opinion . . . ? Understand me, his friend's wishes are in a sense in conflict with an honorable course of action. . . . I am prepared to submit a few questions of this tenor to the high court of friendship wherein let Mr. Justice Taft and Miss Justice Herron to determine such questions."

In the same letter Will gently pressed his views on the proper "home life" for a young man. He used the example of the dissolute lives of two of their wealthy male friends, but Will was really laying out his hopes for his own life. And they struck a remarkably similar tone of idealism to Nellie's diary: "I suppose . . . such men could find companions in their idle, objectless lives. . . . I doubt if either of them read a book a year. The stock reports of the newspapers are their chief literary muse. . . . That is not my highest idea of 'something to do.' . . . They could do so much good. . . . Their . . . idleness is little better than a sin. To seek to become husbands is not occupation of great public benefit but it is much to be preferred. . . . If all the wealthy were of their kind, I should become a communist."[8]

In her personal letters to Will, Nellie did not reveal herself as fully as she had in her teenage diary. In that document, she had flatly stated that she wanted to be a professional writer and earn her wages by crafting a novel. Will, however, showed a deft skill with the language. Spoken or written, he handled words like clay to make tangible shape of his conceptual notions on justice, freedom, equality, and morality.

Over the course of their near half-century together, Will and Nellie exchanged thousands of letters, and both made the effort to save those sent from the other. There are long periods where there seems to be no break in the ongoing narrative and exchange of news and information between them. While not as voluminous as the correspondence of John and Abigail Adams, the correspondence between Will and Nellie Taft is just as fascinating. It readily attests to their having created that rare balance between a husband and wife: equality and respect. Nellie kept more of the letters she received from Will than he kept of hers; the number of his predominate the collection. Either Will decided to burn those letters from Nellie that were too painful for him to have read by others, or she decided to do so herself later in life. She left no documented remark, spoken or written, as to if and why she might have done so. Considering other potentially embarrassing remarks in family letters permitted to be donated to the public, it is highly unlikely Will and Nellie's children would have destroyed any documentation.

Thus, it is largely the voice of Will through which their courtship is personally chronicled. Judging from the tone in some of his letters, Nellie's must have been fairly harsh at times. No period of Taft's writing more acutely reveals his deepest, inner emotions and his willingness to be vulnerable to a woman than do his courting letters to Nellie.

Throughout the autumn of 1884, Will seized on any opportunity to draw Nellie out with him. In October it was a large political meeting at the Music Hall, where Senator Joseph B. Foraker, among others, was to speak. In November he got her out to a play called *The Secretary*, which some friends said was poor but her company would "cure any defect in the play for me." In December, Nellie finally reached out to Will, giving him an unexpected Christmas present of a tie and stickpin as tokens of friendship—not love. He responded exuberantly that her gifts filled "a long felt want" for him, and while he acknowledged that it was all in the context of friendship, he also predicted that "each returning Christmas will find the influence of that friendship on my life as great." He made sure to sign off as "friend."[9]

He gently persisted. When he ran in to Maria Herron and learned that Nellie had decided to back out of a spring dance, he immediately wrote her: "I intended to ask you to go with me. . . . Can you not be persuaded to change your mind and make one night of it?" Sensitive to her anxiety of large crowds, he assured her that if she felt "sticky," he would protect her and that her attendance would diminish his own "terrors" of a crowd. "You can see now the position I am trying to force you to," he wrote, hoping she would "have pity on me and change that determined will of yours." He concluded that "self sacrifice is the great requisite of friendship."

Shortly after, Will again drew her out, this time challenging her pride in being individualistic. "We are prepared to test your unconventionality and Bohemianism," he wrote in inviting her to the rough world of a dog racing show, followed by a chophouse dinner of beefsteak and onions and, if time permitted, some roller-skating after that. If she felt she needed a chaperone, Will promised to invite Annie, who was eager to encourage the romance. Will often asked that Nellie respond to his invitations by walking across Pike Street and giving her answer to Annie, who had a telephone and could call Will at his office. She was also sure to nudge Nellie into accepting Will's request for her company.[10]

Music, reading, and opera were the ways to Nellie's heart, and Will did his duty, but as she sat enchanted by *Tannhauser*, he sat fixated on her. He fed her a steady diet of books on a variety of subjects, mostly nonfiction—a book on Russia, for example, another on the Ottoman Empire in Europe—either for her to discuss in her weekly lecture or for her to read and explain to him! It was all just a ruse to see or write her. He met her at the library to walk her home, took her to the opera and dances, and even invited her to join him to see a new government building. In the last week of April he could no longer hold himself back. He proposed marriage.

Nellie responded with shocked anger and told him never to again raise the subject. It was not an indifferent reaction, and Will had clearly hit a hot nerve with Nellie. Sure—she wanted to marry a man who could be elected President, but was emotionally ambivalent about making the life commitment of marriage.

Forced to repress himself in person, he poured his heart out in a letter—and again blurted out his proposal of marriage:

> *Last Sunday I promised not to bother you for another week. I understand that promise to refer only to personal importuning which is wearisome to you because it requires an answer or rather seems to require one. It will not I hope be a breach of my promise if I commit to paper feelings that press on me for expression. They interfere so much with my work that to let them flow in ink seems the only way for me to quiet them. What I want to say is not in the nature of news to you and my saying it finds no justification on such a ground. I love you Nellie. I grudge the intervals between the times of my seeing you. I called you up yesterday to hear the sound of your voice, formulating in my mind an elaborate excuse for such an unnecessary and therefore impolite interruption. I thought*

perhaps you were going to Miss Sparman's Saturday afternoon and,
as I was going to the tennis ground, I might succeed in walking
home with you. . . . I went home Wednesday night from your sweet
presence with my heart swelling with pleasure. . . . It grew out of a
strong hope that I might soon win the love of her whom I loved and
out of the consciousness of a well formed and virtuous purpose to
live such a life as to make myself worthy of that love. . . .

The thought of what it is that I am asking you to do made me
blue all yesterday afternoon and evening and this morning. And yet
Nellie such a prospect only makes me yearn for you the more. With
your strong noble character and your sweet sympathetic nature you
would strengthen me where I may falter and make my family life a
deep well from which I could draw the holier aspirations for a life
of rectitude. Oh Nellie, in spite of what I have written, I believe
you could be happy with me and could have a life of long pleasure
in the thought that the influence of your character and society and
(I hope) love has made a good and just member of society out of
one whom indifference and lassitude was likely to make only a poor
stick among his fellows. Oh Nellie, it is an awful question for you to
solve whether you will put yourself in the keeping of a man for life.
I ought not to hasten you in making a conclusion. But I love you
and I can not but plead for myself.

I never have been certain that marriage was the happier state for
women. I know it is for a man. Then too a mistake with him does
not involve his entire life. With a woman a mistake is worse than
death for in marriage she gives her all.

I ask you for everything Nellie and offer but little. I offer the
strong pure love of a man which may not be unselfish, indeed can
not be. I know it is not enough for what I ask. But Oh Nellie try to
love me. Your very love will make me worthy of it.[11]

Nellie immediately replied to Will. She turned him down and again
forbade him from raising the subject, only this time she meant not just in

personal conversation but also in his most emotionally satisfying venue of writing. It showed a particularly cruel streak in her, since she knew from experience how important an outlet it was for her.

Being so halted meant only another long stretch of emotional pain for Will. He also refused to back down. About two weeks after his initial proposal, he tried again when they were in her parlor, after visiting some friends. He would recall this night as that when "I forced a forbidden subject until by an unwilling admission I was able to win the reluctant prize." She did not absolutely turn him down but did not accept, either. He returned home and immediately wrote her again:

> *My dear, dear Nellie: I was a brute to weaken and exhaust you as I did tonight with the long walk and importuning conversation I had with you. I was hurried into what I said without thinking of the consequences to you by the overwhelming force of my own feelings. My mind and heart were full. I could talk or think of nothing else and so I poured it out. What I said first I had thought over long, had lain awake nights over, and I made the resolution that whenever I spoke, that must come first. It was an awful scourge for me to bear, to tell to that woman whom I love as my life and in whose esteem and love I would rather stand high than in that of any person on earth that which might well dash all my hopes to the ground. But I love you Nellie. I love you for all that you are. I love you for your noble, consistent character, for sweet womanly disposition, for all that you are, for all that you hope to be. I know my faults, I know my weaknesses. I cannot justify or make light of what I confessed against myself.*
>
> *But, Oh Nellie, I know I could make you happy. I could not live with you for whom I have such deep love on the firm foundation of respect and admiration without developing the best that is in me in a continual striving to make myself worthy of you.*
>
> *Oh Nellie, argue for me, not against me. Take those feelings, if you have any in your heart, which speak in my favor. Do not*

dissect them but believe that they are love. Do not coldly reason
away every vestige of feeling you may have for me. If the stain of
which I spoke is insurmountable then I bow before your just
decision.

   It was with the idea that you should know the truth and give it
proper weight in answering me that I told you. But I beseech you
Nellie to consider that foul as it may be there is no stain which can
not be wiped out, that no stronger evidence of the horror in which I
now hold it could be given than my forcing myself to tell you it.
You said tonight you believed me when I said I loved you. I might
go on and tell you how it came about, how I have done nothing in
six months knowingly (how long unconsciously I do not know)
without thinking what you would say about it, what you would
think about it. You reflected a light, the light of your pure and
noble mind, over my whole life.

   Oh Nellie, do say that you will try to love me. Oh how I will
work and strive to be better and do better, how I will labor for our
joint advancement if you will only let me.

   You will be my companion, my love and my life, and . . . I'll
become worthy of the trust. I write this tonight and shall send it to
you tomorrow morning. I shall wait with impatience until tomorrow
night with hope that you will give me a chance to live for you.[12]

This time, at least, Nellie said she would think about it. She did not
think for long. The next day, grudgingly rather than gratefully, she accepted his offer as if she had granted a favor she was still reluctant to relinquish, weary of his entreaties. Will responded with a willful optimism.
Every time he went to the salon, it "only confirms the certainty I had in the
beginning and increases my happiness with the thought . . . that you were
losing some of the doubts which you had five weeks ago."[13]

   There may have possibly been one other, more subtle pressure in
Nellie's mind. Her elder sister Jennie married Charles Anderson, the millionaire's son who grew up in the mansion across Pike Street from the

Herrons. One of the two houses that Nellie long romanticized about had been successfully stormed by a Herron. There was only one mansion left to storm, if only by marriage: the one next door, owned by Charley and Annie Taft. And it was Nellie's turn to wed. While her mother and sisters Jennie and Maria were all hoping for Nellie to marry Will, none of them quite understood her hesitancy. They accepted her unconventional ways, but they couldn't relate to a woman with such unusual ambitions about a potential husband. Before completely giving in to him, she held out until he declared that he truly loved her for her substance.

He responded with a tinge of exasperation:

> *Would it please you better or give better security of your happiness if I had fallen in love with you without reason? My love for you grew out of a friendship, intimate and of long standing. That friendship of course was founded on a respect and admiration for your high character, your sweet womanly qualities and your intellectual superiority over any woman I know . . .*[14]

Nellie's acceptance of marriage came with a strange caveat. He was not to tell anyone. She insisted that it remain a secret. There is no explanation: Either she wanted the option to change her mind or to have time to process how this decision would direct the course of her life. Will complied but was hurt that she wasn't proud enough to announce the news immediately. She relented only in giving him permission to tell his parents, by mail to St. Petersburg where a few months earlier Alphonso had arrived as U.S. minister. He took great pride in Nellie's earning a salary for three years now as a teacher so that she would not be financially dependent on her father:

> *[S]he persists in thinking that I was precipitate. . . . For nearly a month she held me in suspense and then with some hesitation consented to our engagement. I know that you will love her when you come to know her and will appreciate as I do her noble*

character and clear-cut intellect and well-informed mind. . . . She
had been no expense at all to her father. . . . She has done this
without encouragement by her family, who thought the work too
hard for her, because she chafed under the conventionalities of
society which would keep a young lady for evening entertainments.
She wanted to do something in life and not be a burden. Her
eagerness for knowledge of all kinds puts me to shame. Her
capacity for work is just wonderful.[15]

Several weeks after she agreed to be his wife, Nellie left with her mother and sisters for the Adirondacks, to Lowville, the small town of her maternal origins. Eight weeks from the day she had accepted his proposal, Will wrote her how he missed her dreadfully. He went to the post office where a clerk sorted mail. Will recognized Nellie's handwriting on letters sent to friends. There were none for him. He later returned to the post office on the chance that a letter from her might have arrived in the afternoon packets. Knowing her dislike of his profusion of romantic superlatives, he made certain to emphasize her intellect, recounting how he saw a couple on a front porch, the husband reading while the wife just sat there, "certainly thinking nothing. A horror of such a match seized me at first and then a deep sense of joy and relief at the thought of how different . . . my married life was to be." Meanly, it seems, she failed to write him regularly, and when she did, her responses lacked warmth and encouragement—judging from his responses.

Will decided to join the Herron women on July 23 and stay until the eighth of August. "It will be full moon about that time," he wrote her. "Oh how I wish I could sing Nellie! There are lots of things I could say that way that I can not express now. I have always envied men with good voices and a knowledge of music but never so much as now."[16]

It was a tortuous engagement. Will felt guilty when he ran into the unknowing John Herron on the streets of Cincinnati, and Nellie felt guilty when Will told her that he felt guilty. He bought her the two-volume *Geology of the State of New York,* which she was studying at the time, as a literary bribe that she not back out. "Oh, Nellie, you must love me. I rely on time to help me. My great good luck must not desert me now," he wrote her, begging for reassurance. "I believe you will be happy with me. The consciousness of having made me a better and truer man which you can not fail to have when you shall have become my wife will make you happy."[17]

That Nellie had already "accomplished" something by somehow making Will "better" and could make a lifetime of such work appealed to her. Before he joined her at Lowville, Will got what he felt was a true sign that Nellie's commitment had not been coerced, for she took a step on her own. She finally broke down to share her news. "I am glad you have told your Mother," Will gratefully wrote her. More secure, Will's tone began to change. He was less a victim of Nellie's whims; his voice was now that of a stronger protector, "willing to assume the responsibility over everything in your life, that you regard as errors," he wrote her. "[In] law a man is liable for the torts of his wife. . . . " He still hadn't told his siblings.[18]

Will joined Nellie in Lowville. "Each day found Nellie and me on the lake and in the woods. She sews or sketches while I read aloud to her," he wrote his mother. He also came to know his future mother-in-law, who thought he could handle Nellie's "sensitive nature." Will and Harriet got on well, walking through town as she recalled her childhood there. "I greeted with respect the ghosts of your grandfather Collins and your grandfather Clinton," he teased Nellie. "Oh, you are a blue blood and no mistake."[19]

As he was courting her, Will also begin to fill her in on the uglier aspects of local and state politics. Besides maintaining a law practice with Major Harlan Lloyd, Will tried civil cases as assistant solicitor for Hamilton County. When he attended a Republican primary convention, he confessed to Nellie: "[A] number of votes went into the box for our tickets, cast by men who had no right to vote," and he "protested against that mode of doing things but to no purpose. . . . It is a victory perhaps but I do not feel very proud of the methods that were resorted to obtain it." Will was troubled by it all, revealing an honor that was admirable to those who knew him personally, but which worked against him in politics. The whole experience led Will to a rather prophetic reaction, that he felt "almost cured" of "any desire to take part in politics." It was an inclination he did not follow.

Against his own personal desires, Will recognized that he was actually inching toward politics rather than the bench. One case he won, against a local boss, Tom Campbell, provoked an attack on Will's father in the *Cincinnati Telegram*—of which Campbell was copublisher. This criticism of "my family," as Will put it, was an aspect of being a Taft that he feared Nellie might abhor. "I felt as if it were too much to involve you in a life of such heartburning and sorrow. . . . You, as you are, a pure woman, whom no one would molest, if you were to become my wife must share with me the life which I propose and shall have to lead in a war of self defense and offense against evil."[20]

By September, Nellie had relented and permitted Will to tell the rest of his family. Will described Nellie to his aunt Delia as "not a girl of many friends nor one who makes them easily. She is rather reserved in manner, self-contained, independent, and of unusual application." He soon learned that Nellie was much more. In preparation for the June wedding, Nellie stopped working in the winter semester, and after the new year, she began to take financial matters in hand. Will had debts and insurance to pay off, yet he also thought that by living in a boardinghouse they could survive their first year on half of his $5,000 salary. His family doubted Will's ability to manage his money. Nellie simply announced that they would build a house and may have had a hand in guiding her father's choice of a wedding present—a lot in the Walnut Hills section of town, on McMillan Street, with a river view. Of the $2,500 that Will had saved from his 1885 earnings, he realized it would all go to furnishing a house and the European honeymoon that Nellie had long been anticipating. The couple needed money to build the house, and Will borrowed some $1,500 from Aunt Delia. Yankee that she was, she charged 6 percent interest.

Nellie was withering in her assessment of Will's haphazard notions on how to build and furnish a house, pay off debts, and go to Europe. She soon tried to soften her attitude by being willing to concede to Will in one of her few surviving premarital letters to him: "My opinion is the same still, but I might have given it . . . more deference for your opinion and feelings. . . . I don't blame myself with the fickleness usually ascribed to women. . . . I am quite ready to be as economical as can be, when we are once started." Her opinions, however, had finality. She wanted them to cut costs on furnishings, only buying quality furniture, piece by piece as money came in, rather than cheaper pieces they would later want to get rid of. She also cared more about "traveling than I do the house," although she was willing to shorten their itinerary; at least they could spend quality time in fewer places. She also refused to use the hefty amount that Charley would give Will as a wedding gift for furnishing a room; instead she wanted to use it to buy the finest household items, such as washbasins. Perhaps feeling more competitive with Charley and Annie than she did with Will's mother, Nellie finally told him, "Don't understand this to decline your mother's offer of the furniture. . . . Mothers are different, you know, from wealthy brothers."

Will conceded on financial matters to Nellie, and on the matter of her anticipatory anxiety about so many small matters in life, his sunny disposition worked wonders. When Nellie began fearing the sea voyage and whether she would get sick, he offered rational thinking and humor: "I would not make up my mind to be sick until I couldn't help it. There is this to be said if you are sick and can't get on deck [—] you will be indifferent to your surroundings and it will not make much difference whether we have a large room or a small one." He was also the one to always remind her of the big picture and provide the warm acceptance for which she had long yearned: "[W]e could be happy even if we did not go abroad or build a house, or furnish one if we have that in us which assures us that we can make each other happy. . . . I love you, my darling dearly and with all my heart and shall not be or feel myself until I can fold you in my heart and tell you so again. Goodnight, dearest sweetest girl that ever lived. . . . Let me know that you are close to me and that I am dear to you."

As traced through the letters between them over the decades, the dynamics of Will and Nellie's balance of power began emerging during their courtship. She would chide him in what observers often saw as a condescending manner. Will was actually buoyed by her commands and judgments, found them endearing, and responded with irreverence. It is a mistake to assume, however, that he always followed her advice. In fact, he often responded with advice of his own. When she reprimanded him for not exercising at the gym, for example, he retorted with concern for her caffeine consumption. "The very idea of your drinking coffee at night—allow me to scold you as you have the right to the same privilege with me for missing the gymnasium today and yesterday," he wrote. "I filed my excuses for yesterday. Today I was in court." If the humor touched a nerve of truth, Nellie tended to sign off without an expression of love. "I am sorry you object to the end of my letters. I will endeavor to change it," she admitted in one. When they argued, Will came around to make the peace. In his eyes Nellie would always be "her, who is all the world to me." It was Will who was always overcome with sentiment about special dates and anniversaries.

Despite the fact that she did not feel comfortable expressing her emotional love for Will—or anyone else—either in writing or words, it didn't mean she didn't feel it. For her it was a love that would unfold and grow, that was green at the time of their engagement. In her inimitable manner of always seeking to improve, Nellie Herron wrote herself a list of seven rules, kept in her diary, to being a good wife. It was a curious mix of docile tradition, moral perfectionism, and progressive self-esteem:

I. Be very particular in toilette—to examine the first of every month.

II. Break yourself of any little peculiarity of habit that may prove annoying.

III. Preserve always a certain amount of personal dignity and reserve.

IV. Exert myself to be agreeable to him as the person most important to please.

V. Cultivate an intelligent interest in everything in which he is interested.

VI. Above all never permit him in anything to have reason to look down upon you. I consider this essential ["most important" was crossed out] with a person of his character to keep his admiration and respect.

VII. With people with whom you live so intimately I believe it is better to be scrupulously truthful about the smallest matter.[21]

Will also discovered that when he plied her with intricate details of his legal cases, she responded sagaciously. Nellie had studied some of her father's law books and even considered going into law herself when she was young; she was certainly more familiar than most women with the intricacies of the legal system. Her two uncles, her two brothers, her father, and now her fiancé were all in the profession.

In minutely explaining all that he was doing, Will was absorbing her into his life, encouraging from his perspective their stated mutual desire for a genuine partnership. From her lectures at the salon he also knew of Nellie's knowledge of local, national, and global politics. She never hid her ambitions from Will to return to Washington in an important role of some kind, though there is no evidence she had yet revealed to him her dream of marrying a future President. Still, he did jokingly call her Miss Justice Herron. When she went to Washington, her second trip there, to buy her wedding dress, Will wrote her only half-jokingly: "I wonder, Nellie dear, if you and I will ever be there in any official capacity? Oh yes, I forgot, of course we shall when you become Secretary of the Treasury."

To Nellie it was no joke. "You know, a lot of people think a great deal of Will," she had told her mother when revealing her engagement that previous summer. "Some people even say that he may obtain some very important position in Washington."[22]

Four

Working Wife (1886–1890)

*In all my acquaintance she is the girl I would have picked for
you long ago and ever since and you are the one I would have
chosen for her. What a pair you will be!*

—HORACE TAFT

It was in the gray Herron house on Pike Street that Will and Nellie
had their June wedding. The June 20 *Cincinnati Enquirer* chronicled
the bride's "superbly fashioned satin robe with embroidered front,
and veil caught with sprays of white lilacs," and her bouquet of sweet peas
and lilies. A three-hour reception began at five in the afternoon. "The
wedding," John Herron noted to Hayes, who was unable to attend but sent
a gift of $30, "passed off very pleasantly." "No complaint, everybody satis-
fied" is how Horace described it.[1]

After a few days at the Jersey shore they sailed from New York for
their honeymoon, keeping a diary together. Will had been to Europe in
1883, but for Nellie, seeing firsthand the sites and art she had studied, it
was the fulfillment of a long-held dream. The diary notes historical, artistic, and architectural details of a well-educated American couple touring
England, Holland, Belgium, France, and Scotland, but is more revealing in
illustrating the chemistry between them in the first test of personal interac-
tions for a sustained period of time.

It was clear from the start that Nellie intended to prove that they would do the whole trip on her budget. She kept an account book while Will noted that they climbed to a fourth-floor hotel room "from economical reasons," endured third-class train seats with a feeling of "virtuous economy," and that the prices at an antique-filled inn "were very modern and not so much to my lady's taste." She finally decided to buy a London sideboard after weeks of considering its value, including shipping costs. They sat in decent seats at a performance of *The Country Girl*, Will recorded, only "because Nellie was not with me when I purchased the tickets." In Paris she wrote, "While Will went to the bank I went with fear and trembling to the dressmaker" because of the anticipated costs.

Along these lines, Nellie decided they could see as much as possible as quickly as possible if they first thoroughly studied their guidebooks. Intense in their curiosity, they absorbed everything they swiftly saw. "Nellie shows much greater powers of endurance in sightseeing," Will wrote. "[We] carried away from South Kensington . . . much valuable information . . . in one day." There were dozens of churches (Nellie said, "French Cathedrals . . . did not impress me so much as the English"), every sight associated with Shakespeare (Will said they "came away with our faith in his authorship of the plays attributed to him"), art galleries, and a wide breadth of theater (in London it ranged from Faust to *Adonis: A Perversion of Common Sense*). Throughout the trip Nellie evinced enough curiosity about European politics that she took in a session of the Dutch parliament, engaged a local citizen "who explained to us the political situation," and, Will noted, "read Gladstone and Parnell's speech in Parliament on the Queen's speech and the address and the proposals of the Tory government while I read the railway advertisements."

Nellie had planned on taking in a session of the House of Commons and had requested tickets from the American legation secretary, Henry White. None were available. Instead, Nellie noted sarcastically, "we visited Royalty in her stables," meaning the Queen's horses and equipage. She took it as a mortal insult, but Will recorded that White called and left his card. The incident was to have curious repercussions years down the road.

After leaving their initial stop of London, they crossed to Rotterdam. Nellie was aghast at the rudeness with which everyone pushed for a berth on the ferry and found herself in a tiny room with three Germans, one of whom was "very sick all the early morning." It was worse in Paris. "One of my chief recollections of Paris will always be of waiting on street corners when I was nearly ready to drop, for a bus that was more often than not full," she wrote. "The Parisian omnibus is always slow, crowded and filled with a class inferior to that in London. They do not stop for you to get in or out, but oblige you to run and jump on, or nearly break your neck." So trying was getting around that she even dropped her "economical plan" and took cabs. Wandering through the city court's criminal room, "We stood in a dirty garlic smelling crowd." She sourly noted that emerging from Notre Dame was a "bride . . . not very interesting and twice as large as her husband." On their last day in Paris they went to Versailles, walking through the labyrinth of rooms. She felt "a dearest gratitude" that she "would never have to see it again. It is a great bore to 'do' it."

Inevitably there were moments of tension between two people who had never before spent so much time alone together. Will's habits and humor irritated Nellie. "Will would carry the red covered guide book in full view which distressed me much," she wrote. Will wrote the next sentence, beginning, "The disposition to conceal our real mission to this country developing in my wife I can not approve of and shall do as much as possible to oppress." As they prepared to sail home, the Tafts had their first real argument, Nellie displeased with the books he bought for them to read on the voyage. "They were the cause of a little bit of a fight between us," he wrote.

The new bride had also been more than a bit blushing, and it may have been the cause for some resentment of Will, no matter how irrational. She seemed almost humiliated when she wrote her mother on June 22 in New Jersey that they had been "marked here as a b. and g." That others would know they were newlyweds with all that suggested about sexual intimacy and physical affection was embarrassing to her. She felt "a little strange" when they were "found off by ourselves" in some narrow castle archway and met her old teacher Edith Nourse. "But we pulled up and tried to be natural. . . . We have not seen anyone else to speak to but each other for two days, except the waiter." A morning scene of rustling leaves, she admitted, made them both feel "called upon to be sentimental, which of course, we very seldom are." Will, unashamed, wryly referred to their intimacy. "The advantage we have found in traveling second class is that . . . we are more often alone. . . . There are certain advantages somewhat with being the only occupants of the railway carriage, which it is not necessary to enumerate or describe but which we shall not soon forget. Perhaps Nellie may not confirm my view of the advantages but I must maintain it in spite of any different opinion of hers."[2]

"I saw Harriet and the bride," former President Hayes observed to his wife shortly after the newlyweds returned to Cincinnati. "Mrs. Taft never looked better. She is brown with travel, better looking than usual, and very happy." Will and Nellie lived with his parents until their new home was ready at the end of November, the senior Tafts having returned from Russia in October 1885. Between the stress of living with new in-laws and moving into a new house, Nellie was suddenly confronted with an illness that struck hard at her mother: a stroke. "Yesterday morning, Harriet awoke with one side of her face drawn out of its proper relations, and suffering a good deal. The Drs. say it is simply facial paralysis," John Herron reported to Hayes. After rushing down to see her, Hayes wrote in his diary that Harriet was still "very beautiful notwithstanding."[3]

During those difficult weeks an important alliance was forged between the two primary forces in Will's career: his father and his wife. Under one roof Alphonso and Nellie became extraordinarily close. As she later wrote: "My husband's father was 'gentle' beyond anything I ever knew. He was a man of tremendous firmness of purpose and just as set in his views as any one well could be, but he was one of the most lovable men that ever lived because he had a wide tolerance and a strangely 'understanding sympathy' for everybody." Where Alphonso left off, Nellie would pick up.

Alphonso's influence was felt even in Nellie's new house. The most impressive room in the couple's new McMillan Street house was Will's library. Here, walnut bookshelves held the nucleus of what would become one of the nation's premier private collections of law books, some of them Alphonso's. The house was shingled in redwood and had numerous porches. Among their first guests was former First Lady Lucy Hayes. The couple was entertaining her in March 1887 when word came by messenger that Will was named by Governor Joseph B. Foraker to fill the vacancy left by Judge Judson Harmon on the Ohio Superior Court. "Everybody is wild," reported young Jack Herron, "and also very much pleased since it is such a splendid position for a young man like him."[4]

Nellie was less than "wild" about the appointment, although she initially considered the judgeship an honor "to us." There is no record of when Will learned of Nellie's ambition to marry a President. Certainly as a remark made either in passing or as a humorous prediction, Will probably knew of it back in their salon days and teased her about it gently. Nellie did not raise the ambition when Will went to serve on the superior court. It was only to fill a vacancy, she realized, and only for one year. There was no pushing or urging to be done for that period of time. Nellie made a practical decision. She would use the year to return to work not for money but for engagement.

Will's judicial salary was $6,000 a year, so it was not necessary for Nellie to also earn a salary for their survival. While she would always find a reason to need more money, Nellie's decision this time was simply fueled by her desire to be productive. There is no record showing that she received a salary; it is almost certain that she was a volunteer. With Harriet still weakened by her stroke and unable to mount a protest against her now-married daughter's decision, Nellie returned to teaching.

This time she taught in a kindergarten, perhaps with the thought that experience with young children would be good preparation for motherhood. Most likely she took the job as a strategic move to gain some credibility with her mother-in-law, a driving force in Cincinnati in the Charity Kindergarten movement. Nellie and Louise Taft were never close. Before the wedding the older woman had insulted her when she wrote to Will that she would not stand in the way of his marrying a Herron despite the fact that they had no money. Nellie immediately assumed that Will had, as a family chronicler put it, "reasoned himself into loving her but that his family did not consider her a good match." The resentment went deeper than that, however. Like Alphonso, Louise believed that her boy Will was better suited for the bench than any executive position— a direct threat to Nellie's ambitions for Will. Over time, Nellie would gently pull Will away from his mother's influence, but Louise relented only when she saw proof that her daughter-in-law would take proper care of her son.

The movement to educate preschool children in basic social skills and behavior started in Germany but gained widespread American popularity in the Gilded Age. Charity kindergartens were established for underprivileged children, part of the social reform prompted by the swelling city populations of poor rural migrants and foreign immigrants. In a *New York Tribune* article that Nellie clipped, the positive effects of the Charity Kindergarten were treated as a modern marvel of noblesse oblige: "[T]he most vicious children, those taken, in fact, from the gutter, become good and sweet under the benign influences of the Kindergarten. The first few days, it is like a menagerie of little wild beasts, tearing, pounding each other, talking profane and obscene language, rebellious, selfish. . . . In a week's time order has dawned, for delightful occupations have chained attention . . . lovely sentiments set to music have charmed eye and ear and heart, harmonious . . . plays have been organized, kind words and caresses have wakened a new sense of enjoyment, and in less than a month, it is a little, orderly, docile compliant company."

Louise Taft had persuaded Edith Nourse to begin a Charity Kindergarten in her school, and here at her alma mater Nellie Taft began her stint as a working wife. In 1887, taking her responsibility with absolute seriousness, Nellie wrote her own instructional notebook, culled from lectures or education manuals, on the intricacies of how even the smallest art projects were vital to the development of the minds and abilities of young children. In her "General Statement" and "Rules" she outlined the principles she followed and the concepts they were based on:

> *The basis of the kindergarten system is the idea of organic unity. The salient characteristic of the kindergarten method is the emphasis it places on creative activity. The law which binds all the gifts [objects given to them] and occupations with a connected whole is the law of the connection of contrasts. These contrasts are not in things themselves, but in the qualities common to all things. Every object used in the kindergarten must be considered first as a key to the outer; second as an awakener to the inner world. In other words, each object must interpret the external world and rouse all the activities of the child. . . . Appeal to the threefold nature of the child—to his thought, by your suggestion and explanatory words, to his feelings, by the association of each gift and occupation with his experience and affections, and by music, to his activities by requiring him to handle, divide, reconstruct, transform and create.*

Nellie led her class in sewing, drawing, folding, cutting, and clay and cardboard modeling. Part of the process she taught was cutting paper into shapes and reconfiguring them, and playing with colored balls kept in a box—to teach the concepts of shapes, sizes, and color differentiation. She worked with saltshakers, tablecloths, vases, sailboats, and cigar cases as objects to be studied for spatial form and use. "The objectives of the kindergarten occupations," she wrote, "are to give technical training, to develop the creative power." Nellie even found great psychological power in the simple ball. She believed that its purpose was to "stimulate observation" and "lead to self expression," since it "offers the first basis for the classification of external objects." She concluded that the child's ball "by its extreme indefiniteness and wide adaptability . . . is the best medicine for the expression of the child's indefinite ideas."[5]

At the same time Nellie was beginning to shape and define her marriage the way she wanted to. In the new house she worked with an architect to make sure there were numerous of her favorite bay windows and fewer walls, so the house was roomy rather than formal. She managed Will's $6,000 per annum, scrimping and saving. Alphonso considered her an "economical and excellent calculator." She saved enough to pay off their debts, purchase more household furnishings, and make a second trip to Europe in the summer of 1888, this time exploring Germany, Switzerland, Austria, and Italy. Her first trip to Europe had been riddled with expensive accommodations and inconvenient transportation arrangements, but it had also been Nellie's honeymoon—a time of high stress for her. She had not seen all of the Continent and wanted to give it another try.[6]

The tone of the 1888 diary Nellie kept and that written by both her and Will on their honeymoon was markedly different. Married two years now, she had relaxed. She could even joke at her own expense. While making their crossing in July, for example, Nellie came down with an eye infection and comically went about with a pirate-like black patch fashioned by some German women. Although she claimed that her eye patch prevented her from reading—and so Will read to her in the public salon—she was just fine when it came to writing. She just enjoyed being waited upon. "Will was gratified," she noted cheekily, "to give a very exalted idea of his perfections of a husband to all the lady passengers, by reading aloud to me. . . . He is more anxious to wander than he was two years ago, and if he can get me safely planted somewhere, is not averse to the society of the smoking room. This is the opinion, alas, of a Jewish friend on board, a Mr. Makalowitch, who condoled with him one day on his confinement and remarked that he never brought his wife when he came on a pleasure trip." She even poked fun at her own moodiness: "I have been feeling well the last few days. Before that—about as mean as usual."

Some of Nellie's social insecurity also seemed to abate. Although one shipmate, a Mrs. McFadden, was "not especially refined," Nellie enjoyed her company as a "jolly woman . . . good fun and good hearted." When she met a pair of newlyweds on the voyage, Nellie found the wife to be "a perfect case—not caring what she said . . . the most extraordinary bride I ever knew. They fully expected to be teased and seemed to enjoy it and we all had a good deal of fun together." Knowing that her husband would later read her diary, Nellie repeatedly scribbled in a small phrase here and there: "I love Will."

Still, Nellie had her moods. When she learned that Will had agreed to give a July 4 oratory, her dread of his delivering a speech that was less than perfect left her so nervous that she couldn't bring herself to hear it: "I was such a goose that I could not go and hear him, which I was very sorry for, as it made a very good impression and a great many people complimented me about it." Her feistiness did not abandon her, either, and she was quite enraged at a "queer old party" who said "the future of America was in great danger because the women were not trained as they were in the days of Abigail Adams."

Nor had she lost her girlhood love of drinking. The morning she arrived in Europe, Nellie was "drinking beer." In Bremen, the first city they stopped in, she strolled the farmer's market and found some preserved mummies to be "ghastly and unpleasing" but found a rathskeller "very interesting" when she sat down for some wine from an ancient cask. They were "quite tired out" after touring Berlin "but not too tired," she noted, to go to a "beer garden where we heard Strauss from Vienna play his orchestra."

They went to the same beer garden the next two nights as well. "It seems impossible," she declared, "to go through Germany without drinking beer, for water is never to be had, and wine costs more. I am very fond of it. What they call Pilsner (bohemian beer) is delicious." In Munich she "found the restaurants not particularly good, but the beer delicious."

Venice was their first stop in Italy, and Nellie uncharacteristically swooned at the sight of San Marco, loving it as much in the sunlight as at night. They took gondola rides, found the island of Murano "disappointing," and raved about the food. At night Nellie immersed herself in the culture by reading a biography about the artist Giotto, while "Will read Mark Twain with which he is so happy, that he forgets me entirely, except to be mad with me for not appreciating him." In Florence she thought the Duomo interior "hideous" and Michelangelo's statue of David "very much more pleasing than the others in design."

Rome was a "beautiful city, clean and bright." Recording that the "grace of figure" of the Capitoline Venus was perfect, she cracked that "Will said he wanted to kiss her so he sympathized with this view." They went north, then to Switzerland, back to Germany, and finally Belgium. Sick of hotel food and cathedrals ("There is nothing that wears me out sooner than looking at churches"), she was ready to go home at the end of August. If her exposure to new cultures and peoples was exhilarating and further fueled her desire to travel, it also solidified her negative perceptions about her own people. Nellie Taft found American tourists to be "great bores" who were "doing Europe with a vengeance." One girl was "snippy," another woman "unaffectedly American," and yet another "murdered the King's English."[7]

A week after the Tafts returned from Europe, Nellie resumed teaching for the fall 1888 term, but just after the new year she learned that she was pregnant with her first child. There is no record of how well Nellie withstood pregnancy, but her mother—apparently recovered substantially enough from her stroke—was on hand when she gave birth to a boy on September 8, 1889, in the McMillan Street house—an eight-pound "splendid bright looking boy," as his grandfather Herron called him, with blond hair and large limbs. His size probably meant a difficult birth. Crying endless hours to the distress of his nervous mother, one senses in Nellie a curious detachment from her firstborn. Perhaps he had not been entirely planned in the midst of Nellie's return to work or perhaps the cost of raising a child worried her. She pointedly told her husband not to brag about the child. He wanted the boy named after his father, but Nellie insisted that it be "Robert," and so it was. The name was not that of any family member; it seems as if Nellie insisted on the name to affirm the fact that motherhood was not a sign she was transforming into a docile wife.[8]

Life was just right for Will Taft. He was happily married, a new and extremely proud father, living in a house he owned, and working in the field of his first great love: the judiciary.

Will's one year on the superior court had shown that he had become more conservative when it came to defending the rights of industry over labor. The very thing that Nellie had feared about his having accepted the appointment seemed to be happening: He was drifting off into the life of an old man. The alarm bell went off for her in April 1888, just before their second European trip, when Will ran and was elected in his own right to a full five-year term on the superior court. His place on the bench, however, "was not a matter for such warm congratulation" from Nellie's viewpoint.

At thirty, a teacher, wife, mother, and housekeeper in Cincinnati, life was all wrong for Nellie Taft. She loved Will fully and affectionately, and there were no marital problems. She did not pine to be single again—she wanted to share her life with her husband—it was just that while her husband was content as a judge, she wanted a larger life. Their courtship had already shown, however, that he was willing to take her advice seriously and weigh her concerns, opinions, and ambitions when it came to decisions about his own life.

As she frankly recalled: "I dreaded to see him settled for good in the judiciary and missing all the youthful enthusiasms and exhilarating difficulties which a more general contact with the world would have given him. In other words, I began even then to fear the narrowing effects of the Bench and to prefer for him a diverse experience which would give him an all-round professional development. He did not share this feeling in any way. The appointment on the Superior Court was to him the welcome beginning of just the career he wanted."[9]

The young Mrs. Taft did not despair. Rather, fusing her need for the security that came from familial love with her ambitions for the larger life of Washington, Nellie recognized ever more acutely that it was Will who would be her ticket out of a routine, if respectable, existence in upper-middle-class Cincinnati. Perhaps unconsciously Nellie Herron's talents for order, discipline, management, strategy, and even patience came together as skills for a new, far more subtle "career." Now securely and respectably identified by conventional society as "Mrs. William Howard Taft," she rather unconventionally determined to turn this label into a professional title. Her job would now be to guide Will, whether that meant bragging about his accomplishments or boosting his confidence. His career became her career. While she might raise a few eyebrows by criticizing her husband as a male business partner might, she could get away with doing so under the guise of Mrs. William Howard Taft. Underneath it all she would always be Nellie Herron, the young woman fueled with determined ambition and an impossible goal, chronic insecurity about money enough to live well, bottled anger at society's presumptions about a woman's abilities, and a confident, humorous sense of daring to try practically anything and even break taboos. She would always be the debutante bohemian who loved champagne as much as she did beer.

In many respects the timing was perfect for her to assume her new unsalaried role. The greatest influences on Will had remained his parents. The judicial career Will wanted was, of course, the position that had eluded his father and that Alphonso wanted for his son. "To be Chief Justice of the United States," he had once written to Salmon P. Chase who held that post, "is to be more than to be President, in my estimation." Dutiful, obedient, respectful Will was on the path of honoring his father's wishes. Although the most important decision he made during his tenure on the superior court—an 1890 ruling in favor of industry over a striking bricklayer's union—would haunt him politically, it would do no permanent damage. Will loved the court and hoped to stay on it forever, moving up, rung by rung, until he got to the Supreme Court. He was titillated that one of the old judges he served with, the now-retired Hiram Peck, and the wily Governor Foraker both recommended him to the new Republican President, Benjamin Harrison, as a potential appointee to the Supreme Court. He knew it was highly unrealistic that he could be named to the post without more judicial experience on the bench, and he had no longing to leave his "harbor" of the superior court. So when he received word from Washington in February that the President was offering him the position of solicitor general of the United States, Will was suddenly threatened. What was he to do?

The offer required an immediate answer. At that moment, however, Alphonso was not on hand, nor in the frame of mind, to advise Will or guide him on how best to stay on the judicial track. His health in rapid decline since his return from Russia, Alphonso was in California, that paradise of warm winter and fresh citrus where many wealthy Midwesterners retreated to rest. Will's first instinct was to turn down the offer, and remain on the superior court, serving out his full term. He did not want to resign, but neither did he want to insult the President and the patronage of Foraker. He did not know what to do. In the absence of his father, Will found a new figure to which he would report his activities and seek to please, a person of authoritative nature to whom he could be held accountable: his wife.

The solicitor general was essentially the counsel of the Justice Department. While the position was not officially "judicial," it would provide Will with legal expertise that would improve his abilities and thus his chances of being named a future Supreme Court justice. In recalling the situation, Nellie said nothing about having pointed out the other facts. A solicitor general was one rank away from the President's Cabinet. It would plunge Will Taft into the stream of national political figures. He would come to know Cabinet members, senators, congressmen, and Republican Party officials, and Nellie would come to meet a circle of wives just as ambitious for their husbands as she was for hers. It would provide executive experience as much as it would legal and judicial. While certainly no man who held that position had ever been elected President, being solicitor general was as valid a path to the chief executive as it was to the chief justice. With the dawn of the last decade of the nineteenth century, Nellie Taft's dream at least seemed back on the right track.[10]

Long years later Maria Herron suggested that Will "would not have" resigned his judgeship if not for Nellie. With "more than a suspicion that she could mold this marital clay into a really important figure," Maria asserted that Nellie—as one chronicler gently put it—"persuaded" him to do so. Even after his resignation, Will found his decision "rather overwhelming" and turned to his father, by letter. Whether or not Alphonso suspected that Nellie had influenced Will's decision, the old man realized there was nothing left to do but forgive his son's fears that he had perhaps ruined the chances of obtaining what Alphonso had always wanted for him. The job, Alphonso conceded, was "Herculean," but Will must "go ahead and fear not." Will did as told, but he did so with—as Nellie put it—"regretful glances at his beloved Bench."

Once she became First Lady, Nellie Taft was circumspect about appearing to have manipulated her husband. She would "confess only" to an "active interest" in his career, but no more. In her later memoirs she would neither deny nor confirm her influence on this first important decision of Will's career. Nellie did make it abundantly clear that it was the decision she favored, characterizing the solicitor general position as an "interruption . . . in our peaceful existence" that was "welcome," she wrote, "at least to me."

Besides, she seemed to suggest, being solicitor general would teach Will to push for himself, a situation in which "his own initiative" could be "developed." As for what the new job did for Nellie's determination to get Will onto a professional groove that could lead to the presidency, she put it bluntly: "I was very glad because it gave Mr. Taft an opportunity for exactly the kind of work I wished him to do. . . . I looked forward with interest, moreover, to a few years in Washington."[11]

Five

My Dearest and Best Critic

*Perhaps it is the comfort and dignity and power without worry
I like.*

—WILL TAFT, JANUARY 28, 1900

Will came to Washington first, renting a three-story turreted brick town house at 5 Dupont Circle. He put endless hours into outfitting his second-floor office where "the trees, the grass, the flowers make it a delightful outlook," he wrote his father. Here he lost himself, surrounded by walls of bookcases eight shelves high, filled with his library of law books that he arranged himself. "I look forward with the greatest pleasure to the use of my books at night at home. I was talking with Senator [William M.] Evarts about it, and he said he thought it was a mistake to lumber up a man's house with law books. I did not tell Nellie what he said about it, as I was afraid that she . . . may sympathize with the remark." Throughout his life Will's need for his own retreat, however small it might be, was central to his well-being; there were times when he felt he must be utterly inaccessible. Nellie otherwise ruled the roost. She assigned, for example, a beautiful large room for "Robbie's" nursery. "[A]s I have no jurisdiction over the subject matter," Will wrote, "my protests amount to nothing."[1]

Nellie was exhausted during her first months in town, anxious about getting the house settled and pushing to get it done, all the while nursing her baby. Will soon got her off with the baby to join the Herrons on their summer sojourn in coastal Magnolia, Massachusetts. "The sea has always done her a great deal of good," Will remarked. Despite her activity and the early onset of Washington's humid summer, Nellie had already enjoyed the city. On their fourth anniversary, for example, she and Will took off for an evening carriage drive through the woods into Maryland. "Words cannot exaggerate the beauty," Will wrote. If an event interested her, Nellie also made public appearances with Will in his official capacity. She went out to tour a reform school with him, for example, where President Harrison and his wife's niece, Mamie Dimmock, joined them. Her grudge against the President's daughter, Mary McKee, however, was permanent after the woman snubbed her.[2]

Another promising young couple had already hit the capital, beating Will and Nellie by a year. In 1889 a wealthy and bright pair of sophisticated New Yorkers with Colonial pedigree and name recognition had arrived and been welcomed into the most elite circles. The Harvard-educated commissioner of the U.S. Civil Service vigorously pressed on for absolute reform, shocking party elders and garnering great publicity. His dynamic image was as calculated as his brilliance, foresight, and confidence were real. He had a personal magnetism that beguiled just the sort of "big shots" Nellie had wanted Will to cultivate: Senator Henry Cabot Lodge and British ambassador Cecil Spring-Rice. The man's wife was a snob acolyte of the king of this elite circle, author and biting social commentator Henry Adams. Their names were Theodore and Edith Roosevelt.

Precisely when Will and Theodore first met is not recorded, but they were already acquaintances by the time Nellie arrived in Washington in February 1890. What she made of them is not known, but it was clear that Theodore had that blend of élan and unctuousness that Nellie was able to create within herself when she wanted to charm or ingratiate. It was easy to see how she could be jealous of a wife like Edith Roosevelt, whose husband was so driven that he didn't need her to encourage his ambitions.

Nellie knew Edith Roosevelt early on and well enough to list her in her Washington address, but it was immediately clear that the budding friendship between Will and Theodore "never ripened into intimacy so far as the wives were concerned," as journalist Charles Selden gently put it. To Nellie, sensitive to regional superiority, her Cincinnati insecurity soon made her determined to somehow show up the Roosevelts.

It was, however, nothing personal.

Nellie could not have known the extent of Edith's condescending diffidence toward many of those she met in Washington, for she revealed it openly only in letters to her mother and sister. Even had she extended herself to Nellie, they had little in common. Edith had no interests beyond those defined by her class and gender. She did not drink beer, play poker, or smoke cigarettes. Her coldness even extended to her stepdaughter, Alice, born in 1884 on the day her mother died. In that case Edith was probably only following the lead of Theodore. To everyone else Roosevelt was a gregarious hail-fellow-well-met. Toward Alice, however, he created a permanent emotional wall by refusing to ever verbally acknowledge the existence of her mother, his first wife. Nellie would quickly recognize what she believed to be duplicity in Roosevelt's character.[3]

She was not quite so focused yet on those she might perceive as being in Will's league and thus competition. What was important to Nellie was the fact that she and Will rated high enough in Washington to receive the greatest social plum awarded in town: a White House state dinner invitation. Harriet Herron's daughter could not help feeling a bit superior about dining in the White House. Progressive, intelligent, unconventional, adventurous, egalitarian—Nellie Taft was all that and more. The snobbery she learned at her mother's elbow did emerge, however, when she felt challenged, making her downright imperious.

There was no great principle or political issue behind Nellie Taft's strangely early sense of competition with Edith Roosevelt. The rented house that Edith presided over in Washington, her friendships, her gowns, and even her Puritan genealogy did not intimidate Nellie or rouse her jealousy. The basis of her eventual intense dislike of the Theodore Roosevelts was nothing more than some deeply personal insecurity. She remained silent about it and Will never implied it, but could Nellie have been jealous of Edith for having the sort of husband she did? Had Nellie assessed Roosevelt with the eye of a manager and found his personal qualities attractive enough to imagine him on the path to the presidency—and perhaps even make her wish that her Will had those qualities? This would certainly account for both her general jealousy of Edith and her later mistrust of Theodore's motives. From the start of her association with the Roosevelts, Nellie made remarks about or asked questions regarding them in her letters to Will, somehow keeping track of their progress. Later she bluntly confessed in a letter to her youngest child, "I don't like Mrs. Roosevelt at all. I never did."

What affect Nellie's frequent visits to the White House had on her youthful ambition to someday live there is hard to know. By this point in her life Nellie had begun to meld her own ambition with what she believed was the best course for her husband. Thus, pushing him toward the presidency was all for Will's sake. While this was what certainly motivated her in part, it was still a course she was charting and he was not. Yet what gentleman or lady of political society could not respect the loving endeavors a wife undertook for her husband? This was the cloak that would permit Mrs. William Howard Taft to remain largely unchallenged by others who might think her a trifle pushy about Will.

In telling counterpoint, the first invitation to a White House state dinner was important to Will because it was honoring the entire Supreme Court. Everyone, including President Harrison, knew how much Will Taft adored the world of the Supreme Court. Was there something telling in Harrison's inviting Will to the annual judiciary dinner instead of the annual Cabinet dinner?

For Will, any chance to see the justices outside of the court and perhaps even socialize with them was of vital importance. His grand obsession was making a lasting impression on them. When any of them retired, they might just suggest his name as a replacement. Before them, he felt that as solicitor general "my rank is humble." Yet while he increasingly proved his skill and memory with the law, his confidence sometimes slipped unexpectedly. His parents, brothers, wife, and friends might all insist and argue with him that he was "great" enough to rise to national prominence, but Will frequently doubted this. When he lost his otherwise assured poise, he flustered. Days after the White House dinner, Will made his first oral argument before the Court. It was a disaster. His argument came in late afternoon, and the drowsy justices practically ignored him. It flustered Will and he lost his concentration, fumbled, and froze. His appearance, he told Horace, "did me no credit." A week later it got no better. As Will began to talk, the justices began to read their letters and even "to eat lunch."

For Nellie, Will's work at the Supreme Court had only one purpose: to draw Washington's attention and respect for him. Thus she was, wrote Will, "disappointed that I have not had more speeches to make in the Supreme Court." Barely hiding her contempt for his infatuation with the bench, she was "not much impressed with the appearance of the justices' wives."[4]

Even Will's appearance became an issue for Nellie to manage. She was as angered at him for getting fat as she was at those who ridiculed him for it. She answered Horace's crack that an old coat Will gave him was a "limitless" size with a "contemptuous silence." She began a lifelong battle to shame Will into dieting—and always lost. Commenting on the corpulence of his sister Fanny's fiancé, she quipped, "Dr. Edwards must look worse than you do because he is not so tall." Will dutifully reported on his eating: "I find that hotel meals are not nearly as healthful for me as those at home," he wrote from Nashville. "We have lunch late and I eat too much." Nellie especially curbed his love of sweets. "I fear from the paper that you indulged in too much taffy . . . which is a little fault of yours."[5]

When they were apart, Nellie's letters took on a maternal chiding. She laughed at his poor efforts to care for himself. "How I would have laughed to see you making your own bed!" she wrote before launching into precise instructions on where to find bedding in the house. If he decided to stay instead at a hotel where he would be taken care of, she reminded him to stay at the cheaper Ebbitt and not the Willard. Learning that he had fainted in the heat and wasn't eating properly, she was "wild" with fear, chastising him as "perfectly crazy to walk home. . . . How many times have I told you . . . keep quiet if you do not feel alright in your stomach. . . . For my sake darling do send out for a sandwich or go and get a glass of milk, and eat less at the other two meals."

Nellie closed one letter to her "sweet precious darling" by confessing she was "not a bit happy without you," concluding with a touch of manipulation again: "It worries me to think of you there without anyone to look after you. I wish I could come home tomorrow. Would you like to see me walk in?" Rarely did she admit the real reason for hating the separations. Since her ambivalent courting days, she had grown to love him deeply. "Do you think you will be so wedded to your bachelor mode of living that you will not welcome me back?" she wrote him. "I would come home tomorrow if I believed it. A thousand kisses my own sweet darling and any number of hugs for you tonight."[6]

She wasn't so sweet when it came to money. Will swallowed his pride to ask Charley for a loan, but Nellie was humiliated by the appearance of neediness and wanted to pay Charley back promptly. She went through a lengthy justification for buying a new dress that she promised to wear all through the fall social season in Washington. Working on the bills one morning, she told Will, "It is so close a squeeze as usual. . . . I don't know where the money will come from." After realizing they hadn't canceled a monthly church pew rent, she complained, "How aggravating it is to have all that money thrown away." When he was away, Will wrote Nellie that he "feared you are much cramped" on "money matters." She bore down on him to get his traveling expenses reimbursed immediately.[7]

Although she sometimes had a part-time cook and nursemaid, Nellie had constant trouble with them. "I hope your cook will turn out all right,"

Will wrote her in one note. "I would not put a whiskey or wine bottle under her nose." On other occasions the problem was not having enough money to pay for help, and Nellie cooked, cleaned, and changed diapers. When they entertained, she planned menus down to the penny and always kept a detailed daily household account of every expense. It was not a minor role to allow Will to stay in low-paying public service. Somehow she managed to keep appearances up without running large debts. She learned to be notoriously tightfisted, rarely indulging her family or herself except at Christmas. She was always looking for a bargain.

As a mother, she also struggled. Bobbie was a "determined little cuss" at times, "so hard to manage that I am beginning to be disturbed by it." There was another child when Nellie gave birth in Cincinnati on August 1 to her only daughter, namesake Helen Herron.[8]

Nellie kept herself fully abreast of the details of the cases that came across his desk at the Justice Department. She was "disgusted," she wrote Will, when President Harrison asked the Justice Department to consider possibly withdrawing a case it had wanted to press in Minnesota. "It is inexcusable conduct in my opinion, on the part of the President, and endangers the whole prosecution. The Attorney General [W.H.H. Miller] must have felt mad about it, I should think. Perhaps on looking over the matter the President may conclude not to interfere. Perhaps it is partly owing to his desire to trust to his own opinion in every matter." When Will wrote her that Miller had suddenly become uncommunicative, Nellie said it was simply "embarrassment" on the Attorney General's part because he "realizes what we must think." Will, who could fret more than Nellie when he felt he was facing any sort of professional disapproval, was reassured by her "not worry about it."

Nellie Taft was naturally drawn to political debate and let no societal taboo prevent her from discussing it with men other than Will. In recalling for him details of a lively dinner she had with some conservative southern "mug wamp" [sic] Democrats, Nellie didn't hesitate to hold an opinion at odds with his: "We have spent all the evening in a discussion on politics. As we [sic] none of us get excited, we had a really interesting talk. They are Mugwumps but I don't find them bitter on the subject. . . . The principle part of our talk was on the Negro question [how best to overcome the legal obstacles created that prevented southern African Americans from voting]. I am afraid that I rather agree with them that it is better to leave it alone, which I am sorry for as I know you feel so warmly on the subject."[9]

Political debate was interesting to Nellie not because of policy but for the art of debate itself. She was never motivated to try out new ideas on legislation or laws, as Will was. For Nellie Taft the joy of politics was in creating a successful strategy for winning. The importance of issues and policy found their place in her mind only after she had figured out how well or poorly it would help to win. This is not to suggest that she was not highly principled and was not invested in the value of fairness and equality, for she was, but mastering the political game was the priority. Nellie focused on finding a way to get Will into the presidential game and then to win it. Once he was there, he could apply all the principles and initiate all the policy he wanted to; she would finally sit back and do whatever it was she might wish to do when that time came. Her time in Washington was serving to familiarize Nellie with the rules of the game as she bided her time at the fringes of the power elite. Nellie eagerly returned to the capital in the fall of 1891 for the upcoming social season, but before this second one ended, she would find her path obstructed again.

She could not have been caught entirely unaware by the message that came from the White House in February 1892. Will was ecstatic; Nellie was devastated. A year earlier, Congress had created an appeals court in all of the nation's nine circuits, and Will had told Nellie he was going to push for one of the appointments to the Sixth Judicial Circuit Court, which included parts of Ohio, Kentucky, Tennessee, and Michigan. Perhaps because nothing happened for several months, Nellie did not seem overly concerned, but when the news came that President Harrison had made the appointment, her capital life was abruptly halted. Will resigned his Washington job on March 21.

The return of the Tafts to Cincinnati in 1892 suggested an important element in their marriage. Will had taken the solicitor generalship as Nellie had wished; it was only fair that she now acquiesce to his joyous return to the bench. That they both had the power over each other to make such determinations was witness to the foundation of trust and respect that their marriage was built on. Still, Nellie had made her best effort to persuade him to see it her way. In the interim between his application for the job and his being offered it, Taft had made a government junket with his superiors. "Think of your going off on a trip with two Cabinet officers!" she flatteringly wrote him. "If you get your heart's desire, my darling, it will put an end to all the opportunities you now have of being thrown with the bigwigs."[10]

Back on the judicial path he had feared leaving, Will was "greatly pleased," Nellie recalled in her memoirs, and he "enjoyed the work of the following eight years more than any he has ever undertaken." Now it was Nellie who seemed pained. Will would again be in the company of older men that she felt prematurely aged his sense of self, and "fixed in a groove for the rest of his life"—the very circumstance she had all along "feared."

With her tendency to see her life in black-and-white chapters that ended and began, rather than a flow of experiences, Nellie seemed to resign herself to a fate out of her control. Her surrender was all the more isolating an experience because Will was always away, traveling the circuit, and they had to first board with friends and then rent a house—their own home being under a longer term lease they had signed before leaving for Washington.

The separation affected Will as well. "It seems to me that every time I leave home on the circuit I feel more and more impatient to see you and the children again," he wrote her. "My love for you, Dear, grows each year and you become more and more indispensable to my life and happiness. This is not the enthusiasm of the wedding journey but it is the truth deliberately arrived at after full opportunity for me to know."

Another reality had also set in for Nellie. She could no longer seek to find a happy compromise between what was best for her and best for Will. Children now factored into how her time and money were spent. "I would be glad to go about with you if there were no children at home," she wrote, "and we had, as you say, our expenses paid."[11]

As she later confessed, during those years in Cincinnati "life was tranquil; quite too settled, I thought, and filled with the usual homely incidents." Nellie cast about for some personal fulfillment besides her role as mother. She soon signed on to the board of directors of a local hospital foundation, increasingly drawn into the management, fund-raising, and finding, leasing, and equipping a downtown site. "This morning I went to a Hospital meeting," she reported to Will in November 1893, "and some of us who were decided put through a motion to make the offer for the Huntington houses on the terms formerly offered by Mr. H. . . . This will involve an Emergency ward in town which I fear will be a great expense but the doctors seem to think it essential and hold out a very attractive picture of what it might be." Nellie made her own excursion downtown to inspect prospective buildings and inquire about rental prices but after she found property owners unwilling to negotiate with her, she acquiesced that "it would be well to negotiate the matter through some men." She also helped to train and certify the nursing staff, determining medical charges and the qualifications of the resident physician.

She turned down the presidency of the local International Kindergarten Union chapter, but continued her support of the preschool movement. She attempted to re-create her salon, forming a reading club with women friends and relatives. "We would like to have a Current Event Class," she reported in confidence to Will, "but with these people I don't believe it would work. Annie [Taft] always makes a jest out of everything, so that she is rather hard to manage, and Mamma gets snappy and offends the others unknowingly."

Finding herself just the sort of woman she had feared becoming as a teenager, Nellie ruminated on some of her early life ambitions. At tea with a friend she expressed her frustration "that there were so few people we ever saw who cared for conversation on the social graces in art and music." It was a first inkling of the new direction Nellie Taft's life was about to take.[12]

In the summer of 1893 the Tafts were able to take a full vacation together. This time, however, they went farther north than Massachusetts and west of New York, to Murray Bay in Canada. They had come across the small village the previous year while sailing the Saint Lawrence after attending a family wedding. Just over one hundred miles from Quebec, Murray Bay was a rural spot where several hundred French Canadians lived year round. The cool air, scented pines, and invigorating waters of the river they overlooked made Murray Bay the one place Will and Nellie always called home. After a season in an inn, they rented a small house, which, after buying it, they continued to expand. A later friend described the home as a "simple cottage, with its single partitions of rough boards and a place for Mr. Taft's desk at the back of a small and constantly traversed hall." It was "a happy summer home," where "the entire household could hear the contents of his letters as he dictated them to a secretary in the early morning hours." Restless, Nellie golfed, swam, and even tried tennis but seemed to have lost the brief burst of enthusiasm she had enjoyed as a teenager for such activities: "I must confess that I don't particularly enjoy athletic sports. Probably I did not begin early enough."[13]

When the Tafts returned, Nellie discovered a new outlet for her restlessness. Thinking along the same lines as Nellie—from whom she may, in fact, have gotten the idea—one Helen Sparrman organized seventeen other Cincinnati women to create a music club. Sparrman and Emma Roedter served as president, and Nellie was secretary. Within weeks, Nellie's letters to Will were sprinkled with news of her Ladies Musical Club. Their first goal was to have a small winter concert and determine whether there was enough interest to support a regular series.

"The recital is coming out well," she wrote Will in early 1894. "There is a great demand for the tickets and by sending notes to all requesting them to return their tickets or the money, we shall know pretty well by Wednesday just how many are sold."[14]

Unlike most husbands of his class and era, Will never discouraged Nellie from pursuing her own interests. Still, he depended on her support for his career, albeit by correspondence. His greatest insecurity was public speaking. Whenever Will "did not feel satisfied" with a speech, she invariably responded that it must have been "better than you think." When he didn't reveal how a speech went, she would always ask about it, but end on a reassuring note, "You can make a[s] good [a] speech as any one, and I hope it was a success this time." It did not mean she found many of his speeches to be good. "I was very much pleased with the note from the Lincoln Club about publishing your speech," she wrote him in February 1894. "I hope you will go over the proofs carefully and correct those parts that I thought undignified." He knew that Nellie's harshness ultimately stemmed from her desire for him to make the best possible impression. "I am so glad you don't flatter me and sit at my feet with honey. You are my dearest and best critic and are worth much to me in stirring up my best endeavor," he wrote her a month after their ninth anniversary.

One thing Nellie refused to do, no matter how much it would have lifted Will's spirit, was indulge his continuing dream. He followed any slight or perceived movement on the Court as if it were a chess game. "My impression is that Judge Lurton thinks that Judge Jackson's days are numbered and that he is becoming interested in the succession," he reported to Nellie in February 1894. "I have noted two or three circumstances that bear out my suspicion. My impression is that Cleveland will have to go to the Fifth Circuit for Jackson's successor if he ever has the opportunity of appointing one, and that will shut out Lurton. I have not quite made up my mind whether Lurton is made of Supreme Court material or not. . . . Mrs. Lurton is very ambitious and keeps up a'thinking and a'suggesting." In reaction to talk of the slight possibility of Will being considered for the Supreme Court by Democratic President Grover Cleveland, Nellie retorted,

"You seem to have a very gay prospect ahead, but some way a good deal of it does not sound very attractive to me."[15]

Nellie Taft's focus was not on men of judicial potential but, rather, of executive ability. She had her eye on one with which Will was infatuated. After a trip to Washington, during a session of the House of Representatives, Will reported to Nellie that he "saw Mr. and Mrs. Roosevelt in the reserved gallery and called them over." Mrs. Taft had already been keeping score. Three weeks after she had given birth to Helen, she read in the paper that Edith had also had a child. "I see that I got ahead of Mrs. Roosevelt," she wrote Will, "and feel quite proud."[16]

Six

Managing the Music (1893–1899)

I consider obedience the first virtue of a husband.
—WILLIAM HOWARD TAFT, JULY 14, 1896

I n the two years following her return to Cincinnati, Nellie Taft had adapted to the life that Harriet Herron had always hoped she would lead: wife of a prominent son of a socially prestigious family. It was not a bad situation. While certainly not wealthy, Will and Nellie now had enough money to hire a nursemaid for the children from time to time. At the very least Nellie could count on her mother or sisters Maria and Lucy to watch Bob and Helen, while she devoted herself to her volunteer work for the local hospital foundation. During this period, Nellie made no further mention of her ambitions to make a President out of Will. Yet it was not long before her desire to participate in a world larger than that of motherhood and housekeeping emerged. Being back where her initial aspirations were born provoked her. Even before she had hoped to marry a President, Nellie Herron had dreamed of a musical career.

Nellie Taft may not have been the sole creator of the Ladies Musical Club that she and other prominent socialites were putting together, but it was soon obvious to all that no one had as much enthusiasm for the idea and the driving determination to make it a professional organization as she did.

On February 10, 1894, the Ladies Musical Club held its first ticketed concert, in Pike's Opera House. Nellie felt it was an "assured success." With 360 tickets sold, it turned into a "great jam," enough to cover expenses and turn a small profit for the next concert. Right then and there, Nellie created an immediate and challenging goal for herself: turning her city, within a few years, into a place as renowned for the quality of its music as were Boston, New York, and Chicago. Cincinnati already had a zoo and an art museum, but almost no musical presence. The first effort by professional musicians, the Philharmonic Society, had presented only three seasons. An opera festival lasted seven years. Starting in 1878 there was a May Festival of music, but it was only one week long. In 1894 the massive brick Music Hall was dedicated, becoming the primary place for touring performance groups. Smaller programs were presented at the older Pike Street Opera House. Many large cities already had symphony orchestras. That's what Nellie Taft now wanted to create. As Nellie explained: "We had not a good symphony orchestra in the city . . . but with our music loving population it was only necessary that somebody should take the initiative and arouse definite enthusiasm and keep it going. There were many public-spirited citizens, some of them true music-loving Germans, and I saw no reason why I should not get strong popular support for my project."[1]

The Cincinnati Symphony Orchestra Association was born out of the Ladies Musical Club; although the latter's founder, Helen Sparrman, did not come along, her copresident Roedter did become one of the fourteen members of the board of directors. Nellie made it clear that all of the board "shall be women." She was elected president—and would be every year until 1900. First to join the board and come to her financial aid was her sister-in-law Annie, an important backer. Nellie's old friend Sally Woolley was also on the board, as was the treasurer Isabel Jelke. Once the incorporation papers were filed, governing regulations were drawn.

To finance the orchestra, Nellie estimated that they would not only draw on box-office receipts but also secure some $30,000 annually. Pragmatically realizing that big money was still largely in the hands of businessmen, an advisory board of "seven gentlemen" was enlisted and through them leading families—Fleischmann, Schmidlapp, Ingalls, Ault—soon made generous donations. Several financial forecasts were drawn up, with numbers being moved around to estimate potential costs and income. To what extent Nellie conjured up projected numbers is uncertain, but she had to understand not only the big but the small financial scenarios because she was required to make her own educated opinions known. During the first board meeting, Nellie addressed the value of the various plans, musical union requirements of thirty weeks' work at $18 a week, and the fact that the orchestra couldn't count "on getting the men off [to] the theater as frequently [as the women]."

Nellie and her board furthermore asserted that every single musical venue in the city, whether festival or school, should pledge to help find part-time employment for the musicians or promise to use them in their own concerts. Despite some ruffled feathers, institutions promised to do so. On April 30 a list of shareholders of capital stock in the association was drawn, reflecting the same Jewish, German, and Anglo-Saxon Protestant mix of the orchestra's other committees, subscribers, and supporters. Nellie held one share herself. In her own hand, with Will providing the legal technicalities, Nellie wrote out all of the association's bylaws, organizing more than ten committees to handle everything from making lighting and seating arrangements in the hall, selling ad space in programs, selling subscriptions, maintaining box-office receipts, and collecting on delinquent accounts. She secured guarantors of large four-year loans that allowed the orchestra time to get on its feet. These included Charley Taft, Nicholas Longworth, Charles Fleishmann, Joseph Levy, Joseph Schmidlapp, Thomas Egan, the law firm of Frieberg & Workum, and thirteen other individuals.[2]

There was also the longer-term goal of an endowment fund that would, ideally, ensure the orchestra's continuation for decades. Potential donors to this fund were not cultivated until the orchestra was in its fourth season. She resisted suggestions that she immediately approach David Sinton, Annie Taft's millionaire father ("There is the least chance of it," she said of his giving), and a Mr. Hinkle ("He likes to manage the thing himself"). She would do so in time.

Nellie and her board took an active part in building subscription ticket sales for the whole season and for individual concerts—matinee and evening performances—with names culled from other local music organizations. Each person approached upper- and middle-income friends, colleagues, and associates. Nellie came up with close to one hundred, most of whom bought season seats for matinee performances. She even sent her sisters Jennie, Lucy, Maria, and Eleanor to solicit their friends. Commitments came in rapidly, sometimes even for several years in advance, thanks to her strong arming of women and men alike. "Sally and I went up to the Courthouse to tackle Hol [Howard Hollister] for a subscription this morning, but as he was in the court room . . . we decided not to disturb him. We went down to Judge Harmon and got him, and then tried Mr. Warrington but he was out. I dislike extremely going about, but I fear there is no other way of reaching the people. Dividing the afternoons and evenings is going to make it difficult to get a large subscription for either. It is so long since people have been accustomed to going to concerts that the price seems high, though it is in reality so cheap."[3]

Officially, her responsibilities included presiding at board and stockholder meetings, signing all contracts and stock certificates, and delivering an annual report. She must also "in general, perform all the duties usually incident to such office." That vague description was, in fact, a vast catchall; for although there were specific committees established to cope with individual processes, Nellie Taft was a hands-on president, as the orchestra's files proved. All this "organization and management" fulfilled just what she had sought since her teenage years. "I found, at last, a practical method for expressing and making use of my love and knowledge of music," she later wrote.

Throughout late 1894, Nellie scouted talent. After auditioning one soloist, she told Will, "His price is high and he did not create the furor we expected, so we feel in some doubt," although she still declared him "a very fine human." Hiring individual musicians, however, was not a task for even the most active president. Professional guidance was necessary, and there was one potential musical director Nellie was implacably determined to hire. It was her opinion, she wrote, "that we must make every effort to secure [conductor Frank] Van der Stucken."[4]

Born in 1858, in Fredericksburg, Texas, of German and Belgian parents, Van der Stucken, like Nellie, had loved music since childhood. At eight years old he was enrolled at the Antwerp Conservatory of Music, studying violin with Emile Wambach from 1866 to 1876 and composition and theory with Pierre Benoit. By sixteen he had written two major original works. After a visit to Wagner's Bayreuth Festival in 1876, he settled in Leipzig. For two years he studied there with Carl Reinecke, Victor Langer, and Edvard Grieg. From 1879 to 1881, Van der Stucken traveled throughout Europe and worked with Giuseppe Verdi, Alexis-Emmanuel Chabrier, and Jules Massenet. He was appointed *Kapellmeister* of the Breslau Stadttheater in 1881 and, as part of his duties, composed incidental music for Shakespeare's *The Tempest* in 1882. The next year Franz Liszt sponsored a complete program of his works at Weimar.

He came to New York in 1884 as the director of the Arion Society, a male chorus founded in 1854. During his tenure, which lasted until 1895, the society became the first American musical organization to tour Europe. He also worked with other German musicians who sought to bring their training to the American ear, establishing festivals and training singers. Notably, Van der Stucken encouraged American composers to create their own original movement in music and fostered appreciation of past American music. In 1885 he conducted the first United States concert of works entirely by American composers, and in 1889 he conducted the first European concert with an entirely American program at the World Exposition in Paris. Nellie Taft was determined to get him as musical director.

Van der Stucken, however, could also be an obstinate prima donna and was, in the words of one friend, "an ambitious man." To her first inquiry, in February 1894, he responded that her "proposition cannot be accepted."

Many Cincinnati music lovers didn't want Van der Stucken. William Hobart, president of the May Festival and a kind supporter of Nellie's, said his inquiry showed that Van der Stucken, while he was "the best in New York," was "an unknown quantity as a choir master. . . . It would be a good deal of a leap in the dark to take him and I should be somewhat afraid of a long contract with him." As the summer of 1894 began, there was also a concerted effort by Cincinnati musicians to have local Henry Schradieck chosen as the permanent conductor. Nellie resisted.

She successfully approached the College of Music to have them hire Van der Stucken as a part-time professor, thus providing further income to him to compensate for the lower salary that the orchestra was able to offer. Nellie again approached Van der Stucken. He had two words: "Cannot accept."[5]

Meanwhile, someone leaked the story of Van der Stucken's refusal to the press, and Nellie was flooded with unsolicited aggressive offers and testimonials on behalf of numerous other conductors and musical directors. Nellie held out for Van der Stucken. Other pressures built. The summer pops concert committee wanted to make sure their series would be "perfection," but nothing definitive could be determined about what role the Cincinnati Symphony Orchestra was to have in it until there was a conductor. The Cincinnati College of Music president began to have second thoughts about a professorship; Nellie found his attitude "antagonistic," and was advised not to commit her conductor to teach there. She also discovered that CSO musicians were being discouraged from making themselves available to commit as potential orchestra members. Schradieck sought to exploit the uncertainty by manipulating key figures to push for his appointment, suggesting that he had helped spur the city's interest in an orchestra.[6]

Nellie continued to negotiate for Van der Stucken through her friend, the association's subscribers trustee Lucien Wulsin, who was in Europe where Van der Stucken was conducting at the time. "I hate to acknowledge that I am beaten and yet, as I look over the situation," Nellie wrote

Wulsin, "I see very little hope that we will get Van der Stucken, and I wonder whether we should give him a hint that the situation has changed." If the conductor would not reconsider, Nellie promised to "pocket my pride." She even offered to resign. The board, she said, was "pressing me to take some more active steps about a conductor."

This time Van der Stucken blinked: He wanted more than the $4,000 salary that she offered. Wulsin infused some competition into the mix, telling him that the board was considering Anton Seidl as conductor. Nellie, "anxious to clinch the matter as soon as possible," wrote to Will that "Van is very insistent that negotiations must be kept entirely private." This suited her. "After our experience in failing once, or rather twice," she wrote to Wulsin, "I don't want to have it get out again unless it is certain to go through." Van der Stucken stayed firm. Two members voted no to Nellie's plea to raise the conductor salary by $1,000. Others questioned her judgment. "There is great impatience on the part of all to have some one chosen," Nellie next wrote Wulsin. Van der Stucken's hand was suddenly weakened, however, when Wulsin learned that the Arion Society was "discontented" with the conductor "because of his recent behavior and that perhaps we could now get him."

Meanwhile, Seidl was boldly pushing himself into the scene as the great unheralded talent who could save the day. Nellie went through the motions of requesting his credentials but only because he was "a good drawing card" in her battle to lure Van der Stucken; otherwise she thought him not up to snuff. Nevertheless, she was panicking. "There is a general feeling among the public that we have fizzled, and we all feel that if we hope to keep our subscriptions we must have a conductor this winter. Schradieck is still to be had." Still "anxious to make every effort" to get Van der Stucken, she finally got the College of Music to commit to giving him a salary of $3,000.[7]

Nellie finally devised a unique approach that not only deferred the salary issue but also got Van der Stucken's partial commitment. In what she called the "experimental" concerts, Seidl, Schradieck, and Van der Stucken would each give two consecutive concerts. Nellie thought it a great concept. Not everyone did. Mrs. Taft had her first full blast of negative national press in the November 14, 1894, *New York Musical Courier*:

> *The first principle of a permanent orchestra is certainly a*
> *permanent conductor . . . who . . . drills the body into one compact,*
> *homogeneous mass that must follow his will. . . . An orchestra such*
> *as the proposed Cincinnati organization, which we learn is still*
> *short of about nineteen important players, and which will therefore*
> *require a great deal of drilling to enable it to perform . . . need have*
> *this single head long before the first concert takes place. . . . Will the*
> *men [musicians] selected by the Cincinnati ladies . . . [or] Seidl*
> *please Van der Stucken or the reverse, and how would Schradieck*
> *view them? If Cincinnati had a permanent orchestral body,*
> *complete and in playing order, it is questionable if even then it*
> *could afford to dally with such a peculiar plan. . . . We would be*
> *surprised if all these three conductors would be willing to undergo*
> *such an ordeal.*

There was one humorous consolation: In the article, the "other" Mrs. Taft—Annie the heiress and, now, congressional wife—was mistakenly assumed to be the president, thus unfairly blamed.

Under the direction of conductor Van der Stucken, the Cincinnati Symphony Orchestra performed their premier concert on January 17, 1895, with selections from Bach, a Mendelssohn violin concerto, Dvorak's symphony "From the New World," and Liszt's symphonic poem "Les Preludes." In that first season there were forty-eight musicians in the orchestra, and the association sponsored nine concerts. In contracting with Pike's Opera House, Nellie had gotten the $100 per evening concert fee lowered by $25.[8]

As the "experimental" season progressed, Nellie found Schradieck imperious. "I have now changed the programs according to your wishes," he haughtily wrote, but then insisted on restoring some of his choices to the programs. Whether she seriously considered him or Seidl as candidates is doubtful. The latter never satisfied her, and if the former was as imperious as "Van," he lacked Van der Stucken's talent. She steadfastly determined to make Van the permanent conductor. However difficult he was, she recognized his genius and public appeal. "Under his baton the orchestra plays as one instrument with the same precision of attack, the same strength in the fortissimo, the same delicacy of nuance, with the same article ensemble that is explained only by the feeling of union among the men," she wrote, "the feeling of an 'esprit de corps' that must exist for all successful interpretation." Vulnerable to feminine flattery, Van finally relented to the indomitable Mrs. Taft. She got Will to draw up the six-year contract. Van got $7,000 per year, $4,000 from the CSO and $3,000 from the music school.

Satisfied, she then heard nothing for two weeks and "almost gave up hope." An article in the *Musical Courier* stated "positively" that Van was "not coming." He had to wrangle out of his Arion Society contract and feared that its board "will try to hold out." Exasperated, Nellie contained her temper, writing Wulsin she "suspected that he was not working very hard for his release." In fact, the Arion forced Van to resign immediately, before his season was done, and withheld $1,000 of his $4,500 salary. Now Van asked Nellie to please get the orchestra to pay the difference, since they had solicited him. She sent an encouraging telegram, while delaying an official answer. Trustee Schmidlapp adamantly opposed this and expressed his outrage at Van's arrogance. Nellie felt that it was only fair to pay, though "this may be a sentimental and not a business view." In the end, several trustees, including Charley Taft, shelled out the cash.

On April 22, 1895, Nellie Taft received the letter she had longed for from Van: "I feel happy to have been released, although the Arion are very sore about it. I leave many good friends in this great city of New York, but hope to find a compensation of affection in my new home. If an earnest purpose and work can do it, the Cincinnati Symphony has to be a success."

Nellie and Van signed his contract days later. She declared soon after that the orchestra "already reflects credit upon the city" and "can not but restore" its "musical prestige."[9]

The following season the orchestra moved from the Pike Street theater to its permanent home in the Music Hall. The hall had recently undergone a $100,000 renovation, complete with a proscenium arch stage, permanent seating on a pitched floor, steam heating, and electric lighting. The number of musicians was increased to sixty, and they began to give Nellie problems.

As president, Mrs. Taft signed off on each musician's contract, writing in the instrument to be played, the salary, and any special conditions. She had warned Van to make certain that any musicians he brought from Europe became union members, which required six months of residency prior to performance. In the contract of a Signor Tirandelli, for example, she noted that it could be canceled not only due to "incompetence, insubordination or intemperance," but also "failure to comply with the rules of the local union." Nellie would have a running battle with Van over his inclination to ignore union rules and bring European musicians over to join the orchestra, rather than using local ones. He played on her emotions, admonishing, "Do not forget that the vitality of your enterprise depends on the way we increase the quality of the orchestra. . . . After five years of work, we must be able to go to concerts in New York, Boston & Chicago." Finally, he also managed to insult her musical choices: "Your list of orchestral works is not great. . . . When I have made up the programme for the season, I will invite more about this matter."[10]

Nellie plunged full tilt again into work. She expanded advertising outside of the city, persuading places like A. Beaugurcau's Emporium in Oxford, Ohio, and McCoy & Kitchen Drugs in Middletown, Ohio, to display "a nice attractive" poster with concert dates and to also sell tickets. Ads were placed in the German newspapers like the *Daytona Volks-Zietung*. She obtained free advertisements in the *Lebanon Patriot* by giving the editor free tickets and persuaded the "Big Four" railroads, the Cleveland,

Cincinnati, Chicago, and St. Louis lines, to reduce their rates for passengers with CSO concert tickets. As the professional reputation of the orchestra grew, Nellie began to receive requests for it to perform in the region. Within three years Van felt they were ready to do so—which meant Nellie oversaw hotel bookings for the musicians, arranged rail schedules, reviewed expense accounts, wrote advertising copy, and signed more contracts.[11]

Nellie also created an outreach to the Cincinnati public school system, asking every principal to pass out circulars to music students and offering them discount balcony seats. She had the CSO give free summer concerts and perform an Alms Society benefit, and she subcontracted musicians to the Cincinnati Orpheus Society and United Sangerbund for their performances. In the office she had a daily flood of paperwork across her desk: chair rental contracts, program and poster copy to be read carefully, far-flung newspaper subscriptions, envelope orders to be printed, comparative prices on messenger services. Amid the minutia, Nellie Taft maintained her intention of making Cincinnati's orchestra the rival of Boston's and New York's. In the process, Nellie Taft had become an expert in business and negotiation, comfortable with exercising power in a world dominated by men.[12]

Not everyone was happy with the new Nellie Taft, but then the aging Harriet Herron was becoming embittered. Feeling herself abandoned by her daughters and workaholic husband, she wrote in one letter: "I don't care for people." Harriet had time to criticize everyone: neighbors, her own sisters, the "toothless crone" she paid a dollar a day to for cooking. She was openly hostile toward Nellie's new life. "Your mother was low in her mind last night and delivered a diatribe on the 'new woman,' her of Boards and Meetings, and she would not be comforted. . . . One thing your Mother regarded as an evidence of decadence in woman was the present small families," Will reported to Nellie, mother of two.[13]

Although she could needle Will when she didn't get a letter on her most important day of the year—"I suppose you will not remember this is your anniversary"—the newly confident Nellie surely took some secret pleasure that it was now Will who missed her. Working in Cincinnati while she was at Murray Bay in the summer of 1896, he wished he "could step from here to the [summer] kiosk and catch you in my arms." He was particularly wistful in her favorite city. An evening spring stroll down Connecticut Avenue made him "think of you and our Washington life." He knew she would like it there, but when he remarked that there were many "questions as to why you were not with me," he unfortunately mentioned that it was the Supreme Court wives who had done the asking. He also kept his ear to the ground on presidential prospects. Despite the fact that they were both Ohio Republicans, Will considered Governor William McKinley a "timid statesman" who would "ride to a great victory only to demonstrate his incapacity."

Will was as stubbornly determined to get onto the highest court in the land as he had always been. "Almost every person [I met] spoke of my coming there to sit on the Supreme Bench as a certainty," he reported. With the "growing prospect of McKinley's nomination," however, he feared otherwise, thinking that McKinley was "prejudiced against me." He promised Nellie that he wasn't running around with his pipe dream: "I only allude to what is said to me on this subject as to indicate . . . the friendly feeling at Washington for me. . . . Perhaps you think that this is very weak on my part but when the thing is dinned into one's ears every day, it is hard not to think of the possibilities. Most of the Supreme Judges seem to regard it as very probable and they are as much interested as anyone."

Will's news of his time in Washington could not have entirely pleased Nellie when he reported, "I have some calls to make—I want to look up Roosevelt. I hear they are going to legislate him out of office but I hope not." In fact, Roosevelt would continue to climb up the very executive track that Nellie wanted Will on—encouraged by Will himself.

Roosevelt directly approached Taft to try to help him get a job in the new administration. Having done his part to get McKinley elected and tired of his post as New York police commissioner, Roosevelt wanted to be assistant secretary of the Navy. Roosevelt's friend Henry Cabot Lodge recorded that Taft, "one of the best fellows going," got Ohio political boss Myron Herrick to talk to McKinley about Roosevelt. Taft also did so himself when the two Ohioans met at the White House. "The truth is, Will, Roosevelt is always in such a state of mind," said McKinley. Indeed, Roosevelt could barely conceal his voracious ambition. In the end Will recalled, "We got Theodore into the Navy Department." After just one year in the sub-Cabinet, Roosevelt would be elected governor of New York. It was as governor that he began to make national news, rattling his saber as he "demanded war with Spain." Taft later cracked, "I think McKinley wished he had been anywhere else."

As if not to lose Nellie's focus on his career, Will began returning her attention back to national political issues. Americans, he thought, had a "startling . . . ignorance" of the silver standard currency debate. "I think we ought to take a course ourselves on the question," he wrote her, proposing that for their summer respite in the Murray Bay kiosk they "get a volume or two to read aloud."[14]

Nellie, however, could not ignore her work—especially when, on February 10, 1897, the Cincinnati Musicians' Protective Association Union sent her official notice that some of her orchestra's musicians were not in the union, in violation of local codes, and that the forty-four other union musicians would "refuse to play in any more concerts" with the violators. A union representative even threatened to halt all rehearsals until union dues were paid for those in question. As a result, the salaries of the four German immigrant musicians in question were withheld and their union dues paid out of the amount. Two of the men, a Robert Koehler and a Mr. Schippe, claimed that nonpayment for past work was a contract violation and refused to play the forthcoming work period unless they were given full back pay. They hired lawyers. Nellie fired back that they had violated their contracts with "insubordination" by refusing to pay their union dues; she threatened to dismiss them but agreed to pay a small advance, in good faith. The attorneys replied that Koehler and Schippe would play only if they first received full payment, but Nellie retorted that since they "would not hesitate to break your contract with us by refusing to play the last concert"; she was justified in "withholding your salary until the services for which it is paid have been rendered." Koehler and Schippe gave in.

Nellie Taft not only kept the laws of the unions uppermost in her dealings with the musicians, but she developed a good working relationship with the local shop. Her colleagues on the various boards equally respected her. At the end of the successful 1897 season, one of them declared that "a big laurel wreath should be yours for the work, time and thought you have given." For the girl who had once confided to her diary her frustration at not being able to make something of herself in the music world she loved so much, heading the CSO was an experience of liberating triumph.[15]

The 1897 season had been made all the more challenging by Nellie's pregnancy. Her third and final child, Charles Phelps, was born on September 20, 1897. Coming as he did in the midst of her busy joy with the orchestra, he was the recipient of the full measure of her love. Engaging from an early age, he was the one child that Nellie showered affection upon unconditionally. "Charlie" shone with optimism, humor, irreverence, and warmth that charmed everyone who came in contact with him throughout his life. When Bob got into trouble, he was reprimanded, but Charlie would be laughed off as a rascal. "He has just gone out now looking as sweet as a peach," Nellie reported from Murray Bay when he was one. "If I had a Kodak I would show you how he looked a while ago." Charlie grew to be extraordinarily closer to his mother than his siblings. "I am still without a nurse," she told Will of the child she loved to spoil, "and as baby will not go with any one, I am very much confined." Nellie seemed to enjoy sharing adventures with her children once they could care for themselves. Their love of baseball, in general, and the Cincinnati Reds, in particular, spurred her lifelong interest in the spectator sport, for example.[16]

With the outbreak of the Spanish-American War, William Howard Taft was a rare voice of dissent to McKinley's eventual decision to take the

Philippines as U.S. territory. "There had never been any unusual interest in our family as to the result of the Spanish-American War," Nellie recalled. "Like most patriotic Americans we . . . had discussed its every phase and event with a warmth of approval, or disapproval." Will was more focused on the action closer to the States, in Cuba. "The fighting has demonstrated the bravery of our troops," he wrote Nellie of the battle at Santiago, adding, perhaps to her chagrin, that "Teddy Roosevelt, although in the thick of the fight, has thus far escaped unhurt." Indeed, although it was something of a stretch, Roosevelt as "the Colonel" of his "Rough Riders" cavalry that charged up Kettle Hill would soon be linked in the public imagination to the "liberation" of Cuba from its longtime mother country Spain.[17]

Such news must certainly have stung Nellie. Having managed to make herself something of a big fish in a small pond, her life, if not as she had envisioned it, was certainly fulfilling. But it was certainly not anything on the scale of importance that she had longed for. Not only had Roosevelt managed to elbow his way into McKinley's government and then get elected as the youngest governor of New York, but now he was hard at work building his image as a war hero. Roosevelt's rise must have shaken Nellie Taft back into a certain nervous reality. She had not entirely given up on her ambitions for a larger life. The Spanish-American War seemed to be the perfect opportunity to shake things up to make a change.

Out of the blue Will was called to Washington in the first month of the first year of the new century. The President wanted to see the Fifth Circuit judge. Taft returned to Nellie three days later with a shocking proposal. McKinley wanted Will to head a second commission to the Philippines, to structure and build its civil government. He also promised that if an opening on the Supreme Court arose, Taft would be chosen to fill it. Will said he couldn't accept unless Nellie approved. He feared her reaction.

"Well, are we going to Washington?" she asked half-hopefully, resigned to the idea of Will being offered a Justice Department position that would at least permit them to return to the capital. He told her about the assignment in the Philippines. "Want to go?" he asked her.

"Yes," she shot back without hesitation.

Nellie knew nothing about the Philippines, but she knew that she "didn't want to miss a big and novel experience. I have never shrunk before any obstacles when I had an opportunity to see a new country and I must say I have never regretted any adventure." She had achieved her goal of working in music. Another goal in life was to explore the far reaches of the world. Seeing new places, she thought, was "more fun than anything else."[18]

Breaking the news to Harriet that she and her children were moving halfway around the globe to such a mysterious jungle nation—and taking along her younger sister Maria as a companion—was difficult. Nellie went to have lunch at the Herron house with her mother, but Harriet was busy cooking and washing dishes on cook's day off. Nellie had "no opportunity of talking to her." Meanwhile, she got the children their vaccinations, did all the packing, sold or stored their possessions, and devoured magazine articles on the Philippines and a novel set in Manila, "a trashy thing and stupid in the bargain, but giving some idea of the life [there]."

Leaving her position at the CSO would prove to be as difficult as leaving her intensely attached mother. It had fundamentally altered her, providing confidence and audacity that went against the grain of the refined Victorian lady.

For one, the outwardly proper Mrs. Taft had become a great scheming publicist. "An event of unusual interest in the musical annals of our city will be ushered in," Nellie hyped in one ad she wrote for the Detroit papers. "[A]n event no less in importance than the coming of the Cincinnati Symphony Orchestra. . . . The opportunity of having this famous band is now presented. . . . The orchestra . . . has attained a degree of excellence equal to any in the country. That this orchestra exists at all is due to the untiring efforts of a few devoted women who, in the face of meager financial support and little enthusiasm, has succeeded in arousing a local feeling of pride."

She had also seemingly learned to placate the talented but egotistical Van der Stucken and work with him in hammering out her goals, however often they clashed. In the end she had tremendous respect for "Van," describing him as "a man of unusual strength of intellect and force of character."

In the opening statement for each season's program, Nellie implored Cincinnatians to keep the CSO financially flourishing so that, if for nothing else, it could compete with Boston, New York, and Chicago. "Without this the orchestra will fall to the level of the band to be found in any provincial town; with further assistance it will be one of the great orchestras of the country . . . and will give Cincinnati a great name in the musical world. . . . Otherwise, the work . . . has reached a lame and impotent conclusion." As time proved, she had laid the foundations of great success.

As she prepared to head for the Philippines, Nellie admitted that "more than anything" she regretted leaving the orchestra. It had not been a period without stress, she often physically pushing herself to keep a manic schedule of not only work obligations but the demands of her children as well. Still, it was a time in Nellie Taft's life of genuine self-discovery, confidence, accomplishment, and joy. Before departing, the board gave her a silver bowl once owned by the Lord Mayor of London, and the membership gave her a silver coin. She kept those items with her forever. They would even be mentioned in her obituary.

Yet, typically, once she had crossed another one of the large accomplished ambitions from her list, it was a closed chapter. There was no sentimental looking back. As she did throughout her life, Nellie Taft plunged ahead into the next adventure.[19]

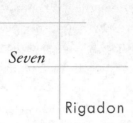

Seven

Rigadon

We insisted upon complete racial equality for the Filipinos.

—NELLIE TAFT

It was in the bright and clear first hours of an August morning that Nellie Taft headed to the deck of the *Kasuga Maru*. Her bags were weighed with the "bright and artistic objects" of a shopping frenzy through Japan. On deck she caught her first glimpse of Manila Bay.

The vessel pulled into the channel straight ahead, flanked on either side by formations of small rock islands, which broke the pounding surf into white sprays. "Corregidor!" the skipper yelled, gesturing toward the mossy hill behind the rocks. As the ship moved toward the harbor, Nellie scanned the vista. On one side of the bay she was able to identify Meriveles mountain, which sloped into the sea from the clouds. Squinting to the south she discerned Cavite Province, buried under low trees in the distance. In the bay itself, as the ship plugged along, Nellie solemnly took in the ghostlike wrecks of the Spanish fleet, masts and hulks rotting in the sun, partially submerged in the shallow shores—a stark legacy of the arrogant Spanish who had conquered and ruled this land, only to be conquered in turn by what even some Americans considered an arrogant United States. Dead ahead some twenty miles she made out the red-tile-roofed convent houses and whitewashed church domes and spires of Manila, framed in a haze of hills the color of delphinium flowers.

The rolling China Sea had left Nellie Taft sickened, but not enough to dampen her "feeling of intense curiosity." The morning glare reflected off the bay so blindingly that the nerves in her eyes hurt, but she was "too interested to seek shelter in the darkened cabin." Soon enough she made out a fleet of harbor launches approaching the *Kasuga Maru* and then a comfortingly familiar rotund figure in the bow of one. It was Will, who had gone on ahead to Manila while Nellie remained in Japan.

There was the rush of customs questions from American soldiers, laughter, bags being rushed off to the launch, children shrieking excitedly at their father, and a welcome reunion of husband and wife—the "busy, bustling, delightfully confusing hours of landing in the farthest orient," as Nellie put it. Steaming up the mouth of the Pasig River, Will pointed out Fort Santiago, the corner structure of a massive graystone wall that stretched down the shoreline and up the riverside, protecting the seventeenth-century Spanish "Old Walled City." In the river itself were blond wood canoes and straw-roofed boathouses in pinks, greens, blues, yellows, and purples, carrying sugarcane and coconuts, and piloted by shirtless men with bamboo sticks.

As the launch docked at the Custom House, overrun with American soldiers and sailors, the Tafts were escorted into a miniature victoria by two native men dressed in flimsy white shirts, the tails hanging outside their white pants, quite dishabille, Nellie thought. Even stranger were the shaggy-maned and -tailed miniature ponies hitched to the carriage. The couple stepped in, the children and Maria in a vehicle behind them.

Suddenly the carriages were darting through the wild streets of Manila, over the shopping district cobblestones, between carts pulled by water buffalo, and near a rushing swirl of natives in red and yellow muslin. Nellie's "heart was in my mouth" as they averted collisions and raced out past scruffy weeded park areas. The speeding continued through narrow streets overhung with house patios covered with green mold from frequent flooding, past windows covered with bamboo. Nellie glimpsed the huts of the impoverished built in the free spaces of the fashionable neighborhood. Finally, at the last house at the end of a street, the victoria pulled through the gate of a high stone wall onto a driveway lined with guards sporting bayonets and under a porte cochere, a rubber tree limply hanging over it. Stepping out onto the marble steps, Nellie Taft was home.

The sights and smells, the food, water, and air, and—as Nellie would constantly comment upon—the servants were a long way from Pike Street. She had taken Bob, ten, Helen, eight, and Charlie, two, by train from Cincinnati to New Orleans to Los Angeles to San Francisco, where they met Will and sailed out on April 17. She had no regrets about leaving America. "I may say," she confessed, that she had only had "happy preparations for my adventure into a new sphere. That it was alluring to me I did not deny to anybody."[1]

During their first stop, Hawaii, Nellie in her wool bathing suit went surfing at Waikiki Beach, a rarity for white women at the time. "In the first place, the surf there doesn't look as if any human being would dare venture into it," she wrote, "but when you see a beautiful, slim, brown native, naked except for short swimming trunks, come gliding down a high white breaker, poised like a Mercury, erect on a single narrow plank—it looks delightfully exhilarating." She considered the venture more daring than eating poi.

On May 10 the U.S. Army transport *Hancock* reached Yokohama Harbor. The six commissioners and their families spent a week in Japan, the men given an audience with the Emperor, the women with the Empress. When the Empress gave Nellie an extravagant tapestry, Will insisted it was government property. Nellie would not turn it over to the American consulate office. She was keeping it for herself. It took President McKinley's decision that it was a private gift to Mrs. Taft for Will to finally concede the point and let his wife keep the tapestry.

Will had realistic fears about bringing his family into Manila: There was a public call for an uprising when the commissioners landed "to convince us of the hopelessness of our mission," he wrote Nellie. One of the servants he hired had what was suspected to be bubonic plague. He wrote

Charley that he had not "bothered Nellie" with news of the threats made against his own life. While the commissioners steamed off for Manila, Nellie, Maria, and the children stayed in Japan for several months, renting a house on a high bluff overlooking the Pacific.

Her respite began Nellie's love affair with all things Japanese. "I can hardly realize that we are so far away from what we are accustomed to consider civilization, when we are living in the greatest comfort you can imagine," she wrote her mother-in-law. She was most taken with the delicate landscape that she described as, "well, peculiarly Japanese." On the inland side of her cottage, nestled in a valley of rice paddies and pine groves, was a Buddhist temple. The sounds lingered with her forever, the "ceaseless drone of a priest repeating over and over an endless invocation to the constant, measured tum-tum accompaniment of little wooden drums," while at night "the single low tong of a great temple bell set the hills to vibrating."

Among the most consequential of acquaintances Nellie made in Japan was with the sister of a member of the American legation, Eliza Ruhamah Scidmore. She was an expert researcher and writer on Asian life and culture, and her particular passion was the white and pink blossoms of the smallish trees native to Japan known as the "cherry blossoms." A harbinger of spring celebrated with elaborate tea ceremonies, "cherry blossom time" had ended just weeks before Nellie arrived in Japan. Nellie and Maria visited Nikko, Kamakura, and Kyoto, led by what Will called his wife's "fascination of travel." As the summer heat began, they moved to Miyanoshita in the Hakone Mountains, to which they traveled by a two-hour rickshaw ride in the dark rain. Once in the mountains Nellie began exploring again. Carried in a chair to Lake Hakone, she was startled at the water, "still and bright as a glass-plate mirror," at the base of Mount Fujiyama and the endless temples and teahouses dotting the mountainside.[2]

Nellie and her entourage sailed for Manila on August 10, with stops first in Shanghai and Hong Kong. Her new home was novel: garish windows, heavy Spanish furniture, mosquito-netted high-canopied beds with cane bottoms, and white wicker everywhere. The children's rooms were on the second floor, away from the ground-level moisture. The main floor had a dining room and reception room on one side and Will and Nellie's rooms on the other, closed off by sliding doors. Chinese servants ran the house. Nellie advised, "We must have no mats or curtains or anything to shelter the insects. They say that keeping things dry is half the battle in being well." Overhead were large ice-cream-parlor fans that Will insisted were his lifesaver in the heat. He would later tell people that even Nellie came to like them—"but I never did," she clarified. He also gave fair warning that Maria would often see him in pajamas because he kept all the doors open at night to let breezes in. There was a breathtaking view of the bay and mountains, often marked by a rainbow.

Ever optimistic, Will said the typhoons helped the grass grow.[3]

■

The island nation where Will and Nellie Taft would live for the next four years had a complicated, tragic, yet rich past.

Will had bluntly told the President to his face that he hadn't approved of the United States taking the Philippines, but McKinley used that fact as part of his argument: He would "trust the man who didn't want them better than I can the man who did."

The peace protocol between the United States and Spain specified that Cuba would be free from Spain and given its independence. The United States would also get Guam in the Pacific and take the last piece of old Spain's colonial empire—Puerto Rico. The American and Spanish peace commissioners would debate the fate of the Philippines, however. The Spanish did make the case that Manila had not even been taken until after the armistice was signed. They could not be part of the war booty. Yet the Americans knew that the defeated Spanish could not continue to rule the islands it had seized hundreds of years earlier from Japanese control. If left to stand on their own, there was as great a chance of anarchy breaking out on the islands as there was that a European aggressor like Germany might seize it and create a world war situation that would surely involve the United States.

The ultimate decision rested with President McKinley. Originally, McKinley himself had not wanted to annex the islands upon the conclusion of the short war. At best, after listening to the U.S. military's view, he wanted to take the northern island of Luzon to use as a military base in Asia. But every newspaper editorial, every adviser, every American citizen, it sometimes seemed, had an opinion on the Philippines. Moralists claimed that expansion begat despotism, and that taking the islands stood for everything that America did not—paternalism, repression, imperialism, racism—and violated the Declaration of Independence and "consent of the governed." A diverse collection of national celebrities belonged to the Anti-Imperialist League—union leader Samuel Gompers, Mark Twain, steel magnate Andrew Carnegie—to fight the President's decision to retain the islands. "Goddamn the United States for its vile conduct in the Philippine Isles!" declared the Harvard professor of philosophy William James.

Wall Street, of course, immediately focused its eye on the main chance. Business leaders, exporters, importers, and manufacturers began suggesting that keeping the islands could brilliantly launch the American economy as a global power, especially as a profit base for trade with China. Manila was the next Hong Kong, industry began to chatter. Although the immigration flood in America would keep labor cheap in the States, there were new, rich natural resources to be explored and plundered. Annexing Hawaii a few years earlier, for example, prompted a boom there for U.S. production and export of sugar, not to mention the farming of that most exotic of fruits that was beginning to show up on the tables of the wealthy—pineapple.

The average, upper-middle-class American family—striving to get those status symbols of electricity and the telephone installed into their home—felt that the islands would prove to be more trouble than they were worth. They might, however, have heard something about the work of the ladies of their churches who were trying to help the poor ignorant island people, the wildest of whom ran around with little to no coverage of their most unspeakably private parts. From many a Protestant pulpit, ministers declared that it was "Christian duty" to convert, and save the alleged "savages" that lived in the brown jungle.

First Lady Ida McKinley, for one, obsessively caught on to the notion that missionaries of her Methodist faith would best do the converting and saving. She would not relent in persisting that the President retain the islands for this reason. McKinley's military aide, Benjamin Montgomery, affirmed that, ultimately, it was the First Lady's argument that pushed the uncertain President—who, at one point, had gotten down on his knees and prayed to God "for light and guidance"—to do so. In the end, the United States decided not to let the islands return to the control of Spain, but rather to purchase it for $20 million.

In all this, nobody had bothered to fully consider that what the Filipino people themselves wanted was complete freedom, not continued subjugation, this time by a new nation that would only promise that the day would come when they were "ready" for "self-government."

Thirty years had almost passed since the first major Filipino revolt against the Spanish had been suppressed by that colonial power, in 1872. Rage toward the oppressor, however, simmered. Twenty years after the first revolt, a native hero had emerged to lead his people toward their independence. If the name of Jose Rizal seemed to be held as high in esteem on the islands as a saint, there was good reason.

Born on the island of Luzon the same year as Nellie, 1861, Rizal was educated in Europe. He could read Greek, Latin, Sanskrit, Arabic, and Japanese. He spoke most of the European languages and the different Filipino dialects. When he came back to the islands, he began to intensely study its political situation. With superb literary quality and a manipulation of facts into propaganda, Rizal's writings were the first to point out the horrors and abuses of both the Spanish government rule and the Catholic priests who were, essentially, feudal lords. Rizal, however, was all the more beloved for his rationality. He called not for revolution but resolution and reform. He believed that the young native Filipinos could lift *themselves* with education, even those who were poor. He called the movement "Liga Filipina." Although deported, his ideas had caught fire with the people, especially among a group of young, idealistic acolytes who now gathered in revolutionary form, poised to challenge Spain's rule of their native land. For spreading such ideas, the Spanish government in the capital city of Manila put Rizal on trial for inciting the people. And he was executed.

The shock of the Filipinos over the gruesome and brutal murder of their beloved Rizal found an outlet for some of its rage in the radical, underground terrorist group "Katipunan," which demanded that the Spanish government initiate immediate and sweeping legal reforms and expel the Catholic friars who owned much of the land and treated its tenants with harsh cruelty. In response, the Spanish government initiated torture and mass execution of those identified as leaders of the movement for independence. One of those who escaped capture and rose as the new spiritual leader of the revolt was General Emilio Aguinaldo. He went a step further and simply declared the islands to be independent and named himself president even though there was no government, no infrastructure. It was simply an emotional declaration, but it had moved the people.

Despite the fact that the Americans had never officially agreed to give the Filipinos complete and immediate independence as its own true nation, this was certainly suggested as a real possibility when U.S. officials convinced Filipino land owners, intellectuals, lawyers, and other elitists to help summon support for the U.S. forces as they were fighting to "liberate" the Filipinos from the Spanish. Interested in making sure their own wealth and status was preserved through to the outcome, they eagerly collaborated with the conquering United States.

General Emilio Aguinaldo, who advocated real Filipino independence, also supported the Americans. He expected that he would be a political power, if not the nation's leader, in the new government that the Americans promised to help establish for the Filipino people in a plan that McKinley called "Filipinization." In December 1898 he learned that the Americans were going to indeed establish the government for the people but still control it and put off "self-government" until the conquerors determined that they were "properly prepared" for it. Aguinaldo believed—and he rallied most of the native population to believe—that the Americans had simply replaced the Spanish as the new imperialists. There was now a genuine concern in the American military that the "liberated" Filipinos would organize a guerrilla war against the occupying troops. When an American troop learned that gathered nearby was a group of Filipino soldiers organized by Aguinaldo, they feared imminent attack, approached their site, and opened fire. It was February 4, 1899. Eighteen days later, a Filipino uprising took place in the capital city of Manila where guerrilla fighters went through the streets and buildings with the declared intention of murdering all white people—Americans and Europeans. It was the beginning of the so-called Insurrection, during which some 600,000 Filipinos were killed. While the ragtag Filipino troops soon took refuge in the outlaying jungle areas, their tactics were at a level of murderous atrocity that the U.S. military had never experienced. Tens of thousands of miles away from home, surrounded by guerrilla forces that knew the lay of the land, the American military establishment there was understandably paranoid and tense, regardless of whether they personally believed that the United States should be fighting such a war. In reaction, they resorted to more repressive measures than needed. McKinley immediately sent off thousands of more soldiers. The more gruesome of the skirmishes and raids persisted for three years until 1901 when Americans successfully plotted the capture of Aguinaldo in a guerrilla camp. Despite some continued but small excursions, the hard fist of the American military, under the direction of General Arthur MacArthur, crushed the *insurrecto* rebellion.

The chairman of McKinley's Philippines commission was Cornell University president Jacob Gould Schurman, and although he had first arrived in Manila in the opening salvo of the insurrection, he did manage to gain support from the Filipino elite, assuring them that once the hostilities ceased, the Americans had no plan whatsoever of behaving as the Spanish had. He issued a proclamation for all the people of the islands saying that much of the new form of government—democracy—they were seeking to put into place would be run by Filipinos. He also made clear that the American principal of justice would rule all government decisions. In all legal matters, a judicial system would be established that promised Filipinos the same due process Americans received in the States. Furthermore, Schurman drew up a variety of recommendations he felt should be adopted by the civil government that was scheduled to begin its work in tandem with the skeptical, bloodied, and defensive military leadership. A few weeks after Schurman completed his commission report in January 1900 and went back to Ithaca, New York, William Howard Taft arrived.

▪

"I long for the time when you shall come with your knowledge of things and how to do them," Will wrote to Nellie in Japan after his nearly three months alone in the Philippines, the longest separation their marriage had ever had to endure. "I cannot tell you how helpless I feel without you." In June, on their wedding anniversary, Will wrote longingly that "every year I feel more dependent on you."

Will's time alone in Manila had been hard. He immediately discovered that the greatest resistance to his establishing a civil government was not the scattered bands of *insurrecto* guerrilla fighters who were ostensibly still marauding for independence and terrorizing the Americans out of the islands, nor even the unmerciful Catholic friars who, through their vast real estate holdings, held financial and political power over the great majority of working poor. It was the American military, personified by the harsh and unyielding General Arthur MacArthur, who lived like Caesar in the old Spanish Malacanan Palace, that would mount the toughest opposition to Taft.

In a nation of six million people, MacArthur had some sixty thousand American troops at his command. In addition, when the Tafts first arrived, MacArthur had the overall executive control of what was already a large, civil force of American government workers. "This," Nellie tartly quipped, was "apparently, not enough." No, MacArthur wanted to control Taft and the commissioners. The general not only resented the appointment of these new commissioners, she noted, but felt "personally humiliated" by having to share power with them.

MacArthur was particularly angry that Taft refused to agree with the military assessment that there continued to be genuine danger from the Filipino insurrectionists. Behind every bush, MacArthur imagined *insurrectos* about to hack white people with machetes. There *were* just such raids, the grisly details making for exciting filler in the newspapers back home, but in reality the attacks were sporadic, minor, and brief. MacArthur believed that the only way to absolutely wipe out such attacks was to grind not only the *insurrectos* but also the civilian Filipino population into a subjugation that would keep them timid but unthreatening.

Deeply ingrained racial bigotry left MacArthur unable to fathom those who believed that the further submission of a conquered people by a foreign military force was undemocratic and inhumane. Like many of the men who composed the American military forces in the Philippines—like most Americans, in general, of that era—MacArthur was largely uneducated. (Taft would soon snobbishly report to Nellie that the general neither spoke nor spelled properly.) From the perspective of such Americans, the "inferior" races should never be granted civil rights because they could never be equal—that they were genetically incapable of rising to the same intelligence and capability levels of the Caucasians. For MacArthur, then, a harsh, unrelenting American presence would not only be what kept more white people from being killed by the "orientals" (as all Asians were then referred to by white Americans), but also serve as active proof that the Filipino was naturally inferior to the Anglo-Saxon.

Along these lines, MacArthur made two decisions that, comparatively, seemed more benevolent yet were intended to humiliate: He ordered the arrests of all Filipinos thought to be aiding the terrorists by secretly raising and dispersing money to them. As supplies and arms quickly diminished, wearied *insurrectos* surrendered en masse. Those who refused to pledge obedience to the American government were deported to Guam. While it was not as bloodless an operation as it should have been, MacArthur had managed to prove to the political decision makers back in Washington that he was succeeding with his "occupation" if not yet quite bringing "freedom" to an oppressed people. He argued that he must continue with his strategy, keep the military in charge of the Philippines, and remain in charge of everything. MacArthur avoided addressing a specific timetable for just when the promised "self-government" on democratic principles would begin by stirring up fears of more imminent guerrilla raids. Thus, before he had even arrived on the islands, Will was at absolute odds with MacArthur.

Will claimed MacArthur and his fears were ridiculous and that his efforts were especially useless since it was the poorer masses that the general most focused on. As usual, Will and Nellie Taft would rely on the "better citizens," the "better class." Education, intelligence, and wealth would always lead the way for a general society, regardless of its race or religion, the Tafts believed. Besides, Will sniffed, the Filipino landowners, the "ladrones," and other native capitalists, were "tired and weary of this murder and assassination policy," welcomed the American presence, and wanted to get started on creating their civil society; their support was key to any successful control.

The truly peaceable, kind, and warm qualities that marked William Howard Taft's private character emerged more publicly during his years in the Philippines than at any other stretch of his life in public service. With his naturally sunny disposition, Will saw a bright new world that would emerge someday in the Philippines. For a man who had experienced winter as only the visiting grandson of a Vermonter could, the Philippines were delightfully balmy or intensely hot, like a perpetual spring and summer. This enchanted him at least initially. The red-tile roofs, the emerald-colored palm trees, the gold reflection mirrored by the sea—everywhere Will suddenly seemed to notice bursts of color, as if in some magic world. In the end, however, it would be his own unanticipated affection for the uniquely hybrid culture and people, his faith in the capability of their elite class for leadership, and his intrinsic belief that no system was superior to that one which guaranteed legal, economic, and political equality and humanitarianism that forged his commitment to the Phillippines.

MacArthur was threatened by Taft's eloquence, comfort, and confidence with the Filipinos. To every suggestion for the slightest improvement of native life that Will made, MacArthur was dismissive. Technically unable to veto commission decisions, the general acted on their orders only slowly and obstinately. To every issue the commissioners raised, he only saw military solutions, convinced that the Filipino people must be broken with rigid order to truly submit to America as a colony. Will had shared details of the MacArthur machinations in correspondence with Nellie. Weighing in on military matters for the first time, Taft wrote her that "as long as this terrorism is not suppressed" it would naturally go away, for *insurrecto* leaders were increasingly surrendering; he believed that this was how to "make them active agents of peace." When Nellie learned that the general was wiring Washington to undermine Will, she was outraged. She arrived soon after.[4]

There were new faces of power in the halls of Washington by the end of 1900. Elected as McKinley's Vice President, against his own personal desire, was none other than Will's great friend Theodore Roosevelt. Governor of New York before the election, he had wanted to stay in that position but immodestly declared that the "feeling for my nomination was practically unanimous."

However self-absorbed, Roosevelt genuinely liked Taft for both his amiability and his intelligence. As governor he had written a mutual friend that "Will Taft is a very fine fellow. I wish there was someone like him here in New York, for I am very much alone. I have no real community or principals or feelings with the machine." Will and Theodore regularly corresponded. "I would a great deal rather be your assistant in the Philippines," Roosevelt claimed despite his thirst for the presidency. "The kaleidoscope will be shaken, however, before 1904," he forecasted to Will of the next presidential election; "some new men will come to the front."

McKinley's November reelection went a long way in convincing Filipinos that the Americans were there to stay. Insurgents were soon imprisoned, deported to Guam, or pressed into declaring oaths of allegiance. A swell of support from the general population soon helped Taft as much as the election.

Although Taft himself specifically focused on drawing up the nation's judiciary system and code of laws, he oversaw the efforts of the individual commissioners and was responsible for the overall governmental structuring. Will instinctively realized that Nellie could serve an invaluable political role by dealing with those who would live in such a civil society. Her forthright personality, considerable power in assessing people, and essential lack of bigotry all converged to make her an excellent partner to Will in his work, first in dealing with the American military and then with the Filipino people themselves.[5]

Nellie began to get a full sense of the diversity of the Filipinos as Will created a system for organizing the first layer of government, on the provincial level. Each province was asked to send its delegates for local rule to each provincial capital on a specific date where Will or a commissioner would read the new provincial code. Every aspect of the provincial government structure was explained, including the appointments in each province of a governor, treasurer, and secretary.

Will and the commissioners made an initial trip on February 23, 1901, just across Manila Bay to Balanga, the capital city of Bataan Province. Nellie went along, and the presence of a female in the party of commissioners "greatly pleased" the Balangains. "They were not slow to grasp its significance," Nellie recalled. It was, she said, "the beginning of my long acquaintance with Filipino hospitality."

In immediately noticing how the Filipinos responded to even the slightest social gesture, Nellie took the simple but vital step of shaking hands with those that Will famously called "my little brown brothers." She did so, she noted, "much to the disgust of the [American] military authorities present." MacArthur, and many of his immediate subordinates, were repulsed by even small gestures of social equality among the different races in the Philippines. Some soldiers sang a tune which included a line that natives "ain't no brothers of mine." Still, Nellie claimed she got concessions from some of the top brass that her "friendliest kind of attitude . . . had an extraordinary effect on the general tone in Bataan."

It was a formula that made her "distinctly useful" Will thought when she joined him on March 10 for "one of the most unique expeditions of my life," as Nellie described it, through the southern island provinces. It was "only through direct contact," she thought, "that anything like sympathetic understanding" could be reached. As they began the journey, Will received the news from Washington that the military government was being replaced with a civil one, and Will was to be inaugurated in several months as the new governor-general.

Over seven thousand islands comprise the Philippines, with their population at the time nearly six million, representing various influences of Spanish, Japanese, and Islamic cultures. Over the next two months the commission party (a total of sixty) inspected each provincial capital to understand the unique problems and conditions of the individual regions. It opened Nellie's Anglo-Saxon sensibilities to the subtle differences between the indigenous peoples. In Moro, for example, she was fascinated by what she called "the Mohammedans," Islamic fundamentalists who had resisted Christian conversion and the Spanish culture by "religious fanatic outbreaks" of violence. In her best imperialistic judgment, Nellie thought them "unruly and independent" but that the "wisest among them recognized the necessity of obedience for the sake of the general good."[6]

One characteristic of the culture seemed consistent to Nellie wherever she went: a love of celebration. Indeed, in each province the local people would see the visit as an opportunity to fete the Tafts with dinners, parades, fireworks, and a ball. As far as sampling all the unknown foods served to her, Nellie did not want to insult her hosts and so—with what she called her "cosmopolitan attitude toward food"—she did. At the ball came the most important part of the day's ceremonies, the native quadrille known as "the Rigadon." The dance was a metaphor for Will and Nellie in the Philippines. To the eye it was a free-flowing dance requiring quick, light steps. In reality the "intricate but stately" steps, as Nellie put it, had to be done precisely. A Filipino could always tell if it was done incorrectly. "I'm afraid we made but a poor display in our first attempts," she wrote, "but by dint of watching others night after night both my husband and I became very proficient at it."

On her own, Nellie Taft undertook a historic trip to the northern Luzon territory where, she stated rather proudly, "no white woman had ever been." Led by General J. Franklin Bell, it would be weeks on horseback into the thick jungle. While "anxious to go," she had "considerable trepidation," especially since she had little experience with horses. Will told her to make the trip, and although she would "have gone without this advice," she found it "comforting" that she could "blame it all on him." When no ladylike sidesaddle could be found, she wore pants or, as she put it, "divided skirts."

One day after her fortieth birthday, June 3, Nellie and Maria set sail for three days to Vigan, where Bell was headquartered, on the steamer *Salvadora*. Maria was a reassuring presence but an emotionally explosive spitfire. "We all fight with each other on every subject and manage to keep up a running debate," Will wrote his mother-in-law during the Filipino years. The only unmarried Herron child, Maria's streak of independence reinforced a feeling of liberty in Nellie. A second mother to the Taft children, she encouraged them to be independent as well.

The expedition also included the general's daughter, nicknamed Bubbles, a Major Rice, a Major Stevens, a Captain Shearer, a Captain Haight, as well as a dozen or so natives serving as aides, twenty cavalry horses, and thirty-seven pack mules. By sailing down rafts with bamboo awnings, being carried in sedan chairs, and riding along treacherously narrow mountain trails, Nellie went deep into the Luzon. Endless nights were spent in pup tents and abandoned huts with driving cold rains dripping on their clothes and food. She confessed to Bob that she cried on the trip, missing her family. "I dread very much leaving," Nellie wrote Will the day before she headed north, "where I can not be reached if it was necessary." Will and the children were fine and he delighted in the role of single parent for a spell.[7]

As Nellie and the group ascended to the highest mountain elevations, they came in contact more frequently with the isolated Igorrote tribes. While she thought they were "the dirtiest people I ever saw," she took to the natives as they took to her. She found them physically attractive, thinking that "their features are stronger marked" than the Filipinos of the south and that "they are very kindly and friendly." She noted everything about them, from the men's "bright-colored G-string" to their musical gong handles made of human jaw. "This is a form of racial pride," she noted of the handles, "and deserves respect." As headhunters she thought them "naked savages," yet seemed to take pride in their amazing engineering of rice irrigation. She made food exchanges for samples of their spears and headgear, and even learned to do a dance of one tribe.

"The natives gathered around in curious groups," she noted early on, rather uncomfortably. Soon enough, Nellie Taft relaxed and blossomed into the lightheartedness of a playful teenage girl—the sort she had never really been. Her diary of the trip had a joyous sense of adventure: "We had a jolly dinner enlivened by the most terrible native band I ever heard.... [T]he rapids were quite exciting...a jolting army wagon over a road rough in many parts and yet we did not seem at all exhausted." Nellie bathed in the river. She played a backgammon game of elimination called Freeze Out. She took delight in observing the flirtation between Bubbles and Captain Haight. She slept on a dirt floor in a room with the men, separated only by blankets on a string. One night at the hacienda of one Don Jose Mills, Nellie recorded, "[We] sang all our songs, followed the leader, sat on the floor in the corner of the vestibule, danced to a harmonica... played grand opera and cut up generally." When she came across a bed of fragrant mint, she "didn't do a thing but make juleps." By the end of the trip a comfortable routine had set in: "We made ourselves comfortable at once. . . . [We] sat around a fire and drank scotches."

"Down in the heat and the political turmoil of Manila, I was taking things much too seriously," she admitted. "[U]p in the far-away north there was nothing to do but dismiss all worry and accept things as they came along. . . . So I enjoyed myself." The trip only buttressed her considerably grown self-confidence. "I wish you could see what a hiker I have come to be," she wrote proudly to Bob, "always in the lead." She noted of her riding skill: "I have become very expert at climbing and descending and can hang on to the horse's mane on the side of a precipice without turning a hair."

In cool Baguio, being developed as a summer capital, Nellie received a telegram that said Will was to be inaugurated as governor on July 4. The old nervous sense of control and responsibility rushed back to her, the news filling her "with something like panic." The ceremony would take place just two days after her return to Manila, and she had to plan a reception for the two thousand people that Will had invited to their house after the ceremony. The next morning the Tafts would have to move into the mansion that would be their new home. Despite the American intent to base the new government of the Philippines on democracy, the name of the mansion has remained the Malacanan Palace. Nellie made no effort to have the word *palace* changed or removed. After all, this was where she was now going to rule.[8]

Although the transfer of American power from a temporary military rule by a general to a civil government overseen by a governor-general had long been the intention of those in the U.S. government who believed in the retaining of the Philippines, the actual decision to make that transfer had been successfully delayed by the still-wary MacArthur and his military establishment. On March 21, 1901, Congress finally passed an amendment sponsored by Wisconsin senator John Spooner to end the military regime and put the civil government into place. Twenty-one days later, the independence leader Emilio Aguinaldo and Mariano Trias, the general Aguinaldo handpicked to succeed him in case he died, were captured. It was just a matter of paperwork—and getting MacArthur out of the

Palace—before Taft became civil governor (the more familiar title of governor-general was not used until 1905, after Taft was gone).

Will's new job would prove to be no small task. He was ultimately responsible for building a new system of executive, judicial, and legislative branches of government, based on the blueprints laid out by him and his commissioners, and incorporating some of the recommendations of the preceding commissioners. Still, it was a job he would love, for it largely involved judicial reasoning and decisions.

In large part, Will had already won over the confidence of the well-educated class of people he had always placed great faith in, those of "the best stripe." Practically all of the leading Filipino lawyers and wealthy landowners spoke English flawlessly, were educated in Europe or America, and had so long imitated Anglo-Saxon customs and manners that it was natural to them. By his diligence—and his tacit promise to remove vast friar landholdings from the Catholic Church—Will had the necessary support in all his efforts from this Filipino upper class.

The great challenge that now faced him and would determine the success of the American government's colonial effort was winning the trust and determination of the common man—the millions of uneducated, suspicious yet proud native people, many of whom maintained such divergent cultures that they could not often understand the regional dialects of their fellow Filipinos. Gaining their full support would require more than just implementing new laws or building new roads. It would call upon a deeper insight into the unique cultural customs of the Filipino people and an extension of the most sensitive and personal of gestures. It called for new leadership that managed to respect the customs of the common people, be considerate of their opinions and concerns, and extend an unmistakably warm, generous, and effusive hospitality. This being more a Latin sensibility than an Anglo one, it still needed to retain enough of a regal character to command a respect not unlike that given to royalty.

This, Will Taft knew, was just the job for Nellie Taft.

Eight

Queen of the Palace (1901–1904)

*I had not been brought up with any such destiny in view and I
confess that it appealed to my imagination.*

—NELLIE TAFT

*Every year I feel more dependent on you; every year I grow
more lonely in your absence, and every year, my Darling, I love
you more.*

—WILL TAFT, JUNE 18, 1902

Following Will's inaugural as governor-general on July 4 and the
mammoth lawn reception Nellie hosted—a torrential storm forcing it indoors—she took hold of her palace.

On twenty acres, Malacanan was larger than even Charley Taft's
mansion. Outfitted with Spanish furnishings and grass rugs, Nellie's room
opened into Will's, forming a suite. Once every two weeks a doctor came to
ascertain the sanitary conditions in the house, which was always damp and
often flooded due to the fact that it sat beside—and its veranda overhung—
the Pasig River. "Not that I wasn't well pleased with the idea of living in a
palace," she later wrote uncomplainingly of her new home, "however unlike the popular conception of a palace it might be."

Once Nellie managed to decipher what the Chinese cook (who spoke
no English) needed for meals, she went off to buy them at the U.S. Army

commissary. She had some twenty other servants to manage as well. "It is astonishing how time flies by, and how little one accomplishes. Here especially you get very little done in a day," she told her mother, "and as we don't get home [from the commissary] until nearly lunch time, we consume the intermediate time in idling over a cocktail. You must try them."

Entertaining consumed Nellie Taft in the Philippines, but not as a personal indulgence. In fact, it was a vital political role that she took intense care in planning. "Even in our daily round of social affairs," recalled Nellie, "we dealt with tremendous problems whose correct solution meant the restoration of peace and prosperity to what . . . we knew could be a great country." Although she kept the twenty rooms of the main level, all with beautiful wood floors, opened to guests, she preferred garden parties that began as the sun was setting. "I began to love the tropical nights and to feel that I never before had known what nights can be like," she recalled. There was constant music, two or three bands playing and relieving each other, and twinkling electric lights and Japanese paper lanterns were hung on the palm and other tropical trees. She served light foods buffet style, including flavored ices and, of course, her favorite treat: champagne.

She enjoyed ruling a palace. "You would be amused to see Maria and me frisking around with youths years younger than we are, and dancing cotillions with the best of them," she wrote their sister Jennie. "Of course, the position gives us a great deal of attention which I for one would never have otherwise; and of course we feel we might as well make the best of it while we have the opportunity. We are really so grand now that it will be hard to descend to common doings."[1]

Whatever the type of entertainment, Nellie was constantly asserting to the Filipinos that they were not only welcome but encouraged to attend the events in the house and that it was, in a sense, theirs. In this way the Tafts consciously sought to win firm support for the new government. "Nellie and I expect to give an afternoon reception to the members of the Federal party who constitute the local committees in the various parts of Manila and vicinity," Will reported to his mother-in-law. "An entertainment like that or any entertainment they regard as of the utmost importance and they noted the absence of entertainments with great emphasis." Will made this social-political role explicit to Nellie: "One of the things we have to do here is to extend hospitality to Filipino families of wealth and position. The army circles definitely and distinctly decline to have anything to do with them. . . . I need your assistance in taking a different course. . . . Its political effect will be very considerable."

Mrs. Taft placed a notice in the local newspapers, inviting all of Manila to her weekly Wednesday open houses. In time she often had about two thousand guests show up for parties, but at first it was hard to get the natives to attend. Nellie poignantly recalled the first time she ever received a social call from Filipinos in her home: a husband, his wife, and their four daughters. Nellie warmly shook their hands and then gave them a tour of the house, but they were silent and extremely nervous, uncertain if they were genuinely welcomed. When she complimented their clothing, however, the women suddenly opened up and lavished praise on everything they came across—including the Taft children.

That the natives presumed there was a blanket sense of white racial superiority troubled Nellie, and she determined all the more to integrate. "The Filipinos had to have a little coaxing," she wrote. "But by asking many of them personally and persistently to 'be sure and come Wednesday' we prevailed on a good number to believe they really were really wanted; and after a little while there began to be as many brown faces as white among our guests." Such racial integration shocked the military community, whom Nellie never liked. Will wrote Charley that Army wives "regard the Filipino ladies and men as 'niggers' and as not fit to be associated with."

Integration became a dogged principal for Nellie Taft. "We insisted upon complete racial equality," she wrote. It was her personal point of pride that she had friends and guests who were of entirely different races from her own. "We made it a rule from the beginning that neither politics nor race should influence our hospitality in any way," she went on. "We came thus to have a very wide and diverse acquaintance." Nellie's belief in racial social integration was made all the more personal because she often used her own money, an early inheritance from her mother, for her entertaining. For a woman as tightfisted as Nellie Taft, it was not only a patriotic statement but the display of a kind spirit that, while rarely displayed to those outside her family, could burst out generously.[2]

To later generations there was racist condescension in the noblesse oblige of Americans like the Tafts toward the Filipinos: Such "savages" were the "white man's burden" and required American control to live better. Certainly, the primary motive of the United States in taking the islands was to have a Pacific base, regardless of what race the conquered were. That imperial Americans would "improve" colonized Filipinos was an afterthought and even a front for those who sought military power. The unfortunate truth was that many Americans at the time believed it was a scientific impossibility to "uplift" to white standards what they considered an inherently "inferior" nonwhite race. There is not even a suggestion of this belief behind Will and Nellie's initial opposition to taking the Philippines.

In the context of their era, the fact that Will and Nellie Taft even believed that the native Filipino was capable of being "uplifted" was the single greatest proof that they did not believe in inherent racial superiority or inferiority. Issues of race, however, were at the heart of their experiences in the Philippines, where the composition of the population was, in every respect, radically different from any known to the United States.

Race and religion were factors in every layer of the Philippines saga. Protestants who had wanted to "Christianize" the natives overlooked the fact that the large, solid majority of Filipinos were already Christian. They were Roman Catholics, a faith many a Pope-fearing American Protestant felt was not Christian.

Within the native Filipino population itself, there was a religious bigotry. Some 90 percent of the population was Catholic, but the other 10 percent were Muslim. These were the Moro tribes of Mindanao and the Sulu archipelago. These peoples were, in the words of Taft's most eminent biographer, "hated, feared and despised by the more orderly Filipinos who had embraced Catholicism."

The original tribes of the island had most likely come from Indonesia about six thousand years ago. Subsequent waves included the first Malaysian migration between 800 and 500 B.C., followed by Indian Hindus, Arabs, Chinese, other East Asians, and Europeans. Evidence suggests the first human inhabitation to be twenty-two thousand years ago. At one point, the Philippines were taken over by the Japanese. And then the Japanese were overtaken by the Spanish. There had been a thorough intermixing of the Asian and European races, and the Filipino emerged as a truly unique and proud race. Consequently, there was snobbery against those people who were either pure European or Asian blood. To be of mixed blood was to be superior, and genuinely Filipino.

William Howard Taft was peculiarly positioned to understand intolerance. Although he was the descendant of old New England English ancestors, he was also an adherent to the most liberal and controversial of all organized Protestant faiths, Unitarianism. While Taft believed firmly in the tenet of one universal Creator and that Jesus was a prophet, he did not believe in Christ's divinity. Unitarians were, at the least, derided for this view by most other Christians, with fundamentalists declaring that Taft and his ilk were blaspheming heretics. The issue of his religious beliefs would rise once he entered elective politics, and the fact that he also maintained extraordinarily close and supportive friendships with national Catholic and Jewish leaders made Will Taft all the more suspect to conservative Protestants.

Furthermore, Will had matured with a deep sensitivity to the suffering and intolerance experienced by Russian Jews. Alphonso Taft, while U.S. minister to Russia, not only had the courage of his convictions to become the first American official to stand up to the Czarist government on its egregious violations of human rights against its Jewish citizens, he also personally helped to arrange the immigration out of Russia of many of them. The legacy of fighting anti-Semitism was an important value in his family that was passed on to Will, and later, his son Charlie. William Howard Taft and Nellie Taft would become the first incumbents of the executive mansion to attend a seder, in 1912, while visiting the Glenham Street home in Providence, Rhode Island, of Colonel Harry Cutler, first president of the National Jewish Welfare Board. Such a background—of experiencing a sense of inferiority because of a religious faith inherited from one's family, and standing up for the respect and equality of a minority to which one did not belong—made all the difference in the way William Howard Taft reshaped the Filipino nation.[3]

Nellie Taft treated all people with genuine equality; there is not the slightest suggestion that at any point in her life she took an action against someone based on their racial or religious background—as long as they were part of the upper-class of their ethnic group, or at least what she called the "better class." A great point of pride for her was telling the story of how, as a young bride, she had laughed at her father-in-law's fear that she might be offended sharing the dinner table with an African American friend of his—and she was quick to point out that he was a "bright man" who had "made a great success as a porter." Her friendship and respect for African Americans Walter Loving and, later, Arthur Brooks, was based not only on their intelligence, sophistication, and authority, but on the fact that the former was a classically trained musician and the latter had commanded the first separate battalion of Washington's National Guard; local government had refused to permit black men to be part of its Spanish-American War quota in the two-hundred-thousand man volunteer army. Her close working relationship with Brooks is a telling illustration of her views on class. Seeing to his appointment during the Taft presidency as a manager of the White House, she relied on his advice and entrusted him with the most discrete assignments. A later suggestion by historian Constance Green that Nellie was demeaning Brooks by referring to him by his last name fails to mention that she did so with Cabinet members as well.

As a debutante Nellie Herron had casually dated Tom Mack, who was Jewish. In organizing the orchestra, she had befriended the wealthy Jewish Fleishmann, Levy, and Freiberg families. She socialized often with Will's judicial, political, and legislative colleagues, such as Simon Wolf, Alfred Cohen, and Frederick Spiegel. The children and grandchildren of Cincinnati rabbi Isaac Mayer Wise, founder of the Jewish reform movement, were close to Nellie and her children. While a reference in her diary does reflect anti-Semitism in her supposition that a Jewish friend might not pay for his share of a meal, she readily admitted to being wrong in her assumption. If not entirely free of stereotyping, she also knew bigotry was hurtful, a point illustrated in an 1893 letter to her husband. "Will [her brother] went on a coaching party yesterday," she recalled. "He said that Harry Levy came in to the office and invited him. He had a vision of himself starting out from the St. Nicolas [hotel] with a whole party of Jews, and was about to plead a previous engagement, but he saw a look in the eyes of his would-be host which seemed to say, 'Now we'll see how far your friendship goes' so he accepted."

Nellie's Jewish friends in Cincinnati, however, had been of the upper class, with German and English ancestors. References she made to the lower-class eastern European Jewish strangers she encountered aboard ships as she traveled between America and Europe were offensive, the sort of vague comments made in passing that were treated as tacitly permissible affectation of both the Christian and Jewish upper classes. For their part, many German and English American Jews, "looked down on these newcomers as social inferiors and felt ambivalent toward them," according to the eminent American Jewish historian Jonathan Sarna, "and worried that the East European would never assimilate." Nellie Taft would never entirely shake her pronounced consciousness of class, and sense of her own superiority as a result of it, a view inadvertently revealed in her quip that the Secret Service were "like the poor—always with us." On her first trip to Europe, for example, she had disparaged a group of Americans not of her class—with no suggestion of their race or faith. To her, there was no inherent inferiority with Catholics, but the Roman counts she befriended had nothing in common with the faithful peasants who blocked her view of a Vatican ceremony. She even applied this snobbery to herself, eagerly dropping the Presbyterian faith of her ancestors when later offered membership in an elite Washington Episcopalian church.

If, as a teenager, she had first been exposed to the lower-class white German(s) in the working-class bars of Cincinnati, as a middle-aged woman in the Philippines, she encountered her first real challenge in dealing with a different class and race simultaneously. Her closest friends among the Filipino people would indeed be the well-educated, powerful, and wealthy. Still, her zestful embracing of the native culture, an element much more a part of the daily life of the poor, was unprecedented.

In the Philippines, Nellie came into more frequent, daily contact with the impoverished, the illiterate, the superstitious and unwashed. Thrown into an entirely new culture, one can either reject or embrace it. Situated as she was, the governor's wife could have withdrawn into a closed white society of Americans. Instead, she went out daily to learn and experience Filipino life. Rather than see the native world as being there to entertain and amuse her, Mrs. Taft sought an overtly active role in public life that would take her far from the guarded palace salon and the bored conversation of the many military and other official wives who chose to remain in racial isolation.

The single fact about the culture that seemed to most fascinate her was the interracial Spanish Asian ancestry of most Filipinos. In her memoirs, Nellie commented, "It is the only country in the world that I know about—certainly the only country in the Orient—where the man or woman of mixed blood seems to be regarded as superior to the pure blooded native."

Ultimately, her progressive racial attitude supported the objective of winning the trust of the Filipinos, but the Tafts' desire to improve health conditions and diminish mortality rates; upgrade agricultural efficiency standards; widen scientific, cultural, and economic knowledge; provide basic and higher education; introduce fairness to legal rights; and encourage a fullness to civic life for the poor Filipino was genuine. Unlike those who wanted to "Americanize" the native, Nellie Taft, like her husband, respected the native culture. She initiated no reform campaign, overt or subtle, to get native women into western clothes or shoes, as white Christian women had done in Hawaii (she was instead amused when they took to wearing hats, which she'd always considered to be a burden to women). She introduced no Anglo foods or cooking styles. She conversed in Spanish and some rudimentary Filipino—not English.[4]

■

Will pointedly mentioned that Nellie was particularly "anxious that the abrupt methods of military government should cease . . ." MacArthur's idea of controlling the Filipinos by "pin[ning] them down with a bayonet for at least ten years" seemed most to enrage her. Nellie was not in the least intimidated by the military. "This afternoon, I rode with Major Stevens, a dried up old bean that I have picked up, but a very useful one, as he is chief quartermaster and so has everything at his disposal," she confessed to her mother. She had influence with them, too, when she decided to use it. As Charlie recalled, "It was she who persuaded the Army engineers not to destroy the medieval walls of the old city of Manila, which were threatened with demolition by army engineers in the interest of efficiency and sanitation." Among the few in the military Nellie liked was a thirty-six-year-old Georgian bachelor whom she called "a great society beau . . . very good looking." A former reporter who had volunteered during the war, and was then commissioned to the quartermaster department in Manila, Major Archibald Willingham Butt would come to play a key role in the lives of the Tafts.

In every act she took, Nellie always conferred with Will, and he made her a complete confidant in all matters, political and military. "Of course, Dear," Will said in one letter, "what I write about the situation you must be careful to keep secret." To what extent she influenced policy is hard to know; since they were together, there was no correspondence. Several years later, however, Nellie would tell a reporter, "The situation in the Philippines, while I lived there, was most interesting and I became familiar with every phase of it. It meant more than politics. The questions involved real statesmanship. Mr. Taft held his conferences at our home, and, naturally, I heard these matters discussed more freely than one would in Washington. It was politics 'over the teacups,' as it were."[5]

Mrs. Taft's first newspaper publicity appeared in the Manila daily *El Progresso*. A reporter who dined with her wrote of how she spoke in French and Spanish to guests on everything from "the favorite musical composer of the Hispano-Filipino society" to "the charitable work she expects to undertake."

Outside of the palace, Nellie Taft made Manila's high infant mortality rate her "own problem." Her first obstacle was resistance from native mothers who feared accepting food and medicine provided by the American government. Many wild rumors spread through the country about how the Americans might kill off the people. After a few women trusted her enough to accept the food and medicine for their infants—and the babies lived—Mrs. Taft introduced a nutrition campaign. Called "Drop of Milk," the program distributed sterilized milk to thousands of children. She literally saved lives. Later, the healthy toddlers would affectionately flock around her at receptions. There are no statistics on just how many children were able to reach adulthood because of the program, nor were Nellie's papers regarding the creation of the organization preserved, but the program flourished. Within a dozen years Drop of Milk built its grand and architecturally significant headquarters in downtown Manila. Eventually the program became a model that was copied in some South American nations where a similar need existed.

Nellie Taft also became something of a maternal figure to many young and single women working in the Philippines. Kathryne Withrow, an American teacher in Manila, recalled her "many kindnesses and her example and inspiration as an American woman [who] helped me over the hard lonely places." When it came to the wives of American officials, however, Nellie generally found them "a most uninteresting set," who lacked her sense of adventure and interest in native culture and politics. She sought to engage native women but noted that "very few Filipino women go out here in society, not nearly so many in proportion as do in the provinces. We can not make out whether it is because they are resentful or not."[6]

At all of her entertainments Nellie had music, usually drawing upon one of her two favorite bands—the Constabulary Band, or the Jose Rizal Band, which Will had named after the native hero. This had great significance since Rizal was the idealized hero of the Filipino people, but also one who had urged a slow, patient, and careful easing into self-government without revolution. The Constabulary Band was an even greater symbol in conveying the message Taft wanted the natives and white Americans alike to realize. Created and assembled at Taft's direction, whenever the band appeared to perform, it made an immediate and powerful statement: The musicians were all native Filipinos, and they were led by African American Captain Walter H. Loving, who had been classically trained, and shone brilliantly among his fellow musicians at the Boston Conservatory of Music. Certainly, in her review of the world's leading conductors and musicians, Nellie would be familiar with Loving and his skill. No records exist of how or where Will Taft—who knew little about music—went about putting the band together, but it is impossible to imagine that it was not Nellie Taft who had sought out Loving, even if she did not conceive of the very idea of the band itself.

Created in 1902, the Philippine Constabulary Band consisted of numerous musicians from different regions of the Philippines, who brought their own local experience and ability to be trained as one unit by Loving. Dressed in crisp uniforms, playing nationalistic American military marches, later even sent on a U.S. tour including such diverse venues as the 1904 St. Louis Fair, public hippodromes, and the stately Boston Symphony Hall, the band was fraught with racial symbolism on many levels. Just after the war, the American military establishment had recruited natives to serve as "Scouts" to help in the promise to self-government and fight the "insurgent bandits," using some regional rivalries as a way of spurring their enthusiasm. With his civilian government being put into place, Taft wanted a similar quasi-military force of native men, proving to Americans back home that not all Filipinos were against the U.S. takeover and that they could also be "civilized." Some would dismiss the band members as simply "mimicking" white music—but accusations of racist intent failed against the reality that it was an African American man who was leading them. Perhaps this was part of the thinking behind Nellie Taft's choice of Loving, yet there is no suggestion that she was racially conscious in the decision; his training and his talent, however, stood out, and it was that excellence that made her invest him with not only the musical responsibility but the symbolic visibility. Indeed, Loving and his musicians spoke for themselves: At the St. Louis Fair, for an entirely white audience, they performed *The William Tell Overture*—even through an electrical blackout—and beat out distinguished American and European concert bands to win the grand prize. Mrs. Taft had a role in the band's subsequent training for orchestral music, her particular area of interest and expertise.

Nellie got her daily dose of music at the Luneta, a sparsely landscaped public park. With bandstands at either end, overlooking the bay, the Luneta was a popular gathering place for all of Manila's classes and races. It was Nellie's favorite spot in all of the Philippines. As the sun set and the music began to play, she recalled that "everybody in the world came and drove around and around the oval [drive], exchanging greetings and gossip." The Taft children particularly loved going there to play with their friends.

The Taft children attracted almost as much attention as their parents in Manila, and realizing this, Nellie made conscious choices about their education there. An especially staunch supporter of the educational system being implemented in the islands, she later wrote proudly that "in no enterprise which America has undertaken in the Philippines have we received such enthusiastic support and co-operation from the Filipinos as in this." As a sign of personal faith in the system, she insisted on enrolling Bob in a model public school taught by Frederick Atkinson, who had come to the islands to head the new educational system. Will had wanted to send

Bob to Horace Taft's boarding school in Connecticut. Equally symbolic, Helen was initially sent to a Catholic school, the Convent of Santa Isabel. With his own cart and pony and two monkeys, "Baby," as she still called Charlie, was "spoiled," according to his mother, and a "tornado," according to his father. "He plays with the little Tagolog children on the place," Nellie added, "and his language is not always choice." He was still too young to attend school, so Charlie and his nurse were often the companions of his mother and aunt Maria. It further intensified Nellie's relationship with him beyond that which she had with her two eldest children.[7]

News of the Tafts' successes with the Filipinos resounded in America and Europe, and rebounded back to Nellie with speculation that made her gleeful. On March 27, 1901, for example, *The London Press* asked "Is Taft a Possibility?" and conjectured that McKinley's original promise that Will's role in the Philippines would "elevate" his career was intended to mean that the President would see to Will's nomination for the presidency in 1904 and not nominate him for the Supreme Court. The *New York Herald* was more certain: "William H. Taft May Be Mr. McKinley's Candidate." Indeed, Harry Taft wrote Will that the boom was real in Ohio, pushed by the same circle that helped make McKinley President and revealed by the state Republican executive committee chairman. "I leave it to your discretion," he added, "to disclose as much as you think fit to the feminine branch of the family."

If Nellie found Harry's news promising, she was suspicious of the intentions of journalist Joseph B. Bishop's letter to Will recounting a talk with Vice President Roosevelt: "He is full of 'strenuous' enthusiasm for you, and said . . . 'By George! I wouldn't ask any higher privilege than to be allowed to nominate Taft for President in the next national convention. What a glorious candidate and President he would make!'" Nellie highly doubted the sincerity of the story; many in the elite circle around Roosevelt, especially Henry Adams, knew that he wanted to be President himself. Although he was Vice President, however, there seemed little chance of his being nominated in 1904. Besides the fact that rank-and-file Republicans looked at him with mistrust, he was fighting historical precedent.

Will summarized his reaction to his brother Charley: "To me such a discussion has for its chief feature the element of humour." He felt that his history of judicial decisions against organized labor forbade any realistic presidential run, and the "horrors of a modern Presidential campaign" stopped him cold. Besides, as always, he asserted that he had "but one ambition." He still wanted to be chief justice. Charley felt that Will's work in the Philippines actually gave him a better chance at the nomination than many others who wanted it—he didn't mention Roosevelt by name. Nellie Taft, however, made it clear that such "speculation . . . did not seem at all unreasonable." Certainly she could not have been pleased with Will's remark in a January 1901 letter to Roosevelt: "I have no doubt that you will be the nominee in 1904."

Roosevelt was equally flattering to Will. In one note, after giving his "warm regards" to Nellie, he signed off like a lover: "I wish I had a photo of you." In his contributory essay on Will for an *Outlook* magazine profile, he wrote that the Philippines governor "ought to combine the qualities which would make a first-class President of the United States with the qualities that would make a first-class Chief Justice of the United States" and "the only man . . . who possessed all these qualities was Judge William H. Taft."

All things being equal, however, Roosevelt would rather see himself as President and Will on the Supreme Court. The quality Nellie would later identify as duplicitous in Roosevelt seemed to first display itself in written form for her in a letter Roosevelt wrote to Will that certainly was contradictory to his public comments about the presidency:

> Let me at the outset say one thing about myself at the risk of seeming even to you of being in the position of the lady who doth protest too much. Of course, I should like to be President, and I feel I could do the work well; but . . . I have seen too many men . . . suffering from the effects of the presidential bee, ever to get it into my head. Moreover, it would be simply foolish for me to think seriously of my chances of getting the office. . . . I cannot see that there is any but the smallest chance . . . to make me seriously spoken of as a candidate . . . I should like to be President. But . . . I should

throw up my hat . . . if I had the [power of] naming of either of
President or Chief Justice, I should feel in honor bound to name
you . . . . I think that you are of all the men in this country the one
best fitted to give the nation the highest possible service as president,
and yet also . . . Chief Justice.[8]

There was little time for Mrs. Taft to indulge her White House fantasies. On July 20, Nellie received a letter from her sisters in Michigan. Her mother had suffered a stroke in June. "We all feel so unhappy and uneasy, dearest Mamma, to think of you being even a little bit helpless, but perhaps even now you can go about again, and I am sure the Michigan air will do lots for you," Nellie wrote lovingly to her mother. "Of course, Maria will not be contented to stay when you need her to entertain and amuse you. . . . Oh my dearest Mamma, how I do wish I were where I could run in and see you every day!"

Recalling her acrimonious parting from her mother, Nellie was now wracked with guilt and frustration. "It is very hard to be so far away, but I try to keep up my courage by remembering all the cases I have known where people have rallied completely and lived some years," she wrote Jennie. "How long it does take to communicate." Maria departed on August 15, leaving Nellie "exceedingly lonely." She had hoped Lucy would now come join her, although there were no men for her there except "Army men who are not eligible, of course, though some are very nice." She had also hoped that her mother might go to Europe the next summer, where they could meet. Now all such plans were on hold.[9]

Waiting for news of Maria's progress toward America, Nellie was thunderstruck by the news that a white-faced Will brought to the lunch table on September 7. President McKinley had been shot the day before, and died eight days later. "Truly it was as if the foundations of our dear world had crumbled under us," Nellie recollected the feeling among Americans in the Philippines. At some point soon after, of course, Mrs. Taft would fully consider a new reality: Theodore Roosevelt had become President of the United States.

To War Secretary Elihu Root, Will was full of optimistic cheer about the new President: Roosevelt's "rugged strength . . . courage . . . intelligence" meant a "pure, honest and straightforward Administration." To the unctuous reporter Bishop, Taft would only say that fear of Roosevelt's "impulsiveness and lack of deliberation" were "unjust," but even if it were true, such characteristics would be naturally subdued by the nature of his ascension.

Privately he felt otherwise. On October 21, Will fired off angry letters to two of his brothers and his mother regarding Roosevelt. To Horace, Will confessed that he had received two brusque cables from the President. "The tone of the dispatch was by no means satisfactory," Will wrote. Later, he wrote Harry that Roosevelt lacked "the capacity for winning people to his support" and wouldn't be able to control Congress. "It does not necessarily follow that [he] will be nominated; such a thing has not occurred in the history of the country." Finally, also that day, he told his mother that Roosevelt "does not use the same tact in dealing with his subordinates that McKinley did."[10]

If Roosevelt's assumption of the presidential throne threatened Taft's political future with sudden uncertainty, it was a concern soon overwhelmed with word that Company "C" of the ninth infantry was massacred by armed Filipinos in a surprise attack at breakfast time near Balangiga on Samar Island. While "absolute panic" broke out in the streets of Manila among all the Americans, the governor-general and his family made such obvious targets that Nellie was quite rational in her fear that they might "be murdered in our beds any night."

To Americans the famous Balangiga revolt was viewed as an insurrection of rebels against the new civil government. For many Filipinos, however, it was the last gasp of a freedom fight to prevent another nation from ruling them as Spain had. While the actual attackers were guerrilla fighters, there was much sympathy for their losing cause. The feeling that the United States had actually betrayed the Filipinos was strong, especially outside Manila. There were numerous examples of the American government having been duplicitous in the process of taking the nation; Balangiga came to represent the most emotional and heroic—albeit the last—effort of the Filipino people to stem the tide of colonization. Almost exclusively at this point, the wealthy, enlightened class among the Filipinos had shifted their allegiance to the Americans. Now, they too were vulnerable to attack and could offer little in the way of comfort to the American community.

To even the most understanding and altruistic Americans, Balangiga utterly destabilized the delicate calm that was just vaguely starting to settle in the islands. It would be months before a sense of security returned, but it so set Nellie off emotionally, especially without Maria's presence, that she later confessed she was about to "suffer a nervous breakdown." Will and she decided it would be best for her to "run up to China" and get out of the heat. On the voyage there on the S.S. *Hamburg*, Nellie delighted in drinking "the best beer on draught that I have tasted since I left Germany." It was certainly one time, at least, when she probably did drink to soothe her anxiety.

And so, Nellie Taft was off to adventure to yet another foreign land. This time, however, she was all alone and going to explore the most mythical of "oriental" lands for an American of that era.

Depressed, fearful for Will's safety, and worried sick, Nellie still pushed herself to make the most of being in a new country. She explored China, starting from Shanghai and proceeding to Peking. In Peking she found the streets narrow and smelly, and a hotel employee tried to steal her watch. But even with high anxiety, she remained fascinated by all she saw. "This place is very much out of the world," she wrote. "There is some allurement in the idea of bargaining for priceless porcelains, ivories, silks and Russian sables behind closed and double-locked doors in the dark depths of some wretched Chinese hovel." She was given a three-foot brass Buddha and blue porcelain dog as gifts from American officials, and after eyeballing different European soldiers in "brilliant uniforms," she concluded that those Eastern Asians of the Sikh faith were, "by the way, stunning looking men." Upon her return to Shanghai in early November, there were two cables waiting from Will:

"October 25. . . . Come dear am sick."

"October 26. . . . Much better don't shorten trip."

Confused and alarmed, she wired back: "What is trouble love?" In her absence, on October 27, Will had undergone emergency surgery for fistula rectal abscess. He wired back that the surgery had been successful but he needed weeks of recovery. Nellie would return on the next available steamer, but with time to wait before sailing, she went ahead with a planned houseboat excursion down the muddy Yangtze River. Because she was obsessively worried about Will and the boat was constantly getting stuck on clay mounds—that Nellie soon learned were graves—her Yangtze cruise was a grim disaster. Raising her anxiety level even higher, she soon learned that there had been an earthquake in Manila. Shortly after she arrived in Manila in early November, Will learned that Roosevelt wanted him back in Washington to testify before Congress on Filipino matters and also to confer about his political future.

The Tafts received a three-month leave to return to the United States, but could not depart before Will had a second surgery on Thanksgiving.[11]

Making matters worse were letters to Nellie from home. Her father complained that she just "dropped out of the world" since she hadn't written them. He was embarrassed to be stopped in the street and asked about newspaper reports of Will's health, as if "we ought to know by telepathy." He and Harriet were "greatly troubled about Christmas this year. Our efforts last year were such failures that we do not wish to repeat them." And just when was Maria arriving home anyway? Eleanor was waiting for her in New York, which meant that he and Harriet would have no family for Thanksgiving. As if that was not enough guilt to load on Nellie, Harriet scribbled a piteous note. She was sorry she could not send Christmas gifts but none of her children "would look after the matter for me," and "it seems too bad that the children so far away should not have something from home to make the day merry." And for good measure she predicted that "Thanksgiving will be a failure."

The Tafts embarked for the States at the end of the month, celebrating Christmas and New Year's Day as they crossed the Pacific. They landed in San Francisco and rushed by train for Cincinnati but were delayed for hours in Utah by a severe blizzard. As winds rocked the train and the water pipes froze, and Will and Nellie shivered under layers of blankets, Harriet Herron died. The Tafts received the news in Omaha.

McKinley's murder, the Balangiga massacre, Will's illness, and now Harriet's death did Nellie in. "I found it no longer possible to brace myself against the inevitable collapse," she wrote. Although they arrived in Cincinnati the day before her mother's funeral, Nellie's exhaustion was so complete that she was unable to attend. As if the fates sought to crush her completely, her father also suffered a stroke. On top of this, medical exams soon showed that Nellie had malaria.[12]

Will, beckoned to Washington to begin his congressional testimony, first settled Nellie and the children in her father's home. At the end of January when he arrived in Washington he reported that the President had immediately telephoned him. Within hours Will and Theodore (or "Teddy," as the nation's newspapers and soon the public nicknamed him, much to his displeasure) were together. Taft seemed to find no evidence that Roosevelt had changed any of his forceful, charging manner to the more restrained modus operandi that Will believed was more effective for a chief executive dealing with the legislature. "He was just the same as ever and it is very difficult for me to realize that he is the President," Will told Nellie. "He greatly enjoys being President and shows not the slightest sign of worry or hard work in his looks or manner."

For whatever motive, if any, the Roosevelts fussed over Will in Washington. The next day Edith Roosevelt even got involved, inviting Will to lunch at the White House. Whether or not the President had asked her to invite Will, Edith certainly discussed with him what she might talk about with Taft. "Mrs. R. is not changed at all," he rather enigmatically confided to Nellie, and she "asked after you and expressed great sympathy in your sorrow and illness."

The new First Lady then invited Will to the Army and Navy Reception and a private dinner with congressmen several nights later. "Write me something more about Mrs. Roosevelt," Nellie instructed. "Is she one of the advanced women? I see she dresses on $300 a year, or did do so." There was no evidence that either Roosevelt had as much curiosity about Nellie as she did about them. Both Theodore and Edith would still view Nellie Taft in a social, not political, context.

There was also a new Roosevelt for Nellie to watch. "I met also Miss Alice Roosevelt, the eldest daughter who is nice looking except for her complexion," Will wrote just days short of Alice's eighteenth birthday. Alice smoked cigarettes, eschewed religion, danced atop cars, and sliced up fools with a malicious wit. Darling of the press, her behavior nevertheless masked a myriad of insecurities. In earlier days her stepmother could make her feel uncomfortable in her brood of four boys and one girl, and they had an antagonistic relationship. Devotedly in love with her father, he kept his emotional distance from her, still refusing to acknowledge the existence of her birth mother. It was easy to understand how Alice's neediness at that time in her life induced her to be strongly and quickly attracted to the soothing, parental warmth that came naturally to Will. And he found her not only witty but beautiful.

To others Will professed the "warmest and most sincere confidence" in Roosevelt's "earnestness" and "high ideals," and the hope that he'd be nominated as President in 1904. To Nellie, however, he seemed almost consciously to feed her doubts about "Teddy," as she began derisively calling him. "His impulsiveness is likely to get him into many troubles and errors which the public will forgive because they think he is honest.... The difference between him and McKinley in dispatch, in dignity, in judgment, and in tact, only the Cabinet know." Nellie rapidly replied, "I was much interested in what you wrote about the Cabinet opinion of Teddy."[13]

Being back in Washington stirred up Will's own dream again. It was "more expensive" now than when they had lived there, but—he slipped in—the Senate raised the chief justice salary to $13,000, while Cabinet members received only $8,000. "I would not for a place on that Bench give up the work in the Philippines," he rushed to reassure her, "at least for a year & a half longer." Nellie parried with a vague reference to her dream when she learned that he had attended a White House dinner with key Republican leaders. "Altogether your stay in Washington has brought you in contact with all the best men," she wrote, "and will be a great help to you."

Will told Nellie that they must be "prepared for onslaughts" from Congress after his testimony. "I do not enjoy . . . the prospect of the abuse to which I shall be subjected," he added. Neither Taft had experienced either political scrutiny or the histrionic diatribes of legislators trying to get in the news. "I hope that your sessions with the Senate Committee have not been so unpleasant as you feared," she wrote on February 1, answering his need for encouragement but withholding her opinion that he had endured a "hostile cross-examination." Within two days of her letter Will showed confidence again: Despite "disputes with the Democrats," the Senate hearings "have not been unpleasant." To this she boosted him more: "I am glad that you do not seem to mind the attacks on you. That of Senator Patterson was most uncalled for, it seemed to me." She also couldn't help provoking politics: "I fear you were disappointed in the tariff bill, and was not Senator Hoar's amendment about the Sedition Law discouraging? I fear its effect on the law will be bad."[14]

Will did, however, come in for some attacks. The goal of his testimony was essentially to make airtight the Republican Administration's case that the United States must continue to hold the Philippines and that the colony was not yet ready for self-rule. In the first bleak winter weeks of 1902, Will was grilled for an average of two hours a day on details about the true conditions in the islands. He told the truth. Asked about American military cruelty to some Filipinos, Taft said yes, there had been some isolated instances. He talked for "as much time as the Democrats do not consume in asking fool questions," he wrote his brother Horace on January 30. His testimony resulted in a continuation of U.S. policy on the islands and also left Will relatively unscathed. Still, he would reflect on April 18 to Nellie, that his "thin-skinned vanity" in regard to being publicly questioned on issues that reflected his competency and decision-making skills "shows my unfitness for public life." Nellie ignored such talk, chalking it up to depression over his health.

Despite her own physical ailments resulting from malaria, Nellie took charge of arranging Will's third surgery. She settled on Cincinnati's Jewish Hospital because "it could be done perfectly well here, and much more cheaply" than in Washington. After his successful surgery and return to the capital, Will flooded Nellie with details of how the Roosevelt women embraced him. "I have just come back from the White House. It was a regular family dinner. Alice Roosevelt came and sat with us for a while," he wrote. "Mrs. Roosevelt is very sweet in manner and asked after you."

Nellie did not react to the Roosevelt news. She was focused on getting out of Cincinnati as soon as possible. The "old gentleman," her father, was "despondent" because he was deeply in debt, having made bad investments for himself and clients. He considered selling all his assets, but Nellie felt that Eleanor's and Lucy's impending marriages would relieve some of his financial burden. Maria was now his constant companion and caretaker. Nellie was also preoccupied with the news that Will was going to the Vatican to begin negotiating the transfer of the Philippines friar lands. Afraid "that I may not get well enough to go," Nellie grandly reported that she simply "told the doctor this morning that he must fix me up by that time." Her old self was returning.

At 137 pounds, Nellie's weight was nearly back to normal, and she was set to sail for Europe on June 4 until Bob contracted scarlet fever and the voyage was delayed. "The worst of all is the idea of visiting here in Cincinnati six weeks longer," she complained. "I really feel as if I could not stand it." In the meantime, Will took his mother to Rome.[15]

Nellie had longed to return to Italy ever since her initial visit in 1888. This time, she made the most of her entrée to counts, princesses, marquises, cardinals, and bishops, attending magical dinners in castles—the ladies in costumes, the men in uniforms, and liveried servants lighting the way to carriages with flaming torches. "Nellie is not at all timid," Louise Taft wrote of her daughter-in-law, who breezed into Catholic masses and festivals at Saint Peter's. "Unshaken though we were in our religious affiliations," Nellie wrote, "we appreciated the real beauty of the ceremonies." In black veil, she and her children were even received by Pope Leo. When the pontiff predicted that Bob would someday be President, the boy said he wanted to be chief justice.

Taft's task was a delicate one. He had to show sensitivity to the Filipino people, yet respect the Catholic hierarchy's right to protect their private property. The Catholic friars had physically fled the lands they still held title to in the Philippines during the fight for freedom by Filipinos. Many natives and even some Americans now simply wanted to seize that property and claim it, so deeply did the resentment toward the friars run.

In his personal interview with the Pope, Taft was able to negotiate an equitable situation. Pope Leo sent an appraiser of the lands. Will eventually persuaded the Vatican to sell and remove itself from the lands for $7.5 million. The negotiations, however, had a lingering effect. Nellie claimed the deal was able to "soothe" American Catholics without shocking Protestants. In fact, conservative Catholics believed the deal was an attack on their faith—that the American government was sanctioning the systematic destruction of the Catholic Church as an institution of Filipino life, and trying to undermine its global influence—as if Taft and his commission were all just a cover for a massive, government-sanctioned, Methodist missionary project. Many fundamentalist Protestants weren't pleased, either, highly suspicious that an American official and friend of the President would be meeting privately with the Pope in the Vatican, making arrangement where U.S. tax dollars were paid to the Roman Church for some useless jungle lands.

As Will's negotiations continued, Nellie took rooms in a Florentine castle and enjoyed walking through pine forests, visiting museums, and strolling along the Arno. Will broke away to join his family only once, in mid-July. On the twenty-first of the month, he left for the Philippines, where a cholera epidemic was raging. Nellie lingered in Florence for the rest of the summer, then headed to Venice, Vienna, and the Swiss Alps. She sailed for Manila on September 3, but not before receiving an extraordinarily straightforward letter of appreciative love from Will:

> *I can not tell you what a comfort it is to me to think of you as my wife and helpmeet. I measure every woman I meet with you and they are all found wanting. Your character, your independence, your straight mode of thinking, your quiet planning, your loyalty, your sympathy when I call for it (as I do too rarely), your affection and love (for I know I have it all) all these Darling make me happy only to think about them and make me fearful to have you encounter the dangers of this long trip alone without me. I love you Dear and if I can only make you happy and bring up our children well, it will be enough.*

After stopping in Hong Kong, Nellie and the children arrived in Manila on October 7. Eleven days later President Roosevelt wrote a letter to Will that would shake Nellie to her core—however momentarily.[16]

"On January 1st, next, Judge Shiras is to resign, and on the whole it seems to me that it would be wise for you to go on in his place."

It was that simple. Roosevelt laid before Will the one thing, the great dream, the driving ambition of his life: a seat on the Supreme Court.

"No one can quite take your place where you are," Roosevelt said, beginning a stream of flattery on Will's work in the Philippines. "Of course there is no telling," he added with a sense of immediacy "whether there will be another chance for me to put you upon the Supreme Court, and moreover, I feel that we do need you on the court. . . . Nothing can be more important than to strengthen in every way the Supreme Court." Roosevelt baited Will a bit, too; the offer was contingent on the understanding that Will did "not intend to go into active political life." He concluded with a mixed message, saying he honored Will's right to guide his own destiny while making it seem like an emergency: "If you do not accept I shall have to at once select some one else." Eight days later Roosevelt was more demanding: "I feel that your duty is on the court."

Nellie's initial response, interestingly, was conflicted. "I had always been opposed to a judicial career for him, but . . . I yearned to be safe in Washington, even though it did mean our settlement in the 'fixed groove' that I had talked against for so long." Despite the fact that no Supreme Court justice had ever been elected to the presidency, Nellie felt reassured when Charley Taft suggested to her that taking a seat on the Court would probably not legally or politically prevent Will from later resigning and then running for public office. She might have also questioned the motive of Roosevelt's persistence.

Will felt, however, that it would be an utter abandonment of his work and a betrayal of the Filipinos. He responded to Roosevelt: "Great honor deeply appreciated but must decline. . . . Look forward to time when I can accept such an offer but even if it is certain that it can never be repeated I must now decline." Two days later Roosevelt gave in, saying he was "disappointed" in Will's decision but admired him all the more for putting his responsibility before his ambition, and adding, "No one can quite take your place as the new member of the court."[17]

In truth, Roosevelt was not done. "I am awfully sorry," he wrote Will one month to the day of his initial offer, "I find that I shall have to bring you home and put you on the Supreme Court. . . . I have the greatest confidence in your judgment; but after all, old fellow, if you will permit me to say so, I am President and see the whole field." Whether he was specifically referring to Will or to Nellie or even Charley Taft, Roosevelt added emphatically yet enigmatically that he would not "yield to anyone else's decision if my judgment is against it." Realizing that Will did have the conviction to resist the offer, Roosevelt directly contacted Commissioner Luke Wright and Judge Henry C. Ide, telling them that they would be appointed governor-general and vice general, respectively. He furthermore instructed the Supreme Court that he would be appointing Taft and told Shiras that he must delay his resignation, because Taft couldn't return to Washington until after the Court adjourned in May. "I am very sorry if what I am doing displeases you, but as I said," Roosevelt wrote Will, "this is one of the cases where the President if he is fit for his position must take the responsibility." He closed by stating that he was submitting Taft's nomination on February 1.

Stunned, Will told his wife. "Nellie was quite disappointed that I should be 'shelved' on the bench at my age," he reported to Charley. Indeed, she considered Teddy's edict to be "quite unanswerable" and "heaved a sigh of resignation." Will cabled Roosevelt "to make one more appeal" to permit him to stay in the Philippines. Slowly, Nellie was becoming "reconciled" to the idea of the Court if only because "we may all get home alive now anyhow." She did not promise to stop urging him toward the presidency, but even if Will had to serve some stint in the judiciary branch, at least they would still live. More than 100,000 would die from the cholera outbreak that hit the islands at that time. Will would soon be suffering from amoebic dysentery.

Before Roosevelt could reply, however, he received an urgent telegram from the other commissioners urging Taft's "retention. . . . He has unequalled confidence and affection [of] Filipino people and complete grasp [of the] situation." Word rapidly spread through Manila from officials down to the public streets that Governor Taft was about to be taken away from them.

In the meantime, Harry Taft met with Roosevelt and reported back to Will that he found no "ulterior motive" behind Roosevelt's being "extremely anxious" for Will to be on the Court. To Nellie's suspicious thinking, however, an "ulterior motive" may have been linked to information in a second letter from Harry. The *Washington Post* and other national newspapers were carrying stories that the "opponents of Roosevelt" were planning to draft Taft as a candidate against Teddy in the primaries; the more conservative Ohio forces in the party who had put McKinley into the

White House were uneasy about Roosevelt and his threats to overturn the political status quo. Taft was seen by party fathers as less aggressive and independent-thinking, more controllable than the wild-eyed, unpredictable reformer Teddy with his gnashing teeth and bravado. Roosevelt, after all, had been "bumped up" to the vice presidency because many New York Republican leaders—seeking to preserve their patronage system and ties to business—wanted him and his reform crusade out of the governorship of New York. Nobody had anticipated his ascending to the presidency. Taft was briefly considered one possible way of replacing Roosevelt.

While it would be ridiculous to think that Will would challenge President Roosevelt or that the incumbent would not be nominated, such talk could damage the public perception of Roosevelt as invincible. Nellie Taft became convinced that Roosevelt would never have encouraged Will toward the Supreme Court if doing so ran contrary to his own purposes.

Will dismissed Nellie's paranoia about Roosevelt's ego and ambition, but she held firm in her view. She was not alone. Will's mother dined at the White House with Roosevelt and wrote her son: "I do not think his personality is agreeable and his manners are explosive and so demonstrative as to seem like an affectation." Louise registered her opposition to the Court offer. "Nellie was especially pleased to see that you and Harry and Horace agreed with her that I ought not to go on the bench," Will wrote her. Despite having his mother and wife both against his accepting a potential Court seat, Will affirmed to Louise, "I venture to differ with you and her."[18]

Both Will and Nellie were overwhelmed, however, by the massive march around the Malacanan Palace on January 10, with chanting natives carrying signs and posters demanding that Taft stay in the Philippines. One speaker even compared Will to Jesus. Among the most astounding of all the reactions was that of the Filipino members of the commission who wired their protest to the White House that Taft must remain. When the

American civil commission was being put into place, Taft had been more adamant than his fellow commissioners in insisting that five native leaders be named to the new commission, which functioned as a cabinet. Three were ultimately appointed, and although they were in the minority and voted with their American counterparts, their presence was an important sign that Taft would make good on his promise of "eventual" self-rule. "We hold the Philippines for the benefit of the Filipinos," Taft would reiterate some years later in a public speech, "and we are not entitled to pass a single act or to approve a single measure that has not that as its chief purpose." This, of course, ignored the glaring reality that self-rule was not immediately granted. In sum, to most Filipinos, Taft was the best man in the worst situation. Replacing him with anybody else would probably be worse. Roosevelt was shocked. "Will has sprung a surprise on me. He must have given the contents . . . of my letter to a number of natives." Teddy wired Will: "All right, stay where you are. I shall appoint someone else to the Court." When she read the curt reply, Nellie laughed. But Teddy did not relent.

On March 27, Will received a heartfelt letter from Roosevelt informing him that War Secretary Elihu Root was returning to the private sector at the end of 1903. Both he and Root "urged upon him," as Nellie put it, to take not only the place of Root as war secretary but become an unofficial presidential "counselor and adviser." In his offer Roosevelt warned him twice not to share this news with anyone. That was impossible. Nellie was determinedly ecstatic.

In perhaps the most overtly written admission by a political wife to having a driving ambition to control her husband's career, Nellie Taft recalled in her 1914 memoirs to the offer of the war secretary position. "This was more pleasing to me than the offer of the Supreme Court appointment, because it was in line with the kind of work I wanted my husband to do, the kind of career I wanted for him and expected him to have, so I was glad there were few excuses for refusing to accept it." She told Will that he must absolutely take the job.

Heading off any excuse about his Philippines work that Will might claim as the reason he must to turn this post down, Roosevelt asserted that as war secretary Taft would oversee all matters related to the islands. Will retorted that he and Nellie couldn't afford to entertain as a Cabinet member would be expected to on the $8,000 salary. Roosevelt wrote that Nellie should just do as Edith had once done—entertain on Sunday evenings and just serve tea, "and she never minded our not having champagne." To this idea Will privately quipped to a friend, "You should see Nellie's lip curl at the suggestion of Sunday high teas and dinner parties without champagne." In the end, Charley came through again with a supplement to the Cabinet salary monetary promise of $6,000 annually.

The Tafts spent several weeks in the cool mountain air of the summer capital, Banguet. Living with them was Will's devoted but obsequious secretary Fred Carpenter. "He is a very nice quiet fellow, and fits in like an old shoe. I rather hated the idea of having him at first, but now we don't mind him a bit, and he makes himself very useful," Nellie wrote. In fact, she discovered early on that Carpenter would bow and scrape at her beck and call. She liked that. She also found a visiting Senator Beveridge to be unctuous and annoying.[19]

Upon her return to Manila in the fall, Nellie's correspondence makes clear her eagerness to leave the tropics, especially after enduring another cholera epidemic. She completed final business, seeing to it that one of the Chinese servants who had worked for her and wanted to enlist in the American Navy was given a position as a steward on a gunboat, and also planning a gala Venetian Carnival costume ball for her farewell. When the family arrived in San Francisco in early 1904, Will proceeded directly to Washington. Nellie, Helen, and Charlie, however, went to spend the winter and early spring in Santa Barbara. Painfully thin and exhausted, Nellie took immediately to southern California's warmth.

In Washington, Will took quickly to the new social scene. His friend, Cincinnati congressman Nick Longworth, a rogue of a bachelor, loved scandalizing Will with gossip of the fast women in his crowd. His domineering mother, Susan, lived with him and had Will in for Sunday suppers. Taft was the special pet, however, of the Roosevelts. He went to the symphony "and sat in a box with Mrs. Longworth and Mrs. Roosevelt was in the next box." A week later it was dinner at the White House where "Alice R. did the honors." Three days later the First Lady "invited me to go to the opera."

Will tried to coax Nellie from California to share the high life. He related that a Senate wife told him "that the wife of a War Secretary who did not hate Washington would be very gratefully received. So you see your opportunity." Nellie was not amused. "Your letters have been rather cross," he responded, "when you hear of my spending afternoons with young women." He spent money easily—$500 for a new wardrobe. She tartly scolded him: "You have not begun to practice economy, and I want seriously to remind you that it is now necessary." Will reassured her: "I do love you Darling whether you love me or not."

Whether Nellie resisted coming strictly because of her poor health or some resentment is unclear. If she was spiting herself, she certainly made sure Will knew it: "I am very lonely all day. I subscribed for the *Los Angeles Times* today as I felt out of the world. . . . I am anxious to hear all the news and will like typewritten letters for the sake of hearing more. There must be so much to tell that of course I will be sure to miss a great deal."[20]

As the weeks went on, Nellie's ennui turned into depression again. "I have a letter from you tonight in which you say 'somehow though I don't seem to enjoy anything very much,'" Will wrote to Nellie. "Why do you suppose you feel that way? Is it because I was not with you for my absence does not usually affect you that way. I am afraid it is that you are still far from well. I have been glad to think that you are gaining flesh and so gaining strength both muscular and nervous; but you must not let the blues rob you of this benefit."

Will, on the other hand, was enjoying himself despite his frequent tiredness due to a nasal-throat blockage that made him sleep poorly. He had grown to 325 pounds. To keep his weight in check, he took up a new sport with a vengeance. "I am glad you have tried the golf and like it. I suppose with your usual extravagance that you bought a new set [of clubs]," Nellie quipped that summer. Money kept her fretting. Scrupulously ethical, Will not only turned down free rail passes but even diamond cuff links. "I fear if you had been here and had seen how nicely the stones would have fitted into your present necklace that you would have used your influence against the right course," he teased her.[21]

Although charged not only with overseeing the Philippines but the new Panama Canal Commission, Will confessed that most of his time was spent stumping for the President's 1904 campaign. Besides praising Roosevelt's policies he fed the cult of personality that had grown up around Teddy. "The issues chiefly will be personal attacks against the President," Will told Nellie, "his extravagance in the White House. It will be easy to defend and it shows the paucity of issues that the Democrats have. We never had a president whose family life has been better than Roosevelt's. The people know it. That is why they like him." Will was out speaking throughout the country—April 9 in Chicago, April 27 in Pittsburgh, May 30 in Topeka. "These things I do by direction of the President."

"The President seems really to take much comfort that I am in his cabinet. He tells me so and then he tells people so who tell me. He is a very sweet natured man and a very trusting man," Will wrote, persistently trying to convince Nellie. "I am growing to be very fond of him." He claimed Roosevelt was "amenable with change when reasoned with." Even Bob got the bug, writing his mother after a visit with the Roosevelt sons that "I like Kermit better . . . but I am just as big as Teddy [Jr.]."

Will was utterly under the Roosevelt spell. "I hope you will agree with me when you have fuller opportunities of observation," he wrote to Nellie. She remained unmoved. If she calmed herself by thinking that she had at least diverted Will from his judicial groove into an executive one— perhaps with her eyes on 1908—she was mistaken. In her absence, Will yet again began to feed his grand obsession. "Spooner was talking of my going on the bench. He said he proposed to make up a crowd of influential men who would force my appointment as Chief Justice. . . . He thinks that after Roosevelt's election the Ch. J. would retire to give me the place." A month later he was kibitzing with Associate Justice Brown who, Will wrote Nellie, "wished to see me Chief Justice." Brown said Chief Justice Fuller was "getting old" but wouldn't resign. Was Mrs. Fuller "anxious to have him stay?" Will asked. "Women usually do," retorted Brown.

"You must not be too confident of Teddy's giving me the Chief Justiceship," Will seemed to backpedal to Nellie in another missive. Mrs. Fuller died soon after, and Fuller stayed on as chief justice. But even before the 1904 election, Nellie was more interested in Will's taking the chance of running for President than being assured the chief justiceship. Protecting that chance was her objective. One can only imagine her reaction to the news that Will unloaded on August 3. "I went over to see the President," he wrote her. "He says he told Root that he would in all probability be in the line of succession to the Presidency in 1908. . . . He said that so far as I was concerned I was out of it because my ambition was to be Chief Justice as he knew."[22]

Jealousy over the Roosevelts, losing a chance to get free diamonds, overcoming her loneliness and depression, keeping a tight rein on finances—none of those worries quite motivated Mrs. Taft to go to the capital as did the terror that Will would lose his chance at the presidency. By early fall she got quite well and hurried to Washington.

Nine

"Teddy, Nellie, and Will" (1904—1907)

Politics makes me sick.

—WILLIAM HOWARD TAFT

I n many ways, her years in Washington as a Cabinet wife proved to be the period of her marriage when Nellie Taft was more physically apart from yet emotionally enmeshed with Will. They would involve themselves in a strange sort of political version of a love triangle with the man who was to one a nemesis, to the other a hero.

Nellie Taft arrived in Washington, Helen and Charlie in tow, on October 1, 1904, staying one night at the Arlington House hotel before moving into their new home at 1904 K Street. Nellie saw to all the mind-numbing details: furniture, crystal, china, linens, clothing, decor, and staff. "Charlie induced me to clean the bookcase this morning instead of going to church," she wrote Will who was out on the road campaigning for Roosevelt.

It seemed that Nellie's life was doomed to be dominated by the Roosevelts. When Will was back in Washington, he was basically on call to the President, bidden at a moment's notice. Helen enrolled at the National Cathedral School where Ethel Roosevelt was a student, and Charlie attended the same public school as Quentin Roosevelt.

Only Nellie resisted befriending her counterpart. "Have you called on Mrs. Roosevelt?" Will goaded. "Don't you think you ought to write to her Secretary and make an appointment?"

With his campaign responsibilities, Will spent most of 1904 apart from Nellie. After a spring respite in Cincinnati during which she met Prince Heinrich of Germany, they came together briefly at the St. Louis Fair at the end of May. From St. Louis Nellie went to Murray Bay, where Will stayed only long enough to be feted at a surprise birthday party by about one hundred of his Quebecois neighbors. Immediately afterward Will was back on the campaign trail, stumping for Roosevelt's election.[1]

As usual the Tafts kept in touch on political matters. Will sent Nellie correspondence he had with the American and Filipino commissioners, and Nellie requested his intercession for a friend for a federal job. After reading his numerous letters to Teddy, Nellie warned that their length undoubtedly "bored" the President. In sending a draft speech for Nellie to look over, Will admitted that it was "more partisan in tone than anything I have written. . . . It will subject me to attack and criticism." Although he recognized his own lack of confidence in his speech writing and public speaking abilities, he was sensitive to even her gentlest criticism. When he complained that people walked out on one of his speeches, she replied, "I could not but smile, my dear, at your saying some of the people went out when you afterwards added that you spoke an hour and three quarters. If you confine it to an hour I think people will stay." Remembering the sting, Will later wrote her defiantly about another speech that "took me an hour and a quarter to read . . . and nobody left."[2]

"I wish you could go with me on some of my excursions," Will sheepishly wrote Nellie from the campaign trail. "I think you might regard them as good fun." Never liking to be shoved off with women's committees, Nellie refused. Without her, he flailed, exhausted, and was even more uncertain about his own speaking abilities. "I wouldn't run for President if you guaranteed the office," he wrote. "I am rather tired of campaigning and am still more tired of my speech but I must go on with it. . . . As your Mother used to say your father would say when things were gloomy and monotonous—'Time will pass.'" Nellie had heard this before, but she urged him on: "How glad you must be that this week ends it. The Democrats seem to be putting some life into them[selves]." Will, however, was dead serious, confiding to a friend, "I have not the slightest ambition to be President, and believe it utterly impossible. . . . A national campaign for the Presidency is to me a nightmare."

Nellie was invited with other Cabinet members and spouses to the White House on election night, where Roosevelt learned that he had won. Whether or not she noticed that Edith was "seen to flinch" when the President impulsively announced to the press that he would not seek another term under any circumstance in 1908 is not known. If it upset Edith, it must have relieved and even delighted Nellie. The road ahead seemed clear.

Mrs. Taft had a brief reprieve from her dull life as a Cabinet wife when she accompanied Will to Panama. Roosevelt had formally recognized the Republic of Panama after that territory had revolted in 1903 from Colombia, and he then took control of the isthmus, where his plans for a canal linking the Atlantic and Pacific oceans were already under way. There were internal political problems in Panama, however, and Taft oversaw financial, agricultural, trade, canal engineering, public health, and jurisdictional matters. This was all in addition to his duties as war secretary. Will's responsibilities in Panama were similar to those he had as governor-general in the Philippines, although the new republic was more autonomous and Nellie played no substantial role there. Before leaving for Central America, she had stopped in Cincinnati and took in an orchestra performance; her sister-in-law Annie was now president of the orchestra. "We met Charley in the intermission and he took us to get beer," she wrote. Nellie's career as founder of the orchestra was far behind her now, and she was satisfied that wealthy, popular Annie was now the "Mrs. Taft" associated with financially saving it. For herself, Nellie had bigger plans.[3]

As 1905 opened, Nellie was frantically planning a dinner for the Roosevelts on January 24, which Will said was "growing in importance in the mind of Nellie until I think it absorbs everything else." A month later her house was jammed with guests for the Roosevelt inauguration, and she was bored by the obligations associated with it. Everywhere she turned, Roosevelts dictated—her husband, her children, her social life. That domination would only increase in the coming months and years.

From May to September, Will would return to the Philippines, stopping in Japan, Korea, and China, with none other than Alice Roosevelt. ("Princess Alice," the press had dubbed her.) It left Nellie "lonely" and "anxious . . . very blue especially when I think of this summer. I have nothing else in prospect," she told him. Newspapers were packed with news of "Mr. Secretary and the Princess." Nellie even received unsolicited letters from people who wanted to go as her aide, but more likely they were hoping to be in the presence of the Princess. "Yet that, I presume, is one of the penalties one willingly pays for being the wife of a public and celebrated man!" one woman unctuously wrote her.

Nellie would not compete with the star of the show and told Will she was taking Charlie and Helen to England for the summer. She left angrily, bitterly reporting her voyage on the "shabby looking" S.S. *Zealand*, again making a distinction of her fellow travelers not only by race but class. She found the deck where the poorer passengers who paid the least for their tickets to be packed to the gills, describing it as "very crowded, two tables and two lines of steamer chairs, and mostly filled with Jews." This particular excursion, she soon discovered, was a cheaper voyage with accommodations not much above second class. Of those making the crossing who were "pleasant looking people on board"—a euphemism for the upper-class passengers—Nellie knew only Mrs. Slater, from a Jewish German Cincinnati family. Even this woman, Nellie noted, however, "keeps to her bed. When she is up, growls mostly. I do hate travelers that can not make the best of things," she wrote Will without irony.[4]

Will's reports were filled with joyous humor and reams about the President's daughter. The forty-five-year-old war secretary was titillated and even smitten with this beautiful, bright, yet cutting young woman who jumped fully gowned into the pool on board the *Manchuria*. Among the political, army, and naval officials, wives, and friends also on the junket,

Will thought his roguish friend, Cincinnati congressman Nick Longworth, "attracts Alice" because "he likes the prestige." From Japan Will observed: "Alice . . . seems to be so much taken up with Nick . . . pays little attention to anybody else. She is however amenable to persuasion and has quite winning ways when she devotes her attention, so that I think the Japanese generally thought she was . . . gracious . . . [I]n the Philippines . . . Lord knows what she may do."

The next day he went on: "Alice tells me she is engaged to Nick. They are a curious pair. . . . She is very young, childish and underdisciplined. . . . Nick's influence over her is not good. . . . Alice likes to smoke cigarettes. Indeed she is quite nervous unless she has a chance after a meal. She likes a strong drink occasionally and Nick always helps her, though such a habit ought not to be formed in one as highly strung as she is."

Life was not as interesting in England. Nellie outlined the sights she saw but concluded, "You get such poor food. . . . I almost got sick."[5]

Alice stormed Nellie's old palace in Manila, was given a suite there, and was feted by Filipino women at a dance, a reception, and a dinner. If such news steamed Nellie, Will pointed out that he arranged this because the new governor-general's wife and daughter had a "contempt for the whole race" of Filipinos and refused to integrate their entertainments. "I knew no way but the direct way of making Alice the guest of the leading Filipino with me to show that we had no sympathy with the apparent desire to exclude Filipino hosts." To Will's way of thinking, if the daughter of the President—feted at home and abroad as the "American Princess"—upheld and recognized the racially integrated social precedent established by the Tafts, there was a greater chance of setting a social custom that the military wives and other white women might seek to follow.

Back in England, Nellie's excitement ran to having lunch with the American artist Francis D. Millet; their fates would later be tragically linked with what would be considered one of the great disasters of the century.

By this time Will and Alice had grown fond of each other, and she confessed to being "really devoted" to him. "I do not think that I have ever known any one with the equanimity, amiability, and kindliness of Mr. Taft. . . . I never saw him really cross or upset. He was always beaming, genial and friendly . . . never out of temper, possibly he was just a little too good humored. I never had the least awe of him. I always felt that I could 'get away with' whatever it was he objected to." As the trip neared its end, Will recorded his thoughts:

> *Alice is . . . frank in the same degree that her father is. . . . Her associations with Nick Longworth and with girls of a fast set has made her very rapid. . . . She and Nick indulge in conversations on subjects that are ordinarily taboo between men and women. . . . I don't thinks she loves Nick and I don't think he loves her. . . . His attentions to her are . . . for prestige and notoriety . . . She seems entirely aware of Nick's cold, selfish nature and of his coarseness. . . . Alice . . . seems to have a . . . Doctor Jekyll and Mr. Hyde arrangement. . . . She made an excellent impression on the Filipinos. . . . In some instances I had to take a good deal of care to prevent her shocking some of our Filipino brethren. . . . She did seem to be oblivious to the comforts of other people, but . . . considering what she is, what she has gone through and who she is, I do not feel that she is subject to great criticism.*

There was, however, a hostility to her that Will found terrorizing. When Congressman Bourke Cochran showed interest in her, "she attacked him in a way that I cautioned her against. . . . She hates him because he attacked her father."[6]

On the Asian trip Will met another debutante to whom he took a liking. Her name was Mabel Boardman, and her interests were political, her personality sober, and her sentiments toward Taft sincere. She would later become a lifelong friend of both Tafts, but Will's initial description of her "high character" did not ring in Nellie's ear quite so much as the fact that he said she was "quite attractive to me." It certainly does seem as if Will was in some way trying to tease Nellie to the point of inciting a sort of humorous jealousy. "I fear the ladies on board have been so fascinating as to prevent your writing," Nellie wrote. "I love you very much even if you don't write to me as you used to do." Guilt always worked on Will. After all of his reports on Alice's questionable behavior, Will seemed to backpedal, condemning the trip's true hussy, the betrothed Katrina Wright who "wears her dress so low as to be indecent . . . walks like a bowery girl," and locked herself in a cabin with a man "drinking cocktails and smoking in there and lord knows what else."

After mentioning that he dined with the "very pretty" Ethel Barrymore, Will rushed to assure Nellie that "notwithstanding all the pretty ladies and attractive women I have met or traveled with I am longing for your society. . . . I can not hold myself until I [have] gotten you in my arms and kiss you dear and tell you how I love you and how I have missed your company and advice." When Nellie sailed into New York on October 10, Will made sure he was there to fetch her on a government revenue cutter.

Although it was rarely expressed, the Tafts had their bouts of marital jealousy. Except for a peculiarly alarming yet vague letter Will wrote to Nellie just a year and two months after their marriage, suggesting some unfounded gossip about Will and another woman, there was not the slightest suggestion that Will was ever unfaithful. Still, with fame Will was a fixation for some young women, and he wasn't immune to flirtatiously encouraging them. His gestures even suggested romantic sentiment, over which Nellie teased him. "A lady called Monday afternoon who was very enthusiastic about you—you had been congenial souls from the first moment. Her cheeks were much rouged but otherwise she was not bad looking," she wrote Will sarcastically a month after she had returned to Washington and he was out on the road again.

Nellie did not identify the woman in question by name, but after a few years of the innocent flirtation, Mrs. Taft's good-humored patience wore thin.

> [Y]our girl came to see me the other day. She said that she had
> given you her picture and had I seen it. I replied that I had. She
> then proceeded to tell me how you had asked for her picture and she
> had shown you all she had, but that you protested that none of
> these would do for you, and that she must have another one taken,
> so that she had had this taken just for you. The more I think of it,
> the madder I get at her cheek in telling me such a rigmarole, and as
> for you, I hereby retract everything I have formerly said about the
> safety of leaving you alone. She evidently has more excuse for her
> attentions than I supposed she had, and wanted me to know that
> she had.[7]

While Will was gone, Secretary of State John Hay died, and Roosevelt replaced him with Elihu Root, thus returning Root to the Cabinet. Nellie was angry that Will wasn't given the higher post and blamed it on his taking the junket with Alice Roosevelt. Will responded airily, "I doubt this." Nellie's regret barely veiled her jealousy of Alice; sensing this, Will made a pitch on behalf of Edith Roosevelt: "Mrs. Roosevelt does not like Mr. Root, so Alice tells me, and preferred to have me as Secretary of State, but of course she yielded to the judgment of the President."

Teddy himself sought to convert Nellie to the Roosevelt cult. A few weeks after their return to Washington, the Tafts were invited to dinner at the White House. Teddy and Nellie had met at large events but never had the chance to closely observe each other in private for such a long period. After dinner Teddy took the Tafts into the library for what would prove to be a defining episode in the Taft saga, a story often repeated to show the power that both Teddy and Nellie had over Will.

The President hammed it up, saying he saw a silver string above Will's head—he couldn't make out whether it said "chief justice" or "President."

Nellie stood her ground and shouted, "Make it the presidency!" Will then piped up, "Make it the chief justiceship!" As a result of his later actions, Roosevelt clearly felt that he could sway Will more than could Nellie. He quickly learned that he was wrong.

Just after New Year's 1906, the Tafts were in New Jersey with their friends the John Jay Hammonds when the phone rang. It was the President, and he had more than holiday cheer to offer. Will took the call in another room, returned with a smile, and told them that Roosevelt had again offered him a Supreme Court seat that was certain to open that year. Will said he might accept. "You didn't!" Nellie yelled. Restraining her temper in front of their hosts, she then went to work on Will, joined by John Hammond, emphatically making the case that an assured seat on the bench was not worth losing a good chance to become President.[8]

The incident only deepened Nellie's frustration with Will and her mistrust of Roosevelt. "The subject of my husband's appointment to the Supreme Bench cropped up with what seemed to me to be rather annoying frequency," she wrote flatly. "At this time, Mr. Taft was all but impervious to any friendly advice which, being followed, would have tended to enhance his own political advantage." Nellie took it upon herself to make up for the ambivalence on Will's part.

Someone else may have weighed in on Roosevelt's third effort to remove Will from the presidential field and sit him on the bench. Edith Roosevelt had insight and perspective on the strengths and weaknesses of political figures and shared them with—and perhaps even influenced—her husband. She thought that Will was not presidential material, and she had greatly resented Theodore's impulsive declaration on election night that he would not seek another term. Mrs. Roosevelt loved the White House but perhaps not as much as Mrs. Taft craved it. The primary difference between the two women was that Edith respected her husband's power to guide his own destiny. Nellie refused to acknowledge Will's own great dream and his hesitations and outright discomfort at the prospect of a campaign and the presidency. "If the Chief Justice would retire how simple everything would become," he said to her to no avail.

Impatient, Roosevelt called a meeting with Will, who afterward recorded: "I also explained . . . that Nellie is bitterly opposed to my accepting the position and that she telephoned me this morning to say that if I did, I would make the great mistake of my life. The President has promised to see her and talk the matter over with her and explain the situation."[9]

The problem was Will. He could not decide whom to please. He could tell Teddy that he wanted the bench but could not tell Nellie that he would not run for President. He was now saying, as he had when previously offered the bench, that his current work had to be seen through. He was sincere, but it was also a noble excuse to avoid commitment. Roosevelt could be guided by ego and manipulate flawlessly, but he wanted Will in a position where he would thrive. Nellie had long recognized that Teddy was her rival in the struggle to control Will's political destiny. Now Teddy recognized her as his worthy adversary. To clear the air he called Mrs. Taft in for a West Wing conference. The meeting was intended to clarify for Roosevelt just who his ideal successor might be.

The truth, however, was that Roosevelt never really lost his own desire for another term. No matter how personally close and affectionate he might feel toward his anointed Republican successor, Roosevelt could never think as highly of that person's ability to be President as he thought of his own. Regardless of whether people adored or despised Teddy Roosevelt, there was no denying the fact that he was a dynamic personality with a wide variety of interests, a man with a spirit of adventure who took a deep interest in the global community, and a leader the likes of which the nation had never experienced. Nobody sensed this more than Teddy Roosevelt—except, perhaps, Nellie Taft.

Through the weeks and months that Teddy, Nellie, and Will would play a game about the 1908 nomination, Roosevelt was testing Taft to determine just how *Rooseveltian* he could be as President, just how far he would go in terms of defending the Roosevelt record. Whatever he might express privately to Nellie about Teddy, Will refused to disagree with Teddy on policy or any element of the Administration's legislative agenda. To Will, less nuanced in politics, even if he disagreed with Roosevelt's aggressive tactics to achieve what he wanted, he would never dare speak out against the President publicly or even confront him in private. To Will, this was not about politics; it was about personal loyalty and gratitude. By the time he would complete his next foreign mission—to Cuba—Will Taft would essentially be an available presidential candidate, however reluctant.

While not unhopeful for a popular drafting for the 1908 nomination, Roosevelt realized he would not be President again. In his second term, he had become so progressive in his views on business reform that Congress declared that the Executive Branch had never been so assertive and perhaps even unconstitutional in its push for regulation. Roosevelt had also become more sensitive to the needs of the common farmer, factory worker, sweatshop immigrant, and even to a certain degree, the suffragists. Having a popular public persona certainly fed his ego, but Roosevelt believed intensely in his principled promise to deliver what he later called a "square deal for every man and every woman." As the nominating process neared, Roosevelt began to recognize that if he wanted to guarantee a successor who would continue his agenda, there was no real choice but diligent and judicious Taft. At the very least, he owed Will: It had been William Howard Taft who had personally gone to President-elect McKinley in 1896 and asked that the police commissioner of New York be given the federal post he most desired at the time, the assistant secretary of the navy.

It was, however, in this state of deep-seated ambivalence about trusting someone else with his own agenda that Teddy called his meeting with Nellie. Could this woman stand in the way of a President Taft pushing ahead with Roosevelt policy? He must have realized, instantly, in this first one-on-one meeting that Nellie Taft was not a spellbound acolyte to be manipulated easily. He proceeded graciously, no doubt, but cautiously.

From her viewpoint, Nellie believed the meeting was a ruse; Roosevelt wanted all of the men who were seeking his support to get nominated as the Republican candidate to promise to carry out his agenda for one reason only: Roosevelt. Nellie Taft was, early on, convinced that the unspoken objective of President Theodore Roosevelt was to rule again. She saw his remarks about supporting Will, or Hughes, or anyone else, as a well-crafted farce. By having them tell the public about how they would continue his policies, the candidates would be stalking horses making the best possible arguments for why Teddy was the best man to continue the Roosevelt agenda. According to journalist Mark Sullivan, this theory seemed to fit with her uncertainty as to why Roosevelt had been so insistent that Will accept a seat on the Supreme Court—that Teddy was just manuevering to be unanimously drafted for Republican renomination and wanted to shelve anyone who could pose a genuine threat to that plan.

The tête-à-tête between Theodore Roosevelt and Nellie Taft is unprecedented in presidential history—a powerful incumbent President conferring with the wife of his potential successor to discuss the candidate's viability. There is no precise record of what transpired in the meeting; both Tafts were in town at the time and thus there was no need for them to communicate by correspondence. In all probability Nellie outlined her reasons that Will could and should be nominated for President—reasons Roosevelt would agree with. Roosevelt also probably told her he would back Will as a candidate, privately at first. Certainly Roosevelt saw for himself just how formidable Nellie's power was over Will. In that sense she could be a potential challenge to his own effort to shape Will's speeches and his stand on the issues and, if he became President, policies. The extent to which Roosevelt could influence a potential President Taft would always be filtered through Nellie. Whether Nellie Taft left the White House that day with a promise from Roosevelt to withdraw the Court offer is uncertain, but she clearly left with that impression. The very next day, however, Roosevelt double-crossed her, asking Will to keep open the possibility of accepting his offer to sit on the Court and thus forgo a run for the presidency.

The President opened with a reference to the fact that he "had a half-hour's talk with your dear wife" and that it had resulted in a conflict of facts: "I have been in error as to your feelings. . . . I gathered [that] what you wanted to do was to go on the bench, and that my urging was in the line of your inclination." Roosevelt pointed to "what your dear wife says," specifically that she wanted Will to run for President. Stung by Nellie, he added gently, but affirmatively referring to her, that nobody else "can take the responsibility of deciding for you what it is right and best for you to do. . . . No one can with wisdom advise you." Roosevelt dutifully claimed that he wanted Will to do what he wanted, even listing the pros and cons of going to the Court or the presidency. However, he attempted to lure Will to the Court by pointing out that his dream to be chief justice could be achieved if he was already on the Court as an associate justice, and that if the chief justiceship opened during the remainder of Roosevelt's term, he would make the promotion.[10]

Will asked Teddy to delay naming a new justice until the end of the year. His play for time left Nellie hanging. With all the angst she shared with friends, all the talk among the Cabinet, and all the letters Will wrote his brothers, word got out to the press about Taft's dilemma, and he soon received letters from friends and strangers weighing in on the issue. To a letter from a Mr. Washburn, Will responded by promising to "show it to Mrs. Taft, who deeply sympathizes with your view in regard to the Supreme Court." To Dodd Brannan at Harvard Law School, who supported Will's going on the Court, he wrote, "Mrs. Taft, however, is very bitterly opposed to it."

Two months later Will was as uncertain as ever, but after a May 3 meeting with Roosevelt, Nellie seemed to have won the battle. Will reported to her: "He was full of the presidency and wanted to talk about my chances. He wants to talk to you and me together. He thinks I am the one to take his mantle and that now I would be nominated."

Roosevelt indeed wanted yet another meeting on the issue, this time with both Will and Nellie. Not only would this unprecedented meeting seal the decision, it would also illustrate to Roosevelt just how personally persuasive Nellie was over Will. Chief Usher of the White House Ike Hoover came into the room as the trio were talking, Roosevelt apparently raising the Court question one last time. Hoover recalled: "[I]t was only through the pleadings of Mrs. Taft that he was not appointed. I can remember the exact hour of the famous visit when Mrs. Taft, in the face of both the President and her husband . . . , carried her point. From that time on the President seemed to feel that Mr. Taft should be his successor." According to her son Charlie, in the end it was Nellie who was definitively "influential in persuading President Theodore Roosevelt that her husband should be a candidate for the presidency rather than accept appointment to the Supreme Court." Will finally agreed.[11]

The issue settled, Nellie dropped back into what she called the "rather monotonous stress" of being a Cabinet wife, or "a nobody" as a woman at a luncheon insultingly told her. Something fundamental had changed, however. Not only Roosevelt but the press now knew what the Taft family and friends had known for years: Helen Herron Taft was the most powerful personal influence on William Howard Taft. At one party Nellie rather proudly announced that one justice—who she assumed had not even known she existed—"deplored that I had kept you off the bench, and I disclaimed any influence."

Most of all Mrs. Taft dreaded Mrs. Roosevelt's tense teas for Cabinet wives. These were nothing more than weekly gossip sessions during which the First Lady pontificated on the private lives of public officials, passing her moral judgment on those who behaved in what she considered a socially undesirable manner. These weekly gatherings, Nellie said sardonically, were "supposed to be of interest to us all."

Nellie Taft was understandably slighted when she was specifically *not* invited to join Will at the presidential summer home at Oyster Bay, Long Island, ostensibly for a private cruise on the presidential yacht *Mayflower,* which included the First Lady. She was suspicious. "I feel that your going could not have been imperative," she wrote, getting no response.[12]

Three days later Nellie read in the newspaper that Will had been dispatched to Cuba to prevent a bloody insurrection against the personally honest but corruptly elected president Tomas Palma. The Cuban constitution and its treaty with the United States provided for American intervention when it was deemed requisite to a continuance of peace and stable government there. The American consul general there had urgently cabled Washington for help as the island nation's government went to pieces. "I was perfectly aghast at your running off to Cuba, and it seems to me rather a hopeless job though I don't know the arguments you are to use," Nellie wrote Will.

When Congress approved the Spanish-American War, Cuba's freedom from Spain was promised. Like the Filipinos, Cubans had expected self-rule. This delusion was abruptly ended in 1901 with its pacification, an army appropriation act stating that Cuba couldn't sign treaties that turned over control in any aspect of its trade to foreign nations, nor could it contract debts over a certain amount. The fledgling Cuban government agreed that the United States could—"for the preservation of Cuban independence, the maintenance of a government adequate for the protection of life, property and individual liberty"—intervene. And, there was some $20 million in property in Cuba, owned by large American business interests. Unlike the Philippines, Cuba was not technically a colony of the United States, but its direction was dictated by the American government that had "liberated" it from Spain. Palma had constructed a Cabinet of both Moderate and Liberal members, but when he decided that the former political faction would see his legislative agenda through more readily, he cut off the salaries of the latter faction. On the heels of this came Palma's reelection—with some extra 150,000 voter names, most of them Moderates. The Liberals prepared a revolt to take down Palma's government. Disgusted, Palma was only too relieved to turn over his leadership to anyone the American government thought could halt the prospect of bloodshed. Roosevelt turned to Taft—who actually had sympathy with the Liberals—on September 20 to, in Nellie's words, "forestall a state of absolute anarchy."

After his arrival, Taft was told by Palma that he couldn't guarantee protection of life and property, thus clearing the way for American intervention, and he furthermore asked the war secretary to request American naval forces. Taft tried to negotiate, initially unsuccessful in his effort to find common ground between the Liberal guerrilla fighters and what was left of the Palma government. Roosevelt wanted Taft to avoid any use of the word *intervention*. That looked impossible. Ever worried about the 1908 election, Nellie felt the need to add the obvious: "This may change our plans somewhat." Such a vote of lack of confidence from his greatest booster may well have been what sent Will into the tailspin he experienced.

Taft had had no time to study the situation there, and he felt at loose ends. With a perfectionist tendency, he worried that his years of toil and success in the Philippines would be lost sight of in the wake of what he assumed would be inevitable failure in Cuba. Unlike the Philippines—where he knew that Nellie would be at his side as he ruled—Will found himself slipping into a pit of self-doubt. From Havana, he confessed in a letter to Nellie that he had fallen into an immobilizing depression. "I am in a condition of mind where I can hardly do anything . . ." He suffered from insomnia and could not think "with sequence." For the first time in his professional life, William Howard Taft faced the potential of a great public failure, and it was affecting his mental health.

Feeling utterly powerless, Will finally made an overt call for her emotional support. "I would give a great deal to talk it over with you my own sweet Darling," he wrote her in Canada. "You could help me so much with your sympathy. . . . I did not think it would prove as bad as this. I wake up in the morning at three and four o'clock and do not sleep any more. My appetite ceases to be sharp." As he looked onto Havana Bay, a massive thunderstorm roared overhead. ". . . were it not for you and the children . . . I should not regret it if one of the bolts now flashing and resounding struck me." Within two weeks, Nellie was in Cuba at Will's side. Her strength seemed to be just what was necessary to calm him down enough so that he was able to focus on the task at hand. Without calling it an "intervention," Taft assumed the position of "provisional" governor under the congressional law that permitted—and the Cuban government had agreed to—temporary control, if necessary.

With his calm, judicious, and warm qualities restored to him, Will

Taft was again able to negotiate confidently with both Moderates and Liberals, and by persistent tact he convinced the Liberals to have their guerrilla fighters turn in their arms. Cuban political leaders realized that the United States had no intention of annexing the country. In the end, there was no bloodshed, Taft was able to work out a peace agreement, the Liberals took control, the American government left, and Cuba regained its stability.

In the aftermath of the Cuban crisis, however, Taft's dread of just the possibility of criticism of his public record proved most revealing. Harsh, unrelenting political criticism would be inevitable in the presidency. Yet he had so become the protégé of Roosevelt, while also indebted to Nellie's wise counsel, that William Howard Taft had essentially allowed himself to be convinced that running for President in 1908 was his fate. At times, he would even work up enthusiasm for running and a conviction that he might make a good President.

While it was true that Taft had accumulated excellent executive experience as governor of the Philippines, much of his decision-making had been in establishing a government, rather than running one that was already firmly entrenched. His relationship with the legislature in the Philippines had developed and shaped that body; in the White House, however, he would be assuming a historically adversarial dynamic with the Congress. Finally, his decisions had been largely judicial in nature, which came more naturally to him than any other. In the White House, however, he would need all the political skills of manipulation and deal-making that had helped to make Roosevelt so successful.

If those he had great faith in—Teddy, Nellie, his brothers—believed that Will would do well as President, he now at least seemed open to making a run for it. Through it all, however, Will would always feel uncomfortable being so scrutinized by the press, politicians, and public. He dreaded having to curry favor by doing and saying things he did not entirely believe in. He was simply not a politician. More than anything, Taft hated the idea of speaking on his own behalf, yet that seemed to drive him all the more to make a convincing and powerful case on behalf of other candidates: Taft became the best promoter of himself by being the best booster of Roosevelt and the Republicans.[13]

As soon as they returned to Washington from Cuba, Will instantly repacked his bags and campaigned for Republican candidates in ten western, southern, and midwestern states. Roosevelt was so taken with Will that he declared that he admired Taft as much as any public figure of the past or present "bar Lincoln and Washington." It is hard to imagine Nellie buying such hyperbole, but even she seemed under Roosevelt's spell when she was with him at the White House in Will's absence, delighting in his mimicry of Senator Albert J. Beveridge. "The President was in high feather that night," she reported to Robert, "and was very amusing."

She quickly returned to her cynical attitude within one week, after she "got a bid" to the White House, ostensibly to lunch with the President, the Roots, the Mexican War minister, and a Harvard German professor. Edith was out on a cruise. Nellie recorded the encounter for Will:

> It was rather slower and more forced than usual. . . . After lunch the President said he wanted to talk to me and drew me off to sit down in the window. As usual, it was about you, but on a new tack.
>
> He seems to think that I am consumed with an inordinate ambition to be President and that he must constantly warn me that you may never get there. And he now says that while you are his first choice, that in case you are not persona grata to the powers that be, it may become necessary for him to support some one else, like [Republican candidate for the U.S. Senate Governor Charles Evans] Hughes, for instance, should he win in New York. I felt like saying 'D— you, support whom you want, for all I care,' but suffice it to say I did not.
>
> He began by saying that his Kentucky friends had [said] . . . that you had [said] . . . coldly that you were not a candidate. He had told them to go ahead . . . but he could not always do that . . . and

you must be more encouraging. . . . Root sat on my other side at
lunch, but as he is perfectly uninterested in me, I can never talk to
him. Metcalf was more calfy than ever.

After mailing the letter Nellie "had a panic for fear that it was indiscreet considering the uncertain address." Her remark that Roosevelt assumed she had an "inordinate ambition to be President" was written without irony—or correction. Roosevelt had called Nellie on the one question no other person had dared pose to her through the decades since her teenage years when she announced her ambition to marry a President: If it was that Nellie pushed Will toward the presidency all these years, to satisfy not his personal ambition but her own, was she not actually more interested in being President than a President's wife? At some point Nellie must have given consideration to the fact that the sort of political partner she had been to Will would translate into being a politically active presidential wife—with none of the actual accountability that came with the responsibilities of the presidency. It was hard not to see such a scenario as rather selfish and, ultimately, unfair to her husband. One may only speculate, but perhaps Roosevelt's remark to Nellie about her own ambitions touched the nerve at the root of her driving ambition, forcing her to face a less than admirable element in her character.[14]

Will responded calmly:

Interested in your conversation with the President. I think what the
President is anxious to do is to stir you up to stir me up to take more
interest in the presidential campaign with a broad intimation that
if I did not take more interest he would not. He evidently thinks
that I am not sincere in my statement that I don't take any interest
in it, at least not enough to go to work setting up the pins for the
nomination. The truth is what I find out here is what I have
written him, that is a very earnest desire for his renomination, and
the people who speak to me do not hesitate to put it that way, with

the statement that if he cannot be induced to run, then they are
willing to take me as a substitute and as near to him as they can
probably get anyone.

At this point Nellie had come so far in pushing Will that she had
long trained herself to tune out his genuine lack of interest. Instead, his
remark about a popular call for another Roosevelt term planted a greater
fear in her mind. Her instinct that at the last minute Theodore Roosevelt
would somehow pull strings to get nominated for another term deepened.
She especially mistrusted him now after he had, in her mind, called Will
a poor politician. Will worsened the situation by immediately writing
Roosevelt:

> *Mrs. Taft writes me that you are disposed to lecture me for not*
> *being more cordial . . . with . . . friends who want to organize a*
> *campaign for me. . . . [I]n my state of indifference about it the or-*
> *ganization is not likely to follow me. Mrs. Taft said that you said*
> *you might have to support Hughes for the presidency. If you do*
> *you . . . will awaken no feeling of disappointment on my part.*
> *While I very much appreciate your anxiety that I should be*
> *nominated . . . you know what my feeling has been in respect to the*
> *presidency, and can understand that it will not leave the slightest*
> *trace of disappointment should you change your views.*

Roosevelt replied:

> *Mrs. Taft could not have told you that I said I might probably have*
> *to support Hughes for the presidency. . . . What I said to her was*
> *that you must not be too entirely aloof because if you were it might*
> *dishearten your supporters and put us all in such shape that some*
> *man like Hughes, or more probably some man from the West,*
> *would turn up with so much popular sentiment behind him that*

there would be no course open but to support him . . . [and] wholly
powerless to support you.[15]

If believing that Roosevelt was pining for another term worried her,
Will's letter to him left Nellie feeling infuriated and betrayed. "I was quite
put out with you for writing the President all I said," she wrote Will, "and
Carpenter also showed me his reply. He did not use the word 'probably,'
but said that he might find it best to do so, and I thought I so represented
it." And if she was insulted that Roosevelt essentially called her a liar or fool,
she was more concerned about his reference to "some man" who would have
"so much popular sentiment behind him" that his nomination would be inevitable. Could Roosevelt be obliquely referring to himself? Would Roosevelt
step in at the last minute on the pretense that Will did not have the necessary
support to win? She might have given up her effort had she seen one particular sentence in a letter Will wrote Elihu Root: "It would be a great thing for
the country to have another term of Roosevelt."[16]

Ignoring Will's pleading hesitancy, Nellie simply began functioning
as a campaign adviser, starting with her critique of his speeches. She began
by waging war against his mentioning the unpopular and convoluted tariff:
"I shouldn't wonder if your dragging the tariff into that Maine speech
would cost you the nomination." Will responded to her concern in a way
that could not have pleased her: "You say in your letter that I talk too much
about the tariff, and I probably do, and you are quite right in supposing that
this will be another ground for opposing me on the part of powerful interests, but it is relevant. . . . I hope it won't give you the blues to think about it,
because you must put aside any hope in the direction of politics." The one
suggestion that Taft was thinking as a candidate was his assertion that Republicans didn't fear the presumed Democratic rival William Jennings
Bryan even in his home state. This news did not deter Nellie's point: "I am
sorry you keep bringing up the tariff as it seems to be unnecessary and not a
special issue at this time, and cut down comments. I thought you had
decided not to refer to it. The Washington papers give so much prominence

to it, that you would suppose it was the principal point of the speech."

Besides his speeches, Nellie also began judging Will's decisions as war secretary in terms of how they would play with voters. "I hope you will go slow on General Humphrey and be sure that the sentiment of the Army is with you, for I don't believe it is," she warned him about a man about to be dishonorably discharged. "I don't see what right you have to disgrace a man who is in some respects very competent and has done excellent service. In his place I should refuse to resign under such circumstances and unless you have proof positive, I don't see what right you have to remove him without a trial. If you are relying on what that Charles Baker says I would not believe him under oath." Will defied Nellie's advice when he wanted to—but at the risk of angering or upsetting her, a state he dreaded. Nellie could use this at will. When he reported his political prospects pessimistically, she moaned that it "gives me the blues," implying that he must be confident.[17]

With Will's constant absence a reality of life now, Nellie was alone in Washington for weeks on end. When she could escape luncheons, teas, and bridge parties, she indulged new interests. Always a voracious reader, she now "read so fast" through library books that she had a hard time finding new ones. She learned how to drive the new "machines" replacing horses and carriages, gleefully relating one particular "automobile picnic" where two tires blew out. She became as gossipy as Will, reporting that she "examined" a friend of theirs "about his love affairs. He didn't get the young woman, though he insinuates that she allowed him to get pretty far." Her passions remained intellectual and artistic, and she often went to lectures on subjects she knew nothing about, even attending one on the "Bahaire Religion, whatever that may be." Still, she confessed to Bob, she wished "I had something I really had to do."

The holidays that year were joyous for Nellie. Not only were her father and unmarried Maria (who lived together) visiting, but for the first time in several years, Will and all the children were home. Bob was a stellar freshman at Yale, and Helen a student at the Baldwin School in Bryn Mawr, Pennsylvania. Charlie remained the terror—fishing so late into the night that Nellie was "nearly wild" with fear, dominating a Halloween party, and skating with a spoon and cough medicine tucked in his pocket.

After making sure that her military escort to the White House New Year's Day Reception was in full-dress uniform and after receiving for several hours with the Cabinet wives, Nellie accompanied Will on their first trip to Charleston, South Carolina. They were feted, attended Red Cross meetings, toured Fort Moultrie and Sumter, and had "a thoroughly enjoyable time." It would become a favorite city of theirs, and Will returned in the early spring, on his way north from golfing in Augusta, Georgia, reporting on the blooming live oaks and azaleas. He added to Nellie that her absence was felt but she was remembered fondly with two of her favorite topics—champagne and the future: "We drank [to] your health as the next lady of the White House."[18]

When Will went back on the road in the spring of 1907, he was barnstorming as a presidential candidate, undeclared and reluctant. As always, his letters to Nellie expressed love and longing but were now packed with every detail of political news and his opinions and projections. "His letters to me were dictated," she recalled. "I get the impression that I was made the victim of his thinking processes since he poured into them all the politics and turmoil of the hour, together with lengthy comments which kept me very much alive with interest in the campaign." She was swift to respond with advice. Meanwhile, Will's brother Charley established an office with two expert political operatives—Arthur I. Vorys and Charles Dewey Hilles—who began scouting and contacting national Republican committee members, seeking to give job patronage to potential Taft supporters, and taking the offensive on press accounts of the war secretary's speeches and accomplishments.[19]

The first emerging threat to Will's nomination was Republican Ohio senator Joseph Foraker. Rabidly anti-Roosevelt, particularly on railroad regulation, Foraker unrealistically wanted the nomination as Ohio's favorite son. Will did not respond to Foraker's attacks on him. Unfortunately,

Charley Taft did, in rambunctious editorials in his newspaper, the *Cincinnati Times-Star*. "The papers are still full of the Foraker row," Nellie wrote Will. "You must take more responsibility and muzzle Charley." The Foraker-Taft dispute raised the issue of the campaign a year in advance, and Nellie worried that Will might appear too much the politician and not enough the statesman that he still ostensibly was. "It was all precipitated, it seems to me, long before it was necessary, by his announcements, and I fear it will be very injurious to your chances — besides being disagreeable." When Foraker then proposed that Ohio choose its candidate by direct primary, Charley wrote an editorial undermining the idea, not having first checked with Will.

It enraged Nellie:

> *I am not at all in an Easter Sunday mood after reading Charlie's [sic] defiance to Foraker in the morning paper. You have got yourself in an awful position by allowing him to take his own way. It makes one cringe, just the way his old effusions in the* Times-Star *used to do, but that now it comes home more nearly. I think this all came from being under money obligations to him [Charley]. It never does [work], even with one's nearest relations.*
>
> *I telephoned [Interior Secretary] Jim Garfield to know whether he knew if the President knew of this latest. . . . He thinks not. . . . The [New York] Sun has one of its editorials on Roosevelt. How they hate him and they go farther than I, in insinuating that this is all part of his scheme to get himself nominated as the only man, and greets you as "a martyr and scapegoat."*

She added a postscript several hours later:

> *I have just had a long talk with Jim Garfield. He says that he talked with the President day before yesterday. . . . They both agreed that Foraker's proposition was absurd and impossible and that no notice ought to be taken of it. That you had nothing to gain in any case*

from such a thing and much possibly to lose. Jim therefore was
dumbfounded by Charlie's statement this morning and can not
think it anything but a bluff—and an ill-timed one. Do, therefore,
cable Charlie to say nothing more till you get here, and then,
possibly, you can get out of it on the ground that you were not
consulted or even to prevent him from saying anything more, would
perhaps enable the thing to die a natural death.

When, however, there were strong suggestions that having the open primary would work in Will's favor and the Republican State Committee
declared its support for Taft, Nellie changed her tune:

I am sorry I wrote such disturbed letters as I have calmed down
now. The articles in the papers here have not been at all bad . . .
which indicates, I think, that Charlie was very sure of his ground
and that you would have a walk over. If only he would be a little
more dignified. Papa writes that the local papers are full of it. . . . I
don't mind it at all so long as it is local, but hate to have it here
[Washington].[20]

At Roosevelt's suggestion Will made a western speaking tour that
summer to become better known to the public. Now that Will had committed to seeking the nomination, Nellie relaxed her goading. She knew
instinctively when to use criticism or support to make him see his potential as she did. His letters to her in Murray Bay throughout the summer
focused on the length, content, and delivery of his speeches. He worried
that "when I read I read rather faster" than "an audience on a hot night"
would be able to endure. She responded with loving support—and only
a touch of guilt: "It makes me blue to get such blue letters from you
about your speech. I am sure it will go off all right and it does not seem
to me that an hour and a quarter will be too long for an important speech
like that. Never mind if you can not get off fireworks. It must be known

by this time that that is not your style, and there is no use in trying to force it."

As crowds got larger and stayed longer, and the polls looked up, both Tafts grew confident. After Will delivered a detailed speech, outlining exactly what Roosevelt policies he would continue, she was pleased it was "safely delivered" and that newspaper "notices were good, while not perhaps enthusiastic. At any rate, it is a relief to have it over, and I fancy the other speeches will be of a more popular character."[21]

Perhaps Nellie was also bracing for the possibility that her dreams would be dashed, commenting, "If people don't want you as you are they can leave you; and we shall both be able to survive it." Still, she viewed everything through a political lens. Although she liked a new country club in Quebec, for example, she feared the potential negative press about belonging to a foreign club and told Will, "If you are not nominated I shall surely join it." Playing bridge in a lodge that autumn, she became paranoid when she realized it was a Sunday, fearing voter reaction to her gambling on the Lord's day.

That Hughes or any other potential candidate would be nominated she could grudgingly accept. What she could never abide, and what now flared up with even more alarm, was the specter of Theodore Roosevelt slipping onstage and seizing the nomination. The first suggestion came in an endless letter from Roosevelt to Will. While Teddy thought "at the present time" that Will would be nominated, he added that "no one could foretell the events of the next nine months, and that as the convention came nearer it was always possible that I should have to alter my judgment." He talked about western state party leaders who "preferred to be for me and were not willing to believe that I could refuse a third term." Then there were "various men of prominence" in West Virginia and Michigan who "were going to be for me anyhow." It was a "real difficulty to prevent certain people declaring for me." Roosevelt claimed he did not want to be "in the ridiculous position of seeming to want the nomination" or accused of "insincerity, double-dealing, self-seeking" or that "I am merely using you as a stalking horse to gratify my own ambition." Two days later, however, in response to those who had questioned his decision to send the naval fleet to the Pacific, Roosevelt took the opportunity to assert his power in a letter to Will, declaring, "But I am commander-in-chief!" Teddy seemed to want to be seen as modest and omnipotent simultaneously.

Privately, Will and Nellie later learned that Roosevelt had been less diplomatic. In conversation with one James B. Reynolds (who then told Taft supporter Jim Garfield who reported it to Hilles), the President said he was "disappointed" that Taft's "boom has not held . . . [I]t lacks spontaneity and resilience. He can't supply these." Hilles further reported that Roosevelt also stated that one of three ways to stop a roll for Hughes, Taft's primary rival, was "by permitting the third term flower to flourish and thus make the President himself the 'favorite son,' " in the crucial New York primary. In "the last analysis if Taft can't win, the President will take the nomination."

No longer "shy or nervous" about winning, Will, having been out across the country for so long and spoken with so many operatives, felt that Roosevelt was wrong. Nellie, on the other hand, was "out of patience with the President's letter." To her it seemed all the more a game tactic by Teddy to Will for the nomination, since the President also wrote, "As Mrs. Roosevelt said, my effort at the moment is to be positive in my declination in the West, and Delphic about it in the East; and to combine both attitudes and yet not be hypocritical." Her mistrust of Roosevelt solidified into hostility.[22]

Shortly after this upset, Nellie was forced to distract herself with preparations for the lengthiest trip she was ever to make. Built around Will's promise to attend the opening session of the Filipino assembly, they would be on the road for three months straight, literally traveling around the world: Japan, China, the Philippines, Russia, Germany, and France. Sailing out on the Pacific on Friday the thirteenth, "which I am superstitious enough not to like at all," she made the acquaintance of a Buddhist prophet with sixty of his disciples on the voyage.

They landed in Tokyo on September 30 and visited the Emperor, where she found "servants galore in livery and very good food." She also "drove out to see one of the gardens on the Cherry Blossom drives but the flowers didn't amount to much. It is between seasons." After a group photo, during which they "nearly sank into the mud," and a look at a private museum of Buddhist idols, Nellie found Will's "fine speech," the important point of the trip, "well noticed by the press" and "cabled home [in its] entire 1800 words." They proceeded to Kobe, Kyoto, and Nagasaki, then headed to Shanghai and Hong Kong. She rode in rickshaws and bought silk and, as she had in Japan, delighted in the presents of silver given to her. But again it was Will's speech that she pleasingly noted was "very well received and mightly advertised . . . as being the beginning of a new epoch."

For the first time since her trip to Luzon territory, Nellie was keeping a diary, a process that always seemed to calm her. Her proudest moment seems to have been in Manila, at the assembly opening. "Will's [speech] was a great success and hit the people just right. . . . Everybody was glad to see us." She also decided she was "too old" to ride Filipino ponies anymore; her "knees got terribly stiff and hurt badly." Being back in Manila so relaxed Nellie that she even took part in a childish night of pranks at a hotel, joining friends who burst into the room of poor Carpenter, Will's secretary, and pulled him from his sleep, where she saw that "his costume was hardly adequate"; they also threw wet towels and sponges from a balcony on departing guests. It was such a release for her.

From Manila the party went into the "cold north wind" of Vladivostock. In Russia, Nellie dressed in sailor socks, fur capes, and gloves to cope with the frigid air—and drank "cherry vodka." On a train crossing Siberia, protected from robbers by armed Cossacks, she was enchanted by the frozen dark land. On a dare one moonlit night, she took off in the sleigh of a mayor of a small village to go to his house, and "though this seemed rather extraordinary," Nellie "did not want to lose the opportunity to see a Russian home." She had tea from a samovar and wine, altogether "delighted" by the experience. At another stop she "drank in turn to the health of all the monarchs whose consuls [were] present, in champagne."

In Moscow she attended Russian Orthodox services and the ballet; toured the Kremlin; marched through furrier shops to buy a supply of pelts that would furnish her with a lifetime's worth of coats, jackets, wraps, stoles, hats, and muffs; "invested in a lot of the Russian lace"; bought aquamarines at the flea market; and relaxed afterward with some Madeira wine. "If only I lived there I should go all the time," she remarked of the flea market. "I wish I had bought more things now." At St. Petersburg she was given access to the Winter Palace, the Hermitage, and Peter the Great's cottage, but Czarina Alexandra was too ill to receive her.

In April, Will's mother had publicly defied Nellie's ambitions by declaring that Elihu Root was *her* candidate for the nomination. "I do not want my son to be president," she told reporters. "He is not my candidate. His is a judicial mind and he loves the law." Nellie refrained from criticizing her mother-in-law in front of Will, but when news reached Russia that Louise Taft had only a few days to live, Nellie's true feelings emerged in her diary: "This has altered my plans as I could not invest in a wardrobe as I had intended and Will thinks I should go home with him. It is a disappointment as I counted [on] this [shopping opportunity] the whole trip." She came up with a scheme to break off from Will in Berlin, rush to Paris for two and a half hours to shop, and then catch a train to rendezvous with Will at the port. He thought it "exceedingly foolish." She pulled it off.

When they came home, Nellie Taft heard the good news that Hughes had made little political headway in their absence. "By the way," Helen wrote Bob about their mother, "have you any idea about a Christmas present for her? If we could think of something that she would really like we might get it together. Unfortunately, I can't think of anything."[23]

Everyone who knew Nellie—even her children—seemed to now understand that there was only one thing she would like.

Ten

Precedent and Mrs. Taft

*I had a little secret elation in thinking that I was doing
something, which no woman had ever done before.*

—NELLIE TAFT

She was lithely elegant. In the stifling heat of a June day in Washington, Nellie Taft's trim figure moved briskly in a bleached white shirtwaist dress and cartwheel "Merry Widow" hat. After ascending the baroque, curving stairwell of the State, Navy and War Departments Building, she sailed determinedly through the carved-wood halls and across the marble black-and-white squares toward her husband's office suite.

At forty-seven years old, her graying brown hair perfectly groomed into her trademark geisha style, her bulging brown eyes serene, her manner was both grand and gracious, and her appearance marked by a balance of the aristocratic and straightforward, a demeanor she seemed to have perfected in the Philippines. This is evident even in the short glimpses of her in the moving picture newsreels that captured the Taft party's arrival at the Canal Zone in 1908 or as she was descending the White House steps or strolling down the gravel drive. Nellie's gestures included a wide, slow, circular welcoming motion of her arm; smooth, long nod of approval; and a way of floating across a drawing room. This afternoon, however, she was not so much stately as stiff, unable to mask her natural nervousness. She was hurrying. The Republican Convention in Chicago had already begun.

As usual she marched through the reception area, past the desk of Will's harried secretary, Fred Carpenter—always a bit frightened by the ferocity of the boss's wife—and straight into the war secretary's office. He was out at the moment, with Root. Senator Frank Hitchcock was on the phone long distance from Chicago, shouting blow-by-blow details to Taft friends in the room. This was the second day of the convention, June 17. There was nothing of real importance this day; all the same, Nellie wanted to know everything that went on. Bob and his uncle Charley were in Chicago on the convention floor. In a reserved box sat Nick Longworth's bride of two years, Alice Roosevelt. They had married just six months after the Asian junket. Nick wanted Will to win. Alice just "seemed" to. "No one will ever know how much I wished, in the black depths of my heart," she later confessed, "that 'something would happen' and that Father would be renominated."

The convention chairman, Senator Henry Cabot Lodge, droned on, and when he routinely made reference to the President, it provoked a thunderous, spontaneous roar through the hall. It would not die down. Lodge tried to halt it, unsuccessfully. It kept going, with foot-stomping and screaming, but the chant of "Four—four—four more years!" was audible above the din. It went on for forty-nine minutes.

This was just the horror Nellie Taft had predicted—that Teddy would somehow steal the nomination from Will at the very last moment. "I am almost feeling as if I would go to the convention myself," she had written days earlier, as if her sheer willpower would control the outcome. Hitchcock reassured her: Relax, Roosevelt wouldn't be renominated.

The next day she was back in Will's office, hanging on to every moment of the day's progress. Late morning stretched into afternoon as nominating speeches began. When Ohio senator Theodore Burton was called to nominate Will, at about 5 p.m., a staged Taft demonstration erupted with banners waving and delegates singing. Will was seated at his desk, the phone to his ear. Helen and Charlie stood with their mother, the boy momentarily pausing from running bulletins over from the telegraph room. Nellie eyed the clock. The silent anticipation in the war secretary's office suddenly broke, and Will turned from listening to the murmur of the demonstration over the phone to the noise Nellie was making.

"I want it to last more than forty-nine minutes," she commanded. "I want to get even for the scare that the Roosevelt cheer of forty-nine minutes gave me yesterday." It lasted only twenty-five minutes.

And then came word that a silk banner with the face of Teddy was carried onto the convention platform. Another burst for Teddy rang out. This time, a witness back in Washington recalled, Nellie Taft's face literally drained of blood. Lodge immediately quieted it down to start the roll call. Nellie again expressed her jealousy and mistrust of Teddy. Will shot an angry look at Nellie, chiding her: "Oh, my dear! My dear!" She fell silent. Just before 5:30, with 702 delegates for Taft, the nomination was won. Reporters in the hall were given the good news.[1]

Will confessed to a friend that a "nightmare for me" would be not only a campaign's speaking and traveling schedule and political attacks but also having "one's family exposed to all sorts of criticism and curious inquisitiveness." Even before Will's nomination, however, Nellie had found herself a public figure, fully complicit in the limited use of her image and those of her children for the public relations purposes of the primary campaign. By the week of the convention she had approved photographs of herself, Bob, Helen, and Charlie to be released to newspapers and eventually to be reprinted in thousands of city and county newspapers around the country. On March 30, 1908, the war secretary sent a "Memorandum for Mrs. Taft" or, as Will dictated, "respectfully referred to my better half." It was a letter from a supporter to Arthur Vorys, making the case that voters "want the human side.... That's the secret of Roosevelt's popularity.... Pictures of Taft in the Philippines, Japan, China . . . excite the imagination." Vorys agreed and got friend, photographer, and writer Robert Lee Dunn to rush *William Howard Taft, American* into print. The informal biography carried photos of Nellie with Filipino children, riding a pony, posing with Japanese officials, in her Vladivostock furs, reading a book on the porch at Murray Bay, examining hot springs, and sitting casually on some steps with Charlie.

In February, Mrs. Taft was able to see Caruso in *Pagliacci* at the Metropolitan Opera House completely unrecognized and then go to the Plaza Hotel. She found it "most entertaining to see the people who came there for tea and late supper." That sort of anonymity would now change.

Nellie's one great fear was public disclosure of her gambling obsession, known to many in social Washington. Several months earlier, before the convention, Helen had written to Bob about the family dispute: "The talk about politics was more exciting than ever. Maria and Papa had an animated discussion as to whether Mama ought to give up bridge for money. Maria claims that she does not think it is wrong and that it is hypocritical to pretend that she does. Papa seems to think that she ought to be able to say that she does not gamble. I shouldn't think myself that it would influence the nomination however much it might mean in the election. And I think that even if Mama drank it wouldn't enable Bryan to beat Papa." Nellie worried about the public somehow discovering that she gambled at cards even more so *after* the nomination. She told Will that a friend of theirs "thinks it is you [who] should stop playing bridge. She does not even mention me." Will shot back—with strained humor—that he didn't play for money. Luckily for the Tafts, the first public suggestion that Nellie was "good at cards" did not hit print until the period of rosiness toward the President-elect and his family that usually follows Election Day.

The details of Nellie's life began to circulate in lengthier profiles of Will, and local newspapers mentioned how involved she had been in his political career. That fact began to dictate her emerging public persona. In response, mail began to trickle in, such as a request from the Galena Kansas Elks Club asking her, as "one of our best known people," to donate a handkerchief to a fund-raiser bazaar. Democrats used her in a minor anti-Taft whispering campaign, claiming that she was a secret Catholic who was wed to Will by a priest. Charley Taft then got Will to join the Masons and Mr. Herron to certify that it was a Presbyterian ceremony.

During the primaries there had even been a cartoon of her appearing around Valentine's Day, presenting Will with the primary win of Minnesota. For permitting her life to be publicly divulged, a State Department official even wrote Nellie that she was a "dear good sport."[2]

That season there was also a full-blown cartoon series in the *American Journal Examiner* called "King Kazooks." In one frame "Prince Taft" gleefully reaches for a newsboy who shouts that the only "radical reason" that could stop the King from "goin' huntin' in Afriky!" was "RE-ELECTION." The final caption said Taft was suspicious about "ye intentions of ye king." Will did warn Nellie that there was "an outbreak in Nebraska in which the Lincoln County convention instructed their delegates for Roosevelt." He also reminded her that "the people are for me because Roosevelt is for me." This reality continued to irk her, especially when Will lavishly praised the President in his speeches. She was particularly upset at his likening Roosevelt to Lincoln, adding, "I do hope myself that you are not going to make any more speeches on the 'Roosevelt policies' as I think they need to be let alone for the present—and you are simply aiding and abetting the President in keeping things stirred up." Taft's discussion of Roosevelt's trust-busting further irritated her. "Let the corporations rest for awhile. It is soon enough to talk about it, when something needs to be done, and whatever the West may be, in the East it has an aggressive air."

Through the spring Nellie had managed polite relations with the Roosevelts. In one day she attended a garden party and dinner at the White House, lunching with the President's sister in between. Her fear of Roosevelt had even waned in April. "[I]t is hard to see how your Father could be defeated now, as none of the other candidates seem to have any strength whatsoever except in their own states and the Negro conventions in the south," she wrote Bob. "I can see nothing to defeat him except a possible stampede for Roosevelt, and that does not seem at all probable."[3]

If Roosevelt did not unnerve her that spring, everything else did. When Will was away, she couldn't "help being afraid of anarchists" who might threaten him, and when he was "busy seeing politicians" at home, she was rattled by talk of threats to the campaign. "He will probably get the solid Ohio delegation," she reported to Bob, but "Foraker has tried to steal two in Cuyahoga county." At home, she hated a house full of visitors. "When I have guests and don't get any time to myself, I always get flurried and do things wrong," she explained as the reason she confused theaters, and saw a variety show instead of an intended performance by the actress Nazimova. Nothing distracted her, however, from tracking Will's political scores, and she was especially proud that he helped to get a bill passed that established a Philippine bank despite opposition from the House Speaker.

As the deadly Washington summer began, Nellie escaped to the Virginia countryside, visiting Monticello and Montpelier but longing for Murray Bay. In February she had declared that if Will was nominated, he couldn't spend the summer in Canada but that "whatever happens" she would go. Ultimately it was decided—probably by Will and Nellie, and perhaps Charley—that she was now enough of a public figure that she should not spend the campaign in a foreign country, either. She was thinking ahead to the next summer—as First Lady. "I am rather in favor of trying the [Massachusetts] North Shore some where as it might prove to be more convenient another year."[4]

Archie Butt, who had just come into service as the Roosevelts' military aide, began to make personal notes on the Tafts, both astute—and petty. "She had on a fearful looking greenish gown," he snidely assessed of Nellie's clothing one night.

Butt even gossiped about how Will, now that he had resigned as war secretary, had no income and that he and Nellie were depending on Charley Taft to get them through the campaign. Indeed, Charley made them flush with cash for whatever they needed. Beginning with the massive public Notification Day ceremony, he even gave them their official Cincinnati "home" for the campaign. The event took place under a tent of flags extending from the front steps to the sidewalk gate of what was now christened the "Taft mansion." The implication that it was the home of the presidential candidate was certainly not corrected by the campaign: A souvenir postcard sold that summer with superimposed pictures of Will, Nellie, and their children at the mansion.

Nellie felt uncomfortable there. It was not her home, and her father lived in genteel poverty right down the street. Starting on July 1, Will planted himself in Cincinnati for the duration of the summer. Nellie returned to their rented cottage in Hot Springs, Virginia, pleased to be joined by her old cook, Alvina, "the one who ran after Charlie with a carving knife but was otherwise quite satisfactory."[5]

Besides taking baths for her rheumatism, Nellie's primary task in Hot Springs was coping with the flood of mail sent to her. She received a touching note from one Eli Freeman, a Kansas school principal, who told her that many blacks supported Will despite their anger at the Brownsville affair (in which Taft, following Roosevelt's orders, discharged black soldiers accused—but not convicted—of murder). There was the Brooklyn nurse who wanted Nellie to lend her money to attend classes and improve her medical skills. The Ladies Social League of Mount Tabor asked her to send a doll. *Extension* magazine requested that she write an article for them "to define what it means to be a wife and help-mate," with the promise that it would be quoted in all the nation's Catholic newspapers. She also received her share of nut letters. "Unless you feel the heart of truth, patriotism and unselfishness . . . you will destroy it," ranted one woman, who also took on socialism and "disgraceful" Alice Longworth.

There was also considerable press on "Master Robert," "Miss Helen," and "good old Charlie." They, too, became objects of public requests and gifts although neither Will nor Nellie thought about the harmful effects of publicity on the children. Ten reporters and one photographer chronicled the Tafts in Hot Springs, especially Will's endless rounds of golf. Before Bob—who hated publicity and completely retreated—left Hot Springs, a series of group and individual portraits were made of the nominee and his family. Helen, in her natural and rational manner, found it all amusing but let none of it go to her head. She was more focused on entering her freshman year at Bryn Mawr College and soon joined her uncle Harry at Murray Bay. Will, Nellie, and ten-year-old Charlie went back to Cincinnati. "His mother continues to think he is the perfect boy," Will told Mabel Boardman. "Charlie is utterly oblivious to any adequate responsibilities of life due to the selection of the Chicago Convention."[6]

Whether in Hot Springs or Cincinnati, Will was hit with a barrage of advice from Teddy: "I believe you will be elected *if we can keep things as they are;* so be very careful to say nothing, not one sentence, that can be misconstrued, and that can give a handle for effective attack." Two days after practically ordering Will to stop playing golf, because "hundreds" of voters wrote him about it, Roosevelt reminded him as if he were a scolding father: "I suppose there will be none until after the election."

By Notification Day not only Nellie but Charley was uncomfortable with Will's continuing to solicit Roosevelt's advice. On his own, however, Will decided to take to the stump on the whistle-stop train. A year earlier, when the Tafts had taken the train from Wyoming to Seattle to leave for their world tour, Nellie got her first "taste of real campaign work and always thereafter enjoyed a full realization of its difficulties." While Will shook hands with the throngs and spoke from the caboose, her "political enthusiasm waned slightly," Nellie confessed—"though temporarily."

Although she attended Will's speeches when she was with him and was part of the whistle-stop campaign from Michigan's Middle Bass Island back to Cincinnati, she found herself bored and ignored on the trail. "The reason I do not enjoy accompanying Mr. Taft on trips is . . . [h]e is taken in charge by committees and escorted everywhere with honor, while I am usually sent with a lot of uninteresting women through some side street to wait for him at some tea or luncheon." She decided to stay off his whistle-stops, although some thought this more stressful for her. "I hear there is some chance of Nellie going with you after all," a friend wrote Will. "I can't help hoping it may be so. . . . It will do her no good, nor her nervous condition, to be separated from you and fret and worry as she naturally will."

During the campaign Nellie broke precedent as a candidate's wife willing to speak on the record with a reporter. As the notification ceremony was breaking up, she spontaneously engaged in a conversation with a *New York Times* reporter: "Hasn't it been glorious! I did not know that so much was to be done, and the demonstration here in our own city showing such good wishes and goodwill towards Mr. Taft has made me very happy. Everything has been perfect. I have been so interested. I love public life. To me this is better than when Mr. Taft was at the bar and on the bench, for the things before him now and in which he takes part are live subjects."

To avoid being seen as a suffragette, because she was so engaged in Will's political direction, she backpedaled, adding, "The law is more in the abstract and harder for a woman to understand." More pragmatic and willing to play the games and stretch the truth than Will was to win politically, Nellie swallowed her pride and even fibbed about her view of Roosevelt. "My opinions are the same as those of Mr. Taft, and I, of course, am also an admirer of President Roosevelt." Realizing the many stories that had already circulated about her political role and alleged views on the issues, she made a blanket denial of influencing campaign policy. "There is one thing I dislike, and that is to be misquoted, and it has brought many letters to me," she admitted. "Some have approved of my supposed opinions, and in other cases I was informed that I had caused Mr. Taft to lose votes." Nellie tied the interview up by declaring her interest generally, without naming specifics. "I am greatly interested in the campaign, but not in any especial plank in the platform. There are so many and all important."[7]

Nellie sought relief from the pressures of the campaign in New York, staying with her in-laws Harry and Julia Taft, who, like Charley and Annie, lived "quite grandly." She thought it "convenient to have such a good boarding house to go to," but quickly discovered just how severe Julia's depression was: "She was verging on the suicidal mania." Harry, with his "indifferent New York view about everything," was no bargain, either.

He had a habit of "repeating any bad news" from anti-Taft newspapers. Nellie found in New York an "even more depressing atmosphere than Cincinnati."

Will, on the other hand, wrote confidently about his campaigning through eight of the Plains and upper midwestern states. Nellie's moods swung according to what she read in the newspaper. "Cheerful this morning, quite like a different person," she told Will after reading that he was "making such a success with your speeches," especially those that left voters "full of enthusiasm." When she read the next day that his voice was giving out, she began to worry all over again. Hearing nothing from the campaign on his condition, she became "anxious." That he would have to stop campaigning because of his voice "has frightened me from the beginning. . . . I have never believed in throat specialists." Even when he was in good health, Nellie worried just from habit. "Isn't it pathetic?" she admitted. "I lay awake three hours last night and worried because I had heard nothing since the article I read of you in the newspaper." She insisted that Carpenter and other staff "continue to wire me, as I am frightfully nervous."

She seemed relatively unfazed when an organized smear campaign by fundamentalist Protestant churches made an issue of the fact that she'd sent her daughter to a Catholic school in Manila and that she herself had socialized with the Vatican elite—and even wore a veil as a sign of deference and honor of tradition to be received by the Pope. In contrast to her reaction when Will was attacked, when Nellie found herself dragged into the campaign she was full of self-defensive confidence. In September, Senator Foraker jointly criticized her and Will for having taken the Middle Bass Island vacation as a gift from those who had government contracts pending. "Wasn't Foraker's attack pointless," she wrote Will. "[I]t seemed so to me. I thought we were the guests of the whole club at Middle Bass . . . and to drag in the poor Richardsons for lending us their boat. The whole thing has a ridiculous side to it." Attacking a candidate's wife would not garner any votes for the opposition, she believed; attacks on the candidate, however, could lead to the loss of the election, and were worth fretting about.

Foraker had begun to create more trouble. While continuing to attack Roosevelt, he made supportive overtures toward Taft, who cautiously welcomed them. Then the news broke that Foraker had been taking money from Standard Oil while doing their bidding in Congress. In reaction, Taft pointed out that he had never solicited the senator's support and publicly denounced him. "Your answer to Foraker was just right. I suppose he will drop it now, as there doesn't seem to be anything more to be said," Nellie reassured Will. "I can't see any way of getting around your plain statement of the facts."[8]

Roosevelt, however, told Will to "fight" with "more energy," because the public might assume that all Republicans "are tarred with the same brush" as Foraker. It came across like an edict to Nellie. "I was so depressed yesterday morning by the President's cross letter, plain cross it was, nothing else," she wrote. Still, she was pleased when he publicly hyped a new report that Democratic committeeman C. N. Haskell had also been in bed with Standard Oil. "I must say for Teddy however that he has made a fine diversion from Foraker in turning the attention to Haskell."

Nellie's hostility toward Teddy now stemmed from the reality that he had as great a vested interest in Taft's election as she did. For his part, Roosevelt now recognized just how potent Nellie was in manipulating Will's thinking and emotional state. The President bid Mrs. Taft to the White House alone a second time—again while Will was out on the road. She complained that "it is very inconvenient to go" from New York and resented what she viewed as his attempt to control her. "I can't imagine what Teddy wants," she wrote Will, "but probably only to complain of something."

Nellie apparently responded to the White House by asking just what Roosevelt wanted of her. "I have a letter from Corbin saying that the President only wants to see me to encourage me. That he is most optimistic," she wrote Will more calmly. No notes of what was said were kept, but Roosevelt somehow wanted to excite Nellie by telling her he foresaw that Will would win and get a sense of Will's true state of mind. She reassured him that Will was just fine and, as proof, passed along a confident telegram that Will had sent her.

"My dear Mrs. Taft. That is fine," Teddy responded in the only known letter he wrote her. "I believe everything is all right. It was such a pleasure to see you!" If he didn't thank her for coming, neither did Nellie thank him for the beneficence of his confidence. She told Will it was a "delightful visit." Will telegraphed Teddy to say, "I am sure that you gave her courage and hope."

In early October, Nellie found it traumatic to enroll Charlie as a boarder for his first year at the Taft School. "I fear I shall never get him back. He is already talking about 'next year.'" A visit with Bob in his Yale dormitory room was also wistful. She found him lonely for his family, rereading old letters from his father. "I do wish you would send him just a short line or two by Carpenter," she admonished Will. "He does enjoy it so much." Sitting on his windowsill, she thought him "quiet as usual," unable to get him to discuss his thoughts about the change in his family life.[9]

Nellie returned to Cincinnati just in time to see Will off, back to the campaign trail from which he would not return until Election Day. In one day he had twenty speeches to give. He told her that if he were to stay in Cincinnati another week, he would be "down in the dumps," but she told Bob that "I don't find it nearly so depressing here as in New York" because the press there was skeptical of a Taft victory.

She and Will reunited on Election Day at the Taft mansion, where they got the expected good news. Bob would gravely reflect on the responsibility to come to his father; Helen wired, "I was never so happy in my life"; and Charlie took instantly to fame, getting his first letter to a newspaper editor published. Will seemed strangely detached from any sense of excitement, momentum, or vision. On the surface he acted as if he was relieved to be keeping a government job that would let him save money and play golf. Immediately after the election he persuaded Nellie to return to Hot Springs with him so that he could play golf. In truth, he was nervous about the awesome responsibilities he was about to be saddled with, and the golf helped him relax and escape.[10]

In Hot Springs, Nellie was inundated with an "awful" pile of public mail and began looking for a secretary. There were now three Secret Service agents trailing the couple, she wrote, "and electric lights all over the place." In making potential Thanksgiving plans for the children to join them there, she was shocked that security now required them to engage a full section of a railroad car—and cover the cost of it all. Nellie had finally achieved the dream of her girlhood, the highest ambition any woman to whom being a political wife was a full-time profession could ever imagine. A woman who drank alcohol regularly, smoked cigarettes occasionally, and gambled obsessively was now "First Lady–elect," and she wouldn't take guff from anyone—not even the President-elect. She left him to his golf and got to Washington as soon as she could, in the last days of November. Within 120 days the White House would be hers, and she would not lose a day in planning her takeover from the Roosevelts.

In Washington she met with military aide Archie Butt, who would oversee her transition. Having so long anticipated this moment, she knew just what she wanted. She would no longer have local caterers bring in food for state dinners—the White House kitchens would do it all. She wanted a fashionable fleet of automobiles, not horse-drawn carriages. She would do away with receiving lines; instead, she and Will would enter the Blue Room and move from one assembled group to another, à la Buckingham Palace. She would hire a housekeeper to run everything. And that was just for starters. Usher Ike Hoover growled that she had a "disposition to change things for the sake of changing." Nellie would counter that a new First Lady had "absolute authority . . . and can do exactly as she pleases."

Archie Butt was the President's military aide, but he had especially befriended Edith and Alice. A lifelong bachelor, he lived with artist Francis Millet (whom Nellie had met in England in 1907) while Mrs. Millet lived mostly in Europe. There were frequent remarks in the Washington social crowd of how fond women were of Archie, but he never married. The closest he came to it was romanticizing about how his fortune would change if he married an heiress. Mannered and courtly, hypersensitive to style, in Edith Roosevelt he found his perfect mistress: betraying no emotion, morally superior, subtle to the point of being vague. In private letters to his aged mother and sister-in-law Clara he recorded every bit of gossip he heard. "Bad temper I can stand," he said, "but not bad taste."

Archie didn't think Nellie would prove to be "as considerate" as Edith. "She is an intellectual woman and a woman of wonderful executive ability," he wrote before her official call on him, on December 7. He was more pointed after their meeting. "Mrs. Taft is very blunt in her manner and comes to the point at issue without much diplomacy. But she generally knows what she wants and how to carry out her ideas," he wrote. He was shocked at how she began using him as her aide when, in fact, he was still beholden to the Roosevelts.[11]

There were more abrupt changes. She was firing Belle Hagner, Edith's social secretary. The woman had crossed a line, Nellie thought, in becoming a friend to the Roosevelts. She just wanted a good stenographer and eventually hired Alice Blech, a Bureau of American Republics clerk. She wanted as much of the entertaining and other costs as possible to be picked up by Uncle Sam. "She is anxious to keep her expenses down," Archie wrote, "and did not hesitate to say so, for she frankly said they had nothing on the outside. . . . She is an able businesswoman. She has had to become so for the President-elect has not the slightest idea of saving money or of its relative value. All this has come direct on her shoulders in the past, and if they are to save anything in the future it will depend on her."

And in the most controversial act of reverse race snobbery she was to commit, Nellie ordered four black men in liveried uniforms to replace the white ushers who stood around in frock coats—two on the portico and two inside the entrance. To the working-class white majority of 1908 America, this act had the effect of altering the status of the servant class: In the context of her times she was seen as demoting white men and promoting black men. Archie knew it would "run counter to a very deep-seated prejudice in this country" and that "Mrs. Taft must be prepared for criticism of a severe character." She was still "intent on doing it." Nellie was praised, however, in the nation's most respected newspaper, *The New York Times*: "Colored footmen in livery lend as great an air of distinction to the doorway of a house as frock-coated doorkeepers of Caucasian descent." Edith Roosevelt, for one, was quite upset.

December 11 was the first time in history that an outgoing First Lady gave a tour of the mansion to her successor. Nellie overcompensated for her nervousness by acting high-handed. After lunch, as the two walked into the Green Room, Nellie quipped in a whisper loud enough for Edith to hear, "I would have put that table over there." Edith sweetly slipped her arm into Nellie's and guided her to sit and chat. "It is merely the case of the setting sun, but the sun must at least set with dignity and self respect" was her only allusion to having her way of doing things being upset by Nellie. Alice— who soon joined the women and had her first chance to size Nellie up as a future First Lady—was unsubtle in her reaction. Not long after, sitting beside the coachman and taking the horses' reins, she tucked in her chin and bulged her eyes to mimic what she called Nellie's "hippopotamus face." Then, to gales of laughter from her siblings and stepmother, and in her best Nellie Taft inflection, Alice airily shrieked, "This, my dears, is what is coming after you!"[12]

Teddy was focused on what kind of President Will would be. Taft told Roosevelt that he viewed the presidency "with much hesitation and doubt." Teddy had no doubts: Will would back issues "for which I have fought" and initiate policies "in which I most firmly believe." As he bluntly told a friend, "In short, Taft will be me!" When Will failed to keep most of the Roosevelt Cabinet as the outgoing President believed he had promised, he now confided to a friend that Taft was "weak." Will tried to dismiss gossip of tension between them by writing Teddy: "People have attempted to represent that you and I were in some way at odds during this last three months, whereas you and I know that there has not been the slightest difference between us, and I welcome the opportunity to stay the last night of your administration under the White House roof to make as emphatic as possible the refutation of any such suggestion. With love and affection, my dear Theodore."

In mid-December, Nellie went to New York. She bought her White House trousseau and commissioned her inaugural gown, "perfectly appalled at the cost." She also inspected cars. Archie had already managed to wangle a $12,000 appropriation from Congress for the fleet, but noted, "Mrs. Taft wants to get four motors out of this amount. There is only one way to do it; that is, to take the cars at a reduced rate and permit the makers to advertise the fact that their cars are being used for the White House." While in New York, she also interviewed Elizabeth Jaffray at an employment agency for the job of housekeeper. When the woman decided it wasn't for her and stood up, Nellie yelled at her, "Sit down!" The "winning persistency" of "this rather outspoken, determined lady" convinced Jaffray to accept. Nellie also snapped at her host and brother-in-law Harry when he teased that Will "didn't work too hard." Horace reported, "The discussion began innocently enough, but before we got through we had Nellie defending you against the charge of laziness."

The year 1908 had stressed Nellie considerably. "The ups and downs of such a campaign, the prophecies, the hopes, the fears aroused by favorable and opposing newspapers were all new and trying to me, and in a way I think I was under as great a nervous strain as my husband was," she later reflected. After the election she still "went so constantly that I am a wreck." Nellie finally confessed to Will that she "was not feeling at all well" and that she "did too much" in New York. Yet she then proceeded to North Carolina for a meeting, returned to Will at Hot Springs, and went with him to Asheville, Charleston, and Augusta, while continuing her work with Archie via mail.

Nellie did not relax in Augusta. She was frustrated that she couldn't find an appropriate Christmas present for Bob, and she had no friends there. She finally bid Archie to come down to her to confer. She snapped to Will that "it is the silliest thing to come away down here where you can't be in it or know what's doing." Will sarcastically wrote in a letter to his brother that such an attitude "leads to continual pleasant conversation." There was genuine tension with Nellie, who, he said, "criticize[s] my efforts at cabinet making." He was enjoying himself "exceedingly," but Nellie was causing "domestic complications."

She also felt he was neglecting their children, to whom she always wrote, even in the midst of her pre-inaugural frenzy, making sure they had enough money and winter clothing. Having been led by Nellie into an awesome responsibility he never wanted, Will typically buried his anger but showed his resentment by studiously ignoring any sense of obligation. The children were clearly stressed, Bob suffering breathing problems, Helen back problems. "Papa shows poor taste in preferring Georgia to Cincinnati for Christmas," Helen confided to Bob. "I think that he is developing extravagant tastes to want to go south for the winter. I am much disturbed for we only have two weeks and I should like to see something of our parents so that I suppose I shall end by quietly remaining in Georgia." Charlie put it on the line, writing Will: "Could you please tell me where you are now. . . . I'd like to keep a better track of my father."[13]

In January, Nellie returned to Washington for one day before leaving to join Will at the Panama Canal. "The engineers have been working hard, starting out at 6:30 every morning," she wrote Bob. "The work is most interesting. I went all over it with your Father and it makes you proud to see how perfectly organized it is and how well it is going on. On the isthmus there is only one opinion as to the type of the canal. They all consider that the lock canal is the one adapted to the place and conditions, and there was absolutely nothing found to induce the engineers to change the plans."

By the time she returned, Washington was in full swing preparing for the inaugural. The Tafts were given use of Mabel Boardman's mansion on the corner of P Street and 18th Street. Tafts, Herrons, and Cincinnatians such as the Andersons and Longworths would soon arrive for the festivities, and Nellie had the overworked but dutiful Carpenter getting tickets, making hotel reservations, and providing transportation for them. "I think it better to entertain all the relatives as soon as possible for they will all expect to be entertained at the White House sooner or later," she decided in composing a post-inaugural ceremony luncheon. She had no intention of inviting officials to the luncheon but did invite Alice Longworth, hardly an act of generosity since most of her in-laws would be there. When Alice mentioned she would first see her father off at the train station, Nellie said a ticket would be set aside for her. The remark broke Alice's pent-up resentment at being "expelled from the garden of Eden." She went about town galled that Nellie would so "quickly become possessive of the White House." Her anger turned to malice. She told Mabel Boardman she would be appointed "Pompadour of the Taft Administration," and when told that Nellie was having all the male servants shave their beards, Alice wondered loudly what the new First Lady would do about those of her women friends who were "bearded ladies."

Alice was her father's best spy. Now he sent her to find out if it was true that their friend Henry White, ambassador to France, would be replaced. Stories circulated that when White had been at the embassy in London, he had gotten the Tafts tickets for only the royal stables and not the House of Commons, and Nellie would now mete out his comeuppance. White was not reappointed. It was the first official act that the Roosevelt camp seized on as proof of ingratitude. "To hear them talk," even Archie Butt said of the Roosevelts, "one would think that . . . Mrs. Taft was not even civil." Whether this prompted Roosevelt's decision not to accompany Taft back to the White House after the ceremony is not known. However, Nellie turned this break with historic precedent by Roosevelt to her own advantage—and into a chance to set a new precedent.

When Archie came to see her at the Boardman house, Nellie conducted the meeting from her side of a bedroom door, slightly opened. He noted that "occasionally she would get excited or greatly interested, and appear to full view. She did not look bad, quite the contrary I thought, for she wore a richly colored Japanese kimono, which is very becoming . . . especially to her." When he suggested that *she* ride with the new President back to the White House, Nellie seized the idea: "Since Mr. Roosevelt has seen fit to change the order of things, I see no reason why the President's wife may not now come into some rights on that day also." While she was at it, Nellie also added a sentimental touch that harked to her own past. She commissioned Van der Stucken to compose an inaugural march to be played at the outdoor ceremony. Unfortunately, the elements did not cooperate, and the ceremony had to be moved indoors.[14]

Roosevelt invited Will and Nellie to dine and sleep over at the White House on inaugural eve. It was a maudlin event, with Edith deeply sad and Nellie uncomfortable. "Neither Mrs. Roosevelt nor I would have suggested such an arrangement," she recalled. After dinner the women repaired to the library. Alice looked out the window, and suddenly her mood lifted. "That will take care of the inauguration, I thought," she later recalled. Shouting, "It's snowing!" she then enigmatically slipped on a scarf and went outside.

That night Nellie tossed and turned in the Blue Bedroom, where she and Will were put up. Through the night, as snow and ice covered the city, she would wake to the sound of an icy branch tapping on the window, ruminating that her gown had not yet arrived and over a thousand other worries for the great day. In the dark room she felt "surrounded by ghosts."

The next morning, after Roosevelt and Taft headed out by horse and carriage to the Capitol, Nellie rode up in her new automobile. The streets were covered in snow and the air was so cold that it was decided to move the ceremony indoors. Arriving at ten-thirty and escorted to her seat in the Senate gallery by the Senate sergeant-at-arms, Nellie was reunited with her children, who had come directly from the Boardman house. In defiance of the official schedule published by the Inaugural Committee, Nellie had informed the press that she would make her ride from here with Will in the parade.

Dressed in purple, with a large matching hat, she betrayed no reaction when Will finally placed his hand on the Bible, repeated the oath, and became President. In reality, said Archie, she was in a "state of nerves" and "trembling all over." She was focused on meeting up with Will on the abandoned outdoor inaugural stand where some of the apparently drunk crowds waited for the new President's promised greeting. As she made her way down, some men started irreverently whistling and singing. "Are they trying to gay [make light of] us, you think?" she asked Archie. Nellie had left before Will completed his inaugural address, which Alice Longworth said was "noted for an abundance of lack and shortage of luster."

For Nellie Taft the day she had so long dreamed of reached its zenith in "that ride" down Pennsylvania Avenue in an open coach, her "proudest and happiest" moment. A woman not easily given to smiling, during the procession she beamed radiantly at the hearty crowds who cheered her and President Taft from the rented seats on raised platforms and storefronts. It was, she said, "all that my fancy had pictured it." For those forty or so minutes she dropped her anxieties. "I was able to enjoy, almost to the full, the realization that my husband was actually President of the United States and that it was this fact which the cheering crowds were acclaiming." Despite some inaugural committee men's disapproval, Nellie could say, "I had my way." When she stepped over the brass seal in the middle of the entrance hall floor as she entered the White House and read "President of the United States" around the border, she felt like "Cinderella," as if "the whole thing was unreal." Inside were her new housekeeper and liveried doormen to greet her.

She had done it. The man the former Miss Helen Louise Herron had married had become President. After the luncheon and parade, Nellie, "eager to roam around the house, to familiarize myself with the mysteries of my new home," walked through each room of the private quarters. Only then did she get her hair done and get dressed for the ball. Her hair had to be fixed twice and was still not right. It made her "more nervous than anything else" that day. She was deeply relieved when she saw her gown of heavy white satin, glistening with silver embroidery and trimmed in lace and rhinestones. It had been stranded for several hours on a train coming from New York, along with thousands of inauguration-goers paralyzed by the snowstorm. At the ball, Nellie Taft promenaded regally on the arm of her Will, a diamond clasp in her hair, down a wide aisle made through the thick crowd by silk ropes in the national colors. They walked halfway down the length of the mammoth Pension Building, around a fountain, and back again. However serene she appeared, she confessed to "frequent spasms of anxiety lest my gorgeous length of train be stepped on." Then, just like the royal families of Europe, the Tafts appeared in a box below which hung a large flag, and waved to the thousands of attendees in gowns, uniforms, and white tie and tails.[15]

What she had most longed for, Nellie Taft now had. Even the Roosevelt threat seemed to vanish, with Teddy soon to be on another continent, Africa, for big-game hunting and Edith tucked away in her cozy Oyster Bay nook. One of their tribe lingered in Washington, however, and Archie Butt predicted that Alice Roosevelt Longworth "would be just as popular after the fourth of March as she has been, if not a little more so."

Alice, in fact, had already cast a spell of sorts on the Tafts. The night before, when Nellie and Edith talked in the White House library after dinner, Alice had been down on the South Lawn, clearing snow and digging a deep hole in the dirt. There she buried a "bad little idol," a voodoo to bring ill fortune. "I helped to make bad blood," she later confessed somewhat proudly.[16]

Eleven

Ragtime

*Entertainments work most smoothly, especially if the lady of the
White House has, as mine had, executive ability and understands
where to put her fingers on the reforms needed and to give every
one to understand that she is really in control.*

—WILL TAFT, "PERSONAL ASPECTS
OF THE PRESIDENCY"

Nellie instantly took to being First Lady. "Yesterday I presented over three thousand persons by name to the President and Mrs. Taft," Archie Butt wrote three days after the inaugural, "and she, by the way, acted like a trump [trooper] in receiving this heterogeneous mass of out of town folks. . . . [S]he was really a brick in accepting the situation."

Her changes in White House custom, her ride in the inaugural parade, her civic and social reform efforts, all converged to make Mrs. Taft a presidential wife of more than the usual fascination in the national press. The title "First Lady" was first used in 1848 in reference to Sarah Polk, but until 1909 it still largely meant White House hostess. Nellie had read Abigail Adams's published letters and had known First Ladies since Lucy Hayes. She was all for honoring tradition, but she had some new ideas of her own.

If her decision to make the historic inaugural ride was calculated to garner attention, it worked. Photographs of her on that day appeared throughout the nation's newspapers in the following Sunday's rotogravure sections, and numerous profiles of the new First Lady opened by referring to this act as a sign of her desire to figuratively take her place next to the President. *The New York Times*, for one, said Nellie's action would "smash all precedents." This was coupled with her open declaration that she was politically astute and the already legendary tales of how she had been the one to guide Will's career away from the judiciary and toward the presidency. She was also portrayed as being not only an intelligent and educated woman but one who found nothing unfeminine about exercising her intellect. "Mrs. Taft has brains and uses them" went one article that emphasized her love of George Eliot's works, her connoisseurship of master woodcarvings, and her skill at whist.

In one of her few interviews, with George Griswold Hill for *Ladies' Home Journal*, Nellie honed the familiar points of her persona: adept at budgeting, fond of music, experienced with protocol, and friendly to different races in the Philippines. Most of all her political role was completely revealed, but without detailing the specifics. Hill wrote that

> . . . *she is the close confidante and companion of her husband . . . ever animated with an intense ambition. . . . The companionship . . . is like that of two men who are intimate chums. Mrs. Taft defends her own opinions and wishes with almost masculine vigor.*

Nor did Hill portray her in the Victorian tradition of modest femininity:

> *On meeting her for the first time one is impressed with her dignity, her capability and her reserve. A person of keen perceptions and of more than average intelligence, she surveys the man or woman presented to her with a look so calm and deliberate that strangers sometimes are wont to describe her as cold. . . . There is a steadiness . . . that look[s] straight into your [eyes] which at once bespeak her genuineness. Her frankness and hatred of insincerity constitute one of her attractions. She is a woman who thinks and*

thinks well, who draws upon an unusually wide experience for her
comparisons, and expresses her views with an originality. . . . Under
the calm exterior, and the perfect savoir faire is the real Mrs. Taft—
emotional, of keen sensibilities, in fact, as sensitive as a girl. But so
perfect is her self-control . . . that few discover these characteristics.

It was keenly accurate.[1]

Nellie believed "a public office [is] a public trust." In changing the social order in the White House, "the highest and broadest democracy" was her guide, and the press praised her egalitarianism in contrast to the exclusive Roosevelts. She would not invite any guest to an event more than once a season, so she could invite more people who had never been to the White House before. Then she expanded the calendar of White House social events beyond the official dinners held in honor of the Cabinet, Senate, House, Supreme Court, and Army and Navy and diplomatic corps during the "social season" from January until the start of Lent.

Nellie added four musicales held during Lent and then four spring garden parties after Lent. She could thus invite larger numbers of guests who might not otherwise have ranked high enough to get a dinner invitation. Instead of focusing on Washington society, Nellie and Will especially wanted congressional families—whose often middle-brow qualities made them verboten to the Roosevelts—made to feel included. There were also more of the lower-ranking and lower-paid members of the military and their spouses in evidence at the house.

All of these people still represented "official" Washington, but they largely came from the middle and, in some instances, the lower class. Even snobbish Archie Butt thought this an astute part of the Taft dictum, that "the White House is a big political asset when used wisely." Nellie integrated the smart set and the rubes, as opposed to Edith who "segregated." Because of her years in the Philippines, Mrs. Taft was vitally aware of the sacrifice and patriotism made by military families, and as a Cabinet wife she certainly knew what it felt like to be deemed "unimportant." It had been more than a decade since a First Lady had displayed such sensitivity toward a more general population—when Frances Cleveland held Saturday receptions for working-class women on their day off. Even for tourists, Nellie would have more rooms opened and even displayed personal family items for public glimpsing.

All of this brought praise for Nellie in *New York Times* editorials, "The Lady of the White House" and "Washington Official Society." One *Washington Star* article declared that "Mrs. Taft is a woman of distinctive personality. . . ." Some took issue with the fact that, unlike the more fashionable set in New York, the First Lady refused to host teas, receptions, and other events on Sunday. Finding this trend of sophisticates to be too debauched, however, Nellie intended to set the example of "family Sundays," a day set aside for the exclusive socializing of families and relatives.[2]

Nellie Taft was in the process of changing, growing into the larger-hearted woman that a First Lady was idealized to be. While she certainly didn't revive the mob scene open house receptions that were popular in the pre–Civil War days of the White House, nor seek to expose herself physically to the masses, Nellie's common touch was more apparent at the traditionally public events—the New Year's Day Reception, the Easter Egg Roll party on the South Lawn, assorted military band concerts on the lawn—where seats, refreshments, rest areas, first aid, and other services were amply provided for the citizenry's comfort.

If recognized while she was out conducting her own private business, Nellie was gracious and receptive to strangers, but when she was "on duty" as First Lady in the mansion, she radiated a lively warmth and engaged people in conversation. There is also no indication that she permitted any of Edith Roosevelt's racial or class filters to weed out those "undesirable" citizens who requested an invitation to her "At Home" receptions, simple events where tea was offered and a dozen or so visitors were invited to meet her more privately, usually in the Red Room. In time, her efforts to help the hundreds of anonymous citizens who wrote to her for various sorts of aid, support, or intervention would also serve her impulse to help those who were primarily of the working class.

If Nellie Taft's perception of the working class had grown more sympathetic, her imperious nature emerged even more strongly in dealing with the White House domestic staff. Judging from the memoirs of the chief usher, housekeeper, a mail clerk, and a housemaid, she was efficient, vocal, demanding, appreciative, but hardly beloved. The staff, it seems, generally found her more autocratic in the planning of her private entertaining. The commanding manner she had assumed in the Philippines had not left her. It must also be said, however, that the domestic staff was composed of servants who were largely unworldly people who believed that their way of running the house was the best and a form of change suggested an insult to them.

As a chatelaine "demanding good service, but showing appreciation of the labor of the least of her servants by fair wages and fair treatment," she made another internal change. Nellie did away completely with the class system that Edith Roosevelt had created for the servants, in which the domestic staff was divided into "upper" and "lower" distinctions, even being served different grades of food. Now they were all served the same food and given the same privileges. In the kitchen, black and white workers still gathered at separate tables, but no longer would a butler be treated better than a charwoman. Her replacement of the male steward she viewed as a sort of reverse sexism. She wanted a woman housekeeper because the work involved what she saw as details that "no man . . . would ever recognize."

Before the inaugural, rumor ran rampant among the staff that Nellie had a "very bad temper," and many were rushing to be transferred to other government jobs. Even Archie Butt felt uneasy about reports of her mood swings. There is no record of Mrs. Taft ever losing her temper with the staff, but she would not abide disorder. With her experience at the orchestra, she structured the staff functioning with herself as a sort of corporate head. A flowchart showed Nellie's authority over housekeeper Elizabeth Jaffray (who oversaw maids, butlers, cooks, pantrymen, kitchen maids, chambermaid, laundresses, and house cleaners), custodian Arthur Brooks (accountable for silver, china, glass, linens, wine, liquors, and cigars, and responsible for coatrooms during receptions), and chief usher Ike Hoover (who directed the doorkeepers, police officers, doormen, footmen, electrician, engineer, fireman, and florists). Jaffray, who lived in the house, reported to Nellie every morning to review accounting records, menus, and upcoming events. Hoover had a direct phone line to her, over which came her orders. Brooks, who had the closest relationship with Nellie dating from the War Department years, had as frequent contact and absolute access to her as he wished.

Nellie made it clear through Jaffray that none of the staff was to roam about the halls. The cooks resented the constant presence of a First Lady in the kitchens. With her exquisite and long-developed taste for quality foods, she would look under pot lids and in the ovens, second guessing the cooks. She was especially sensitive about the quality of terrapin soup, finally hiring a special cook for $5 a night to prepare it. The waiters thought that her introduction of exotic foods, such as Mediterranean artichokes, was continental snobbery. Ike Hoover ridiculed Nellie's al fresco entertaining. Especially offensive to him was her replacing white globes covering electric lights on the outdoor west terrace with garish red shades. Potted palms, flowering shrubs, tables, and chairs were placed outside, but Hoover considered it "a complete failure," plagued with bugs, mosquitoes, and dampness. Whenever she gave garden parties, it seemed inevitably to rain—which meant the waiters had to dash out and carry everything inside.[3]

Mrs. Taft sought to make the historic old mansion in every way her personal home, using the state rooms for family purposes at night. The footman at the front, north door—an entrance now used only for guests, not those on executive business—enhanced the feeling of a private home as opposed to an institution, even though police guards were just inside the door. In the evening the Tafts entertained friends in the Blue Room, many dancing around the white bearskin rug to music cranked out on Will's Victrola. Although Will had a large collection of disks that included his favorite opera singer, Caruso, Charlie later recalled that he, Nellie, and their children also loved the new syncopated sounds of "ragtime" music that emerged from African American pianists in Storyville. It was a rage that had begun nearly a decade earlier but now seemed to define the Progressive era, enjoyed by all classes and races except evangelicals, who equated it with immorality. A bar was set up near the entry hall, at the usher's office, and guests wandered in for cocktails. Hoover recalled that while the guests "cut up generally," the President would "sit to one side of the room and watch the antics of the company. His laughter could be heard all over the house."

The chief usher thought it was all too much like a royal court. Whenever Nellie received in the Red Room, as she did nearly every day, she wanted the fireplace scrubbed and a fresh fire lit so she could "hold court" elegantly. She and Will maintained a regal Edwardian suite in pale pink, with twin beds, perhaps the first presidential bedroom apparently outfitted by a professional, decorator Elsie DeWolfe. The family's West Hall was done up with palm trees, wicker and teakwood Asian furniture, and grass floor mats; the staff ridiculed it as the "palace." This was the site of Mrs. Taft's command post, her office desk placed squarely in the center of the West Hall, where she could see straight down the hallway through to the other end of the building, or turn around in her chair to see who was entering and exiting the West Wing.

To the largely southern domestic staff, used to the soft-voiced and smiling Edith Roosevelt, this new First Lady appeared coldly efficient with a near-fetish for order and precision. Soon maids and gardeners were cracking one another up with Nellie Taft impersonations: "They don't do things at the White House the way we used to do them at the Malacanan Palace!"

The chief usher claimed, however, that as soon as she issued one edict, she was apt to reverse it. "When I told General [Clarence] Edwards [Taft friend from Philippine days] that Mrs. Taft was not the decided character I had been led to think, he laughed," recorded Archie. Edwards said, "No, she gives the opinions as if she were delivering a valedictory but she changes her mind with a rapidity which would startle Shakespeare in his most cynical mood." Her early efforts to change protocol so she could enter a room on equal status with the President was reverted to the older way after her first dinner for members of Congress when she "bolted in ahead" of the President and "rather assumed his place."[4]

The public learned everything they knew about the new First Lady through the nation's newspapers and magazines, who sold Nellie as a new kind of First Lady, independent and pro-suffrage. Her first brush with what she viewed as press intrusion was not so much a request but an order from the *New York Herald* for the "color, material and style" of her inaugural gown so sketches could be made and published. She did not cooperate. Following the custom of royalty, she often had friends speak to reporters who requested interviews with her. During the campaign, at the notification ceremony, she had exuberantly talked to a *New York Times* reporter in plain English. Now, the same paper reported, she was "refusing to be interviewed." Here Nellie emulated Edith Roosevelt, who felt that being quoted compromised her public dignity and personal status.

Like Edith Roosevelt, Nellie took no pride in having her clothes described in detail in the press—including the fact that a friend of hers estimated that she spent about $6,000 a year—astronomical in 1909—on all her clothes. There was much made of the fact that she did not take to the new look and was, thus, "unhobbled" in her gait by the fashion rage of "hobble skirts," which wrapped tightly around women's legs. Beyond the traditional social notices of her clothes and parties, Nellie Taft received a larger share of political coverage and speculation than her immediate predecessors. Marie Corelli, a celebrated novelist, declared in one newspaper interview that "It is not President Taft but Mrs. Taft who really rules America. She simply takes her husband along with her. To be able to do this is a greater woman's triumph than the gaining of universal suffrage." One story had leaked that Nellie had declared that if she became First Lady she would "work for a uniform divorce law" in the nation, creating a national standard to stem the increasing ease afforded by some state laws. Mrs. Taft offered no reaction to the initial report, but when the Austrian Baroness Hengelmuller publicly recounted a conversation with Nellie in which she said she would "not tolerate the presence at her White House receptions of divorcées," the First Lady was livid. Regardless of her personal belief that social acceptance of divorce would undermine family life in America, she retorted that she had never threatened to ban divorcées; indeed, she never did, as Edith Roosevelt had. The First Lady did not believe she had a right to impose her judgment on other people. Mrs. Taft proved good copy for the nation's readers and when one Ohio newspaper seemed to be limiting its coverage of the First Lady, there were protest letters to the editor demanding more news about her. The *Mansfield News* defended itself by saying it was protecting her personal privacy.

"Publicity is dreadful to a woman of refinement," Mrs. J. P. Morgan sniped to one reporter, while also warning him not to use "snapshot photography" on her. On this Nellie concurred. She tried in vain to control her public image by releasing a series of beautiful, well-lit portrait photographs of herself as a regal First Lady in evening gowns, diamonds, and even a tiara, formally posed in the Green Room. She was not successful. Her snapshot appeared just weeks after she became First Lady, ambling down the steps at Carnegie Hall, glowering in vain at the persistent photographer. Soon enough she became a recognizable figure in the streets of the eastern and midwestern cities she frequented. Although able to ride trains without being disturbed, and usually escorted only by Butt, there were times her celebrity became annoying. While shopping with her sister in a Pittsburgh department store, a salesclerk recognized her and asked for an autograph. A customer overheard the exchange and asked for one as well. Soon, two hundred people besieged the First Lady, and management had to rush her out.

With examples of photography no longer confined to posed portraits family and friends exchanged with one another, the power of the image had increased dramatically during the Roosevelt years. Photography had proliferated into numerous aspects of American life—magazine covers, billboard advertisements, art exhibitions, postcards, travel brochures. Certainly the nation had come to know and love its youngest woman celebrity—Alice

Roosevelt—through her beautiful portrait photographs that were reproduced in endless formats.

While Mrs. Taft was not the sensation that the young White House
bride Frances Cleveland had been, like her, her image was soon appearing
on commercial products, ranging from stereoscopic postcards to china
plates. The First Lady, along with the rest of the Tafts, was even parodied
publicly in a Philadelphia Mummers Burlesque Parade as "The Whole
Daft Family."[5]

Generally, Nellie managed to live an orderly life. The three Secret
Service agents on the premises—Sloan, Wheeler, and Jervis—were never
assigned to her, and she never requested them as escorts. She breakfasted
with Will in the small Family Dining Room between eight and nine, then
returned to the West Sitting Hall in the private quarters. There, for an
hour, she conferred with Jaffray and dictated public correspondence to
Alice Blech. Before lunch, Nellie got her daily exercise in a vigorous hike
along the city streets and through its many parks. Afternoons she shopped,
socialized, held meetings, and kept up with a laborious handwritten correspondence, largely thank-you letters to politically important figures. Dinner was always with houseguests and, when he was home, with Will. It
was at evening theater or music performances that Nellie most frequently
saw friends, official wives, and socialites that she had known either in the
Philippines or during the Cabinet years. Brigadier General Clarence Edwards, whom the Tafts had disliked as a militarist during the Philippine
years but whom Will took to when they came to personally know him,
served as an unofficial adviser to them. Will and Nellie were also befriended by millionaire engineer and founder of Uniroyal John Hays
"Jack" Hammond and his wife, Natalie. Hammond had put $100,000 into
Taft's campaign and became president of the National League of Republican Clubs. Another friend that Will and Nellie shared was Mabel Boardman. Spinster, philanthropist, Republican, Mabel took a serious interest in
domestic and international politics. In 1905 she helped oust founder Clara
Barton as the president of the Red Cross and assumed that role herself.

Mabel was extremely efficient, taking a group of trained volunteer nurses and turning them into the world's premier emergency relief force. Under her leadership the American Red Cross became a bureaucratic philanthropy, and Mabel began efforts to create an endowment fund that would enable the organization to prepare in advance for emergencies. Will always said the Red Cross was her child. He and Mabel had become close during his years as war secretary, in conjunction with his department's joint efforts with the Red Cross. Nellie and Mabel were similar in their serious nature, but Miss Boardman always had an extra, often humorless nature.

Nellie's only true intimates remained her sisters, Lucy Laughlin, who lived in Rhode Island; Maria Herron and Jennie Anderson, who both lived in Cincinnati; and Eleanor More, who lived in Pittsburgh—especially the last two. Archie sized up the sisters by saying, "They look well bred, some very elegant, and none shoddy or vulgar. She will have no need to feel ashamed to present them to any class of people. . . . As a rule her relatives would strike one as possibly a hard and unsympathetic type . . . but far above the average as relatives and connections go."

Whenever a Taft or Herron visited—and almost always there was a relative in residence—Will and Nellie were lavish. Neither did they stint on their private parties or even public events. Again, Archie observed of the Tafts: "[T]hey have entertained more people and more elaborately than any couple ever in the White House. . . . [T]heir way of entertainment . . . [is] on the best scale and in the best form. . . . [T]he most critical old gourmets . . . pronounce the cooking at the White House the very best in Washington. I know the tobacco is the best and the wines are above average and to Mrs. Taft's credit be it said she never entertains with punch or cheap wines."[6]

The Tafts covered the cost of all meals served to their family servants and guests; any clothes or personal items they bought; the Christmas turkeys expected by each staff member; and all wine, cigars, and other liquors served to even official guests. Taft was the first President to be salaried at $75,000 a year with an additional $25,000 "traveling fund," which was sometimes used to cover other official costs. Nellie rigidly kept the books, reviewing all accounts and making certain that Mrs. Jaffray purchased food in bulk and, if possible, at discount. She pinched pennies everywhere she could, even convincing Will to accept the crates of whiskey offered each holiday season by Andrew Carnegie.

Nellie fretted about whether to rent a summer house in light of the fact that she and Will were anticipating a congressional appropriation for a summer junket to Alaska. He told her it "makes no difference" and to "take the house for four years." Nellie sighed. "Do you wonder that we have only saved in all this time $5,000? And we should not have that now, had I not worried over expenditure." Will sarcastically quipped, "My dear, how much do you think you have added to our income by worry and trouble?"

"I fear nothing," Nellie hit back boldly, "but I have made ends meet, and you have been able to make moves when they were necessary without borrowing money. You might have been sued or arrested for debt, who can tell?" Nellie Taft would save $100,000 from her White House years, the first real money she and Will had, and invested heavily and successfully in real estate.

Nellie's concern over money was reflected in her obsession for gambling. She loved playing poker, bridge, and whist for stakes, and managed to accumulate enough for a pin money fund. Her housekeeper called Nellie a "bridge addict" and said she "loved to have her friends in, even in the morning, to play a game." None outside her family and closest friends knew the extent of this, a sole newspaper reference to it being her playing it as a "scientific game" with partners who "take the game seriously." The only public reaction was that Nellie received two free packs of silk-finished cards from an admirer, who feared that "when you get down to governing, you'll not have so much time for cards."

Cards were just the start of the loot Nellie Taft gleefully bagged as First Lady. The Pianola Company sent her the piano she quickly accepted and used in the Blue Room. To cut dairy costs she announced that she wanted a cow to provide fresh milk, cream, and butter. "Mooley Wooly," a

Jersey cow from a New Hampshire farm, was offered by Hood & Sons dairy. "Mrs. Taft will accept the cow," Archie Butt scribbled on a memo, and Mooley arrived, was kept in the stables, and grazed on the South Lawn. Mooley died after a year and a half, but Wisconsin senator Isaac Stephenson, on behalf of his dairy state, bought a new cow, "Pauline Wayne," for her.[7]

Not only befitting the presidency but herself, Nellie's demand that the First Family have the latest technology of the automobile became a reality in her first weeks as First Lady. Although only the congressional appropriation of $12,000 was approved, Nellie got her four cars out of it. Primarily, the President used the first car, a Pierce-Arrow convertible in three shades of dark green. The black touring car, also a Pierce-Arrow, was used mostly by the First Lady and seated seven people.

Besides the two large Pierce-Arrow limousines and a White Steamer, she determined to get her own special car, a Baker electric Victoria, the smaller "runabout," which looked like a buggy. The day it arrived, April 24, the press reported how the First Lady "took her first spin in it, handling the levers and steering bar herself." Having taken driving lessons for about a month, she was called one of the capital's "most enthusiastic drivers." Such unprecedented independence—she was the first presidential wife to drive—earned her another laudatory editorial: "No greater contrast can be found between . . . a European court and the democracy of America than to see the wife of the President driving her own automobile in the streets of Washington."

As far as commercializing the presidency was concerned, she raised no protests and soon there were advertisements that showed the Tafts in a Baker or Pierce-Arrow, although there was no printed "appointment to the President" endorsement. Annually, she got her new fleet and was exacting in how they must be tailored. Referring to the color of upholstered cloth for her limousine's interiors, she wrote Pierce-Arrow, "the samples you sent are not TAN, which I specified in my letter to you, but BROWN." And because "Mr. Taft is so big" she wanted wider seats for his car. Nellie quite loved her cars. When she learned that the King of Siam owned forty cars, mostly Packards and Renaults, Helen observed, "Mama was quite indignant because he didn't have Pierce-Arrows."[8]

The fact that Nellie Taft played cards, drank and served alcohol, urged girls to go to college, supported "partial" suffrage, and, most of all, drove a car marked her as modern. "The telephone, coeducation, wireless telegraphy, motor cars, millionaires, bridge, whist, women's rights, Sherry's, cocktails, four-day liners, pianolas, steam heat, directoire gowns, dirigible balloons, and talking machines," author Francis W. Crowninshield wrote the same year as the Taft inaugural, "have all contributed to an astonishing social metamorphosis." This was immediately visible by the First Lady wearing women's suits that were raised inches from the ground to allow her rapid movement without having to lift the hem of a long dress, and evening gowns that form-fitted her bust and had square-cut necklines that revealed her skin.

Nellie quickly adjusted to spending her own money on lavish, stylish clothing. She never stepped out of the house without one of her signature cartwheel hats, the popular "Merry Widow" hat of the era, often loaded with ribbons and fake flowers. After she showed Archie her new outfits for her garden parties, he marveled that "I don't know any woman who dresses better or with more taste than she does. . . . [S]he will never be willing to go back to the old simple way of gowning herself."

While her gowns were usually in white, light blue, or light pink and embroidered in silver thread, Nellie's suits were usually in her favorite shade of violet, or gray tweeds, always with her trademark spray of violets pinned to her lapel. As for jewelry, she found a further trademark in diamonds always set in silver, particularly pinned on a collar of white silk and pearls or a regal hair clasp. Although she never wore spectacles regularly, she used a gold or an amber and diamond lorgnette at Will's speeches or at any of the performances she attended. Diamond rings, diamond bangles, and even a diamond tiara were usually part of her ensemble.

"[Y]ou have no idea how lovely she can look when handsomely

gowned with her hair well done," Archie observed. "She really looks ten years younger since she entered the White House, and I think she has become more gracious and kinder toward all the world." Indeed, it seemed as if having reached her goal, Nellie was finally learning how to relax, with which, said Butt, "she has always had a struggle." While she still had "contempt for herself" when anyone caught her being sentimental or even crying at the theater, "she possesses a nature which I think is going to unfold and enlarge itself as it adjusts to new and broader surroundings," the major concluded.

As for the President, other men made other predictions. "If he makes good, he will be renominated and re-elected! And if he does not make good," said President Theodore Roosevelt privately, "I'll come back in 1912 and take it myself!"[9]

Twelve

Blossoming

*She is uncompromising in all matters of honesty and where
principle is involved, and never deceives herself, and in
consequence never tries to deceive anyone else.*
—WHITE HOUSE MILITARY AIDE ARCHIE BUTT

The level of sophistication of the dinners, the wine, the champagne, the cigars, the musical entertainment, and the First Lady's gowns and diamonds combined with the fact that Nellie Taft was the worldliest First Lady up to that time all served a political purpose. That she had seen more of the globe than any past President, let alone First Lady, symbolized a level of international interest just when the United States was establishing its place among nations as a world power equal to the British and Japanese empires. To Americans such an unusual background lent itself to accepting more of the untraditional activities that the First Lady focused on in her first two months as she began to respond to national and civic issues.

After just a few weeks Nellie showed signs of boredom of the limitations of being merely a hostess. "We had two large dinners of 32 here, almost entirely Congressmen. They seem to enjoy them very much, but I find them rather stupid. The dinners are so long that if you get uninteresting people next [to] you (and it is arranged entirely according to rank) it is pretty hopeless."

As a Cabinet wife, Nellie Taft read about the McMillan Plan to create order and beauty in the nation's capital, to coordinate in an overall scheme the buildings, parks, districts, and monuments of Washington, part of the "city beautiful" movement then popular with urban planners. She had clearly been searching for a part of the city in which to realize her own vision of urban beauty. Her love of pomp and promenade combined with her egalitarian principals, made Manila's Luneta Park, where concerts were held for all classes, an ideal. As spring began in Washington, she set her sights on a muddy patch of land beside the Potomac River. A road had recently been cut there and was informally called "the Speedway," perfect for the growing number of car owners to drive their machines at top speed. Early on the morning of April 1 in her White House car—always getting the right of way and not being held to any speed limits—Nellie went alone to the Speedway "to look at it in the light of a possible Luneta." Upon her immediate return to the White House she bid Archie to "come up at once." He recalled:

> *I found her quite excited. She said that the thought had come to her. . . . I was surprised that no one had ever thought of it before. She was unwilling to discuss the matter with anyone else, but ordered the automobile and together we drove to the Speedway, and in less than one hour she had chosen the place for the bandstand, fixed upon the day to inaugurate the scheme, which is to be the fourteenth of April, and settled upon Wednesdays and Saturdays as the two days of the week for the concert. By noon I had given the orders from the President to Colonel [Spencer] Cosby [Public Buildings and Grounds Superintendent] to have the bandstand erected, and to the Secretary of the Navy for the Marine Band, and I understand to popularize the idea through the press. In consequence, everyone is looking forward to the opening. . . . [T]he method of putting it into effect is also hers.[1]*

Cosby's landscape architect George E. Burnap immediately drew up plans for the First Lady's approval. She already had a unique idea for how the area might ultimately look in the springtime—flanked by an "avenue" of pink and white clouds of flowering Japanese cherry blossom trees. It was not Nellie's original idea but one she quickly adapted from an idea in a letter from Eliza Scidmore. Scidmore, the only woman on the National Geographic board of managers, author of seven books on Alaska and Asia, and *New York Times* correspondent, had lived in and loved everything about Japan. For some twenty-four years she had tried to sell the Superintendent of Public Buildings and Grounds on the idea of planting the delicately beautiful Japanese cherry blossom trees known as Sakura when they were in bloom. A non-fruit-bearing variety of numerous genuses, they would grow well along the reclaimed swamplands beside the Potomac River. Eliza Scidmore and Nellie Taft had first met, briefly, in Japan in 1900. Scidmoore knew that a First Lady could get the cherry blossom tree grove planted with the snap of her fingers.

Seven months earlier, however, the U.S. Agriculture official and horticulturist David Fairchild, who had imported and planted cherry trees for his Chevy Chase home and about three hundred others in the area, had given local students a cherry sapling each to plant in their schoolyards on Arbor Day. He further suggested—and newspapers noted—that a "sakura-na" (field of cherry trees) be planted at the Speedway. Scidmore, in attendance, agreed. When the press announced the plans for Mrs. Taft's bandstand, public concerts, and landscaping in the area around it, Scidmore gave the idea to the First Lady, who replied on April 7: "Thank you for your suggestion about the cherry trees. I have taken the matter up and am promised the trees, but I thought perhaps it would be best to make an avenue of them, extending down to the turn in the road, as the other part is still too rough to do any planting. Of course, they could not reflect in the water, but the effect would be very lovely of the long avenue."

Mrs. Taft was working quickly. On the same day she wrote to Scidmore she had already met with Cosby's landscape gardener George H. Brown to discuss where the trees should be placed. Not only did she want the trees along the drive, but she wanted them to encircle the oblong greensward that cradled the bandstand at the south end of the drive, paralleling the Potomac. Cosby immediately scoured regional nurseries, and a total of about ninety cherry blossom trees were purchased for $106 from Hoopes Brothers and Thomas Company in West Chester, Pennsylvania. Within a week of Mrs. Taft's orders, the cherry trees were planted, in time for the second concert. On April 12, Nellie held a meeting with Eliza Scidmore and a Filipino friend, Mr. Legardo, who apparently had worked on the Luneta, to begin the next phase of her plan and get more trees. Coincidentally, famed chemist Tokicho Takamine was in town along with the Japanese consul in New York, Mr. Midzuno, when they heard this news. Takamine suggested they immediately offer the First Lady dozens of native trees. Midzuno agreed, further suggesting they be an official gift from the city of Tokyo. They got an appointment with the First Lady.

"How are your cherry trees getting along?" Midzuno asked her about those transplanted from the American nursery. "Doing well," she said, suggesting that she hoped to create a full park of them. Midzuno and Takamine mentioned the gift idea, and Nellie reacted excitedly. Tokyo's Mayor Ozaki was contacted and agreed to the idea. Midzuno wrote her on April 29 to say that "the formal notification will come from our embassy in the course of time. . . . [T]he trees can not and will not arrive in Seattle until some time next winter, to be planted in Washington early next year." Fairchild also offered to make a donation of imported trees—but those arranged by Takamine were the ones accepted, serving an obvious political purpose. Secretary of State Philander Knox and the Japanese ambassador saw tremendous symbolism in the gift that Mrs. Taft would learn in August was to total two thousand trees that were uprooted in the Tokyo area.

Nellie even pushed Congress to do its part. Will took Senator Penrose of the Finance Committee for a Speedway drive and let him go on some about why Taft must make a certain appointment. "Penrose," Will said with a smile, "what a beautiful park the Army engineers have made of this old bottom. I only wish Congress would be a little more generous and give to the Superintendent of Public Buildings and Grounds more money for further improvements." The Tafts received $25,000 in federal funds.[2]

Meanwhile, in the area just northwest of the Tidal Basin—where a chlorinated man-made bathing "beach" was in place—a canvas-covered wood octagonal bandstand, painted white, was being rapidly built under Cosby's direction. When the press reported that a temporary stand might have to do, Cosby was pushed—by the First Lady, it is safe to assume—to make sure the permanent wood bandstand was finished for her first concert and done up with flags and evergreens.

At 5:00 p.m., on Saturday, April 17, the first of Nellie Taft's Potomac Park public concerts began. Sentimentally, she had the Filipino Constabulary Band perform for the premiere. Led by her friend, the conductor Walter H. Loving, the program opened with a march, "The Flag of Victory," followed by the overture "Poet and Peasant." Seven pieces were played, including "Songs of the Philippines" compilation by native composer Escamilla and "Reminiscences of all Nations."

About ten thousand people were in attendance; they came by car, buggy, horseback, canoe, and on foot from a nearby streetcar stop. Earlier that day the *Washington Star* had announced the anticipated gift of cherry trees from Japan, and the novel experience seemed further enhanced by its future possibility. The Tafts drove in without much fanfare, Cosby and Butt, in black suits, riding their black horses beside the presidential car.

Its top was down, and the throngs got their first close glimpse of the new First Lady. Many came over to speak to her. Dressed in a black dress trimmed with white lace and wearing a large purple hat with purple ribbons, she did not disappoint, smiling and waving her white-gloved hand widely in acknowledgment of cheers as Will tipped his top hat. The First Lady, who had "worried herself almost sick" that no one would come, was flush with joy at such a "terrible crush," and Will lovingly smiled at her. Said Butt of the proud Nellie, "It was the result of her own idea and she has really provided a long-felt need here in the Capitol City." She officially renamed the Speedway "Potomac Drive."[3]

Not everyone was so pleased. There was a smattering of rowdy drunks creating trouble at the concert. The only seating for the public was that provided by one's automobile—which only the wealthier society crowd could afford. Finally a group of citizens wrote the First Lady demanding that seats be made available for the vast number of middle-class families that had not the wealth to own a car, as the upper class did, and were not rowdy and drunk, like many of the lower class. *The New York Times* concurred: "That the public is not expected to interfere with society's weekly meet was indicated today by the conspicuous absence of benches, or seats for . . . those who had plodded wearily the long distance to the affair." Alice Longworth complained that her fine clothes became windswept and sooty from the automobile fumes. At future concerts there were seats—and no Alice.

In the next few weeks the First Lady drove out to attend subsequent concerts, all by the Marine Band. The Wednesday and Saturday evening concerts continued through October. Mrs. Taft became a permanent fixture at the Tidal Basin.[4]

At the summit of her self-confidence and determination, happier than perhaps at any other time in her life, Nellie Taft began laying further tracks for an activist role in public affairs, drawing upon her own executive skills and opening her heart with a generosity to the masses in a way that she had rarely done. Whether embroidering a handkerchief for a Salvation Army auction with a handwritten note wishing "success for the venture" or donating a doll in a blue dress that she cheekily named "Alice" to raise Christmas funds for poor New York children, she fulfilled the traditional First Lady charity role. But she was eager to do more and to do it outside the White House.[5]

Mrs. Taft's interest in civic improvement had a larger context. With masses of American cities swelling with immigrants, as well as rural citizens moving into urban areas for employment, there was a rise in charitable efforts funded by private interests to meet increased educational, health, and welfare needs. Will was on the executive council of the National Civic Federation, serving as the Public Employees' Welfare Committee chair.

The foundation was already part of the fabric defining the Progressive era, from civic improvement to sanitary housing and working conditions, child labor laws, workers' compensation, immigrant education, corporate capitalism, and the churning machinery of mighty American industry.

An organization of the corporate establishment, yet with a genuine altruistic agenda, the National Civic Federation (NCF) was an ideal berth for both Will and Nellie Taft and what might be termed their "conservative progressivism." They believed strongly in their obligation as people of privilege to help those less fortunate, but not to press for radical or sudden change, no matter how beneficial it might prove to be for certain constituencies or even the President's own political popularity. If Taft did his part for the working man by continuing to reform industry through antitrust cases and by reducing the cost of household goods through the promise of reduced tariffs, Nellie would do her part within the context of a socially respectable organization like the NCF.

By the time Taft became President, the NCF was already deep into conducting research and lobbying for progressive policy reform. Its basic tenet was that the government must take the lead in creating public policy that met the growing needs of the nation's weakest and most vulnerable workers. Its founder, economist and journalist Ralph Easley, also saw it as the best way to combat acts of terror and the menace of a socialist revolution. In its broadest purpose it was a way to convince the nation that big business was not evil and could be counted on—through conservative reform—to support the unionized worker. With its judicious approach to "fair" compromise, with an emphasis on collective bargaining but absolute protection of property, the NCF fit perfectly with Taft's own philosophies. However, the NCF was attacked on both sides. The militant socialists, who believed it was a ruse to propagate capitalism, rejected it. The *Daily People* declared that the National Civic Federation was just "malignant" and referred to its "impotency and treachery." The National Association of Manufacturers, on the other hand, claimed that NCF advocated "the most virulent form of socialism, closed shop unionism."

As they had conducted themselves in the Philippines, much of what Will and Nellie sought to do through the National Civic Foundation was class-based paternalism. Should the suffering masses be "uplifted" at the charitable whim of the ruling elite? Was it genuine altruism that motivated John D. Rockefeller to work with Samuel Gompers of the American Federation of Labor, or a grand scheme to ensure that privileged status went unthreatened? Mrs. Taft's history of working with the musicians' union as well as her creation of postnatal care organization in the Philippines indicates, however, that she was not resigned to a permanent class system for anyone, and that there was opportunity to improve the quality of life for all people. Events were provoking issues that obviously would sweep up Will. What involved Will involved Nellie. During her tenure there would be labor tragedy, violence, and calamity—the Cherry Hill mining disaster, the Triangle Shirtwaist Factory fire, the Lawrence mill strikes. During the Taft years, Gompers's AFL membership would double to two million, primarily with immigrants and women.

Nellie Taft had no record of strident activism that in any way challenged the status quo. Still, her motivation to publicly involve herself in the National Civic Federation was a bold move and a complete departure from her past. It was one thing for society women to do charity work, but there was no history at all of a First Lady publicly associating herself with a national organization of public policy and some controversy.[6]

It was Nellie Taft who opened the National Civic Foundation's 1908 convention on the morning of December 15. Before a crowd at the Astor Hotel in New York, she made her first public speech on the working conditions of federal government workers. In inviting her to do so, Ralph Easley had written that her status would give the NCF "a great opportunity to put before the country the work of the Women's Department—not only the needs of industrial workers but the needs of public employees including the army, navy, and all public institutions."

The issue had come to her attention seven months earlier, when she was more absorbed in the machinations of Will's nomination. She had attended a meeting of the Washington women's committee of the NCF with

Mabel Boardman, who sat on the executive committee. There, Nellie heard Ruth Hanna McCormick point out that although the issues of the "working people" in New York were centered on sweatshops and factories, the equivalent problems existed in the nation's capital in the government department offices. Here, hundreds of workers of both genders and all races faced deplorable health conditions—no sanitary restrooms, dim lighting, and poor ventilation, no lunchrooms or even water fountains. At that meeting, Nellie had agreed to accept the post of an "honorary" vice chair of the Washington NCF branch, along with Mrs. Oscar Straus. As First Lady, Nellie Taft would now have the resources to make a difference on the issue. And she took to it with vigorous activism.

While the text of her speech is no longer extant, newspapers did report that she "proposed many additional reforms" to change the federal government's treatment of its employees. At the closing session of the NCF convention dinner, Nellie Taft sat beside Samuel Gompers, deep in conversation. Unanimously elected the honorary national chairman of the NCF's women's division, she accepted. As Easley put it to her, "The moral effect of having the working people of the country know that you are giving consideration to their welfare will be tremendous, and will be used not only by the press in this country but in Europe."

A week and a half later, after stopping in Washington, Nellie Taft went to Spray, North Carolina. She decided to make this stop herself because there were numerous cotton mills employing children in dangerous working conditions. "To evidence her interest in the movement," reported the *Washington Star*, "she arranged the first meeting in the South." There, with a Mr. Mebane of the NCF, Nellie visited a model factory welfare department, and the press noted that she was "deeply interested in this feature of the federation work." A meeting was then held in the Mebane home, where Nellie again "presided," among Virginian, Carolinian, and Georgian reformists, "to organize welfare work in the Southern States."[7]

As marked in the White House diary books of both Ike Hoover and Archie Butt, 11:00 in the morning on March 15 marked the First Lady's one-hour appointment with Mrs. Samuel Spencer of the NCF. That day

Nellie "promised to lend her efforts to the betterment of the conditions of working women" and announced her commitment to working locally, with the Washington branch of the Women's Division of the NCF. The announcement was made to anticipate a meeting of the local Bookbinders Union, with the news that the First Lady "promised to support the objectives of the bookbinders" for a demand for safer working conditions.

The initial result of the White House meeting was the plan for Nellie to visit "every department of the government" and investigate working conditions. Mrs. Spencer already had made an initial visit to the money- and stamp-making plants of the Bureau of Printing and Engraving, and a report was being prepared on the findings. The First Lady's stated support was already enough to prompt a promise from the new Cabinet secretaries to all "cooperate in the movement for the betterment of the condition of the women employed by the branches of the federal departments."

By indication of her follow-up four weeks later, the First Lady anticipated an active role. On Wednesday, April 28, she again met with Mrs. Spencer and a Mrs. Wainwright for two and a half hours. The next day they returned, bringing about twenty members of the women's committee, and met with Nellie for three and a half hours in the Red Room. It was too early to know how the public would react to the radical idea of a First Lady involving herself in labor policy–related concerns. Archie Butt, for one, did not approve. "If we can only keep her from making speeches and hold her down to the simple duties of First Lady, I shall be content," he wrote, "but I fear she has a leaning towards the betterment of the working class girl through the lecture platform."[8]

If Nellie was not bothered by any potential criticism of her involvement on such welfare issues, she was also overt in the political advisory role she now played for the President. Between her schedule of Civic Federation meetings, car "joy drives," as she called them, dinners, teas, luncheons, and theater and concert outings, the official schedule books had the unusual notations showing that the First Lady spent long hours over several days taking in U.S. Congress debates and votes on what would prove to be the earliest and most important policy issue in the Taft administration: the tariff. As Ike Hoover recorded for Monday, April 5, "Mrs. Taft at Capitol from 10 am to 1:30 & 2:30 to 5:00 pm," for the House debates on the tariff. Along with her sisters Eleanor and Jennie, Nellie sat in the first row of the Executive Gallery. Archie Butt was with them and made notes on how agitated the First Lady became when House Speaker Joseph G. "Uncle Joe" Cannon appeared on the floor. Like Will, like even Teddy, she detested Cannon because he proved to be a troublesome block to progressive Republicans:

> *Mrs. Taft was keenly interested in every move. . . . Since the Speaker was the author of the rules and was in so many other ways objectionable, she thought they should make every effort to defeat him and change the rules later. . . . She was quite excited and did not want to take time to go to the House café for lunch.*

In response to consumer concern for the cost of living, Taft wanted to rapidly fulfill his promise of a lower tariff schedule. Industry, successfully pushing them upward, was adamantly opposed. Taft did his best to fight their call for continued protectionism, but it would be a struggle for him to get through Congress any substantial lowering. Nevertheless, the day after he called on Congress for the "prompt revision" of tariff rates, New York Republican Sereno Payne sponsored a bill.

The New York Times made note of the fact that the First Lady returned four days later for two and half hours, watching the House vote, "perfectly quiet, evidently impressed with the importance of the occasion." The bill of tariff schedules passed with a final vote of 271 to 161, with petroleum products remaining on the "free" list after much debate. In the Senate, Nelson Aldrich, Rhode Island Republican senator and chairman of the Committee on Finance, followed through with his bill. Nellie Taft was back at the Capitol on April 26 from 1:15 to 4:25 in the afternoon, according to the White House diary, for "Senate debate on Tariff, Senator Bailey speaking."

In the White House, Nellie's focus on the first important effort of the administration was intense. Almost certainly she reported to the President nuanced details of both the effort to get rid of Cannon and the progress of the Payne-Aldrich Bill. His letters to her during the bill's progress are filled with minute intricacy, particularly on rates of individual materials. To one friend he even specified the "revision of the tariff" as a primary issue on which he was depending on her for advice. There is also the eye-witness account left by the chief usher of a typical White House tableau in the spring of 1909:

> *A familiar sight about this time was to see Speaker Cannon or Senator Aldrich . . . consulting jointly with the President and Mrs. Taft. Sometimes it was a conference of the four. But Mrs. Taft seemed always to be present and taking a leading part in the discussions. At large gatherings, principally social, different people would entice the President to a corner for the purpose of a talk on some subject. Failing perhaps to have had the time granted them through regular channels they would without exception be joined by Mrs. Taft immediately upon her discovery that such was the case. The conversation begun before her arrival would continue with her taking a full share in the discussions. . . . It was no uncommon thing to see Mrs. Taft taking part in the conferences and the deliberations . . . that were held for the political and official purposes they might have in the country.[9]*

Roosevelt had had Senator Henry Cabot Lodge as a political confidant and sounding board. Will had Nellie. She was his ultimate protector and remained vigilantly defensive of him, ever on the lookout for threats, real or perceived, to his political success. One night at dinner a guest mentioned to President Taft that a *New York Sun* article carried an interview with ex-President Roosevelt in Naples in which he said that if Taft didn't carry out his policies, Roosevelt would "return and put him aside." Archie Butt immediately said Roosevelt "never said any such thing."

"Oh, I don't know," Nellie said, breaking the polite silence. "It sounded just like him. It is just as well to recognize what has got to come sooner or later, and let people and papers like the *Sun* take sides."

Butt was stunned by the remark; it was the first time Nellie Taft betrayed her real feelings about Roosevelt to his former, devoted aide.

"She is very decided in her opinions and there is no sidetracking her when her mind is made up," he concluded. Archie confessed to his sister-in-law that he was still "unblushingly flying the Roosevelt colors" but had a growing attraction to Nellie. "I cannot but admire Mrs. Taft's honesty and directness," he wrote.

The new roles she assumed as First Lady, however, were consuming her. Will was elected. Politics had been the means to that end. Now she focused on making the most of that achievement for herself. "My very active participation in my husband's career came to an end when he became President," she reflected. "I had always had the satisfaction of knowing almost as much as he about the politics and the intricacies. . . . But in the White House I found my own duties too engrossing to permit me to follow him long or very far into the government maze which soon enveloped him." She evidently had not shared this feeling with Will. During the same period she wrote about, Will had confided to a friend that "with the troubles of selecting a Cabinet and the difficulties in respect to the revision of the tariff, I feel just a bit like a fish out of water. However, as my wife is the politician and she will be able to meet all these issues, perhaps we can keep a stiff upper lip and overcome the obstacles that just at present seem formidable."

If Will were to find himself in dire need of goading, Nellie would have given it. But he could soon ask for help only at the risk of threatening her health.

Perhaps as the weeks passed and some of her resentment burned off,

Alice Longworth had whispered to Archie Butt the silly story of her plant-ing an evil idol on the lawn, to curse the Tafts. He did record his supersti-tious fear that some kind of "hoodoo" had settled over the White House.[10]

"Mrs. Taft taken ill," the Chief Usher wrote boldly in his date book for Monday, May 17, 1909, underlining the words. It signaled something far more ominous than just another day in the White House.

▪

"I am very proud of the way Nellie has taken hold of things at the White House," President Taft told Archie Butt on May 12 as they drove through the rain. Indeed, despite her history of nervous tension, the new First Lady seemed to almost revel in her frenetic schedule.

Will was not the only one who took pride in the new First Lady. A far more objective *New York Times* gloriously praised her: "Mrs. Taft has done more for society than any former mistress of the White House" and her afternoon receptions were "the most successful and brilliant . . . known in all White House history." Nobody—not her children nor her husband nor her friends and sisters—would have wanted to dampen Nel-lie's excitement. And nobody, not even Will, seemed concerned about whether her increasing nervousness was excitement or anxiety.

One event more than any other, however, seemed to have triggered overwhelming emotions within her. On May 10, 1909, accompanied by Nellie's sister Eleanor More, a white-haired and bespectacled eighty-one-year-old man shuffled up the front steps of the North Portico of the White House. Once a Cincinnati lawyer, he had bounded up these same steps more than thirty years earlier when his friend Rutherford Hayes was Pres-ident. John W. Herron was returning to the White House, but this time the old mansion was in the family, ruled by his own daughter. It certainly trumped the mansions across Pike Street from the gray house where he still lived.

Helen Herron Taft left no record of her thoughts as she first wel-comed her father to her new home, the White House (he had been too ill to attend the inaugural). It certainly must have been an emotionally wrought moment. He had so long been a factor behind her drive to someday live in this place where he had first brought her in 1877 when they were overnight guests of Ruddy and Lucy Hayes. In Nellie's eyes John W. Herron might have become President himself—if only he had had the money of the Hayes or Taft families. In fact, he was now penniless, living on "loans" from her and Will.

Still, the fact that she had managed to fulfill her outrageous ambition and to far exceed the standards of anything the grand Harriet Herron could possibly have imagined must have given Nellie a deep sense of accomplishment. The "old gentleman," as she now called her father, was safely ensconced in the famous Lincoln Bedroom Suite. There being no formal dining facilities in the family quarters, the Tafts descended to the State Dining Room for their nightly supper; here John Herron presided at the head of the table.

Two days after her father's arrival in Washington, on May 12, Nellie ordered up her new White House touring automobile with the open seats and sat beside the "old gentleman." They were driven out of the black iron gates of the mansion and down near the riverside, coming onto the new driveway beyond the Washington Monument, flanked by a stiff row of the freshly planted cherry blossom trees. Certainly, taking her father to one of her Potomac Park concerts that night filled Nellie with pride. Already, one newspaper had called the musical series so successful that they alone were "enough to have made her famous."

Reporting to her eldest son about her father, Nellie noted that the "old gentleman" had finally "settled down now." After a few days in residence at the White House, she recorded that John Herron "sits in the grounds and on the portico, and [drives out in the car] some, but he is really quite feeble." In taking stock of just what sort of character the "old gentleman" was made of, Nellie decided that he was "inclined to overdo [it] at first." Like father, like daughter.

On May 11, the day after her father arrived, Nellie hosted the fourth of six formal dinners, a series to which every senator and congressman would ultimately be invited. May 12 was her park concert. May 13 was the fifth congressional dinner. On Friday the fourteenth, Nellie held the second of her four garden parties. The first one had been rained out, the decorations "sopping wrecks," and the entire enterprise rushed indoors. The weather held for the second, and male guests wore white suits, women carried parasols, and teenagers in tennis whites played on the clay courts. On Saturday, May 15, and Sunday, May 16, the First Lady would have some private time with the "old gentleman," and they would be joined by her favorite child, Charlie, who was home from the Taft School in Connecticut for an indefinite and not entirely welcome stay. He was having surgery to remove his adenoids early on Monday morning, the seventeenth.

The next morning—her fragile father in residence and her youngest son in surgery—Nellie was also overseeing the sixth and final congressional dinner to be held that night. In between the surgery and the dinner she would be hosting an informal cruise to Mount Vernon on the presidential yacht *Sylph*, another privileged experience to share with her father.[11]

Charlie went into Episcopal Hospital at ten in the morning for his surgery. Nellie was at his side, "looking pale and evidently worried," according to Butt. The boy was put under with ether, and the operation went well, though it lasted several hours. When he awoke, however, Charlie became hysterical at the sight of so much blood. Nellie had to calm him, but the scene upset her. She was fuming that Will had not yet arrived at Charlie's bedside, but the President was, as usual, running late. Exasperated when he finally arrived, they rushed back to the White House in time to change clothes and get down to the Navy Yard, board the yacht, and— with her sister and father and Archie Butt—greet their guests, including Attorney General George Wickersham and his wife.

On the Potomac River the air was thick and muggy. Nellie began to sweat profusely. At one point Wickersham turned to speak to her, and she did not answer. He turned away for a moment, and when he turned back to her, she had fainted.

The captain revived her with whiskey, and Archie got ice for her temples. The blood had drained from her face, but she came to. She said nothing. Archie wanted to get her to lie down on a nearby chaise longue, and she staggered to it, half-carried by him. The yacht was immediately turned back to Washington, a short distance, but the minutes seemed endless. Once docked they had to wait for the limousine. The ride back horrified Will. "No one could do anything, and she made no motion and did not seem to be more than half conscious," Archie observed. He carried the limp First Lady up the steps of the North Portico, passing the stunned, silent African American valets in livery. He guided her through the door she had entered boldly weeks earlier, down the Cross Hall, and to the elevator, which whisked her up to the family quarters.

The state floor, meanwhile, was buzzing with busy servants; they were preparing for an official dinner less than four hours away. Luckily, Eleanor More was willing and able to substitute as hostess for her sister that night. She quickly decided what to wear and was ready to descend the grand staircase on the arm of Will, in his tuxedo. The presence of one of the Herron sisters seemed to steady the terrified Will throughout the dinner as he went through the motions of laughing, smiling, and eating—and assuring guests that Nellie was simply exhausted from the day's activities. Archie had urged this fib because it would "humiliate her [Nellie] terribly to feel that people were commiserating with her." Scheduled to depart early the next morning for Petersburg, Virginia, and then head to Charlotte, North Carolina, he was further convinced by Archie to keep to his schedule or else it would publicly suggest the seriousness of the First Lady's illness. Unsuspecting congressmen, senators, and their wives made their way out onto the West Wing terrace, enjoying Nellie's champagne punch after dinner and the balmy air of an early May night. Their enjoyment made the night "all the more ghastly" for the President.

Just one flight above the party on the terrace, pacing through the presidential bedroom, Major Matthew A. Delaney of the Army Medical Corps had already taken immediate charge of the First Lady. For the next sixteen hours, without any sedatives, she would lie motionless in a deep sleep.

All of this must have been especially painful to the gentle old man who had been the impetus of Nellie's early life, but John Herron left no record of his reaction to his daughter's sudden collapse. There had to be some irony, certainly at least to Eleanor More. For so much of her life the articulate, intelligent, and outspoken Nellie Taft had been driving herself and Will to this pinnacle to, in part, somehow redeem all that her father had sacrificed for his family. And now the First Lady of the United States, this powerful political partner of the President, had suffered a stroke that had rendered her utterly speechless.

Thirteen

The Stroke

To be stared at is not pleasant because it keeps one self-conscious all the time.

—NELLIE TAFT

The First Lady's indisposition made the front pages of newspapers across the country the morning after she was stricken. It had come out in a press statement released by the White House that further suggested her absence at the congressional dinner was simply a matter of exhaustion, a result of her hectic spring activities: "The excitement, heat and exertion were too much for Mrs. Taft's nerves. . . . The doctor says that after a few days of complete rest, Mrs. Taft may be able to resume her social duties." Unknown to the public, the President had carefully composed the statement himself.

A day later an even rosier picture was painted, the entire incident chalked up to "excessive heat." It was claimed that she was resting so easily that "she expects . . . to receive her guests invited for next Friday's at-home as usual," and a weekend voyage to Hampton, Virginia, was "expected to aid greatly in re-establishing Mrs. Taft's shattered nerve forces." She made no such voyage. When she failed to show at the following week's Potomac Park concert and White House garden party, the press realized she was far from well. A newspaper headline reading "Mrs. Taft Can't Greet Guests" came closest to the truth, but the public was never to know just how severe the illness was.[1]

Will revealed to Bob what was known of her medical condition:

You know she has had these attacks which seem to proceed from nervous exhaustion, and in which her heart functionates [sic] very feebly. It is not an organic trouble of the heart, but it seems to be some nervous affection. . . . She did not lose consciousness, but she did have a very nervous attack, in which for the time being she lost all muscular control of her right arm and her right leg, and of her vocal chords, and the muscles governing her speech. . . . Dr. Delaney . . . gave her some stimulant for her heart which was very weak. . . . She recovered some control of her leg and arm, but she has not yet been able to speak. Of course, these symptoms were very alarming, because they indicated paralysis—that is, a lesion in the brain. The doctor soon reassured us all, and her as well, because she could hear all right, that there was nothing of this kind—that it was a mere attack of nervous hysteria rather than a bursting of a blood vessel in the brain, which is true paralysis. She slept well last night, had a good appetite, and slept well all day today.

In fact, based on Nellie's inability to speak, it seems that the doctors may have either misdiagnosed her condition or mistold the President about it. Evidence suggests that Mrs. Taft's brain was affected, that a blood vessel had broken there and the effect was "aphasia," the partial or total loss of the ability to speak, a result of a small stroke.

As soon as Nellie awoke from her long slumber and realized what had happened to her, she reverted to form, refusing to give in to any weakness. "Her old will and determination asserted itself today," Archie wrote of the day after the stroke, "when she arose from the bed without warning and attempted to walk." Will's going on with his schedule seemed to throw off the press from learning "the serious side of her illness entirely." She was able to make audible sounds within three days, but not words. Less than two weeks after the stroke, Helen arrived home, her spring Bryn

Mawr term finished. She soon joined her aunt Eleanor in reading constantly to Nellie, so the First Lady could, however slowly, practice learning to speak again by repeating the words. Helen wrote of the rapid progress—and the continuing media cover-up:

> *She gets up every day and walks around upstairs a little but doesn't*
> *attempt to go downstairs yet. She talks a little better each day but*
> *she can say very little unless she repeats after you. She can repeat*
> *almost anything and can read out loud quite fluently though not*
> *very distinctly. But her improvement is quite noticeable and the*
> *doctor says it is merely a question of time and rest and practice until*
> *she regains her speech entirely. We have managed to keep it out of*
> *the papers that she lost her speech at all, as she is very sensitive about*
> *it for reporters are getting around already.*

Anxious about making a perfect impression as First Lady when she was well, Nellie was now mortified over her speaking problems. Still, she was determined not to miss White House life entirely. The day before her forty-eighth birthday she made her first, brief appearance in front of others at a private ceremony where Will turned a key that opened the Alaska-Yukon-Pacific Exposition in Seattle. She was escorted to the elevator, walked the hall on Archie's arm, and sat in the front row before a group of seventy-five Cabinet, diplomatic corps, and congressional officials. Attempting to speak or respond to greetings, however, would betray her secret. Apparently it did not go well: Eight days later she did not go down again when Will presented the aviators Orville and Wilbur Wright with Aero Club gold medals. She even tried to avoid the servants, going into the halls only when no one was there.[2]

Each morning the family doctor checked on the First Lady and tried different therapies on her, reporting the progress afterward to the President. In early June, for example, he experimented with a machine that applied electricity to her throat, "in order to facilitate the return of the control of the muscles and nerves governing vocal expression."

For the President the situation was doubly upsetting because he so relied on his beloved wife as a sounding board. Although he had fought for a congressional appropriation extending his summer western tour to include Alaska, he withdrew his request on June 5, Helen said, because "Mama could not go with him and it would worry her to have him go without her." Instead he would go to the Pacific coast and then rush back to Washington. His confidence on passing the tariff also flagged. "The tragedy," Archie wrote, "has entered his administration." In front of Nellie he "laughs all the time and tries to amuse her," but the sight of her paralyzed attempt at a smile "unnerved" him, "his great soul . . . wrapped in darkness over the continued illness of Mrs. Taft." At the season's last garden party, although Archie and Eleanor More kept up the charade about Nellie being nearly recovered, Will disclosed the extent of her incapacitation to some of the guests. Upstairs, Nellie sat at her open bedroom window, sadly watching the festivities below. "We then came to what might be called the administration of four years of strife," the chief usher put it bluntly. "Mrs. Taft's illness from almost the very beginning put a damper on things generally." Hoover also noticed that over time Will's uniformly considerate treatment of the servants eroded into unpleasant ordering about.[3]

The effect of the stroke on Will's relationship with Nellie was more complex. At times, he had depended on her as a child does on a mother. In those moments of quiet desperation, such as the situation he had found himself in when serving as interim governor of Cuba, Will needed to know that Nellie was there for him, even if he ultimately did not call upon her. Now, there was no way he could count on her as he formerly had without further jeopardizing her precarious health. At the same time, he could not show panic, for then she would likely feel compelled to do something to help him, and end up all the more frustrated because she really could not.

Initially, this seemed to leave Will with a sense of being trapped, in terms of facing the tough choices a President must make. There was no escaping total responsibility, not just for his decisions and successes, but also for the inevitable public criticism that would come to a President. At first, except for occasional lapses into bitter sarcasm, he would just learn to act as if it did not upset him. Yet it was obvious that he was in his own world of frustrated pain: Throughout the following months, he gained exceedingly unhealthy pounds of fat from gross overeating to the point that he would become the only dangerously obese President of the United States. While no medical records document the long-term effect of this, modern science makes plain that there would have been inevitable damage to his heart. Certainly he must have felt some rage at Nellie for getting him into the presidency, for promising that she would be there for him, and for not being able to be there for him—and most certainly he would repress it, only leading to bouts of depression.

Yet his devotion to her well-being overrode all other instincts. He treated her gently and lovingly. He wanted nothing brought to her attention that could upset her. If she insisted on something to the point where Will could detect that it was important to her, he seemed perfectly willing to acquiesce as long as it did not affect the public good. Over time, with Will now taking the part of the parent in control of a willful child, he began to realize that he was quite capable on his own as President. While it made him exceedingly happy to have Nellie's support on a public issue or decision, it was not really necessary. As he grew into his presidency, Will Taft became independent of Nellie's advisory role—to the point, actually, where it may have damaged his chances for a second term.

Nellie Taft had always excelled at the details of public presentation and scrutinizing the human motivation behind the games of politicians. In contrast, Will remained loathe to see the negative in anyone—most especially the man he loved as a mentor and to whom he felt loyal obligation, Teddy Roosevelt. It was the one issue that Will would continue to defy Nellie on: There was no way that Roosevelt would ever double-cross him, Will would insist. It turned out to be the one issue that he shouldn't have defied her on.

As for Nellie, she seemed to be in a state of perpetual frustration. On the one hand, she had always managed to rise above any setbacks and serve as the great filter on Will's decisions, a sort of salve for his political battles, and certainly a harsh judge of his every public utterance and appearance. She could not simply rise above a stroke, however, regardless of how mild it was. For the first time since she had married, Nellie Taft had to somehow look inward and find the strength to do something she had never done: Detach herself from Will's fortunes and stay calm no matter what crisis he found himself in. She would attempt to do this in fits and starts and succeed only partially—until she was struck down in health again.

Nellie Taft had not fought to get herself and her husband into the presidency just for the sake of getting there. Throughout her years abroad and the transition period, she had awakened to a deeper sense of social responsibility. She knew her husband to be rational, fair, and honest. She had every great hope of being a partner to a great and good presidency, perhaps not as flashy a tenure as Roosevelt's (and certainly not as meek as his wife's), but one that made a definitive improvement in American life nonetheless. Now, there was nothing but uncertainty and seeming defeat. How could she play an active role either in public or with Will when she had trouble simply communicating and was immobilized by her disability?

As Helen told Bob, Nellie "gets pretty depressed about talking. She can say almost anything by herself now if she tries very hard but it seems to be such an effort that I hate to make her." She wanted no sympathy, Helen urged and yet warned Bob, "Mama seemed to think you had better not [visit]. It seemed to disturb her frugal mind . . . [but] come down here for I'm sure Mama would be glad to see you in spite of what she said." The family hoped that two months of summer rest would restore her.

In March, Nellie had made a trip to Massachusetts's North Shore to look at summer homes with Mabel Boardman. When word got out that there was to be a "Summer Capital," she was besieged with letters, blueprints, photographs, and testimonials from homeowners and civic associations boasting of their properties and locales. She finally settled on a home on Woodbury Lane in Beverly, renting it for $2,000. Nearby were the summer homes of the Boardmans, Hammonds, and Longworths. It set off a realty boom; rentals went up 20 percent and two large hotels were planned.[4]

If citizens, tourists, and renters thought they would be regularly rubbing elbows with the First Family, however, they were sorely disappointed. Will, Nellie, Charlie, Helen, and Eleanor arrived by private train car on July 4, but at the President's orders no speeches were made at the train station and they were whisked away to the house. Nellie remained in seclusion, the house surrounded by Secret Service agents. Two days later the White House issued a statement that Nellie "will not entertain or be entertained." Will left the next day, via Boston, to return to work. Every slight movement of Nellie was watched—an auto trip, a sea voyage to Gloucester—the press even reporting "Mrs. Taft Much Improved" when Eleanor and her husband, Louis More, made an overnight trip away from Beverly.

Life at the Summer White House was uneventful. Nellie pored over her monthly magazines with Eleanor. She took up German language studies again and was "quite enjoying it." Her mental faculties were fine; her right arm had fully recovered, and with slow care she could write fairly legibly. She had a good attitude. "I saw Mrs. Stanley Rome the other day and she and I compared notes about how lonely we were," she wrote Robert. "Her loneliness, however, has been complicated by sinus trouble this week so she is worse off than I am."

Still, she was embarrassed by her speech problem. Around the servants Nellie fell silent, depending on Eleanor to give instructions. "I am tolerably well and you see how I take to this word. I do not like this thing of being silent, but I don't know what else to do about it," she wrote to Will in July. "The doctor insists I will get well, and says that it is a long time to do so. Eleanor is well. She takes so much interest in what the doctor is doing that it amuses me."[5]

The only unexpected benefit of her condition was that the First Lady had a public excuse to skip Sunday religious services. According to Will, she felt few activities were "as stupid as going to church." Since her youth she had disliked windbag ministers and made light of her irreligious ways. "I have been to church," she had written four weeks before becoming First Lady, "and this being somewhat unusual, feel very virtuous."[6]

Nellie's sustenance, as always, was political intrigue. Initially, Will thought news would agitate her and withheld it. After dictating a letter to his brother detailing the minutest of his tariff negotiations with her in the room, he added that she "got more information by listening to my letter to you than she has gotten out of me for the last three or four weeks." Realizing his letters would help them both, he was soon writing her endlessly detailed letters on his ongoing tariff battle when they were separated. In one he gave her just the opening she was looking for. "If I had more of a technical knowledge," he confessed to her, "I should feel more confident." As in days of old, she began bucking him up: "With renewed trust that you will come through the tariff all right." . . . "I will breathe easier when you get this tariff finished." . . . "How interesting all your talk[s] about the tariff are. I see today that you made a statement as to what you were going to stand for. I hope you won't have to back down on it." . . . "This morning I got your letter full of tariff talk, and I hope you will come out of it well."

Will's letters also had annoyingly frequent references to the one Washington couple that he rarely saw when Nellie was in the capital. Alice Longworth first came to dinner at the White House on March 16, 1909, and she never seemed to leave. Nick and Will maintained their friendship based on not only personal but politically expedient ties. While it was true that Alice was a representative of her father, her connection to Will went deeper. Their affectionate friendship had continued to grow. Although she delighted in flouting protocol, when Alice discovered that Nick had gone to a stag White House dinner in an informal linen suit, she was enraged that he so insulted "Dear Mr. Secretary" (as she still called President Taft) and made him apologize. According to Archie, her "indignation" at Nick was "not feigned, for she is truly fond of Mr. Taft and will not allow any criticism of him in her presence."[7]

In early July, although Alice and Nick had been right in Beverly near

Nellie, they had not called on her, left their card, or made a telephone call as a sign of welcome. It was different with Will, however. "Alice Longworth and Nick have returned from Beverly," he wrote Nellie on July 11, "and Alice has invited me over to dine at their house sometime during the week." He accepted. Several days later they dined together again at the French embassy, Alice arriving after the President, ignoring protocol. Will merely laughed when she came in with absurd apologies. "Alice, if you will only stop trying to be respectful to me I believe you would become so." She shot back, "And then I would bore you to death as the other women do." In reality, said Archie, "the President enjoyed himself very much, especially the vivacious conversation of Alice Longworth. While he does not approve of her, he simply delights in her wit and her brilliant repartee."

And it went on. Three days after the embassy dinner, Will informed Nellie that he was hosting a private White House dinner for Nick and Alice—and even Teddy Roosevelt, Jr. That night Will told Archie Butt that, given the unlikely chance that Longworth would win reelection, he "wanted to take care of Nick and Alice before they were humiliated by defeat. I do not care so much about Nick, but she is Roosevelt's daughter, and I always want to look out for Nick on her account. I would like to give him a mission abroad if they would like it, or I would make him Governor of Puerto Rico, and what a queen she would make there! Until she got tired of it! Or I would send him to Cuba. . . . I shall sound Alice at the first opportunity as to what she would like in the case of an emergency." Four days later Will wrote Nellie that he had eaten at the Longworth table yet again. It was probably at this dinner that Will talked to her about what ambassadorial post she'd want Nick appointed to, for Washington was soon gossiping that the Longworths were poised to leave for Peking, China—a place that intrigued Alice.

On July 28, the President, Archie, and others, including Alice, went out to Fort Myer, Virginia, to watch the breathtaking sight of Orville Wright soar in his airplane for upward of fifteen minutes per flight. Cabinet members, Senate leaders, society folk, and government workers alike crowded the field to witness the historic exhibition. Alice was there every day, running a secret bar. Friends nearing her open car were invited to have lemonade—only to find out it was spiked with gin. When she saw Will, she told him that his latest portrait made him look pudgy. "But I am pudgy," he told her. "Not as pudgy as that, Mr. President, and I would not have it." It was more backhanded flattery, which Will fell prey to easily.

From Nellie's perspective, the fact that it was Alice who celebrated the first Taft political victory with the President was the last straw. During the day a message had been sent to the President from congressional conferees requesting him to capitulate on his position on lumber and gloves tariffs. Will responded firmly that he would not approve the higher duty on gloves that had been contained in the Senate bill, nor permit lumber to carry a duty of more than $1.25. He had earlier managed to bring it down from the $4 duty the House had originally proposed and would not now give it up. Congress buckled. That night at a private dinner "Alice Longworth fairly danced before the President in her delight," Archie recorded.

The First Lady knew that Archie Butt was a strong bond between Will and the Roosevelts. He had even visited Edith Roosevelt in Oyster Bay and revealed all the details of Nellie's illness to her ("She thought it tragic," he noted). He also wrote Teddy about it, adding that Will was too optimistic about her condition, "and I dread the awakening for him." Had she known about Archie's revelation to the Roosevelts, Nellie would have been appalled. Archie's indiscretion went further when, in a letter to Roosevelt, he quoted Taft's promise to Nick and Alice: "I want them to feel that they can have any post in my power to give and whenever they want it." This much Nellie would soon learn herself.

Nellie ignored Will's constant nattering about his doings with Alice by simply not responding to it. After one more of his unctuous remarks about Mrs. Longworth's great ability and wit, however, Nellie let loose with a jealous cut. "I read all the accounts of your dinners," she wrote, and then added a rhetorical but sarcastic question about the wondrous Alice's many talents. "I wonder whether *that Alice* 'does it all'!" There were no more letters about Alice.[8]

The President signed the Payne-Aldrich Bill on August 5. It cut only 5 percent off the overall rates, but ultimately 650 tariffs were reduced. It also saw other rates rise on 220 items such as iron, coal, and hides. More than 1,000 tariffs were unchanged. Democrats and western progressive Republicans, called "Insurgents," claimed it was no real reform, but Taft considered passage of the bill a success for his administration and left for Beverly.

Making some marital amends, he devoted his afternoons to Nellie. Their mutual affection was evident; reporters even witnessed him kissing her. Each morning he played golf, and the day he broke one hundred, Nellie was so proud that she went up and openly kissed him in front of onlookers, "a mark of great favor from Mrs. Taft," said Archie, "because she is not demonstrative as a rule in public." When Nellie protested that the children were using the White House limousines too frequently, Will calmed her. "Let them have a good time while they can. In four years we may all have to become pedestrians again," he told her. "I want them each to look back upon this portion of their life with the keenest relish. They are not children to be spoiled by a little luxury now." His love of Nellie was in great evidence that summer. When someone told him that the "New Thought" movement then being espoused by Christian Scientists taught people to rely on themselves and might benefit his wife, he quipped that Nellie "must have tried the New Thought years ago, for she was about the most self-reliant person" he had ever known.

Not all of the summer was pleasant, however, especially within the Herron clan. First, John Herron suddenly succumbed to an illness that, although unstated, was serious enough to make him permanently bedridden. Then there was the embarrassing newspaper story that the First Lady's brother Will, a lifelong Democrat, was not only running for vice mayor of Cincinnati but had not voted for Taft in 1908. Eleanor's husband, professor and scientist Louis More, went to Beverly to cajole

Eleanor into returning to her own family. He was becoming irritated at his wife for returning to her sister so frequently and was finding his own substantial scholarly reputation overshadowed by his famous relations. Eleanor took a break with him in Maine but would not leave Nellie's side until the fall.

In the evenings the President reviewed with the First Lady the decisions and issues that crossed his desk. "He sits with her and talks," wrote Archie. It was at such a conference that Nellie Taft influenced a decision that would prove to be irreparably damaging to Taft's political life. Will had not made an official announcement about appointing Nick as minister to China while he was in Washington because the tariff consumed nearly all of his attention. It was only while he was in Beverly that he focused on it, and like all his diplomatic appointments, he discussed it with Nellie. It was from Beverly that it was announced that the new minister to China would be Charles R. Crane.

Nellie made no effort to mask her veto power. "She told me that Nick had asked to be sent to China and was willing to resign his seat to accept the mission, but that she simply would not have it, as she thought neither Nick nor Alice fitted for this post," Archie Butt recorded. "I suppose the President put it on different grounds, but the real reason for his refusal was the opposition made to it by Mrs. Taft." To Alice it was jealousy, pure and simple.

How was it that Taft did not stand firm on the Longworth ambassadorship when he knew how important it was to maintain goodwill with the Roosevelt interests? Certainly he and Nellie had argued over any number of issues, and despite her strong disagreement or protests, if Will felt strongly enough he would do as he wished. While Taft left no record of the Longworth incident, either one of two factors came into play: Will Taft privately agreed with Nellie but would not verbalize it, yet found her "bad cop" reputation an easy excuse to explain the decision, or Nellie was so persistent in her veto that Will might have feared that denying this to her might raise her stress levels and jeopardize her health. Indeed, Nellie

Taft's insistence that Will withdraw the Longworth appointment proved to be the first and most personal in a series of what the Roosevelt camp took as high insults lobbied at them from the Taft contingency. Whether intended as insults or not, the new friction would eventually fissure the Republican Party and change the course of American political history.[9]

The second insult came three weeks later. Before President Taft left for his two-month thirteen-thousand-mile trip to the West Coast, his fanatical conservationist chief of the Forest Service, Gifford Pinchot, publicly rebuked him. A Roosevelt appointee and close confidant of the former President, Pinchot called on Taft to fire Interior Secretary Richard Ballinger. Pinchot alleged that Ballinger had committed improprieties in allowing private interests to buy huge Alaskan coal fields. Taft refused to do so, and Pinchot attacked him for backing Ballinger. Will raged to Archie Butt that Pinchot had no concept of collegial work; as President he would "not stand for such insubordination as he has been guilty of." Will determined not to fire Pinchot, however, because he believed that was just what the Forest Service chief wanted in order to create a breach between Roosevelt and Taft loyalists.

From the road Will kept Nellie informed of the Pinchot-Ballinger situation and other matters. On his western tour the President angered Democrats and Insurgents alike when he declared that the tariff bill had been "the best" ever passed by Republicans. The remark was ridiculed as a sign of Taft's naïveté; it would be used by Democrats a year later, in midterm elections, resulting in the loss of the Republican House majority and making it difficult for the administration to initiate legislation. Whether it was interstate commerce, railroad regulation, corporation and income taxes, or conservation, the President poured every detail about his western speeches and the public reaction to them into his letters to Nellie. Writing to her on October 3, Will fired off his first private attack on Roosevelt, saying he and Pinchot, "have more of a socialistic tendency." The remark was music to her ears.

That Will was so explicit with his wife also made the news. Reporting that the President sent telegrams about the progress of his tour to the

First Lady, *The New York Times* added that he "has interspersed the daily messages by wire with long letters detailing the most minute happenings of his trip." When he met with Mexican President Porfirio Diaz, Will only half-jokingly asked him if he thought that either of their wives "know to what extent they affected the affairs of the public." Taft went so far as to say that while Nellie "appeared to interfere very little" in the presidency, none was as conscious as he "as to what a factor she really was." He confided to Diaz "it was largely through the influence of Mrs. Taft" that he had forgone the Supreme Court for the White House.[10]

If the fact of the First Lady's political influence garnered coverage, there was not widespread public knowledge of the specifics, such as the Longworth veto. In the arena of what was still considered the traditional prerogative of First Ladies, however, she was vulnerable. When Nellie returned to the White House with Eleanor on October 16, she found herself publicly criticized when the White House announced that alcohol would be served during its upcoming social season.

The issue had been brewing for nearly a year. In her post-election *Ladies' Home Journal* interview, Nellie made it clear that alcohol "will be served at dinners" and lied when she claimed that she "personally does not use wine." The issue thus focused on alcohol being served in the mansion, but the public was never to learn just how much its First Lady enjoyed drinking. From her teenage diary to letters at the end of her life, Nellie's writings are peppered with references to her taste for alcohol. "There was a very fine punch," she reported after one tea, "strong enough to make your hair curl." Just four days before she returned to the White House from Beverly, she reported to Bob that prior to going to lunch and a matinee she went "to the hotel for a cocktail before starting out. It was very good fun." And the First Lady wanted to make sure that no liquor she paid for was left behind. When a lieutenant from the *Mayflower* found some bottles of wine onboard, he was instructed to "please send them to Mrs. Taft."

The *Ladies' Home Journal* article had unleashed a flurry of signed petitions, protest letters, and editorials. "I do not know whether you are a

Christian," pondered the author of one letter to the First Lady from the United Presbyterian Manse in Argyle, New York, further wondering if she "realized the terrible influences" she was having "on our entire American world." The Ohio Women's Christian Temperance Union hoped that as one "of our most thoughtful, progressive people" she would follow the Lucy Hayes example of banning all spirits. Twenty thousand Pennsylvania Women's Christian Temperance Union members petitioned Will; they were happy that at least he would not drink. It did no good when it came to influencing the First Lady.

The controversy had subsided with the First Lady's May illness, but an autumn newspaper article headlined "Punch Bowl Reappears" prompted a concerted national lobbying effort by prohibitionists. "Just now you are in a position where your influence is so great, won't you please throw it on the side of good," one person wrote in response to the story that Nellie's "champagne punch" would be served to the diplomatic corps. The First Lady's policy was not to ignore the sharpest protests and respond to the rest simply by restating Will's campaign stand that prohibition was best left as a local issue. The protests of an Indiana women's group finally prompted an editorial defense of Nellie's right to make her own decisions: "Doubtless Mrs. Taft ... will receive patiently and graciously the demands. . . . If she obliges them to the extent of banishing wine from her table, they may as well ask her to dismiss her man cook and do her own housework." The controversy would flare whenever articles such as "Refreshments . . . One of Mrs. Taft's Innovations" appeared. Not only would she never relent, she would take fiendish glee in her defiance of the drys. "The musicale went off very finely," she would write Bob early in the next year. "I had champagne at it!"[11]

In the White House waiting for Will's return, the First Lady resumed her speech therapy sessions. "I have my 'Instructions,' a person that I have got to come in and talk," she wrote Bob. "We read articles and then I try to tell her about them. It is very slow work though." She took odd pride in the latest diagnosis from a Johns Hopkins specialist. "He says it is not paralysis at all, but something weird which strikes people now and then. It is very safe to know it, but I wish it would strike other people now and then."

When the President finally returned home on November 10, Nellie was eager to renegotiate her summer promise to a complete rest from any official tasks. She had been making brief public forays. On October 20 she attended the last of the year's Potomac Park concerts in her car. Some Cabinet wives and close friends made short calls four days in a row at the end of the month. Nellie even made a four-day excursion, a private shopping trip, to New York, returning on November 6. Will, however, discouraged her from resuming her former active role. Her doctors had told him that if she insisted on taking part in public life in the coming months, they would release themselves from any responsibility of a feared relapse. She had greatly improved, and now she wanted to take up her activities as First Lady again.

"Now, my dear, you have agreed to retire for this season—"

"—I don't care," Nellie interrupted him. "I am going to have a voice in this household."

Obstinate in moments of vulnerability or insecurity, she was invariably won over by Will's loving understanding. When, for example, she refused to invite former President Harrison's daughter Mary McKee to dinner because she had once been rude to Nellie ("I have not forgotten it"), the President coaxed her to change her mind. If her judgment was questioned by others, the First Lady got "on the defensive" and simply responded with a cool "Well!" refusing to explain herself, but Will could often get her to change her mind, observed Archie Butt. Ultimately she "still objected" to being socially inactive but admitted she would "have to yield." Eleanor More went home to Pittsburgh after seven devoted months at her sister's side. Sister Lucy Laughlin arrived and assumed the role of White House hostess, presiding at a state dinner on December 16.

The First Lady's routine now had her down to breakfast at 8:30, after which she returned upstairs to have her hair done and work on correspondence until 11:00. After lunch she would "go right to work" with her pathologist. "I read some article every day, because at three o'clock my 'instructoress' comes, and I talk with her about it. It takes me an hour, or something over, to do that." As her regular physical exercise, Nellie took a daily brisk walk, accompanied only by Lucy. Avoiding at all costs any person she might be expected to give more than a few carefully rehearsed words of greeting to, Nellie walked "down [a side] street usually, because I meet loads of people if I go the other way [on a main cross street]." She was still embarrassed about her speech impediment.

Yet she would not be left out of things entirely. She insisted on joining a voyage to Norfolk for a presidential trip but remained on the yacht with her doctor while the official party deboarded for public activities. When she joined Will in New York, she stayed at his brother's home while Will gave a speech, then joined him for Christmas shopping. Sometimes her eagerness to enjoy her brief moments in the sun failed miserably. After insisting that she sit onstage while Will addressed some ten thousand Methodists, her appearance in a pink satin gown with slits "for such a strait-laced meeting" was deemed inappropriate, so she took a wrap. Throughout the speech she sat onstage tugging on her wrap "to keep the flesh underneath from peeping out at the bishops."[12]

The Tafts' first White House Christmas was a peaceful day, the children home to join their parents for turkey and mincemeat pie. The next day, like young lovers, Will and Nellie took an hour stroll through the quiet snow-filled streets, the Secret Service following at a discreet distance. The enforced rest had cost Nellie her trim figure, and it would be a year before she regained it, but some pedestrians thought that she looked robust, "a contradiction of the numerous reports about her ill-health." At the annual New Year's Day reception, 1910, some of official Washington got a closer look at the First Lady in her white satin gown. In flat shoes, managing to repeat a routine greeting—but clutching a bouquet of lilies of the valley to avoid handshaking—Mrs. Taft stood to welcome the diplomatic corps and congressional leaders for nearly an hour before retiring. She had hoped to withstand the entire day but simply did not have the strength.

The state of her health distressed her enough, but she soon got more depressing news from Colonel Cosby. The two thousand cherry blossom trees, a gift from the mayor of Tokyo, had arrived in Seattle from Japan on December 10. The next day Mrs. Taft had signed her approval of Burnap's new landscape design, expanded to include the two thousand trees. The trees arrived in Washington by train on January 6. Two days later, examination of the trees on the grounds of the Washington Monument revealed that the roots had been severely hacked and the trees were in danger of dying. Eleven days later a USDA inspection team discovered that the trees were so deeply infested with wood-boring worms and other insects that fumigation would not help. Mrs. Taft's cherry trees would have to be destroyed. On January 28 they were all burned.

On January 8 another of Nellie's sisters, Jennie Anderson, arrived to serve as hostess for the five large official dinners of the winter social season. Fine foods and wines were served, conversation sparkled, and the best music was played. Unknown to the guests in gowns and diamonds, and white tie and tails in the State Dining Room, however, behind a screen that blocked the jarred door of the smaller Family Dining Room sat the First Lady who had planned it all, eating the same meal and listening in. "It makes her feel less lonely," Archie poignantly recalled, "and she never has anyone appear with her on these occasions." Only when alone with Will did Nellie dine in the state rooms. These tête-à-têtes were bleaker. On one occasion Archie found "as lonely a picture as I have ever seen." Next to each other on a sofa in the Blue Room sat Will and Nellie, she "wan and pale," and he asleep.[13]

Nellie Taft's parents. Classmate of President Harrison and best friend of President Hayes, lawyer John Herron (left) was equal to the presidency himself, but had to work unceasingly just to support his eight children. Lonely for marital company, nervous, demanding daughter of a congressman Harriet Collins Herron formed a romantic friendship with widowed former President Hayes, whom she stands behind. Next to her is daughter Eleanor; seated in front of her is daughter Lucy. (*Rutherford B. Hayes Presidential Center*)

ABOVE: Resembling the White House, the "Taft Mansion" was incorrectly assumed to be owned by Will and Nellie Taft–a fib propagated on campaign postcards. In this picture, Nellie Taft is under the central awning with other women on Notification Day in the background. Will speaks to the crowd in the center, foreground. That day, she could look across the street to see ...the cramped row house (left) where she was raised with seven siblings. *(Library of Congress; Recollection of Full Years, 1914)*

Not wanting the same type of life as her mother, teenage Nellie
Herron determined to become a self-supporting, working woman—
but also to become First Lady. On vacation with friends in Newport,
she (seated far left) wrote in her diary that she'd probably end up a
single woman because the men she met weren't intelligent enough for
her. At her salon of friends who gathered to debate economics,
literature, politics, and philosophy, she fell in love with an enlightened
man who respected her independence—Will Taft: he is seated, center.
Nellie Herron is seated at far left, her sister Maria is standing behind
her, far left; Will's brother Horace is seated at far right. *(Craig
Schermer Collection/National First Ladies Library National
Historic Site; Library of Congress)*

Nellie Taft managed the family finances and raised her first two children, Bob (at right) and Helen, essentially alone; Will was largely absent from home as a circuit court judge. *(William Howard Taft Birthplace)*

As president of the Cincinnati Symphony Orchestra (which she helped found), Nellie Taft learned business management, advertising, fund-raising, and labor relations. *(Taft Papers, Library of Congress)*

En route to Japan, 1900. Nellie Taft made no secret of the fact that Charlie was her favorite child, lavishing unabashed affection and attention on him. He became her sole confidant in widowhood. *(Library of Congress)*

As the wife of the Philippines' U.S. governor-general, Nellie Taft was a crucial factor in convincing Filipinos to accept American implementation of education, health, and social services. Besides racially integrating all of her events at the presidential palace, she also created a postnatal program to stem the high infant mortality rate. Here with Filipino students, Nellie is third from left, Charlie at center, and Will at far right. *(Schermer Collection/National First Ladies Library, NHS)*

Nellie Taft (second from left) and her sister Maria (far left) were the first white women to explore the northern Luzon territory of the Philippines. A fearless adventurer with a passion for exploring new cultures, Mrs. Taft honored and respected the native culture and customs of the islands. *(Recollection of Full Years, 1914)*

As a cabinet wife, Nellie Taft pushed Will toward the 1908 Republican presidential nomination and away from his dream of being appointed to the Supreme Court, doing all she could to get President Theodore Roosevelt behind Taft's nomination. Openly acknowledged as political partners, they are seen above in Will's home study. Responsible for overseeing the Panama Canal's construction, Will brought Nellie to inspect it—complete with his and her guides (below). *(author collection; Harper's Magazine, 1908)*

During a 1905 junket to Asia, War Secretary Taft chaperoned Alice Roosevelt, the world-famous daughter of the President (second from left). They became close friends, despite her dislike of Nellie Taft. On the trip, Will was alarmed by Alice's open flirtations with his friend Cincinnati congressman Nicolas Longworth (in top hat, far left), who married her in the White House in 1906. *(Burr McIntosh photograph, Library of Congress)*

In one of the first political cartoons portraying the political influence of a presidential candidate's wife, Nellie Taft is shown as coming from Minnesota to give Will that state's support for his 1908 nomination as a Valentine's Day gift. Less amusing were the anti-Catholic attacks on Taft, who was parodied in this cartoon as a pope while Roosevelt parades before him as a crusader. *(author collection)*

Roosevelt (left) and Taft (seen here on Taft's inaugural day) were genuine and affectionate friends, but Nellie predicted that "Teddy's" ego would drive him to challenge Will for the 1912 nomination. When President Taft finally forced himself to publicly criticize Roosevelt, he broke down in tears. *(Library of Congress)*

Inauguration Day 1909 realized Nellie Taft's life dream to become First Lady. Relishing the chance to create a new tradition, she rode next to the President in the inaugural parade, the first First Lady to do so. The event became a symbol of her activism to the press. *(William Howard Taft Birthplace, National Historic Site)*

The first public project fostered by a First Lady, Potomac Park was created by Nellie Taft as a place for citizen promenades, drives, and concerts—all to be outlined and shaded by blossoming cherry trees she ordered planted there. The first of the trees are behind the bandstand. Tokyo would donate 3,000 cherry blossom trees to fully landscape her park. The Tafts arrived for the first concert in April 1909 in the new limousine Nellie Taft insisted upon having for her use. *(William Howard Taft Birthplace, NHS; Schermer Collection, National First Ladies Library)*

After her stroke, Mrs. Taft was initially unable to speak. Her family (encircling her at the summer White House) helped her to practice reciting to regain her speech. *(author collection)*

Initially, a speech impediment inhibited the First Lady's public interaction but on those occasions at which she was absent, she was either listening from behind a screen off of the State Dining Room, or watching a lawn party (at which the President acted as host alone) from her open upstairs sitting room window, located above Taft's head in the picture at left. *(Library of Congress)*

Seated beside Senator Henry Cabot Lodge as the only woman on a dais of political figures, Nellie Taft's primary political role in her husband's administration was in reviewing and listening to his policy and campaign speeches. Charlie smiles behind her. *(Pilgrim Monument and Provincetown Museum)*

Besides smoking cigarettes and drinking beer, champagne, and hard liquor, the First Lady (seen here with Will and two aides) also gambled for small stakes at bridge and poker. *(Library of Congress)*

The Tafts ascend the gangway for the August 1910 dedication of the Pilgrim Monument in Provincetown, Massachusetts; the day was an important turning point for Nellie—her first appearance at a day-long series of public events since her stroke. *(Pilgrim Monument and Provincetown Museum)*

The happiest day of Nellie Taft's tenure as First Lady was her silver wedding anniversary, celebrated in a massive White House lawn party, lit up by electricity, at which the Tafts received hundreds of silver gifts. Seen here are members of the Taft and Herron families gathered on the South Portico for the party. Standing, left to right: Robert Taft, Maria Herron, Will Taft's brother Horace, Helen Taft, Will's brother Harry, and Charlie Taft. Seated, left to right, are Jennie Herron Anderson; Nellie Taft; Will Taft; Will Taft's maternal aunt Delia Torrey; and Harry Taft's wife, Julia. *(Library of Congress)*

Standing behind the President: military aide to Roosevelt and then Taft, Archie Butt would find his loyalties conflicted as the 1912 election got underway and drowned with his companion, artist Francis Millet, on the S.S. *Titanic*; Alice Roosevelt Longworth, whose dogged devotion to her father turned her against her "dear Mr. Taft." *(Library of Congress)*

ABOVE LEFT: Both baseball fans, Will and Nellie Taft attended opening day in 1912, an event symbolizing the end of *Titanic* mourning and start of Will's aggressive campaign against Roosevelt. Taft threw out the first baseball on opening day in April 1910 at a Washington Senators game, starting the presidential custom. *(Library of Congress)*

ABOVE RIGHT: Flanked by Democratic friends Mrs. Mack and Mrs. Francis, Nellie Taft was the first incumbent First Lady to attend a national presidential convention and the *only* one to attend that of the opposition party. *(Collier's, July 13, 1912)*

Will and Nellie (seated, second and third from left) in retirement with family at Murray Bay. When Will finally became Chief Justice in 1921, Nellie created a separate life. As his heart disease progressed, she put her globetrotting plans on hold to care for him until his death in 1930. *(Seth Taft)*

Of all her successors, Nellie Taft (second from left) shared mutual interests with worldly Lou Hoover (third from left). Along with Elsie Grosvenor, wife of the National Geographic Society president (fourth from left), Nellie also attended numerous educational films, lectures, and concerts. (Supreme Court Chief Justice wife Antoinette Hughes is at far left.) *(National Geographic Society)*

The former First Lady attended the 1940 Republican national convention in Philadelphia with her daughter Helen when her son Bob, a senator, was an unsuccessful candidate for the nomination. Nellie publicly defied Bob when she signed a 1941 petition demanding Republicans allow a vote on FDR's lend-lease bill. *(William Howard Taft Birthplace, NHS)*

Fourteen

Return of the Comet

*I am bound to say that his [Roosevelt's] speeches are fuller of the
ego now than they were, and he allows himself to fall into a style
that makes one think he considers himself President.*

—WILLIAM HOWARD TAFT

The greatest stress and distraction that President Taft experienced
and that ultimately damaged his administration was due to Mrs.
Taft's condition. Archie Butt said, "[A]s the weeks go by and
there does not seem to be any permanent improvement, his hope sinks
pretty low at times." After a Sunday afternoon when she had happily gambled at cards, Charley Taft warned his brother that such occurrences
would be politically damaging if leaked to the press. "I will not forbid anything," Will responded, "which gives Mrs. Taft any amusement and takes
her mind off troubles."

"Gradually," Will revealed to Roosevelt in Europe, "she has gained in
strength and she has taken part in receptions where she could speak a formula of greeting, but dinners and social reunions where she has had to talk
she has avoided." At "safe" events the First Lady made carefully orchestrated appearances. She sat in the Blue Room nodding to diplomats at their
reception, and after a February dinner she materialized for a moment before coffee-sipping guests in the Green Room. As always, Will nervously
hovered. At a March 11 musicale, for example, he escorted her into the
State Dining Room to see guests, careful to grasp her right, weaker side.

Nellie's sisters were equally devoted to her. When Lucy Laughlin, who had come to help Jennie, had to leave in March to look after her depressive husband, Eleanor returned. When they were away, Nellie felt discomfort. "It is hard when you have not some one to fall back on," she wrote Bob. She was terrified of being left alone in a crowd. After sallying forth with Will at a spring 1910 garden party, she recalled, "I became separated from your Father, and had, after a time, which was pretty awful, to get ahold of Captain Butt and go into the house." Still, she took pride in even the smallest gain. Carefully seated to be seen at only a distance at a building dedication, Nellie noted, Andrew Carnegie "paid me a compliment. He said from the platform that he was so delighted to see me out and doing again."

Nellie acted as if all was well, but the facts painted a bleaker picture. Ike Hoover recorded:

> She was unable . . . to ever take her place again, properly, in the affairs of the White House. . . . As time went on there were material signs of improvement, but never were [was] there even a partial return to the spirited and unusual doings that we planned. . . . This condition was a severe burden during the entire four years, not only to herself but those about her. . . . Especially so as time went on and her physical condition improved only to leave her awkward in her speech and other slight deficiencies. It was with the greatest care and tenderest labor that she was in any wise permitted to the rightful place in the doings of the household. . . . [H]er peculiarities were pointedly noticed by all. Numerous were the occasions when the President especially was embarrassed. . . . [Her] affliction was principally in the region of her throat and affected her speech. It was very hard, almost impossible at times to understand her. She seemed mentally affected also for [she was] so different from what she had been prior to the affliction. . . . Unfortunately as she improved she insisted upon taking her place at the head of affairs when it was so clearly evident she was in no condition to do so.[1]

The First Lady remained equally persistent in controlling all social aspects of the house. When her secretary Alice Blech left in April to get married, the press hoped Nellie would reconsider the role of social secretary and hire a young matron able to focus on "persons of a certain class" and "recognize by name and sight the thoroughly accredited members of polite society." They seemed to be pining for the days of Edith Roosevelt when the upper class and "smart set" were made to feel as if the White House was their privileged dinner club. The position of social secretary had quickly developed on the Washington scene. Many wealthy political families wanted someone to direct their social functions and make certain that the important people were invited to their homes—and the unimportant ones left off their guest lists. The job was best filled by one of the city's numerous young, unmarried socialites who were high on breeding but low on cash. No social secretary position was thought to be more powerful and prestigious than the one found at the White House.

Instead, however, Nellie hired tall, blond Mary Dandridge Spiers, a Navy Department clerk who lived in a boardinghouse. She reported to work at nine, took an hour for lunch, and left at four-thirty like other government workers. Nellie alone decided whom to invite to White House events.

At Will's insistence, nobody was invited more often than Alice Longworth. Her name appears as a constant on guest lists for dinners, receptions, and musicales. When Alice did call on Nellie, it was as a congressional wife, not a friend. "Alice is really wonderful," Butt mused on her "art" of insult. "The only person she cannot entirely placate is Mrs. Taft. The President is as much under her influence as any of the rest of us. He gets dreadfully put out with her at times and then comes around completely when she is nice to him. . . . She makes a mistake in not placating Mrs. Taft, as she underrates her influence with the President."

Neither did Nellie placate Alice, who remained irrationally jealous. "The reception to the Diplomats last night," wrote Archie Butt, "was pronounced by everyone, save Alice Longworth, as being the most beautiful reception ever held in the White House." Frankly, he said, Alice was "green with rage" that Mrs. Taft hadn't asked her to receive guests in the Blue Room. "She is very angry," he wrote, "and while I cannot agree with her openly I think as many do that she should have been asked to do so. After all it was her home for eight years. . . . But I think it very bad taste in Alice to talk of it as a slight and show her resentment as she is doing. She and Mrs. Taft do not like each other and Mrs. Taft cannot dissemble her feelings. Nick says never a word and is discretion itself but he cannot keep Alice quiet when she has anything to say." As the link between the Roosevelts and Tafts, Archie now recognized that they were on the brink of estrangement and that the schism between Nellie and Alice could have political consequence. He felt that Alice's unwillingness to mask her feelings "only gives the faction which is trying to bring about a rupture between the President and her father an opportunity to make a great many ill-natured remarks."[2]

There were other signs of a split in Will and Teddy's friendship in the first half of 1910 after the former President's comrade Pinchot so brazenly defied Taft. Will still believed that Pinchot *wanted* to be fired in order to have a pretext for accusing Taft of being anti-Roosevelt. Will did not want to make Pinchot a martyr or alienate Roosevelt. He held out as long as he could—so long that many thought it made him look weak and indecisive. On January 7, 1910, Taft finally dismissed him, with a legally reasoned statement of Pinchot's insubordination. Pinchot ran off to Europe to confer with Roosevelt. To the paranoid or the astute it seemed that Pinchot was trying to poison Roosevelt against Taft.

When a friend posed the far-fetched scenario of the former President running for a third term, Will seemed cowed. "I don't think he will want to, but the country may demand it of him; and if he does, he will most certainly be elected." Taft had "not heard from him" and was as uncertain as everyone about just what Roosevelt would do when he returned to America. In late spring, as plans were made for Roosevelt's welcoming ceremony on his return, Will impulsively decided to greet Teddy. Butt made him see that it would appear as if he was "trying to placate Mr. Roosevelt, if the latter has been disgruntled with him for any cause." Besides, as Roosevelt's assistant said, "It will be a T.R. day and there will be no other note sounded."

If he didn't want to seem to be placating Teddy, he certainly did so with Alice. A large facet of politicking has nothing to do with policy and everything to do with personality. This was the dynamic in which Alice Longworth's antagonism toward Nellie, but also her affection for Will, played out. "The Roosevelts believe that the Tafts are in the White House solely as a result of their father's predetermination to put him there. The President agrees to this, and he thinks he has done everything in his power to pay that debt," Archie wrote. "From his standpoint he has shown every honor to Alice and Nick, and in Mrs. Taft's condition it was not possible for her to do more in the way of entertaining them."

Clearly Will had let the Roosevelts and Longworths know—most likely through Archie—that it was not he but, rather, Nellie who had insisted that he rescind Nick's nearly certain ambassadorship to China. What he failed to recognize (and what must surely have made Will seem stupid to the Roosevelts and Longworths) was that he could not blame the First Lady for what was ultimately a presidential decision. He had chosen to please Nellie above Teddy.

No matter how much Alice resented the fact that Nick didn't get the ambassadorship, she could not quite bring herself to openly deride or otherwise belittle the First Lady to her face. It was not just that she cherished her access to the White House and the President of the United States, she also wanted to remain personally close to Will. Alice grew jealous when he focused on other women, such as opera singer Mme. Luisa Tetrazzini. "Alice Longworth accused him of having a flirtation with her," recalled Archie. She enjoyed not only the shock she caused when she smoked in the White House but the knowledge that the President protected her. Will's reactions were always more like a finger wagging than a reprimand.

If Alice feared losing her access to the President, Will feared losing his connection and standing with Teddy if he provoked Alice's disapproval in any way. He knew that however seemingly she was enamored with the social world, Alice was a political operative, and her remarks bit all the harder at foes of her father. "There is always a sting in Alice's wit," he remarked. After her tantrum about Nellie not asking her to receive at the diplomatic reception, Taft rushed to invite her to a judicial dinner as consolation—without telling his wife. "Do you think it will pacify Alice?" he asked Archie Butt. In order to please Alice, and thus Teddy, Will was willing to undermine Nellie.

For now, Alice and Will doted mutually, but the oversensitive President's fear of confrontation and criticism was leading to depression. He continued to overeat and approached the four-hundred-pound mark; a mammoth bathtub had to be installed in the White House to accommodate him. "I get rather tired of hearing from his friends that I am not carrying out his policies," the President growled about the complaints of congressional Insurgents whose loyalties had remained with Roosevelt, "and when I ask for one instance they cannot name one." Taft never publicly voiced or leaked his view to the press.[3]

If talk that the increasingly powerful Insurgents were plotting against him hurt him, Will was in for a ruder shock when he spoke on April 14 at the Arlington Hotel gathering of the National Woman's Suffrage Association Convention. He had been cheered when he first entered the hall and was introduced. When he stated that the "unintelligent class" of women was unqualified for "self-government" and not until the majority of women wanted suffrage should it be granted, the President was booed and hissed.

At a presidential speech a month later, when the First Lady made an appearance onstage, Will led her to the podium and introduced her as "the real President, my wife." It got immediate applause and laughter. Mrs. Taft's well-publicized interest in politics did not translate, however, into any public belief that she could or would convert the President to supporting immediate national suffrage.

Ever since her famous inaugural ride the press had sought to tie Mrs. Taft to the movement to give all American women the right to vote. "Mrs.

Taft Sets Suffrage Pace," the *Washington Star* had headlined their story. An article that was published during the 1908 campaign about Miss Helen taking part in a mock political event behind the slogan "Let the Women Vote" said it was done so "in deference to the supposed sentiments of Judge and Mrs. Taft."

There was good reason to suspect that Nellie supported suffrage. In a curious listing of the First Lady's opinion of who were "the greatest women the world has produced," Nellie showed a breadth of interests. The only contemporary figure was scientist Marie Curie. All except one had made professions for themselves in politics, literature, social reform, education, medicine, religion, music, astronomy, art, and abolition. Two felt that their work would be more respected if they appeared to be men. Interestingly, however, particularly with the issue of suffrage so divisive in American life at the time, she also chose the most famous of suffragists, Susan B. Anthony and Lucretia Mott.

During the campaign Mrs. Taft had made her first statement on suffrage. She obfuscated her belief in the right of women to vote by making the right of a woman to run for office part of her definition of suffrage, attempting to please both the pro- and anti-suffrage public. "I am not a sympathizer with the woman suffragists," she stated blankly, "for though it may be all right for women to vote, I do not believe in their holding office. We are not ready for women to vote, as not enough of them take an interest in political affairs, and until the majority of women want to vote they will scarcely be given the right. I do not question that they should have the privilege of casting a vote, but it seems to me that they should not hold office, as that forces them to neglect other duties that they cannot possibly shift to others." As First Lady she held firm that it was "impractical" for women to hold office just yet, but her belief that women were ready to vote was firmer. "I favor bestowing upon women every civic right," she said. "I can see nothing unfeminine in women casting the ballot."

Nellie further clarified that she was a "limited suffragist." She opposed the concept of "universal" suffrage, favoring instead some national exam that would prove a potential voter's aptitude with the views of political candidates and issues. She was quick to emphasize, however, that she wanted this applied to men, as well as women. She believed that both genders must inherently "possess equal political rights," and did not favor "universal suffrage for either sex." As had her seemingly dichotomous freedom from racial and religious bigotry yet categorizing of all peoples by their levels of education, intelligence, and achievement, her notions on suffrage were based on class judgment. So strongly did she feel on this point that, although she would headline a prominent suffrage gathering to show her general support, she would later join an anti-suffrage association when no effort was made to adopt the provision she favored.

Nellie Taft had always been wary of formally joining women's organizations. While she had sat on a women's board at the Cincinnati Symphony, her work tasks in the capacity of president of the organization were conducted largely with men in business, advertising, and organized labor. Having been accepted by men in business and political circles, she felt no natural draw to efforts on behalf of the female masses. There was also the stinging example of the one time she had sent a letter to an organization of Serbian women involved in political and social reform among their people.

The Serbian women had asked her to support the American branch of their group. She politely declined and wished them good luck. Her response was misconstrued as what Will called "sympathetic expression with Serbians in general." As Nellie recalled, "I was proclaimed the warm friend of the young State and an enemy to all her enemies." Considerable publicity ensued and angered the Austrian-Hungarians, who read it as a shift in American policy. The ambassador registered a complaint on behalf of his government. The Secretary of State responded that Mrs. Taft had not intended to "express any opinion as to the difficult issues arising out of the Balkans." Finally, recalled Nellie, "it took a bit of the suavity of the State Department to extricate me from the tangle in which my alleged active participation in the trouble in the Balkans had placed me. It taught me a lesson." Indeed, she would no longer respond to any politically active women's groups pleadings that she support their petitions.[4]

If the Serbian incident was to falsely suggest to the American public that Nellie Taft was interceding in State Department policy, printed suggestions that she had a direct role in the staffing of the executive offices provided only a superficial glimpse of her quite real imperious tendencies in the West Wing. In June 1910, the First Lady found herself in a political context in the press again when it was announced that the President's secretary, Fred Carpenter, was being "promoted" to ambassador to Morocco. "When Mrs. Taft expressed disapproval of things in general or in particular," a newspaper profile of the secretary read, "Carpenter's teeth chattered. . . . Had Secretary Carpenter possessed as strong a champion in Mrs. Taft as Mr. Loeb had in Mrs. Roosevelt, it is quite likely that he would have found his pathway smoother and would not have fled to Morocco." A forty-two-year-old bachelor art collector, Carpenter had first worked for Will in the Philippines. Leaving his San Francisco home, he loyally followed his boss around the globe, but enduring Nellie's demands tested his quiet politeness.

Whether it was having him fetch "dress goods" from her bedroom bureau and sending them rush delivery, wiring money to her children, or her excoriating him for beckoning the servants and chauffeurs too soon from Beverly, Mrs. Taft treated Carpenter shabbily. "What arrangements have you made for getting us home? Does the car come here, or in town? What time does it come here? In time for supper? Or do we get supper somewhere else?" she condescendingly fired off in one missive. No matter how much he did for her, he just seemed to annoy the First Lady. "We have had Carpenter and Uncle Jack for meals," she complained in one letter. "Carpenter went with us to the theater every time." Mrs. Taft was a prime factor in his leaving.

"It seems that they think aides were made for the role of domestics," Butt wrote of the Tafts. "I remember seeing Major Noble when he returned from the Philippines and he certainly looked cowed and hacked. I have heard that Mrs. Taft did not hesitate to skim him well if he did anything she did not like." When Butt recommended that Will's friend General Edwards deal with Nellie's automobile demands, he was "quite short about her." Edwards grumbled, "I expect to make no more suggestions to her. You get no thanks for anything you do."

As Archie had predicted, she "in a short time" had "not only . . . the White House but the offices as well entirely under her control." Nowhere was Nellie Taft's freedom from societal expectations of feminine demeanor more evident than in her dealing with the executive staff. Her word was as final with them as the President's. "Mrs. Taft played a prominent part in framing up the affairs of the Administration," recalled Ike Hoover. "Her influence and weight of position went even into the office side of the Administration." Nellie could always frighten the President's mousy but loyal stenographer Wendell Mischler, but she would find a challenge in charismatic, ambitious Charles Dyer Norton, who replaced Carpenter.[5]

Owner of a Chicago insurance firm, Norton had been made Taft's assistant secretary at the urging of Treasury Secretary Franklin MacVeagh. Married to the wealthy niece of *New York Post* publisher Oswald Garrison Villard, Norton seemed just the man Taft needed. Carpenter's softness was a liability, Norton's aggressiveness an attribute. One thing Nellie must have found attractive was his open antipathy to Roosevelt. She felt that Will was still too trusting of the former President, and Norton's attitude would certainly back her own. What she had not counted on, however, was Will being pushed around by Norton. Recalled Ike Hoover, "[Norton] declared himself as Assistant President, all with the approval and sanction of the President." Butt thought Taft "talks most freely with him, far more than he would to some of his Cabinet." When Norton demanded higher protocol status, the President immediately gave it to him.[6]

Spring brought other changes more personal to the lives of the Tafts. In March there was a great tragedy surrounding the death of Thomas Laughlin, the chronically depressed husband of Nellie's youngest sister

Lucy. The first press report stated the cause as cerebral hemorrhage, but Nellie told the truth to her son: "In the morning he was found in the cellar. He had put a bullet through his head. They tried to hide it but it was no good." Nellie could not bring herself to attend the funeral. Then came the news that her father was dying. This time the First Lady quickly got herself to Cincinnati and the bedside of the "old gentleman." After nearly two weeks at death's door, however, John Herron seemed to rally, and Nellie returned to Washington, not sure whether she would again see her father alive.

There were some light moments. Like many Americans, the Tafts were gripped by news of Halley's comet; visible that spring it came only once every seventy-five years. On May 23, Will, Nellie, and Charlie went to the Naval Observatory "to see the comet," but after two hours of looking through telescopes, she concluded, "It was not very much." Two weeks later Will and Nellie took a "joy ride" to glimpse it from the countryside— while arguing over her refusal to invite more guests to a dinner because she would have to order more chickens; she thought the guests were too lackluster to justify the extra cost. "We can invite the comet," Will quipped, "which does not have to be fed chicken," cracking her up enough that she relented.[7]

Something far less amusing was on the horizon. In New York Harbor on June 20, two days before the First Lady left for Beverly, a naval fanfare, two Taft Cabinet members, cheering fans, and Archie Butt welcomed Teddy Roosevelt home from Europe. At Archie's urging, Will had written welcoming letters to Roosevelt, one sent to him in England and another that Archie handed to him in New York. To the first, an invitation to the White House, Teddy responded from London asking "to let me defer my answer until I reach Oyster Bay." In the interim, Butt pushed Mrs. Taft to write Mrs. Roosevelt and emphasize the invitation because then, he explained to Will, "you and Mrs. Taft have left nothing undone, and it can never be charged in the future that there was the slightest discourtesy toward Mr. or Mrs. Roosevelt from the White House." Nellie grudgingly did so. Privately, however, Archie had little hope it would persuade Edith to bring Theodore down to the Taft White House. "I don't know that it will be altogether welcomed," he wrote his sister-in-law, "for when women get at cross purposes it is hard to get them straightened out again."

Upon his arrival, Roosevelt was hero of the hour; newspaper columns were crammed with details of his adventures and triumphant return. Once he was home, however, Edith pulled her husband aside and showed him the letter from Nellie—a woman she had never criticized but never particularly praised, either. She also evidently exerted her influence on him, for Teddy soon after wrote to Will that although his invitation "touches me greatly, and also what Mrs. Taft wrote to Mrs. Roosevelt," he didn't "think it well for an ex-President to go to the White House."

If the Tafts took the Roosevelts' rejection personally, they might have found comfort in the reaction of several men who knew and loved Roosevelt well. Senator Lodge, Navy Secretary George Meyer, Roosevelt's secretary William Loeb, and Archie Butt all felt Roosevelt was strangely different. After some discussion Archie said that they agreed it was "an enlarged personality . . . capable of greater good or greater evil." He showed a mean streak even toward his Taft-loving son-in-law. When *Outlook* magazine, which Roosevelt wrote for, ran a questionnaire that seemed to have an anti-Taft slant, Nick Longworth asked his father-in-law to please disavow it. Teddy and Alice's reaction was to "laugh very much." Nick felt further belittled when Alice told him that her father had said he was a child "in the game of politics."

When Butt sat with Roosevelt, he told him about Mrs. Taft's illness and "how she dreaded to see anyone whom she had known in the past." Roosevelt "made no comment either then or anytime." Former President Roosevelt said about President Taft only that he had "heard much" that "distressed" him but would make no public comment for at least two months.[8]

Nellie didn't care what Roosevelt thought of Will. She settled in Beverly for a quiet summer. Will did not come until a week later but dutifully wrote her about a River and Harbor Bill, antagonism from Insurgent senators, and his statement on labor boycotts that he feared would anger unions. Two days after Nellie had gone, however, he invited Alice to dinner. "Tell her to bring Nick and her cigarettes," he told Archie, hoping the dinner invitation would somehow melt any frost between him and the former President. Will decided it was better not to raise the question of any resentments her father might have toward him. And Alice never did. Finally, on June 30, days after Will arrived in Beverly, Teddy finally paid a "friendly" and "private" call.

Roosevelt consciously readied himself for the meeting. He asked his longtime friend and ally, Massachusetts senator Henry Cabot Lodge, to accompany him to the meeting on the condition that he not say anything to Taft that Roosevelt didn't want to say and to make absolutely certain that he wasn't left alone in conversation with Will. Once they went up the steps and onto the wide wood veranda of the summer White House, it was clear to Teddy that he had no reason for such concern. There was Will with their mutual friend and liaison, the loyal Archie Butt, as well as Taft's "assistant president," as Ike Hoover sarcastically dubbed Charles Norton. The five men gathered together in the back portion of the house, an enclosed porch that overlooked the water at Beverly. They were chatting amiably about the New York gubernatorial race when the First Lady of the United States made her entrance.

Knowing Mrs. Taft, Roosevelt did not seem at all unprepared for her orchestrated drop-by at this "friendly" and "private" call. In fact, he had probably anticipated it. Roosevelt, said Archie, had been "primed not to ask Mrs. Taft any questions, so he did the talking which put her very much at ease." Without Nellie's knowledge, Roosevelt knew just how vulnerable her illness had impaired her—courtesy of Will. The former President expected the incumbent President's wife to be so self-conscious of her slight speech impediment that she would sit silently throughout the visit. Instead, she managed a few choice words for him.

The conversation began with gossip about the power machinations of the European monarchs, King Edward of England and Kaiser Wilhelm of Germany, and then evolved into an analysis of the English and

German naval buildups. President Taft raised the subject of an international peace conference; he had wanted Roosevelt to head it. "No, no, I wouldn't take it," Teddy said, backing away. Then he chuckled. "Why not name [Andrew] Carnegie? He would certainly finance the commission, and if you could seal his mouth so that he would not be talking about what we think and so on, he might do fairly well."

At this—after a brief pause for her to gather her words—the First Lady spoke up with crisp clarity for the first and only time during the meeting in a gently confrontational rebuke of Teddy Roosevelt: "I don't think Mr. Carnegie would do at all."

It was a miracle Roosevelt didn't start sputtering. He had been effectively shut up by a woman who, though perhaps lacking the vigor of earlier times, had not lost her capacity for manipulation. He immediately changed the subject, led into a lighter topic or two, rose, and then shook hands with Will, Archie, and Charles Norton. Nellie left, put on her vast white hat and motoring veil over it, and went for a drive. She did not shake Roosevelt's hand.

In the years that followed, Nellie Taft remained especially vague about what had happened that afternoon. What is clear, however, is that she and Will had a rather firm disagreement about Roosevelt's visit. It had not been a warm meeting of old friends Will and Teddy, but neither had it resulted in an open breach. Nellie seemed to wish it had. At worst it was a standoff. For Nellie, however, there was no doubt about Teddy, and the sooner Will agreed with her view, the better it was for him in the effort to win a second term in 1912. Will, she said, "resolutely refused to believe that it could ever be anything but friendly." She made clear that she "did not share his complete faith." For public consumption she would only write that the meeting was "pleasant and entertaining" and that she tended to be "unwarrantably suspicious." She privately told friends, however, that she "became impressed with his [Teddy's] unfriendliness which she declared, 'Will will not see.'"

The summit on the porch would prove to be the last time Nellie Taft and Teddy Roosevelt ever saw each other.[9]

For his part, Will remained plagued by his uncertainty as to where he stood with the man he now sarcastically called "the sage at Oyster Bay." The former President was nevertheless nursing numerous resentments towards Taft. Roosevelt was insulted that Will gave some of the credit for his 1908 victory to his brother Charley. To make matters worse, the Pinchot firing still rankled him. Roosevelt listened to all the anti-Taft Insurgents who sought him out. On his western tour he spoke proudly of Taft's tariff reforms without crediting the President and proposed policies that could be enacted only by abrogating the Constitution. In September he wrongly blamed Taft for running Vice President James S. Sherman against him as temporary chairman of the New York State Republican Committee Convention. When Charley Taft's paper editorialized that even Roosevelt's help couldn't get Jim Garfield elected Ohio governor, Roosevelt was outraged. And although he had left unexpressed his wish that Taft retain his friend Henry White as a diplomat, he took umbrage at White's dismissal.

"It looks a little bit as if he were hunting reasons," said a bewildered Will, "justifying his attitude towards me." He soothed himself in believing "the coolness will wear away and our old relations will be restored." He was also reassured by Nick Longworth, who said it was just newspapers misrepresenting Roosevelt's speeches and others trying to break up the friendship by using Roosevelt for their own agenda. Will decided to "sit tight." A mid-September meeting between Teddy and Will went well enough, but the so-dubbed "assistant president" Charles Norton told reporters that Roosevelt needed advice on New York politics. This, of course, insulted the old lion further. Teddy now implied that *both* Norton and Taft were liars.

Nellie lost no love over Roosevelt, but Norton's open hostility in the press wasn't going to help the Taft cause. And Norton's acting as if he were a secondary chief executive irritated her. "Will," she angrily argued, "you approve everything—everything Mr. Norton brings you, everything Captain Butt brings to you, and everything everybody brings to you."

"Well, my dear," he laughingly retorted, "if I approve everything, you disapprove everything, so we even up on the world at any rate."

Nellie wouldn't let it go. "It is no laughing matter. You don't want to fire Ballinger, and yet you approve of Senator Crane and Mr. Norton trying to get him out. I don't approve of letting people run your business for you."

"I don't either, my dear, but if you will notice," Will said calmly, "I usually have my way in the long run."

She was not finished—and would have the last word: "No, you don't. You think you do, but you don't."

The Roosevelts—Teddy, Edith, and Alice—were creating tension in the Taft marriage. Mrs. Taft finally opened up to Archie Butt. "I have not asked him anything, and he has not talked to me," she said of Will. "But this Roosevelt business is perfectly dreadful. I lay awake all last night thinking about it, and I don't see what is going to be the outcome."[10]

Shortly after their October return to the White House, Will and Nellie got into another row, about his upcoming trip to Panama. She insisted on going. "I am hopeful that Nellie will not go," Will wrote his brother Horace. "I am rather inclined to think that the voyage is too severe for Nellie. . . . Nellie, however, has her mind made up that she wishes to go with me, and as you are familiar with that member of my family, you will know that it is an even thing whether she wins or not." Nellie knew the real reason: "Your Father thinks it would be too much of a junket." Indeed, Will feared the political fallout from what he called the "presence of petticoats." The argument persisted until forty-eight hours before the trip. "We're in a great state now about going to Panama," Helen wrote Bob. "Mama is very indignant about it. I don't know why she is so eager to go, unless because she can't see why she shouldn't, which is, really, a very good reason." A day before the trip, Nellie finally gave up and rode to the station with Will. "She has been lonely and rather depressed since Papa left," Helen wrote Bob again days later.[11]

Nellie no longer feared being stricken ill while Will was gone. The summer had gone so well that she was comfortable enough to speak to strangers. Most notably, she had endured endless speeches in the sun; receiving politicos; and walking up hills, gangways, and in and out of carriages at the August 5 dedication of the Pilgrim Monument in

Provincetown, Massachusetts. On and off the reviewing stand, greeting the citizenry, sitting on public display at a luncheon, the seven-hour experience had proven to be a turning point in renewing her self-confidence.

On October 22 she also presided at a state dinner for the Tokyo mayor and Mrs. Ozaki. Ozaki had uplifting news for Nellie. After the initial gift of cherry trees had been destroyed, the Japanese government and the chemist Tokicho Takamine, who had underwritten the donation of those trees, decided to give several thousand more trees to Mrs. Taft. It was officially announced in December.

Nellie had even lost her fears about the personal safety of the presidential family. The day after Will left for Panama, one James Downs of Geiger, Alabama, was apprehended at the White House gates. "Worrying, want[s] relief" was the entry in the White House diary about the "insane" man who had come to see Mrs. Taft. None of it flustered Nellie. When she learned that a certain former resident was coming to visit former colleagues in the White House executive offices on November 19, however, the First Lady practically fled the premises.

"Mama and I are going to New York," Helen wrote her brother. "Mama is going chiefly to avoid Mr. Roosevelt's visit to Washington."[12]

Fifteen

The Stars and Silver Forever

*No fundamental superiority or inferiority between the two
appears plain to me. . . . [S]ome wives are superior to their
husbands, and some husbands to their wives.*

—NELLIE TAFT

When Will returned home, Nellie said she was "glad to see him notwithstanding that I didn't go to Panama." The President, however, was mortified that neither of them had been at the White House to greet Roosevelt during his return. "I was particularly sorry not to see Mrs. Taft the other day. I had no idea she was not in Washington until I myself reached that city," Roosevelt wrote Taft. In fact, unknown to the Tafts, Roosevelt was lying. Wrote Butt, "He knew that Mrs. Taft had left." Will again invited the former President to visit, this time on the pretext of his attending the Gridiron dinner. If Roosevelt was coming, he must stay at the White House. He wasn't coming, and he pointedly added, "I cannot say that I think [things] are satisfactory from the political standpoint."

Will *again* invited Roosevelt—and more rejection, writing him to bring Edith so they could "resume in some way our relations of yore." Reporting on the Panama Canal and predicting its completion date by July 1, 1913, he also predicted that he would lose the election and seemed to warn Roosevelt not to run against him for the nomination; it was "a date at which both you and I will be private citizens." As early as September 1910,

Taft seemed to concede loss. The "prospect of a second term" was "discouraging," he had "given up any hope of it," and he would be "beaten like a gentleman," he told his brothers. He had never wanted to be President, and he knew that he was not the sort of person who could innately thrive in that role. He also seemed to have finally caught enough of his wife's anti-Rooseveltism, however, to think that Teddy should not be President either.

Ever worried about Nellie relapsing, Will chose not to lean on her as he always had. Yet she could still overwhelm him with unsolicited advice. She began to sense that Norton's open belittling of former President Roosevelt violated Will's sense of dignity about the presidency and thus hurt his public reputation. It also made Norton look more like the protector of a weak President, perhaps a man with a political future of his own. It was not long before Nellie wanted Norton axed. "He said the other evening that Mr. Norton was very fresh," she told Butt, "so I think he sees through him now, but it may be too late." Norton would be gone by early 1911, replaced by Assistant Treasury Secretary Charles Dewey Hilles, who would stay until he left to work on the reelection campaign.

Christmas was particularly festive that year: The house was filled with family, the first public Christmas tree was put up in the Blue Room, and there was caroling from the St. Paul's Catholic Choir on the North Portico. On New Year's Eve there was another great party and even an exhibition of billiards in the Blue Room, "champagne and coke [Coca-Cola] served at midnight." The highlight of the season was Nellie's hosting of her daughter Helen's debutante party in the White House. Helen had taken time off from Bryn Mawr to aid her mother, as her aunts had, as a hostess. "Helen's coming this winter is giving her something to think about and to make plans for," Will wrote a friend. For the First Lady, 1911 opened with a sense of new hope.[1]

Miss Helen Taft would exercise considerable influence over her strong-willed mother. Nellie wanted Helen to be a "first daughter" in the mold of Alice Roosevelt. When Helen first broached the idea of taking a western camping trip with Bob, Nellie reacted by chastising him: "I don't think it is the thing for her to knock around unchaperoned—in this position. I mean, of course, before it was quite different than it is now." The president's daughter cared little, however, for making a social splash. Helen revered education and was determined to contribute to society. Archie called her "a nice girl and very intelligent without being a prude." Her gratitude and thoughtfulness to the staff for whatever was done for her was remarkable. When the White House limousine failed to fetch her, she just took a streetcar. In fact, she liked taking public transportation. Visiting New York, she "spent a small fortune riding in the Fifth Avenue bus."

Most of all she had a great sense of humor. "I have to lead a Christian Union Meeting next Wednesday night," she wrote from school. "This reflects no glory or any Christian character." When she did poorly at field hockey she joked, "Even a remarkable family like ours has its failings." She was the subject of newspaper profiles, and some of the attention garnered was unwanted—as when a lovesick lunatic sent her a diamond ring and press tales about her poodle, Caro, a gift from the Italian king. She was bemused by the fuss: "[N]othing very dreadful ever can happen to me because too many people feel responsible for my welfare. On the other hand, of course, much more is expected of me."

Helen welcomed some of the expectations. She taught Girl Pioneers, an afternoon school program in southeast Washington's Noel House for needy children, taking them on outings such as picnics, museum trips, and House hearings, where she and her students slipped quietly into the public gallery. She was troubled by the inequities in society and wrote of going to the theater one night with escorts who "became frightfully excited because a woman who looked like a negress was sitting next to me." One of them "finally insisted on changing seats with me—to keep me 'uncontaminated' I suppose, but I thought that I could much better stand it than he. I was thankful that neither of them called on an usher to turn her out."[2]

Just when Helen was presiding with her mother in the White House, the nation's attention was focused on the horrors of women's working conditions. The Triangle Shirtwaist Company fire occurred on March 25, 1911; 150 girls and women, mostly young immigrants, perished in the crowded, unsafe factory fire. Many jumped to their deaths rather than burn. Public outrage eventually led to reform, and in the process Helen became an even more ardent advocate for workers' rights. A year earlier she had landed on the front page of *The New York Times*, in January 1910, for her interest. Listening to the testimony of shirtwaist factory strikers, she sat with activist Fannie Cochran, taking notes and talking freely to a reporter:

> *I felt sorry for the little Russian girls who had to live, or starve, on 89 cents a day. I certainly sympathize with the poor little girls. I never knew they were so downtrodden. Really, I'll never put on a shirtwaist again without a shudder. . . . But to think that these poor creatures have to work ten and twelve hours a day, suffer agonizing headaches because they have to watch a dozen needles flash up and down a thousand times a minute, and then get but $5 a week is too awful. . . . I am going to know more about this affair. . . . I am coming, too, hereafter. I read the story about the girl who was told by her employer: "If you do not work you do not live." The girl told him "I live not much on 89 cents a day anyhow." That was one of the little incidents that won me to the cause. Besides, I was down at the pickets' headquarters and heard all about it from the girls themselves.*

Helen then mused about picketing herself. "I'd like to," she said. "Oh suppose I were to be arrested. . . . I certainly shall speak to papa about the terrible conditions under which these poor girls are compelled to live."

Whenever asked to gain presidential support for a cause, Helen told her father, "I am divided between the dislike to bother you . . . and the effect they produce on my feelings." Thus, she remained true to her own feelings, without compromising her father. Helen continued her support for labor reform and often headlined meetings of groups, such as the one in the home of a Wilmington matron, who were seeking Delaware state regulation of working conditions for women who worked both day and night shifts.

Helen, a charter member of Bryn Mawr's Suffrage Club, was an unabashed feminist. She wrote with displeasure to Bob about the twenty-fifth anniversary of Bryn Mawr that 140 "distinguished" delegates from male colleges attended. "Yale, I am sorry to say, did not show its proper appreciation of this great occasion for the cause of the education of women," she wrote, "and only sent one 'undistinguished' delegate." When suffrage stamps appeared, Will used the first one he got on a letter to Helen. Her conviction eventually induced Nellie to back full suffrage—even for those women who lacked education or who intended to run for political office, two conditions she had previously held out for. Over time, Helen would also interest Nellie in reform issues.[3]

Mother and daughter were devoted to each other. "Do write Mama often because she is so lonely," Helen admonished her brothers. As George G. Hill had discerned after his interview with Nellie in 1909, "good enough" was never something Nellie would say to her children: "Nothing short of the highest honors has satisfied the mother for her daughter and son at college." Nellie was especially proud of Helen: "She worked very hard at school and won a scholarship at Bryn Mawr College." Helen's example expanded Nellie's feminism. When girls graduated from local schools, the First Lady rewarded them with invitations to the White House. In a rare interview she made clear her belief in the intellectual equality of women—although she held steadfastly to the belief that even educated women best served society as homemakers:

> *Higher education for women? My daughter has elected to take a full college course. . . . I believe in the best and most thorough education for everyone, men and women, and it is my proudest boast that all of my children are studious. My idea about higher culture for women is that it makes them great in intellect and soul, develops the lofty conception of womanhood; not that it makes them a poor imitation of a man. . . . No fundamental superiority or inferiority between the two appears plain to me. The only superiority lies in the way in which the responsibilities of life are discharged. Viewed in this light, some wives are superior to their husbands, and some husbands to their wives, some girls to their brothers, and women to men in varying circumstances.*

Halfway through her year as an assistant White House hostess, Helen was bored. "I wish that it weren't such a worry to have people to visit," she complained about the effort required to have friends drop by. She "decided definitely" to "put down all the vanities of the world behind and return to my cloistered existence" at Bryn Mawr in the fall of 1911. Her father encouraged her to do so, while Nellie was "merely acquiescent." Days later Helen informed Bob that "Mama seemed to be so sorry about it, that I changed my mind." Now she thought she would stay out of school through all of the 1911–12 school year "unless Papa seems likely to be re-elected"— in which case she would not feel pressured into taking advantage of what would be their last social season in the winter-spring of 1912.[4]

In the winter and spring of 1911, mother and daughter received more guests than at any other time in the administration. Another social season got under way with the help of a Miss Letterman, Nellie's third social secretary (Miss Spiers left after her request for a raise was denied). Mr. Tiffany of Steinway and Sons contracted the performances at Nellie's annual four Lenten musicales, ranging from soloists to the Boston Symphony quartet, and often featuring world famous vocalists and musicians. Selecting the music to be performed at other events, however, was an aspect of being First Lady that always brought her satisfaction; she actively scouted talent by attending musical performances each month. The varied programming reflected Nellie's wide knowledge. At one concert of her favorite Philippines Constabulary Band, she worked with the conductor Walter H. Loving to choose the selections ranging from Rossini and Donizetti to Beethoven and Paderewski and two Hispano-Filipino composers, Escamilla and Hernandez. She also had a unique evening with a Hawaiian quartet performing native music and song for the Prince of China.

With her professional experience in music, Nellie Taft had a deep respect and appreciation for those who made a living by it. In an age when women pianists were paid and worked less than their male counterparts, Mrs. Taft chose nine women pianists among the eleven that she had perform during her tenure. She also instituted an early form of the Presidential Medal of the Arts, having small gold medals struck by Tiffany with the presidential seal on one side and the musician or singer's name on the other. She presented the medals, hung from red, white, and blue ribbons, in the Red Room as a symbol of respect for the artist from the government.

Perhaps her greatest White House social legacy was that she always hosted musical entertainments after state and other formal dinners, thus setting another precedent for administrations to come. From musicians all over the world she received requests to perform. "Since we have noticed by the newspapers that Your Ladyship is especially interested in music and a patroness of song, I take the liberty to ask that you take a favorable view of the German male chorus," the director of a Rhine choral society wrote Nellie. "People who are fond of music and song are always good-hearted and are always ready to help advance the art."

Nellie expanded her musical presentations to include concerts during her annual slate of four spring garden parties. At one, for example, she had 130 singers of the Mozart Society of New York perform on the South Lawn together with the eighty-piece Marine Band.

The night of June 17, 1910, had been an especially historic night on the South Lawn—the only time Shakespeare was performed there. Nellie had invited the local Coburn Players to perform *As You Like It*. That afternoon they had done *Twelfth Night*, as suggested by her. An amphitheater was set up, with the sky and Washington Monument as backdrop. Both productions were fund-raising benefits to create playgrounds for poor local children who had no healthy open spaces in which to play, a program endorsed by the First Lady. Among the guests sitting on clacking wood chairs that night were dozens of local schoolchildren. Despite a summer rain, the Tafts remained transfixed to the end, encouraging many more of the audience to sit through the brief downpour than might have otherwise.[5]

Spring in Washington also signaled the second season of blossoming cherry trees, about one hundred of which were thriving. On May 1, Will and Nellie took their first drive of the season to Potomac Park. "Mrs. Taft actually clapped her hands in delight when she saw the cherry blossoms," Butt recorded. Familiar with West Potomac Park and the area around it (thanks to her role in its expanded landscaping plans), she noted the large greensward that the trees bordered remained undeveloped. Will sat on the Lincoln Memorial Committee, planning the building tribute to the six-teenth President. The site he recommended was Arlington Cemetery. The Fine Arts Committee recommended the bank of the Potomac. It ended up being on the Potomac Park greensward. Will's acquiescence to this site may well have been at Nellie's urging. The memorial certainly formed an apt balance to the expanse of cherry blossoms.

Seemingly better than she had been at any time since her stroke, Nel-lie sailed through the social season. It was all a dress rehearsal for the event she seemed to have been planning since election night 1908. Her first White House visit had been as a guest at the silver wedding anniversary of President and Mrs. Hayes, and, as one newspaper observed, it was at that event "Miss Herron hitched her wagon to the stars, and chose for herself the position which at some time in the future she resolved to make a real-ity. She determined . . . that she should some day preside over the mansion as the First Lady of the land. She determined that she would marry a man capable of being President and help guide his course toward the White House."

Now Nellie Taft was going to host her own silver anniversary in the White House on June 19. It was a full circle in many ways, even after her stroke and the struggle that ensued, a sort of second inaugural, a second chance to shine. The Hayeses had invited the original wedding party and friends and family as their anniversary party guests. Nellie Taft would repli-cate that event "at which her ambition was born" and invite her wedding party, friends, and family—all eight thousand of them. It would be the grandest garden party the mansion had seen in its 111-year history.[6]

The First Lady had also begun to make day trips again with the Pres-ident, mostly to hear his speeches. She was with him in New York at a din-ner for the Academy of Political Sciences at the Hotel Astor on the night of Saturday, May 13. Seated at the table of one William Ivins, she was particu-larly chatty. Her speech had improved to the point where the impediment was so slight that it went undetected. She and Will left at 11 p.m. and headed to their usual headquarters in New York, Harry and Julia's home. Nellie was there just a few minutes when she collapsed.

Harry immediately sent for his family physician, E. M. Evans. The First Lady was suffering again from a "nervous attack." By the next morning Evans had assured Will that the stroke was mild compared to the one she had suffered exactly two years before to the day in 1909 and told reporters gathered outside the house that there was "no cause for alarm." Helen decided to come to New York "whether Mama wanted me or not." Nellie claimed that she was "cheerful," but Helen noted, "She isn't able to articulate clearly or to find her words. The doctor seems to think that the attack is similar to the first one but much less severe. . . . She seems to be improving rapidly now. I suppose that she has been overdoing and having the garden party one day and coming on to New York the next, in the heat, was too much for her. I don't think that she ought to have so many people visit. . . . Mama is insisting that she will go straight home."

By Thursday she was well enough to travel by train, even enduring the extreme heat well. All of the First Lady's scheduled appearances were canceled since the new attack was "probably the result of the trying season of social events in which Mrs. Taft took a leading part." There was some thought of sending her immediately to Beverly to rest for the next five months, but she would not hear of it. She was staying in the White House.[7]

As soon as Maria Herron heard that her sister had fallen ill, she went to her, leaving their feeble father whose senility made him unaware of her absence. While Maria was in Washington, John Herron suffered a severe stroke and was not only in pain but delusional, believing he was lost and starved. Helen took the first train to Cincinnati to check on her grandfather. Maria had "a fit of hysterics" when she first heard the news, but Nellie predicted that he would live through it. He did.

Once again Nellie was confined to her room, watching another garden party from her window, listening to her daughter's stories of the receptions and dinners she was missing. Will was anxious to get her out into the fresh air "due to a faintness" she had in the house, and on June 11 she joined him for a drive to Great Falls, Virginia. It was the hottest day of the year; there were reports of several sunstrokes, and Archie Butt took note of a "very pale" Nellie. Eighteen miles out, Archie wrote that "the most astonishing case" of a recovery he had ever seen took place. "As strange as it seems she appears to be so much more normal than she did before the second attack. While her tongue is very thick and her speech very poor, yet mentally she seems to have a grip on her faculties which she never had between the two attacks."

The most glorious moment of her tenure was just a week away. Still, her doctors insisted she could not revel in this moment. She must have continued rest. To make it firm it was even announced by the White House to the press that "Mrs. Taft will not be present, for the physicians still wish her to avoid excitement." Helen would substitute. For a woman accustomed to doing as she pleased, it was just the challenge Nellie needed.

Will was determined to make the day special for Nellie. When Bob told his father that exams might prevent him from coming, the President replied, "It would gratify your mother very much if you could be with us. We don't like to have a wedding [anniversary] without the presence of our three children." Helen wrote that he must come "to stand in a line with Charles and me as the proof of the real success of our parents' twenty-five years of matrimony." Bob did attend, escorting his great-aunt Delia from her home in Massachusetts after Will insisted that she come as well.[8]

The first sign of the spectacle to come began about a week before the great day. Delivery wagons, messengers, carriages, and cars were stacked along the nearby approaches to the White House, all bearing silver. The mailroom was deluged with boxes of all shapes, all containing silver urns, plates, loving cups, dishes, candlesticks, vases, punch bowls, olive forks, tea caddies, photo frames, skewers, umbrella handles, fruit stands, teaspoons, jewelry boxes, trays, and cake stands. There was a silver-cased watch for Nellie and a book covered in silver and inscribed in silver ink. There were silver tea services, coffee urns, salt holders and salt spoons, and beer steins.

Army wives gave the First Lady a silver chain and a pearl necklace and diamond pendant. There were silver cigar lighters and cigarette cases. As the day got closer, the shower got heavier. The Vice President sent a silver case; the Supreme Court, the House, and the Senate all sent silver tea services. Maryland sent a silver ladle. General Corbin's widow sent pickle dishes. And still the gifts continued: water pitchers, bread baskets, ice cream dishes, and a centerpiece. Even more exquisite gifts came later from overseas, including English silver baskets engraved with the royal coat of arms from 1755. Meanwhile, a New York baker was decorating a gigantic cake; caterers were carrying in punch bowls, buffet boards, tables, and chairs; and poles to be covered in green-striped tenting were rising on the South Lawn.

National fascination with the Tafts' anniversary ran high. In-depth articles retold the now legendary story of Nellie's determination to become First Lady and her guidance of Will to the presidency, accompanied by photographs of many gifts and old family snapshots. "A popular desire throughout the country to participate" in the event brought an avalanche of lumpy envelopes. In them, less wealthy American citizens of all kinds— newsboys, farmers, traveling salesmen, and Yalies—also sent silver: dimes, nickels, quarters, and dollars. There was even paper currency. Nellie had a tidy cash sum—until Will ordered all money returned, thinking it unbecoming. Others just sent good wishes—in poetry and biblical quotes. Congratulatory cables from the kings and queens of Denmark, Spain, Italy, Sweden, England, the Emperor of Japan, the Kaiser of Germany, and the Sultan of Turkey clogged the telegraphs at the old State, War and Navy Building next door to the White House. No matter how ambitious she had been for her husband, it is hard to imagine that the former Miss Herron could possibly have imagined that twenty-five years later Czar Nicholas of Russia would be wishing them the happiest returns of the day.

There were also gifts from powerful industrial giants such as Henry Frick and Andrew Carnegie. John D. Rockefeller, Jr., sent a slew of silver tea caddies. Judge Elbert Gary of U.S. Steel sent an $8,000 antique soup tureen. A "worried" President advised the First Lady to hide "certain ones" away in cold storage and not permit them to be displayed. "It is hideous to see such a profligacy," Butt thought. "It begins to look as if this feature might be the occasion of considerable embarrassment."

A broad cross-section of eight thousand guests received White House invitations with the presidential seal embossed in silver, including ambassadors, ministers, consuls, all of the diplomatic corps, House, and Senate, the Supreme Court, and the highest-ranking Army and Navy officers. Anyone who entertained the President on his trips around the nation was invited. Eminent cardinals, bishops, rabbis, and ministers were on the guest list and would surely tell their congregations about the occasion. Past first family members were invited, among them sons of Lincoln, Hayes, Garfield; daughters of Grant, Arthur, and Cleveland; and the most famous of the small group: Ethel, Kermit, Theodore Jr., and Alice Roosevelt. The judiciary and governors of every state, the mayors of all major cities, and every state Republican committee member were included. And then there was the entire National Republican Committee and the official Notification Committee that informed presidential candidates of their official nomination. After all, the presidential election was just a year away. And of course an invitation was sent to Theodore and Edith Roosevelt, but the White House had not yet heard whether they would accept.

Meanwhile, Nellie had made some progress with her doctors. The White House let it be known that she could now "appear" but "will not stand the strain of receiving very long." It would be Miss Helen Taft who would "stand by her father's side and act as mistress of the White House."[9]

On June 19, as the hour of nine approached, a thick sea of citizenry clustered around the gates, curious to watch the arriving guests. When the early summer sun began to set, however, attention turned from who was going through the gates to the scene within. It was called "mesmerizing," a "fairyland," a "magic sight." The White House and its lawn had been made fantastical by the modern wonder of electricity.

During the previous week, two dozen electricians had been scattered all over the lawn and even in trees and bushes. They had been on the roof, terraces, and every "cornice, angle or gable" of the mansion itself. Now the White House looked as it never had. Everywhere was light. Colored lights beamed on the fountain, transforming it into a splashing rainbow. High-voltage searchlights, positioned on the roofs of the Treasury Building and the War, State and Navy Building, flanking the White House, spotlighted the bright green lawn itself so that guests could see clearly. Interspersed with hundreds of red Japanese paper lanterns in the trees and bushes encircling the lawn were strings of thousands of little twinkling white lights, seeming to match the star-filled sky. A huge flag of red, white, and blue lights hung from the portico, flashing every few seconds. Under a large elm tree, above a mound southwest of the portico, "1886–1911" was spelled out in shining white bulbs. The most spectacular sight of all was the mansion, entirely outlined in white lights, from corner to corner, across the roof and the base, and along the portico fencing and the east and west terrace balustrades.

Just before nine o'clock the presidential party descended by elevator from the family quarters to the state floor and walked through the Cross Hall and into the Red Room. The ragtime and other popular music stopped, the party stepped onto the South Portico, a huge cheer and applause broke out, and the band struck up the "Star-Spangled Banner." Suddenly the crowd noticed that it was not the President's daughter Helen but the First Lady who was on the President's arm as they descended the curving portico stairs to Mendelssohn's "Wedding March." Dressed in a square-necked white satin gown embroidered with silver flowers and a long train, walking briskly and beaming a confident smile, Nellie looked revitalized. The original wedding party followed: Maria Herron and Horace and Fanny Taft.

Once the Tafts had stationed themselves under the "1886–1911" electric bulb canopy, police and Secret Service formed a receiving line. Throughout the formalities Nellie warmly greeted her guests, repeating several phrases flawlessly. She and Will shook hands with guests for two hours, then went into the East Room to watch the dancing. On their way to the State Dining Room they stopped in the Cross Hall. There the multi-tiered wedding cake sat in splendor, ornamented with spun sugar hearts, cherubs, and flowers. One layer was studded with fifty miniature American and presidential flags (the latter being a monarchical navy-gold-white standard). After the Tafts had cut the first piece of cake, servants took charge of slicing it up as the couple made their way into the State Dining Room, circulated among the crowd, and then joined their family and Cabinet members on the west terrace. The terrace was filled with small trees and dotted with ferns and palms, and a line of lights under shades resembled "monster poppies."

The Tafts remained at the party until nearly one in the morning, Nellie only briefly having to receive seated. It was one of those rare times when the First Lady lost all self-consciousness and was so convivial that she eagerly accepted compliments, relishing her position as the center of affectionate attention. As Archie had recorded months before, "When she allows herself to be loved, she is very lovable, but as a rule she keeps herself buried down deep within herself."

As if hoping the night would last forever, Will did not go to sleep. From an open window in their darkened bedroom he watched the dwindling crowds and listened to the last strains of the final songs. Before retiring, he and Nellie decided that the lights must all be kept up for another night. Tomorrow, Will announced, the general public would be invited onto the lawn and into the mansion to enjoy the splendid display. Although she did not personally greet guests during the encore performance, the First Lady stood on the portico for an hour, waving to crowds.[10]

On that night open to people of all colors and classes, one guest who had been unable to attend the night before, the painter, muralist, illustrator, and writer Francis D. Millet, took in the scene. His wife, Elizabeth Greely Merrill, and their children lived in England indefinitely, but Millet shared an active social life and his home with Archie Butt, twenty-one years his junior. Millet had befriended Nellie in the summer of 1905 when they met in the English countryside. Francis wrote of his experience to Will:

> *I went into the White House grounds last evening with the "livi polloi." A happier company of people I never saw and I am sure you would have felt as I do now, if you had heard them talk and had seen their happy faces. I hope some of them will write to thank you for the pleasure you gave them. If they do not, it is because they are shy and not because they do not recognize the sympathetic interest, which prompted you. . . . I was so touched by the spirit of the evening . . . of what you have so gracefully done to win the hearts of those who accepted your hospitality.*

To Will and Nellie the event provided deep satisfaction. It was a celebration of Taft not only as President but as a human being, and it seemed to ignite within him a sense of his worthy gratitude. As he wrote to a friend, reflecting on the event:

> *It is perhaps of doubtful expediency to celebrate publicly and officially such a domestic event as that of a silver wedding, and yet the expressions of good will and kindly feeling that the silver wedding has brought out are so full of pleasure to Mrs. Taft and me that it would have been a real self-denial to have taken any other course than we have. It seems to introduce the touch of nature that makes the whole world kind and breaks down party and other limitations and instills in one's heart a self-searching gratitude for all that has come to one of a kind that cannot be but useful influencing one's future conduct.*

More practically, the event potentially widened his political base. To those influential invitees who regretted, Will made sure to send thank-you notes, along with a little politicking. To Bishop Edmund Dunne of Peoria, Illinois, for example, he regretted his absence but assured him that "I count on being a guest of the Knights of Columbus in your city sometime this fall." Still, even if a "great throng of friends" made Will and Nellie "merry for more than four hours," as he put it, the endorsement was far from universal. Conspicuous among the absent were Theodore and Edith Roosevelt. Teddy, just an hour away in Baltimore, turned down Will's personal invitation to the party. He sent a silver bowl but no explanation or apology.[11]

Since their meeting the previous summer, Roosevelt had not personally made antagonistic or critical remarks in public about Taft, but he met frequently with Insurgents who courted him as if he were the ideal presidential candidate in 1912. Nevertheless, Will still resisted seeing Roosevelt negatively and Nellie still resisted seeing him as anything *but* negatively. Even when reporting that she and Will attended a traditional annual charity ball, she got in a dig: "Roosevelt was the only President who did not do it."

Two weeks before the anniversary, Taft and Roosevelt had chatted in a corner "about Mrs. Taft's health" at a Baltimore ceremony honoring the Catholic clergy. It was cover for a problem that promised to be the point of departure between them. It was personal and involved Roosevelt's ego. Will told Teddy that as an ex-President he should refuse to testify before Kentucky Democratic congressman August O. Stanley's committee investigating U.S. Steel's acquisition of the Tennessee Coal and Iron Company.

The acquisition had occurred with President Roosevelt's approval. Claiming they had acted to avoid a major Wall Street panic and financial disaster because Tennessee Coal and Iron's stock shares dropped below its loans, U.S. Steel's J. P. Morgan, Elbert Gary, and Henry Frick offered to buy the company's stock at twice its value. To make sure they didn't violate the Sherman Anti-Trust Act—and be subject to prosecution—Gary and Frick rushed to Washington in their private railroad cars to breakfast with Roosevelt in the White House and made the case that their motive was patriotic. Roosevelt told them it was "no public duty of mine" to object, and U.S. Steel walked away with a valuable acquisition at a good price. Criticism had been unrelenting, and now with the Democrats in control of the House, the Stanley Committee was essentially claiming that Roosevelt had been duped by the greedy magnates or complicit in their plan. To Taft's suggestion that he not defend himself, Roosevelt took umbrage, as if he could never be so unmanly.

Notions of manliness were behind Roosevelt's own attack on Taft's proposal for a global arbitration treaty with England and France. The idea was that a world court would seek to resolve disputes where negotiations had failed. On Memorial Day, Taft had declared that anything was better than "internecine or international strife." When the National Rifle Association president sent to Roosevelt the organization's attack on Taft's antiwar stance, Teddy agreed, writing, "To me there is something unspeakably humiliating and degrading in the way in which men have grown to speak in the name of humanity of death as the worst of all possible evils. No man is fit to live unless he is ready to quit life for adequate cause."

Family may have been a factor at keeping the two men from overt bickering. The children of Will and Teddy behaved so much more maturely than their fathers that they had remained genuine friends. On New Year's Day, 1911, for example Ethel and Kermit had joined their friends Helen and Bob. At Helen's debutante party, Ethel was an honored and convivial presence, and she danced joyously with the delighted President.

Still, Helen paid especially close attention to her father's reactions to the increasing number of editorials harkening to the better days of the Roosevelt years, trying to detect if he perceived Roosevelt as any sort of rival or threat. In reporting on them to Bob, she slipped just long enough to suggest that Nellie's prediction that Roosevelt would somehow challenge Taft for the 1912 nomination had become, at the very least, a subject consciously cloaked in humor with the President. "Papa reads all the editorials on his illustrious predecessor aloud at the breakfast table and seems to regard the situation with great amusement," she reported. "Several people who have been here seem to think that all this excitement will help Papa by throwing the Democrats into the shade and giving him the prestige of a victory of Roosevelt."

If the first bit of rumbling about a potential Roosevelt challenge to Taft was being heard, it was not in any way being goaded by the First Lady, however anti-Teddy her sentiments were. Such an open break so early in game would jeopardize not only a second Taft term—enough time for her to potentially achieve some of the goals that had been derailed by her stroke—but the nomination itself.

Thus, Nellie took the most incredible of steps forward and put on a polite façade to Alice Longworth. Alice called on Nellie several times during 1911, and Nellie tried to patch things up for Will's sake. "Tuesday, I went up the Monument with Alice. I did everything that she wanted me to, even walking in the garden on a very cold day."

Alice still gushed and cooed over Will. "It was too dear of you to think of me, and a cigarette holder is just the very thing I need," she wrote, thanking him for his most recent Christmas present. "I will come and see you on an official call and thank you in person, so don't be surprised if you see me marching into the office before very long!" She signed off "ever affectionately." True to form, once Nellie was in Beverly, Will invited Alice to dinner. She loved to scandalize him, pulling her dress into trousers and doing a "Dance de Vent." Said Archie, "She danced it for the President . . . and he ordered her to stop it. . . . She still gives a motion or two at him . . . but she does not get very far before a look stops her." Despite their easy friendship, Alice was no longer giving Will any sense at all about her father's thinking.[12]

That summer the Tafts rented a different home, "Parramatta," on Corning Street in Beverly. Nellie survived the silver anniversary "only a little tired," and, except for "insist[ing] on superintending the packing of the silver," was forced to rest by Helen. Will wanted his daughter to return to college that fall, but Helen decided "I really ought not to." She sensed that her mother would feel needy if one of her sisters had to return to aid her as hostess. "My being there is so much more natural," she wrote Bob, in Europe that summer. Her decision left her "feeling rather sad," but her father wrote her with "praise for my unselfish attitude." She didn't let Nellie read the President's letter because "Mama can't bear to have people unselfish on her account." Still, she thought Nellie was secretly "glad to have me."

Although the "perfect quiet" of Beverly strengthened Nellie and her speech continued to improve she said it was "rather boring." Fearing political fallout, Will refused to let Nellie and Helen use the *Mayflower* for pleasure trips that summer. Nellie was "rather depressed" that Will had to remain in Washington, dealing with Congress. Besides numerous congressional investigations involving the Food and Drug Administration and the Alaskan state comptroller, Will was battling Senate support on the wool tariff. When a coalition of Democrats and Insurgents passed the wool bill, Will's resolve to veto hardened, though he knew "it would do him harm politically," and he became, said Helen, "depressed about the next election." Opposed to the recall of the judiciary proposed in the Arizona Constitution, he planned to veto the bill granting statehood to Arizona and New Mexico, a measure coupled to the recall provision. The Senate also opposed his arbitration treaties, feeling their war powers would be diminished.

The Senate finally struck out Arizona's recall of judges' clause, and Taft signed the legislation making Arizona and New Mexico the forty-seventh and forty-eighth states, but he did veto the wool tariff bill. The unpopularity of the veto was offset by press praise for his veto of cotton, metal, and chemical tariff schedules, and things looked up for Taft again. "Everyone is making fun of [Progressive Republican senator Robert M.] La Follette [*sic*] and as he is the only rival mentioned for the nomination, Papa seems sure of it [the nomination]," Helen reported. On the heels of this, Will's autumn tour to western and midwestern states that were considered insurgent—or progressive, as they were increasingly called—was announced. It would be the opening of his 1912 campaign, and the President was the undisputed leading candidate.[13]

In August, however, Roosevelt was back in the news, testifying before the Stanley Committee that U.S. Steel's "predominant motive" in acquiring Tennessee Coal and Iron "was of no consequence." It made the man who built an image as a trustbuster look like a hypocrite. On his birthday he was enraged by news accounts of Taft's Justice Department pursuing a suit against U.S. Steel and claims that "Roosevelt was deceived" by the U.S. Steel magnates. He made Will his target. As a member of his Cabinet, Will had also approved the transaction. To Roosevelt it worsened matters even more that Taft did not first know that his attorney general was going to file the suit. A "responsible" President, Roosevelt stated in a private letter, must know everything. Meanwhile, his self-defense in *Outlook* magazine became such hot copy that the issue sold out and had to be reprinted. Corporate industry, now wondering if Roosevelt might be a better defender of their interests, began sending envoys to Oyster Bay. The former President puffed up when he noticed the "very strong undercurrent . . . of talk about my nomination for the Presidency." When representatives of both Taft and La Follette asked him to declare that he would not run, Roosevelt refused, saying he might have to respond to "duty."[14]

On October 14, Justice John M. Harlan died, and Will named yet another man to sit on his beloved Supreme Court, Mahlon Pitney—the sixth man he had nominated for the Court. Except for George Washington, no President had put more justices on the Court. On December 13, 1909, Taft had nominated Horace Lurton an associate justice. On May 2, 1910, his second associate justice, Charles Evan Hughes, had been confirmed. On December 12, 1910, Willis Van Devanter and Joseph R. Lamar had become his third and fourth associate justices, but William Howard Taft had also named Edward D. White to the job he most desired for himself—chief justice. Had Will not given in to Nellie urging him to run for President in 1908 and had Roosevelt gone ahead and accepted the nomination, they would not only have remained friends, but before the end of Roosevelt's second term, Will would have been chief justice. It made him resent all the more those justices who retired only when extremely ill and pushed to the end. There was bitter irony to this, as if somehow Will was paying for not following his own heart.

At Van Devanter's and Lamar's swearing-in ceremony, all eyes had been on Mrs. Taft, who shattered another precedent by sitting within the bar of the Supreme Court. That she—who had for years demeaned Will's desire to sit on the Court as a place of old fogies—was now seated closer to them than any woman in history must have seemed curious to Will. It was typical of him to tease her gently about it, because he could not directly express resentment toward her. Still, his emotions emerged, however obliquely. When they were in public, he now often referred to her influence openly, and mortified her. After they were toasted at a massive dinner of national journalists, Will mischievously thanked them for her, "the real President." When Nellie persisted on joining him for a drive, then ordered the route changed, he silently acquiesced. "The President enjoyed her discomfort every time we got bumped for she insisted that she knew all the good roads," Butt recalled. He loved going to dances away from her judgmental eye, and, "in fact, the President discourages her from going to these entertainments with him." Nellie no longer hesitated in scolding Will in front of strangers. As they were receiving guests, she argued with him to get rid of his derby hat—and got an aide to take it away and bring a top hat. She was critical, too, of his tardiness, complaining to Butt that Will was thoughtless of others.

Earlier that year, in March, as the President was pushing his reciprocity trade bill with Canada through Congress, he thought that by courting the representatives at a huge and expensive dinner, the traditional one honoring the House Speaker, he would win their support. Nellie angrily disagreed. The very afternoon of the dinner honoring him, House Speaker Joseph J. Cannon began attacking Taft's reciprocity bill by trying to hold up a vote on it. "So you see this entire dinner is wasted," Nellie bickered. "Twenty-five [guests] would have done just as much good as seventy-two. Now I do wish you would consult me before you do these things. I could have told you that nothing will move that old Cannon when he gets his head set, and it is a waste of good material to lay a dinner before him." Until the Rules Committee finally agreed to bring it to a vote, Will called her hourly to say the dinner had to be delayed. His side of the conversation was a snapshot of their relationship—at once combative, caring, and compromising:

> *Come closer to the phone, dear. Is that you, Nellie? It would be a little more grammatical to say "It's I," but I don't care what pronoun you use. . . . Yes, "me" does sound more natural, but we can't change the English grammar. I couldn't at least but I don't feel so sure about you. . . . Don't hurry me so. I thought you might be interested in the good news. They have got the reciprocity bill up in the House and are now voting on it. Yes, I thought it would interest you. I am afraid it will make some of the members who are coming to dinner late. No, I don't see how we can help it. Would you mind having it . . . at a quarter to nine? Too late, is it? Well, I don't want to upset your plans. . . . All right, then, we will say half-past eight.*[15]

The marriage, however, endured the squabbles. "Well, I don't see what you can do now," Nellie quipped during an afternoon "joy ride" in their car, when he mused about having another child, "unless you get another wife and you will have to give me alimony if you do." It was a wonderfully rare light moment like the past, before the stress of the presidency had enveloped their lives. Nellie and Will were still the best for each other.

Nellie was also proud of him, especially in one aspect of his career that she consistently focused on—his speeches. "She loves to hear the President speak and to see the enthusiasm he arouses, and I think it makes her very happy and takes her thoughts from her own troubles," Butt observed. "She is a good sport." Throughout 1911 her letters to Bob were full of praise: "Your father had to write his Chicago speech (a very good one it was, too)." "I went with your father to a Peace Meeting down in the Pan-American Building . . . very interesting. . . . Your Father made a very good speech." "Your father made a great speech on Reciprocity. I think it was the finest I have heard." Attacks on Will upset her, since she "had formed the habit of thinking there was nothing to criticize him for except, perhaps, his unfortunate shortcomings of not knowing much and of caring less about the way the game of politics is played."

If the public perceived Mrs. Taft as being less political as a result of her stroke than when she assumed the First Lady role, they were mistaken. She was still advising Will, taking in Senate debates, surveying editorials, and studying official documents. When she accompanied Will to Cincinnati to vote in November 1911, she vigorously disagreed with his voicing an opinion on local politics. "Mama and I were very sorry that Papa got mixed up in it [local elections] by announcing that he was going to vote the Republican ticket," Helen explained.

While she was home, Nellie visited her father, lifting his spirits by gathering his children and grandchildren around his bed. The Herrons remained a tight, loyal tribe. Upon her return to Washington, for example, Nellie's brother Will, his wife, and children were often at the White House. Despite the fact that Will Herron was a Democrat, Nellie saw to it that he was made an assistant attorney general. Other Herrons, too, enjoyed the benefits of having their sister as First Lady. Jennie Anderson's son Thomas, a captain in the Seventh U.S. Infantry, was named as a White House social aide, and Will offered the White House for her daughter Harriet's wedding. When Maria Herron made a seven-nation tour of Asia, she was given presidential letters of introduction to ambassadors, diplomats, and military officials. Will did the same thing for Will Herron's wife when she visited Italy.[16]

Will Herron and his family spent Christmas 1911 with the Tafts in the White House. Will and Nellie took delight in escaping the watch of the Secret Service to tramp through the rain for two hours on Christmas Eve, visiting friends in their homes and bringing little gifts of presidential stickpins. The President especially loved giving out gifts at Christmas. For every person who worked in the White House—in any capacity—the Tafts annually gave a Christmas turkey. Whether or not Will realized how it could be taken, along with the bookmark he gave Alice Longworth that Christmas he also sent along a knife for opening letters. Perhaps with witty malice as she anticipated the coming election year, Alice responded, "It is going to be so useful."

Nellie could communicate by code, too. When, at the end of 1911, she gave her aforementioned list of "the greatest women the world has produced," the one name that didn't seem to fit with the others was that of Prussian Queen Louisa. She was certainly not on par with the British monarchs, Elizabeth or Victoria, whom Nellie also named. But there was something encrypted in her obscurity. An impassioned foe of the French Revolution, Queen Louisa openly declared her hatred of the egomaniac emperor, Napoleon Bonaparte. In fact, the Queen had goaded her husband to go to war with him.[17]

Sixteen

Titanic

I told you so four years ago.

—NELLIE TAFT

As 1912 began, the Tafts cultivated a public image geared to winning four more years in the White House. When England's Duke of Connaught visited, for example, the First Lady and her daughter refused to curtsy, and the President walked home after calling on him at the British embassy, underscoring his democratic convictions. To artificially boost the President's popular public image, the number of callers at the New Year's Day reception given to the press was inflated to eight thousand to put him in the same league as Roosevelt.[1]

One man not in Roosevelt's league was Senator Robert LaFollette, the leading Progressive Republican, who made clear his intention to run for the nomination against Taft. At a February 2 press dinner, however, after New Jersey governor Woodrow Wilson, a leading contender for the Democratic nomination, spoke, LaFollette got up and ranted hostilely at the press. Half the audience left, and the other half sat to witness his self-destruction. His followers soon joined the Roosevelt bandwagon and added grassroots support to that of the politicos and financiers. Roosevelt knew that if he simply announced his intention to run—after four years of persistently saying he wouldn't—his campaign might backfire. When several governors urged him to run, Roosevelt hatched a scheme: "If four or five

Governors wrote me a joint letter . . . which I could respond to . . . such procedure would open the best way out of an uncomfortable situation." The letter was written, seven governors signed it, and it was sent to Roosevelt. Without irony, Alice cracked that "it did not take Father by surprise."

The first suggestion that Teddy would in fact run came from his perturbed son-in-law. Nick Longworth declared himself completely for Taft. At the Ohio Constitutional Convention on February 21, after a visit to Oyster Bay, he told reporters, "I have learned nothing that will cause me to change my attitude towards President Taft . . . [A]nd for Mr. Roosevelt's attitude, you'll have to ask him." It was also at the Ohio Constitutional Convention that Roosevelt made his famous declaration regarding his plans for the 1912 Republican presidential nomination: "My hat is in the ring!"

Instead of making a direct and immediate response to the challenge thrown by Teddy, Will decided to focus on Roosevelt's unconstitutional proposal that voters be allowed to reverse judicial decisions if they were "in defiance of justice." Will took what he believed to be the high road with his "saner view of our government" than Roosevelt's, and vowed to uphold the Constitution "whether beaten or not." He believed that if Teddy was to win the nomination, he would lose the election based in part on the "safe tradition" of no man being elected to three terms. In response to Kentucky senator William O'Connell Bradley, who said Taft was at a "disadvantage" for "having advised my friends not to attack" Teddy, Will was adamant. "I believe the arguments [of constitutionality] pro and con will force themselves upon the electorate," he wrote Bradley, "without the use of denunciation and personal attack." The ideas of Roosevelt could be attacked, Will avowed, but never the man himself. Taft may have been terribly fair in deciding this, but he didn't stir much public attention talking about constitutionality—certainly not as much as Teddy did with his colorful challenge.[2]

The one year that most required Will and Nellie's focus and attention ended up being the most strangely disjointed one of the Taft presidency. The unprecedented challenge to an incumbent President by his mentor and immediate predecessor was punctuated with other disparate distractions, both equally tragic and triumphant. Nellie Taft had always preferred to cast her life and the events that affected it in the high relief of either all good or all bad, but 1912 would insist on being both for her.

The immediate issue at hand was how to deal with the preposterous idea that had become a reality—the mad challenge of Teddy Roosevelt.

Emotionally, Will could no more turn on his old mentor than he could on a loved one, yet he recognized that because of this the aggressive Roosevelt "has me at a disadvantage." While he faced the reality that a "devoted friendship [was] going to pieces," he would rather lose than "lend myself, in any way, to a personal controversy with him." Nellie opposed this strategy. Her old prediction that Roosevelt would run was coming true, and she wanted Will to do everything—including attacking by name—to crush him. "Well," she had decided after yet another report of a Progressive powwow at Oyster Bay, "I suppose you will have to fight Mr. Roosevelt for the nomination, and if you get it he will defeat you. But it can't be helped. If possible you must not allow him to defeat you for the renomination. It does not make much difference about the re-election."

With Helen now monitoring her fiercely, there was less chance of the First Lady's getting herself worked up with tension and then relapsing, however concerned she became about the election. "I had quite a fight with Mama and Papa yesterday," Helen confided to Bob, "because Mama insisted on spending our afternoon before the Diplomatic Dinner, from two-thirty until six-thirty, in going to the Senate and the House, and then to a long concert. I couldn't induce Papa to urge her to rest a little. He just encouraged her. She does seem well, but I am in terror of overdoing in these two months."

Unable to make speeches, Nellie could not work actively with the National Civic Federation, but she met with Charlotte Hopkins, the local chapter's new and activist president, lent her name to their efforts, attended their annual meeting, and held a garden party for the entire membership. She strongly maintained her association with politically moderate women or, as she described them to Will, women "somewhat between the suffragettes and the women who don't believe in doing anything."[3]

Safeguarding her health, Mrs. Taft did not accept many of the fundraiser invitations she received. Instead, for charity auctions she sent autographed White House prints and handkerchiefs. It was also by mail that Nellie Taft exercised some government influence. Although she could not make inspection tours of government working conditions as she had originally planned, Nellie kept abreast of hardship cases of government workers, enlisted men, and private citizens. The initial press about her influence over the President prompted citizens to appeal to her. "You are so associated in my mind with all that is strong and vigorous," a Caroline Hastings wrote her. A Mrs. Remel wrote Nellie because she had "the good influence a woman usually has over her husband," and so asked her to "use your good offices with him."

With her practical, even pessimistic nature, Nellie Taft recognized that anything was possible in politics—including the defeat of an incumbent. Once she felt herself restored to reasonable health, she returned to consider what she was doing with what might be a limited amount of time in power. She did not have to seek a cause to exercise a degree of influence that could benefit those less fortunate than herself. The situation thrust itself upon her.

Certainly advertised to the public as the most politically involved of the First Ladies to that time, Nellie Taft became a natural target for the general public in need. While each case was simply an individual one and did not necessarily accumulate into some larger, specific "cause," other than helping the suffering or aggrieved, judging by the number of pleas and requests and "beg letters" that she received, Nellie Taft was to, in fact, aid more American citizens in a personal manner than any of her predecessors.

Every angle was used to get her attention. A novelist hoping to get a government job to support his writing ambitions appealed to Nellie because she was "very devoted to music and because of the artistic temperament which I believe you must possess." A request to get an applicant into the

Annapolis Naval Academy was made on the basis of an alleged but unsubstantiated distant kinship to the First Lady, and a Texas woman tried to get her husband retained as a postmaster because, like Nellie, she was "not [in] very good health." A Mrs. Evans begged for help for the "sake of American Womanhood" and a Mr. Jabs because he was the "most unfortunate individual civilian" in America. Some resorted to extreme measures, such as the man who claimed to have sent a chain to the First Lady as a gift, then applied for a job—for which he was rejected—and demanded the nonexistent chain back. She was asked to feed the poor of China, honorably discharge sailors, reinstate a U.S. Surveyor General's office clerk fired for forging mining field notes, appoint a Filipino as representative to the Argentina centennial celebration, and prevent a Turkish immigrant's son from having to serve in the Turkish army.

Although she avoided causes with a potential for controversy—such as the effort by the Daughters of the American Revolution in Baltimore to stop a government plan to use historic Fort McHenry as a port for immigrants—the First Lady directly intervened in numerous cases. Among them, she got West Point cadet Jewett Casey Baker a yearlong leave of absence to help his family, Louise Leland a job in the local Washington government, and Elizabeth Sloan a government job transfer when she moved to Montana. Often, by a minor act, she greatly altered a person's life. When a Mrs. Duvall stopped her at a social function, Nellie listened: Her husband, a former local policeman, suffered from nerve damage due to exposure to the elements on his job and had been let go. Mrs. Taft had the man hired as a White House guard. "Through your intercession," the woman wrote, profusely thanking the First Lady, "he has improved in health and God only knows how grateful I am to you for it."[4]

Individuals who sent appeals to Nellie would eventually receive a response over her secretary's signature with a copy of the government investigation and decision on their cases. A referral from the First Lady expedited decisions, and nothing fell through the bureaucratic cracks when an inquiry was forwarded from her desk. If she already knew an answer, her office would respond directly to the applicant rather than route the plea through government channels. In the case of a Pennsylvania man seeking to replace the local postmaster, for example, she wrote that he needed his senator's and congressmen's endorsements first. While the law might be stretched from time to time, it was never broken. No matter how strongly Mrs. Taft felt, if an applicant could be helped only by circumventing civil service rules or other laws, it was not done.

Some also wrote Nellie after trying the President and receiving no response or fearing that if his secretary opened it, "the waste basket would be the next place." It certainly worked at times, as in the case of a Mrs. Kratz who was reinstated in her old War Department job. Neither Will nor Nellie, however, ever presumed to obligate the other. "I have written this person that if she would like to see the President she will have to communicate with you first," Nellie's secretary wrote Will's. "Mrs. Taft will not see her." Nor did the President's secretary make assumptions when letters intended for the First Lady first came across his desk. When he initially prepared a form letter to turn down a Mrs. W. W. Brown who sought the First Lady's patronage, he soon learned that Mrs. Taft wanted to help the woman. He struck out the words "She does not . . . care to avail herself of your kind offer" in his first draft and replaced them with "She will be glad to . . ."

There was a good line of communication between the First Lady and the President's office. In the situation of John Dougherty, for example, who took the civil service exam and wanted to be a clerk at the Panama Canal, her secretary wrote the President's secretary, "Mrs. Taft would like to know if anything can be done for him." Typical of the routing, it went directly from the President's office to the Civil Service Commission. On another occasion, in the case of Rose Mary Ball, who needed temporary employment, a clerk noted that "Mrs. Taft is interested in case and thinks President ought to issue order if necessary." At the President's order, Ball was given a temporary Census Bureau appointment.[5] While certainly these were modest gestures that shifted no policy or led to any great revelation about her influence, on a small personal basis they illustrated the positive impact the First Lady could have on the lives of individual citizens.

The First Lady was personally friendly with the War Secretary, Treasury Secretary, and Attorney General, but there is no hint that she ever directly lobbied a case to them; her requests were always routed through the West Wing. Based on her correspondence with some members of Congress, she appears to have supported passage of three pension bills: for former Civil War nurses, volunteer officers and soldiers who served in the Philippines, and the widowed second wife of the late President Benjamin Harrison. Any lobbying, however, was done covertly. Only one story on her political intercessions broke publicly—a *New York World* story, "President Heeds Mrs. Taft's Plea for Mercy for Condemned Man," that was picked up by other papers. A Russian named Perrovich, convicted of murder in Fairbanks, Alaska, was sentenced to death, a punishment supported by the Attorney General. Intercessions to save the man's life were on the President's desk, where the First Lady often poked about.

> *Actuated by his wife's pleas that mercy be shown the condemned man, the President had commuted the sentence to life imprisonment, although it is said he was not inclined to interfere with the carrying out of the death penalty until Mrs. Taft intervened. . . . The incident has served to illustrate the part Mrs. Taft plays in at least one phase of the work of the Chief Executive. The President considers all pardons and commutation cases in his study in the residential part of the White House. . . . Mrs. Taft takes a keen interest in these matters.*

Nellie took an active interest in political appointments, too. She was inordinately proud that her old friend from the Philippines days, a Mrs. LeRoy, now widowed, was named Land Office clerk, a position not covered by the civil service. Archie recounted how Nellie dismissed one of Will's potential appointments because "he is perfectly awful and his family are even worse." She was even more intent on protecting Will from "pickpockets" than getting even with those she disliked. In reference to Mr. and Mrs. Robert Ferguson, she wrote, "They seem to take the stand that [Will] is obliged to do something for Mr. F. who has never been loyal to your Father, but has openly spoken against him as we hear from everyone." There is testimony to her patronage control in a cover memo from Will regarding her successful placement of a friend in the Justice Department. Written with humor, it nevertheless reflected the power the President gave her. "Memorandum for Mrs. Taft—the real President from the nominal President: If you are going to give Gist Blair a place in this Administration you had better talk with the Attorney General about him. He has the power of appointment over in his Department. Don't come to me, who have very little influence in this Administration."[6]

The cases that most appealed to Nellie were those where children were in need of protection or aid. A moving letter from a Mrs. Pincus Schein related how her son was not only refused admission at Ellis Island because he was thought retarded—when he was only "badly tongue-tied"—but was about to be deported to Europe where he no longer had anyone to care for him. In less than a week eleven-year-old Solomon Schein was released from the "mass of strangers" at Ellis Island and given to his mother. As the Commerce and Labor secretary Charles Nagel wrote the President, "The case is one of unusual hardship and the family has Mrs. Taft to thank for the decision."

With tens of thousands of immigrants unable to speak English and lacking practical skills pouring into the country, efforts to teach them and their children were springing up throughout the country. When such groups appealed to the First Lady, she generally lent her support. For example, Mrs. Taft accepted honorary membership in the M. M. Society, a group of Jewish teenage girls who "sew for the poor, distribute flowers to the sick and also aid one another through studious efforts and literary culture."

Although her name could help, Nellie knew that direct support from the President was even more effective. Consequently, although she supported The Little Mothers, a program that gave the daughters of working mothers lessons in homemaking and child care, hosted outings and holiday parties, and maintained nurseries, kindergartens, and a library, she got the President to help their fund-raising. In another instance the First Lady found the International Sunshine Society's work especially pioneering. The society focused on teaching blind infants and children rather than just adults, so they could begin life with an ability to communicate. Mrs. Taft got the President to speak at their fund-raiser in New York.

African American teacher Anna Murray was one person for whom the First Lady directly got the President's aid. When the president of the Cincinnati branch of the International Kindergarten Union, recalling Nellie's work with that group, forwarded a letter from Murray, who was seeking to "spread the kindergarten work in the South among the colored children," to the First Lady, not only did Nellie "induce the President" to meet with her in the White House, making her the first African American to confer there with a President since Roosevelt met with Booker T. Washington, but Will also sent a letter of support for her cause to be read to potential supporters in the capital.

Interested in child welfare, Mrs. Taft naturally took pride in the April 1912 federal appointment of Julia Lathrop, social worker and colleague of Jane Addams, to head the newly created United States Children's Bureau, the first federal office to investigate and report on matters relating to child welfare and child life, especially among the poor. Suffragettes praised Will for the appointment. While no correspondence between Lathrop and Nellie is extant, the First Lady's attendance several weeks earlier, in the first week of March, at a congressional hearing attested to her genuine interest in child labor.[7]

In January 1912 one of the nation's most dramatic confrontations between industry and the labor movement took place in Lawrence, Massachusetts. Some thirty thousand mill workers, mostly immigrants, went on strike to protest unsafe working conditions. Half of the town's young people aged fourteen to eighteen were employed at the mills. Fourteen-year-old Camella Teoli was among the sixteen children who testified before a

House Rules Committee hearing on the strikes and ensuing violence, and the First Lady listened to her entire testimony. Throughout, reporters kept their eyes on her: "[A]n interested observer of the proceedings . . . Mrs. Taft spent some time listening to the charges of cruelty, of the alleged clubbing of women and children by the police of Lawrence, the huddling of strikers' families in jails, and of children being taken from their mothers to the Lawrence poor farm after the authorities had stopped wives and children being sent to other cities to be cared for by sympathizers." Especially gruesome was Teoli's tale that predated the actual Lawrence strike when earlier in her factory employment a machine pulled out her scalp and left her hospitalized for months. So gripped by it all, the First Lady returned for two subsequent sessions.

Mrs. Taft's presence at the hearings fostered more publicity about the testimony, and although she had come to the hearings because of her interest in child welfare, she may have inadvertently increased public sympathy for organized labor. In fact, Nellie gave Bob her honest reaction: "Kitty and I went to hear [the] House Committee investigate the Lawrence strike three times—but my inclination [she struck out the word *sympathies*] was with the employers."

Several days later, however, Helen acted as a guide at the National Consumer League's Industrial Exhibition in Washington. The President's daughter, "an enthusiast in the reform movement," had become an expert on sweatshop conditions and now showed the press specific items made in sweatshops, while explaining the work involved, the paltry wages, and the living conditions of the workers.

A week later, perhaps in a coordinated campaign effort to suggest that the President's family supported working women, the First Lady was the guest of honor at the Women's Industrial Exhibition in New York. Nellie spent several hours inspecting booths and exhibits—from the Widowed Mothers Fund to the National Consumer's League. She was surprised to discover the variety of industries that women were employed in, but she skipped the National Suffrage Association booth. It was said to have been an "accident" that she wasn't allowed to stop there, and she "didn't mean to pass them by." The missed opportunity and the later explanation certainly permitted the First Lady's current view of suffrage to remain undefined.[8]

Had the First Lady's usual escort, Archie Butt, been present, such omissions would have been avoided. Butt, however, had suffered something of a nervous breakdown while accompanying Taft on his western trip in the fall of 1911. The journey had been the longest in presidential history to that time, some thirteen thousand miles, and Archie became ill on the trip and spent much of his time bedridden. Back in Washington he was still weak, but whenever the President had appearances Archie was in attendance. Sometimes there were two dinners in an evening, and the physical strain became tremendous. "It got the best of him," Hoover said of Butt. "He actually broke down." For four years, since coming to the White House in the last year of the Roosevelt presidency, Butt had not had a vacation.

His breakdown was as much the result of the mental anguish caused by the Roosevelt-Taft schism as physical exhaustion. Save for Nick Longworth, Butt was the only person who had each man's trust, understood their quirks, and tried to preserve their friendship against all odds. In a matter of weeks Archie would have to choose between Roosevelt and Taft, but for the time being his presence seemed to suggest support for both Roosevelt and Taft, preventing the open attacks typical of primary campaigns. Yet he had to make the next move.

The sad situation of Archie Butt and the ensuing tragedy that soon involved him and consumed the fascination of the world might manage to briefly and poignantly distract Will and Nellie Taft from returning their focus to the Roosevelt problem, but it ultimately only intensified it into a genuine political crisis.

During the holiday season Alice Longworth delivered her father's ultimatum. "I was lunching with him in New York," she told Archie, "when he said to me . . . '[t]ell Archie from me to get out of his present job.

And not to wait for the convention or election, but do it soon.'" Alice added her own opinion: "The President can't be elected, and it looks doubtful if he can even be nominated." Weeks later Roosevelt's sister Corinne told Archie that Teddy "would never forgive the President for introducing or allowing his name to be introduced into the Steel suit."

Archie grasped at any small bit of news that he thought might suggest the Tafts still cared for the Roosevelts. When he visited the Roosevelts with the hopes of patching up the friendship, he piped up that instead of having a new china pattern, Nellie had decided to simply order more pieces of the Roosevelt pattern. Edith tartly remarked that it showed "a good unprejudiced mind." She sent "love" to Will. Theodore did not. Archie was paralyzed: If he went to work for his beloved "Colonel," he would be "cowardly" for abandoning Taft. Above all he liked to think himself chivalrous.

On February 25, Archie and the Tafts were dining at the White House before heading to the theater for a comic monologue from Buffalo Jones on how he caught live animals—making, Will cracked, "animal hunting in Africa ridiculous." A bulletin was brought to him at the table. Roosevelt had released his response to the letter from the governors urging him to run. If it was the "genuine rule of the people," he said, he would "accept the nomination if offered." Furthermore, he said the "rule of the people" could only be determined "through direct primaries."

Now that all the speculation was reality, there was the feeling of a dam finally having burst. For the First Lady it was a perverse point of pride. "I told you so four years ago," she harped to Will about her long-simmering suspicions about the Roosevelts craving for another term, "and you would not believe me." The President shot right back at her: "I know you did, my dear, and I think you are perfectly happy now. You would have preferred the Colonel [Roosevelt] to come out against me than to have been wrong yourself."[9]

Four days later, at the insistence of Francis Millet, Archie Butt obtained a surgeon's certificate attesting to his weakened state and took a leave of absence for fifty-four days. Their mutual friend Richard Watrons recalled the fervency with which "Millet pleaded with Major Butt to go to Europe with him for a rest and the manner in which Millet pleaded with the President to order Major Butt to go with him when the President demurred."

Francis had been in Rome superintending new American Academy of Arts buildings. Upon his return he detected the change in Archie. "No Damon and Pythias friendship could have been closer than the friendship of Major Butt and Millet," Watrons said. "The two kept quarters together and were inseparable when both were in Washington. . . . Millet noticed that Major Butt was looking paler than usual, and generally run down. He announced to us his determination that Major Butt should rest." Still Archie vacillated. He was overwhelmed with guilt as he lay awake at night, thinking, "This is the time" to be of "any real comfort" to Taft. "I really can't bear to leave him just now." The next morning Butt told the President he was canceling his trip. Taft, Archie Butt recalled, "would not hear of it and insisted on my going."

Archie and Francis were to go directly to Rome and would then proceed to Berlin, Paris, and England. From there they would sail home. Butt was scheduled to be back at the White House on April 22. President Taft gave Archie a letter of introduction to the Pope as well as many Vatican officials. When American reporters in Rome spotted Archie on his way to the Vatican, stories began appearing that Archie had been sent on a secret mission to confer with the Pope on the state of Catholicism in America. The tip had likely come from a cardinal seeking good publicity for the Pope, but the result was the reintroduction of the 1908 campaign claims that Taft, who denied Christ's divinity, was undermining American Protestantism, especially with his inclusive attitude and policies toward Catholics and Jews. None of this was helped by the headline news that Harry Taft's wife, Julia, had converted to Catholicism and that Will and Nellie had attended a Catholic "peace" mass at Washington's St. Patrick's Church on Thanksgiving Day. When word of the President's letter of introduction to the Pope for Archie became known, Taft feared "an inquiry by Congress as to whether I am opening diplomatic relations with the Vatican."

In reality, Archie's two letters from Rome—dated March 19 and 23—did report polite and somewhat substantive discussion of the relationship between the U.S. government and the Catholic Church. Despite the fact that Taft was *not* attempting to establish a secret link to the Vatican and that Butt's letters might prove embarrassing but ultimately exonerate Taft of the charge, the missives were not made public at the time. Nor were similar ones such as that from Pastor Baugher of the Indiana First Christian Church, who wrote with outrage that if Will was reelected, "this American nation of ours would be turned over to the Pope." Regretting that he had given Butt the introduction to the Pope, Will refused to provide one to his sister-in-law Julie Taft for her imminent trip to Rome. He was determined not to lose the nomination to Roosevelt on any account—however trivial, rooted in bigotry, or utterly baseless.[10]

Perhaps the most welcome of distractions from the antagonism of Teddy came for Nellie Taft with the warm winds that signaled the arrival of spring in the capital city. During Butt's absence the First Lady had a day of triumph over adversity. The three thousand cherry blossom trees that the mayor of Tokyo had promised her at the end of 1910 were, this time, chosen carefully and nurtured throughout 1911 and early 1912. Free of all infestation or any other fungus, they were shipped to the United States and arrived in the capital on March 26. As Yei Theodora Ozaki, the Tokyo mayor's wife, wrote Nellie, the trees would be "a memorial of national friendship between the U.S. and Japan. . . . We hope to hear of their blooming in the salubrious Washington climate reminding you all of Japan's faithful devotion and admiration for her old friend and tutor, America."

The next day, with Eliza Scidmore, Colonel Cosby, and the Japanese ambassador watching, Nellie Taft planted the first cherry blossom tree, a Yoshino, in a simple ceremony. The ambassador's wife, Viscountess Iwa Chinda, planted a second one, after which Nellie gave her an American Beauty Rose bouquet. There were no photographers, but plaques later marked the trees. Within four years the entire Tidal Basin would be ringed with the donated trees, near those that had been initially planted in 1909 in Potomac Park.

West Potomac Park would not, however, prove to be the only lasting legacy of Nellie Taft as First Lady. Under the headline of "Aided by Mrs. Taft," the March 17, 1912, *Washington Post* reported that executive order number 1498 providing for the systematic inspection by the Bureau of Public Health and the Marine Hospital Service of all executive branch government buildings and offices to standardize and maintain the sanitary and hygienic conditions in all executive department workplaces in Washington, D.C. had been issued by the White House two days earlier. It "has revealed the interest Mrs. Taft is taking in the welfare of the men and women who serve in the numerous government departments."

Executive order number 1498 came after several years of prodding by the First Lady and NCF findings and recommendations. President Taft's order called for overall supervision by the surgeon general. A board of health experts would continue surveying conditions on a monthly basis in executive branch government buildings in Washington, determining precisely which required structural changes to get up to proper ventilation code. Many buildings had only windows and chimneys to let any air into crowded rooms; in others, all that was needed were mechanical ventilators. Proper lighting and plumbing would also be provided. Although many foreign governments had laws requiring healthy conditions for workers, the executive order prompted by Nellie Taft was "the first time that a systematic effort has been made to improve sanitary conditions and improve the health of the employees" of the U.S. government. For a woman whose judgment of people was colored by their class, this first-documented instance of a First Lady effecting official government action on public health was a proud illustration of just how far she had grown in her commitment to those less fortunate than her.

Proud of her accomplishments, Mrs. Taft was eager for a second term to build upon her accomplishments. She seemed confident and ready for the fight that she and Will faced. After two years of stressful speculation about whether former President Roosevelt would challenge Taft, the First Lady was greatly comforted by the fact that at least Butt had *seemed* to decide to cast his lot with the Tafts—and not the Roosevelts. "He was champing at the bit to get back to Washington and declared if he ever did get back he would never go away again," Butt's last host in London wrote to President Taft. "Strange enough he was very melancholy part of the time and talked again and again of death and declared he would not have much longer to live. We chaffed [teased] him about it, but somehow he had the feeling in his system."

From England, Archie wrote to the President what he called "this final letter." He told Will how hard it was for "everyone who formed the link between the Colonel and yourself." He also had letters from friends to deliver to Taft. While he was in Europe, Archie had received a letter from Edith Roosevelt asking him to visit her once he set foot back in America; certainly it was also a veiled invitation to confer with Teddy. He was "anxious to be home," but Archie would neither visit Roosevelt nor give Taft his letters. And he would never choose either man over the other.[11]

With Francis, Archie set sail for home on the S.S. *Titanic*. From Southampton they traveled on the enormous luxury vessel in their first-class quarters, crossing the Atlantic at a clipped rate and dining on the finest cuisine and champagne. They rarely, if ever, had contact with the masses of poor immigrants from numerous nations—Finland, Ireland, Italy, Syria—who stayed below in steerage. First class was an English-American crowd, but Francis was not impressed. "Queer lot of people on the ship. There are a number of obnoxious, ostentatious American women, the scourge of any place they infest and worse on shipboard than anywhere. . . . Many of them carry tiny dogs, and lead husbands around like pet lambs." His letter was mailed from Queenstown, the last stop of the *Titanic* before it headed out to the open seas.

On the night of April 14, Francis joined Archie as guests of the Widener family at a private dinner in the A La Carte Restaurant. Afterward, they went to drink at the Café Parisian, a watering hole for first-class passengers. It was here, at about 10:30, that they might have felt a slight bump: The *Titanic* had hit an iceberg. The captain, who was with the party, told them that the ship could sink. Archie instantly left to help keep order.

As the ship began to take in water and the lifeboats were being lowered, there was panic. Many men tried to get into lifeboats, but officers—and Archie—prevented them from doing so, permitting only women and children in. Will later called him a "shining figure . . . on the deck of the great ship, helping others to safety and facing death with the calmness of one rejoicing in an opportunity to sacrifice self to duty."

Throughout his life Archie was an appalling class snob who made open and frequent bigoted remarks against blacks, but in the moment of truth, Butt redeemed himself. He made no distinction in his efforts to save lives—except against the stronger, privileged white male. One *Titanic* survivor, a Mrs. Harris of Washington who knew Archie, pointed out that he saved the lives of "ever so many women from the steerage. . . . Major Butt helped those poor, frightened people so wonderfully, so tenderly, and yet with such cool and manly firmness." She recalled Francis's "little smile" as he waved to another woman in a lifeboat being lowered and how Archie had yanked back the collar and cracked on a railing the head of a man who tried to get on a boat. "Sorry, women will be attended to first, or I'll break every damned bone in your body" were Archie's last known words. A Libyan teenager emigrating to America in steerage was yelling for her brother, who had been placed in the last lifeboat, about to be lowered. Archie swept her up in his arms and rushed her toward her brother. "I noticed he was weak, and I could understand he was praying for strength to get me to the lifeboat. I was praying for him and for myself," the girl would recall.

In the darkened Chase Theater, Will and Nellie were laughing at the Pole Players's production of *The Nobody Widow* when military aide Lieutenant Rockwell was led by the Secret Service to their box. Rockwell whispered to the President, and he and Nellie left immediately. Will sat up in his new office, the Oval Office, late into the night, waiting for news of Archie's survival. He even wired the White Star line but received no reply.

The last credible sighting of Archie and Francis had them giving their life preservers to women just before the *Titanic* sank entirely into the icy black North Atlantic waters. Francis's body was eventually recovered.

In the following days the Tafts attended several memorial services for Archie and all those lost. The President—who had insisted that Archie go to Europe—was overwhelmed with guilt. He admitted that he couldn't "go anywhere without expecting to see his smiling face or to hear his cheering voice." At the memorial service for Archie in his hometown of Augusta, the President spoke without notes and allowed tears to openly stream down his face. "He was loyal to President Roosevelt and his family while he served him and retained their love and affection always," he remarked. "Then he came to me and to my family and became one of us and was as much interested in the welfare of each one as if he had been a son or a brother."

Typically, while Will gave way to his emotions when they were too much to bear, Nellie contained hers all the more. In no letter or statement did she express her true feelings. Two weeks after the sinking, however, Natalie Hammond contacted the First Lady to propose that the women of America raise a $500,000 memorial to the men who gave their lives. Nellie immediately responded, sending the first dollar of the fund-raising drive and saying she was "[G]lad to do this in gratitude to the chivalry of American manhood." Donations were limited to one dollar so more women could contribute, and Nellie was "sure that every woman will feel that the smallness of the contribution will enable her to do the same." Some months later she would preside at a benefit performance on Broadway from a presidential box, where those who contributed $1,000 could sit with her. Debutantes sold souvenir theater programs at Broadway shows and raised $10,000 for the cause. Gertrude Vanderbilt Whitney was chosen as the memorial's designer.

The memorial created a backlash, however, when it became clear that wealthy white ladies intended to honor only those "brave" English and American men of first class. Numerous references in witness testimony and newspaper stories belittled the working crew, men in steerage, and any but the "Desirable Immigrants" from northern Europe. Archie and other society gentlemen were contrasted with the "miserable specimens" in the third class. Attacks on the memorial—and, by association, Mrs. Taft—came swiftly. Many suffragettes felt that women, given the opportunity, could be as brave as men and would have given their lives for husbands and children. Why didn't it also honor the heroines of the tragedy or engineers who realized the danger but stayed on the job to the end? Many of the first-class men who saw to it that women got into the lifeboats were themselves unaware of the actual danger and may not have been as chivalrous as the First Lady believed them to have been. As one poem published in an Indiana newspaper put it, "A monument for millionaires, a monument for snobs, No marble shaft for the men on the craft, who simply did their jobs."

The *Titanic* tragedy carried a potential second wave of disaster for President Taft. Nellie's support of the monument to the heroic men not only alienated suffragettes—who could vote in some western states and now had Roosevelt supporting their cause—but associated the President, through her, with elitists contemptuous of the workingman, which was hardly helpful to winning over progressives.

With his usual tin ear for what the public wanted and needed in the way of symbolism compounded with his distracting grief, Taft had failed to see the immediate need for a *Titanic* investigation or even lowering flags in national mourning. He never even issued a proclamation. His presentation of the Congressional Medal of Honor to Captain Arthur Henry Rostron of the *Carpathia* for his response to the *Titanic*'s distress signals only bolstered the impression that he dealt only with prominent figures tied to the tragedy. It was one missed opportunity after another to connect with the electorate. "I do not know whether Taft or the *Titanic*," wrote Henry Adams, "is likely to be the furthest-reaching disaster."

Yet, as he considered the fragility of life and the value of fighting for it, William Howard Taft seemed to liberate something within him that Nellie had long hoped he would. As Will said of Archie Butt, but might have said as well about himself, "Occasions like the sinking of the *Titanic* frequently develop unforeseen traits in men. It makes them heroes when you don't expect it."[12]

Seventeen

"If They Don't Win, It's a Shame"

You have the worst luck.

—NELLIE TAFT TO WILL TAFT,
THREE DAYS BEFORE THE ELECTION

I f Nellie Taft had been waging a personal battle against Teddy Roosevelt long before the 1912 election, it was always based more on his personality than on any principle he stood for or policy he proposed. Once she became the wife of the incumbent President, Nellie became all the more vigorous in her partisanship and made certain that Will said or did nothing to bite the hands—the National Republican Committee members—that fed them. When Will disparagingly said Republicans were attempting to use a conflict with Mexico as an excuse to unite the party, for example, she considered him disloyal to the party for making such a cynical remark—however true.

By the time Roosevelt challenged Taft for the 1912 Republican nomination, however, Nellie Taft had developed some political principles beyond the mere promotion of her husband. She wanted Will to win, but no longer at any cost. "Papa got off the Reciprocity message," she had written in early 1911 to Bob. "He has a great notion of its harming him running for the Presidency again, but I don't care if it does or not, as long as he thinks it right." That was a remark in sharp contrast to 1908 when she advised Will not to mention the tariff, for example, because it would work against his nomination. Her personal dislike of Roosevelt hadn't been replaced by a high-minded regard for the issues of the campaign; rather, they were forged together. She believed strongly that the greatest threat to the American system of government that Roosevelt posed was his proposed "reform" to permit federal judges to be recalled. She "had been urging him [Will] to come out openly against this fallacy in governmental reform for some time," according to friends.

As far as the Progressives were concerned, Nellie—as Butt had said—went "to the center of things." She was outraged at one such "coward" senator who was willing to call the President "weak and vacillating" but without attribution; she found this more contemptible than political disagreement. She was also doubtful that Progressives could be brought to support Taft. After hosting a lavish dinner for freshmen Republicans in the Senate whose support Will hoped to win, Nellie cut to the chase: "Well, you have had your new Senators, and I don't think you made much headway with them." She could even joke about it. After she permitted an inferior violinist, who was a constituent of a Progressive senator, to perform at the White House, she said she would "do a great deal to propitiate the insurgents" but would henceforth "draw the line on admitting their musical friends."

Will had again begun to rely on Nellie, especially her keen memory, telling an aide, "[I]t was marvelous how she could repeat things accurately after days had elapsed." In one instance, after conferring with Senator Reed Smoot of Utah about who among the potential Democratic rivals would be the easiest to defeat, "someone came up and began to speak to Mrs. Taft of the political situation, and she repeated word for word what Smoot had said." When Will retreated into the fantasy that Roosevelt would not try for the nomination, she returned him to reality: "I think you will be renominated, but I don't see any chance for the election." The extent of Nellie's public role in the campaign was descending the South Portico steps and walking down the gravel driveway with Will for "moving picture machines" on February 14, producing fodder for newsreels. To what extent she reviewed the convention and campaign strategy of the professionals now advising Will is not clear, but she certainly supported using any evidence coming in to show Roosevelt as a habitual liar.[1]

The proof was being accumulated by the Taft forces. There was a May 19, 1911, letter in which Teddy declared that his own potential nomination in 1912 "would be not only a misfortune to me, but undesirable from the standpoint of the Party and the people. . . . I expect every real friend and supporter of mine to do everything in his power to prevent any movement toward my nomination." There was also substantial data tracing paid patronage. "If anybody doubts the intention of Theodore Roosevelt to make himself perpetual President of the United States," wrote Leroy Vernon of the Taft campaign to a White House operative, "let him ponder well over the facts herein set forth." Another Taft supporter wrote of an encounter in which a legal scholar had told Roosevelt that the Constitution gave the Executive Branch far greater powers than any of the past Presidents had taken, and how Roosevelt was "entirely carried away" with the possibility of exploiting any such loopholes and began conjuring up the circumstances in which he could eliminate "the power of both Houses of Congress when [those legislative bodies were] in opposition to the will of the President."

Taft publicly rebuked any suggestion that Roosevelt was an alcoholic, but privately he seemed to consider that Roosevelt's mental health might be unstable, in light of what the Tafts viewed as Teddy's erratic statements and driven ego. One New Yorker confided to Will that two "alienists" (psychologists) diagnosed Roosevelt as suffering from paranoia. The First Lady received such a letter in regard to Roosevelt, asking, "Why isn't there a doctor for maniacal hysteria?"

Nellie had long ago laid out her view of Roosevelt. Now, less directly involved in Will's political fortunes than at any previous time, it was up to the man himself. Here was a chance for Will not only to fight for reelection but to counter attacks, defend his revered principles, and finally grant himself the validation he had always sought from others. At first, he hesitated, while former ambassador Henry White carried out a last-ditch effort to save the Taft-Roosevelt friendship. It failed. As Elihu Root said of Teddy, "When he gets into a fight, he is dominated by the desire to destroy his adversary completely."[2]

Taft picked up eighty-three delegates in the March New York primary and, he said, Teddy, with only seven delegates, was "beside himself with rage." Roosevelt accused Taft of "receiving stolen goods" and corruptly winning delegates by giving them political jobs in the federal government (in fact, it was Roosevelt who had given most of the delegates who were officeholders their jobs) through "dirty instruments"—the corrupt political boss William Barnes, Jr. (who, Roosevelt failed to mention, had allegedly helped him in 1904). Finally, Roosevelt called Taft's New York victory a "fraud."

By late April, Will finally realized "that the time has come when it is necessary for me to speak out in my own defense. . . . I cannot longer refrain from refuting his false accusations." The chief usher's notes reflect the personality change that came over Taft in the months leading to the convention:

> [W]hen the contest for re-election [was] hot, President Taft seemed
> to get quite mad. He took issue with what Mr. Roosevelt was
> preaching and in angry tones said . . . he would get out and tour the
> country and make speeches in reply. . . . The preparations for these
> speeches . . . necessitated a lot of work on the part of the President.
> He was mad and angry all through and his dictation could be heard
> all over the house. . . . His suspicion of those about him who had
> served under Mr. Roosevelt increased as the days went on. So much
> so that it really became an issue in his mind as to who was loyal.

Taft was especially suspicious of the Secret Service. While the President spoke from the caboose on a whistle-stop tour, an agent at the other end of the train praised Roosevelt to several citizens. When Taft learned of this, the agent was immediately fired.[3]

On April 29, the day before the Massachusetts primary, Roosevelt and Taft barnstormed the Bay State. To ten thousand Republicans that night Will passionately shouted his speech from the podium in Boston's Arena. Point by painstaking point he made the case that Roosevelt was wrong in charging that "fraud and violence" had been used in the primaries and state conventions or that he had abandoned progressivism. Roosevelt, said Will, was suggesting that he was a "puzzlewit"—a befuddled thinker with no logic. Taft showed that he had initiated more progressive reforms than Roosevelt and had functioned scrupulously within the Constitution. Emotionally, it was a cathartic experience; in essence, he had practically declared Roosevelt a liar. Afterward, sitting in his railroad car, Will held his head and moaned to a reporter, "Roosevelt was my closest friend." Then President Taft began to cry.

In Massachusetts the next day Teddy flew into a rage when he learned that Taft had quoted from their letters to make his case. Roosevelt threw away his prepared speech and pummeled the air with his fists, shrilly claiming that Will had been disloyal to "every canon of decency." Will didn't blink. He called Roosevelt an "egotist" and "demagogue."

"I had nightmares for two nights in which I came suddenly upon papers with 'Roosevelt sweeps Massachusetts' in headlines," Helen wrote with relief when she finally heard that her father had narrowly won. "I suppose the nomination is about safe now unless something unexpected happens."

Then came Ohio. Roosevelt called Taft a "guinea-pig brain." Taft called Roosevelt a "honeyfugler" for his trying to sweetly gloss over a glaring discrepancy. President Taft raised the question none others had yet dared: What about Roosevelt's famous 1904 promise not to run for a third term?

Teddy dissembled; well, he meant no consecutive third term. On May 23, Helen focused on the good news before the bad news. "The twenty-four delegates from Texas cheered him a good deal," she wrote, keeping tight score of the delegate count with her mother. "Papa got back this morning and doesn't seem blue. But," she reported despondently, "I heard about Ohio." If Nellie had been upset when Teddy won Pennsylvania, she went into high alarm when he took her Buckeye state. "Roosevelt put three hundred thousand dollars in Ohio—your Father expected to break even with him there, but he only got seventeen votes and he thought [that] had he not gone out there, the whole thing would [have] gone for

Roosevelt," the First Lady wrote to Bob. "I hope it will be better in New Jersey—but I don't know. Roosevelt seems to have captured the working man." He *did*—as well as New Jersey.

Teddy said he would attend the National Republican Convention in Chicago if a "grave emergency" of "unfair play" seemed likely. Many states had disputed delegates. Which were legitimate would be determined by the national committee, which an incumbent President's supporters traditionally dominated. The Taft forces would seat delegates they decided were "right." Alice Longworth would attend under the guise of neutrality. She was both the wife of Taft's most vigilant friend and supporter and the daughter of Taft's adversary, but she could declare her support of her father only at the risk of jeopardizing Nick's congressional seat and being banished to Cincinnati, an outcome she dreaded. Such "bottled-up savagery" caused a "chronic cold and cough, indigestion, colitis, anemia and low blood pressure—and quite marked schizophrenia."[4]

In the weeks prior to the convention Nellie assiduously clung to routine. Her activities seemed trivial and disconnected from the larger drama of the imminent Republican nomination. After a short respite to Charleston, where she declared southerners "strange" for "always tak[ing] half an hour to get ready for anything," she had her garden parties and attended Potomac Park concerts. On May 21 she welcomed Rose Hoes and Cassie James, a team of society women who were creating a Smithsonian exhibit of clothing worn by First Ladies throughout history, and eagerly donated her inaugural gown, thus immediately validating what would endure as a compelling tourist sight in the capital. She grudgingly paid for a wedding gift after being convinced she couldn't palm off a piece from her silver anniversary surplus. The bride, she sighed, "does not want silver." Three weeks before the convention Nellie was simply "reading and sewing." It was, said Helen, "a very quiet life." It was purposeful distraction to preserve her health. "Except for the nervousness that Nellie feels from the present contest, and her reluctance to read Roosevelt's attacks on me," Will wrote, "she is very well."[5]

The greatest distraction came on June 18 when she joined Will to watch the Washington Senators beat the Athletics. It was a delayed "opening day," for when the season opened in April, the President had been preoccupied with the *Titanic*. Now he came to throw out the ceremonial first ball.

"Father and all of us regarded baseball as a mollycoddle," Alice Longworth had declared. In contrast, the Tafts loved the game. Nellie was the first baseball enthusiast in her family, initially drawn to Cincinnati Reds games for her children, then going on her own with women friends. In 1910, Taft had become the first President to throw out the first ball, Nellie taking it from him briefly so he could remove his gloves before pitching. "Take Me Out to the Ball Game" was even the hit song that year. With the Senators on an amazing sixteen-game winning streak, having moved up from last place, the day became one of hope over adversity, especially in light of the *Titanic* disaster. Will and Nellie, warmed by the crowd's welcome, seemed almost indifferent to their political fortunes, as if a "Take Me Out" lyric—"if they don't win, it's a shame"—was a metaphor for their fatalistic attitude toward the Republican convention, which opened that same day.

Teddy was the star of convention week. Alice—who lost her luggage and had to wear the same suit for several days—was usually at his side and predicted to a reporter that "the result [of this convention] is going to be the same" as the one in 1904. Meanwhile, Teddy declared that thievery had forced him to come to the convention but that he was strong: "I'm feeling like a bull moose!" He had already planned a rally to address his disgruntled supporters with a speech Alice had helped him edit. The address took on religious tones, with Teddy declaring that the nomination had been stolen from him, that he was "cast aside and left to die" as he led a "battle for the Lord."

Unlike 1908, Nomination Day 1912 found Will and Nellie subdued. Taft played golf. Nellie planned a quiet family dinner to mark their twenty-sixth wedding anniversary. Throughout the convention balloting they and Bob were in the family rooms, while Charlie relayed bulletins that came via telephone in the West Wing. Will was so blasé about his renomination that he never made use of the phone in the family rooms that was hooked up directly to his convention headquarters for his convenience. When the nomination was secured, Taft made it clear that it was less a personal victory than a vindication for "constitutional representative government." It was even publicly acknowledged that he cared less whether he "wins or loses in November" than the fact that "Rooseveltism," a "most serious menace to our Republican institutions, has been averted." Rather than refer to the convention as that which renominated her husband, Nellie sarcastically called it the one at which "the party was divided."[6]

In the end, as she most desired, Taft beat Roosevelt for the nomination, and yet despite her claims that Will's being the Republican standard-bearer was her only hope that election year, the First Lady turned her sights on the Democrats. In a two-way race of Taft against the Democratic candidate, her hopes for four more years in the White House rose. Shattering one precedent after another, 1912 saw Nellie Taft become the *first* First Lady to attend a presidential nominating convention. Four days after Will was nominated, she took the train to Baltimore and shocked the Democrats by appearing at *their* convention. No other First Lady would ever attend the opposition party's convention.

If part of her strategy was to blunt the inevitable Democratic attacks on Taft, the First Lady succeeded. William Jennings Bryan confessed, "In introducing the anti–Wall Street resolution on Thursday I had planned a reference to President Taft and the Chicago convention. Just before that resolution was presented I was escorted to the part of the hall where Mrs. Taft was standing and was introduced to her. I didn't have the heart then, and the resolution as introduced did not have any reference to the interests that nominated Mr. Taft at Chicago. I am not sorry that I spared the feelings of the President's wife."

Nellie Taft still knew how to make an entrance. At 11:35 on the morning of the convention's fourth day, she swept into the hall, took a front-row seat in one of the boxes that abutted the platform, and was the center of attention for the half hour before the chairman appeared to open the session. She sat through the hot tedium of reports on credentialing, delegates shouting for a vote, a demonstration for House Speaker Champ Clark, and a protest against permitting the Philippines to vote since the Supreme Court had ruled they were not part of the United States.

During the recess she went out to dinner but returned at eight for the night session. She heard Bryan rail against the "privilege-seeking class," naming J. P. Morgan and August Belmont in particular, but not Frick, Rockefeller, Carnegie, or any of the industrial captains friendly to Taft. When Senator LaFollette appeared and was escorted to a platform seat near Nellie's, she did not acknowledge his presence because of the part he had played in fostering the Progressive Party. She was coy with reporters: "It's very interesting, isn't it? I don't suppose I could expect them to en-dorse the administration of a Republican president, could I?" To the pub-lic she declared that she was just there as a guest of women friends and, reported the press, to "see nominated who will oppose her husband." In fact, with her remarkable memory for political intelligence and discourse, she was trying to get a sense of Will's chances of winning the general elec-tion. When Woodrow Wilson won the nomination, however, Nellie's hope seemed to fade rapidly.

Settled in Beverly for the summer on July 3 after several days back in Washington, newspaper editorials soured her optimism. A year earlier she had admonished Will to read the opposition press so he would "know what the other side is doing." Now she felt there was "unfairness and in-justice" in most of the press and confessed, "I stopped reading the accounts of the bitter political contest because I found that the opposition newspa-pers made so much more impression on me than those that were friendly to my husband that I was in a state of constant rage which could do me no possible good."[7]

Nellie's frustration was compounded by the fact that she had nobody as informed as herself with whom to discuss the campaign. Will was mostly in Washington, and Helen and Bob were camping out west. While he certainly enjoyed many privileges as the President's son, Bob resented the interference the publicity created in his life. When he went to Europe the summer before, his hope of doing so incognito was dashed the moment the ship's captain invited him to dine at his table. There were the usual nut letters (one of which he naively answered himself) and the weird case of one Charles Baker, a "thorough scoundrel" who assumed Bob's identity until the police caught the imposter. Before he even made the head of his first year law school class, he was offered a position in the Manhattan local district attorney's office; he was unsure whether it was based on his deserved merits or the fact that the President had told the D.A. that working in his office would benefit his son's legal experiences. Obedient and dutiful, it could also not have been easy to have a mother who, in response to one of his letters, told him, "Don't sign yourself 'sincerely.' Sign 'affectionately.' "[8]

From Beverly, where Charlie was her sole companion, the First Lady kept in nearly daily touch with the President on campaign developments. He tried to calm her fear of the popular idea of Roosevelt running as a third-party candidate of a Progressive "Bull-Moose" Party. "They have fallen out about electors and various things," he wrote her, "and on the surface the third party movement does not seem to be gaining a great deal of ground." It would prove to be a gross miscalculation.

The First Lady was planning to return to the White House for the notification ceremony that would take place there, which Will took charge of arranging. Beyond the Notification Committee and some party officials, Nellie wanted no more guests, considering it a waste of money. "Not over seventy-five to lunch," she wired Will. Hours later she sent another warning, "The committee is sixty-five. Invite a few women to go with them. That is all you need." He shot back, "I don't think you quite understand"; he must invite the entire National Republican Committee, all Republican House and Senate members in town, and other supporters, "because it is a festal occasion. Therefore, we must have a buffet luncheon, and must expect to entertain 400 to 500 people."

Nellie relented, arriving with Charlie on the last day of July. The next day she welcomed the politicos as they gathered in the East Room for the ceremony, marching over in assembly from the West Wing. Will came down as the band played "Hail to the Chief." When Nellie walked in, she was heartily applauded. With three women friends, she sat in the front row. The Cabinet sat behind her, all the chairs in a semicircle facing the platform flush against the east wall. After the ceremony the Tafts received in the Blue Room, music played, and lunch was served.[9]

If Nellie's mood was momentarily lifted by the ceremony, it was lost four days later when word arrived from Cincinnati that her father had died. Nellie had not seen him since the previous November. She, Will, Charlie, and her brother Will went out for the funeral in the old Herron home, the President and Charlie serving as pallbearers. Will returned to Washington the next day, leaving Nellie and her siblings to distribute John Herron's possessions and bid adieu to their childhood home. At eighty-five John Herron had been in pain for two years, and, as Will said, his end was "a relief." The old man, Will continued, had his "chief pleasure" in "continuous labor" as an attorney well into old age and in knowing that he had provided for his children's educations. He left no assets. His home was sold to pay off his debts, and Maria moved into an apartment. In mourning, Nellie and Charlie returned to Beverly with Nellie's sister Lucy.

In the midst of such sadness came plain bitterness. Two days before Herron's death, Roosevelt was nominated as the Progressive Party candidate. Now Nellie "anticipated" Will's defeat due to what she euphemistically called "developments in the campaign." Any hope of Will's defeating Wilson was gone. "I wanted him to be re-elected, naturally, but I never entertained the slightest expectation of it and only longed for the end of the turmoil," Nellie claimed. "During the last campaign I was at Beverly alone a good part of the summer, but when Mr. Taft did join me for short intervals he brought Republican Headquarters with him, more or less, and a few political supporters were sure to follow for consultation with him." One of them, unbearably upbeat, insisted to her that Will would win. "Well, you may be right," she retorted, "but just the same I intend to pack everything up when I leave Beverly, and I shall take the linen and silver home."[10]

Will, in contrast, believed he still had a chance of defeating Wilson. Then came October 14. Late in the day he received word that Roosevelt had been shot—wounded but not killed, the bullet slowed by a metal spectacle case. Roosevelt's skin was punctured, but he suffered no lasting harm and was quickly out of the hospital. Will wired his wishes for a full recovery, but realizing "sentiment plays a great part in elections," he knew sympathy votes for Teddy would only help Wilson. Instead of bottling his anger, however, Will continued to vent it. "I have a sense of wrong in the attitude of Theodore Roosevelt towards me," he had written that past May. "The fact is that I do not think I ought ever to get over it." He still believed that "the hypocrisy, the insincerity, the selfishness, the monumental egotism, and almost the insanity of megalomania that possesses Theodore Roosevelt will make themselves known to the American people." Before October was over, Nellie would leave Beverly for New York. As if nothing else could possibly go wrong, Vice President Sherman suddenly died, making Taft the lone candidate on the Republican ticket. "Sherman's death was very unfortunate coming just at this time," Nellie wrote to Will three days before the election. "You have the worst luck." She was not hyperbolic. When the polls closed on November 5, Taft won only Vermont and Utah, and he came in last on the popular vote, not quite three and a half million.

Like 1908, there was no great overriding crisis to be dealt with by the man who won the 1912 election. The primary issue was the question of not whether reform should continue, but rather to what extent and at what rate. Roosevelt offered the most radical agenda: suffrage for women, stronger labor unions, greater federal government power and regulation, public health services, minimum wage laws, "social" insurance, inheritance tax, occupational safety standards, direct primaries, ballot recall of elected officials, full public disclosure of and limitations on personal campaign contributions, child labor protection, a six-day work week of eight-hour days, social security, workman's compensation, requiring lobbyists to register, publicly open congressional hearings, and no labor injunctions.

If Teddy seemed to have a promise for everybody, there were two that stunned and then motivated Taft to do all he could to see that Roosevelt was defeated: a less time-consuming manner in which to amend the Constitution than the required ratifications by statehouses and, most egregious of all to Taft, national referendums to reverse Supreme Court decisions. This was all the proof Taft needed to make his claim that Roosevelt wanted to destroy the democratic system of checks and balances and replace it with some Yankee-fangled socialism.

In comparison to Roosevelt's ferociously delivered declarations, Wilson's lofty, inspirational language made an equally heartfelt case for progressivism, but in more rational, smaller-bit reforms: the economic and political systems should be favoring the small businessman, entrepreneur, and the individual enterprise while held in balance by strict antitrust regulation. This, he claimed, would provide for the necessary social welfare reforms that Roosevelt wanted to come from the government. In comparison to Roosevelt and Wilson, Taft came out on the conservative side of reform, keeping the protective tariff in place, creating a powerful federal trade commission, increasing civil service, liberalizing banking laws, and ending campaign contributions from corporations.

With the Roosevelt challenge to the Taft candidacy, it had been a foregone conclusion to many that Wilson would win, if by math alone. Wilson only took 41 percent of the popular vote—smaller than Bryan had as the Democratic candidate in the last three elections, even with the population growth. Supporters of the Republicans got a total popular vote of 50 percent, but it was split between Taft and Roosevelt. As one Republican leader sighed, "The only question now is which corpse gets the most flowers."

Had Roosevelt run against Wilson alone, he would have won. Had Taft run against Wilson alone, the results are debatable. Taft would likely have lost, since the Roosevelt progressives would have gone for Wilson. On the other hand, Republicans who were more firmly entrenched in the

Teddy cult might have stayed loyal to the Republican Party, even if they didn't entirely agree with Taft. Wilson had a total of 6,296,547 popular votes. Roosevelt had come in second with 4,118,571 popular votes. Wilson, however, took 435 electoral votes, while Roosevelt got only 88, and poor Taft, the paltry eight from Utah and Vermont.

Overall, the voters wanted more reform than less (the Socialist candidate, Eugene Debs, managed to get 900,672 popular votes—nearly a full-third of the President's 3,486,720 popular votes). They found their answer with the man in the middle who seemed to offer just the right amount of reform—Wilson. Sensing his victory, Wilson further trampled the Grand Old Party by vigorously campaigning for Democratic candidates for Congress. He ended up delivering for himself a greater gift—a Democratic majority in both houses of Congress that would work closely with him to pass great amounts of progressive legislation, much of which Taft and Roosevelt would both manage to see as positive changes, in retrospect.

Another factor, however, had played into the election. It was one in which, had she been as active and vigorous as in years past, Nellie Taft could have potentially had a great influence upon. It had practically nothing to do with the real issues and policies that Will loved to bore the crowds with. It was rather something that could emerge by giving the campaign a title (Roosevelt had "New Nationalism," Wilson had "New Freedom"), or rephrasing his speeches for some unforgettably vivid phrase ("We stand at Armageddon," Roosevelt had implored his followers), even adopting a symbol (Roosevelt, again, had the Bull Moose).

After the Progressive convention, Taft had become a passionate man on a mission to defeat what he feared were Teddy's revolutionary impulses. "Death alone can take me out now," he had even declared of his determination to see Roosevelt thwarted. A consciously executed and revamped translation of the complacent President into a fiery, principled constitutional defender would have helped make Taft not only more accessible to the common man but appealing to them as a "character," not unlike the way that little, funny "Tramp" from England, Charlie Chaplin, had done in the Taft years. For a person who stayed as current with public sentiment as she had upon entering the White House in good health, the stroke and subsequent weakness that Nellie Taft had endured was all the more tragic in its final effect. She had been forced to become too absorbed in her own well-being to fully recognize the cultural changes that had shifted her favorite game of politics. However much she had made overtures and begun to open her view toward the needs of the middle and lower classes, she had become distracted. She failed to recognize that the masses—even those millions of immigrants who did not speak or understand English—were responding with a great universal emotionalism to the power of a good story and a great picture.

By 1912, the "illustrated newspapers" had largely shifted from creative renderings of factual events to real pictures. The shiny-sheeted magazines were now able to print dozens and dozens of photographs in just one issue. The moving picture had progressed from clips of a few dozen seconds watched individually in a nickelodeon viewer to reels that could be projected in small theaters.

Among the candidates themselves, only Roosevelt seemed to be keenly, acutely conscious of this, slipping into his manically waving persona punctuating his appearances with his crowd-pleasing signature line, "Bully." No matter that Taft had stopped millions of western acres from desecration by the coal industry and water-power plant developers and created the Bureau of Mines to ensure preservation of natural mineral resources, Teddy had fought his children against having a Christmas tree because it killed a tree, and he saved a baby bear in the wilderness. While the Bull Moose publicists did not refresh for the public's memory the details of why Taft fired Roosevelt's old forestry chief, they certainly made Will appear far more anticonservation than he was. And when rumors reached Roosevelt that love letters from Wilson to a woman other than his wife could be used against the Democrat, Roosevelt dismissed this tactic, not on the basis of fairness, or modesty, or abhorrence of dirty politics, but it too dramatically conflicted with the public persona of Wilson, already cast as a prim Presbyterian. An "apothecary" could never be recast as a "Lothario," was the way he put it.

That Teddy Roosevelt won more of the popular and electoral votes than Will Taft did was essentially a moot point to the President. The point was simply that America had been rescued from potential anarchy: Even a prudish professor was better than the hostile hunter. If Taft's pummeling had left him wiser about so-called friends, and more cynical about the press and the political system, it was also proof of his highest-held value, being true to oneself. If being a dull speaker, who bored the public with the facts rather than stirred their imaginations with a utopian vision of the future, meant that Taft's caution was his downfall, he was proud to be cautious. It may not have won him enough votes to win an election, but it got enough votes to save the country from the Bull Moose.

Taft would always rather err on the side of caution. He did not want to provoke any strikes, any unrest, anything that could accumulate into socialism and a destruction of the capitalist system. He recognized that labor and technology were transforming that system, but he decidedly sought to change it from the government's viewpoint in gradual steps, punctuated with pauses, when necessary. And it was in this regard that William Howard Taft was able to view his four years in the White House as successful. The greatest accomplishment of his term as President, he would repeat (most always in private conversation or, occasionally, correspondence) was protecting the country from a man whose radical progressivism would have dangerously weakened the Constitution.

It was a Pyrrhic victory also savored by the First Lady, but in an entirely personal context. Teddy may have beaten Will, but Wilson beat Teddy. The chief usher thought it "strange to hear the satisfaction expressed that Mr. Roosevelt had failed. That seemed to be the crowning pleasure." In truth, she was conflicted. Being First Lady had largely proved to be personal trauma, but having four more years to try again would have been welcome.

"I have been seeing people every day condoling with me, on account of the election, as though your Father would have had a Democratic Congress. . . . I am very glad that he was not elected," she wrote Bob, adding, "which is making the best of it." The chief usher soon realized that despite her saying all year that Will would lose, she had secretly hoped he would win, and became genuinely depressed when the results came in. "Plans were made for leaving with regret. Mrs. Taft had not improved, in fact seemed to have a setback after the election for she honestly believed the President would be re-elected. She had made plans for the second term. Interest seemed to be lost in everything." However ignoble vindictiveness might be, surely Nellie felt some: Alice Longworth was also leaving Washington. Nick had lost his bid for reelection.[11]

There was a curious epitaph to the 1912 election in which Nellie Taft figured far more directly in the ultimate loss of her husband's presidency than most people knew or, among those who knew, would openly admit. Not until fifteen years later did a reporter, Charles Selden, pick up a lead on it and dare to suggest it in print, and gently at that. "It is just possible that if Edith Carow Roosevelt and Helen Herron Taft had become fast friends in their early Washington years," Selden wrote after speaking to Helen, "the political history of the country would have been different and no Bull Moose would have taken up temporary habitation with the Elephant and the Donkey in our political zoo."

The idea that former President Roosevelt might not have contended with Taft for the Republican nomination and in the general election had their wives been friends was ludicrous; it was larger issues and policy disagreements that drove the two men into their far corners from each other. Yet it was on just such a sensitive personal quirk that Roosevelt seemed to turn on Taft. Edith Roosevelt had never extended herself to Nellie Taft, who never forgot it. Evidence suggests that the spiteful slights that Nellie inflicted on the Roosevelt women had more than the effect of a social snub.

"I don't know what I have done to offend Theodore," President Taft had pondered to his brother Harry at the end of 1911. "I have heard that he is offended because we did not do more for Mrs. Roosevelt while he was in

Africa. . . . *What else could it have been?* [author emphasis] I offered to appoint anyone he named. But he didn't ask me to appoint anyone." Surely, Will decided, the Roosevelt vendetta could not have been based on something so "trivial."

In fact, the social slights had so enraged Roosevelt that he put his anger in writing, to Henry Cabot Lodge. Lodge replied to him in Africa that both he and Nick Longworth were "hurt and galled by the attitude of the White House towards Edith and Ethel of which you speak." Nick wrote to Teddy, however, that the indifference to Edith was not due to Will, who always liked her, "but is Mrs. T." Will had also been correct in stating that Roosevelt hadn't asked him to make any specific appointments—including that of Nick Longworth to China. The desire for that possible appointment had been conveyed by Alice to Taft while Teddy was in Africa. Again, not for political but rather for social reasons, Nellie insisted on blocking that request.

After the election, Will wished no one poorly. Others did that for him. "Having accomplished your purpose animated by a feeling of cruel jealousy and desire for revenge and standing as the most colossal liar of the time," wrote one L. A. Ault to Roosevelt, "many former admirers are now trusting you will subside." Will would stay active in politics, he told one correspondent, Samuel Carr, to "end the Rooseveltian menace to our government and keep him harmless."[12]

What would he do now? He and Nellie briefly considered a world tour. In February, he had said that Cincinnati was "where I expect to live and die," but Nellie would not go back. Offered the Kent Professorship at Yale Law School, he happily accepted: It was honorable for a former president, yet allowed him to make money writing and lecturing. He did not feel it was proper to accept, and thus turned down, a pension offered by Andrew Carnegie. He had no bitterness. "The nearer I get to the inauguration of my successor the greater the relief I feel. . . . I am content with the opportunity that has been mine. . . ." He still longed, however, for his old dream. "My tastes had been, and still are," he wrote nine days after the election, "judicial."

As Will prepared to make a final inspection of the nearly completed Panama Canal, there was no way of talking Nellie and Helen out of accompanying him. Helen was given the honor of opening one of the giant gates of the Gatun lock for the first time, pulling a lever that set the electrical equipment in motion. On their return, once they had landed at Key West, the Tafts rushed by train to Washington in time for their last New Year's Day Reception.[13]

As 1913 began, Nellie proceeded with the last of her entertaining. Even at the eleventh hour she managed to break another precedent when she hosted the first comedic performance in the White House, inviting monologist Ruth Draper to entertain on January 7. There was a National Civic Federation meeting, a Visiting Nurses Association reception, and a visit to help a local first-aid effort. A group of society women led by Mabel Boardman presented Nellie with a parting gift—a $100,000 chain of white diamonds set in platinum and with a hanging pendant of a pear-shaped diamond. There would be a unique dinner honoring her predecessor, the widowed Frances Cleveland, and her fiancé, Thomas Preston, as well as Mamie Dimmock Harrison, President Harrison's second wife and the niece of his first wife, who had scandalously married her older widowed uncle. Alice Longworth even came to dinner, under the polite protection of Nick's sister Clara de Chambrun, on February 7. When Will wrote a letter to the incoming First Lady Ellen Wilson, praising Elizabeth Jaffray and Arthur Brooks, and urging the Wilsons to keep them on, he scribbled below, "Mrs. Taft has read this and approves it." By the third week of January, Nellie was in New Haven complaining that there were few choice houses to rent. They would eventually buy a Victorian house on Prospect Street, not far from the campus.[14]

Then came the inevitable. At six o'clock on March 3, when the Wilsons called, Will and Nellie were, said Helen, "as practical and cheerful as possible. Papa seemed to delight in being beautifully cordial to the Wilsons, which annoyed Mama a little. They had a very amusing quarrel as to whether they should receive them . . . in the Red Room . . . invitingly arrayed in candles and tea table or in the Green Room . . . cold and gloomy. . . . We received them in the Green Room."

On March 4, Nellie Taft left the White House, walking slowly and sadly over the same presidential seal she had so excitedly noticed four years earlier. Will, delayed in joining her and Helen at Lucy's house, met them at Union Station. They were headed to Augusta for three weeks of golf. "People seem so sorry to have us go," Nellie wrote Bob in her last letter written from the White House, "and many are coming to the station to see us go."

Nellie would never disclose what she felt as she had to relinquish this house. Getting into the White House had been the driving force of so much of her life. She lingered as long as she could, writing letters on White House stationery. The chief usher reminded her that Frances Cleveland's husband had been defeated for reelection only to win and return her to the White House four years later. At this, Nellie seemed to brighten with hope, and walked out.

Yet her sole public appearance the day before she left was the clue to the new kind of person she would become. At three o'clock Nellie Taft sat front and center on a parade stand on Pennsylvania Avenue to review five thousand marchers in white dresses with yellow and purple sashes—the largest parade of suffragettes in history. When a reporter asked Helen if, in leaving the White House, Nellie had felt a great sense of relief, the ex-President's daughter sighed, "Well, Mother was never very much for relief. She always wants something to be happening."[15]

Eighteen

Elba (1913–1921)

Well, we live to learn.

—NELLIE TAFT TO WILL TAFT, MARCH 27, 1895

The black outfit Nellie Taft wore on her arrival at her new home, a cold New Haven hotel, obviated the need to ask how she felt.

Before leaving the White House she had stashed a supply of official letterhead into her handbag. Although she did cross out the words *White House* by March 25, she was still using the stationery two months after she was no longer First Lady. And she quickly learned what it meant to no longer enjoy the privileges of that title. "My maid left me in New York, so I had to do all the unpacking myself, which took me about three days," she reported to Bob on April 6.

Nellie, however, had always been quick to requisition whatever she needed—even from Will. She continued in her letter, "Your father has gone out for golf every day and takes Romaine along—his new valet—but Romaine is useful in other ways, opening boxes and trunks so that I do not complain—though I have to open the door myself, to the numerous callers who come in." When she couldn't get the car going on her way to the Harvard-Yale football game, Nellie got a group of boys to push it down some hills and she arrived by halftime. Nor had the weeks of "rest" in Augusta been much help: "The moment he got here, your Father went to play golf, as usual. . . . I go around terribly."

In contrast, Will was happier than he had been since his days on the circuit court. Relieved of the expectations of others, he lived on his own terms, teaching a few days a week, making dozens of speeches each year, and rapidly losing weight. He was rarely in their hotel suite, where they lived until their home was ready in the fall. When he was there, she admitted it was "dreary, dull." They rarely went out, and in one letter Nellie told Bob, "I occupied my time mending and sewing a white silk shirt waist in the newest style."

Life was also cramped, especially since Helen and her dog Caro were in residence, too. Helen was returning to Bryn Mawr in the fall, but she was often out with friends or making lengthy visits. Nellie was left caring for the dog, and once Helen had gone, the dog became Nellie's. Despite the fact that her first pet came to her so late in life, she grew exceedingly close to her new companion. Nellie took Caro with her everywhere she could, even marketing. The dog drew out a great tenderness in Nellie, and she was soon protective of her time alone with Caro.[1]

Concerned that a lack of stimulation might spur her tendency to depression, her husband and daughter were soon gently pushing Nellie into breaking yet another precedent. Will was soon negotiating Nellie's memoirs, working out advance and royalty payments and magazine rights with literary agent and editor Eleanor Egan. Nellie, who hated ruminating over the past, was initially reluctant, but it proved healthy for her, affording the chance to dispel the frustrated anger of her White House years before it could turn into bitterness. Helen did the writing while Nellie reminisced and tweaked the narrative. If reliving her happy days in the Philippines and poring through family letters seemed to clear the mental slate for the next phase of her life, her resentments of Roosevelt remained fresh, and although she displayed ironic humor when writing about him, her dislike is clear. She was equally frank in the book about her political interests: "I am not trying in this narrative to pose as a woman endowed with an especial comprehension of such problems of state as men alone have been trained to deal with. I confess only to a lively interest in my husband's work which

I experienced from the beginning of our association and which nothing in our long life together, neither monotony, nor illness, nor misfortune, has served to lessen."

"Her Home: Mrs. Taft Tells How She Felt and What She Did When She Entered the White House as First Lady of the Land" was the tag of the May 1914 *Delineator* magazine cover, complete with a diorama image of the White House front doors held open by two African American butlers. Given further coverage in *The New York Times, Recollection of Full Years* not only sold well, it set another of Nellie Taft's prized precedents: *the first* First Lady to write her memoirs.[2]

Nellie Taft was now really on her own in a way that she hadn't been since before her marriage. Helen returned to Bryn Mawr in the fall of 1913; Charlie entered Yale in 1914, but he was constantly absorbed in campus life—debating team, basketball team, and mandolin club.

Bob remained aloof. He wondered to his fiancée, Martha Bowers, if his family was really going to spend money on a planned South American voyage, but he couldn't simply ask them. Nor could he bring himself to tell them of his engagement. "I know she thinks we are engaged," he said of his mother, "for she is very quick to jump to that kind of a conclusion. And very often she is right fortunately." At the end of 1913, Bob passed the Ohio bar with the highest score in the state. When he moved to Cincinnati to practice law, Nellie urged him to accept the offer of Charlie and Annie to live in the mansion. "You will like it, all in all. You will have to be attentive and useful, much more so than if you stayed with my family, but I think it will be good for you. I think that you had better write and accept." Robert did as his mother advised.

Even after Bob and Martha married in October 1914, Nellie meddled. "You did not write to Aunt Delia about your wedding present. Your father discovered that. She said it did not make any difference though, but I think you must write." When she pushed him also to write a note of thanks to the Harry Tafts for their gift, Nellie got into trouble. Harry had relayed the initial slight to Nellie's sister Jennie who had also not gotten a thank you. Now Jennie was hurt that Nellie hadn't also told Bob to write one to her. "That," Nellie wrote her son, "is where the trouble came. I am very sorry about it."[3]

When Martha gave birth to a son, Will and Nellie were in California. Named after the former President but always called "Billy," the baby was the first Taft grandchild. Nellie, "crazy to see the baby," was just then taking in the exhibits of the Pan-American Exposition. In September 1915, Will and Nellie, with Helen and Maria, drove from San Francisco to Monterey, then took the train to Los Angeles and San Diego. In San Diego they were guests of the exposition, staying at the famous Hotel Del Coronado. "A committee of the fair met us there and we went in motors, troops marching ahead to the Exposition. There we had a formal lunch, then went over to another building where we shook hands with four hundred people," Nellie reported. "We came over across the ferry to the Hotel (another free hotel). . . . The bathing is not very good here. . . . [T]he undertow is so strong in the ocean."

Such public excursions and celebrations might remind Nellie that she was still a public figure, but these occurrences were indeed rare. Back in New Haven she was rather like Napoleon condemned to Elba. "The days go and I don't know what becomes of them," she wrote, "reading, sewing, housekeeping, and caring for Caro, who is a large part of my day."

Will was constantly on the road: Ithaca, Philadelphia, Cleveland, Wilkes-Barre, Kansas City, Chicago, Hartford, Toronto, Portsmouth, Boston, New York, and Trenton. He spoke to the YMCA, DAR, and the Knights of Columbus. He became a national leader on the issues of a world court and Palestine as a Jewish homeland. Nellie invariably began her letters with a report of his speaking engagements and travels—and how much he was paid. She gleefully reported that "he has made eight hundred and fifty dollars, speaking five times!"

While she certainly enjoyed keeping account of the lucrative speaking fees that a former President could command, Nellie was largely removed from Will's new life. He had a personal secretary who made all his necessary arrangements, and there no longer existed any reason for her to feel she must manage his appearances and speeches. She also felt that his activities were dull and routine—travel, dinner, speech, and travel. Nellie stayed home, but she seemed lonely at times. "Your father came home yesterday from Dartmouth at half past one and he just had time to say good-bye again, and went off to New York," she wrote sadly, "so he did not have time to tell me of his experiences at Dartmouth."

Being alone in New Haven left her miserable. She found the New Haven Symphony to be "perfectly awful," and as for all the young students in town, she confessed, "I don't think I get on with Freshmen at all." The feeling in town was mutual. "I came home to receive calls," she recorded of one of her open house reception days, "and did not get but one."[4]

Nellie gradually opened herself to new experiences. Among other things she became an avid Yale sports fan. "It is the third time that Yale has not beaten," she complained about a football game, "which is very rotten playing." She was happier with a 1915 Yale-Princeton baseball game, reporting, "It was very slow until the 9th inning, but Yale woke up then and it was very exciting until the end." Nellie Taft even attended her first basketball game. She also began a friendship with her cousin Carrie Collins, who lived nearby. A member of the Colonial Dames, Carrie coaxed Nellie out with her to meetings and into membership. Although she had no interest in her genealogy ("I don't know anything about it"), Nellie did develop an interest in Colonial American culture, attending lectures and concerts where music of the period was performed and explained. Most of all she was fascinated by Colonial architecture. After attending the annual Colonial Dames convention in Hartford, for example, she motored through Stratford, Old Lyme, and New London for a week, accompanied by an architectural historian.

While such activities were certainly trivial in comparison to her earlier life, they spoke of her delayed evolution. She would never have made time to attend sporting events in the past, and doing so forced her to relax. She had never previously made a conscious effort to develop a personal relationship with another woman such as her cousin, especially one who served no ulterior political purpose. It must have been a refreshing experience for Nellie to be liberated from the constant planning and conscious cultivation of powerful figures that had consumed so much of her earlier life. The excitement of enlarging her interests as well as the novelty of exploring and discovering an entirely new subject such as Colonial culture joyously absorbed her.

In was in this same period that a long-term pastime became a full-time passion. On any excuse she ran off to the theater, though "New Haven is a 'bum' place to see shows." She didn't go just for distraction. Beginning with her post–White House years, Nellie Taft was to become as observant and as insightful a New York theater critic as any found at a newspaper. In many ways the theater gradually replaced her obsession with politics; she often attended several performances of the same piece, analyzing plot lines, comparing actors, and judging musical and lyric quality. Initially it seemed simply an excuse to get out of New Haven, but soon it became a preoccupation. Her love of the stage even overcame her love of economy. "When I think of the money it costs, going to the theater so much," she wrote, "I ought to stop." But she kept going.

Nellie took in all forms of theater: classics, dramas, comedies, musicals. At first she usually caught matinees—"Wednesday and Saturday afternoons, if I have not anything else to do"—but she was soon staying in New York over several days, catching as many as ten performances a week. In the process the former First Lady was also rebuilding her independence, liberating herself from older notions of "improper" social behavior. "Friday I went to the theater to see 'The Girl from Utah.' Uncle Charley was there and came over to speak to me," she reported. "I felt rather foolish going by myself to the theater at night, but he did not speak of it, and neither did I." Escorted or not, Mrs. Taft kept right on stepping out in Gotham.[5]

There was only one other place Nellie enjoyed going to more than New York: Washington. It was the one place she insisted on accompanying Will. In the capital she was still queen bee. "All the people that I knew best were there," she reported on a lunch, "and those that were not there came to Armide's [McClintock] to tea afterwards." The Patten sisters, Mabel Boardman, and Evalyn McLean all honored her at receptions, dinners, and luncheons. "I had a magnificent time," she wrote giddily, "parties all the time." Always a connoisseur of cuisine ("You don't like food the way I do," she told Bob), Nellie found her palate best satisfied in private homes there. She waxed ecstatic about one dinner where she was served her favorite terrapin, "with a delicious sauce and cauliflower alone, with a nice dressing with cheese."

Nellie used any pretense to visit Washington. Although she had long scheduled a trip to Cincinnati to see her grandson, when she heard that Martha was bringing the baby to Washington, Nellie decided there was "no sense in my going west" and rapidly offered: "I will go to Washington and stay with Lucy." Her motive was all the more transparent since the family knew she'd disapproved of Lucy's 1915 marriage to Rhode Island senator Henry Lippitt. Nellie readily confessed: "I love to go to Washington."[6]

Increasingly, Will was in the capital consulting with the man who had defeated him in 1912. Elected to a second term in 1916, Woodrow Wilson shared Taft's vision of a world court to resolve disputes. "Your father went to . . . Washington, where he spoke with the President on peace—though affairs are broken off with Germany," Nellie wrote Bob two months before the United States entered World War I.

Even before Congress declared war on Germany in April 1917, Will and Nellie supported American involvement. Will had remained a staunch supporter of the Red Cross, and Wilson named him to the organization's council that was formed to prepare for the inevitably heavy demands brought on by the war. Once the war began, he and Nellie donated some of their stash of "silver gifts" to the aviators' fund of the National Special Aid Society. One of the dramatic changes the war brought to their life was Wilson's naming Taft as joint chairman of the National War Labor Board on April 8, 1918. It meant that Nellie Taft would return to Washington, at least temporarily. "The New Haven ladies seem to have stepped out as soon as they discovered you were about to leave," Charlie teased her, knowing how unpleasant her social life had been there. "[W]hen you get all moved in down in Washington you'll have a pretty good time, better than in New Haven."

The second great change made for mixed emotions. "Charlie-Boy," as his sister called him, enlisted as a private in the Third Field Artillery, eventually becoming a sergeant. It was hard on Will and Nellie. "You are the apple of our eye," Will wrote him. Two months before he sailed for Europe, in December, Charlie married witty, kindly Eleanor Chase from a wealthy Connecticut family. Weeks after Charlie's departure, Caro died. The loss hit Nellie harder than she expected. Caro had drawn out a gentle sensitivity in her, and as a daily companion the dog had taught her a patience she had never had. Will wrote with gentle sympathy to her: "My heart goes out to you, dear." The sudden absence of her favorite child and the vacuum left by the passing of her beloved pet were compensated for, in part, by the close relationship she developed with her grandson Billy Taft, who came to live near her in Washington after his parents relocated there. Bob had taken a position as assistant to the Food Administration's director, Herbert Hoover.

If Nellie had finally relinquished her hold on Will's career and the direction of his life, she still held firmly to her own destiny. However her ambitions had shrunk—theater, lectures, concerts—Nellie Taft remained in charge of her own agenda, but now with far less aggressiveness or frustration when she did not achieve it quite as perfectly as she envisioned it. This was perhaps the greatest lesson of the 1912 defeat for Nellie. As difficult as her first months and years were after the White House, she had regained her old sense of fun. The war, however, forced Nellie to confront the possibility that she might lose the greatest love of her life next to Will—her "Charlie-Boy." She buried herself in writing letters to him and going back to work. In Washington, the former First Lady became a volunteer waitress, pouring coffee for sailors at the Navy Lunch Room. She even gave what is known to be only the second public remarks she made, delivering a "patriotic speech" at the Washington Club. Sometimes she went with Will on trips, like one to Georgia where they inspected a munitions factory, "and afterwards to see the machine guns firing." To ward off anxieties about Charlie, she quietly rolled bandages, worked the canteen, or knit socks and skullcaps.

Even summer in Murray Bay, her most pleasurable constant, was shadowed by Charlie's absence. She had expanded the house—decorated with Philippine souvenirs—and improved the property. "[W]e arranged the armor in the hall, which is a grand place now, and later we fixed the rugs which we had brought from home, and put the hooks in every closet and the shades up," Nellie detailed to Bob. "We stained the floors, upstairs and down. They don't look very well." To her Murray Bay news Charlie responded irreverently: "It is great to hear of the same old crowd of people allowing you to win all the bridge prizes from them in the same old way."

From the front, Charlie began a lifelong habit of sending his mother single-spaced typed letters, running up to six pages on occasion, and sharing the minutest details of his life—with his humor. When his aunt Maria Herron, a Red Cross volunteer, was driven out of her post by the Germans, Charlie piped up, "You can't beat her for seeing the war." When his wife, sister, and mother sent a Christmas package, Charlie cracked, "I wish I could have seen you and Helen and Eleanor fighting over what to put in." Even Will got a jab. "I never saw anything like that father of mine. Not only is he talking everywhere, but he seems to be raising all kinds of money, even his own." The letters calmed Nellie and drew her even closer to Charlie.[7]

Both mother and son were as wary of Wilson's ego as they had been of Roosevelt's. When Charlie read a copy of a letter Wilson wrote to Taft, he thought it a "little too carefully drawn" and told Nellie, "I'll bet you made some disparaging remarks about it after you read it." Edith Wilson, the President's second wife, had Nellie to lunch at the White House, but there was a strained politeness between them. Both Tafts supported Wilson's

League of Nations, articulated at the Paris Peace Conference following the November 1918 armistice, and Nellie even joined Ladies of the League. In one week, for example, she participated in a conversation at home with Will and Charles Warren who "wanted to talk about peace" and attended several pro-league speeches given by Will and others in Boston. When Taft went out on a western speaking tour, Nellie noted disparagingly, Roosevelt progressive and U.S. senator from Idaho William E. "Borah is trailing him, speaking against the League of Nations." Following Wilson's stroke, Edith's secret stewardship of the presidency, and their effort to keep Vice President Thomas Marshall from assuming office, however, Nellie turned on the Wilsons. Lois Marshall "should" have been First Lady, she wrote, "but Mrs. Wilson kept her out!"

As for Roosevelt's reconciliation with Will, Nellie remained silent. "Mrs. Taft, I may tell you, never returned to the familiar 'Will-Theodore' status with their one-time friend," Washington socialite Nelle Scanlon noted. When Roosevelt died suddenly in January 1919, Will attended his funeral and sobbed at his grave site. Miffed at being seated with the servants at the private funeral, he stoked Nellie's dislike of Edith Roosevelt by reporting, "Mrs. R, you know, is exclusive and it was her idea." Nellie stayed home and made only passing reference to the fact that Will had just "got back from the Roosevelt memorial." She gave no sign of mourning, loss, or regret. In the Taft home, it was observed, there was not one picture that recalled Roosevelt among the many mementos that celebrated their life in politics.[8]

The Tafts kept their Washington apartment until the end of September 1919 and returned to New Haven that winter. Nellie, who had been planning to sell some real estate she owned in Washington and buy in Cincinnati, decided to hold on to it. Apparently she had not given up hope of returning.

Meanwhile, the work in all fields that women had done during the war had turned both Tafts into full-fledged feminists on numerous legal, political, and social issues of gender equality. In a lengthy, thoughtful article in *Ladies' Home Journal*, Taft became the first President—incumbent or former—to seriously address the need to break "prejudices of society" against women. "Custom and habits have a powerful effect always to restrain reasonable and needed reform," he wrote. "Convention has heretofore had a great deal to do with the restriction on women's opportunities to earn their own livelihood."

He especially affirmed that women should work before marriage, gain their own financial strength, and not be forced to marry out of material necessity. He and Nellie made a fundamental shift from their previous view that wives should not work: They no longer saw a career as necessarily interfering with marriage and motherhood. As a member of the National War Labor Board, Will publicly called for all American industries and unions to embrace the principle that "women engaged in the same work as men should receive the same pay" and called for legislation to that effect. "Women who can work have just as sacred a right to earn a living by the sweat of their brow as men. The Constitution secures it, and it is one of the chief elements of civil liberty."[9]

The primary reason for the shift in Will's and Nellie's attitude was the example of their daughter. While Nellie would be quick to exercise her right to vote, she had been apprehensive when Helen became a national spokeswoman for suffrage, worried that it might hurt her academic career. Helen, however, was full of confidence. During the war she had focused on the farm labor shortage and the increased need of canned food supplies in Europe. She worked on a farm—planting, hoeing, harvesting, and canning. She became a speaker for the Women's Congress of National Service, outlining practical ways women could "help solve the war problem" on the home front. Helen had come to feminism by experience, not theory.

After graduating from Bryn Mawr in 1915, with honors and the Literary Prize, she entered a Yale graduate program in history, earning her Ph.D. in 1924. "Helen does not come home to lunch at all," Nellie complained. "She takes her lunch down to the library. She says that it interrupted her [—] coming home." Helen would surpass the academic and professional accomplishments of most women. In 1937, at age forty-six, she would even earn a law degree from George Washington University. At Yale, Helen met Frederick Manning, a 1915 graduate, who had his doctorate in history and then served as a lieutenant in the war. While Fred began his career as a history instructor at Yale and then went to Swarthmore, Helen ascended the academic ladder rapidly at Bryn Mawr. Breaking tradition, neither she nor Fred asked Will's permission to marry—they announced their intention. Will responded with touching gentleness. He hoped she would delay marriage, fearing she might not finish her thesis or secure her degree, but concluded, "You are a woman of poise and level headed. . . . You and I are a good deal alike, more so I think than the boys and I." He promised to supplement their small income, and if he survived Nellie, Helen would inherit a full half of his estate, the boys getting a quarter each. If he died first, Nellie would inherit everything, and "I know she will deal generously with you." When she married in July 1920, Helen was already Bryn Mawr's dean—at twenty-nine years old. She broke even newer ground within the family when, after giving birth to their two daughters "little Helen" and Caroline, she continued to work, achieving tremendous respect in academia as an educator.[10]

For a woman who in her youth had been torn between having a family or a career and living her life according to her own terms or those of society, Nellie held her daughter in high esteem and was extraordinarily proud of her accomplishments. Helen was managing the sort of life that Nellie had wished for herself. Her reluctance, however, to vigorously support suffrage, despite Helen's involvement in the fight, seemed to have more complex origins. As a wife, Nellie had been welcomed by her husband and his brothers into their circle as a political adviser, regardless of her gender. She had enjoyed an access and exercised an influence as a woman that was rare in national politics in the early twentieth century and had pragmatically decided that derivative political power was better than none at all. Her experiences certainly didn't match those of the masses of less educated and less privileged women who were fighting for the right to vote, and, thus, she was less sympathetic. She had never needed the vote to be involved in politics.

There is no record of Nellie Taft's stating that she had relented in her belief that women should not run for political office. Considering the changes she would see in the coming decades and her ability and even eagerness to adapt, it is hard to imagine that a woman elected to political office would offend her. Had she been born later in the nineteenth century, Nellie Taft might very well have been a candidate for political office herself. In many ways the choices that Helen made with her life became instructive to Nellie. Despite the fact that the former First Lady would always be registered as a Republican, her daughter and son-in-law's activism in the Democratic Party broadened Nellie's sensibilities to such a degree that she became less of a hardened partisan.

A month before Helen married Fred, Ohio senator Warren Harding was nominated as the Republican presidential candidate. Taft and Harding got on well despite their differences on the League of Nations—which Will refused to abandon. Once Harding won, he invited Will to visit him in Marion, Ohio, and the former President reported his impressions of Florence Harding. "She is a little disposed to be anxious not to be backward, but she will readily adapt herself," he wrote Nellie. "I think she tries him sometimes but he is very considerate." In fact, the new First Lady from Ohio was like the last one: Florence even revived Nellie's favorite entertaining venue—the gigantic garden party—and took her advice to retain the housekeeper.

The most promising aspect of the alliance, however, was Will's future. Harding asked Will if he was still interested in the Supreme Court. "I said it was and always had been the ambition of my life," Will reported to Nellie. He affirmed, though, that at this point in his life he would accept only the chief justiceship. "He said nothing more about it and I could not make out whether . . . he did not further wish to commit himself. . . . I don't feel at all confident it will work out as I would like it, but it is more favorable to my hope and life ambition than I thought possible." Word soon reached Will that Harding would make the appointment if Chief Justice White resigned.

At the end of June in Montreal, Will received a phone call tipping him off that the Attorney General was sending over, for the President's signature, the nomination papers for Taft's appointment as chief justice. Excited and fearful, he wrote instantly to Nellie: "I don't know how long it would take for confirmation in the Senate. When I nominated White, Hale moved immediate confirmation . . . but I don't suppose my enemies in the Senate would permit this, and anyone by an objection could block it. There are many things I will wish to write you after the nomination goes in, if it does go in but I wait until the golf ball is in the hole." He wired her joyously the next day: "Nomination went to Senate four o'clock today. Love and kisses." Will was ecstatic, nervous, and full of energy and hope.

"Well, that has happened which I have always doubted coming true. I am Chief Justice of the United States lacking only the qualifying oath. . . . The immediate confirmation of the Senate was unexpected. . . . I have tried to call you up twice today but the line is out of order. I hoped to be able to tell you over the line what the change in my plans is." He had a lot to do: go to Washington and be sworn in, find a house there, confer with the Attorney General, resign an editorship in Philadelphia, and sell the house in New Haven. Having received the good news while he was in a Montreal restaurant, Taft even indulged in a rare glass of champagne.

Nellie never recorded her own reaction to the news that Will had finally achieved his great goal. In the years since the White House, however, Nellie had developed her own rhythm of activities, and Will never sought to control her. Interestingly, however, at the moment he achieved the position she had detoured him from pursuing, he seemed to distance himself from her, as if she might somehow talk him out of it, perhaps.

Will received hundreds of congratulatory telegrams, but none from Nellie. Whether he sensed a hesitation at her coming down to the celebration of his confirmation at the White House or was genuinely concerned, as he wrote her, about "throngs" of well-wishers bothering her and her having to bring "many clothes for functions at the White House" he did not encourage her to rush down to Washington and be by his side to share his joy. Nellie Taft, however, had never avoided a momentous occasion that celebrated her Will because of well-wishers or clothes.

Mrs. Taft may, in fact, have felt a degree of guilt over the difficult path she had led Will. "She realized afterwards," Helen later recalled to historian Will Manners, "that he hadn't enjoyed the Presidency as much as she thought he would."

When Will lost the 1912 election, he had first reverted to form—more concerned about his wife's feelings than his own. He confessed to Horace that he had "more sorrow at Nellie's disappointment and yours than I did [for] myself." The years since he left the White House, however, had greatly changed William Howard Taft. In fact, the process had begun when he became President and Nellie suffered her stroke. Will had gradually learned to make his own decisions without consulting her first. As a former President, this was truly put into action. There is no record at all of his depending upon or asking her for advice. As a former First Lady, Nellie clearly was relieved that she no longer carried such a burden of responsibility for her husband's public career and personal well-being.

As a consequence, however, they had grown bolder in making their own decisions with less regard for how it would affect each other. Will's acceptance of the Chief Justiceship was not a decision he had felt any need to consult Nellie on. Nor did he encourage her to share this day with him. He was finally going to Washington on his terms, not hers. "Have been thinking it over," Will wired Nellie. "Strongly advise against your going."[11]

Nineteen

In His Court (1921–1930)

*The truth is that in my present life I don't remember that I was
ever president.*

—WILL TAFT, DECEMBER 29, 1925

Returning to the White House in 1921 for a state dinner, as an honored guest with a new protocol ranking, must have seemed strange for Nellie. Her Will was no longer the President but finally the chief justice. Another overtly political Republican woman from Ohio was now reigning in the mansion—and she'd made her own history by becoming the *first* First Lady to vote for her husband and drive *to* the inaugural ceremony with her outgoing predecessor.

President Harding and his wife, Florence, were eager to welcome the Tafts back to the White House in the autumn social season of 1921. Taft was the only living former Republican President, and his new position further boosted his celebrity. Upon his swearing-in as chief justice, William Howard Taft became the only man in American history to serve as head of the executive and judicial branches. With this came an immediate shift in the public perception. Never a particularly popular or happy President, his joy at being chief justice was evident to all, even on the streets of Washington, as he swung his walking stick to acknowledge the waves of passing admirers as he took his brisk morning walk to work. He had studied and revered the history of the Supreme Court. He had waited a lifetime for this experience. Taft, said editor William Allen White, was just like "one of the high gods of the world, a smiling Buddha, placid, wise, gentle, sweet." Judging by the tone of the major newspapers around the country, Taft was beloved and cherished, and the appointment met with general approval.

Will's appointment, however, further altered the relationship that he and Nellie had created in their immediate post–White House years. Now she was no longer physically separated from him as much, since he stayed close to Washington, but she was more removed from his work and activities than at any point since his first judicial appointment to the circuit court in the 1890s. Will's new job, in fact, permanently ended the active partnership of the Tafts. Nellie had not learned to appreciate or find in any way interesting the judicial process or the world of law. That her spouse was now chief justice made no difference. At the same time, she came to utterly respect the bench in a way that she never had, and certainly supported Will in his avid devotion to his work. He rose just after five in the morning, got to work at six in his study, and ate breakfast with Nellie at eight. He then returned to his study for more work. At a quarter to eleven, he began his three-mile walk to Capitol Hill. The court was in session from noon to four-thirty. He was driven home, worked from five to seven, then worked again until ten. He would work himself into broken health, but Nellie did not dare to stop him from working as he wished to. It was as if he was making up for a lifetime of being denied his great love of the judiciary. While she never verbalized it, there must have been some degree of growing resentment toward the court for the toll it would take on her husband.

At the very least, however, it was the Supreme Court appointment that finally grounded Nellie in the city she loved most and into her first permanent home in a quarter of a century. As Will wrote, it was for them, "a return home. . . . We have been wanderers on the face of the earth and it will be good to be anchored in a city we like and where we have so many friends."

At the age of sixty, Nellie Taft finally settled into a house that became her true home. She would live in the three-story Georgian-style brick mansion on Wyoming Avenue longer than any other place. It was in the Kalorama section, and the Wilsons, Herbert Hoovers, and young Dwight Eisenhowers were neighbors. The Hardings and Franklin Roosevelts had moved out of the neighborhood just six months before the Tafts arrived.

Will had continued to defy Nellie when she argued that he had every right to accept the annual $25,000 offered to him by Andrew Carnegie before he left the presidency. Before leaving the White House she had made her point clear by describing a dinner where she sat next to Carnegie. "He was very nice," she wrote Bob, "seeing that your father has refused his $25,000." When Carnegie died in 1919, his will promised Taft $10,000 a year for life, and upon his death the sum would continue to be given to Nellie. This time she insisted he take it. "Mrs. Taft wishes me to do so," he wrote, "and she is an interested party." He capitulated. Now serving as chief justice, however, criticism of his continuing to take the money grew strident. There was even a call for a hearing on the potential conflict of interest of the Justice taking money from a U.S. Steel managed fund. Socialist leader Eugene Debs even called for Taft's impeachment or resignation. The publicity seemed hardly worth it, but on Nellie's account he rode out the attacks and kept collecting. Taft had also built on the $100,000 they had saved when they left the White House as well as his Yale salary and speaking fees. They still owned a valuable lot in Washington and several in New York's borough of Queens.[1]

Financial security was matched with professional bliss. "Your father has court duties all the time and work in the evenings," Nellie wrote Charlie two years into the Taft court. "He says that he is going to take Saturday night and Sunday for recreation, but I don't see any signs of it yet." Plunged happily into his work, lighter in weight than he had been since he was in college, Will felt free. As chief justice he would no longer collect speaking fees and lectured solely on what he wanted to, primarily international peace and fighting anti-Semitism.

Taft was among the first public figures of national stature to educate

American Christians on Judaism. He was passionate about fighting religious bigotry in America. "Henry Ford has attacked the Jews and they are in arms and are very anxious for me to make a speech for them," he wrote Nellie. "It is an outrage that Ford should make such an attack. As if we did not have [such] feeling enough without making more. If I can do this, I'll go into it con amore." Nellie often joined Will at Jewish venues, and on one occasion she even filled in for him, accepting an award for his support of Jewish causes and, in the same evening, taking in a Yiddish theater performance. Despite the class-based snobbery she had earlier expressed in regard to the masses of poor, largely uneducated Jewish immigrants from Russia, Poland, and the Slavic states (as opposed to her wealthier, well-educated Cincinnatian, German-American Jewish friends), Nellie shared Will's outrage toward religious intolerance, considering it to be the antithesis of "Americanism." In fact, both Tafts had been so vigorous in their view that they influenced their son Charlie to make a lifelong commitment to interfaith councils and organizations on the national, state, and local levels.

While Will wrote and spoke out in support of the Jewish homeland in Palestine, he was never able to fulfill his dream of seeing the Holy Land. In June 1922, however, he and Nellie went to England, their first transatlantic trip together since 1907. Most of the events honoring Will were restricted to men—jurists, political figures, and society. Hemmed in by her husband's schedule and looking bored by officiousness, it would be the last time they went overseas together. From then on she would go on her own.[2]

After being presented to King George, Will wrote to Helen that they "returned to the embassy, and your mother and the ambassador took some bottles of beer." It was a sore subject between Will and Nellie. The Chief Justice angrily resented her continuing to drink and serve alcohol during Prohibition, although many people defied the Eighteenth Amendment, including President Harding. "The truth is that Nellie and I differ on prohibition," Will confessed to his brother. "We might as well face that, because I am utterly out of sympathy with her and she with me." Prohibition or not, the chief justice's wife or not, Nellie still liked her cocktails. She seemed to delight in her defiance, proudly writing Charlie about a "gay cocktail party" she had attended at the time.

Mrs. Taft didn't care what anyone—including Will—thought about her continuing to enjoy drinking and serving alcohol. In 1915 when she had accidentally returned to Bob a mislabeled gift, she wrote him frantically, "Send the cocktail shaker on again. I want it very much—I am getting along [with] the other one now and it is not good at all." She was aghast when she checked into what she sarcastically called a "unique place" at Lake Mohonk: "They don't allow any drinking, card-playing or dancing." During a trip to Bermuda when a friend sent them off with three bottles of whiskey, "which your father says I can not bring home," Nellie confessed to Helen, "I have only drunk one bottle of Scotch and have to begin on Rye and Bourbon—as he sent one of each. . . . [T]he way that the Governor put away champagne was a caution." In consideration of Will, however, she was discreet. "I liked better the old Welsh rarebit of plain cheese and beer," she admitted to Charlie after trying the dish with a watery near-beer substituted for the real brew, "but I did not say anything to the others."[3]

From England, Nellie went directly to Murray Bay for the entire summer of 1922, and in October she joined Will in Washington. Suffering from extreme fatigue, Will underwent a battery of tests in December and January. Nellie reported, "Last Sunday your father was in the hospital and every day I went to see him. He got out Wednesday feeling well but not walking very much. Friday and Saturday I went to walk with him round the bridges, which he likes very much. . . . We had dinner alone." During their first fall and spring social season back in Washington, Will and Nellie were feted about twice each week. In late 1922, however, Nellie's brother Will, who worked at the Justice Department, suffered a heart attack and died. His death, "just when he had everything to look forward to," hit her hard. She plunged into mourning and rarely went out, perhaps comparing her own Will's capacity for enjoying life despite questions about his health.

Nellie didn't go to the funeral in Cincinnati. She still resisted returning there despite the fact that her sister, sons, and a growing number of grandchildren lived there. Her boys were attorneys at Taft, Stettinius & Hollister. Bob, increasingly conservative, was elected to the Ohio House of Representatives in 1921 and would serve as speaker and then go to the state senate. Charlie was the liberal president of the Cincinnatus Association, a group seeking to restructure the corrupt city council. "In our family we have one vote for the practical good and another vote for the ideally good," Will cracked. Fearing that Charlie's "radical action" might jeopardize Bob's political career, Will tried and failed to persuade Charlie to resign from his club. If Will looked out for Bob, Nellie still favored her "Charlie-Boy," usually staying with him when she did visit.

Elected county prosecuting attorney, Charlie soon put notorious bootlegger George Remus on trial for the murder of his wife. With a lifelong fascination for criminal stories, Nellie was gripped by the case all the more because there was said to be a hit out on Charlie from the Remus gang. "I sympathize with you about the bootleg cases and the 'crime wave,'" she wrote him, worrying if he was "satisfied with the jury." Charlie lost the case but ran again for prosecuting attorney. Nellie advised him to: "I know it is hard running again this year, but you have to do it. If you let down, all the party could complain, but do not run again." Several days later she added, "I hope your campaign is going along successfully, but don't be too hopeful." She was glad he lost. With his growing family she didn't want him struggling on a public servant's salary. "I am glad that the Community Chest went off tolerably well," she told him, "but I think you will wonder whether it is well [worth] while or not—working so hard, and not anything to show for it." She never stopped doting on and advising him.[4]

Nellie claimed that she preferred boys, but that wasn't the case with her first granddaughters, Charlie's eldest two: Eleanor, called "Nonie," born in 1918, and Sylvia who came two years later. Not only did she impulsively buy clothes for them, but if she saw outfits she wanted them to have, Nellie ordered Charlie to get them with admonitions she rarely made: "Send the bill to me . . . and don't pay attention to the price." She "enjoyed exceedingly" their visits. "How is Nonie? Is she as cute as ever? And Sylvia? I long to see them!" Nellie was equally loving with Helen's two daughters, Caroline and "little Helen," but as a full-time working mother and often low on cash, Helen Manning had less chance to bring them to Washington for visits. Although interested in the progress of Bob's sons, there was a distance with their parents. "We never hear from Bob and Martha, so we depend on you," she wrote revealingly in one letter to Charlie.

It was at Murray Bay, with all her grandchildren gathered about, that they most strongly felt her presence. As Seth Taft recalled of those August days, "It was full of family and she was very much in charge." The chief justice, however, spent much of his time in his books. Nellie created a private suite for him there of bedroom, bathroom, and library, "way off by himself and he keeps the door shut! And it makes him private."[5]

The setup at Murray Bay was a metaphor for the new direction that the Taft relationship had turned. Ostensibly, as a member of the Supreme Court, Will was now nonpartisan. Still, he tended to be conservative in his decisions; if there was any one emerging theme to his years as chief justice, it was his protection at all costs of private property. He helped to weaken, for example, the Clayton Anti-Trust Act by invalidating a tax approved by Congress on interstate products that had been manufactured by companies that used child labor, allowing injunctions in secondary boycotts, and making unions open to lawsuits. When his health began to deteriorate, Taft determined to stay on the Supreme Court as long as possible because he wanted to "prevent the Bolsheviki from getting control of it," he wrote a friend. He was not referring to real Communists, of course, but rather any potential appointees that might be made by President Herbert Hoover who, despite being a Republican, was a Progressive—a dangerously liberal faction of the party to Will's thinking during the massive unemployment and unrest of the Great Depression.

Interestingly, as chief justice he was far more in favor of expanding the duties of the chief executive than he had been when he himself had served in that position. He was generally well-regarded by associate justices. "It's very difficult for me to understand why a man who is so good as chief justice," Justice Louis D. Brandeis remarked, "could have been so bad as president." The reason, Felix Frankfurter retorted, was because Taft was happy on the court and had been unhappy in the White House.

Nellie, on the other hand, became increasingly less interested in politics and partisanship. Had the coincidence that she was the chief justice's wife under three successive Republican administrations been otherwise, she would have been just as cordial and frequent a guest at the White House. With Will pursing his great love, however, she occupied her life largely with theater and music. "She is youthful and she is very active, and her figure is such as to make some of the younger dames a little impatient about it," Will reported to Helen about her mother, in 1929. "She goes without hesitation everywhere, accepts all the invitations that she wishes to accept, goes out at night when there is anything that is attractive to her."

While she took an active interest in the current events of her day, especially since she knew many of the newsmakers in Washington, Nellie Taft lived in a political vacuum, much more so than she had since before she was married. Of his Republican successors, Taft was closest to Coolidge. Will was at Murray Bay in August 1923 when he received word that President Harding had died. He rushed to the funeral in Marion, Ohio. "I saw [Calvin] Coolidge today," he wrote Nellie of the new President. "He looked cool and self-possessed." Nellie frequently attended the White House musicales that fellow pianist Grace Coolidge hosted, including a famous concert given there by Rachmaninoff. She was less enthusiastic about her successor's voguish fashions. Returning from a memorial service, Nellie told Charlie, "Mrs. Coolidge was there in a red raincoat—which was not a thing I would have gone in!"

Six months after Harding, Woodrow Wilson died. As the only living former President, Will received unwelcome publicity when he was unable to attend Wilson's funeral. He had suffered severe chest pains and sent Nellie in his stead. She recalled of the day: "I went to ex-President Wilson's funeral yesterday, but his [Will's] attack came on in the morning, so though he was honorary pallbearer, he could not go. It called attention to it, and reporters were calling up all afternoon. . . . The funeral was at the house first, and then went out to the Cathedral, perfectly plain funeral without military aid. . . . Mrs. Wilson and Margaret, Florence Harding, President Coolidge and his wife, and I sat down in the house. . . . I was fourteen in the line of carriages. I thought it was a poor funeral."[6]

Insisting that his "attack" of chest pains was not serious, Will encouraged Nellie to go ahead with her long-anticipated adventure to southern Europe. She left in April for what would be their lengthiest separation. Unknown to Nellie, her absence depressed Will. He wrote Charlie: "It is hard to realize that she is gone for four months. It will come on me with more and more force as I live all alone in the house. We have had our sitting rooms next to one another, and I don't remember that we have ever been absent from one another for four months since we were married. It is easy to agree to such an arrangement, but it is hard to bear it."

In Spain, Nellie's meeting with the King at a polo match made news when he raced up to her on his pony. While she "hated to leave" Madrid, she was anxious to experience Barcelona and Montserrat, "going up in the mountains where I have always longed to go." Although Will fretted when he discovered that she was briefly laid up with the flu, it was his health that rapidly failed during their separation. In reporting to her that he had "another palpitation of the heart," Will dismissed it as nothing more than a "little setback." In reality he was so weakened by the declining condition of his heart that he was ordered to bed. Again by letter he tried to reassure Nellie that "the trouble with the heart" was simply due to "nervousness," that the doctor thought there was "nothing organic" in the dysfunction of the organ, suggesting somehow that it would pass and that there was no chronic condition. He would diet down to 240 pounds. "I think that will help," he cheerily wrote her. By May 5, however, he had to report truthfully that the problem was serious enough for cardiac experts to "photograph" his heart with the new "x-ray" machine at Johns Hopkins Hospital.

Will had planned to meet Nellie in England and escort her home. Now she had to sail the Atlantic alone, arriving at Murray Bay in mid-August. Her feelings about being apart from him when he was ill were certainly anxious, but she hadn't been told the details. When she landed, she learned that the Johns Hopkins cardiologists had discovered Will had suffered two mild heart attacks—one in late April and one on the morning of Wilson's funeral. He had an enlarged heart and had to give up his daily three-mile walk to work.[7]

It was clear that despite his positive attitude, Will was weakening. Forgoing her hopes for more adventures, Nellie determined to stay beside Will for the rest of his life, and they would now rarely separate. When they had to be apart, they wanted to be together. "I hate to have you worried by the old strikes," Nellie wrote him from Murray Bay when the court had an unexpectedly long session. "I love you darling and wish you were here—ever your loving Helen."

"I go down the street every morning to do marketing or shopping and then come home at eleven o'clock to read and do tapestry work," Nellie wrote of her now-typical day to Charlie. "And then in the evening at about half past five I go motoring with your father in the park." Things had come full circle: They had done the same thing—in a buggy—in Washington in 1890. If their driver Tom Ford was occupied driving Will, Nellie just hopped on a streetcar to do her business.

Every Saturday morning, Nellie drove the car herself to the local public library. There she would check out the latest detective novels for herself and Will and return the one from the previous week that he had finished reading. While she continued to pursue her own interests, Nellie found herself willingly absorbed again into Will's life. As he began to slow down, she began to run about anticipating his needs, whether it was escorting him to an event she would otherwise rather not attend, or forgoing a Sunday concert just to sit beside him and share a quiet luncheon. While it was for entirely different reasons than when they were younger, Nellie was again the one looking out for the well-being of Will Taft.

Staying in town, Nellie rediscovered the city she had loved since her youth. She most enjoyed motoring through "my" Potomac Park, sometimes taking her Kodak to events there, such as the unveiling of a John Erickson monument, and always at cherry blossom time. Occasionally she lent her name to local events such as a Catholic charity concert of Vatican choirs and Roman churches. Besides continuing to support the Red Cross, Nellie also interested herself in the struggles of local policewomen, often attending lunch lectures and other meetings on their behalf. "I like the Policewomen very much," she teased Charlie. "I am going to join up with them." Rarely did she permit herself to be a prop. Only after she arrived at a Congressional Club tea, for example, did she learn that she was to receive with Edith Wilson "as the former wives of Presidents."

Whatever she did, Nellie stayed focused on Will. They spent their evenings alone together, reading in the study for several hours. When officials came to the house to confer with him, Nellie often joined in discussions, as she did at a meeting held to consider which of the potential nominees for the Filipino governor-generalship would best "carry out [outgoing governor] General Wood's policy." She and Will did not discuss cases before the Court, but they did weigh potential justices together. Nellie, for example, expressed her strong dislike of Minnesota senator Frank B. Kellogg when he was being considered as a potential associate justice. Both Tafts remained strong proponents of a world court, despite opposition from President Coolidge, and Nellie attended Senate debates on the issue and reported back to Will. "Senator Swanson had the right to speak and he presented his subject in favor of the World Court and his speech was three hours long," she wrote after one session.[8]

Despite his flagging energy, Taft persisted in working full tilt, bringing work home with him in the evenings. It was becoming an uphill battle. In October 1924 he suffered a mild heart attack on a Sunday and called for Nellie, who sent for a doctor. In two hours he seemed fine. He went to work the next day, was well all week, and then had another attack on Saturday. He no longer traveled at the hectic pace he had thrived on. Even on holidays they stayed home, one Thanksgiving inviting as guests his secretary and clerks and several assistant attorneys general, including Mabel Willibrandt. Will's new walking route was on flat ground on his own street and then north on Connecticut Avenue over a bridge later named for him, just two blocks north of the Taft home.

In June 1926, however, Nellie reported to Charlie that Will had another heart attack after climbing "four flights of stairs to an oratorical contest. . . . I went with him and [when] he came home he had trouble. He has been in bed ever since." This time the attack prevented the Tafts from going to Murray Bay. "He does not get over it, the way that he did former attacks," she told Charlie. Nellie had an elevator installed for Will, who was no longer permitted to climb the stairs. "We are all well notwithstanding your father's bad heart," she soon reported. "He has not walked at all up hill yet."

Living with Will's precarious condition changed Nellie. She no longer sought to control what she realized she couldn't and managed to keep a matter-of-fact attitude without letting anxiety overcome her. If anything, she tended to be optimistic about the usual elderly fears of illness. When Maria told her that Charley Taft was "failing rapidly" and "unconscious most of the time," Nellie wrote Charlie: "I think she takes a gloomy view of it."[9]

Nearly seventy, Nellie was in excellent health. Learning to let go of the stress that had provoked her earlier attacks, she was even calm when she fell ill. "Something that I ate disagreed with me," she wrote. "I had to retire and lie down and go home in the auto. The next day I had a cold. . . . I sent for Doctor Delaney in the end and spent two days in bed. I had a slight attack of ptomaine poisoning but I was up Thursday, going to lunch. . . . I could not eat anything, but I drank cocktails and white wine, which I enjoyed." If she still delighted in her cocktails, gambling had lost some of its appeal. After a long losing streak, she finally declared, "I came out even, which is all I dare hope for now." Her love of theater, however, continued to broaden. She would take a streetcar downtown, take in a matinee alone, and be home in time to meet Will on his return from the Court.

The former First Lady kept a dizzying theater schedule. In one week, for example, she saw *Beggars, Go to Bed, Play the Game, Young Woodley,* and *Lady Fair*—which was "too long as it always is if it is new." She also took in the era's popular musicals: *Gentlemen Prefer Blondes* was "common but very funny." *Showboat* had "singers and chorus [who] were good as they always are in Ziegfeld productions," and she saw *No, No Nanette* a number of times. In drama, she thought of *Abie's Irish Rose* that "the first part was very funny but it got tiresome after awhile" and Shaw's *Jilla's Atonement* was "very good, but it had some of Shaw's queer sayings." Despite the fact that the segregated capital city had many white residents who wouldn't even consider attending productions with African American themes or actors such as *Porgy and Bess,* Nellie "enjoyed it very much" and over the years would see various productions of the operatic play.

Only to Charlie did Nellie admit that she also explored a genre new to 1920s theater known as "sex plays." She liked *The Czarina,* about Catherine the Great's love life, but called it "not a play that little boys and girls could see." The *Green Hat,* she thought, had value because it was "well-acted" although "risqué." Managing to slip into such plays, which could often be raided, the chief justice's wife seemed to take delight in shocking her son. "Saturday I went to the theater to see *Ladies of the Evening.*" She told him about a dramatic portrayal of prostitution, "a sex play that had some interesting points."[10]

On New Year's Day 1928 the Tafts held an open house at which, Nellie recorded, they had "more [guests] than we have had any time since we have been Chief Justice." Vigilantly monitoring his health, Will slightly improved that year. Nellie thought it a great moment when he was able to greet her up at Union Station—he hadn't been able to do so in four years. At the end of 1927 she had declared that "Will and I are very well and happy, and Will is working hard." Apart from his court work, the chief justice had endless dinner meetings with the Public Building Committee on plans for a new Supreme Court building. He hoped, said Nellie, "to have the building on its way when he retires."

That Will was talking about retiring indicated his realization that his health could hold out only so long, yet he couldn't imagine doing anything but staying on the bench. As Nellie put it, he didn't have "any hobbies. . . . I don't know what he will do if he stops being Chief Justice." He was also paranoid concerning any leaks about his condition. The pat remark to inquiries was that he was "as well as his health allows." Helen and her family spent Christmas 1928 with her parents, but when Nellie learned that Charlie and his family could not join them, she was particularly sad. She had an urgent sense that time was running out. "Next year we will see about it!" she scolded. Several months later, after attending the funeral of Justice Holmes's wife at Arlington National Cemetery, Nellie bluntly addressed her mortality. "We want to be buried there," she told Charlie.[11]

Nineteen twenty-eight also brought another Republican President, Herbert Hoover, who had been commerce secretary under Harding and Coolidge. The Tafts first used their new radio that October to hear Hoover's Madison Square Garden rally speech days before the election. Nellie had intended to vote in Connecticut, where she still claimed residency based on property she owned there—Washington residents couldn't then vote for a President—but Will thought it wrong. "Your father said at the last minute that I could not vote in New Haven," she told Charlie. The Tafts used their radio a second time to listen to election returns until nearly ten at night. "It looked very much as if Smith was going to be elected. Connecticut had the cities and the city of New York was overwhelming and I had [to] go get away before I realized that Hoover had the states that counted." Of all her successors, Nellie was closest to Lou Hoover, with whom she attended lectures and the theater. As neighbors from 1921 to 1928 they had begun dining at each other's homes and even had lunch together a week before the election.

Nellie rarely saw Alice Longworth, although Nick was back in the capital, having been reelected to Congress in 1914. At one lunch she reported, "I talked to Alice about Cincinnati people, and the baby [Longworth child]. She said she was going to bring the baby up to see me but I don't think she ever will." The Longworths had Nellie to lunch once—certainly at Nick's insistence—years after the Tafts had returned to town. Nellie attended Nick's "Washington Study on Government" lecture, but her mistrust of Alice and her Roosevelt tribe endured. "Even now there is a kind of Igorot head-hunterish look in her eyes when some one refers to the dark days of 1912," a socialite wrote in 1925.

Nellie was more drawn to Elsie Grosvenor, wife of the National Geographic Society president. They also attended lectures together on topics ranging from George Bernard Shaw to Women of the Renaissance. Elsie was one of the few Washington women who had also explored the world beyond Europe, appreciated other cultures, and thought nothing of discussing such issues as international law with Nellie.[12]

Three months after Hoover's inaugural, Will visited Cincinnati, reporting to Nellie on relatives and such remarkable civic improvements that it "looks like another city." The rest of the year was less pleasant. Just days after his return, Will was back in the hospital. He was out two days later, but back again the following week. He left Murray Bay in a sad state at the end of the summer, the spread of infantile paralysis forcing the cancellation of his annual September birthday party for the townspeople. Upon their return to Washington, Nellie undertook a major housecleaning and disposed of old clothes, eager to "begin leading the life that I did before." It would not happen that fall. Will's spirits sank rapidly in the holiday season when he heard that his brother Charley had died. He returned from the Cincinnati funeral shaken.

On January 8, Will entered Garfield Hospital in Washington. After his release, he and Nellie headed to Asheville, North Carolina, for a planned six weeks of complete rest. Will could ride but little in the car, and Nellie became impatient with waiters who didn't retrieve room service plates promptly. Bob told his aunt Fanny that Will's heart was "not at all good. . . . I doubt very much whether he ever ought to return to the court." Nellie reported the moment of truth to Charlie: "Bob came down to have him sign his resignation. He expressed his willingness to Bob. He said that he was failing and wanted to sign it right away. . . . [T]his morning your father did not say anything, because he was not so clear—but he signed it all right." Her reaction was difficult to read. She had always embraced the truth, never hiding from reality. However, she reported that she was looking for a home in Asheville for herself and Will, but there were none "with room and bath on the first floor." They simply returned home.

On February 8, Will fell and was back in the hospital. Nellie never left his side. He was so "feeble" that she told Mabel Boardman and other friends they couldn't see him. Barely able to sign his last letter on February 15, he was in and out of consciousness. The only word he was heard to repeat was "Darling." He said it whenever he sensed his Nellie nearing his pillow. With Nellie beside him, he died on March 8.[13]

The day before the funeral, Nellie went to Arlington and chose the site for what would be not only Will's burial site but eventually her own as well, next to him. The site reflected the ambitions of both her and Will; it was on a hill with a view of the White House and, in the far distance, the new Supreme Court that was being built. She also chose Will's burial clothes, picking a navy blue suit and a bright red bow tie he'd taken a recent fancy to. That she decided to place the judicial robe he had worn as chief justice in his coffin was a touching way of honoring him personally. All of their life together, from the moment Nellie Herron had first encountered him, Will Taft had aspired for the chief justiceship. That afternoon, in a black dress with no jewelry, hat, veil, or gloves, she read telegrams of sympathy from former First Ladies Frances Cleveland, Mary Harrison, even Edith Roosevelt, and the Coolidges. At the house, she received callers including the President and Mrs. Hoover, and Edith Wilson, who viewed

Taft in an open coffin, placed in the library. Alice Longworth did not visit, or write. One friend said the widowed Nellie had a "calm philosophy" through the day, the reality of Will's demise becoming inevitable in her mind several weeks earlier, upon their return from Asheville.

Neither Nellie nor her children left the house to follow the coffin as the horse-drawn caisson drew it past the White House, up to the Capitol (where the late former President lay in state for several hours), and then past the new Supreme Court building, still under construction, to All Souls Unitarian Church. She had turned down an offer by the Hoovers to have the funeral in the White House, an extraordinary gesture since no former President had been so honored.

In this city that was now more racially segregated due to "Jim Crow" laws instituted under Woodrow Wilson than it had been when Nellie first lived there in the 1890s, came an amazing tribute to the former President. The newspapers took note of the fact that, despite the rain and drizzle all day, people "of every class, creed, and color" came to pay their respects and look in the open coffin at the Capitol. At his funeral, Nellie requested that two poems be read, *The Happy Warrior* by William Wadsworth and *Ode on the Death of the Duke of Wellington* by Alfred Lord Tennyson. Driving in the lead car to the cemetery, Nellie requested that the burial service be private.

In none of her correspondence or that of her children is there any suggestion of whether she was in deep bereavement in losing her life's companion or saw his death as a release from pain. She just kept going on.

In her first week of widowhood, Nellie focused on matters at hand—black-bordered stationery, lingering relatives, and the reading of the last will and testament. "There were very many people at the grave," she wrote matter-of-factly after going to Arlington, "but we went inside the rope." She seemed numb to her sister Jennie's sudden death just days after Will's. Within a month she had gotten rid of Will's clothes and warned Charlie that a week later she was going "to dispose of nearly all" of Will's books. When he asked for some several weeks later, it was too late: "They are gone now." She dismissed a proposal to name an Ohio airport for Will because he wasn't "very strong for aviation." She, Bob, and Helen went to the grave site with the arts commission chairman to decide on a memorial stone. Only once did she seem forlorn. "I am eating alone," she wrote Charlie. "I wish you would come to Washington before I leave."

Nellie was indeed alone—but also independent. She found that she embraced life best when she looked ahead, plotting some new adventure. She told Charlie of herself and sister Maria just days after Will's burial, "We, on talking it over, decided to go to the continent . . . on the steamer that goes to Lisbon and then through the Mediterranean stopping at several ports and to Trieste where we would hire a motor and go through Serbia to Prague and Budapest and then go to England and come home the Canadian way."[14]

This time Nellie had no agenda but her own—to discover, journey, relax, and be herself.

Twenty

Adventures of an Old Lady (1930–1943)

[A]fter his death, I felt that your mother was so occupied that it was not always convenient to have a transient drop in unannounced.
—CHARLES HILLES, FORMER TAFT SECRETARY,
TO BOB TAFT, MAY 25, 1943

Churned up by the Gulf Stream, the Straits of Messina were rolling and tossing the *Saturnia*. Inside, as chairs in her stateroom kept rolling over, Nellie Taft simply "got up and straightened them."

Just a dozen weeks after Will's death, with Maria as her companion, Nellie debarked at Lisbon, then headed for Marienbad, sailed to Naples, and took the train to Pompeii, Trieste, and Venice. From there Nellie rented a car and drove herself and Maria through Krakow and Warsaw, before heading to Vienna. She could easily have stayed home and reigned in the capital as the widow of an honored statesman and jurist—but Nellie ran in the other direction, as if making up for lost time. She had shed the old fears and nervousness that defined her as a younger woman. Most certainly the changes in Nellie were prompted by the devastating loss of the life partner who had always loved and accepted her with all her flaws and fears. Nellie had spent a lifetime worrying nervously. Time was running out. She would now seek to do nothing more than indulge herself completely in the pleasure of adventure. For Nellie, adventure had always competed with ambition for her attentions. Amazingly unconcerned now about what people thought of her activities, the world was her oyster. And she indulged freely. Her favorite meal, she declared, were crepes—with brandy, Cointreau, and Benedictine.

Her first year without Will was not without a certain hardness toward others who might be suffering. Of one hostess, she sharply remarked, "Mrs. Whitney had a nervous breakdown and she could not play [bridge] for which I was extremely glad." After Helen's daughters were in a car accident, Nellie noted with seeming indifference that one was "threatened with a broken rib but I do not know how it came out." Her old social prejudices sometimes emerged again too. On one occasion, she disparaged some Polish citizens; on another, she said that the educated, upper-class Jews whom she met were "very pleasant," but "generally the Jews here are awful, so objectionable." She seemed unconscious that her remarks were anti-Semitic as well as elitist. She would not have made such observations, for example, of poor Lutherans in Germany, or Presbyterians in Scotland.

Nellie wore her lack of sentimentality as a badge of courage. She refused family offers to spend Christmas with them, her first without Will. Had Helen not brought her family down, Nellie would have been alone for the holiday. "It is an awfully big house," Bob thought, "but I think she manages to enjoy herself." Under no circumstances, it seems, would she share her grief or even admit to feeling any. The closest she came to revealing her emotions, even to Charlie, was to confess that she "cried a bit" at the theater.[1]

Never asking for escorts or special treatment from anyone, Nellie unveiled the *Titanic* Memorial in May 1931, but generally insisted on leading the life of a private citizen, not as a former First Lady. She supported causes out of personal interest, not public obligation. After visiting Greece, for example, she signed on to support a project of the Near East Foundation that helped refugee Greek women support themselves and their families through sales of their native crafts. During the Depression, she joined the

Red Cross's National Advisory Committee of Volunteer Special Services. She sympathized with many local actors she had seen perform over the years, and when they had financial difficulties, she gave them gifts of money. "Your mother was a true friend to the troupers of the theater," one of them, George Smithfield, told Bob, "whom we of the theater knew well for her charity and sympathy."

One aspect of her former life still engaged Mrs. Taft. Each spring Nellie proudly took family, friends, and guests to see the cherry blossom trees in bloom. After she had planted the first of the Japanese-donated trees in 1912, annual plantings had continued. By 1920 some eight thousand trees, creating their distinctive pink clouds, drew hundreds of thousands of tourists, becoming one of the most lucrative annual attractions in Washington. On April 16, 1927, a special pageant was held, with Japanese dance performances and other commemorations in honor of the former First Lady whose dedication had brought the cherry blossoms to Washington. Nellie sat on the podium beside the Japanese ambassador, and when a sudden rainstorm hit, she remained staunchly in the drenching rain until the ceremonies were over, "in a blaze of glory," as one reporter put it.

So popular had the trees become that the local government decided to host the First Annual Cherry-Blossom Fete in April 1930. Out of respect for Nellie (Will had died just a month earlier), the event was canceled, and the Park Service placed an inscribed bronze plaque at the base of the first tree she had planted. In 1933 a three-day celebration was held, and a year later civic groups underwrote the first official event that would henceforth be celebrated annually. When the walks were widened, more people strolled down to see the trees rather than drive. When the Jefferson Memorial was built, the dozens of trees that had to be temporarily removed to make room for the edifice were uprooted under cover of darkness in order to avoid public protest. Once the memorial was completed, the trees were replanted in a configuration that actually enlarged the park. Other changes reflected the shifting political realities. After Pearl Harbor Day, the word *Japanese* would be suspended and the trees were described as *Oriental*.

What Nellie thought of the growing perception that Japan would side against America in a world war is unknown. She always had good relations with Japan's representatives. In 1931, she and the wife of the Japanese ambassador together planted more cherry blossom trees in Potomac Park. At the end of the 1930s she was gratified to receive a letter from Yei Theodora Ozaki, wife of the former mayor of Tokyo, directly crediting Nellie for the 1912 Japanese gift of three thousand trees. Nellie had always assumed the trees had been sent simply because she had already had ninety of the trees from an American nursery transplanted there. "I am delighted to hear that my remarks [about wishing there were thousands more of the trees available to be planted there] were responsible for the beautiful gift. . . . I am delighted to hear the truth at last." So delighted, apparently, that the former First Lady was willing to rewrite history a bit. In her draft response to a Mr. Copen who had inquired of her an account as to how the trees first came to Washington, Nellie scribbled a line about Eliza Scidmore being involved in getting the first trees—and then scratched it out. Her legacy was secure whether or not the whole story was told.[2]

At the end of January 1931, Nellie headed to Charleston, staying at the Villa Margherita, which was to become her regular respite each winter. Charlie teased that she was there with "old hens," and she teased back that her indulging in cocktails was "awful." He quipped, "It seems to me as if you had nothing but cocktail parties all day long, but I was also a little surprised to hear you say that it was awful." While Nellie was in the midst of her backgammon lesson, she received a call about the sudden death of Annie Taft. Stunned, she wondered, "Is there any possibility of it being suicide?" There was no evidence that it was. More devastating news came that autumn: Her sister Eleanor had cancer of the spine. "It is awful," Nellie wrote. Perhaps with her own mortality on her mind, Nellie drew up a list of her silver items that she wanted to give to individual family members "after my death." Charlie brought a note of levity in: "You sound as if you are distributing your goods from the casket."

"Christmas is very nice for the people who have families but it has its trials for other persons," she oddly wrote Charlie while again insisting on spending the day alone in Washington in 1931, going out to the movies. Finding the Fox Theater too crowded, she went to the Columbia. "I had to wait a half hour before I got in. And then I saw Jackie Coogan." With her love of murder mysteries, she tried to see all the Charlie Chan series. "Movies are not fit to see and I don't like movies anyhow," she claimed— and then went a week later to see *The Mummy* and "thought it very good." On New Year's Day she went to the theater to see *The Jewel Robber*. She found it "naughty but amusing."[3]

From mid-autumn to mid-winter Nellie was in Washington but rarely in the house. Maintaining a manic pace, she went to lectures on Aristophanes, fossils, and traveling in China. She heard Winston Churchill speak about the parliamentary system and Amelia Earhart on "My Aerial Adventures." At the National Geographic Society she took in films on Mexican ruins and African jungles. She attended concerts with the finest musicians of the era, joining Lou Hoover for a Paderewski performance and going to hear Vladimir Horowitz, whom Nellie considered "the best pianist anywhere." Frequently, she was spotted in her green glass "sun spectacles," searching through bookstores for travel guides to some port of the globe she had not yet explored. Mid-winter to early spring she was back in Charleston, playing driver and tour guide for visiting friends to Fort Moultrie, Middleton Gardens, and Magnolia Gardens. She got "tired of chicken all the time" and unpunctuality, but "that's the way Charleston people live."

From Charleston, Nellie took the train directly to New York, then sailed for England and Wales—exploring Bath, Chipping Cameden, Wells, Glastonbury, and Shrewbury in the summer of 1932. Bob had asked her to stop in Washington and see Will's memorial stone at Arlington, "but I think I will go on," she told Charlie. Nellie still refused all entreaties to make public appearances as the Widow Taft. That spring she had been conspicuously absent from a dinner party where many of her family members joined the social, political, and civic leaders of Cincinnati at a gala in Charley and Annie's "Taft mansion" before it was converted into an art museum. From Europe she went to Murray Bay on August 23, and left on October 16, almost certainly pressured by her children to attend the laying of the cornerstone of the new Supreme Court building. She was supposed to place a box with Will's picture in the cornerstone. "I went alone. They did not call upon me for anything," she reported, seemingly relieved to have been forgotten. Mrs. Taft seemed to take fiendish delight in being unrecognized. When she proceeded toward the V.I.P. seating area above the Senate floor to listen to a debate on monopolies, guards blocked her entry. She "smiled, said nothing and walked away . . . edged her way through the throngs of tourists and sightseers and [took] her seat in the public gallery." Soon enough, someone tipped off the mortified guards that they had just turned away the wife of a U.S. President and Supreme Court justice.[4]

With Will no longer there to object to her claiming Connecticut residency through property she owned, that autumn Nellie returned to vote in the state where she was registered. Some friends, she wrote, "don't like anything President Hoover does. They nearly blame the depression on him." Nellie did not. She had been "anxious to go to Mr. Hoover's speech" at the Garden but suddenly declined, claiming she didn't want to sit on the platform. The reason was almost certainly her discovery that Edith Roosevelt had already accepted an invitation to be there.

When Hoover lost to New York governor Franklin Roosevelt, Nellie attended a farewell luncheon for Lou Hoover, and then, for Thanksgiving dinner, invited Will's old stenographer Wendell Mischler and his wife, "as boresome as usual." She left for Charleston for three weeks and missed FDR's March 1933 inaugural, eager to begin a lengthy visit to Italy and the Middle East. Her two remaining Taft brothers-in-law and her two sons were meeting in New York the day before she was to sail, to discuss the hiring of author Henry Pringle to write the official biography of the former President based on the family papers. Charlie suggested that she arrive a day early to join in the meeting. "I can express my opinion when I come the next morning," she replied. But they could also give her a bon voyage party, he suggested. She wouldn't change her plans.

Nellie let her children and in-laws deal with Will's biography and its author. She did not even grant an interview for the two-volume book. When a studio that had a beautiful photograph of him offered to sell it with the rights to her for $500, she would pay only $200, insisting that her son would have to pay the rest or she'd turn down the offer. When she ran out of pictures of Will to send to the public who wrote to her requesting them, she did not order any more. On one level her indifference to Will's memory was baffling, and her attitude of simply carrying on with the next chapter of her life did not entirely explain it. Her constant activity, staying in the Washington house for only brief periods, and lack of anything but the most perfunctory mention of Will in her family letters all suggest that she simply processed her grief privately and found it too painful to revisit. Rather than live with the dead, she insisted on living alone to the fullest.[5]

Nellie was off again. This time her fellow passengers included Helen Hayes and Norma Shearer. In Rome she went through the Vatican and St. Peter's, carefully examining items she had once rushed past. She hoped to glimpse the Pope during the Closing the Door ceremony, but "the Italians prevented that! Though I had a very good seat right near, the people stood up all around me and I could not see at all. I came home thinking that was a morning wasted!" From Italy she went to Greece. "The Acropolis is the most magnificent in my world!" At seventy-two she even managed to climb the ruins, a "hard job." She went through Haifa, Port Said, Cairo, Nazareth, and Mount Carmel, and she spent Easter in Jerusalem. Disappointed in the pyramids, she liked the Sphinx. "I went up in a pony cart," she wrote, "not liking the whole appearance of ladies that rode camels." She explored mosques, ancient ruins, and mountains. Very little upset Nellie anymore; she was no longer beset by worry or anticipating the worst. When one of her bags was lost, she casually wrote Charlie that she had $5,000 and jewelry in it. Luckily, it was returned to her.

The pattern of her life was set: Charleston in mid-winter, an overseas trip until early summer, Murray Bay until October, and holidays in Washington. At Thanksgiving 1933 it was again the Mischlers, and, again, "they were as boresome as usual." She was still particular about her cars, sending the chauffeur to pick up a new model at the Ford plant in Michigan and then drive it to her at Murray Bay. Although she liked to be driven in the new models, she also kept an old station wagon in Canada that she liked to drive herself. In Washington she had a Packard Town Car—with a glass window that could be raised between her and the driver. In other personal ways, she was utterly modern. As the nation approached mid-century and women's dress hemlines rose, Nellie never appeared in the long, conservative gowns still worn by many in her social and age group. Even at eighty, she would appear fashionable in short dresses that came just below her knees, open-toed shoes, and the polka-dotted, small-veiled, cornucopia-shaped hats of the late 1930s styles.[6]

Besides her cook and maid, Irish immigrant sisters Annie and Margaret McNamara, Nellie was content to live alone with an unnamed Persian cat who stayed in the kitchen. She diverted suggestions from Charlie that she come live with him, taking fiendish pride in her stamina. One day, for example, she left the house at nine-thirty in the morning, went to the market, the theater, a luncheon, and then the theater again in the evening—"which is doing very well for an old lady!" she thought. Rather than get dentures, she insisted on getting fixed those teeth she had left. She was proud that she could still race up the four flights of stairs to her room. Her years of daily, brisk walks left her with a trim figure and a strong constitution.[7]

Nellie felt comfortable revealing her private life only to Charlie. She delighted in detailing her drinking to him, and he never scolded her for it. "Lots of cocktails, but very poor food," she wrote him after one luncheon. Another afternoon with some old friends, she confessed, meant "strong cocktails but not very much lunch." At the holidays she had some "very weak eggnog. I drank three cups without it making any impression on me!"

While Helen also encouraged her mother with love, she sometimes reported her concerns to the sterner Bob. "I hope she finds somebody to go with her, so that she will not be entirely alone," he wrote his aunt before one of Nellie's overseas trips. "She does not seem to mind, but I should think it would get very discouraging." Nellie avoided confrontations with her children by buying her travel tickets before announcing that she was going on a trip. Once she was away, however, she didn't always keep in touch with Helen and Bob. "You are the only one to write, but I don't blame them," Nellie wrote Charlie from overseas, "for I did not tell them where to write and they, Helen particularly, did not have the address. Bob writes only business letters."

Nellie seemed slighted at what she felt was distance from the Bob Tafts. "I wrote to Martha ten days ago," she told Charlie, "but she has not answered." Perhaps it explained Nellie's show of indifference to a friend who was "crazy for Bob to be Senator." Slight fraternal competition may have also been the root of Nellie's reserve with Bob and Martha. Favoring Charlie, she was also a liberal Republican like him. When Charlie wrote to Helen and her husband—the Democrats—about politics, Bob sent a follow-up note to his sister that "the news transmitted is not entirely from my point of view, and I trust that political discussions are taken with a grain of salt."[8]

Nellie was stunned by the shift in the new Democratic era. "The Senate and House is deplorable," she had written in 1933. "I hear there are only nine Republican senators. I don't count the Progressives. They don't vote with the Republicans anyhow." She emerged fearfully from a Republican lecture on the midterm elections, where she learned "how the communists had eleven representatives in the coming Congress, that were 'reds,' just the type of the Russian communists." When she realized that she knew none of the new crowd in town, however, old Mrs. Taft accepted a lunch invitation to the Democratic Club to meet some of them.

Eleanor Roosevelt was considered radical, even socialistic by conservative Republicans, but in none of Nellie's correspondence or known remarks did she criticize her controversial First Lady successor. When Mrs. Taft began attending Mrs. Roosevelt's annual luncheons for Supreme

Court wives in 1935, her presence could have been viewed as an act of polite nonpartisanship. Still, Mrs. Taft's appearances in the FDR White House must have raised some questions by capital observers since Nellie had so firmly abdicated any sort of public role as either a presidential or a judicial spouse.

It was perhaps curiosity that led Mrs. Taft to go to the White House and observe Mrs. Roosevelt, but her presence at a May 3, 1935, breakfast honoring the First Lady seemed to signal admiration for her. Perhaps she empathized with Eleanor's drive to be politically involved. She may even have felt a slight competition with the niece of Teddy himself. When a mutual friend of theirs, Marie Stafford, came to Washington, she accepted Nellie's invitation to be a houseguest instead of Eleanor's. "I had beer and potato chips for her," the former First Lady bragged. Mrs. Taft had, in fact, first met Mrs. Roosevelt in the summer of 1910 and long recalled the pleasant day they had spent together.

It was harder to read Nellie's opinion of FDR. She relished taking guests to the Capitol to hear "Huey Long abusing Roosevelt," and enjoyed *Bring on the Girls* because it was "a play attacking the New Deal." Yet after hearing him preside at the Capitol on the one hundredth anniversary of the death of Lafayette, Nellie decided that "the President was very good" as a powerful and persuasive speaker.[9]

Having seen too much of the shifting fortunes of partisanship to gravely worry about the nation's ability to survive under any one party, Nellie became increasingly indifferent to the parochial world of Washington. No sooner was she back from one part of the globe than she was looking forward to her next trip. "She seems to have unlimited energy, and loves to travel," Bob wrote during Nellie's 1934 adventure through Spain, Greece, western Italy, and southern France. Despite strikes, she prowled the night streets of Marseilles on her own. Driving rainstorms did not deter her from tramping through the gardens of Alhambra. She was indignant at Franco, the new dictator of Spain. "The Easter processions are not allowed now," she wrote, "the government is afraid of processions!"

On the way to Europe in 1934, Mrs. William Howard Taft had had an unpleasant surprise when, walking up the gangway, she learned that the newsreel cameramen gathered at the pier with the newspaper photographers were all there waiting to capture the departure of one of her fellow passengers—Mrs. Theodore Roosevelt. There was a fuss over Edith, but nobody seemed to take notice that Nellie was on board, too—and she liked it that way: "It was Mrs. Roosevelt's party, and I kept out of the way all I could. When I saw that she was going to use the sitting room in the evening I went in the card room. I don't like Mrs. Roosevelt at all. I never did. . . . And they all seemed to think that I was very peculiar."

The Roosevelt women felt likewise. "I was very much amused," she told Charlie, "at Alice Longworth's inviting you to dinner, and inviting Bob the next day—shows what she thinks of the *younger* Tafts."[10]

In 1935, after trying out the swimming at Palm Beach first, Nellie returned to Charleston. There, she relished her solitude, walking each morning along the Battery, sitting to read a book, and dining alone at a favorite King Street restaurant, indulging in "lobsters and highballs." Late spring and summer found her in the British Isles—Plymouth, Oxford, Stratford, Edinburgh—largely for theater festivals.

At year's end she suffered a slight brain swelling with "distinct paralysis on the right side." Within twenty-four hours all such symptoms had vanished, and the incident proved not to be a stroke. Still, Nellie's announcement that she was headed for Mexico in 1936 alarmed Bob, who feared it was "doubtful" that she could endure the sea voyage and rail excursion. As always, she refused to take a "paid" companion; an escort would have to come as a friend and pay her own way. Helen, realizing that she and Bob couldn't make "very strenuous suggestions" to their mother without provoking her, finally contacted some friends in Mexico City to look after the former First Lady. Climbing ruins, swimming, shopping madly in Yucatán, Guadalajara, and Oaxaca, Nellie did it all with flying colors. "I can't think of anything else to worry about except typhoid and dysentery and I am counting on Mama's distaste for water to prevent those," Helen wrote Bob. "I wrote down the Spanish word for beer and if she succeeds in pronouncing it all should be well."[11]

If she didn't want her children telling her how to live, neither did Nellie tell them how to conduct their lives. While she did not interfere in the parenting of her grandchildren, she did have specific ideas on how the younger generation should behave in her home. When "little Helen" visited, Nellie noted, "she did a great deal of telephoning—sometimes it was twice a day—at two dollars a time it was very much—and I pay the bills!"

Mrs. Taft had not been voted the traditional presidential widow's pension. It had to be approved by Congress. She did "enjoy" the ten thousand dollars she received from the Carnegie trust, a continuance of the payment once given to Will. "It enables me to go abroad when I could not [do] it alone, not getting the $5000 from Congress." Whether it was to make her case more appealing to Democrats or not, there may have been some politicking in a minor controversy in which Nellie found herself while in Charleston in the spring of 1936.

Nellie was alleged to have told the *Charleston News-Courier,* "It will be disastrous if President Roosevelt is not re-elected. Although I've always been a Republican I believe that no one except President Roosevelt can fill the place under present conditions." Although it may have been a private remark, it was reported as an "interview" and widely reprinted. Bob Taft quickly "repudiated" it, and his office released a statement from his mother's "secretary" that an interview "had never been given" and that "she did not hold the views imputed to her." Nellie had no such "secretary," but Bob was then planning his successful U.S. Senate bid as an anti-Roosevelt isolationist.[12]

There were, in fact, pro-Roosevelt sentiments in Nellie's family. Helen might ostensibly call herself a "Republican" to those who associated her with her father's party rather than explain that she was really a Democrat. Her husband ran for local office as a Democrat and took "little Helen" to FDR's 1937 inaugural luncheon at the White House. Charlie became overtly pro-Roosevelt when he published the book *You and I—and Roosevelt,* calling for Republican support of FDR. "To talk to him," Charlie wrote his mother about FDR, "you would not know that he had a care in the world."

Ironically, it was the newly elected Democratic congressman from Cincinnati Joseph Dixon who immediately got Nellie her presidential widow's pension after his January 1937 swearing-in. Dixon "set out to show that he could do in two months more than [his predecessors, Republican congressmen] John [Hollister, Jr.] and Nick [Longworth] had done in their whole service," Charlie wrote her. "To produce evidence of this accomplishment, he took hold of your pension bill and pushed it through both Houses." Nellie now received $5,000 a year from the government. "Mama's finances are in excellent shape," Bob told Helen, "and with the pension checks she can do now about what she pleases."[13]

Nellie left on February 10, 1937, for what would be her lengthiest stay out of the United States since her days in the Philippines—seven months. She went through the Azores, Spain, Italy, France, England, Scotland, Turkey, and Egypt. While in Luxor she fainted and cut her eye, and it had to be bandaged. Nellie "blamed it on the heat" but was otherwise "quite vague." Her primary concern was that it meant she had to give up her stay in Florence. At one point she had just cut loose on the Continent, and none of her children knew how to reach her. She had refused to leave a mailing address or itinerary with her maid.

The next year her children insisted that she no longer travel alone and made sure one of them was always with her. The immediate job fell to Fred Manning. "I know the difficulties," Bob wrote in thanking him for assuming the task. With a swollen leg she had some walking problems, but she kept going to card parties, she wrote Charlie, "and try if I can not to be as good as any of them!"

Charlie, on the pretense that she "may get bored in Washington," tried flattering her into a renewed offer. "You certainly are a knockout! . . . Why don't you come out here and stay a while? [Baby] Peter will certainly keep you busy." He even found a house she could rent across the street. "If you get tired of us you can look out the window in the other direction."

Nellie claimed that she no longer intended to keep her home in Washington but did not want to let Annie and Maggie go without warning. She promised to do so a year later and give each woman a thousand dollars, but her focus at the moment was her next trip. In fact, she never gave up the house. "Your mother seems to be in splendid form—packing furiously, all set for Italy," Fred Manning reported. "She eats well, seems much stronger and very clear-headed about any details she thinks important." This time, with the Mannings, Nellie would visit Taormina, Palermo, Syracuse, and San Remo in Sicily, the island of Corsica, the Italian Lake region, the Amalfi coast, Genoa, and Paris. She seemed unable to make a trip to Italy without a stop in Naples, "the most beautiful of any place I have been." As far as her health was concerned, Fred added, "I'm not a bit sure that your mother won't preside at my obsequies instead of you and me at hers! . . . I have never seen her equal!" A doctor found that her blood pressure and circulation had actually improved from six months earlier.[14]

By the autumn of 1938, however, Nellie—forced to slow down after a bad fainting spell—was "very discouraged about her prospects and very lonely." Bob was elected to the Senate in November and planned to look in on her once he moved to town. Just weeks after his arrival in early 1939, however, Nellie was in fine form and out on the road again on her own. "Is my mother in Washington or Charleston?" Charlie had to ask Bob's secretary.

For her overseas trip that year, her children finally persuaded Nellie to take a companion. Since her friend Maria Stafford was planning to visit her family in Denmark, Nellie traveled with her to Madeira, Sweden, Norway, Denmark, and Paris; she didn't have to pay anyone's fare, but she did as her children wanted. The seventy-eight-year-old former First Lady fearlessly made her way around tense European nations increasingly threatened by the growing, dark shadow of Hitler. Her sons nervously anticipated her return at the end of April until they received a radiogram from her ship: "Decided to continue on. . . . Well." The next they heard of her, Nellie was spending two weeks motoring through England. "I am having a grand trip," she began her postcard to Bob. Only to Charlie did she admit that her legs were weak and she walked with a limp, so she went to Windsor Castle "in a bus (!)."

At the end of the year Charlie again appealed to Nellie to stay with him during the holidays. "Come on!" he urged her. Again she refused, though she did decide in the end to visit Helen and her family in nearby Pennsylvania. It was during that visit that Nellie first learned Bob was going to make a run for the presidency in 1940. She seemed blissfully unimpressed. At the same time Helen was stunned to discover that "Mama was preparing to sail . . . in January for what she calls the South Seas." Helen was concerned, telling Bob "it will need a concerted attack and I wish to undertake it next week. . . . You had better write or telegraph to the same effect at the same time. My chief argument will be that as the mother of a presidential candidate she must travel with some stable [companion]." All her children managed to do was convince Nellie to take a companion— whose passage they paid for since she still refused to do so.

Mrs. Taft spent her winter in Hawaii, Tahiti, and Samoa, and pictures of her sitting on a veranda scattered with palm plants appeared in newspapers around the world. After that, in Charleston, Helen found her "very well indeed and most energetic." Her summer in Murray Bay was spent poring over dozens of dime novels and detective stories, which she sent to the Merchant Marine Library once she was finished with them.[15]

The old adage that politics makes strange bedfellows proved true that spring when Alice Longworth was the most vociferous of agitators to get Bob Taft nominated as the Republican presidential candidate. Old Roosevelt and Taft allegiances were now utterly scrambled. The liberal Republican Charlie Taft was an ardent supporter and acquaintance of FDR and Eleanor Roosevelt. As the prospect of America's entry into the European war came closer to reality, Alice Longworth's politics diverged even more dramatically from that of her first cousin, the First Lady, and FDR, toward both of whom she was openly contemptuous. Alice joined the America First isolationist movement and turned herself into something of a Bob

Taft acolyte. Bob was scrupulously honest, open-minded when given new information, and running as a self-described "reactionary" rabidly favoring American isolationism when it came to the war in Europe.

Nellie did not record her reaction to his running for President just two years after being elected to the Senate, but her sister Maria bluntly told him, "I could never wish such a thing as that on you. . . . The nomination was not a desirable thing for any one." All the Tafts, however, pulled loyally together to back the long shot. Accompanied by Helen, the former First Lady even made her way to the 1940 Republican National Convention in Philadelphia, posing for many photographs wearing a large "Taft" button, Bob on bended knee beside her in one picture. It would prove to be her last public appearance.

Love and support did not mean blind loyalty to Nellie Taft. She shocked not only much of the nation but especially her son the senator when, a year later, she joined twenty-nine other women of the Committee to Defend America by Aiding the Allies in a protest against the ongoing filibuster "declared or undeclared" on the Lend-Lease Bill. Senator Taft was, in fact, one of the leading opponents and would vote against the bill, but his mother signed a public telegram to Vice President Henry A. Wallace and Senate party leaders calling for passage of lend-lease. "We regard the right of intelligent debate as inseparable from the practice of American democracy, but to resort to prolonged and repetitious argument serves no useful purpose and thwarts the manifest will of the people." It was the amazing final act of the former First Lady's defiant independence.[16]

Charlie's first sense that his mother was changing must have come when she told him how she planned to spend the holiday season in 1940. She told of inviting the Mischlers yet again, only this time, she remarked, "I hope they will come as it is lonely having nobody come!"

Although she never overindulged, Nellie had retained from girlhood her pleasure in cigarette smoking. One of her 1936 Christmas gifts from Charlie had even been a new cigarette case. By the time she turned eighty in 1941, however, she had circulatory problems, probably tied to smoking.

At the end of 1940, Bob had reported, "She has great difficulty in walking, but keeps going." Ignoring the elevator in the house, "she insists on walking up and down stairs." Knowing how her children worried about and sought to limit her precarious movements, Nellie didn't tell them her plans for her next trip, but her eldest grandson, Billy, who lived with her while teaching at the University of Maryland, felt he had to tip off his father to her latest scheme. An alarmed Bob told Helen that Nellie "has faintly suggested a cruise to South America. I believe it ought to be discouraged, but it may not be possible to do so." Weeks later Nellie seemed to fail. "I think she has given up the idea of a cruise, although she expects to go to Charleston in the spring," Bob discovered.[17]

By the summer of 1941, Nellie was battling a lung illness—and all those fussing over her. A nurse, Miss Eney, was hired, and along with her new maid, Katey, the former First Lady had two people in the house to keep an eye on her—and report to her children. She went with Helen to Montreal for two days before arriving in Murray Bay for the summer. "She gave us a scare on the boat when she fainted quite suddenly in the midst of her post-breakfast cigarette. The nurse was determined that she should be carried off at the Murray Bay dock," Helen wrote, "but of course when I got the bell boys lined up she rebelled and left in great style on the arm of the chief steward."

The week after her arrival, Nellie was "very quiet" and "on the whole asserts herself very little." Her appetite was robust, and when friends came by "she livens up a little." Helen further reported that Maria Herron, "feeling that she has neglected Mama," came to visit. On July 8, Nellie, determined to walk alone, pulled her hand out of her nurse's arm while going to lunch. She fell, broke a bone in her right arm, and bruised her face—but since Maria was coming that night, her spirits remained high. Helen soon reported that Nellie was "very meek and well behaved." Days later she had convulsions, and her doctors said the "effect on the brain would be progressive." Amazingly, she felt well the next morning and recovered from the slight paralysis she had suffered.

That autumn, confined to her home, Nellie ruled the roost, disliking the nurses Bob hired. "Mama became very annoyed at the night nurse, and I have obtained another one . . . who is much younger," he told Helen. "I saw Mama this morning and she did not seem over-pleased, but I think perhaps it will work out." She wasn't "quite as bright as the last time I saw her."[18]

Nellie was at home on December 7, 1941, when the Japanese attacked Pearl Harbor and prompted American entry into World War II. Throughout the 1930s, Nellie still held the Emperor in high esteem, even attending a select Japanese embassy dinner to honor him on his birthday. Still, she was aware that Japan's economy was running a deficit, and she suspected that the nation would do anything—even go to war—to get out of debt. One afternoon two of her friends "had a very hot fight about the Japanese. I like the Japanese too—but Sophie said there was no war debt at all[!]" As for Pearl Harbor Day and early 1942, Bob would write, "My mother was so ill at the time that she could not sign her name."

Bob came to see Nellie frequently, and Helen visited often from Bryn Mawr. Charlie sent her weekly updates on family matters, his views on local, state, and national politics, and accounts of his work ranging from legal cases to Council of Churches and YMCA leadership. Since March 1941 when he went to work for FDR on the War Relief Control Board, he was able to spend a lot of time with her when work brought him to town.[19]

Throughout all of 1942 and into early 1943, Nellie remained ill, bedridden but lucid. She loved visits from her sisters Maria and Lucy. "I think she is rather depressed because there is no change," Bob wrote Lucy, "and I believe that the more people she sees, the more cheerful she is likely to be." In March 1943 she had surgery; the reason is not entirely clear, but likely it was related to her lungs. On April 8, Bob reported, "Mama is still in the surgical ward, and while she seems to be improving slightly, the progress is slow. I think it will take rather longer in the hospital than we had estimated. She came through the operation, but has spent part of her time in an oxygen tent to eliminate that tendency towards pneumonia.

Now she is in it only at night, and hopes to get away entirely in a day or two."

Mrs. Taft returned "home again" on April 23, and Lucy came to be with her five days later. Nellie was able to breathe only with the aid of an oxygen tank. Mabel Boardman recalled that "the last time I saw your mother she seemed very fragile and weary and I was afraid of tiring her and when I [called] again she was not able to see me." As Bob noted, "Charlie is there most of the time."

To the end Nellie enjoyed spoiling her Charlie-Boy. In one of her last notes to him, she enclosed $10 and told him to "get yourself a book or several books if you want them!" Now director of FDR's Office of Defense Health and Welfare, he was at her bedside when she died on May 22, a week before her eighty-second birthday. "We all felt the end was near," Harry Taft wrote to his nephew. "Your mother's death was a relief and it was a release from a condition which permitted no normal enjoyment of life by her and only distress to her family."[20]

■

To a nation in the midst of war, news of Nellie Taft's death harked back to an era of the first automobiles, the Wright Brothers, the *Titanic,* ragtime, and Teddy Roosevelt. In a time when jeeps and bombers were fighting the Axis, radios blared jitterbug, and "that man" named Roosevelt *was* elected to a third term, she seemed like ancient history. But with many women doing work traditionally done by men, there was currency in the story of scrappy, determined Nellie Taft. Her obituary pointed out that "she prevailed upon her husband to forgo the realization of his ambition . . . and her dreams of his political advancement were quickly recognized." Mention of her "painstaking economy" would have made her proud and certainly had relevancy to life during World War II rationing.

Soon the public flooded the family with sympathy and memories, many praising Nellie as an ideal First Lady, most focusing on her legacy of the cherry blossoms. "For more than a generation," Secretary of State

Cordell Hull wrote Bob Taft, Nellie was "one of the outstanding women of the nation." At her funeral Franklin and Eleanor Roosevelt sent calla lilies and carnations. Even Alice Longworth sent pink gladiolas, and one telegram arrived that would have shocked Nellie: "Affectionate sympathies from your old and faithful friend, Mrs. Theodore Roosevelt."

The family gathered in the city that Nellie always considered her true home, Washington, for her funeral in St. John's Church and burial. In death she managed to posthumously break yet one more precedent: the first First Lady to be buried at Arlington National Cemetery. She was laid to rest beside Will (the first President to be buried there). She was the only First Lady so honored until 1994 when Jacqueline Kennedy was laid beside her late husband, John F. Kennedy (the second President buried there).

On April 8, 1987, just four days short of the seventy-fifth anniversary of Nellie Taft's first planting of the Japanese cherry blossom tree at the Tidal Basin, a ceremony was held at her grave site. A military band played some of the selections from her first concert at Potomac Park. Her grandson, Billy, and this author were among the speakers. The highlight was the appearance of U.S. Supreme Court associate justice Sandra Day O'Connor. She was an appropriate choice, not only as a representative of Will's beloved Court but as one who had made a historic "first" of her own—the first woman to sit on the Supreme Court. "With time and nurturing, Mrs. Taft's dream became Washington's most famous symbol of beauty. The trees are indisputably the mark of spring in our nation's capital and the tangible evidence of Mrs. Taft's energy and vision," Justice O'Connor remarked.

She also hit on what might be the single greatest lesson of the life of Helen "Nellie" Herron Taft: Never give up. "Mrs. Taft's hopes were initially dashed [but] . . . the hardy and generous Japanese trees," recalled the Justice, "were as undaunted as Mrs. Taft."[21]

NOTES

NH	Nellie Herron
AT	Alphonso Taft
HHT	Helen "Nellie" Herron Taft
WHT	William Howard Taft
RAT	Robert "Bob" Alphonso Taft
HTM	Helen Herron Taft Manning
CPT	Charles Phelps Taft
TR	Theodore Roosevelt
AWB	Archibald "Archie" Willingham Butt
FWC	Francis W. Carpenter
RBH	Rutherford B. Hayes
WHTP	William Howard Taft Papers
RATP	Robert A. Taft Papers
CPTP	Charles P. Taft Papers
HTMP	Helen Taft Manning Papers

Note: Unless otherwise indicated, all cited primary sources are from the William Howard Taft Papers (WHTP).

Prologue: Being First

Information on the Taft house history is from the Taft Museum of Art, www.taftmuseum.com; Taft Museum, www.daap.uc.edu/library/archcinci/1taftmuseum; HHT, pp. 1–5; Taft mansion layout, www.aroundcinci.com/content/multimedia/ttour/flash/

index2. Longworth quote to Nellie Taft from "Spells Didn't Bring Luck, Good Fortune," *Augusta Chronicle*, March 7, 1999. Other Longworth quotes, Alice Longworth, *Crowded Hours*, pp. 155–56. Other general information on election night from *New York Times*, November 4, 1908, and Henry Fowler Pringle, *Life and Times of William Howard Taft*.

1. First Lady of the Land (1861–1878)

1. Harriet Herron to RBH, December 26, 1892.

2. Francis Herron immigrated to America in 1734 from County Wexford, having perhaps moved there from a northern county. Francis came with five siblings—David, William, James, Mary, and Elizabeth—settling in the Pequa Valley of Lancaster, Pennsylvania, in Chester County. They lived there for ten years. In 1745 they moved to the line between Cumberland and Franklin counties, creating a family settlement near Shippensburg beside a stream that flows into the Conodoguinet River that became known as Herron's Branch or Herron's Run. One of the Herron brothers had enough money to build a mill on Herron's Run in 1793, paying each of the workmen in money, board, and four gallons of whiskey. David became a collector of taxes for the Colonial government and a Presbyterian elder in Middle Springs. When he and his family once failed to appear at a Communion Sunday, the minister came by their house to see why. "Well, pastor," the story has David replying, "we got up very early, did our chores, ate breakfast, and all the family gathered for our usual morning worship. It was the morning to read Psalm 119, and after reading and singing the 176 verses and having prayer, it was entirely too late to go to church."

Francis Herron married a fellow Irish immigrant, Mary McNutt, in the 1750s, and they began acquiring farmland. Their third son, William (who was born in 1750 and died in 1828), married another Irish immigrant, Nancy Reynolds. William and Nancy named their son after his immigrant grandfather, Francis. This Francis married Jane Wills. They were the parents of John Williamson Herron. Herron family history: John Herron to CPT, March 26, 1975; Margaret Hykes to CPT, January 9, 1975; Helen Herron Holland to

CPT, June 27, 1962; CPT to Milton Herron, January 17, 1961; Willa Beall to Helen Herron Holland, July 9, 1962; CPT to Margaret Hykes, December 5, 1974; CPT to Roxie Cain, January 24, 1961; John Herron White to RAT, Borger, Texas, n.d.; quotes at length an article on the Herrons from the *Shippensburg News-Chronicle*, n.d., circa post–March 8, 1930. Internet reply by Diane Sabido to Bill Meyers, www.genforum.genealogy.com/cgi-bin/pageload. cgi?Helen,Taft::herron::344.html. Internet reply by Marjy to JoAnn Cernosek, www.genforum.genealogy.com/herron/messages/1236.html.

3. The Miami University celebration that John Herron presided over was in 1889. CPT to HHT, September 11, 1939; CPT Papers, Box 25; "Helen Taft, June 1939 to May 1944 file"; Dr. Phillip Shriver on the "History of Women at Miami," transcript of a Women's History Month presentation on March 5, 1996, sponsored by the Women's Center, Miami University.

4. RBH diary, January 8, 1850; Nan Card, Rutherford B. Hayes Presidential Library to author, e-mail of December 21, 2001; RBH diary, March 29, 1851; RBH to Lucy Webb, September 19, 1851.

5. Harriet met her husband through her brother Isaac Clinton Collins, a judge and a law partner of John Herron for more than forty years. It was through Collins's membership in the local Literary Society that he first met Herron. It was as much a social center for Cincinnati's leading young legal community as a cultural outlet; besides Hayes, another founding member was Alphonso Taft.

Nellie Taft's maternal great-great-great-great-grandfather, John Collins, Jr., immigrated to Boston with his father and namesake about 1645 and worked as a shoemaker, tanner, and schoolteacher. He was born in Bramford, Suffolk County, England. In the next generation the family migrated to Connecticut and then, in the next generation, to New York.

Ela Collins (Nellie Taft's maternal grandfather) died in 1848. His family migrated to Ohio in either 1850 or 1853. William Collins (Nellie's maternal uncle) served a term as a U.S. congressman from Lowville, from 1845 to 1847, during the Taylor presidency. Uncle Willie went into banking, and although he had been a Democrat in the House of Representatives, he helped found the Ohio Republican organization in 1856. Willie Collins was described as having "a fair and good mind . . . excellent disposition and rather elegant literary culture," RBH diary, August 1, 1878. Nellie was much closer to her younger uncle, Isaac Clinton Collins, a Yale graduate and another judge. Maria Collins (Nellie's maternal grandmother), a native of Massachusetts, lived in Cincinnati until Nellie was in her teens, but there is no record of any contact between them. John Herron to RBH, April 29, 1871. Collins information is from "John Williamson and Harriet Anne Collins," at www.vineyard.net/history/allen/Web%20Cards/WC43/WC43_118.HTM and www.politicalgraveyard.com/bio/collins3.html; biographical information on Ela Collins (1786–1848) and his son, William Collins (1818–78), is from the Biographical Directory of the U.S. Congress at www.bioguide.congress.gov/scripts/biodisplay.pl?index=C000635 and C000644; the Collins Family Papers, 1799–1876 (454 items), located in the New York State Library, Albany; Harriet Herron to RBH, January 11, 1891. Numerous Presidents and First Ladies, prominent New England writers, and scientists represented Nellie Taft's kin on the U.S. side of the Atlantic. Her European ancestors were descended from the royals, warriors, saints, heroes, and legends of Renaissance and Dark Age England, Scotland, Denmark, Italy, France, Belgium, Holland, and Germany, including such colorful names as Ranulph the Rich, Bjorn Ulsuisson, Ulf Thorgilsson, Saint Ida de Boullion, Gerberga of Lorraine, King Cambo Blascon of Italy, Irmangarde of Hesbain, Blithide Princess of Cologne, and King Dux Syagrius of the Romans. Her blood antecedents stretched even further back into ancient times, traceable to the Middle East: Nahshon ben Amminadab born in Jerusalem, Judea; Ram ben Hezron Prince of Israel born in Goshen, Egypt; and Phares ben Judah born in Hebron, Palestine. Clinton history is from "Revolutionary Soldiers Buried in Lewis County, New York," *DAR Magazine*, vol. 48, no. 6, June 1916; www.rootsweb.com/~nylewis/lcrevsoll; Gary Boyd Roberts, *Notable Kin*, volume 1, n.d, n.p., available from www.genealogy-books.com; *Ancestral Roots of Certain American Colonists Who Came to America Before 1700*, edition 7, Frederick Lewis Weis (Baltimore, 1992), as cited at www.kinnexions.

com/kinnexions/cousinst.html; the ancestral chart tracing Nellie Taft back to biblical civilization through her Welles great-grandmother from "House of Midgard: Mark and Mariah's Family Tree, consisting, at present, of 166 generations," can be traced by each generation backward, starting from Maria Clinton at www.mariah.stonemarche.org/famfiles/fam07461.htm.

6. Harriet Herron to RBH, July 8, 1889; John Herron to RBH, September 25, 1862; John Herron to RBH, September 7, 1862. At one point, in September 1862, Herron spent four days as a private in Kentucky, carrying his musket, sleeping in the mud, and eating army rations. John Herron to RBH, September 16 and September 25, 1862; John Herron to RBH, August 6, 1864.

7. Emily Herron married Gustave Swan Parsons in 1878 and had five children: George, John, Elizabeth, Anne, and Lois. Jane "Jennie" Herron married Charles Anderson in 1876 and had three children: Jane, Catherine, and Harriet. William C. Herron married Jane Espy in 1895 and had four children: James, Janet, John William, and Patricia. John W. Herron married Georgia Aldrich in 1896 and had three children: Eleanor, Truman, and John Ogden. Eleanor Herron married Louis More, date unknown (circa late 1890s), and had two children: John and Catherine. Lucy Herron first married Thomas Laughlin in 1903 and had two children: Thomas and William. Lucy Herron married a second time, to Henry Lippitt in 1915, and had two children: Frederick and Mary Ann. Thus, through her siblings, Nellie Taft had a total of twenty-one nieces and nephews. Herron family chart, n.d., CPT Papers, Genealogy File. Will was to become a lawyer like his father. They came to share many professional friends in the law and on the bench and travel together for work, eventually forming a firm together. RBH diary, February 7, 1882. Jack was described as "a fine, strong, promising boy—full of friendly affection"; Emily, Jennie, and Maria as "superior persons"; and Eleanor and Lucy as having "a tender place in the household." RBH diary, February 13, 1877.

8. Eleanor Herron to HHT, August 9, n.d. (post-1891), CPT Papers. Comment on Edith Nourse, WHT and HHT honeymoon diary entry, 1886.

Circular for "Miss Nourse and Miss Robert's English and French Family and Day School," from manuscript collection, Cincinnati History Center. One Nourse student, Elsie Field, later recalled the setting that was to be the primary force in Nellie Herron's lifelong passion for learning and respect for education. The classrooms were on the third floor, dominated by the main room, some forty feet long, twenty-four feet wide, and sixteen feet high. Two smaller rooms opened into it from either end, partitioned by folding doors. With windows facing south and sun streaming in, these were used by the primary students and for recitations. Instead of individual desks in the main room, there were large, long study tables where the girls sat through the day. At the front of the class in front of the blackboards was Miss Nourse's black walnut desk and a gas stove, elevated on a platform. Three recitation benches were placed between her and the student tables. The walls were decorated not with the usual Americana of Washington and Lincoln portraits but scenes of Italy, where Miss Nourse had purchased them: the Colosseum, the Pisa tower, the temple at Paestum near Naples, the Rialto in Venice, the Campagna near Rome, and a view of Florence. Miss Field recalled, "But this is only a poor description of the room as it is at recess, when it is filled with noisy girls, with books and papers scattered about on the tables and two or three girls drumming on the piano." "A Description of our School-Room" by Elsie C. Field, n.d., Cincinnati Historical Society Library.

9. John Herron to RBH, April 5, November 10, December 17, and December 18, 1875; RBH to John Herron, November 11, 1871.

10. Herron as delegate, Robert Harlan to RAT, RAT Papers, Box 3, "Sympathy Letters, G-M" file. Nomination, John Herron to RBH, June 16, 1876. Lucy Hayes famous, John Herron to RBH, November 8, 1876. The disputed election of 1876 provoked further the Herron loyalties to Hayes. Pike Street was "wild with shouts" the day after the election, and Herron was certain Hayes would be declared winner, as he was. July 15, 1876; John Herron to RBH, April 23 and December 15, 1877, August 22 and August 24, 1879. Herron had told Hayes years earlier that he "was not intended for a

politician," August 20, 1856. Harriet as midwife, RBH diary, November 5, 1854. Putting up Rutherford, RBH diary, September 3, 1854. Herron borrowed money and then covered expenses for Lucy, RBH to Lucy Hayes, July 6, 1861. John Herron's mother sick, RBH to Fanny Platt, December 25, 1853. Just married and moved from Cleveland after her sister's death, Harriet found that Lucy "went far to dissipate the feeling of homesickness which oppressed me, and cheered me with the hope of finding another Sister. . . . I have had no other friend . . . ," Harriet Herron to RBH, July 8, 1889; Harriet Herron to RBH, July 8, 1889. The text of Nellie Herron's January 12, 1876, letter to Lucy Hayes: "Mamma wants to know where she shall send the black silk which she is going to get. She thinks it would be better to have it sent from the store right to Columbus or wherever you wish. We are well and glad to know that the Inauguration went off so well. Mamma sends much love to you, and I hope Scott Russell enjoyed his Christmas! Ever your affectionate niece Nellie L. Herron."

11. "Little angel," Rutherford Hayes diary, February 13, 1878. "Can't you give," John Herron to RBH, November 9, 1877. "The prettiest child," John Herron to RBH, November 26, 1877; John Herron to RBH, December 26, 1877; Helen Herron to Lucy Hayes, November 30, 1877.

12. Gilson Willets, "Inside History of the White House," *Christian Herald,* 1908, p. 478; HHT, pp. 6–7; George Griswold Hill, "The Wife of the New President," *Ladies' Home Journal,* March 1909.

2. Beer, Cigarettes, and Gambling (1878–1884)

Unless otherwise noted, all the quotes in this chapter from Nellie Taft are taken from her 1879–1884 diary. She did not necessarily date her entries, but when she did, they are noted in the text.

1. Harriet Herron to RBH, January 3, 1882, RBH Presidential Center. Father drinking, HHT to WHT, August 18, 1890.

2. "My dear Miss Herron: Mr. Sykes and I are to change our class into a school next year, and are to occupy the old Presbyterian church building on McMillan Street, near Kay's Corner, the building to be changed of course to

suit school purposes. To complete our plans it becomes necessary for us to secure an assistant. I have understood that you are regularly teaching at Madame Fredin's and it is this fact which encourages me to think that you might be induced to teach for us. I am sure that nothing could give us greater satisfaction. The assistant will have the smaller boys under her charge, for purposes of teaching, not of discipline: they will sit in Mr. Sykes' room and mine, and be sent for recitation purposes to the assistant's room, of which she will have exclusive use. We offer you for five hours a day, for five days in the week, during the school year, seven hundred dollars." Joseph White to Helen Herron, Park Avenue, Walnut Hills, March 25, no year (1882).

3. Harriet Herron to Nellie Herron, transcript, March 29, 1882, CPT Papers, Helen Taft file; Joseph White to Helen Herron, April 1, no year (1882), CPT Papers.

4. Howard Hollister to Nellie Herron, August 30, 1883, CPT Papers, HHT file; John Herron to RBH, August 19, 1883.

5. WHT to Helen Herron, April 19, 1882; WHT to Louisa Taft, February 12, 1883; WHT to Helen Herron, May 15, 1883.

6. WHT to Helen Herron, November 3, 1883.

7. Henry Fowler Pringle, *Life and Times of William Howard Taft*, vol. 1, p. 72.

3. The Will of Love (1884–1890)

1. Ishbel Ross, *An American Family*, p. 86.

2. Ishbel Ross, *An American Family*, p. 28.

3. Unless otherwise noted, general information on, and short quotes and remarks of WHT as a young man, as well as quotes of and information on the Taft family are from Ishbel Ross, *An American Family*. Alphonso Taft to WHT, July 2, 1879.

4. Nellie Herron poem to WHT and Horace Taft poem, n.d. [1884]; Valentine's Day party invitation to Nellie Herron, n.d. (February 1884), CPT Papers, HHT file; "pleasure," WHT to Helen Herron, February 17, 1884; "An aching void," WHT to Nellie Herron, February 19, 1884.

5. WHT to Nellie Herron, March 12, 1884.

6. WHT to Nellie Herron, April 29, 1884.

7. WHT to Nellie Herron, August 9, 1884.

8. WHT to Nellie Herron, August 18, 1884.

9. WHT to Nellie Herron, October 11, November 21, and December 25, 1884.

10. "I intended to ask," WHT to Nellie Herron, n.d. (circa April 1885). "We are prepared," WHT to Nellie Herron, n.d. (circa April 1885).

11. Activities and reading, WHT to Nellie Herron, April 21, 1885; "Last Sunday . . ." WHT to NH, May 1, 1885.

12. WHT to Nellie Herron, May 10, 1885.

13. WHT to Nellie Herron, June 15, 1885.

14. WHT to Nellie Herron, June 17, 1885.

15. WHT to Alphonso Taft, July 12, 1885. In response, Will received a loving and supportive letter from Alphonso, just the sort of parental approval that Will loved. "I am very happy in your prospects," he wrote. He recalled meeting Nellie when she was in a chemistry class at the university and being told how successful a student she was. He liked and respected the Herron family and foresaw a great future for the couple. Will used the letter to prod Nellie to permit him to soon tell the rest of his family, bringing it to her at home and claiming that Horace already suspected.

16. Missed her dreadfully, WHT to Nellie Herron, July 5, 1885; No letters, WHT to Nellie Herron, July 12, 1885; The husband reading, WHT to Nellie Herron, July 16, 1885; "It will be full moon," WHT to Nellie Herron, July 9, 1885.

17. Ishbel Ross, *An American Family*, p. 91.

18. WHT to Nellie Herron, July 10, 1885.

19. WHT to Louise Taft, August 13, 1885; Ishbel Ross, *An American Family*, pp. 92–93.

20. Report on convention and aftermath, WHT to Nellie Herron, September 1 and September 22, 1885. Campbell case, WHT to Nellie Herron, May 1, 1886.

21. WHT letter ("not a girl of . . . ") to Delia Torrey quoted in Ishbel

Ross, *An American Family*, p. 94. NH stopped working as a schoolteacher, "Nellie has dropped her school; has been at New York and Washington & is home again," John Herron to RBH, March 20, 1886. WHT finances, WHT to Nellie Herron, January 25, 1886, and WHT to Delia Torrey, February 23, 1886. On finances, seasickness, WHT to Nellie Herron, March 5, 1886. "The very idea," WHT to Nellie Herron, March 4, 1886. In one exchange Nellie had the audacity to complain to Will that his endless and numerous letters were too general in their expressions of flattery, that somehow she wanted some clarification on just what he meant by them. He replied in good humor with his own gentle rebuff about her typically cold letters to him. "You criticize my writing of letters on the ground that they are too bold and you want a little qualification," he responded. "Perhaps the criticism is just but when I write, I love you. That seems to me to comprehend everything I can say on the subject. It includes all the qualifications I can think of. But I'll try to shade it all hereafter. I might make a suggestion as to the ending of your letters but I won't." He then returned to his instinctive nature by closing the letter with "I count each day Nellie my darling until your return. Oh I long to see you so and take you in my arms and whisper to you how dearly I love you and how much is missing from my life when I can not go to you. Goodbye, your loving Will," WHT to Nellie Herron, March 4, 1886. "I am sorry," Nellie Herron to WHT, March 5, 1886. "Her, who is all," WHT to Nellie Herron, note, February 22, 1886. "Just think," he wrote her on March 10, 1886, "it is ten months since that night when we walked in from the Scarborough's. . . . The parlor is unchanged, the street is unchanged, the new Custom House is as it was then, but to me they all wear a different look, so different indeed that I almost forgot how they did look before you made silent promise to be mine. The change has gone on gradually ever since our engagement." List of seven rules, Nellie Herron diary, September 22, 1885.

22. WHT to Nellie Herron, January 25 and March 4, 1886; In Washington, WHT to Nellie Herron, March 6, 1886. Henry Fowler Pringle, *Life and Times of William Howard Taft*, vol. 1, p. 108.

4. Working Wife (1886–1890)

1. Maria Herron, Horace Taft, and Maria's best friend—Will's sister Fanny—were the three attendants. Reverend D.N.A. Hoge of Zanesville, Ohio, performed the Presbyterian ceremony, but Nellie soon after converted to Episcopalianism, Will remaining a Unitarian. John Herron to RBH, June 28, 1886. The claim that Hayes attended the Taft wedding is incorrect. Charles Richard Williams, *The Life of Rutherford Hayes,* vol. 2, p. 422; Ishbel Ross, *An American Family,* p. 98.

2. The honeymoon diary is in the Taft Papers in the Library of Congress. On their voyage home, as they crossed the icy north Atlantic in a dense fog, their steamer hit another vessel and broke the bowsprit and rigging. "I was very much frightened," he admitted, "and when the engines stopped as they did at once, visions of a watery grave for both of us rushed before my eyes."

3. RBH to Lucy Hayes, September 15, 1886; John Herron to RBH, October 23, 1886. Harriet Herron illness, RBH diary, December 30, 1886, and John Herron to RBH, November 18, 1886.

4. Jack Herron to RBH, January 30, 1887.

5. There would even be a kindergarten created in the White House for the daughters of President Cleveland in his second term. With the first massive wave of poor immigrants arriving in the United States unable to speak English, many heraldic, patriotic, and upper-class women's groups and organizations sought to "uplift" and educate them in the ways of being American. A focus on the preschool education of young poor children rose in the large cities. It provided advantage to the children of the underclass. Louise Taft led fund-raising efforts to open them in local public schools. Nellie was also probably coaxed to work at Miss Nourse's by her friend Allie Keys, who worked there as a teacher of composition. Although later newspaper stories mention her working as a kindergarten teacher at the time she and Will were engaged, Nellie Taft's instructional notes were marked 1887 and signed with her married name. Notebook marked "Helen H. Taft, December 1887," and *New York Herald* clipping, n.d.; also see Ishbel Ross, *An*

American Family, p. 67. A further quote from the notebook includes: "Present each object alone, to concentrate attention. Present each object as a whole that the idea of unity may precede that of variety, that is, unity should be conceived as the basis from which variety is evolved. Present each object in rest before presenting it in motion that the mind may not be confused by too rapidly recurring impressions. Present each object from many standpoints to give variety of interest and accustom the child to careful judgment. Emphasize salient characteristics that the child may learn to distinguish salient and permanent from accidental and transitory qualities."

6. When her scrupulously honest husband told the county tax assessor that the house was undervalued and that they should pay more property taxes, Nellie was, to say the least, displeased. When the appraisers came, she "hoped that my husband would not be at home." Because of the oddity of the house, however, there was no raising of taxes. Alphonso Taft quote from Ishbel Ross, *An American Family,* p. 105.

7. In Potsdam, Nellie pulled a bold stunt that almost got her and Will in hot water. The Empress was in residence and the palace was closed, but Nellie wanted to sneak in anyway: "[W]e managed to elude the soldiers stationed at the entrances and had my courage not given out, we might actually have called upon her highness—but I made Will return to ask permission of a soldier, and great was the consternation in the ranks. They refused to let Will return to get me, even, but as I then came in straight he beckoned me, and we returned with profuse apologies and explanations that we did not read German." They also stopped in Hanover and Dresden. In Italy they also went to Bologna, Padua, and Fiesoli. Florence seemed to be her favorite: "I could not recommend a lovelier place." She found Michelangelo's statue of Moses "the finest of his works," but Mrs. Taft didn't appreciate his painting: "It is very hard for me to think M.A. a great painter; I wish he had stuck to sculpture and finished some of his things." They went from Rome north to Genoa and Pisa, Milan, Lake Como, and Lake Lugano. The Rhone glacier, Rhine castles, and the Matterhorn most impressed Nellie in Switzerland. They proceeded to Cologne, Heidelberg, and Antwerp. Helen Taft, 1888 European diary.

8. Birth of Robert, John Herron to RBH, September 9, 1889. "There is

something charming about Bobbie that I don't see in any other baby," Will wrote her, "our boy is different from other babies in many most desirable ways." Will eagerly volunteered to push his son in his pram around Walnut Hills.

9. HHT, p. 22.

10. Alphonso Taft to Salmon P. Chase, December 7, 1864. Alphonso—who had vigorously supported and campaigned for Hayes—had hoped that during the Hayes administration his dream of sitting on the Court might be realized. He even wrote this out plainly to Chief Justice M. R. Waite in 1874, in anticipation of the retirement from the bench of Noah Swayne. "But I do not suppose that anything of that kind is in store for me," he wrote. Swayne didn't retire until after Hayes had left office. Ishbel Ross, *An American Family*, p. 62. Maria Herron recollections on Nellie's influence on Will's decision to resign from the superior court and accept the solicitor generalship is from Maria Herron to Henry F. Pringle, February 28, 1935, Pringle Papers, LC. Calming his son's fears of the new position, Alphonso Taft to WHT, February 1, 1890.

11. HHT, p. 24.

5. My Dearest and Best Critic

1. WHT to Alphonso Taft, April 18, 1890. Since the house at 5 Dupont Circle was rounded, its windows all afforded full street views and lots of light. The first-floor rooms were a reception and dining room. Will and Nellie's room was at the back of the second floor. The third floor's back room was for guests, and the front one Nellie established as Robbie's. The house was filled with assorted pieces, including tables given them by Louise, matching mahogany chairs, and cupboard that Nellie bought in New York, and a Chippendale sideboard she got in London. "We have been obliged to spend a great deal of money," Will told his father, "but I think it has been judiciously expended, so that what we have bought will be useful to us all our lives, both in Washington and after we leave it."

2. Nellie's health, WHT to Alphonso Taft, April 18, 1890. Vacation, WHT to Horace Taft, May 6, 1890. "Words" and Harrison event, WHT to Alphonso Taft, June 20, 1890.

3. For Edith Roosevelt letters on Washington of the 1890s, see Betty Caroli's *The Roosevelt Women* (New York: Basic Books, 1998). In Nellie Taft's calling book, "Mrs. Theodore Roosevelt" is listed at 1820 Jefferson Place. HHT Washington name and address directory, n.d. (circa 1890–91). Selden quote is from "Six White House Wives and Widows," *Ladies' Home Journal,* June 1927.

4. WHT to Alphonso Taft, April 18, 1890. "Did me no credit," WHT to Horace Taft, April 23, 1890. "to eat lunch." WHT to Alphonso Taft, May 6, 1890. "Disappointed" and "not much impressed," WHT to Alphonso Taft, April 18, 1890. Certainly Will's position was welcomed by the Herrons. Nellie's father successfully lobbied for him to intercede with the assistant solicitor of the Treasury on behalf of his client, Fidelity Trust. WHT to William Herron, June 18, 1890. Not to be left out, Harriet Herron got Nellie to influence Will to try to talk to the right people to reinstate a local postmaster fired unfairly, she thought. "I don't see why a poor man should be deprived of the means of earning a livelihood for his family. . . . Tell Will to do what he can for this poor fellow." Harriet Herron to HHT, October 5, 1891.

5. "Contemptuous," WHT to Horace Taft, April 23, 1890. "Dr. Edwards," HHT to WHT, September 13, 1890. "I find that hotel meals," WHT to HHT, February 9, 1894. "I fear," HHT to WHT, November 23, 1894.

6. Will caring for himself, fainting, eating, etc., HHT to WHT, August 18, 1890. "Sweet precious," HHT to WHT, August 13, 1890. Love and separation, HHT to WHT, August 30, 1890.

7. Will found it "embarrassing to make ends meet at the present time," WHT to Charley Taft, May 2, 1890. Nellie wrote Will, "I do hope we can pay Charley that two hundred and fifty dollars." Dress, HHT to WHT, September 13, 1890; "It is so close," HHT to WHT, January 3, 1894; "How aggravating," HHT to WHT, August 18, 1890.

8. "Anxious . . ." WHT to HHT, February 9, 1894. "I hope" WHT to HHT, March 18, 1896. One menu she planned was of shaddocks, bouillon, creamed oysters, sweetbreads, boiled chicken, peas, mushrooms on toast,

tomato salad, and orange pudding. Nellie Taft's letters are often filled with the frustration of having to find, interview, and teach new servants. Many of their names are lost to history, Nellie simply recording their first names, but they were often of Irish, German, or English extraction. In the latter half of May 1891, for example, she recorded $6.00 for Beatrice, 10 cents for stamps, $1.80 for butter and chickens, 10 cents for mushrooms, $1.00 each for Mrs. Kennedy and Mrs. Pringle, 24 cents for mailing parcels, 20 cents for liver, 10 cents for lard, and 30 cents for yams. She also did all the purchasing of Will's clothing—three shirts for $3.60, six stockings for $4.38, slippers for $2.50; and her own corsets for $7.75, a fan for $1.98, and two and a half inches of fur trimming for $2.15. Account book from late 1890 to 1892 in HHT handwriting. "Determined," HHT to WHT, September 1, 1890. "So hard," HHT to WHT, August 13, 1890.

9. "It is inexcusable," HHT to WHT, September 1, 1890. "Embarrassment," HHT to WHT, September 4, 1890. "We have spent," HHT to WHT, September 13, 1890.

10. HHT, p. 301. "Think of your going off," HHT to WHT, July 18, 1891.

11. "It seems," WHT to HHT, February 6, 1894. Will was also devastated to be missing much of his children's early years: "I hate to have the years go on to change the sweetness of our present existence with the children in that most interesting and lovely period of budding intelligence and ourselves sufficiently young to enjoy the things of youth. When Robbie came down to the train, he walked along with me to my car, trotting fast for him because he was afraid the train would go before I got on (in which I saw a maternal trait) and when I kissed him goodbye two or three times, he surprised and delighted me by saying Goodbye papa I hope that you have a good time away. I wanted to take him in my arms again and hug him but there was no time." "I would be glad," HHT to WHT, February 8, 1894. Will reported, "There is a true southern shiftlessness in the look of everything," in Nashville. "The legislature is Democratic but populist in its sympathies and of course everything is neglected." He also observed with some

surprise that his messenger "looks like a white man and I supposed he was. His color is sallow and his hair is straight as mine. . . . He is quite intelligent and disposed to talk politics. He has been in two national conventions." WHT to HHT, February 9, 1894.

12. Hospital work, HHT to WHT, November 11, 1893; HHT to WHT, December 7, 1893; HHT to WHT, January 3, 1894. "Life was," HHT, p. 41. Kindergarten presidency, HHT to WHT, May 26, 1893. Reading club and, "We would like," HHT to WHT, November 11, 1893: "That there were . . ." HHT to WHT, May 28, 1893.

13. "The Summer Capital" by Mabel Boardman, n.d., n.p., article in WHTP, clipping files on microfilm version, reel 454. "I must confess . . ." HHT to WHT, July 4, 1895; golf, HHT to WHT, September 22, 1899. Over the years, the rest of the Taft family would go to Murray Bay, though initially Charley's father-in-law did not want him to go that far away, and Horace's wife wanted her husband to vacation in Long Island. "Charlie [sic] is still full of going to Murray Bay and if they could get a house there, no doubt they would decide to go." HHT to WHT, February 5, 1894. Nellie soon found advantage in Will's position. After willfully transporting flammable oils in her luggage across the Canadian border, her trunk was inspected and the border police stopped her. Not only was her doing so a violation of customs laws, but it was dangerous. She immediately phoned Will, who pulled strings to have her released. "I shall not ask any intervention of Spence's good offices in the future if you are going to persist in smuggling in this way," he admonished her. "It isn't right in the first place and it isn't the square thing for me under the circumstances to do in the next." WHT to HHT, June 29, 1896.

14. Ladies Musical Club, HHT to WHT, February 5, 1894. "The recital," HHT to WHT, February 5, 1894. For information on the earliest origins of the Cincinnati Symphony Orchestra, see www.cincinnatipops .com/volunteers.html.

15. "Did not feel satisfied" and "Better than you think," HHT to WHT, November 23, 1894. "You can," HHT to WHT, November 3, 1894. "I was very much pleased," HHT to WHT, February 10, 1894. "I am so

glad," WHT to HHT, July 8, 1895. "I have noted. . . . My impression," WHT to HHT, February 9, 1894. "You seem to have," HHT to WHT, February 9, 1894.

16. "Saw Mr. and Mrs.," WHT to HHT, March 9, 1892. "I see that I got," HHT to WHT, August 22, 1891.

6. Managing the Music (1893–1899)

1. "Assured success," HHT to WHT, February 9, 1894. "Great jam," HHT to WHT, February 10, 1894. Through early 1894, Nellie continued her work for the hospital, inspecting newly completed wings, trying to get underwriting for more beds, and even going down to the site when the first operation was performed there. HHT to WHT, February 8, February 9, February 11, and February 14, 1894. In 1872, the Philharmonic Society gave its first concert as a Cincinnati orchestra but did not survive as an entity. The May Festival was founded by Maria Longworth, who also founded the famous Rookwood Pottery kilns two years later. HHT, p. 30.

2. "Regulations of the Orchestra Association Company." Estimates #1 and #2, CSO, March 28, 1894; undated minutes document of CSO starting, "We have heard from the committee on subscriptions." List of shareholders and one share certificate to Helen Taft, May 18, 1894. Draft of "By-Laws" document, 3 pages. CSO program, third season, 1896–97, list of guarantors.

3. Sinton and Hinckle, HHT to Lucien Wulsin, n.d., Cincinnati Historical Society Library. "List of those who have signified their willingness to take stock in the Opera Festival Association" document, n.d., HHT to Wulsin, n.d., Cincinnati Historical Society Library. List of HHT subscribers, "Mrs. Taft" document, n.d., "Sally and I," HHT to WHT, November 26, 1894. HHT spelled her friend's name as both "Sally" and "Sallie."

4. "Regulations of the Orchestra Association Company," n.d., HHT, p. 30. "His price," HHT to WHT, November 3, 1894. Her opinion, HHT to Lucien Wulsin, October 1, 1894, Cincinnati Historical Society.

5. Background on Van der Stucken from draft of "Cincinnati Symphony Orchestra "Detroit" document, 7 pages. "An ambitious man,"

William Hobart to HHT, June 11, 1984. "Proposition cannot be," Frank Van der Stucken to HHT, February 21, 1894. William Hobart to HHT, June 11, June 13, and June 18, 1894; and "To the Orchestras Association": "We the undersigned musicians," n.d.; Cincinnati College of Music, Peter Rudolph Neff to HHT, June 23, 1894. "Cannot accept" telegram, Van der Stucken to HHT, July 1, 1894.

6. Testimonials: Martin Roeder to HHT, July 30 and September 7, 1894; Ross Jungennickel to HHT, August 5, 1894; Adolph Neuendorff to HHT, August 26, October 9, and November 27, 1894; Henry Mottet to Annie Taft, October 27, 1894; Harmon Hans Wetzel to Annie Taft, November 8, 1894; and "American Applicants" scrap, n.d., Pops series, Edith Loechheimer to HHT, n.d. (1895–97). College of music president "antagonistic," HHT to Lucien Wulsin, n.d., Cincinnati Historical Society Library; Schradieck, Edith Loechheimer to HHT, n.d. (1895–97).

7. Two letters, HHT to Mr. Wulsin, n.d., Cincinnati Historical Society Library. "Van is very," HHT to WHT, September 18, 1894. "After our experience," HHT to Lucien Wulsin, October 1, 1894. "There is great," and "Anxious to make," HHT to Lucien Wulsin, October 5, 1894.

8. Nellie believed that the first concert of the fall 1894 season was unsuccessful only on the basis of seating and subscriptions. She made no comment on the quality of local performers. "We had our first meeting of the Ladies Musical Club on Saturday and it was a great success," Nellie reported to Will. "The full number of three hundred was reached, and some were turned away, which was certainly most satisfactory. The only trouble was that it was necessary to put a good many chairs in the hall and I fear the members will complain unless they can get a good seat. Corinne sang beautifully. I had never enjoyed her so much and Miss Metzger is certainly the finest pianist we have. The orchestra subscriptions are coming on very slowly. I suppose we will get there at the last but it is discouraging not to make more rapid progress. Our system of tickets has been a mistake I fear and is altogether too complicated, but we must do the best we can with it now." HHT to WHT, November 23, 1894. Handwritten program for "1st Concert." Pike

Street Theater, Harry Rainforte to HHT, May 9, 1894. HHT got concert fee lowered. HHT to Frank Hall, January 18, 1895.

9. "I have now changed," Henry Schradieck to HHT, March 1, 1895. "Under his baton," draft of Cincinnati Symphony Orchestra "Detroit" document, 7 pages. In contrast to Schradieck, the great singer Maria Brema sweetly wrote Nellie, "I am happy to inform you that all is right about my engagement." Paying Van der Stucken his lost wages from the Arion Society left Schmidlapp steaming, especially in light of the news that the nasty Mr. Neff had left the Cincinnati College of Music and Van's $3,000 salary there as musical director was assured. Van der Stucken and Arion Society and salary protests, HHT to Lucien Wulsin, May 1, 1895. "I feel happy," Van der Stucken to HHT, April 10 and April 27, 1895. Van der Stucken's contract of April 12, 1895, HHT to Lucien Wulsin, June 24, 1895, and Wulsin contract of March 25, 1895, Cincinnati Historical Society Library. Van der Stucken refused to hire local musicians if he deemed them not to his standards; Van der Stucken to HHT, December 26, 1894, and January 3, 1895. He also forced her to pay top dollar for top performers. Van der Stucken to HHT, November 12, 1894. "Already reflects credit upon . . . " CSO program, fall of 1895.

10. Music Hall rental, J. Blackburn to HHT, April 13, 1896, and signed contract, "To the Executive Committee." See contracts for R. Koehler, Arthur Brooks, Jose Marien, Hippolyte Vinick, signed by HHT, ranging from 1896 to 1999. Van der Stucken's desire to import talent from Europe is suggested in a scrap memo on Hotel Des Reservoirs stationery, dated July 30, 1895. Tirandelli contract, April 21, 1896. Van der Stucken seemed bothered by having to deal with the union. Less than two months after his contract was signed, he wrote Nellie from Cologne that he believed that a "soloist" was "exempt" from union rules and wondered if "the union would be generous enough to give its consent to them when they were able to import a horn, a bassoon, a viola, a second violin, a cello, a bass," considering such musicians "soloists." He hoped "it would be feasible to import a few men without any trouble at all." Under any circumstances Van der Stucken would have known the most basic requirements of the union, espe-

cially since he was so frequently performing in both Europe and America. Or possibly he was such a creative artist type that contracts and business details escaped his focus. Van wrote with strange reference to union laws, "[B]e careful with the Musical Union matter. Speak with [concertmaster] Mike Brands about it, but confidentially." Van der Stucken to HHT, June 3, 1895.

11. A. Beaugureau to HHT, November 6, 1897, and McCoy & Kitchen to HHT, November 15, 1897. *Daytona Volks-Zeitung* to CSO, March 12, 1898. Mary Wilson to HHT, November 5, 1897. Tickets written out by HHT. George Wells, "Big Four," to HHT, January 2, 1894, and November 2, 1897. Nellie was initially urged not to give concerts outside of Cincinnati, on the premise that it would strain the musicians and, ultimately, the quality of their work; W. N. Hobart to HHT, n.d. (1894). December 16, 1897, contract with the Indianapolis May Festival. The Phillips House receipt to CSO, March 17, 1898. Expense Accounts . . . Dayton . . . Columbus . . . Detroit. "The CSO . . . will give a series of concerts in Columbus," document in HHT handwriting, n.d.

12. Handwritten form letter, HHT to "Dear Sir," n.d. (1892–97). She gleefully accepted one patron's offer to buy six hundred tickets at $2.50 each for local students. HHT to Mrs. Allen, November 4, 1897. Van der Stucken to HHT, March 1, 1897. Alms Concert, March 2, 1899. Contract with Cincinnati Orpheus Society, n.d. Contract with United Sangerbund, February 10, 1898; Huber & Co., March 16, 1898; Wolf Brothers, March 16, 1898; The Press Publishing, March 17, 1898; The Evening News Association, March 18, 1898; American District Telegraph Company bill, March 1898.

13. Typical of Harriet Herron was her complaint about a servant who left her in Cincinnati, as she wrote from Europe: "I do not regret losing Maggie. She was most uncertain in her cooking and by no means clean, but she knew my way of managing and would have done better than a stranger. I can't endure the thought of beginning the struggle with those dreadful creatures again when I get home. All that class look and seem so different over here. I do not wonder Americans like to live here." Harriet Herron to HHT, July 6, 1894. While her father could also be judgmental, he had a

sense of humor. He sniped about hotels being "steep," when he got to England after the Continent, and he cracked that while it was "a comfort . . . to hear one's tongue again . . . the English is so badly spoken here." William Herron to HHT, August 16, 1894, and September 13, 1894; Harriet Herron to HHT, August 14, 1898. The other Herron children were also marrying and having children. Jack married Janie Espy, Will believing that the bride and her family would finally give Jack the "hero worship" he never got from his own family. WHT to HHT, March 25, 1896. "Your mother," WHT to HHT, June 27, 1897. There is no record of how Nellie responded. As for her mother-in-law, Nellie still found her frosty. "I asked her to come to lunch today to see the children," she reported to Will, "but she said she preferred to wait till you got home." HHT to WHT, May 25, 1899.

14. "I suppose," HHT to WHT, June 6, 1897. "Could step from here to," WHT to HHT, July 14, 1896. Washington, WHT to HHT, March 18, 1896. "Questions," WHT to HHT, November 21, 1894. McKinley, WHT to HHT, March 18, 1896. "Almost every person," WHT to HHT, March 25, 1896; Roosevelt, WHT to HHT, March 25, 1896, and Henry Fowler Pringle, *The Life and Times of William Howard Taft,* vol. 1, p. 153. Silver standard, WHT to HHT, July 14, 1896.

15. National League of Musicians notice, January 14, 1897; Cincinnati Musicians' Protective Association, February 10, 1897. Koehler, Albresht, Schippe, and Stunr (the four German immigrant musicians) to HHT, March 24, 1897. HHT to Messrs. Jones and Herholz, March 25, 1897. Alfred Herholz to HHT, March 26, 1897. HHT to Gentlemen, March 24, 1897. Musical Mutual Protective Union to HHT, April 17, 1897. Jos. Ostendorf, Assignees of J. H. Brinker vs. Richard Ferrer, Answer of the Cincinnati Orchestra, n.d. Adolph Belz to HHT, October 10, 1898. HHT to Adolph Belz, October 30, 1898. HHT to CSO members, February 7, 1898. When one trustee doubted whether Nellie could truly make the orchestra finally viable, she confronted him at a meeting he called. "He does it with some idea of acting as peace maker apparently, but I hope to convert him just the same. I think he will be more convinced by the business aspect of it than the others," HHT to WHT,

June 8, 1897. For further note of appreciation of HHT's work at the CSO, and her deserving of a "big laurel," see Fred H. Aluca to HHT, March 31, 1897.

16. "He has just gone," HHT to WHT, September 22, 1898. "I am still without," HHT to WHT, July 6, 1899. Mrs. Taft took her role as a mother as seriously as she did her independent work, but she seemed to enjoy her children more once they had matured a few years: "Yesterday I went to another baseball game, and I am going again this week to see the champions. I have been much interested in and I expect to learn all about it to keep up with Bobbie." HHT to WHT, May 25, 1899. Her second child also proved to be a great baseball fan. At eight Helen reported to her father on a Cincinnati Reds game, with childlike coverage of the hits and fouls. HTM to WHT, May 22, 1899.

17. "There had never been," HHT, p. 31. "The fighting," WHT to HHT, July 8, 1898.

18. For this period, see HHT to WHT, December 10, 1899. HHT to WHT, December 20, 1899. HHT to WHT, February 17, 1900. HHT to WHT, November 19, 1899. Philippines offer, HHT, pp. 33, 34. "More fun," HHT to WHT, August 18, 1890.

19. McKinley assured Taft: "If you give up this judicial office at my request you shall not suffer. If I last and the opportunity comes, I shall appoint you." WHT to Henry and Horace Taft, January 28, 1900. Nellie was only too happy to get him out of the judicial groove. She just wanted to make sure about the money he spent on the trip east: "You will get part of it back won't you as expenses . . . ?" HHT to WHT, February 20, 1900. "No opportunity" and "A trashy thing," HHT to WHT, February 17, 1900. HHT handwritten annual report for 1896 and 1898. CSO program, January 1, 1897. Orchestra work, HHT, p. 31. HHT obituary, *New York Times,* May 23, 1943. As far as being a financial success, beginning with the end of the 1896 season, the Cincinnati Symphony Orchestra brought in a small profit (nearly $300 more in receipts than expenditures), although two years later they cleared only $70. The CSO would go on, in Nellie Taft's lifetime, to host some of history's most talented and renowned composers and conduc-

tors, including Josef Hoffman, Richard Strauss, Edward Elgar, Leopold Stokowski, Sergei Rachmaninoff, Jascha Heifitz, Igor Stravinsky, Arthur Rubenstein, Isaac Stern, and, in the last year of her life, Arturo Toscanini. It would disband in 1907 due to labor disputes and lack of funds, but two years later, under the presidency and underwriting of Annie Taft, it was reorganized. The year Nellie died, Aaron Copland's "Fanfare for the Common Man" was commissioned by the CSO. The CSO continues to hold subscription concerts as well as children's, holiday, summer pops, and operatic pro grams throughout the year.

7. Rigadon

1. HHT, pp. 35, 75, 89–100. On board were also the other commissioners who served under Will, including Judge Henry Ide and General Luke E. Wright, and worked closely with him. Nellie was most amused by these men's teenage daughters—the two Ide girls who "displayed no sign of Puritan ancestry or upbringing" and Katrina Wright, whose antics made for good gossip.

2. "To convince us," WHT to HHT, May 21, 1900. Bubonic plague, WHT to HHT, June 10, 1900. "Bothered Nellie," WHT to Charley Taft, n.d. (circa summer 1900). Nellie's first three weeks in Japan were spent quarantined behind a yellow "Diphtheria" placard, since Bob came down with the illness. She had a housekeeper and nanny to help her. She registered Helen in dancing school. Mrs. Patton to HHT, June 1900. Bill for dancing instructions and life in Japan, HHT, pp. 50–66. "I can hardly realize," HHT to Louise Taft, June 28, 1900. "Fascination," WHT to HHT, July 11, 1900.

3. Will warned her that Canton would "not be safe" due to the harassing of foreigners by the Boxers, WHT to HHT, July 11, 1900. She had written Will, "I am tired of visiting temples and Japanese towns without having read up the guide book so that I can intelligently enjoy what I see." HHT to WHT, May 20, 1900. China experiences and Manila house, HHT, pp. 65–90. Chinese servants, WHT to Charles Taft, June 2, 1900. "We must," HHT to WHT, July 6, 1900. Doors open at night, WHT to HHT, July 11,

1900. Will told Nellie that the "mountains on the other side of the Bay are touched at their summits with pink, a beautiful rainbow reaches from sea surface to sea surface and the many graceful ocean-going steamers that lie two miles from shore are outlined clearly by the morning sun against the foot of the mountains behind." WHT to HHT, June 14, 1900. Typhoons, WHT to HHT, August 14, 1900.

4. For background on the history of the Philippines, a variety of general sources on the islands and Taft were consulted, including the accounts by Judith Anderson and Pringle, and *The American Pageant,* vol. 2, 11th ed., Thomas Bailey, David M. Kennedy, Lizabeth Cohen, editors, Boston: Houghton-Mifflin, 1998. *Little Brown Brothers,* Leon Wolff, New York: Oxford University Press, 1992 [reprint]; *Bound to Empire: The United States and the Philippines,* H. W. Brands, New York: Oxford University Press, 1992; *"Benevolent Assimilation": The American Conquest of the Philippines, 1899– 1903,* Stuart C. Miller, New Haven, CT: Yale University Press, 1984 [reprint]; *In Our Image: America's Empire in the Philippines,* Stanley Karnow, New York: Ballantine Books, 1990 [reprint]; McKinley quote, Judith Anderson, p. 66; WHT to HHT, 1900; On MacArthur, HHT, pp. 108–109. MacArthur replied condescendingly: Taft, for example, wanted to create a large police force of Filipinos. Nonsense, said MacArthur, the American military presence is what should be increased. Will said he was "utterly out of sympathy with the military government, its abrupt methods and its intense desire to avoid giving up the supreme power which it now has. They resented our coming and do not enjoy our stay." WHT to Harriet Herron, January 19, 1901. "As long as," WHT to HHT, June 26, 1900. Will thought MacArthur fine on "social accounts," but noted confidentially to Nellie that he "can't write English very well." WHT to HHT, February 17, 1900. Undermining Will to Washington, WHT to HHT, July 18, 1900. "If you were to hear all the conflicting opinions as to what should be done you would think that the persons giving them were talking of different countries. Charges and counter charges of bad faith and of corruption are made with an easy and apparent sincerity which first stagger me and then steel me against believing

any thing until it is proven by the visible evidence." WHT to HHT, June 18, 1900.

5. In California before his departure, WHT had been sought out by McKinley's Democratic opponent William Jennings Bryan, "desirous of catching me in some statement which he could use on the stump," WHT to Nancy Roelker, April 16, 1900. "Will Taft is a very fine," quoted in Ishbel Ross, *An American Family,* p. 123. "I would a great deal ... the kaleido-scope," Theodore Roosevelt to WHT, August 6, 1900, cited in Henry Fowler Pringle, *The Life and Times of William Howard Taft,* vol. 1, p. 190. The aspects of Filipino government that William Howard Taft had to structure were con-siderable and included taxation, civil service, provincial and municipal orga-nization, the new currency, finance, the police forces, roads, railway systems, improvements of the shorelines and harbors, customs, the postal services, ed-ucation, health, public lands, and commerce.

6. In illustrating his genuine ideal for self-government as soon as pos-sible, Will sought to place a native Filipino in the position of governor in every province. Local peoples, in many instances, insisted that the American Army officer then in command of each district be retained for that position. Since the Spanish friars, who had been the sole government rulers known by the people, decided to keep the Filipinos ignorant of their language, most of the natives still spoke only the native Tagalog language. Thus all the Ameri-can speeches had to be translated first into Spanish and then into Tagalog. While Will and Nellie took Spanish lessons, only little Charlie managed to pick up some Tagalog from his little friends in the neighborhood. Social contact in Bataan and military reaction, HHT, pp. 153–57. The first stop was Lucena, the capital of Tayabas Province. They would then visit Boac on Marinduque Island, Romblon, Masbate, Iloilo, Bacolod, Jolo, Moro, and Zamboanga in the Sulu Islands, Cotabato and Davao on Mindanao Island, Surigao, capital of the same-named island province, Cagayan, Misamis, Dapitan, San Jose de Buenavista, Capiz, Cebu, Bohol, Leyte, Samar, Albay, the Camarines, and Sorsogon. HHT, pp. 170–71.

7. Filipino life and Rigadon, HHT, pp. 150–51, 183. "Divided skirts,"

HHT to Mrs. Bell, n.d. (circa June 1900). Keeping a diary, Mrs. Taft recorded of her voyage that her room was "painfully dirty, the thermometer stood at 110!, the beds were without sheets, the pillows like rocks and it opened into a small salon where Filipinos galore sat and slept on the floors, chairs or resting places. The second night I slept on the bridge as the deck was also covered with a miscellaneous crowd. . . . We ate on deck on top of the ventilators and by the end of the trip the string of cabbages that hung from the awning were not so odiferous as they might have been." It was a trip, she scribbled drolly, that she was "not anxious to repeat." "We all fight," WHT to Harriet Herron, January 19, 1901. In contrast to Maria, Nellie received a letter from her sister Jennie who wrote, "You don't know how blue I feel to think that you and Bobby are really gone, and I shall see you no more!" Jennie Anderson to HHT, n.d. (circa 1900–1902). Crying, HHT to RAT, June 15, 1900 (misfiled as 1902). "I dread very much," HHT to WHT, June 6, 1900. Will's role as father while Nellie was gone: Charlie ate bananas and played with Will's mustache. Robert always asked Will to write "I love you Mama" to Nellie, and Helen was putting on weight. "I can not tell you how we all miss you. When I come home, the children look as if much had gone out of their lives and I feel very lonely. I suppose I am silent and uncommunicative, dear, but it is a great comfort just to feel your presence and sympathy. Still, I am delighted to hope that you and Maria are getting a new and pleasant experience," WHT to HHT, n.d. (circa June 1901).

8. HHT, pp. 188–205. Description of natives, HHT to RAT, June 15, 1900 (misfiled as 1902). "I wish you could see," HHT to RAT, June 18, 1901 (misfiled as 1902). Regarding her plans for the inaugural, WHT to HHT, telegram, June 27, 1901.

8. Queen of the Palace (1901–1904)

1. Description of palace and life there, HHT, pp. 206–10. "It is astonishing," HHT to Harriet Herron, July 27, 1901. Tropical nights, HHT, p. 214. "You would be amused," HHT to Jennie Anderson, July 17, 1901.

2. "Nellie and I expect," HHT to Harriet Herron, January 19, 1901. "One of the things," WHT to HHT, July 8, 1900. Among the guests were

many white American and European "derelicts and generally disreputable people" who had come to improve their lot in the islands. "The Filipinos," HHT, pp. 126, 217. "Regard the Filipino," WHT to Charles Taft, June 2, 1900. "We insisted upon," HHT, p. 125. "We made it a rule," HHT, p. 114.

What made the Tafts' efforts at social integration all the more admirable was that they paid personally for most entertaining. Will's salary was less than was originally promised him. Both branches of their families believed that his work there was important not only in terms of civic duty but what it would do for his political future. Thus, Charley made such a large gift of money to them that Will was "struck dumb" by the "material benefit which it will do us all." WHT to Charles Taft, June 13, 1901. As a Christmas gift to Will and Nellie, Harriet Herron had also sent a large sum of money that Nellie was to have inherited at her death. WHT to Harriet Herron, January 19, 1901. The Taft salary and finances are further discussed in WHT to Senator Henry Cabot Lodge, October 23, 1901.

3. Certainly, Will and Nellie were products of their class and era when they arrived in the islands. "There is nothing reminds one so much of home as the Episcopal ceremony in this country of Catholics," Will wrote his mother-in-law, explaining his frequent attendance at Army weddings. WHT to Harriet Herron, January 19, 1901. "The population of the islands is made up of a vast mass of ignorant, superstitious people, well-intentioned, lighthearted, temperate, somewhat cruel, domestic and fond of their families, and deeply wedded to the Catholic Church. They are easily influenced by speeches from a small class of educated meztizos [those with Spanish blood]. . . . They are generally lacking in moral character." "They are born politicians; are as ambitious as Satan, and as jealous as possible of each other's preferment," he wrote Nellie when he first arrived. "They are also light fingered and the greatest liars of the world. . . . They are careless and cruel to animals. They are respectful, and polite." WHT to Elihu Root, July 14 and October 1, 1900, and WHT to HHT, July 22, 1900. Native food: "These Filipino meals will be the death of me. They have a dozen courses. Everything is fried in lard with garlic," Will confided to Nellie, "but nevertheless I must eat in order to seem to appreciate the hospitality which is

certainly bounteous and unstinted." WHT to HHT, June 26, 1900. Will refused to make English the official language of the court system also because it would alienate the educated native lawyer class, whose views were persuasive with the masses. "Nothing in all the history of extending sovereignty of one country over another has created such a bitter feeling as forcing a new language upon an unwilling people." Undated typed document of WHT's paper, "Shall Spanish or English Be the Official Language of the Courts?" Not outlawing cockfighting, WHT to HHT, June 26, 1900. Catholic antidiscrimination in schools, WHT typed statement on "substitute for the amendment moved by Commissioner Moses," January 21, 1901.

4. On black guest at dinner table Taft home, HHT, pp. 19–20. "Will went on a coaching party," HHT to WHT, May 26, 1893. American and British attitude toward race in the late nineteenth and early twentieth centuries is taken from George M. Frederickson, *Racism: A Short History* (Princeton, N.J.: Princeton University Press, 2002). Jonathan D. Sarna and Jonathan Gold, Brandeis University, *The American Jewish Experience Through the 19th Century: Immigration and Acculturation*, Teacher Serve from National Humanities Center website. See also Jonathan D. Sarna, ed. *The American Jewish Experience: A Reader* (2nd ed. New York: Holmes and Meier, 1977).

5. As her son Charlie recalled, "She was of great assistance . . . in winning the affection and cooperation of the leading Filipinos; she had very great talents as a hostess, and her receptions at Malacanan Palace . . . were one of the principal means of bringing Americans and Filipinos together." Undated biography draft of Nellie Taft written by her son Charles, CPT Papers, Box 15, HTM, 1962–69 and undated file. "Anxious that," WHT to Charles Taft, June 13, 1901. "Pin them down," HHT, p. 219. "This afternoon," WHT attributed this quote directly to MacArthur in Henry Fowler Pringle, *The Life and Times of William Howard Taft*, vol. 1; HHT to Harriet Herron, July 27, 1901. "It was she," undated biography draft of Nellie Taft written by her son Charles, CPT Papers, Box 15, HTM, 1962–69 and undated file. "A great society beau," HHT to Harriet Herron, September 2, 1901. "Of course, Dear," WHT to HHT, June 26, 1900. "The situation in the Philippines," Gilson Willets, *Inside History of the White House*, pp. 479–80.

6. HHT, p. 117. The article was written by the urbane Juan de Juan, whom Nellie found fun, as Will predicted. WHT to HHT, August 14, 1900. Drop of Milk, Carl Sferrazza Anthony, *First Ladies,* vol. 1, p. 290. Mrs. McClintock to HHT, n.d. (1901). Maria Stafford, a doctor's wife who worked with Nellie in creating a children's ward in the local hospital, reported proudly to her that "the hospital is being praised by everyone." Maria Stafford to HHT, February 10, 1904. Kathryne Withrow to RAT, May 23, 1943. For herself, Nellie was exposed for the first time to working with middle-class women a generation younger than her own, but just the sort of women she imagined herself someday becoming, as she had written in her teenage diary. Nellie found the teachers "for the most part, a fine lot of men and women who had come out with high hopes and ideals and an enthusiastic desire to pass them on. . . . I believe they used to enjoy my parties in Manila as much as anybody in Manila. They were homesick, no doubt, especially the girls, and I suppose the sight of so many friendly American faces cheered them up." Another woman she befriended was a Mrs. LeRoy, the wife of one of the commissioner's assistants. Coming as a young bride to the islands with her husband, she gave private Spanish lessons to Robert. Her intelligence, skill, and genuine grit appealed to Nellie. HHT, pp. 138–39. "A most uninteresting" and "Very few," HHT to Harriet Herron, July 27, 1901.

7. Music and bands, HHT, p. 221; HHT to Harriet Herron, July 27, 1901. HHT also organized a musical presentation by a native all-women quartet, see HHT to Jennie Anderson, August 3, 1901. The Luneta, HHT, p. 98, and WHT to Harriet Herron, January 19, 1901. Children's educations, HHT, pp. 159 and 217, and Ishbel Ross, *An American Family,* p. 131. "He plays," HHT to Harriet Herron, July 27, 1901. Will told his mother-in-law that "Maria criticizes Nellie for spoiling him, and before the words are out of her mouth, she is engaged in doing exactly the same thing. He knows his power with both of them." WHT to Harriet Herron, January 19, 1901.

8. The *Herald* claimed that "the attitude of intimate personal and political friends of the President is such as to warrant the conviction that the President would look with favor upon his nomination." *New York Herald* clipping, n.d. "I leave it to your discretion," Harry Taft to WHT, June 7,

1901. "He is full of strenuous . . . ," Joseph Bucklin Bishop to WHT, June 24, 1901. Bishop wrote for the *Commercial Advertiser*. Only one Vice President, Martin Van Buren, had been popularly elected to chief executive. John Adams and Thomas Jefferson were both Vice Presidents elected to the presidency but not in the same electoral system that existed after 1828. "To me such a discussion," WHT to Charles Taft, August 27, 1901. Charley thought Will would be "a long distance on the road to the White House—much farther than some of the politicians who would like it. . . . It is not best to trouble about this matter just now. That will take care of itself when the proper time arrives." Charles Taft to WHT, July 9, 1901. "Speculation," HHT, pp. 222–23. "I have no doubt," WHT to Roosevelt, January 1901, cited in Henry Fowler Pringle, *The Life and Times of William Howard Taft,* vol. 1, p. 191; *Outlook*, September 17, 1901. "Let me at the outset," Theodore Roosevelt to WHT, July 15, 1901. Roosevelt listed different reasons for his probably not getting the nomination: "My own State will be against me . . . but my present situation [the vice presidency] is one in which I can do absolutely nothing to shape policies."

9. "We all feel so unhappy," HHT to Harriet Herron, July 19, 1901. "It is very hard," HHT to Jennie Anderson, August 3, 1901. Maria leaving, WHT to John Herron, July 19, 1901. Maria had already booked the later passage of August 15 because she wanted the experience of traveling west via the Suez Canal. HHT to Harriet Herron, July 27, 1901. Nellie wanting Lucy to come and to meet her mother in Europe, HHT to Harriet Herron, n.d. (post–July 4, 1901). "Exceedingly lonely": Maria's "cheery interest" had deeply impressed Will and drew a permanent bond between him and his sister-in-law. "I shall always look back upon the pleasantest part of our stay in Manila as associated with Maria," he wrote. He did seem relieved, however, at the end of the stream of criticism that the two sisters indulged in together toward outsiders. WHT to Harriet Herron, November 18, 1901.

10. McKinley's assassination, HHT, pp. 225–26. "Rugged strength," WHT to Elihu Root, September 26, 1901. "Impulsiveness," WHT to Bishop, September 20, 1901. "The tone of the dispatch," WHT to Horace Taft,

October 21, 1901. "The capacity for winning," WHT to Harry Taft, October 21, 1901. He also added a flattering line about Roosevelt, saying "men of talents and character have not generally been made vice-presidents." "Does not use," WHT to Louise Taft, October 21, 1901.

11. Experiences in China, HHT to HTM, October 12, 1901; HHT to WHT, October 20, 1901; HHT, pp. 226–27. Details of Will's illness and surgery, WHT to Harriet Herron, November 18, 1900. It was found that gangrene had set in and required a deep and long incision that would not heal easily; series of telegrams between WHT and HHT, October 25–28, 1901. Associated Press report on WHT, December 17, 1901.

12. John Herron to HHT, November 17 and November 24, 1901. Harriet Herron to HHT, November 17, 1901. Leaving Manila, HHT, pp. 228–30. In their absence the Malacanan Palace was left unoccupied although repairs were made to it; WHT to Edgar Bourne, December 16, 1901. Harriet Herron's death and John Herron's stroke, Nellie's health, HHT, pp. 233–34, and WHT to James Lamberton, February 2, 1902. Malaria, HHT to WHT, February 1, 1902.

13. "He was just" and "Mrs. R.," WHT to HHT, January 20, 1902. "Write me something," HHT to WHT, February 1, 1902. "I met also," WHT to HHT, January 20, 1902. "Warmest and most," WHT to Morris Belknap, January 6, 1902. "His impulsiveness . . . ," WHT to HHT, February 6, 1902. "I was much interested," HHT to WHT, n.d. (circa February 1902).

14. "More expensive," and "I would not," WHT to HHT, February 6, 1902. "Altogether your stay," HHT to WHT, n.d. (circa April 1902, mislabeled 1905). "Prepared for . . . I do not enjoy," WHT to HHT, January 20, 1902. "Hostile cross-examination," HHT, p. 234. "Disputes with the Democrats," WHT to HHT, February 3, 1902. "I am glad," HHT to WHT, n.d. (circa winter 1902). "I fear you were," HHT to WHT, February 25, 1902. She scolded him, too, as in days of yore. Having forgotten to take his formal trousers, she cut him with "I am mortified that you should not have been able to dress for dinner. Of course, all Washington people do. Did you just wear your farmer's suit and necktie?" HHT to WHT, February 1, 1902.

15. Whether Will did so consciously or not, his expressed neediness of Nellie seemed to pull her up out of her own problems. "You certainly are not as devoted as you used to be" she started in on him about his lack of letters. HHT to WHT, February 3, 1902. As Will fretted about the reality that he needed a third surgery, Nellie said she did "feel dreadfully" about him, then casually mentioned that "my spleen has come down wonderfully—it is somewhere nearer now to being normal" and that her current discomfort was simply her "rapid pulse." WHT to HHT, February 3, 1902; HHT to WHT, February 5, 1902. When Will worried about whether to have his surgery done in Washington, New York, or Cincinnati, she first recommended Baltimore, but backtracked because "they might charge you frightfully." As for herself, her physical health was improving but not her "feelings." HHT to WHT, February 6, 1902. Nellie was "very blue" over the pain Will again had to endure (HHT to WHT, February 8, 1902), this time necessitating, as he wrote, "the cutting through the inner sphincter muscle." WHT to Charley Taft, February 14, 1902. "I have just come back," WHT to HHT, March 1, 1902. Will reported on another White House dinner, WHT to HHT, February 6, 1902. "Old gentleman," HHT to WHT, February 6, 1902. "that I may not . . . ," HHT to WHT, n.d. (circa April 1902, mislabeled 1905). "The worst of all," HHT to WHT, April 22, 1902. Arrangements for trip to Rome, WHT to Luke Wright, March 14, 1902; WHT to HHT, telegram, n.d. (February 1902); Louise Taft to WHT, May 4, 1902.

16. Rome visit and ongoing Vatican negotiations on Philippines, WHT to HHT, June 11, 1902; WHT to HHT, July 18, 1902; and TR to WHT, July 31, 1902. Draft of letter from WHT to Pope Leo outlining U.S. views on state and religion, n.d.; HHT, pp. 233–50; Anthony, First Ladies, vol. 1, p. 290. "I can not tell you," WHT to HHT, August 5, 1902. Nellie's return trip to Manila, WHT to J. G. Schmidlapp, October 4, 1902.

17. "On January 1st," and "If you do not accept," TR to WHT, October 18, 1902. "I feel that your duty," TR to WHT, October 26, 1902. "I had always," HHT, pp. 263–64. "Great honor," WHT to TR, October 27, 1902. When Roosevelt got War Secretary Root to telegram Will that staying in the

Philippines would jeopardize his health further, Will retorted that he was fine. He reaffirmed: "I long for a judicial career but if it must turn on my present decision I am willing to lose it." WHT to Root, October 27, 1902. "Disappointed" and "No one can quite," TR to WHT, October 29, 1902. The matter settled, Nellie determined to focus on her own "continued and continuous round of social work and pleasure." She looked forward to "perhaps two more years of it"—which meant leaving the Philippines just as the presidential campaign was beginning. HHT, p. 265.

18. "I am awfully sorry" and "I am very sorry," Theodore Roosevelt to WHT, November 26, 1903. "Nellie was quite disappointed," WHT to Charley Taft, January 7, 1903. Health conditions in Manila, HHT, pp. 266–67. "Reconciled," WHT to Charley Taft, March 2, 1903. In the palace, no water was drunk that was not first boiled, and all fruit and vegetables had to be soaked in antibacterial solution. It prompted Nellie to send for her own small farm of a cow and chickens, providing fresh dairy and meats for the family. HHT, pp. 253–58; H. R. Bogart to HHT, April 17, 1903. "Retention," Worchester, Ide, and Smith to TR, n.d. (January 1903) enclosed in letter of WHT to Charles Taft, January 7, 1903. Will's brother Harry found no "ulterior motive" behind Roosevelt's push for Will to sit on the Court. This was reassuring to Will on two counts: He had feared that his being taken from his post was either because of indignant American Catholics or because Roosevelt felt his work wasn't good. He also reported that Secretary Root, who didn't want to be "disloyal" to Roosevelt, privately hoped Will would not take the Court offer because he was the surest successor to Roosevelt. Harry told Roosevelt that Will "sat down hard" when he decided to sit. Roosevelt laughed. He had "a habit of doing so, too." Harry Taft to WHT, January 10, 1903. "Opponents of Roosevelt," Harry Taft to WHT, January 22, 1903. "I do not think his personality," Louise Taft to WHT, March 11, 1903, cited in Ishbel Ross, *An American Family,* p. 150. "Nellie was especially," WHT to Louise Taft, March 7, 1903.

19. "Will has sprung," TR to Henry Taft, January 12, 1903. "All right, stay," TR to WHT, January 13, 1903. Nellie laughed, HHT, p. 269. TR to

WHT, February 14, 1903. "This was more pleasing," HHT, p. 269. Couldn't afford, WHT to TR, April 3, 1903. "And she never minded," TR to WHT, June 9, 1903. "You should see," WHT to Howard Hollister, September 21, 1903. Charley Taft promised $6,000, Ishbel Ross, *An American Family,* p. 151. Nellie had initially hoped to spend their summers in the Philippines in Banguet and had chosen a site for a home there. HHT to Harriet Herron, July 19, 1901; WHT to TR, December 30, 1902. Nellie wrote to the military supply headquarters in Manila for flour to be delivered in the mountains, HHT to Manila Grocery Store, April 22, 1903. On Carpenter, HHT to Harriet Herron, July 19, 1901. Senator Beveridge, HHT to Harriet Herron, September 2, 1901.

20. Cholera, WHT to Dean Worchester, September 14, 1903. She had also confessed to her sister that "it is tiresome to be always hostess especially when you can not remember people's names." HHT to Jennie Anderson, August 3, 1901. Chinese servant, Quartermaster Robinson to WHT, October 1, 1903; unclear name to HHT, October 26, 1903. As Helen Taft wrote to her brother Bob of the costume ball, "All Manila is going wild [about the costume party]. Everyone has to wear fancy dress and come by the river. Papa is going to go as Doge and Mama as Dogess and I am going as an Italian peasant. Charley will go à la Lord Fauntleroy. Papa will wear a long red robe with white satin cape and Mama's will be made from pink brocade." HTM to RAT, November 30, 1903. Robert Taft preceded his family to America, arriving on October 1 to begin class at his uncle Horace's school. "I was at the edge of a rapid crowd," WHT reported to Nellie. "It seems that the Barney girls are queer that one of them associates with a leader of the demimondaine in Paris and has written a French book of the most unnatural and nastily amorous poetry. This was one of the things that led to Al. Barney's death—Nick Longworth elaborated the story to me." WHT to HHT, February 12 and March 3, 1904. He was over at the home of Nick's mother, Susan, when she read a letter from mutual friends "that caused sidesplitting laughter" at their pretense in Europe. WHT to HHT, March 14, 1904. "Alice R.," WHT to HHT, March 11, 1904. "Invited me," WHT to HHT, March 14, 1904. "The wife of a War Secretary," WHT to HHT,

February 8, 1904. "Your letters have been," WHT to HHT, March 11, 1904. He spent money, WHT to HHT, March 4, 1904. "You have not," HHT to WHT, February 3, 1904. "I do love you Darling," WHT to HHT, March 7, 1904. "I am very lonely," HHT to WHT, February 4, 1904.

21. "I have a letter," WHT to HHT, March 15, 1904. Nellie still felt "rather mopey" as late as August of that year. HHT to WHT, August 3, 1904. Health problems, WHT to HHT, March 15, 1904; WHT to Louise Taft, May 10, 1904. Weight, WHT to Cottrell & Leonard, June 18, 1904. "I am glad," HHT to WHT, August 6, 1904. Rail passes, WHT to A. J. Cassatt, March 24, 1904. "I fear," WHT to HHT, August 18, 1904.

22. "The issues chiefly," WHT to HHT, March 31, 1904. "These things I do," WHT to HHT, March 13, 1904. "The President seems really," WHT to HHT, March 4, 1904. "I like Kermit better," Ishbel Ross, *An American Family*, p. 156. "I hope you will agree with me," WHT to HHT, March 18, 1904. "Spooner was talking," WHT to HHT, March 19, 1904. "Wished to see me," WHT to HHT, April 12, 1904. "You must not be too confident," WHT to HHT, March 31, 1904. "I went over to see," WHT to HHT, August 3, 1904. Will feared Roosevelt's reaction to an impromptu remark at a Yale dinner where Taft was hailed as Roosevelt's inevitable successor.

9. "Teddy, Nellie, and Will" (1904–1907)

1. "Charlie induced me," HHT to WHT, "Sunday," n.d. (circa October 1904). The boy was always underfoot: "I shall be greatly relieved to get him [Charlie] out of the house," she wrote Will, "as he is a perfect cyclone." HHT to WHT, October 2, 1902. "Have you called," WHT to HHT, October 12, 1904. Prince Heinrich, HHT to WHT, May 16, 1904. Will's birthday, WHT to Howard Hollister, September 16, 1904.

2. WHT to HHT, March 30, 1904. Job for friend and "bored," HHT to WHT, August 20 and September 14, 1904. "More partisan," WHT to HHT, August 25, 1904. "I could not," HHT to WHT, October 7, 1904. "Took me an hour," WHT to HHT, February 23, 1906.

3. "I wish you," WHT to HHT, March 22, 1904. "I wouldn't run,"

WHT to HHT, October 12, 1904. "How glad," HHT to WHT, November 2, 1904. "I have not the slightest," WHT to Milton McRae, November 12, 1904. 1904 election night, Sylvia Jukes Morris, *Edith Kermit Roosevelt*, pp. 280–81. "We met Charley," HHT to WHT, November 2, 1904.

4. WHT to Charley Taft, December 30, 1904. Money remained a constant worry for her at this time. "She is at present very much troubled over the cost of things," WHT wrote about HHT to a friend the day before the big dinner. "More troubled because I find it difficult to rouse myself on such a subject." WHT to Therese McCagg, January 23, 1905. Nellie felt she did "nothing but pay calls and go to dinners." HHT to RAT, February 26, 1905. "Lonely," HHT to WHT, May 25, 1905. "Yet that," Anna Weostink to HHT, March 19, 1905. In her memoirs Nellie later claimed that the reasons she didn't go was that she knew she would be making a later trip to the Philippines. Bob was going to Scandinavia. "Shabby looking," HHT to WHT, July 8, 1905.

5. "Attracts Alice," WHT to HHT, August 14, 1905. "Alice … seems," WHT to HHT, July 31, 1905. "Alice tells me," WHT to HHT, August 1, 1905. "You get such," HHT to RAT, July 30, 1905. Nellie would also write, "I do not like England nearly as much as the Continent and shall never feel tempted to spend another summer [here]." Decades later she would spend another summer there.

6. "Contempt" and "I knew no way," WHT to HHT, September 24, 1905. Francis Millet, HHT to WHT, August 24, 1905. "Really devoted," Alice Roosevelt Longworth, *Crowded Hours*, p. 69. "Alice is … frank," and Congressman Cochran, WHT to HHT, September 24, 1905. As the Asian junket drifted back to the West Coast, the spell of the Princess had been cast, and she was being hailed in song by her fellow passengers—including a gleeful Will: "And when she's near you, She's sure to cheer you! And she makes you feel you're glad that she is here! So slyly winkin', we all are drinkin', And whisperin' 'God Bless you Alice dear!'" WHT to HHT, September 18, 1905. Even Nellie figured out a way to profit by the Princess. When she was trying to get porters to move her luggage so she could make her transatlantic voyage, she announced that she was the wife of the man who was just then traveling with Alice Roosevelt. She made her ship on time.

7. Mabel Boardman, WHT to HHT, September 24, 1905. "I fear," HHT to WHT, August 1905, as quoted in Ishbel Ross, *An American Family,* 173. Wright and Barrymore "notwithstanding," WHT to HHT, October 5 and October 9, 1905. Taft was so cryptic in the reasons for his profuse apologies to Nellie—which had upset her greatly—that it is difficult to discern what happened. See WHT to HHT, September 3, 1887. "A lady called," HHT to WHT, November 2, 1904. "Your girl came to see me," HHT to WHT, May 25, 1907.

8. "I doubt this," and "Mrs. Roosevelt," WHT to HHT, September 24, 1905. Will sent Nellie a telegraph from Fort Monroe in Virginia: "Have accepted invitation for you and me to dine with President," WHT to HHT, November 14, 1905. "Make it," H. H. Kohlstaat, *From McKinley to Harding,* pp. 161–62. The exact date of when Roosevelt called his meeting for both Will and Nellie Taft is in doubt. The other known meeting of both Tafts with Roosevelt is recounted in Irwin Hoover's memoirs, and it resulted more definitively in Taft not taking the Court offer. Thus the Kohlstaat incident is more likely matched with the invitation from Roosevelt to both Tafts in November 1905; Hammond, pp. 532–33.

9. HHT, p. 304. Edith not thinking Taft presidential material is from Sylvia Jukes Morris's biography *Edith Kermit Roosevelt*. "I also explained," War Secretary diary, March 9, 1906.

10. TR to WHT, March 15, 1906. Nellie remained absolute in her protest against the Court. Her ultimate power over Will's thinking was even proven to be greater than that of his brother Charley. Charley had proposed an alternative to make everyone happy: Will could take the Court appointment, be removed from the typical attacks of politics, and then, however unprecedented, resign and run for the presidency—if a good prospect for winning was in place. Nellie knew Will better. Once on the Court, it was unlikely he would ever give it up for anything. War Secretary diary, p. 131, quotes the letter of Charley Taft to WHT, March 12, 1906. Interestingly, many years before, Will and Charley's father had considered this option and found it wrong. In a September 10, 1874, letter to William Evarts regarding his eulogy of Chief Justice Chase, Alphonso Taft wrote: "I think it unfortu-

nate for his reputation that after his acceptance of the Chief Justiceship, he did not give up entirely his ambition for the Presidency. Perhaps it was too much for human nature. It may be conceded he never allowed his political aspirations to warp his judicial conduct. . . . Though in some of his letters he disclaimed any strong desire for the office of President, yet it was the current belief he had such a desire, and to many of his associates and intimate friends it was well known that his longing for the Presidency amounted to a passion. It must be admitted that had he not been Chief Justice, a more fit man for the head of the government could hardly have been found."

11. WHT to C. G. Washburn, March 27, 1906; WHT to J. D. Brannan, March 29, 1905. "He was full of," WHT to HHT, May 4, 1906; Irwin Hoover, *42 Years in the White House,* pp. 37–38. Undated biography draft of Nellie Taft written by her son Charles, CPT Papers, Box 15, HTM, 1962–69 and undated file.

12. When she first arrived, a woman turned to her at a luncheon and, referring to Manila, quipped, "Why, out there you were really a queen, and you come back here and are *just nobody!*" HHT, p. 276. Will in the Cabinet was a "promotion" that had "diminished advantages" to her previous life. Now it was spent in endless rounds of formal calls at homes of other official wives, which she found "irksome," and nightly official dinners. Her one great solace in entertaining was Major Arthur Brooks, a prominent African American who had served in the Army as a major and was now the war secretary's messenger. Arthur and Nellie worked closely together on all of the Taft's official entertainments, and their mutual loyalty and affection was one of the few elements of Washington life that she seemed to enjoy during these years. HHT, pp. 276–82. "Deplored that I," HHT to WHT, November 7, 1906. "Fortunately for me," HHT, p. 282. Will invited to Oyster Bay without Nellie, TR to WHT, September 1, 1906. "I feel that your going," HHT to WHT, September 15, 1906.

13. "The Quebec papers had it that you were off to Cuba, so Monday morning I telegraphed to find out and got a prompt response from Carpenter. . . . I was perfectly aghast," HHT to WHT, September 18, 1906. In the

same letter she also tried to lift his self-doubt: "I am quite sure that you will do it better than anyone else could as it seems right in your line." Taft declared a provisional American government in Cuba, installing himself as temporary governor only to last as long as necessary "to restore order and peace and public confidence." Nellie wrote him, "The news in my Sun is bad yesterday and today—likelihood of war in Cuba and Hearst nominated [for Democratic candidate for governor] in New York. . . . It is too bad if your mission was unsuccessful, but I am sure no one else could have done better." "I am in a condition," WHT to HHT, September 27, 1906. Within two weeks, WHT to HHT, October 1, 1906. She enjoyed her three days as Cuba's First Lady in a mansion "as cheerful as a mortuary chapel," with a bedroom of "spacious discomfort," but the goal of her mission was to steady and advise Will. HHT, pp. 294–301.

14. "Bar Lincoln," TR to WHT, August 2, 1906. "The President was in," HHT to RAT, October 21, 1906. Bid by phone to White House lunch; HHT to RAT, October 28, 1906. "It was rather slower," HHT to WHT, October 27, 1906. "Had a panic," HHT to WHT, October 29, 1906.

15. "Interested in your conversation," WHT to HHT, October 31, 1906. "A poor politician," HHT, p. 304. "Mrs. Taft writes me," WHT to TR, quoted in HHT, p. 305. "Mrs. Taft could not have," TR to WHT, November 5, 1906.

16. "I was quite put out," HHT to WHT, November 18, 1906. Indeed, Will nearly matched the President's phrase of "some man from the West" in his letter to Elihu Root, in which he stated: "From everything I have seen in the west, my judgment is that the President cannot avoid running again unless he would resist the unanimous call of his party. There is a ground swell in his favor." WHT to Elihu Root, November 10, 1906.

17. "I shouldn't wonder," HHT to WHT, October 27, 1906. "You say in your letter," WHT to HHT, November 1, 1906. "I am sorry," HHT to WHT, October 29, 1906. "I hope you will go," HHT to WHT, November 2, 1906. "Gives me the blues," HHT to WHT, October 29, 1906.

18. "Read so fast," HHT to RAT, March 11, 1906. "Automobile pic-

nic," HHT to RAT, May 20, 1905. "Examined him about," HHT to WHT, November 2, 1906. "Bahaire Religion," HHT to RAT, March 10, no year (circa 1907–1908). She especially loved opera, reporting on one performance of *Madame Butterfly*, "We all wept, even howled." HHT to RAT, November 25, no year (circa 1907–1908). "I had something," HHT to RAT, October 28, 1906. Christmas 1906 and Nellie happy, WHT to Annie Taft, December 28, 1906; HHT to RAT, December 9, 1906. Charlie's activities, HHT to WHT, October 27, 1906; HHT to WHT, September 14, 1906; HHT to WHT, October 31, 1906. HHT wanting Army escort in full-dress uniform, WHT to Captain T. Bentley Mott, December 31, 1906. Activities in Charleston, "a thoroughly enjoyable time," HHT to RAT, January 27, 1907. "We drank [to] your health," WHT to HHT, n.d. (March 27, 1907).

19. "His letters," HHT, p. 302. Charley Taft also continued to give money to Will and Nellie, FWC to WHT, October 6, 1906. Charley sets up campaign office, Henry Fowler Pringle, *The Life and Times of William Howard Taft,* vol. 1, p. 321.

20. "The papers. . . . It was all precipitated," HHT to WHT, March 29, 1907; HHT to WHT, Easter Sunday, 1907 (April). "I am sorry," HHT to WHT, April 3, 1907. WHT's brother's name was spelled "Charley," although HHT often wrote of him as "Charlie."

21. Will was frustrated with one speech of "horrible length," feeling unable to "make it shorter, though I worked on it hard," but confessing, "I am made this way." WHT to HHT, August 15, 1907. Nellie soothed him this time, sending him a line "to wish you every good luck in the speech. I am sure it will go off well, and that you have no cause of worry." HHT to WHT, August 16, 1907. "When I read," WHT to HHT, August 18, 1907. "It makes me blue," HHT to WHT, August 18, 1907. Will even encouraged Nellie to "keep him [Charley] advised" on issues arising as a result of the speaking tour. WHT to HHT, August 20, 1907. "Safely delivered," HHT to WHT, August 21, 1907.

22. "If people don't want," HHT to WHT, August 18, 1907. "If you are not," HHT to WHT, August 16, 1907. "At the present time," TR to

WHT, September 3, 1907. "But I am," TR to WHT, September 5, 1907.
Roosevelt conversation with Reynolds, Charles D. Hilles to A. I. Vorys, November 13, 1907. "Shy or nervous," WHT to Mabel Boardman, September
11, 1907. Taft was confident that he would trounce Hughes. Even Vorys
thought the letter simply meant that Roosevelt would not "pitch in openly
hammer and tongs." A. I. Vorys to Henry Taft, October 5, 1907. "Out of patience," WHT to Charley Taft, September 11, 1907. Nellie's mistrust of
Roosevelt may have also been spiked by her being told by a mutual friend of
how flatteringly he had spoken of Mrs. Taft. Nellie knew there was no reason for it except disarmament. Mrs. Selmes to HHT, April 22, 1907.

23. Nellie had joined Will for a brief trip to Puerto Rico in April 1907.
See HHT to RAT, April 29, 1907. Nellie Taft's diary of her 1907 travels is
listed as "World Tour Diary." There are no page numbers. Starting at the
end of August, Nellie took a train from Minnesota to Wyoming to join Will
at Yellowstone Park. There they covered fifty miles a day for three days,
spending their first night at Old Faithful. From there they stopped in Seattle,
where she attended some of the local symphony meetings, and then set sail
on September 13. Sleeping in her old room at the Malacanan Palace in
Manila and being feted and showered with gifts of pearl jewelry, Nellie felt
herself just as equal in importance to Will, based on their treatment; she
wrote Bob that "no doubt you have followed our career in the newspapers."
HHT to RAT, October 7 and October 27, 1907. Originally their itinerary
had the Tafts touring Europe, but Nellie reported disappointedly, "For some
reason the President changed his mind and became unwilling" to permit this
so "we shall not see any royalities [sic]." HHT to RAT, November 13, 1907.
The Tafts celebrated Thanksgiving on the train with some women they befriended who worked at Jane Addams's Hull House in Chicago. HHT diary
of world tour, September–December 1907. "I do not want my son," quoted
in Ishbel Ross, *An American Family*, p. 178. Louise Taft explained to Will
that she had done this as a way of stating her opinion once and for all and
then denying all further interview requests. Louise Taft to WHT, April 29,
1907. "By the way," HTM to RAT, n.d. (circa November 1907).

10. Precedent and Mrs. Taft

1. Story and descriptions of Nellie Taft going to the office and the 1908 Republican Convention are from Alice Longworth, *Crowded Hours*, p. 149; Ishbel Ross, *An American Family*, p. 197; Joseph B. Bishop, *Presidential Nomination and Election*, pp. 73–74 as quoted in Henry Fowler Pringle, *The Life and Times of William Howard Taft*, vol. 1, pp. 352–54; Gilson Willets, *Inside History of the White House*, pp. 480–81; videotape from film of Nellie Taft, author's collection.

2. "Nightmare . . . one's family," Henry Fowler Pringle, *The Life and Times of William Howard Taft*, vol. 1, pp. 356–57. Taft had responded as curtly as he could to inquiries of a personal nature sent to him. Asked what maxim had influenced his career, he scribbled, "Do things!" To a question about the essential elements of success he wrote, "Industry and Integrity." The chief causes of failure? "Lack of Industry and Integrity." Typed sheet, "Inquiries," n.d. WHT ended up not sending his responses. His release of the list of pictures on his office wall was crafted to reflect his international affairs career; even the picture of Nellie was one taken "in Havana at the time he was there." FWC to Mrs. Post Wheeler, February 10, 1908. A. Raymond to A. I. Vorys, March 26, 1908, with cover note WHT to HHT, March 30, 1908. "Most entertaining," HHT to RAT, February 9, 1908. "Thinks it is you," HHT to WHT, February 14, 1908. "Dear good sport," L. R. Wilfley to HHT, February 4, 1908. Elks Clubs to HHT, February 3, 1908. Rumors of Nellie being Catholic and married in a Catholic ceremony, Charley Taft to WHT, May 28, 1908. Cartoon of Nellie appears in Taft political cartoons, WHTP.

3. "King Kazooks" cartoon series, in Taft cartoons, WHTP, *American Journal Examiner*, April 25, 1908. "An outbreak," WHT to HHT, February 17, 1908. "The people," WHT to HHT, February 14, 1908. "I do hope myself," HHT to WHT, February 15, 1908. Lunch and dinner at White House, HHT to WHT, May 15, 1908. "[I]t is hard to see," HHT to RAT, April 5, 1908, RAT Papers.

4. "Help being afraid," HHT to RAT, April 5, 1908, RAT Papers.

"He will probably," HHT to RAT, March 28, 1908. "When I have," HHT to RAT, n.d. (spring 1908). Will had "been very busy over the Philippine Bank Bill . . . and succeeded in getting it passed in spite of the opposition of the Speaker which he considers a great victory. It is to establish an agricultural bank for the benefit of the farmers." HHT to RAT, March 3, 1908, RAT Papers. Murray Bay plans for her and Will in light of possible nomination, HHT to RAT, February 23, 1908. Money was also a concern about summering in Canada. Nellie briefly considered opening the Murray Bay house and staying part-time, "but that would be much more expensive, and of course, [Will's war secretary] salary stops," she wrote Robert, op. cit. "I am rather," HHT to RAT, n.d. (late May 1908), also see "It would be better," HHT to RAT, June 1, 1908, RAT Papers. "We had excellent seats at the convention—went early and located many friends." Confidence of WHT's victory abounded in their circle: "The proceedings were well planned and carried out. . . . It was so crowded . . . your sister Mrs. Anderson and one of her pretty daughters and Bob I told . . . must stay with us for the inauguration," Mabel Boardman reported to HHT on June 16, 1908.

5. "He has kept up some life insurance but that is all he has to show after his years of public service," Butt continued to his mother. "It is rather a problem as to how they are going to live this summer and pay campaign expenses, for present they are going to their brother's house. . . . I presume he will simply have to support them while the Secretary campaigns, for they have nothing." Archie Butt to Mother, June 20, 1908, Butt Papers. A year before, Nellie complained to Bob that "duty and freight" were too prohibitive for her to buy necessities in Canada. HHT to RAT, June 2, 1907. Now she told him, "If you need more money let me know, as I don't wish you to give up any pleasure you really want so long as we have the money, which we have this year." HHT to RAT, May 19, 1908. Helen reported to Bob that "finances seem to be looking well for us, by the way. Mama was talking quite seriously of buying an electric [automobile]. It's funny for everyone else is so poor. All our Cincinnati relatives seem to be dreadfully hard-up." HTM to RAT, March 5, 1908, RAT Papers. In fact, Nellie's father, now living alone with Maria, was dependent on

his children for money. The "old man," as they called him, was "tolerably cheerful" but largely confined to his bed, where he "likes to have people sitting around." Nellie had gone to see him in Cincinnati, while also attending the May Festival, "a great success both artistically and financially and, of course, I had a fine time with the musical cranks." HHT to RAT, May 15 and May 17, 1908 and n.d. "Papa has gone back to his idea of going to Cincinnati July 1 and staying there," she had written Bob. "I rather hate to leave him for the entire summer and might go somewhere near like Hot Springs [Virginia] where we could come weekends. In that case could you dispose of yourself?" HHT to RAT, June 10, 1908, RAT Papers. Her old cook's presence was also "a great relief to have someone I know." HHT to RAT, June 6, no year (1908).

6. Note to Nellie, Eli C. Freeman to HHT, June 22, 1908. Nurse needing money, Nellie Clinton to HHT, June 26, 1908. Ladies Social League, M. Ardell to HHT, July 11, 1908. *Extension* magazine to HHT, July 17, 1908. "Unless you feel," anonymous to HHT, July 10, 1908. A fledgling businessman told Helen that her endorsement of his endeavors would lead to success, and Charlie was sent a phonograph and fifty Edison records. A bank president even asked Nellie's old father to get Will to intercede on his behalf with the government. Fledgling businessman, unclear to HTM, July 8, 1908. Records and phonograph, N. C. Durard to CPT, July 28, 1908. Years later when Charlie sought to retrieve the records from his widowed mother, she told him that she had taken them all out of the basement and donated them to charity. Charles Hinsch to John W. Herron, n.d. (July 1908). "His mother," WHT to Mabel Boardman, July 14, 1908. "Charlie is," WHT to HHT, July 26, 1908. Among the general lines of advice Roosevelt told Taft was to accept corporate contributions without guilt, to talk about his own accomplishments, to limit references to the Roosevelt administration, to allow himself to express his anger, and to sympathize with prohibitionists without supporting them. TR to WHT, August 7, July 15, July 16, July 17, and July 21, 1908. Advice against golf, September 14 and September 16, 1908.

7. Advice from Roosevelt, Cincinnati newspaper clipping, n.p., July 21, 1908. Whistle-stop, WHT to Charley Taft, September 9, 1908. Nellie on

campaign stump, HHT, p. 312, and WHT to Mabel Boardman, September 11, 1907. "I hear there is," Annie Zoelkel to WHT, June 22, 1908. "Glorious, Says Mrs. Taft," *New York Times,* July 29, 1908. "[Father] starts on his first tour on Wednesday also and I shall breathe much easier when I see how he gets along. It is proving to be very hard work and I am nervous when I think of it." HHT to RAT, September 20, no year (1908).

8. "Quite grandly," HHT to RAT, March 15, 1908, RAT Papers. "She was verging," HHT to WHT, September 24, 1908. Several days later, after "Julia had another bad day," Nellie happily reported to her husband that "after she has frightened Harry and taken it out on him she seems to settle down and get along pretty well." HHT to WHT, September 26, 1908. "Indifferent New York," HHT to WHT, September 27, 1908. "Repeating any bad news," HHT to WHT, September 25, 1908. Will confidently reported on the campaign, WHT to HHT, September 29, 1908, and WHT to TR, October 3, 1908. "[Papa] is in decidedly better spirits than before," she wrote Robert on October 10, 1908. "He starts again on Monday with three days in Ohio ending Wednesday night in Wheeling, and goes pretty steadily until the election." "Cheerful this morning," HHT to WHT, September 24, 1908. "I am awfully worried about your voice giving out so soon, and don't see how you are going to get through the trip, as it can hardly get better, when it has no rest. I was so jubilant until I saw that." HHT to WHT, September 25, 1908. "Anxious . . . has frightened me," HHT to WHT, September 26, 1908. "I lay awake," HHT to WHT, October 4, 1908. "Continue to wire me," HHT to WHT, September 25, 1908. "Wasn't Foraker's attack," HHT to WHT, September 26, 1908. "Your answer to Foraker," HHT to WHT, September 27, 1908.

9. Theodore Roosevelt advice to WHT, Henry Fowler Pringle, *The Life and Times of William Howard Taft,* vol. 1, pp. 370–73. "I was so depressed . . . I must say," HHT to WHT, September 24, 1908. "It is very," HHT to WHT, September 24, 1908. "I can't imagine," HHT to WHT, September 25, 1908. "I have a letter," HHT to WHT, September 27, 1908. Nellie was invited to stay for dinner and also attend a play with the Roosevelts

afterward. "My dear Mrs. Taft," TR to HHT, September 30, 1908. "Delightful visit," HHT to WHT, September 30, 1908. "I am sure," WHT to TR, October 3, 1908. On Charlie and Bob, HHT to WHT, October 4 and October 5, 1908, and n.d. (circa October 1908).

10. At the end of October, Nellie made a brief trip back to Washington where she had a chance to talk to Carpenter, and, she told Will, she was "so glad" that "your speech is somewhat shorter!" HHT to WHT, October 29, 1908. "I was never," HTM to WHT, November 3, 1908. Will's reaction to winning, WHT to Mabel Boardman, September 1, 1908.

11. Nellie in Hot Springs, HHT to RAT, November 7, 1908, RATP. Thanksgiving plans, HHT to RAT, November 14, 1908, RATP. In the end she canceled the idea; the children didn't want to go there, and she decided that Hot Springs "does not interest me particularly," as golf was something in which, she said, "I don't indulge." HHT to RAT, November 19, 1908, RATP. Butt said Edith had "marvelous character . . . perfectly unconscious of herself . . . perfectly poised and nothing seems to annoy her . . . feminine luminiferous ether." AWB to Mother, July 27, 1908. "Bad temper," AWB to Clara Butt, February 15, 1909. "She is an intellectual," AWB to Clara Butt, November 16, 1908. Butt did recall how, in 1906, among three women who promised to assure his mother that he was fine in Panama, Nellie— the busiest—was the only one to do so. Butt wrote after his meeting with Nellie: "She seemed to expect me to act for her as if I were already an aide to the husband, and this makes it rather difficult for me, for I do not like to do anything which would seem to reflect on any one in the Roosevelt regime."

12. Secretary, *New York Times*, March 14, 1909. Saving money and hiring African American doormen, AWB to Clara Butt, December 8, 1908. When he told Edith, she was stunned. The ushers had been loyal to her family. Finally, Nellie would write Butt to "do nothing about change in men." The old ushers were reassigned within the executive offices. AWB to Clara Butt, November 30, 1908; HHT to AWB, December 31, 1908; *New York Times*, March 9, 1909. The first names of the four footmen cannot be deter-

mined, but their last names were Parker, Dunn, Pusey, and Pannell. December 11 lunch, AWB to Clara Butt, December 12, 1908; Will Manners, *TR and Will,* p.8. During the lunch the President called his Vice President a "transparent stuffed club," and Nellie piped up, "That's just what he is." "It is merely," AWB to Clara Butt, December 4, 1908. "This, my dears," AWB to Clara Butt, December 12, 1908.

13. "With much hesitation," WHT to TR, January 2, 1909. "For which . . . In short," *American Heritage Book of Presidents,* vol. 8, p. 702 (New York: America Heritage Publishing Company, 1967). Tensions on Cabinet, Henry Fowler Pringle, *The Life and Times of William Howard Taft,* vol. 1, p. 392. "People have attempted," WHT to TR, February 25, 1909. Nellie spent $850 on just dresses. She also had to get undergarments, hats, shoes, and so forth. HHT to WHT, n.d. Looking at cars, HHT to HTM, Tuesday, n.d. (December 1908) "Mrs. Taft wants," AWB to Clara Butt, December 25, 1908. WHT proposed to Butt that a new fleet of cars be leased each year from the White Steamer Company and that they only pay the drivers' salaries. WHT to AWB, January 4, 1909. Job of housekeeper, Elizabeth Jaffray, *Secrets of the White House,* pp. 6–7. "Didn't work . . . The discussion," Horace Taft to WHT, December 1, 1908. "The ups and downs," HHT, p. 323. "Went so constantly," HHT to HTM, Sunday, n.d. (December 1908). "Was not feeling," HHT to WHT, n.d. (December 1908). "It is . . . leads to," WHT to Frank Hitchcock, December 22, 1908. Activities in Hot Springs, HHT to RAT, December 4, 1908. Butt to come down, WHT to William Loeb, January 7, 1909. "I am really enjoying our stay here. . . . Since Nellie has become the First Lady of the land she seems to have a yearning for . . . society . . . [which led to] domestic complications." WHT to Jennie Anderson, December 27, 1908. Nellie's concern for her children, HHT to RAT, January 27, 1908, and HHT to HTM, December 4, no year (1908). "Papa shows," HTM to RAT, n.d. (circa November 1908). "Could you please," CPT to WHT, November 18, 1909.

14. Panama Canal, HHT to RAT, January 31 and February 9, 1908. Inaugural plans for relatives, Lucy Herron Laughlin to FWC, February 4,

1909; FWC to HHT, February 5, 1909; HHT to FWC, Saturday, n.d. (circa February 1909); AWB to Clara Butt, February 16, 1909. Alice resentment, Michael Teague, *Mrs. L.,* pp. 140–41. White firing, Carl Sferrazza Anthony, *First Ladies,* vol. 1, p. 314. Butt meeting with Nellie at Boardman house, AWB to Clara Butt, February 28, 1909. Van der Stucken commissioned, HHT to FWC, n.d. (February 1908).

15. "Neither Mrs. Roosevelt," HHT, p. 325. Night before Taft inaugural, Michael Teague, *Mrs. L.,* p. 141. Nellie's announcement that she was riding in the parade appeared in *The New York Times* on March 1, 1909. "State of nerves . . . Are they," AWB to Clara Butt, March 5, 1909. "Noted for," Howard Teichmann, *Alice,* p. 78. Quotes and descriptions of inaugural from HHT, pp. 327–36, and "Ceremonies Connected with the Inauguration of Honorable William Howard Taft as President of the United States and Honorable James Schoolcraft Sherman as Vice President of the United States," March 4, 1909, WHTP.

16. "Would be just," AWB to Clara Butt, February 1, 1909. "Bad little idol. . . . I helped," Alice Roosevelt Longworth, *Crowded Hours*, p. 158.

11. Ragtime

1. Archibald Willingham Butt, *Taft and Roosevelt,* pp. 1–2. According to the *Washington Evening Star,* March 6, 1909, the event took place on March 5, the day after the inaugural, and it was not 3,000 but 4,009 people. "Smash all," *New York Times,* March 1, 1909; see also March 14, 1909. "Mrs. Taft has brains," *New York Times,* November 15, 1909; *Ladies' Home Journal,* "The Wife of the New President," March 1909.

2. Egalitarian plans of Nellie Taft versus the exclusivity of Roosevelts, *New York Times,* March 14 and March 25, 1909. "Family Sundays," *Washington Post,* December 19, 1910. Edith Roosevelt segregated by class, AWB to Clara Butt, June 11, 1908. Edith Roosevelt Cabinet wives meetings, AWB to Clara Butt, January 3, 1909. Congressional families and "the White House is," AWB to Clara Butt, March 5, 1909, and Archibald Willingham Butt, *Taft and Roosevelt*, p. 60. "Opens Whole White House," *New York Times,* July 1,

1910. Personal family items on display in public rooms, *New York Times,* March 25, 1909. Nellie's interest in historic preservation extended only to her placing Dolley Madison's portrait besides James Madison's in the Red Room, HHT to RAT, May 3, 1912, RAT Papers. "Mrs. Taft is clearly going to manage her home in her own way. . . . She is well qualified." Her "tact," "skill," and "wisdom" would result in "less formal" and thus more enjoyable events, *New York Times,* March 9, 1909. "The New Belle of the White House," *Washington Evening Star,* February 28, 1909. "The Tafts Reconstructing Society in Washington," *New York Times,* January 1, 1911.

3. "All Servants Equal by Mrs. Taft's Rule," *New York Times,* October 11, 1909. "No man," HHT, p. 349. Nellie's temper, AWB to Clara Butt, January 27, 1909. "The White House," typed memo in Pringle Papers, n.d. White House employee flowchart, March 28, 1911; "List of Employees at the White House," No staff in halls, AWB to Clara Butt, February 24, 1909. Nellie in kitchens, Lillian Rogers Parks, *My Thirty Years Backstairs at the White House,* p. 108. The first of many references Nellie made to having terrapin soup was in HHT to WHT, August 18, 1890. Artichoke incident is from Archie Butt. Al fresco entertaining, Ike Hoover manuscript on Tafts, Hoover Papers. Raining at garden parties, Parks, p. 109.

4. Use of house as a home, and footman, "Taft Shifts Staff," *Washington Star,* March 3, 1909; "Changes at the White House," *New York Times,* March 4, 1909. Entertaining in the Blue Room, Ike Hoover manuscript on Tafts, Hoover Papers. Staff ridicules look of private quarters, Parks, *My Thirty Years,* pp. 111 and 125. Resentment toward Nellie ran deep because, said Hoover, "There just seemed to be the disposition to change things," Hoover manuscript on Tafts, Hoover Papers. Helen Taft was given the northwest corner suite, once occupied by Alice Roosevelt, and the current kitchen and dining room of the family, while Bob and Charlie were given rooms farther east of it, also on the north side. "When I told General Edwards," AWB to Clara Butt, January 27, 1909. "Bolted in ahead," Archibald Willingham Butt, *Taft and Roosevelt,* pp. 33–34. Most of the staff also disapproved of Nellie's overt public role. Several had apparently been in the rooms during the Roosevelt

years when Nellie had her head-to-head confrontations with Teddy, insisting that Will not be appointed to the Court but rather promoted as a presidential candidate. They gossiped endlessly about it, and whether she overheard or was told that they all perceived her as "pushy," Mrs. Taft soon became hurt and paranoid. Lillian Rogers Parks, *My Thirty Years Backstairs at the White House,* p. 117. "At the very start, precedent was thrown to the winds [when] Mrs. Taft decided to share the honors of the Inauguration," recorded the chief usher. "It but portrayed the shadow of happenings to come and events that were to follow." Ike Hoover manuscript on Tafts, Hoover Papers.

5. Request for information on inaugural gown, Leila Wilson to HHT, n.d. (post–November 1908). Press policy, "The New Regime Within the White House," *New York Times,* part 5, March 14, 1909. Edith Roosevelt press policy, Archibald Willingham Butt, *Taft and Roosevelt,* p. 8. "Unhobbled," *Indianapolis Star,* November 20, 1911; Corelli quote, *Marion Daily Star,* October 22, 1914. Nellie Taft's views on divorce, *Washington Post,* December 19, 1910; "Mrs. Taft and Publicity," *Mansfield News,* April 15, 1910. Mrs. Morgan quote, *New York Times,* December 23, 1908. Another snapshot of Nellie at Carnegie Hall, with Butt, appeared in the *New York Times* rotogravure section, March 28, 1909. "Women Besiege Mrs. Taft," *New York Times,* May 29, 1910; "The Whole Daft Family," *New York Times,* January 2, 1909.

6. Blech was named as Nellie's "personal secretary," as opposed to "social secretary." Salaried by the government at $1,000 a year, Blech's title was made to imply that she might keep invitation and food records and carry out social plans set out by Nellie, but not make them herself. *New York Times,* March 14, 1909; "The Most Intimate Friends of President Taft," *New York Times,* May 29, 1910; Although niece Elizabeth Parsons came to the White House, her mother, Emily, the First Lady's eldest sister, remains mysteriously absent from any guest records. Nellie was not as close to the wives of her brothers Will and Jack, and their visits were less frequent. "They look well bred," AWB to Clara Butt, March 5, 1909. "I don't think we have been close or stingy to our friends," Will told Archie. "They have entertained," AWB to Clara Butt, April 28, 1911.

7. "Principal items of Living Expenses at the White House," with

"Mrs. Taft" written on top, n.d. U.S.S. *Mayflower,* September 13, 1912, invoice for "To entertainment of Mrs. Taft and guests . . ." "A $100,000 Salary for the President: Why He Should Have It," William Howard Taft, *Ladies' Home Journal,* October 1919. Conversation between Will and Nellie over money is from Archibald Willingham Butt, *Taft and Roosevelt,* pp. 22–23. "Bridge addict," Elizabeth Jaffray, *Secrets of the White House,* p. 30. "Scientific game," *New York Times,* November 15, 1908. "When you get down," Frank Jamison to HHT, February 16, 1909. Free piano, "Memorandum for Mrs. Taft from FWC, n.d. (circa 1909). Mooley Wooly the cow, H. P. Hood & Sons to HHT, May 25, 1909; handwritten AWB note, n.d. (May 1909). File on Pauline Wayne the cow, PPF File #6.

8. C. R. Edwards cablegram to HHT, February 3, 1909. "Mrs. Taft Drives New Auto," *New York Times,* April 25, 1909, and "Mrs. Taft New Runabout," *New York Times,* March 27, 1909; "Will Have an Auto," *Washington Star,* March 5, 1909; *Washington Star,* April 18, 1909, item under "Motoring" column; "Mrs. Taft Drives Her Car," *New York Times,* April 25, 1909. Instructions on outfitting of cars, HHT to Charles Clifton, May 11, 1911, as reprinted in *Manuscripts,* vol. 47, no. 3 (Summer 1995), p. 222, and HHT to Charles Clifton, April 29, 1991, p. 220. "Mama was quite indignant," HTM to RAT, January 17, 1912, RATP. Information provided by Michael Bromley. See also his book: *William Howard Taft and the First Motoring Presidency* (Jefferson, N.C.: McFarland & Co., 2003).

9. "I don't know any woman," AWB to Clara Butt, April 28, 1911. Color of clothes, Lillian Rogers Parks, *My Thirty Years Backstairs at the White House,* p. 106. Diamonds and lorgnettes information is from photographs. HHT's official photographs show her always with diamonds; also see RAT to Bailey, Banks & Biddle Company, June 22, 1943, and handwritten list headed "Mrs. Helen Taft Manning" with the diamond jewelry Nellie left her daughter, RAT Papers. Observations on Nellie's personality changes, Archibald Willingham Butt, *Taft and Roosevelt,* pp. 54–55. "If he makes good," page 4A of six pages of handwritten notes of Henry Pringle, record of conversation with TR friend Henry Wise, Pringle Papers.

12. Blossoming

1. "We had two large dinners," HHT to RAT, May 2, 1909, RAT Papers. "To look at it," HHT to HTM, April 1, 1909 (mislabeled 1911). "I found her quite excited," Archibald Willingham Butt, *Taft and Roosevelt,* pp. 40–41.

2. "The Washington Cherry Trees," *Book Digest,* April 1939. David Fairchild, *The World Was My Garden* (New York: Scribner's, 1938). Fairchild claimed that it was he, not Scidmore, who suggested to Mrs. Taft that the trees be planted at the park. *The Washington Greeter's Guide*, 1937. The Japanese Cherry Trees, National Capital Park handout, n.d. "Japanese Spring in America" by Paul Russell, *Asia Magazine,* May 1930. Lori McConnell, Cultural Resource Specialist, U.S. Department of the Interior to author, January 24, 2002. Draft of the NACC Cherry Tree Source Book, release 1, June 1996, courtesy of U.S. Department of the Interior. Roland M. Jefferson and Alan E. Fusonie, *The Japanese Flowering Cherry Trees of Washington, D.C.*, U.S. Department of Agriculture, December 1977. "Twelve Varieties of Japanese Cherry Trees" by Eliza Scidmore, *Washington Evening Star*, March 27, 1921. "Capital's Cherry Blossoms Gift of Japanese Chemist" by Eliza Scidmore. *Washington Evening Star*, April 11, 1926. "First Japanese Tree Planted by Mrs. Taft," *Washington Evening Star*, March 28, 1912. President's getting money from Penrose for Potomac Park, Archibald Willingham Butt, *Taft and Roosevelt*, pp. 51–52.

3. Cosby and the bandstand, "Gayety on Speedway," *Washington Star*, April 2, 1909. Opening concert at Potomac Park, Archibald Willingham Butt, *Taft and Roosevelt*, p. 56; "Mr. Taft to Attend," *Washington Star*, April 17, 1909; "Great Throng Out on Potomac Drive," *Washington Evening Star*, April 18, 1909.

4. Complaints of no seats, "Mrs. Taft's Aid Invoked," *Washington Evening Star,* April 12, 1909, and "Washington Drive Opened," *New York Times,* April 18, 1909. Alice Roosevelt Longworth, *Crowded Hours*, p. 167. Ongoing concerts, "Proceeds with Plans," *Washington Evening Star,* April 3, 1909, and MGy Sgt Mike Ressler to author, May 31, 2002.

5. "Mrs. Taft's Gift for the Poor," *New York Times*, December 3, 1910, and "White House Doll Brings $245 to Fund," *New York Times*, December 15, 1910.

6. The brief summary here of labor and the National Civic Federation and other related subjects is drawn from the following sources: "Whatever Happened to Noblesse Oblige?" by John B. Judis, *The New Republic*, March 27, 2000; "The Chicago Convention" by Daniel DeLeon, *The Daily People*, June 27, 1905; Marguerite Green, *The National Civic Federation and the American Labor Movement, 1900–1925* (Washington, D.C.: Catholic University Press, 1956); Charles Evans Hughes, *The Autobiographical Notes of Charles Evans Hughes,* ed., David Danelski and Joseph Tulchin (Cambridge, MA: Harvard University Press, 1973); Christopher J. Cyphers, *The National Civic Federation and the Making of a New Liberalism, 1900–1915* (New York: Praeger Press, 2002); James Weinstein, *The Corporate Ideal in the Liberal State, 1900–1918* (Boston: Beacon Press, 1968). In later years the NCF director Ralph Easley shifted the organization's focus to ferreting out Bolshevism, real and perceived; John B. Judis, "The Development of Democratic Pluralism," chapter in *The Paradox of American Democracy* (New York: Routledge Press, 2001); Florida Atlantic University Libraries, "Jewish Heroes and Heroines in America, 1900 to World War II" exhibit, Samuel Gompers text by Seymour Brody; "History of International Women's Day," March 8, 2001, at tsinoy.com; 1912.history.ohio-state.edu/reaction.htm; "What Went Wrong?: How Progressive Voices Are Muffled in America" by Townsend L. Walker, Sr., "The Harbinger," February 6, 2001 online. Dolley Madison's work with orphans and Frances Cleveland's with poor children were local charity efforts that could hardly raise eyebrows. Mary Lincoln's work in Union hospitals and support of the Contraband Relief Society reflected the emergency needs of Civil War that all women were expected to fill at the time. Caroline Harrison's presidency of the Daughters of the American Revolution associated her only with an exclusive membership and her fund-raising for Johns Hopkins University Medical School on the basis of admission to women involved only the lending of her name for one event. Although the National

Civic Federation association with Mrs. Taft did not have her responding to a specific constituency, as later First Ladies' work would, it nevertheless was national in scope rather than confined to a regional institution or cause. It was quite different, for example, from her supporting and visiting the Washington Home for Incurables, which cared for the indigent who had terminal illnesses, a charitable cause her predecessor and successors would also adopt. See Carl Sferrazza Anthony, *First Ladies*, vol. 1.

7. National Civic Federation, Ralph Easley to HHT, November 18, 1908. Press notice of Nellie Taft's work with the NCF, "Taft in New York City," *Washington Star*, December 7, 1908; "Will Make Short Stay Here: Mr. Taft Expects to Reach Augusta Tomorrow," *Washington Star*, December 17, 1908; "Mrs. Taft Presides," *New York Times*, December 18, 1908; HHT to HTM, December 4, n.d. (1908); "Child Labor in the Carolina," A. J. McKelway, secretary for the Southern States, National Child Labor Committee, *Charities and the Commons*, January 30, 1909. HHT speech to NCF and accepts presidency of NCF, *Evening Telegram* [Elyric, Ohio] December 15, 1908, and *Reno State Journal*, December 15, 1908.

8. All information on Nellie Taft's initial meeting and statements on the NCF, "Mrs. Taft Volunteers Help: Interested in Uplift of Working Women," *Washington Star*, March 16, 1909. Hoover diary entries, Hoover Papers. HHT White House diary entries, 1909, WHTP. "If we can only keep her," AWB to Clara Butt, February 1909.

9. All the details of Nellie's schedule and visits to Congress are from Hoover White House datebook; HHT White House datebook; Archibald Willingham Butt, *Taft and Roosevelt,* pp. 15–16. "Perfectly quiet," *New York Times*, April 9, 1909. "Revision of the tariff," WHT to H. A. Morrill, December 2, 1908. "A familiar sight," Ike Hoover manuscript on Tafts, Hoover Papers.

10. Roosevelt incident, Archibald Willingham Butt, *Taft and Roosevelt*, pp. 64–65. "My very active," HHT, p. 365. "With the troubles," WHT to H. A. Morrill, December 2, 1908. "Hoodoo," Butt, p. 93.

11. "I am very proud," Archibald Willingham Butt, *Taft and Roosevelt*, p. 85. "Mrs. Taft has done," *New York Times*, May 19, 1909. Dates of John

Herron's activities, Hoover datebook. For HHT's reports on her father, "The 'old gentleman,'" HHT to RAT, "Sunday," n.d. (circa mid-May 1909). For reports on HHT's spring 1909 entertaining, Dinners and garden parties, HHT, pp. 365–68; Butt, p. 86. "The last garden party was a success held out of doors, and made a pretty scene," Nellie had written Robert proudly. "We had some tennis players to add to all the picturesqueness of the scene, but the people did not pay as much attention to them as they did on Easter Monday when you objected so strongly." HHT to RAT, "Sunday," n.d. (circa mid-May 1909).

13. The Stroke

1. The best account of Nellie Taft's stroke is from Archibald Willingham Butt, *Taft and Roosevelt,* pp. 88–89. Also see accounts in *New York Times*, May 18 to May 20, May 22, and May 29, 1909; *Washington Post*, May 18, 1909; *Boston Post*, May 18, 1909; *Los Angeles Times*, May 18, 1909; *Denver Post*, May 18, 1909; *Kansas City Star*, May 18, 1909.

2. "You know she," WHT to RAT, May 18, 1909. "Her old will," Archibald Willingham Butt, *Taft and Roosevelt,* p. 92. "The serious side," WHT to Fanny Edwards, June 25, 1909; however, she was also found to be anemic and also passed renal calculi—kidney stones. Old John Herron returned home ten days after Nellie's stroke, but the next day, the twenty-ninth, Miss Helen arrived. HHT White House diary, May 28 and May 29, 1909; "Successful Speech Therapy for Stroke Patients Available" by Clyde Noel, *Los Altos Town Crier*, May 15, 1996. "She gets up," HTM to RAT, n.d. (post–May 29, 1909), RATP. Private ceremony and Wright Brothers ceremony, HHT White House diary, June 1 and June 10, 1909. "Taft Sends Congratulations: Mrs. Taft Watches," *New York Times*, June 2, 1909. Avoiding servants, Butt, p. 108.

3. The family physician was a Dr. Barker. HHT White House diary, June 1909. "In order to facilitate," WHT to Fanny Edwards, June 25, 1909. "Taft Not to Go to Alaska," *New York Times*, June 6, 1909; Archibald Willingham Butt, *Taft and Roosevelt,* pp. 99–101, 108. It was the right side of Nellie's face that was affected. "We then came," Ike Hoover manuscript on Tafts, Hoover Papers. Hoover wrote that "the President had taken on a

disposition as contrary to the one known of him when he was to come to the place as often during the Roosevelt time. . . . There was an entire change. No more did he seem considerate. The smile was replaced by orders, not always given in a pleasing way."

4. There is no question that Mrs. Taft's continued effort to control every aspect of her White House tenure and then her stroke only worsened her condition through her time there. Five years later she herself would admit, "Perhaps I did make the process of adjusting the White House routine to my own conceptions a shade too strenuous." HHT, p. 347. "Gets pretty depressed," HTM to RAT, n.d. (June 1909). "Mama seemed to think," HTM to RAT, June 10, 1909, RATP. Information on Nellie's search for vacation spots and ultimate decision to rent in Beverly is from the following sources: George Barker to HHT, January 1, 1909, with pamphlet on Islesboro, Maine; George Adams Woods to Henry Taft, January 22, 1909, on Cape Cod home; Mrs. S. I. Powell to HHT, April 13, 1909 on Port Jefferson, Long Island; J. H. Hammond handled the rental details for the Tafts. R. D. Evans to John Hayes Hammond, April 13, 1909; HHT to John Hays Hammond, April 13, 1909; "Tafts Start Realty Boom," *New York Times*, April 19, 1909. She also was solicited by proprietors of all sorts, including "Imperial Laundry," which promised to wash her clothes with "proper sanitary and mechanical conditions." Herbert Saunders, Superior Laundry to HHT, circa May 1909.

5. "Taft on the Way to Summer Home," *New York Times*, July 4, 1909; "Rainbow for Taft in his Beverly Home," *New York Times*, July 5, 1909; "Guarding Mrs. Taft," *New York Times*, July 7, 1909; "The Removal of the Presidential Family to their Summer Home, July 3, 1909," memo, prepared by Butt; "Mrs. Taft Much Improved," *New York Times*, July 30, 1909; "Mrs. Taft Takes Sea Trip," *New York Times*, July 26, 1909; "Mrs. Taft Takes Auto Ride," *New York Times*, August 3, 1909. "I am tolerably well," HHT to WHT, n.d. (July 1909). Eleanor More was Nellie's constant companion; the children were busy with their own activities. In one letter she wrote that Helen had motored to Newport, Robert was playing tennis, and Charlie ran out for lunch. "I saw . . ." HHT to RAT, July 10, 1909, RATP. See also "The

Summer Capital" by Mabel Boardman, n.p., n.d., WHTP and HHT to WHT, July 22, 1909.

6. "As stupid as . . . ," WHT to Jennie Anderson, December 27, 1908. "I have been to church," HHT to RAT, January 27, no year (1909). The Tafts and religion as an issue of public interest: WHT to Harlan Page Lloyd, September 12, 1908; William Hayward to W. H. Pitzer, October 14, 1908; WHT to Magnus Larson, October 9, 1908; *New York Times,* August 4, 1908.

7. "Got more information," WHT to Horace Taft, June 27, 1909; "If I had more of a," WHT to HHT, July 8, 1909; also see WHT to HHT, July 17, 1909; WHT to HHT, July 25, 1909; WHT to HHT, July, 27, 1909; WHT to HHT, July 28, 1909; WHT to HHT, July 30, 1909; WHT to HHT, August 1, 1909; WHT to HHT, August 3, 1909; Will also passed on to Nellie some dispatches from the U.S. Ambassador to the Court of St. James Whitelaw Reid, a Roosevelt holdover. They were unctuous and somewhat silly accounts of London society. Nellie apparently read them, but never responded to Reid. WHT to HHT, July 23, 1909; series of letters from HHT to WHT during summer separation, HHT to WHT, July 13, 1909; HHT to WHT, n.d. (July 1909), and HHT to WHT, July 17, 1909; HHT to WHT, July 24, 1909; Alice Longworth and WHT, Archibald Willingham Butt, *Taft and Roosevelt,* p. 119.

8. WHT reports on his activities with Alice Longworth, WHT to HHT, July 11, 1909; WHT to HHT, July 18, 1909; and Archibald Willingham Butt, *Taft and Roosevelt,* pp. 123, 143, 147, 153, 158–159, 163–164, 177–182; "I read all the accounts," HHT to WHT, July 22, 1909.

9. Taft events during summer vacation, Archibald Willingham Butt, *Taft and Roosevelt,* pp. 173, 175, 176, 187; Maria Herron to WHT, telegram, July 25, 1909; "Herron for Vice Mayor," *New York Times,* July 23, 1909; "Taft Plays Golf in Pouring Rain: Mrs. Taft's Health Good. Devoted Sister Now Feels Able to Leave Her," *New York Times,* August 18, 1909; Longworth appointment, Butt, p. 228; "Summer Capital as Busy as Washington," *New York Times,* August 22, 1909.

10. Taft getting angry, Archibald Willingham Butt, *Taft and Roosevelt,* p. 193; "Taft Prepares for His Trip," *New York Times,* September 14, 1909;

report on trip, WHT to HHT, September 20, 1909; "Have more of a . . . ," WHT to HHT, October 3, 1909; "Has interspersed" and "Taft Home To-day," *New York Times*, November 10, 1909; Diaz event, Ishbel Ross, *An American Family*, p. 67.

11. *Ladies' Home Journal*, March 1909; "There was a very fine punch," HHT to WHT, November 3, 1894. "To the hotel for a cocktail," HHT to RAT, October 12, no year (1909), RATP. Wine on *Mayflower,* Rudolph Forster to Lieutenant Little, September 20, 1912. "I do not know," Mrs. Harry Crawford to HHT, April 7, 1909. "Of our most," Frances En-sign to HHT, April 2, 1909, case file #2999; Pennsylvania WCTU, Emily Clark Scott to WHT, December 3, 1908. For WHT's admission to occa-sional drinking of beer and wine, see WHT to Fred Chapman, August 1, 1908. Mrs. Taft's punch, Taft Presidential Subject File Case, #4133 and #2999; policy on critical letters on alcohol, handwritten instructions on let-ter of Mrs. M. D. Stout to HHT, April 7, 1909, case file #2999; editorial de-fending HHT serving alcohol, "Cats and Cattiness," *New York Times*, March 7, 1909. "Refreshments," *New York Times*, December 12, 1909. "The musicale," HHT to RAT, February 16, no year (1910).

12. "I have my," HHT to RAT, November 30, (1909), RATP. "He says it is not," HHT to RAT, October 28, 1909, RATP; see also "Mrs. Taft Re-turns to the White House," *New York Times*, October 17, 1909. "Now, my dear," Archibald Willingham Butt, *Taft and Roosevelt*, p. 211. Mary McKee, Butt, p. 64. "President Gives Dinner to Cabinet: Mrs. Taft Represented by Her Sister," *New York Times*, December 17, 1909. Daily routine, "I read some," HHT to RAT, December 12 (1909), RATP. Norfolk voyage, Butt, pp. 213–14; in New York, "Taft In Danger at Carnegie Hall," *New York Times*, December 14, 1909; Methodist meeting, Butt, pp. 354–55.

13. "Washington Enjoys White Christmas," *New York Times*, December 26, 1909. "The Tafts Out Walking," *New York Times*, December 27, 1909. "Taft Shakes Hands with 5,575 Persons," *New York Times*, January 1, 1910. De-struction of diseased cherry trees, Jefferson and Fusonie, *The Japanese Flower-ing Cherry Trees of Washington, D.C.,* pp. 9–15. "It makes her feel," Archibald Willingham Butt, *Taft and Roosevelt*, p. 341. "As lonely," Butt, p. 340.

14. Return of the Comet

1. "As the weeks," Archibald Willingham Butt, *Taft and Roosevelt*, p. 313. "I will not forbid," Butt, p. 357. "Gradually," quoted in Ishbel Ross, *An American Family*, p. 239. Sat in Blue Room, AWB to Clara Butt, January 5, 1910, Butt Papers. Will takes Nellie's weaker side and other appearances in the White House, Hoover White House diary, January, February, and March 1910 entries, Hoover Papers, LC. "It is hard," HHT to RAT, April 29, (1910), RATP. "I became," HHT to RAT, May 16, (1910), RATP. Andrew Carnegie, HHT to RAT, April 29, (1910), RATP. "She was unable," Ike Hoover manuscript on Tafts, Hoover Papers, LC.

2. "Miss Alice Blech to Wed," *New York Times*, November 29, 1910. "Mrs. Taft's New Secretary," *New York Times*, March 13, 1910. Reports on Alice Longworth and Tafts, Archibald Willingham Butt, *Taft and Roosevelt*, pp. 227–28 and AWB to Clara Butt, January 5 and 6, 1910, Butt Papers.

3. Pinchot incident, Archibald Willingham Butt, *Taft and Roosevelt*, pp. 245, 255, 312. "I don't think," Butt, p. 327. Roosevelt's return, Butt, pp. 277–78, 281. "The Roosevelts believe," Butt, p. 352. "Alice Longworth accused," Butt, p. 258. "There is always," Butt, p. 329. "Do you think," Butt, pp. 257, 258, and AWB to Clara Butt, January 7, 1910, Butt Papers. "I get rather," Butt, p. 263.

4. "Suffragettes Hiss Taft, Their Guest," *New York Times*, April 15, 1910. "Suffragists Storm National Capitol," *New York Times*, April 19, 1910. "The real President," is from "Taft Addresses World Sunday School Convention," *New York Times*, May 20, 1910. "Mrs. Taft Sets Suffrage Pace," *Washington Evening Star*, March 2, 1909. Helen in mock political event, "The New Belle of the White House," *Washington Sunday Star*, February 28, 1909. "Mrs. Taft's List of Greatest Women," *New York Times*, December 14, 1911. "I am not" and "Glorious, Says Mrs. Taft," *New York Times*, July 29, 1908. HHT's complete statement also included: "I should like to put in a prohibitory clause debarring them from running for office. If women should indulge in a scramble for office, I think that the natural scheme would become disjointed and the aim of the home destroyed . . . but it seems to me for the present that it is impractical to dissociate the right to vote from the right to hold office." HHT quoted in Edna Colman, *White House Gossip* (Garden City, N.Y.:

Doubleday, 1927), pp. 329–30; Nellie Taft's opposition to "universal" suffrage, *Washington Post*, December 19, 1910. HHT joins anti-suffrage association, *Edwardsville Intelligence*, April 11, 1914. Balkans women incident, WHT to TR, January 4, 1909; HHT, p. 38.

5. "Pity the Sorrows of the President's Secretary," *New York Times*, June 5, 1910. HHT to FWC, October 1, October 3, October 6, and October 12, 1909, and telegram, April 14, 1909. "Personal Staff of the New President," *Washington Sunday Star,* April 4, 1909. "Fred W. Carpenter, the New Presidential Secretary," *Washington Sunday Star*, February 28, 1909. "We have had Carpenter," HHT to RAT, n.d. (fall 1909), RATP. "It seems," and Edwards conversation, AWB to Clara Butt, February 15, 1909, Butt Papers. "Mrs. Taft played a prominent," Ike Hoover manuscript on Tafts, Hoover Papers.

6. Norton "declared himself as Assistant President," Ike Hoover manuscript on Tafts, Hoover Papers. Chapter on Charles Norton from Michael Medved, *The Shadow Presidents: The Secret History of the Chief Executives and Their Top Aides* (New York: Times Books, 1979), pp. 123–33. "Talks most freely," Archibald Willingham Butt, *Taft and Roosevelt*, pp. 347, 372.

7. "Thomas K. Laughlin Dead," *New York Times*, March 12, 1910. "President Attends Laughlin Funeral," *New York Times*, March 14, 1910. "Mrs. Taft's Father Very Ill," *New York Times*, May 30, 1910. Nellie's reaction to her father's illness seems cold: "The last Garden party was a great success. We received out of doors and the weather was warm just as it ought to be. Your grandfather is very ill. I don't know whether I will be able to have to last one or not," HHT to RAT, May 23, (1910), RATP. Halley's comet interest, HHT to RAT, May 23, (1910), RATP and Archibald Willingham Butt, *Taft and Roosevelt*, pp. 370–71.

8. "To let me," Theodore Roosevelt to WHT, June 8, 1910. Mrs. Taft's note to Mrs. Roosevelt, Archibald Willingham Butt, *Taft and Roosevelt*, p. 392. "Touches me," Theodore Roosevelt to WHT, June 20, 1910. "An enlarged personality," Butt, p. 396. Nastiness toward Nick Longworth, Butt, p. 403. TR's lack of reaction to news of HHT illness and WHT policy, Butt, p. 402. In response to WHT's letter reporting on HHT's health, however, TR

responded, "the sickness of the one whom you love most has added immeasurably to your burden. We have followed with the greatest concern the news of her trouble, and feel very genuine pleasure at learning how much better she is. Will you give her our warmest regards!" TR to WHT, June 8, 1910.

9. WHT reports on legislation to HHT, WHT to HHT, June 24, 1910 and June 26, 1910. "Taft Enjoys a Quiet Day," *New York Times*, June 27, 1910. "Taft's Vacation Delayed By Work," *New York Times*, July 3, 1910. "Tell her," Archibald Willingham Butt, *Taft and Roosevelt*, p. 409. Dinner between WHT and Alice Longworth, Butt, p. 412. Details of the preparations for, and the eventual meeting of Theodore Roosevelt, WHT, and HHT are from Butt, pp. 417–31, HHT, p. 383, and HHT obituary *New York Times*, May 23, 1943. Details on the Taft family visiting Maine, Massachusetts, and New Hampshire that summer can be found in *The New York Times* of July 8, July 14, July 20, July 22, July 24, July 25, July 27, July 29, July 30, August 1, August 19, August 28, October 3, October 11, and October 12, 1910. HHT refused to let WHT play golf with John D. Rockefeller and trying to prevent his doing so with Frick: Cavorting with such industrialists would only confirm his image as a friend of the capitalists over labor. Butt, p. 443. In her memoirs, HHT briefly recalls her first visit with Eleanor Roosevelt, the wife of Franklin D. Roosevelt and niece of Theodore Roosevelt, at the FDR summer home at Campobello Island in Canada as a pleasant experience.

10. "The sage," WHT to Clarence Edwards, July 27, 1910. WHT private bewilderment at TR is amplified in WHT to Mrs. Aaron Perry, November 3, 1910. Reassured by Longworth, Nick Longworth to Charles Dyer, August 30, 1910. "Sit tight," WHT to Charley Taft, September 10, 1910. Norton irritating TR, Michael Medved, *The Shadow Presidents,* p. 131. Argument between HHT and WHT over TR, Archibald Willingham Butt, *Taft and Roosevelt*, pp. 461–62. "I have not asked," Butt, p. 493.

11. "I am hopeful," WHT to Horace Taft, November 3, 1910. "Your Father thinks," HHT to RAT, November 6, 1910, RATP. "We're in a great state now," HTM to RAT, November 7, 1910, RATP. "She has been lonely," HTM to RAT, November 7, 1910, RATP.

12. WHT and HHT Provincetown visit from Jeffory Morris, Curator of Collection, Pilgrim Monument and Provincetown Museum, booklet, *The Pilgrim and Their Monument*, pp. 165–257, and clippings from private collection of John Dowd. Hoover diary, November 10, 1910, and HHT White House diary, November 10, 1910. "Mama and I are going," HTM to RAT, November 14, 1910, RATP. WHT was also away, WHT to TR, November 5, 1910.

15. The Stars and Silver Forever

1. "Glad to see him," HHT to RAT, November 27, 1910, RATP. WHT return, Archibald Willingham Butt, *Taft and Roosevelt*, p. 564. "I was particularly sorry," Theodore Roosevelt to WHT, November 28, 1910. He knew that Mrs.," Butt, p. 561; see also, "Roosevelt Cheerily Visits White House," *New York Times*, November 20, 1910. "I cannot say," Theodore Roosevelt to WHT, November 29, 1910. "A date at which," WHT to Theodore Roosevelt, November 30, 1910. "Prospect of," WHT to Charley Taft, September 10, 1910. "Beaten," quoted in Ishbel Ross, *An American Family*, p. 240. "He said the other," Butt, p. 493. Holiday season, HHT, White House diary, December 31, 1910. "Miss Taft's Debut," *New York Times*, December 2, 1910. The entire House of Representatives and their wives and daughters were not invited to the debut and registered their outrage with the White House. It was alleged to be a mailing error at the House mailrooms, rather than from political motivation, see "Vexed Over Taft Party," *New York Times*, December 8, 1910; "Helen's coming this," WHT to Mrs. Aaron Perry, November 3, 1910.

2. "I don't think it is," HHT to RAT, "Sunday," n.d. (spring 1909), RATP. Limousine incident, White House case file #502, December 15, 1910, WHTP. "A nice girl," Archibald Willingham Butt, *Taft and Roosevelt*, p. 53. "Spent a small fortune," HTM to RAT, November 7, 1910, RATP. "I have to lead," HTM to RAT, n.d. (November 1908). PPF #3, "Taft, Miss Helen," see 240 for memo re: J. P. Hawkins who sends diamond ring, January 7, 1912. "Nothing very dreadful," and Girl Pioneers, HTM to RAT, April 2, 1912, RATP. Helen referred to the group as "Girl Pioneers" but a newspaper

article identified them as "Campfire Girls." "Became frightfully excited," HTM to RAT, October 23, 1910. "Crowds Cheer Taft As He Leaves City," *New York Times*, March 5, 1913. HTM's description of her debut party is amusing, see HTM to RAT, December 21, 1910, RATP. She also unveiled the Lafayette Square statue of Baron von Steuben, HTM to RAT, December 4, 1910, RATP; see also, *The Sunday Star*, "The New Belle of the White House," February 28, 1909.

3. "Miss Taft to Aid the Girl Strikers," *New York Times*, January 16, 1910. "I am divided," HTM to WHT, n.d. (1909–12), HTM to WHT, n.d. (January 1910), HTMP. Wilmington event, Margaret Hilles to Charles Hilles, December 6, 1912. PPF #3, WHTP. "Yale, I am sorry," HTM to RAT, October 23, 1910, RATP.

4. "Do write Mama," HTM to CPT, n.d. (1909–12), CPTP. Hill interview, "good enough," from "The Wife of the New President, *Ladies' Home Journal*, March 1909. "Higher education for," Edna Colman, *White House Gossip,* pp. 323–24. "I wish that it," HTM to RAT, n.d. (spring 1911), RATP. "Put down all the vanities," HTM to RAT, March 10, 1911, RATP. "Mama seemed to be," HTM to RAT, n.d. (spring 1911), RATP.

5. HHT daily routine, HHT to RAT, January 15, 1911, RATP. Miss Letterman earned $1,800 a year. White House employee flow chart, March 28, 1911, WHTP. Philippines Constabulary Band, Program for Concert at White House, Tuesday, April 6, 1909. HHT idea of arts medal, Elise Kirk, *Music in the White House*, pp. 188–91. "Since we have noticed," Joseph Dierdorf to HHT, January 21, 1909. Mozart Society, HHT to Lily Grosvenor, October 24, 1910, Grosvenor Papers, LC. Shakespeare at the White House, "Play on White House Lawn," *New York Times*, June 18, 1910. For a review of the musical performances that Mrs. Taft hosted in the White House, see various programs in the Hoover datebooks, Hoover Papers, LC and HHT White House diaries, 1909–13, WHTP.

6. "Mrs. Taft actually clapped," Archibald Willingham Butt, *Taft and Roosevelt*, p. 638. West Potomac Park, Lincoln Memorial Committee, WHT to HHT, July 26, 1911. PPF #301, Memo to HHT office, February 16, 1911,

and Lincoln Memorial Commission meeting notes, July 26, 1911, WHTP. HHT admitting to ambition for presidency since her first White House visit; see *New York Times*, June 11, 1911.

7. "Whether Mama wanted me," HTM to RAT, May 15, 1911, RATP. "Mrs. Taft Ill Here," *New York Times*, May 15, 1911. "Mrs. Taft Better," *New York Times*, May 16, 1911. "Mrs. Taft Reaches Home," *New York Times*, May 19, 1911. "Mrs. Taft Will Rest," *New York Times*, May 20, 1911.

8. Maria Herron offer to help, Maria Herron to WHT, May 14, 1911, WHTP. John Herron illness, "a fit of," Maria Herron to WHT, June 27, 1911, PPF #157, WHTP, and Archibald Willingham Butt, *Taft and Roosevelt*, p. 681. Tragedy seemed to follow the family. Helen went out for a night cruise on the *Dolphin* on May 28 and it hit and sank a motor boat, drowning a man who had been onboard. HTM to RAT, September 6, 1911, RATP; "Taft Regrets Drowning," *New York Times*, May 29, 1911. Drive to Great Falls, AWB to Clara Butt, June 11, 1911, Butt Papers. "It would gratify your mother," WHT to RAT, June 7, 1911, RATP. "To stand in a line," HTM to RAT, May 31, 1911, RATP.

9. Accounts of the preparations for the Silver Wedding Anniversary party are from: Archibald Willingham Butt, *Taft and Roosevelt,* p. 679, "Tafts to Ask 4,000 to Silver Wedding," *New York Times*, June 13, 1911; "Kin of Presidents Invited," *New York Times*, June 17, 1911; "Presents to Tafts Flood White House," *New York Times*, June 18, 1911; "Czar and Sultan Congratulate Tafts," *New York Times*, June 19, 1911; "Taft Returns Money Gifts," *New York Times*, June 25, 1911; "The Silver Wedding Anniversary of the Tafts," (photos) *New York Times*, July 1, 1911; "Congratulations Sent to the President and Mrs. Taft," and "Gifts Presented to the President and Mrs. Taft," n.d. typed memos, reel 601, WHTP.

10. Details of the anniversary party are from: Archibald Willingham Butt, *Taft and Roosevelt*, p. 494, "Tafts Receive 5,000 on Lawn," *New York Times*, June 20, 1911; descriptions from guests, *Washington Post*, June 20, 1911; *Washington Evening Star*, June 20, 1911; White House Memorandum, Reporter John Elfreth Watkins request for old photos, May 19, 1911, PPF

#157; WHT to HHT, July 26, 1911 and WHT to HHT July 28, 1911, both PPF #1, WHTP.

11. "I went into the White House grounds last evening," Francis D. Millet to WHT, June 21, 1911. "It is perhaps," WHT to Ambassador Bryce, June 19, 1911, PPF #200. "I count on being," WHT to Bishop Dunne, June 13, 1911. "Great throng . . . merry," WHT to Thomas Emery, June 21, 1911.

12. "Roosevelt was the only," HHT to RAT, January 15, 1911, RATP. U.S. Steel and National Rifle Association incidents from Will Manners, *TR and Will,* pp. 190–99. Roosevelt children at New Year's Day Reception, "Taft Greets 5,625 New Year Visitors," *New York Times*, January 3, 1911. "Tuesday, I went up," HHT to RAT, April 2, 1911, RATP. "It was too dear," Alice Longworth to WHT, December 28, 1910. WHT invited Alice to dinner when HHT was away, WHT to HHT, July 28, 1911. "Dance de Vent," AWB to Clara Butt, June 27, 1911, Butt Papers.

13. "Taft Summer Home Ready," *New York Times*, May 22, 1911. "Only a little tired," HTM to RAT, May 31, 1911, RATP. "Insist[ing] on superintending," HTM to RAT, June 23, 1911, RATP. Helen's decision to extend her absence from college and help her mother, HTM to RAT, July 26 and August 12, 1911, RATP. Instead, to cope with the heat wave, the First Lady joined Helen, Charlie, and her sister Lucy in daily swimming sessions while escaping dead fish and prostrated by the heat. Reports on Nellie's condition in Beverly that summer are from HTM to RAT, July 21, July 25, and July 29, 1911, RATP. Old habits died hard. When she learned that her daughter, on a fox hunt, was not riding hard enough to lead, Nellie was "much upset." HTM to RAT, August 6, 1911, RATP. "Taft to Lay 1912 Wires," *New York Times*, August 6, 1911. "President Goes to Beverly," *New York Times*, August 11, 1911. The only real excitement that summer was another trip to Maine and another automobile accident. This time, Will and Nellie were being driven in the car when another hit them, but there were no injuries. "Taft Party Shaken in Auto Collision," *New York Times*, August 14, 1911. "President Off to Rest," *New York Times*, August 22, 1911. Helen's reports on her father's Senate battles over statehood bill and tariff vetoes,

HTM to RAT, August 26, 1911, and n.d. (circa late August 1911), RATP. She reported, for example: "Everyone seems to think that Papa has come very well out of the mix-up. The veto messages are widely praised. He was able to expose the inconsistencies of the last two tariff bills so well that many of the papers (for instance, the *N.Y. Post*) which attacked him for the wool veto upheld him on these"; "Tafts on Mayflower Sail for Maine," *New York Times*, September 2, 1911. "Taft Returns to Beverly," *New York Times*, September 5, 1911.

14. Information on Roosevelt's reaction to Taft's Justice Department suit against U.S. Steel, his self-defense, and talk of his running for nomination are abstracted from Will Manners, *TR and Will*, pp. 190–203. "Taft Begins Trip," *New York Times*, September 16, 1911. "Tafts Leave Beverly Soon," *New York Times*, October 16, 1911. Lucy Laughlin also joined Nellie and Helen, HTM to RAT, October 30, 1911. "While Resting, Taft Will Plan Message," *New York Times*, November 4, 1911. "None to Welcome Taft," *New York Times*, November 12, 1911.

15. Will resenting justices who retired only when extremely ill, Archibald Willingham Butt, *Taft and Roosevelt*, p. 433. "Supreme Court Bench Filled," *New York Times*, January 4, 1911; WHT to HHT, October 14, 1911. "The real President," "Bosh, Says Taft of Annexation," *New York Times*, April 28, 1911. "The President enjoyed her discomfort," AWB to Clara Butt, April 9, 1911. "In fact," Butt, p. 585. Receiving guests, Butt, p. 641. "He cannot be hurried, and he does not mind whom he keeps waiting or how long they have to wait," she complained. "He likes to go when he wishes and where he wishes, and he does not mind breaking engagements," Butt, p. 6. Cannon dinner and Will's phone call to Nellie, Butt, p. 597. Taft would manage to push the reciprocity bill through Congress, but with great damage to his party support. And then in the autumn of 1911, fearing it was the first step in an American annexation, Canada rejected what Taft had seen as a mutually beneficial free trade reform for both nations. Only to Butt did Will confide his fear that she had been right all along. "Nellie will have another one on me," Will said. Butt, pp. 598–99.

16. "Well, I don't see," Archibald Willingham Butt, *Taft and Roosevelt,* p. 638. She also listed potential successors, finally concluding, "I don't know. Some of your friends are too old to have children and you might get a young one who would not have any. Girls are so queer these days." "She loves to hear," Butt, p. 628. Nellie praiseful of Will's speeches to her son, HHT to RAT, March 10, December 12, and April 30, 1911, RATP. "Had formed the habit," HHT obituary, *New York Times*, May 23, 1943. "Mama and I," HTM to RAT, November 12, 1911, RATP. Will Herron, CPT to Arthur Hoffman, October 13, 1960, CPTP; The Herrons' privileges, PPF #157. Maria Herron to WHT, June 27, 1911; WHT to Maria Herron, July 23, 1912; and WHT to Maria Herron, August 13, 1912; PPF #285; WHT to Jennie Anderson, March 28, 1912; Mary Herron to WHT, n.d.

17. "Tafts Out in the Rain," *New York Times*, December 25, 1911. "It is going," Alice Longworth to WHT, December 27, 1911, PPF #55. "Mrs. Taft's List of Greatest Women," *New York Times*, December 14, 1911.

16. *Titanic*

1. The Duke was making an official trip to Canada and planned on socializing in New York. The U.S. ambassador to England, Whitlaw Reid, had invited the President to attend a dinner, but Taft refused. When Will discovered that Helen had accepted, he made her rescind it. Only after some diplomatic dispute did the Duke call on the Tafts for forty-five minutes. Both Helen and Nellie refused to curtsy. When Will returned the call at the British embassy, he walked back to the White House, underscoring his democratic differences with the British monarchy. No Taft attended any of the dinners or other entertainments given him in Washington. Various stories on the Duke's visit to Washington in *New York Times*, January 26, 1912. "Taft Greets 8,000 at New Year's Fete," *New York Times*, January 2, 1912, and Archibald Willingham Butt, *Taft and Roosevelt*, p. 807.

2. Information on LaFollette's speech and growing support for Roosevelt, as well as his governors' letter, is from "President Choice Named by Governors," *New York Times*, January 26, 1912, and Will Manners, *TR and Will,*

pp. 207–209. "I have learned," "Longworth Cheers Taft," *New York Times*, January 27, 1912. On Roosevelt throwing his "hat in the ring," Will Manners, *TR and Will*, p. 209. Taft's view on Roosevelt seeking the nomination, WHT to Otto Bannard, January 22, 1912, and Archibald Willingham Butt, *Taft and Roosevelt*, pp. 802–803. WHT to Senator Bradley, February 5, 1912.

3. "Has me at" and "devoted friendship," Archibald Willingham Butt, *Taft and Roosevelt*, p. 804. "Lend myself," WHT to Charles Brocker, March 5, 1912. He also wrote, "The campaign is a very hard and sad one for me." "It is hard for me now to be in opposition to him and feel that he is in bitter opposition to me. I do not mean to but of course it will be impossible to keep our respective followers from using language that will irritate and embitter." "Well, I suppose," Butt, p. 436. "I had quite a fight," HTM to RAT, January 17, 1912, RATP. HHT's activities with the NCF are found through the Hoover datebook, May 10, 1910, to March 7, 1912, for example. Special garden party for them and "somewhat between," Butt, p. 642.

4. Handkerchiefs, HHT to WHT, October 29, 1912; Caroline Hastings to HHT, August 10, 1909, PPF #1329; E. R. Remel to HHT, February 23, 1909. "Very devoted to music," Charles H. Harris to HHT, May 10, 1910, PPF #1289. Annapolis applicant, William Dudley Bungert case, Hilda H. Wells to HHT, December 1909. Texas postmaster, Gladys Dodge to HHT, n.d. (April 1909); Mrs. John Evans to HHT, April 19, 1910, PPF #752; J. Jabs to HHT, August 1909, PPF #1649. Man who sent chain, FWC to Alice Blech, January 13, 1910, PPF #1970; G. W. Painter to HHT, September 3, 1909, PPF #2781; PPF #3451, PPF #3452. Oliver Dallas, formerly chief clerk of the Office of the U.S. Surveyor General of Montana, tried to get reinstated after being fired for forging mining claims field notes. Surveyor General of Montana office, Interior secretary to WHT, October 25, 1909, Dallas case, PPF #1544. Filipino friend, Pardo Tavera, to HHT, October 6, 1909, PPF #3726. Turkish immigrant, Mary Hennessey to HHT, n.d. (September 1912), PPF #3834. The local DAR chapter president characterized the immigrants as an "unweeded crowd" of "threatening evil" that "bring but a spirit of unrest, rebellion, anarchism and worse." The initial request was sent to WHT: see Fort McHenry, PPF #852; Louise Casey Baker to HHT,

May 17, 1909, and War Secretary to WHT, May 26, 1909, PPF #99; Commissioner of the District of Columbia to FWC, July 31, 1909, PPF #1975; Mrs. O. E. Duvall to HHT, July 1911, PPF #1855.

5. Example of how the First Lady's office had cases investigated, Lilly Lynn to HHT, March 11, 1910; Navy Secretary to FWC, March 23, 1910, PPF #2101; Pennsylvania man, FWC to HHT, March 12, 1910, PPF #2188. It was the cases of average or impoverished citizens, however, where Nellie helped the most consistently. Such was the case of a young girl who had to drop out of school to work as a government typist and support her brother who returned sick from the Spanish-American War. Maude Dubant to HHT, August 31, 1909, PPF #667. Examples of those who wrote the First Lady after hearing nothing from the President or assuming his secretary would throw the letter out, Mrs. L. W. Gary to HHT, August 19, 1909, PPF #973; Peter Fernandez to HHT, September 24, 1910, PPF #2; Mrs. Kratz to HHT, August 12, 1909; Civil Service Commissioner to WHT, August 25, 1909, PPF #1881. "I have written this person," Belle Kearney to HHT, January 6, 1910, PPF #1779; FWC to W. M. Brown, May 28, 1909. Nothing could be done in the request of Dougherty to work as a clerk at the Panama Canal, and the matter was closed. Anna Dougherty to HHT, March 10, 1909; John McIlhenny, commissioner, U.S. Civil Service Commission to FWC, June 30, 1909; FWC to Anna Dougherty, July 2, 1909, PPF #649. Rose Mary Ball case, White House memorandum, August 30, 1909, PPF #109.

6. The bill for Civil War nurses was S.5251. Senator Scott to HHT, February 18, 1911, PPF #873. The bill for Philippines officers was S.7373. The bill for Mrs. Harrison was S.5130. Correspondence to Mrs. Taft is barely intelligible, but from a member of Congress on the House Committee on Public Buildings and Grounds, circa January 1912, "President Heeds Mrs. Taft's Plea," clipping, n.d., n.p., reprinted from *New York World*. Interest in political appointments, HHT, p. 13; Archibald Willingham Butt, *Taft and Roosevelt*, p. 234; HHT to RAT, January 27, 1908, RATP. Mrs. LeRoy was the only person in the government who was given the responsibility of signing the President's name to land patents. "Memorandum," WHT to HHT, March 25, 1909.

7. Moving letter: Mrs. Pincus Schein to HHT, March 7, 1910; Charles Nagel to WHT, March 15, 1910, PPF #3316. M. M. Society: Marian Citron to HHT, May, 1909, PPF #416. Little Mothers: Marie Burns to HHT, March 14, 1910, PPF #895. International Sunshine Society: Cynthia West-over Alden to HHT Secretary, April 8, 1911, and to HHT, April 22, 1911, PPF #1280; Anna Murray to HHT, March 6, 1910; Annie Laws to HHT, December 4, 1909, PPF #2553. Besides the Lathrop appointment, Will was also praised for his call for arbitration among nations: "Suffragists Praise Taft in Convention," *New York Times*, November 27, 1912.

8. "Mrs. Taft Listens to Strike Charges," *New York Times*, March 6, 1912; "Kitty and I," HHT to RAT, March 10, 1912, RATP. Ultimately, the Lawrence hearings brought higher wages than those that had barely permitted the workers to subsist. Certainly the strikes did not reflect well on Will, as the *Louisville Post* editorialized: "Here we have a picture of the workings of the Payne bill, the best tariff bill that ever passed, as Mr. Taft called it. In the first place, as shown at the mills of the American Woolen Company [where Teoli worked], it secures only a starvation wage for laborers in New England manu-factories. In the second place, the most pauperized labor of Europe has been brought here to work in protected mills and the good of the 'American laboring-man' has been lost sight of. It was an evil day for protection that brought the strike at Lawrence in a Presidential year." "The Lawrence Strike Children," *Literary Digest,* March 9, 1912; Hearings on the Strike at Lawrence, Massachusetts, House Document No. 671, 62nd Congress, 2nd session; "Miss Taft a Guide," *New York Times,* March 12, 1912. At the Women's Industrial Exhibition, Nellie stopped by the booth of the "Little Mothers," which she continued to support, had her silhouette cut at the Widowed Mother's Fund, and was given tulips from the National Consumer's League. She learned about paper bag cookery and box furniture, and even paid homage to Asbestos the guinea pig, and Faithful the cat, which both survived the Equitable Life Insur-ance Building fire and were now advertising mascots for Edna Lewis's insur-ance company. "Mrs. Taft Visits Exhibit," *New York Times,* March 21, 1912; "Mrs. Taft Ignores Suffrage," *New York Times,* March 22, 1912.

9. "It got the best," Ike Hoover manuscript on Tafts, Hoover Papers. The psychological strain caused by the Taft-Roosevelt rift, and Alice Longworth remarks, Archibald Willingham Butt, *Taft and Roosevelt,* pp. 776, 813. Tafts dining when they received bulletin on Roosevelt running, Will Manners, *TR and Will*, p. 215. Argument between Tafts, Butt, p. 850.

10. Watrons' quotes are from "New Version of Butt's Trip," *New York Times,* April 17, 1912. "Any real comfort" and "would not hear of it," Archibald Willingham Butt, *Taft and Roosevelt*, p. 852. Archie leaves for Europe, "Major Butt on Sick Leave," *New York Times,* March 1, 1912. Nellie had converted: "Mrs. H. W. Taft Now a Catholic Convert," *New York Times,* February 7, 1912; "Tafts Attend Peace Mass," *New York Times,* December 1, 1911. The two letters from Rome were AWB to WHT, March 19 and March 23, 1912; S. L. Baugher to WHT, May 17, 1912. WHT refuses to give sister-in-law letter, WHT to Henry Taft, March 25, 1912.

11. Cherry blossom trees: Yci Theodora Ozaki to HHT, February 26, 1912. "Aided by Mrs. Taft," *Washington Post,* March 17, 1912. "He was champing . . . Strange enough," Mr. Rosenkrantz to Mr. Cloman, April 16, 1912, case file #1158. Archie also thought there was a "touch of pathos" in Edith's note when he learned she was soon leaving for South America—"an excuse," he thought, "to be away from it all during the trying days between now and June." AWB to WHT, n.d. (early April 1912). There is some suggestion that the White House made the arrangements for Archie's return trip on the *Titanic,* the President's stenographer writing him of "the White Star [line] matter." Wendell Mischler to AWB, March 6, 1912.

12. "Shining figure," WHT to Arrington Margaret Butt, May 19, 1912. The information from Mrs. Harris of Washington on Archie's last known moments on the *Titanic* and his rescue of the Libyan teenager is from *Jacksonville Times-Union,* May 25, 1912. "He was loyal," *Augusta Herald,* May 2, 1912. Some of the President's other remarks: "I first knew Archie Butt in the Philippines . . . a very active officer . . . very useful and faithful. . . . The duty of an aide to a President is very hard to fill. It calls for great self-sacrifice. A President is isolated. He sees but few people continuously in

a confidential and close way, and his aide has to be with him all the time, when he is out of humor and when he is in humor and when he is silent and when he is talking. . . . Of the many fine qualities he had loyalty was one." During the American inquiry into the disaster one wireless operator claimed the coal stoker who attacked his colleague in a panic was an African American, while a steward said the "coward" men who rushed for lifeboats were "probably Italians, or some foreign nationality other than English or American." The *New York Sun* bemoaned the fact that "Desirable Immigrants" were lost when nearly eighty Finns perished, implying that only the loss of Northern European immigrants was a tragedy. A false story claimed that Chinese stowaways had hidden under the lifeboat seats to live. All sorts of legends also began about Archie Butt: He had been traveling with his teenage lover and their illegitimate child; he was secretly engaged to a Colorado woman; he was involved in some plot to help the Catholic Church take over the American government. None of them was true, but the only one vaguely addressed by the President was that Archie's love for his mother was the reason "he never married." All the information on the *Titanic* disaster is derived from research at the online Encyclopedia Titanica Document Archive, including articles such as "The Butt-Millet Memorial Fountain," "Francis Davis Millet," "Major Archibald Willingham Butt," "Marie Grice Young," "The Illegitimate Daughter (?) of Archibald Butt"; "My Search for Titanic Memorials;" the *Denver Post* article, "Archibald C. Butt Was to Have Been Married This Fall"; all by Phillip Gowan, are all online at current Gowan's *Titanic Site*, as of May 2004; Archie Butt–*Titanic* case file, PPF #303, WHTP. All *New York Times* articles on the *Titanic* from April 15 to May 26, 1912; also "Women Raise $10,000 by Titanic Benefit," *New York Times,* December 1912; Wyn Craig Wade, *The Titanic: End of a Dream* (New York: Penguin Books, 1986). "Occasions like the sinking," "Taft in Tears as He Lauds Major Butt," *New York Times,* May 6, 1912.

17. "If They Don't Win, It's a Shame"

1. "Papa got off," HHT to RAT, January 28, 1911, RATP. HHT on progressives, Archibald Willingham Butt, *Taft and Roosevelt*, 645, 650–51,

667–68. HHT memory and Senator Smoot, Butt, p. 768. "I think you will," Butt, p. 768.

2. TR's May 19, 1911, statement quoted in Victor Rosewater to Charles Hilles, telegram, April 23, 1912. "If anyone doubts," Leroy Vernon to Sherman Allen, April 24, 1912; attached to the letter was a detailing of Roosevelt patronage. Legal scholar "entirely carried," A. B. Colvin to WHT, April 30, 1912. Two "alienists," Alfred Conkling to WHT, May 14, 1912. "Why isn't there," Weir Mitchel to HHT, July 14, 1912. Henry White effort and "When he gets," Will Manners, *TR and Will*, pp. 216–17.

3. New York primary, Will Manners, *TR and Will*, p. 217. However pale by future comparisons, this was shaping up into a "dirty campaign" in the mind of 1912 America. "That the time has come," Henry Fowler Pringle, *Life and Times of William Howard Taft,* vol. 2, pp. 771–74. "The Secret Service especially came in for a goodly share of the suspicion and in their case one of their number was relieved from duty with the President. As to him the thought generally was that he just let his enthusiasm of association with Mr. Roosevelt . . . get the best of him . . . while out on the trips. While Mr. Taft would be addressing an audience from one end of the car and telling why the people should vote for him, this secret service man would be at the other end of the car sounding the praise and expressing the wish that Mr. Roosevelt would be elected." Ike Hoover manuscript on Tafts, Hoover Papers.

4. Although the President told a man who kept yelling to him that Teddy was "a liar" that such a word was not "in my vocabulary" and that he would only talk about "facts," he finally went on the defense. "I am here to reply to an old and true friend of mine, who has made many charges against me. I deny those charges, I deny all of them. I do not want to fight Theodore Roosevelt, but sometimes a man in a corner fights," he repeatedly shouted in a one-day whistle-stop from Springfield to Boston. "50,000 Turn Out to Cheer Taft On," *New York Times,* April 30, 1912. Massachusetts primary and quotes, Will Manners, *TR and Will*, pp. 226–29. "I had nightmares," HTM to RAT, May 4, 1912, RATP. Ohio primary, Manners, pp. 229–30. "The twenty-four delegates," HTM to RAT, May 23, 1912. "Roosevelt put three hundred," HHT to RAT, May 26, 1912, RATP. "Bottled-up savagery . . . chronic cold,"

Longworth, quoted in Manners, p. 231. In contrast to Alice Roosevelt, Helen, Bob, and Charlie Taft had a healthy sense of detachment from the election: Their worlds would not fall apart whether their father won or lost. Helen even sent some lyrics about the election to Robert that she heard when she attended Bryn Mawr graduation: "Oh, when I vote, I vote for Billy, For he knows the game. Though Teddy talks, His talk is silly, And never twice the same." HTM to RAT, June 8, 1912, RATP.

5. For HHT preconvention activities, HHT to RAT, April 26, May 12, and May 16, 1912, all RATP, and May and June entries of HHT White House diary, 1912. "Except for the nervousness," WHT to Delia Torrey, May 12, 1912.

6. "Father and all of us," William B. Mead and Paul Dixon, *Baseball,* p. 20. For an account of Tafts at the 1912 "opening day," see Mead and Dickson, pp. 23–28. Alice's lost luggage: "Longworth Trunks Lost," *New York Times,* June 18, 1912. Roosevelts at convention, Will Manners, *TR and Will*, pp. 235–38, 241. Nomination Day, "Anniversary for Taft," *New York Times,* June 20, 1912. "Taft Plays Golf," *New York Times*, June 21, 1912; "Taft Rejoices That the Party Is Saved," *New York Times,* June 23, 1912; HHT, p. 392.

7. Will seemed to have little confidence of winning in November and had even privately expressed the wish that Charles Evans Hughes had been the candidate "because I believe his chance of election would perhaps be better than mine." WHT to Delia Torrey, June 19, 1912. "Bryan Spared Mrs. Taft," *New York Times,* July 12, 1912; "Tales of Convention as Told in Flashes: Mrs. Taft Is Guest of Democrats," *New York Times,* June 28, 1912. 1912 would be the hardest of all her White House summers, compounded by genuine tragedy when Will's beloved Chevy Chase Club caddy, thirteen-year-old Guy Hurdle, was found in the woods of a Maryland hollow, hanging from a tree branch. He had committed suicide after his mother scolded him: "Taft's Caddy a Suicide," *New York Times,* June 27, 1912. Even her cow died. Pauline Wayne the cow file, PPF #6, Senator Isaac Stephenson to WHT, May 18, 1912. "Know what the other side," Archibald Willingham Butt, *Taft and Roosevelt,* p. 749. "I stopped reading," HHT, pp. 392–93.

8. When some Blackfoot Indians gave Bob the gift of a real live "teddy bear" in Montana, he quipped, "I don't think I dare take this thing home in the face of the strained relationship between my father and one of his old friends." "Young Taft Gets a Bear," *New York Times*, August 7, 1912. Helen thought that the idea of "such a serious minded and systematic person" as Robert taking a European summer with wild classmates was "a good joke." HTM to RAT, December 15, 1911, RATP. His parents held him to high standards and set the path for his career: Yale, Harvard Law School, practicing attorney, and, hopefully, public service. *Ladies' Home Journal*, "The Wife of the New President," March 1909. If there was any straying, Nellie corrected it quickly. "You appear very busy with your golf and all that," she wrote Bob, "but the freshman debating team is the worst ever. I hope very much that you do well." HHT to RAT, April 17 (1911), RATP. "Don't sign yourself," HHT to RAT, November 28, 1911, RATP.

There was considerable expectation from the public on the children, especially the eldest. "I feel strongly that the same wholesome genuine and normal tone that will emanate from the White House," wrote one Taft supporter, "will have its sweet influence on the country." A. L. Roelker to WHT, March 23, 1909. Consumed with his work as editor of the *Harvard Law Review*, Bob would not graduate until 1913 but was offered the opportunity to work for Justice Holmes long before. Although his own inclination was to start practicing in Cincinnati, he would not accept until he had consulted his father about what "you and Mama have planned to do next year" if they were not in the White House. Will wanted Bob to have "experience in the actual drudgery of the practice and procedure in Ohio." He did what his father expected. On the other hand, he took advantage of his position's privileges. He got his father to promise to give the *Harvard Law Review* the first legal article he might write and tried to get the President to drop by a twenty-fifth anniversary dinner of the *Review*. When Bob made his summer tour of an astounding twenty-one nations, presidential letters to all the U.S. embassies ensuring his safety preceded his arrival. The President also began to share the most intimate and intricate of political intelligence with him, as he did with Nellie and his brothers. Bob also interceded for his fellow *Review* board members: Maurice Hirsch got in to see the President and plead for a pardon for someone he thought innocent; Morris Barroll was given a presidential letter of introduction to the U.S. ambassador in Paris. When the *Review* was composing an editorial on the presidential elector's cases and had only the short Kansas Supreme Court decision of July 1911 on hand, he simply got the White House to send him all the documentation they had. And, too, there was something pleasant about being able to remind one's parents of money they promised through the buffer of clerks and secretaries. RAT to Carmi Thompson, November 9, 1912; RAT to FWC, May 31, 1909; RAT to Rudolph Forster, October 20, 1912; RAT to Carmi Thompson, July 19, 1912; John Wilson to RAT, December 1, 1911; Charles Hilles to RAT, March 25, 1912; RAT to Charles Hilles, March 24, 1912; Charles Hilles to RAT, January 23, 1912; RAT to Charles Hilles, January 26, 1912; RAT to Charles Hilles, June 18, 1912; Ezra Thayer to WHT, August 24, 1911; James Brown Reynolds to WHT, December 24, 1910 and January 4, 1911; WHT to RAT, August 27, 1911; WHT to Ambassador Robert Bacon, June 26, 1911; White House memorandum on Robert Taft imposter, August 17, 1912; Richard Sylvester to Rudolph Forster, July 18, 1912; John Halsey to Carmi Thompson, August 15, 1912; memorandum for the President, August 22, 1912; RAT to WHT, November 13, 1912; John Chipman Gray to WHT, November 9, 1912; WHT to John Chipman Gray, November 19, 1912; WHT to RAT, November 19, 1912; RAT to Charles Hilles, January 19 and February 12, 1913; All of case file #2. Charlie, on the other hand, was front and center that summer in the news. He openly enjoyed his life as the President's son. As newspaper stories about him reported, he phoned reporters to deny a story that he was going to give up knickers, carved his name in the dining room table on the presidential yacht, flew airplanes from the White House roof, and substituted for the switchboard operators at lunchtime. "Charlie Taft," *Washington Star,* February 21, 1909; "Charley Taft's Aeroplane," *New York Times,* December 20, 1910; see also Carl Sferrazza Anthony, *America's First Families.*

9. "They have fallen," WHT to HHT, July 20, 1912. On guests for no-

tification luncheon, HHT to WHT, two telegrams, July 22, 1912; WHT to HHT, July 21, 1912, PPF #1. "Furthermore," he informed her, "I have concluded not to invite any ladies. You might ask a few to help you receive, but with that exception I shall not ask any at all. . . . This is especially the case because I shall have to invite four or five colored men, officials about Washington, and I think the presence of ladies among the guests is more noticed and more resented than the presence of colored men." WHT to HHT, July 22, 1912. "Mrs. Taft Returns to Washington," *New York Times*, August 1, 1912; "Taft Talks Issues in Strong Speech," *New York Times*, August 1, 1912.

10. Death of John W. Herron, "Mrs. Taft's Father Dead," *New York Times*, August 6, 1912; "President Taft Pallbearer," *New York Times*, August 7, 1912. Details on John Herron's last years, death, and legacy are from WHT to Charley Taft, August 5, 1912; WHT to Joaquin Mendez, August 7, 1912; and WHT to Franklin MacVeagh, August 7, 1912. "Mrs. Taft Back at Beverly," *New York Times*, August 10, 1912. "Developments in the campaign" is from HHT obituary, *New York Times*, May 23, 1943; "I wanted him to be" and "During the last," HHT, pp. 393–94.

11. "Sentiment plays," WHT to Rufus Thayer, October 17, 1912. "I have a sense of wrong," WHT to Delia Torrey, May 12, 1912. "You have the worst," HHT to WHT, November 2, 1912. That fall the Tafts spent some time driving throughout New England, Will doing a limited amount of campaign speeches, and made one excursion to Pennsylvania. Beverly had not been the happy "Summer Capital" that Nellie had hoped it would be in 1909. "The President's lease on Parramatta expires this year and Beverly does not look for his return," noted a newspaper, "no matter how the November election goes." The President went back to Cincinnati to vote on November 5. "Taft in Beverly," *New York Times*, August 28, 1912; "Taft Motors to Maine," *New York Times*, September 9, 1912; "Taft Completes Tour," *New York Times*, October 13, 1912; "Taft Spends a Quiet Day," *New York Times*, October 21, 1912; "Taft Motors in Rain," *New York Times*, October 24, 1912; Ike Hoover manuscript on Tafts, Hoover Papers. "I have been seeing people," HHT to RAT, November 24, 1912, RATP.

12. Curious epitaph, Charles S. Selden, "Six White House Wives and

Widows," *Ladies' Home Journal*, June 1927. Harry Taft revealed his conversation with Will about Edith Roosevelt to Taft biographer Henry Fowler Pringle, *The Life and Times of William Howard Taft,* vol. 2, p. 760. The Lodge and Longworth quotes are from Will Manners, *TR and Will*, pp. 166–67. "Having accomplished," L. A. Ault to Theodore Roosevelt, November 6, 1912, copy in WHTP. The original correspondence has not been located. "End the Rooseveltian," WHT to Samuel Carr, November 8, 1912.

13. For general information on WHT's post-election opinions, plans, and state of mind see the following: WHT to Charles Fairbanks, November 20, 1912; WHT to Jesse Lilienthal, February 20, 1912; WHT to Anson Phelps Stokes, December 14, 1912; WHT to Elihu Root, November 20, 1912; WHT to J. D. Brannan, "November 25, 1912; WHT to Henry Ide, December 16, 1912. "Statement dictated by the President for Harry Dunlap, for publication in the *New York World*," November 14, 1912, Pringle Papers. Had he been reelected, Taft later said, he "had in mind to go to the Philippines during a vacation of Congress with the idea that the presence of the President in that part of the United States jurisdiction might give to the Filipino people a sense of our interest in them that would conduce to their acquiescence in our rule and our effort to fit them for future self-government." WHT draft of speech, "Personal Aspects of the Presidency," n.d., reel 582. As Helen wrote Bob of the Panama Canal, "It is the most wonderful place for feeling that big things are happening." HTM to RAT, December 9, 1912, RATP; "Miss Taft Tests Canal Gate," *New York Times*, November 24, 1912; "Taft Home To-Morrow," *New York Times*, December 30, 1912.

14. Comedic performance: Among the monologues Ruth Draper performed were her "A French Dressmaker," "A Southern Girl at a Dance," and a "Scotch Immigrant." HHT to RAT, January 25, 1913, RATP. "Mrs. Taft's $10,000 Necklace," *New York Times*, February 18, 1913; "Give Necklace to Mrs. Taft," *New York Times*, February 22, 1913. "Mrs. Taft has read," WHT to Ellen Wilson, January 3, 1913. Although New Haven was their home for the foreseeable future, Nellie still held on to some choice real estate that she had purchased in the gravy years of the presidency.

Listed as "Assets of the President" were one house in the Bronx, New York; an apartment complex, also in the Bronx; and another single home in Hempstead, New York—all in boom real estate areas where middle-class Americans could move to from the city now teeming with millions of poor immigrants, and all paying rent to the Tafts. There was also another property, listed on a separate document headed "Assets of Mrs. Taft." Not only did Nellie hold notes on the National Cathedral Foundation but also on a lot at the corner of Twenty-fourth and U Streets, later to be renamed Wyoming Avenue. On a bluff overlooking the city from the top of the Connecticut Avenue hill, it was a perfect place to build a grand retirement home. It was in Washington, D.C. "Assets of the President, July 10, 1912"; "Assets of Mrs. Taft, July 10, 1912"; James Douglas Campbell to HHT, March 9, 1911; C.H. Kelsey, Title Guarantee and Trust Company, to HHT, March 10, 1911; WHT and HHT to James Douglas Campbell, Esq., March 14, 1911, WHT and HHT to John Hayes Hammond, March 14, 1911. Also among the assets was a note due to be paid by John W. Herron for $9,000, $75.00 of which was paid to WHT by his brother-in-law Louis More, indicating that the President's father-in-law had borrowed the money from Nellie but was too poor to repay any of it; see February 18, 1909 receipt of HHT's loan, signed by Louis More; Irwin, Ballman & Co. Investment Securities to HHT, February 15, 1909.

15. "As practical and cheerful," HTM to RAT, March 11, 1913. "People seem so sorry," HHT to RAT, March 4, 1913, RATP. The suffragette parade was so raucous that it turned into a dangerous brawl, and the First Lady left, disgusted when a mob of "hoodlums" began harassing and cursing at the suffragettes. "Washington Suffrage Pageant," *New York Times*, March 3, 1913. "Well, Mother," Charles A. Selden, "Six White House Wives and Widows," *Ladies' Home Journal*, July 1927.

18. Elba (1913–1921)

1. "My maid . . . Your father," HHT to RAT, November 22, no year (1913–1918), RATP; Augusta, HHT to RAT, March 9, 1913. "Dreary,

dull . . . I occupied," HHT to RAT, May 11, 1913. HHT in New Haven, HHT to RAT, May 25, 1913; HHT to RAT, January 11, 1914, RATP. Typical was her letter to Bob: "Another week has passed by without your Father and I doing a thing." HHT to RAT, May 18, 1913.

2. Helen wrote her mother's book. As she revealed to her brother, "The book begins to come out in the May *Delineator*. I am feeling more cheerful about it now. The *Delineator* will use only a tiny part of the book. Only of course Mrs. Egan and I often differ. We are going to work in Washington at Easter, I hope, and may finish up the last chapters. Dodd, Mead is giving $2,000 advance." HTM to RAT, March 17, 1914, RATP; Dodd, Mead to HHT, November 6, 1914; Eleanor Egan to WHT, n.d. (1913); HHT, p. 182.

3. Bob also worried that Helen "will feel put out," after the news of Eleanor Wilson's engagement to William McAdoo. RAT to Martha Bowers, n.d. Helen didn't know either: "I don't know when we leave for South America if we go. . . . Mama never says." HTM to RAT, March 17, 1914, RATP. Will was hesitant to let Bob spend another summer in Europe, not wanting him to get "the idea that you could drop work and run abroad every year to get foreign habits I think he called it. He was quite indignant when I laughed at him," Helen wrote. HTM to RAT, May 18, 1913, RATP. Nellie, however, prevented the trip because of money: "We have all forgotten how to economize," Helen wrote Bob. "At present we seem to be living beyond our means." HTM to RAT, June 6, 1913, RATP. "You will like it," HHT to RAT, June 4, 1913, RATP. "You did not write," HHT to RAT, January 3, 1915, RATP. "That is where the trouble," HHT to RAT, December 2, 1914, RATP. When his first child was expected, Robert wrote his mother. She responded that she would not tell Will because "I know he will tell it to everybody—just like every man and the woman to hide it." HHT to RAT, March 21, 1915, RATP.

4. California trip: HHT to RAT, February 14, September 19, and November 14, 1915; HTM to RAT, September 20, 1915, RATP. Nellie had first learned that Martha was pregnant but Helen "couldn't persuade" her to tell

Will because "she insisted that he would tell everyone at once." HTM to RAT, April 9, 1915, RATP. "The days go," HHT to RAT, January 11, 1915, RATP. "He has made," HHT to RAT, December 12, 1915, RATP. "Your father came home yesterday," HHT to RAT, March 17, 1915, crossed out to read March 14, RATP. Nellie attended a New Haven meeting debate on whether to "buy property on the common or not for a city hall." HHT to RAT, January 31, 1915, RATP. "Perfectly awful," HHT to RAT, March 21, 1915, RATP. "I don't think," HHT to RAT, November 7, 1914, RATP. "I came home to receive," HHT to RAT, March 7, 1915, RATP.

5. "It is the third time," HHT to RAT, November 7, 1915, RATP. "It was very slow," HHT to RAT, May 31, 1915, RATP. Basketball game, HHT to RAT, March 17, 1915, crossed out to read March 14, RATP. Colonial Dames, HHT to RAT, January 31, May 31, and June 13, 1915 (itinerary of her Connecticut architectural tour), RATP. Membership was offered to Nellie Taft in the Colonial Dames because of her descent from the Colonial governor Thomas Welles. She was later elected an honorary vice president of the organization. HHT to CPT, February 10, 1923, CPTP. When Helen had a friend visiting but had to study, for example, Nellie "suggested going to the theater Saturday night so that I would not be caught [sitting at home] again." HHT to RAT, December 5, 1915, RATP. "New Haven is," HHT to RAT, February 28, 1915, RATP. "When I think," HHT to RAT, March 29, 1914, RATP. "Wednesday and," HHT to RAT, April 4, 1915, RATP. She also went to see mature plays like *Excuse Me* and *Twin Bed*. HHT to RAT, February 14, 1915, RATP. "Friday, I went to," HHT to RAT, May 23, 1915, RATP.

6. "All the people," HHT to RAT, November 28, 1915, RATP. "I had a magnificent," HHT to RAT, January 14, 1917, RATP. Love of food and dinner in Washington, HHT to RAT, June 6, 1915, and January 26, 1919, RATP. "No sense in my," HHT to RAT, March 19, 1916, RATP. Disapproved of Lucy's marriage: "Lucy was married Monday. . . . What [sic] she ever wanted to marry Lippett, I do not understand." HHT to RAT, May 2, 1915, RATP.

7. "Your father went to," HHT to RAT, February 4, 1917, RATP. "The New Haven ladies," CPT to HHT, July 4, 1918, and CPTP. "[W]hen you get," CPT to HHT, May 21, 1918, CPTP. "Patriotic speech," *Indianapolis Star*, May 8, 1919. Other details of Charlie are from Ishbel Ross, *An American Family*. "My heart goes," quoted in Ross, p. 301. Nellie's war activities, HHT to CPT, March 24 and April 20, 1919, CPTP. "We arranged the armor," HHT to RAT, July 4, 1915, RATP. "It is great to hear," CPT to HHT, September 22, 1918, CPTP. Maria in Europe, CPT to HHT, July 21, 1918. "I wish I could have," CPT to HHT, November 23, 1918, CPTP. "I never saw," CPT to HHT, April 6, 1918, CPTP.

8. "Little too carefully . . . I'll bet," CPT to HHT, May 21, 1918, CPTP. Lunch at the White House: "I went to the White House for lunch—the President, Mrs. Wilson, Margaret, Miss Bones and Miss Bolling were there. Janie and myself." HHT to RAT, January 14, 1917, RATP; Edith Wilson to HHT, January 11, 1917, author collection. Ladies of the League, HHT to RAT, February 11, 1919, RATP, and Borah following WHT, HHT to RAT, February 23, 1919, RATP. "But Mrs. Wilson," HHT to CPT, June 4, 1933, CPTP. Nelle Scanlan, *Boudoir Mirrors of Washington* (Philadelphia: John C. Winston, 1923), 206. In agreeing to fill the vacancy left by Teddy on the advisory board of the Dan Beard Outdoor School, wrote, "I am honored by the succession." WHT to Daniel Beard, January 30, 1919. Roosevelt memorial, HHT to RAT, February 11, 1919, RATP.

9. Giving up Washington apartment and returning to New Haven, WHT to Colonel Meekins, October 25, 1919, letter described in Ebay auction listing from May 2002. "Is it not fine that you have a lot on Indian Hill! I have been thinking of buying too—right next to the Williams place—I have a lot in Washington, which the tax returns put at $13,000 and the Williams lots I can buy at $10,000." HHT to RAT, February 11, 1917. Part of former President Taft's case for gender equity read: "Many married women are so situated that without destroying their homes, they may, by earnings from useful labor, add to the attractiveness and comforts of such home. Instead of interfering with happy marriages and homes, greater

opportunities for women to earn their own livelihood will tend to improve present conditions," he wrote. "A most frequent source of unhappiness . . . is the dependence of a woman on marriage for her material future. . . . If she were supporting herself and could look forward to a reasonably comfortable life, independent of marriage, she would be much more likely to choose wisely. The more independent . . . that women become in their opportunity and ability to win their own bread the more sensible and happy their marriages are likely to be. Whatever puts the wife nearer on an equality with the husband should help their association and increase their mutual respect. The wife's independence before marriage is such a help.

"Why is it not fair, if woman's work is in every way as valuable in its result to the employer, that he should pay her what he pays a man? Why should he take advantage of the fact that she can perhaps live on less than a man with a family, and give her less than to a man for the same job? To prevent such unfairness, women ought to organize. Indeed they ought to associate their unions with those of the men engaged in the same work. If the men refuse to unite in this way, they will make a great mistake." All from William Howard Taft, "As I See the Future of Women," *Ladies' Home Journal*, March 1919.

10. Nellie voting and worried about Helen's career, Ishbel Ross, *An American Family*, p. 307. Helen Taft, "The Six Weeks I Spent on a Farm," *Ladies' Home Journal*, June 1918. Women's Congress for National Service, *Ladies' Home Journal*, February 1918. At Bryn Mawr she had complained in her final semester about one teacher who "assumes that everyone in college agrees that feminism is the movement of the age, and then proceeds to relate the views and positions of the leading feminists. I think that I will be an ardent feminist myself by the end of the year just from having it assumed so often that one can be nothing else." HTM to RAT, January 16, 1914, RATP. "Helen does not come," HHT to RAT, March 3, 1916, RATP; "*Baldwin (School) Echoes*, February 17, 1964; Frederick Manning obituary, *New York Times*, December 3, 1966; WHT to HTM, January 13, 1920, WHTP.

11. Report on the Hardings from Marion, WHT to HHT, December 26, 1920; Warren Harding to WHT, January 4, 1921; Florence Harding to WHT, January 7, 1921. Rumor that Harding would name Taft if White resigned, Gus Karger to WHT, January 14, 1921; WHT to HHT, June 29, 1921; WHT to HHT, telegram, June 30, 1921. "Well, that has happened," WHT to HHT, June 30, 1921. Had the former First Lady wired her husband, he most positively would have saved it as he did every scrap of paper she sent him. "Have been thinking it over," WHT to HHT, July 4, 1921. The rest of the note includes: "If you go you just take [have to put up with] throngs [of people] and [take] many clothes for functions at White House."

19. In His Court (1921–1930)

1. More information of Taft's lives in Washington home, decor, etc.: "I hope you have kept [help] Annie and Maggie [McNamara]," Charlie wrote her, "because it would not be like home to miss those gray shoes that Annie used to sport, and I know nobody could make mushroom soup or tomato bisque the way that Maggie could." CPT to HHT, October 8, 1918, CPTP. The reference to "junk" furniture is from CPT to RAT, n.d. (circa 1913–1921). Furniture, HHT to CPT, November 14, 1926, CPTP. Free tickets to events, HHT to CPT, May 1925, CPTP. "He was very nice," HHT to RAT, February 9, 1913, RATP. As late as October 1919, Will pointed out that he was not taking the Carnegie pension; see William Howard Taft, "A $100,000 Salary for the President: Why He Should Have It," *Ladies' Home Journal*, October 1919.

2. "Your father," HHT to CPT, October 22, 1923, CPTP. "Henry Ford has attacked," WHT to HHT, November 30, 1920. Nellie filling in for Will, HHT to CPT, October 16, 1923, CPTP. Information on trip to England is from Henry Fowles Pringle, *Life and Times of William Howard Taft,* and Ishbel Ross, *An American Family*; also the photographs and captions are from an album of the trip in WHTP.

3. "Returned to the embassy," Henry Fowler Pringle, *Life and Times of William Howard Taft,* vol. 2, p. 1001. "The truth is," WHT to Horace

Taft, October 3, 1929. "Gay cocktail party," HHT to CPT, November 2, 1924, CPTP. "Send the cocktail shaker," HHT to RAT, January 11, 1915, RATP. When the cocktail shaker arrived, she was gleeful. "It is large, so that I can make you and Martha cocktails, and six others besides. . . . It is lovely," HHT to RAT, February 14, 1915, RATP. "They don't allow," HHT to RAT, May 21, no year (circa 1914–1916), RATP. Three bottles of whiskey, HHT to HTM, January 14, 1920 (mislabeled 1910), HTMP. "I liked better," HHT to CPT, circa 1927, CPTP.

4. Will's health and tests, HHT to CPT, December 3 and December 24, 1922, CPTP. Will Herron's death, HHT to CPT, October 8, 1922, CPTP. Bob and Charlie Taft's careers and political differences, Ishbel Ross, *An American Family*, pp. 348–50. Remus case, HHT to CPT, August 7, 1927, and HHT to CPT, November 24, 1927, both CPTP, and Ross, p. 356. "I know it is hard," HHT to CPT, June 10, 1928, CPTP. "I hope your campaign," HHT to CPT, July 28, 1928, CPTP. "I am glad that," HHT to CPT, May 13, 1934, CPTP. There was no rivalry with her daughter-in-law. After Eleanor left Murray Bay in 1923, Nellie wrote her, "We felt a vacant spot when you left." HHT to Eleanor Taft, August 26, 1923, CPTP.

5. Nellie claimed: "Is not great that Helen has a girl. I would have preferred a boy, but your papa likes girls." HHT to Eleanor Taft, January 18, 1925, CPTP. Charlie's first son, Seth, was born in 1923 and is also among the most frequently mentioned of all the grandchildren in Nellie's letters. Charlie had more daughters in the twenties: Lucia in 1924 and Cynthia in 1928. After Will's death, Charlie fathered his last two children, Rosalyn and Peter. "Send the bill," HHT to CPT on snowsuits for daughters, n.d. (circa December 1920s), CPTP. Nellie had ordered Charlie to go to Best's where she saw snowsuits she wanted the girls to have. She not only picked the colors ("I like the red and the blue") but insisted they were "no good without the caps." She also bought "little aprons" for the girls, HHT to CPT, December 24, 1922, CPTP. She wrote: "The house was all cleaned, ready for the children when they come. I have two rooms ready if they do not like the

sleeping porch." In another letter she was "anxious Eleanor come again with any children she wants to bring." Nellie signed off to Charlie with more un-abashed sentiment than she had since writing Will during their separations: "Give my love to Eleanor, Nonie and Sylvia and keep a lot for yourself." HHT to CPT, October 8, 1922; HHT to CPT, January 11, 1927; HHT to CPT, November 11, 1922, all CPTP. "How is Nonie?" HHT to CPT, April 1922, CPTP. In one note to brother Bob, Helen wrote, "Thank you for the five hundred dollars. It makes the Mannings solvent once more." HTM to RAT, n.d. (circa 1920s), RATP. "We never hear from Bob," HHT to CPT, April 1922, CPTP. Murray Bay and grandchildren, CPT to HHT, May 29, 1940, CPTP, and Seth Taft to author, e-mails, June 21, 2002. "Way off by," HHT to CPT, June 12, 1927, CPTP.

6. "I saw Coolidge," WHT to HHT, August 7, 1923. Rachmaninoff concert, HHT to Eleanor Taft, January 18, 1925, CPTP. The Tafts also joined the Coolidges on the inaugural parade review stand when the President won a full term, HHT to CPT, December 20, 1925, CPTP. Red rain-coat, HHT to CPT December 18, no year (circa 1923–29), CPTP. "I went to ex-President," HHT to CPT, n.d. (circa February 1924), CPTP.

7. "It is hard," WHT to CPT, April 1924, quoted in Ishbel Ross, *An American Family*, pp. 346–47. "I know you have had experience and know what it is to try to be pleasant to every one," the Queen told her. "Mrs. Taft Meets Spanish Royalty," *New York Times*, April 21, 1924. "Hated to leave" and "going up in," HHT to CPT, May 28, 1924, CPTP. Will wired, "Are you alright? Answer. Love Taft." She was "all right," she answered. WHT to HHT, April 9, 1924; HHT to WHT, April 10, 1924. "Little setback," WHT to HHT, April 24, 1924. Will brushed it off simply, oddly, as the re-sult of eating a large peach that proved gaseous. "Health report, there is," WHT to HHT, April 30, 1924. X-ray of heart, WHT to HHT, June 5, 1924. Will planned to meet Nellie in England, WHT to William Ballantyne, March 31, 1924. "Disturbed, you are," HHT to WHT, May 15, 1924. Will revealed the results of the x-ray exam to his daughter, WHT to HTM, June 8, 1924, HTMP.

8. "I hate to . . . I love you," HHT to WHT, n.d. (circa 1922–28). "I go down the street," HHT to Eleanor Taft, June 7, 1925, CPTP. Potomac Park monument, HHT to CPT, May 30, 1927, CPTP. The concert for the Catholic charity had the Roman Polyponic Society performing, with choirs from the Vatican and other Roman churches. HHT to CPT, December 4, 1927, CPTP. "I like the Policewomen," HHT to CPT, October 21, 1928, CPTP. Receiving with Edith Wilson, HHT to CPT, May 8, 1928, CPTP. "Carry out," HHT to CPT, October 30, 1927; Senator Kellogg, HHT to CPT, January 11, 1925, CPTP. "Senator Swanson had," HHT to CPT, December 20, 1925, CPTP.

9. October 24, 1924, heart attack, HHT to RAT, October 12, 1924, RATP. Thanksgiving guests, HHT to CPT, circa 1927, CPTP. "Four flights," HHT to CPT, June 6, 1926, CPTP. "He does not get," HHT to CPT, June 15, 1926, CPTP. He was in bed for a week. "We are all well," HHT to CPT, October 3, no year (circa 1927), CPTP. Charley Taft's health, HHT to CPT, June 24, 1928, CPTP.

10. "Something that I ate," HHT to CPT, January 2, 1924, CPTP. "I came out," HHT to CPT, November 19, 1922, CPTP. Week of theater, HHT to CPT, October 31, no year (circa mid-1920s), CPTP. *Gentlemen Prefer Blondes,* HHT to CPT, November 24, 1927, CPTP. *Showboat,* HHT to CPT, November 24, 1927, CPTP. *No, No Nanette,* HHT to CPT, December 2, 1928, CPTP. *Abie's Irish Rose,* HHT to CPT, December 24, 1922, CPTP. *Jilla's Atonement,* HHT to CPT, January 14, 1923, CPTP. *Porgy and Bess,* HHT to CPT, April 29, 1928, CPTP. *The Czarina,* HHT to CPT, January 29, 1922, CPTP. *The Green Hat,* HHT to CPT, November 21, 1926, CPTP. *Ladies of the Evening,* HHT to CPT, December 4, 1924. She seemed blasé about other emerging lifestyles, recalling the visit of a sophisticated female relative and "her intimate friend," a woman. While it was possible that Mrs. Taft had intended to imply an extremely close friend, "intimate" was not a word found elsewhere in the hundreds of letters she wrote. HHT to CPT, November 21, 1926, CPTP.

11. New Year's 1928, HHT to CPT, January 8, 1928, CPTP. "Your fa-

ther met me at the station," Nellie wrote to Charlie. "It is the first time he has done that for four years, when he had that heart attack." HHT to CPT, October 7, 1928, CPTP. "Will and I are," HHT to Lilly Grosvenor, October 22, 1927, Grosvenor Papers. Plans for new Supreme Court building, HHT to CPT, December 16, 1928, CPTP. "Any hobbies," HHT to CPT, October 28, 1928, CPTP. "As well as his health," HHT to CPT, June 10, 1928, CPTP. "Next year," HHT to CPT, December 23, 1928, CPTP. "I [don't] know if we can be [buried at Arlington]. Your father being President, was head of the Army and Navy, for four years, but I don't know if that gives him the right." HHT to CPT, May 3, 1929, CPTP. Nellie seemed to have become more conscious of aging in 1928. After attending a concert to hear a favorite singer perform, Nellie sighed, "She is getting old like the rest of us." HHT to CPT, January 15, 1928, CPTP.

12. "Your father said," HHT to CPT, November 6, 1928, CPTP. "It looked very much," HHT to CPT, November 4, 1928, CPTP. Lou Hoover and Nellie Taft lunching a week before election, HHT to CPT, October 28, 1928, CPTP. Other mentions of Nellie Taft seeing Lou Hoover, HHT to CPT, January 11, 1925; HHT to CPT, December 12, 1926; and HHT to CPT, April 22, 1928, all CPTP. Longworth lecture, HHT to CPT, March 18, 1923, CPTP. "I talked to Alice," HHT to CPT, April 11, 1926, and lunch invitation, HHT to CPT, March 25, 1928, both CPTP. Anonymous (Nelle Scanlan), *Boudoir Mirrors of Washington,* p. 205. The name "Roosevelt" no longer carried any special reverence for Will, either. For two years Franklin Roosevelt—the former Wilson Cabinet member and husband of Teddy's niece—attempted to persuade Will to attend fund-raisers for the Boy Scouts. Will claimed previous engagements. FDR to WHT, March 31, 1924. Geographic lectures and Elsie Grosvenor, HHT to CPT, February 19, 1928; HHT to CPT, March 25, 1928; HHT to CPT, April 1, 1928; HHT to CPT, April 15, 1928, CPTP. The Tafts got their first radio as a Christmas gift in 1927 from Elsie Grosvenor.

13. Cincinnati visit, WHT to HHT, June 7, 1929; Murray Bay, HHT to CPT, June 16, 1929, CPTP. "Begin leading the life," HHT to CPT, Octo-

ber 6, 1929, CPTP. Asheville, HHT to CPT, January 19, 1930, CPTP. "Not at all good," RAT to Fanny Edwards, January 13, 1930, RATP; "Bob came down," HHT to CPT, February 2, 1930, CPTP. Finding house in Asheville, HHT to CPT, February 2, 1930, CPTP. Last days of Will's life, HHT to CPT, February 2, 1930, and HHT to CPT, February 8, 1930, CPTP. Reports of former President Taft's death, *New York Times, Washington Post,* and *Washington Star,* March 9, 1930.

14. "There were very many," HHT to CPT, March 16, 1930, CPTP. Jennie's death, Lucy Lippitt to RAT, March 14, 1930, and RAT to Lucy Lippitt, March 18, 1930, RATP. "To dispose of," HHT to CPT, April 12, 1930, CPTP. "You said several weeks ago that you wanted to see them, and I kept them for three weeks." HHT to CPT, n.d. (circa early May 1930), CPTP. "I am eating alone," HHT to CPT, May 11, 1930, CPTP. "We, on talking it over," HHT to CPT, March 16, 1930, CPTP.

20. Adventures of an Old Lady (1930–1943)

1. Rough seas, HHT to CPT, June 10, 1930. Crepes, HHT to CPT, n.d. (June 1930), CPTP. Mrs. Whitney and accident of granddaughters, HHT to CPT, September 28, 1930, CPTP. "Very pleasant . . . generally," HHT to CPT, June, n.d. (1930), CPTP. Refuses invitation for Christmas from Charlie, HHT to CPT, December 18, 1930, CPTP. "It is an awfully," RAT to HTM, December 31, 1930, RATP. "Cried a bit," HHT to CPT, October 25, 1931, CPTP.

2. Helping Greek women, Cleveland Dodge to RAT, May 26, 1943, RATP; George Smithfield to RAT, May 26, 1943. Nellie honored at ceremony and sits through rainstorm, *Washington Evening Star,* April 17, 1927. Plantings after 1912, Paul Russell, "Japanese Spring in America," *Asia Magazine,* May 1930. Bronze plaque at tree planted by HHT, U.S. Grant III to HHT, May 24, 1930, WHTP; "Capital's Famous Blooms," *Washington Star,* March 27, 1938; "Under Cover of Darkness," *Washington Post,* September 17, 1940; "Oriental Is New Designation," *Washington Star,* April 14, 1940. The word *Japanese* was dropped from the festival title in 1940. HHT planting more trees with Japa-

nese ambassador's wife in 1931, HHT to CPT, May 17, 1931, CPTP. "I am delighted," HHT to Yei Theodora Ozaki, n.d. (circa late 1930s); HHT to Mr. Copen, draft, n.d. (circa mid- to late-1930s), HTM Papers.

3. "It seems to me," CPT to HHT, February 18, 1931, CPTP. Annie Taft's death and "Is there any," HHT to HTM, February 1, 1931, HTMP. At the time she heard about Eleanor she also learned that she owed Canadian taxes. "The news about Eleanor and the taxes made Bob's visit a sad one," she remarked. HHT to CPT, November 1, 1931, CPTP. "You sound as if," CPT to HHT, April 28, 1931, CPTP. Christmas day and going to the movies, HHT to CPT, January 1, 1933, and HHT to CPT, January 8, 1933, CPTP. "Naughty but amusing," HHT to CPT, January 3, 1932, CPTP.

4. Concerts and lectures, HHT to CPT, January 31, February 14, and December 18, 1932, CPTP. Touring friends in Charleston, HHT to CPT, March 29, 1932, CPTP. "That's the way," HHT to CPT, April 19, 1932, CPTP. In the weeks after the Supreme Court cornerstone was laid, Nellie plunged back into her rounds of theater—Nazimova in the "very gloomy" production of *The Good Earth,* Ed Wynn in "a very poor show," Tallulah Bankhead in *Forsaking All Others,* Katharine Hepburn in *The Lake*—and movies starring Greta Garbo, Fred Astaire, John Barrymore, and Douglas Fairbanks. Supreme Court building and Nellie being ignored, HHT to CPT, October 2 and October 16, 1932, CPTP; unrecognized in Senate, *Lowell [MA] Sun,* January 11, 1938.

5. "Don't like anything," HHT to CPT, October 25, 1931, CPTP. Nellie on wanting to go to Hoover rally, HHT to CPT, October 27, 1932, and HHT to CPT, October 30, 1932, CPTP. "As boresome," HHT to CPT, November 27, 1932, CPTP. "I can express," HHT to CPT, February 14, 1933, CPTP. Bon voyage party, CPT to HHT, February 19, 1933, CPTP. Studio picture of Will, HHT to CPT, February 19, 1933, CPTP. Won't reorder pictures, HHT to CPT, January 8, 1935, CPTP.

6. "The Italians," HHT to CPT, April 3, 1933, CPTP. "The Acropolis," HHT to CPT, April 9, 1933, CPTP. "I went up in," HHT to CPT, April 15, 1933, CPTP. Bag of cash and jewels lost, HHT to CPT, March 26, 1933, CPTP. "They were as boresome," HHT to CPT, December 3, 1933, CPTP.

New Ford from Michigan, HHT to CPT, May 27, 1934, CPTP. Packard, HHT to CPT, November 1935, CPTP.

7. Nellie's life in Washington, HHT to CPT, December 27, 1935, CPTP. "Which is doing," HHT to CPT, February 12, 1933, CPTP. Teeth, HHT to CPT, November 4, 1934, CPTP. She was irritated that Bob had suggested she give her home to him in her will; she was thinking of selling it if she could make a profit.

8. "Lots of cocktails," HHT to CPT, January 29, 1933, CPTP. "Strong cocktails," HHT to CPT, July 9, 1933, CPTP. "Very weak eggnog," HHT to CPT, January 6, 1935, CPTP. "I hope she finds," RAT to Lucy Lippitt, October 29, 1932, RATP. "You are the only," HHT to CPT, April 16, 1934, CPTP. "I wrote to Martha," HHT to CPT, April 20, 1935, CPTP. "I had a very nice conversation with Mrs. Bolton who was crazy for Bob to be Senator. She did not see any reason he should not. If he should be elected, Senator Fess, she decided, was no good! He said to me that Senator Fess had decided to run and he could not run against him." Bob Taft would successfully run for U.S. senator from Ohio in 1938. HHT to CPT, May 27, 1934, CPTP. "The news transmitted," RAT to Fred Manning, November 28, 1933, RATP.

9. "The Senate and House," HHT to CPT, October 29, 1933, CPTP. "How the communists," HHT to CPT, November 25, 1934, CPTP. "Really I know few people in Washington," she explained. "They have all changed and I have not kept up." HHT to CPT April 7, 1935, CPTP. Mrs. Taft attending breakfast honoring Eleanor Roosevelt, HHT to CPT, December 15, 1935. Eleanor Roosevelt and Nellie Taft had no correspondence, except for the latter's handwritten acceptance to luncheons given for Supreme Court justices' wives. Raymond Teichman, FDR Library to author, June 24, 2002. "Huey Long," HHT to CPT, January 14, 1934, CPTP. *Bring on the Girls,* HHT to CPT, October 28, 1934, CPTP. "The President was very good," HHT to CPT, May 20, 1934.

10. "She seems to have unlimited," RAT to Fanny Edwards, April 11, 1934, RATP. "The Easter," HHT to CPT, March 16, 1934. She wanted to go to the Barbary Coast but didn't have enough time. She also wrote Charlie, in

planning her return, that "if nobody meets me I will get through all right customs all in all." HHT to CPT, April 16, 1934, CPTP. "It was Mrs. Roosevelt's," HHT to CPT, April 16, 1934, CPTP. "I was very much amused," HHT to CPT, December 9, 1934, CPTP.

11. Palm Beach, Charleston, "lobsters and highballs," HHT to CPT, March 10 and March 31, 1935, CPTP. On trip to British Isles, Nellie went with an older Filipino friend, a Mrs. Relyea. "Confidentially," she told her son, "I did not invite Maria, as she does not like plays—while I am crazy about plays!" HHT to CPT, January 27, 1935, CPTP. Nellie's health, Mexico travel plans, and refusal to take paid companion, RAT to HTM, December 17, 1935, and March 21, 1936, RAT to HHT, December 26, 1935. "I can't think . . . I wrote down," HTM to RAT, March 2, 1936, RATP.

12. "She did a great deal," HHT to CPT, December 27, 1932. Nellie also decided not to buy dolls for her granddaughters, returning some she bought because they were of no purpose and "silly." HHT to CPT, November 30, 1930, CPTP. When her grandchildren came to Murray Bay, Nellie enjoyed watching them run about or playing with the phonograph while she sat on the porch. They also came to know their great-aunt Maria, HHT to CPT, May 12, 1935, and HHT to CPT, July 26, 1931, CPTP. Making her home now in the Phelps Apartment in Cincinnati, Maria lived on limited funds. Lucy, however, was now remarried to the wealthy Rhode Island senator Henry Lippitt, with homes in Providence, Newport, and Washington. She and Nellie continued to send money to their brother Jack and his family, he seemingly unable to maintain a steady job and income. RAT to Lucy Lippitt, November 29 and November 30, 1936, RATP. Pro-FDR statement allegedly made by Nellie. *New York Times*, May 19, 1936. "It enables me to go," HHT to CPT, January 27, 1935, CPTP.

13. "To talk to him," CPT to HHT, August 21, 1937, CPTP. "Set out to show," CPT to HHT, June 10, 1937, CPTP. "Mama's finances," RAT to HTM, August 24, no year (1937), HTMP.

14. Nellie in Egypt, "blamed it on . . . quite vague," RAT to HTM, April 12, 1937, RATP. Nellie left no address with her maid, RAT to HTM, July

20, 1937, RATP. "I know the difficulties," RAT to Fred Manning, March 3, 1938, RATP. "And try if I can," HHT to CPT, March 9, 1938, CPTP. Charlie trying to get Nellie to move out to Cincinnati, CPT to HHT, April 12, 1938, and CPT to HHT, May 4, 1938, CPTP. Claim that she did not intend to keep the house another year, HHT to CPT, May 6, 1938, CPTP. Planning trip, HHT to CPT, May 21, 1938, CPTP. Naples, "the most beautiful," HHT to CPT, n.d. (1938), CPTP. "I'm not a bit sure," Fred Manning to RAT and CPT, n.d. (June 1938), RATP.

15. "Very discouraged," Fred Manning to RAT, October 16, 1938, RATP. "Is my mother," CPT to Ruth McConnell, March 24, 1939, RATP. Nellie arrived back stateside in June, just in time to run down to the wedding of one of her grandsons in New York and a granddaughter's graduation at Bryn Mawr. More detail on HHT trip to Europe in spring 1939, RAT to CPT, April 22, 1939, CPTP; Ruth McConnell to CPT, April 26 and May 1, 1939, CPTP; RAT to HTM, May 17, 1939, RATP; CPT to HHT, May 26, 1939, CPTP. "I am having," HHT postcard to RAT, n.d. (May 1939), RATP. Legs weak, has to take bus, HHT to CPT, May 20, 1939, CPTP. "Come on," CPT to HHT, December 5, 1939, CPTP. "Mama was preparing," HTM to RAT, n.d. (marked only as "Sunday"), and December 24, 1939 (mislabeled as 1940), RATP. On how the children finally persuaded Nellie to take a companion, who they paid for, HTM to RAT, February 18 (1940), and RAT to HTM, January 17, 1940, RATP. Nellie's trip to the Pacific in 1940, CPT to HHT, January 24, January 31, and March 15, 1940, CPTP. Reading dime novels and then donating them, Seth Taft to author, e-mails, June 21, 2002. Merchant Marine Library, CPT to HHT, May 29, 1940.

16. "I could never wish," Maria Herron to RAT, April 3, 1940, RATP. One of several photographs of her at the convention, with Bob kneeling at her side, appears in the James T. Patterson biography, *Mr. Republican*. Nellie signing protest petition, "Protest Filibuster on Lend-Lease Bill," *New York Times*, March 6, 1941.

17. "I hope they will," HHT to CPT, December 22, no year (1940), CPTP. Cigarette case, CPT to HHT, December 29, 1936, CPTP. "Has

faintly suggested," RAT to HTM, November 27, 1940, RATP. "I think she has given," RAT to HTM, December 18, 1940, RATP.

18. Reports on Nellie in Murray Bay the summer of 1931, HTM to RAT, July 2, 1941; HTM to RAT, July 6, 1941; HTM to RAT, July 9, 1941; HTM to RAT, July 12, 1941; all RATP. "Mama became very annoyed," RAT to HTM, October 6, 1941, RATP. "Quite as bright," RAT to HTM, October 3, 1941, RATP.

19. Japanese embassy dinner, HHT to CPT, November 3, 1933, CPTP. "Had a very hot fight," HHT to CPT, June 27, 1933, CPTP. The IRS wrote to the Senator that they required his mother's signature on her 1941 tax returns, filed in early 1942. In August of that year he responded with an affadavit and her signature, adding, "My mother was so ill at the time that she could not sign her name, and still has some difficulty." RAT to M. H. Magruder, Collector of Internal Revenue, August 22, 1942, RATP.

20. "I think she is rather," RAT to Lucy Lippitt, February 22, 1943, RATP. "Mama is still in," RAT to Lucy Lippitt, April 8, 1943. "Home again," RAT to Lucy Lippitt, April 23, 1943, RATP. Southern Medical Supply Company oxygen, "Helen H. Taft, debts paid by the administrator," handwritten notes, RATP. "The last time," Mabel Boardman to HTM, May 25, 1943, RATP. "Get yourself a book," HHT to CPT, December 22, no year (1940), CPTP. "Your mother's death," Henry Taft to RAT, May 23, 1943, RATP.

21. "For more than a generation," Cordell Hull to RAT, May 25, 1943, RATP. FDR, Eleanor Roosevelt, and Alice Longworth notes are in sympathy cards, Box 4, CPT Papers. Edith Roosevelt telegram to RAT, May 24, 1943, RATP. Speech of Justice Sandra Day O'Connor, National Cherry Blossom Festival Honoring Mrs. Helen Taft, Arlington National Cemetery, April 8, 1987. Nellie left all of her personal and real property to Helen, who was also named executor. Nellie had stock in Otis Elevator, R. J. Reynolds, and Standard Oil, among others. It amounted to nearly $213,000. She gave the Murray Bay house to both sons, and the Washington house to all three of the children. Pieces of silver were bequeathed to individual friends and fam-

ily members. Nellie Taft left an estate of nearly $1 million. "Last Will and Testament of Helen Herron Taft," signed February 8, 1933; "Codical to the Last Will," signed November 3, 1933; "Deed of Gift," signed September 1, 1937; "Memorandum found with Last Will" signed February 8, 1933. Nellie's real estate holdings were vast—from apartment buildings and homes from which she collected rentals in Brooklyn, Queens, and Long Island to the Aeronautical Corporation Building at Lunken Airport in Cincinnati to Ohio farmland properties. RAT to John More, July 21, 1943; RAT to Frank Ellison, July 21, 1943. Among her corporate investments were Proctor & Gamble, Caterpillar Tractor, and Atchison, Topeka & Santa Fe Railway. RAT to Riggs Bank, August 31, 1943, all RAT Papers. Her survivors included three siblings, three children, twelve grandchildren, and two great-grandchildren. If not as colorful as the Adamses, Roosevelts, Kennedys, or Bushes, the name "Taft" would reach through generations of politics. Bob would fail in his efforts to become President in 1952, but his son would serve in the United States Congress, and his grandson would go on to serve as governor of Ohio in the twenty-first century.

BIBLIOGRAPHY

Manuscript Collections

Daniel Carter Beard Papers, Library of Congress

Archibald B. Butt Papers, Georgia Department of Archives and History

Cincinnati Orchestra Society and Miss Nourse School materials, Cincinnati Historical Society

Eli Collins Papers, New York State Library

William Collins Papers, New York State Library

John Spalding Flannery Papers, Library of Congress

Grosvenor Family Papers, Library of Congress

John Williamson Herron and Harriet Collins Herron correspondence, Rutherford B. Hayes, Presidential Center

Irwin Hoover Papers, Library of Congress

Frances Benjamin Johnston Papers, Library of Congress

Gertrude Lane Papers, Library of Congress

Alice Roosevelt Longworth Papers, Library of Congress

Nicholas Longworth Papers, Library of Congress

Franklin MacVeagh Papers, Library of Congress

Helen Taft Manning Papers, Library of Congress

Victor Murdock Papers, Library of Congress

Henry Fowler Pringle Papers, Library of Congress

Charles P. Taft Papers, Library of Congress

Robert A. Taft Papers, Library of Congress

Robert Taft Oral History Project, Columbia University, Butler Library

William Howard Taft Papers, Library of Congress

Selected Articles

"Mrs. Taft's Plans in the White House," *Ladies' Home Journal*, March 1909

"Mrs. Taft's Home-Making," *Good Housekeeping*, September 1911

"President Taft's Denunciation of Roosevelt," *Literary Digest*, May 4, 1912

"Six Weeks I Spent on a Farm" by Helen Taft, *Ladies' Home Journal*, June 1918

"As I See the Future of Women" by William Howard Taft, *Ladies' Home Journal*, March 1919

"$100,000 Salary for the President," *Ladies' Home Journal*, October 1919

"Does America Need College Women?" by Helen Taft, *Collier's*, January 31, 1920

"Women in Politics" by Helen Taft, *Women's Home Companion*, April 1920

"Chief Justice: A Mistaken Appointment," *Nation*, July 13, 1921

"Six White House Wives and Widows," *Ladies' Home Journal*, June 1927

"Some Impressions of 150,000 Miles of Travel" by William Howard Taft, *National Geographic*, May 1930

Selected Books

Anderson, Donald E. *William Howard Taft: A Conservative's Conception of the Presidency*. Ithaca, N.Y.: Cornell University Press, 1973.

Anderson, Judith Icke. *William Howard Taft: An Intimate History*. New York: W.W. Norton, 1981.

Anonymous [Nelle Scanlan]. *Boudoir Mirrors of Washington*. Philadelphia: Lippincott, 1925.

Anthony, Carl Sferrazza. *America's First Families: Two Hundred Years of Private Life in the White House*. New York: Touchstone/Simon & Schuster, 2000.

————. *First Ladies: The Saga of the Presidents' Wives and Their Power, 1789–1990*. New York: William Morrow, 1990.

Boller, Paul. *Presidential Wives: An Anecdotal History*. New York: Oxford University Press, 1988.

Brough, James. *Princess Alice: A Biography of Alice Roosevelt Longworth*. Boston: Little, Brown, 1975.

Butt, Archibald Willingham. *Taft and Roosevelt: The Intimate Letters of Archie Butt, Military Aide*. 2 vols. Garden City, N.Y.: Doubleday, 1930.

Clotworthy, William G. *Presidential Sites*. Blacksburg, Va.: McDonald & Woodward, 1998.

Collins, Herbert R. *Presidents on Wheels*. New York: Bonanza Books, 1971.

Colman, Edna. *White House Gossip*. Garden City, N.Y.: Doubleday, 1927.

Dunn, Robert Lee. *William Howard Taft: American*. Boston: Chapple Publishing, 1908.

Durbin, Louise. *Inaugural Cavalcade*. New York: Dodd, Mead, 1971.

Felsenthal, Carol. *Alice Roosevelt Longworth*. New York: Putnam, 1988.

Fuller, Edmund, and David A. Green. *God in the White House: The Faiths of the American Presidents*. New York: Crown, 1968.

Furman, Bess. *Washington By-Line: The Personal History of a Newspaperman*. New York: Knopf, 1949.

————. *White House Profile*. Indianapolis, Ind.: Bobbs-Merrill, 1951.

Geer, Emily Apt. *First Lady: The Life of Lucy Webb Hayes*. Kent, Ohio: Kent State University Press, 1984.

Green, Constance M. *The Church on Lafayette Square, 1815–1970*. Washington, D.C.: Potomac Books, 1970.

Hammond, John Hays. *The Autobiography of John Hayes Hammond*. New York: Farrard Rinehart, 1935.

Harnsberger, Caroline Thomas. *A Man of Courage: Robert A. Taft*. Chicago: Wilcox & Follett, 1952.

Hay, Peter. *All the Presidents' Ladies*. New York: Viking, 1988.

Hoover, Irwin. *42 Years in the White House*. Cambridge, Mass.: Riverside Press, 1934.

Jaffray, Elizabeth. *Secrets of the White House*. New York: Cosmopolitan Books, 1927.

Jefferson, Roland M., and Alan E. Fusonie. *The Japanese Flowering Cherry Trees of Washington, D.C.* Washington, D.C.: U.S. Department of Agriculture, 1977.

Kirk, Elise K. *Music at the White House*. Urbana and Chicago: University of Illinois Press, 1986.

Kittler, Glenn D. *Hail to the Chief! The Inauguration Days of Our Presidents*. Philadelphia: Chilton Books, 1968.

Longworth, Alice Roosevelt. *Crowded Hours*. New York: Scribner's, 1933.

Manners, Will. *TR and Will: A Friendship That Split the Republican Party*. New York: Harcourt, Brace & Jovanovich, 1969.

Mason, Alpheus Thomas. *William Howard Taft: Chief Justice*. New York: Simon & Schuster, 1964.

Mead, William B., and Paul Dickson. *Baseball: The Presidents' Game*. New York: Walker Publishing, 1997.

Means, Marianne. *The Woman in the White House*. New York: Random House, 1963.

Medved, Michael. *The Shadow Presidents: The Secret History of the Chief Executives and Their Top Aides*. New York: Times Books, 1979.

Miller, Nathan. *Theodore Roosevelt: A Life*. New York: William Morrow, 1992.

Morris, Edmund. *Theodore Rex*. New York: Random House, 2001.

Morris, Sylvia Jukes. *Edith Kermit Roosevelt: Portrait of a First Lady*. New York: Coward, McCann & Geoghegan, 1980.

Parks, Lillian Rogers. *My Thirty Years Backstairs at the White House*. New York: Fleet Publishing, 1961.

Patterson, James T. *Mr. Republican: A Biography of Robert A. Taft*. Boston: Houghton, Mifflin, 1972.

Perling, J. J. *Presidents' Sons*. New York: Odyssey Press, 1947.

Pringle, Henry Fowler. *The Life and Times of William Howard Taft: A Biography*. 2 vols. New York: Holt, Rinehart, Winston, 1939.

Ross, Ishbel. *An American Family: The Tafts*. Cleveland, Ohio: World Publishing, 1964.

Sadler, Christine. *Children in the White House*. New York: Putnam, 1967.

Seale, William. *The Presidents' House*. vol. 2. Washington, D.C.: White House Historical Association, 1986.

Slayden, Ellen Maury. *Washington Wife*. New York: Harper & Row, 1962.

Smith, Ira T. *Dear Mr. President: The Story of Fifty Years in the White House Mail Room*. New York: Messner, 1949.

Taft, Helen Herron. *Recollections of Full Years*. New York: Dodd, Mead, 1914.

Taft, Seth. *Take on the World! Rules of the Road*. Euclid, Ohio: Williams Custom Printing, 1999.

Taft, William Howard, and James Bryce. *Washington: The Nation's Capital*. Washington, D.C.: National Geographic, 1913.

Teague, Michael. *Mrs. L: Conversations with Alice Roosevelt Longworth*. Garden City, N.Y.: Doubleday, 1981.

Teichmann, Howard. *Alice: The Life and Times of Alice Roosevelt Longworth*. Englewood Cliffs, N.J.: Prentice-Hall, 1979.

Wade, Wyn Craig. *The Titanic: End of a Dream*. New York: Penguin, 1986.

White, William Allen. *A Puritan in Babylon: The Story of Calvin Coolidge*. New York: Macmillan, 1938.

White, William S. *The Taft Story*. New York: Harper & Brothers, 1954.

Willets, Gilson. *Inside History of the White House*. New York: The Christian Herald, 1908.

Williams, Charles Richard. *The Life of Rutherford Hayes: Nineteenth President of the United States*. vol. 2. Columbus, Ohio: Ohio State Archaeological and Historical Society, 1928.

Withers, Bob. *The President Travels by Train*. Lynchburg, Va.: TLC Publishing, 1996.

Wolfskill, Mary. "Meeting a New Century: The Papers of Four Twentieth-Century First Ladies," in Nancy C. Smith and Mary C. Ryan, eds., *Modern First Ladies: Their Documentary Legacy*. Washington, D.C.: National Archives, 1989.

INDEX